THE PROTESTANT REFORMATION

THE PROTESTANT REFORMATION

BY

H. DANIEL-ROPS

TRANSLATED
FROM THE FRENCH BY
AUDREY BUTLER

LONDON: J. M. DENT & SONS LTD
NEW YORK: E. P. DUTTON & CO. INC.

H. Daniel-Rops: *Une Révolution Religeuse:
la Réforme Protestante,* first published in
France by Librairie Arthème Fayard, 1958

TRANSLATOR'S NOTE

M. Daniel-Rops dealt with the period 1350–1622, under the general title *L'Église de la Renaissance et de la Réforme*, in two volumes, from the first of which, *La Réforme Protestante*, this volume has been translated.

CONTENTS

*
vii

MAPS

CHAPTER I

A CRISIS OF AUTHORITY: THE SCHISM AND THE COUNCILS

THE GLORIOUS RETURN

THE SUN was shining fitfully on the morning of 17th January 1377, and there was a gentle breeze—it was the kind of day which is not uncommon on the Roman plain in winter time. An enormous crowd thronged both banks of the Tiber in an obvious state of frenzied excitement. Not far away, among the pines, stood the basilica of St Paul 'without-the-walls,' that selfsame church built by the Emperor Honorius and his wife Galla Placidia in honour of the Apostle, over the place where his grave had been dug, and whose mosaics rivalled those of Ravenna. More waves of human beings continued to stream into Rome along the old flagged road, the ancient Ostian Way, all hurrying to join those fervent folk who had been keeping vigil all night long by torchlight, giving proof of their rejoicing in prayers and hymns. The papal galley was moored upstream, followed by some twenty others, flying the flags of several different realms and cities; the river seemed carpeted by the escorting vessels. At last the man whom all had been awaiting appeared; he came down the gangway and made his way towards the church where Peter Ameilh de Brenac, Bishop of Sinigaglia and prelate of the Curia, was to celebrate High Mass. Everyone fell upon his knees, and then acclaimed the pontiff with tremendous cheers. He was weary and very pale: and he did not look particularly joyful.

The Pope whom the Holy City was welcoming in this fashion was Gregory XI. At the time he was forty-eight years old. He was a frail, spare figure, his features heavily lined, prematurely aged by a lifetime of strife and grief: even at the time of his election in 1370—one of the miniatures in Froissart's *Chronicles* depicts him thus—he had looked about sixty, although then scarcely past his fortieth year. But this fragile scabbard housed a blade of excellent steel. A Frenchman by birth—he was to be the last of the Sovereign Pontiffs born in France— a son of the Count of Beaufort and nephew of Clement VI, Gregory had profited by the strange customs with which the Papal Court at Avignon was, alas, all too familiar; but in his case these scandalous promotions had served to further God's glory. Although created canon at the age of eleven, prior of Mesures, near Autun, and cardinal at nineteen,[1] unlike so many others, he had not decided that his dazzling rank exempted him from the need to study or even to conduct oneself with propriety. At Perugia, where he was a pupil of the celebrated Baldo degli Ubaldi, Gregory had acquired the considerable judicial knowledge that sustained his judgment, which was naturally detached and sensible. Modest, pious and prudent, he showed himself kindly and gracious on every occasion, but he also knew how to demonstrate the firmness, and even the severity, which is sometimes demanded of great leaders. As a reformer of morals, a propagator of the faith and a scourge of heresies, he had courageously confronted countless dangers which were threatening the Church of his day, and although he had not succeeded in breaking the vicious circle of Anglo-French rivalry, he had at least re-established peace in the Spanish kingdoms, and reconciled Hungary and the Empire, and Sicily and Naples. This Pope who lived at one of the decisive turning-points in history was in many ways a great man; so it occasionally follows, in the case of certain individuals, that we find the most unfaltering energy going hand in hand with an indefinable, mysterious frailty.

There was no more striking evidence of this energy than the glorious return whose climax was even now taking place. No sooner had Gregory XI been consecrated as St Peter's successor than he announced his plan. 'The well-being of the Christian religion, the interest of the Church, the Bride of Christ, the state of the papal domains and the public weal, all demand our entry into the Holy City,' he declared. One bishop, whom he had summoned to the Palace of Doms in order to reprove him for abandoning his Church, his mystical Bride, made so bold as to retort: 'Is not Your Holiness even more tardy than I in adhering to *his* Church?' And Gregory replied quite simply: 'I shall be in Rome very soon now.' The intrigues of kings, cities and cardinals managed to delay him, but could not prevent his decision bearing fruit. A saint's voice did the rest. In the bas-relief of his sarcophagus, chiselled in marble by Paolo Olivieri, as well as in the famous panel by Matteo di Giovanni in the hospital at Siena, it is the scene of his return to Rome that the artists have chosen to record as the outstanding achievement of Gregory's life. Even in the middle of the sixteenth century, an epoch when the Church of Christ was stricken by a still more terrible schism, the imagination of artists was fired by the memory of one who had sealed that other breach and put an end to the exile at Avignon.

The procession moved off. The Vicar of Christ was on horseback, riding beneath a canopy which was carried by four bishops, all on foot. Behind him walked the Princes of the Church, their red hats on their

[1] There is some argument on this point: at all events it is certain that Gregory was made a cardinal when still extremely young.

heads, or else slung on their backs, over their cloaks. Raised standards and decorated chargers, tinkling with bells, were to be seen everywhere; the Roman bannerets dashed about like mad things; the *caporioni*, the boatmen and the dancers were beside themselves with joy. Women and children threw flowers, and showered sweetmeats upon the escorts' horses. The Roman nobility rubbed shoulders with the youthful followers of Raymond de Turenne and his brothers, from Provence; folk pointed out the aged Juan d'Heredia d'Emposte, solemnly bearing the pontifical banner, as was his right, and the harbinger Bertrand Raffin, Archdeacon of Lerida, who was bustling about in search of lodgings for the important visitors. It was rumoured too that miracle had played its part in the joyous event: the angels had taken pains to bring the Apostle's chair, so long exiled, back to St Peter's, and, in order that Catherine of Siena, the marvellous nun responsible for this triumphal return, could be present to see it, along with her cloistered sisters, the walls of her convent had swung open, of their own accord, in one fell swoop.

Joy was supreme. All else was forgotten. In this hour men wished to wipe out everything save the glorious present. They were anxious to forget the profound sorrow felt by many of the Pope's French retinue on leaving 'the town whose beauty is like a flower, and which glitters with all the brilliance of ivory,' and the dark forebodings which, thanks to considerable recourse to astrology, very many of their number had had on departing from their beloved Rocher des Doms. They were anxious to forget the frightful hardships of the journey from Avignon, which had taken four whole months, and during which it had seemed that every force on earth was combining to combat the pontiff's vow: violent gales, the sea, human intrigue, rivalry between the various groups making up the escort and, to crown all, the suspect manœuvres of certain individuals in Rome itself. They were still more anxious to forget the dreadful price paid for this dazzling victory. It had been accomplished rather by brute force than by the weapon of love advocated by St Catherine of Siena: the mercenary bands of Bretons and Englishmen sent to restore order in Italy had been guilty of atrocities; Florence, governed by her 'Eight Saints,' was still waging a formidable war, despite the fact that she was under interdict and half in ruins; and within the Church herself, even within the bosom of the Sacred College, there lurked a host of jealousies and hatreds that were now but temporarily lulled. Finally and above all, they were anxious to forget that the situation, fraught with anxiety as it was on so many sides, was in the hands of this tired old man of nearly fifty, who appeared to have one foot already in the grave, and who knew nothing at all about Italy.

It did not do to think of any of these things. It behoved each man

to throw himself heart and soul into the clamorous joy of the bells and
the fanfares. 'Here is the man we welcome! He whom we have waited
for so long! Long live the Pope! Long live Gregory! Hurrah! Hurrah!'
All day long the procession wound its endless way along the narrow
little streets of the city, its order now largely broken. A herald flourished the keys of the Eternal City before the pontiff. At windows and
balconies, in the threshold of every doorway, there was naught to see
save the splendour of many-coloured silks and the glitter of gold
ornaments. Night had fallen, but the procession went on—'and we
were all marching upon an empty stomach,' notes good Bishop Ameilh
in a practical aside to the rhyming account which he composed of the
whole adventure. At last it arrived in front of St Peter's. The saint's
successor advanced as far as the Apostle's tomb, and remained there
for a long time, sunk deep in meditation and prayer. What did this
mind, in whom the Spirit dwelt, sense at that moment? What exactly
did Gregory foresee? The rebirth of violence in the near future; the
abominable slaughter of Cesena, which was to be perpetrated by papal
troops themselves less than five weeks later; the exile to Anagni six
months afterwards; and the final return to Rome, where death would
be awaiting him, impatient to carry him off? Totally absorbed in the
gloomy forebodings which mingled with his acts of thanksgiving the
Pope forgot the passage of time. But his followers, exhausted by their
prolonged singing of God's praises, concerned themselves with less
supernatural matters from now on. They had taken up residence in the
Vatican, and were systematically refreshing themselves there by torchlight. The service was judged to be quite magnificent: the dishes
offered, most rare and precious.

THE LAST AVIGNONESE POPES

Thus ended a long and painful ordeal which the Church had endured
for more than seventy years. The reader may remember its details.[1]
In 1305 Bertrand de Got, Archbishop of Bordeaux, had with some
difficulty succeeded to the Papacy as Clement V. He had considered it
his duty to settle the dispute between the Papacy and the King of
France before being installed at Rome, but had openly proclaimed the
Eternal City to be his 'own See.' Capetian diplomacy, fear of the chaos
then existing in Italy and the requirements of the Council of Vienne
had kept him on the other side of the Alps. Then, after many pere-
grinations, and quite a long stay at Avignon, which he had reached in
1309, Clement had died in 1314, at the start of yet another journey. He

[1] See the author's *Cathedral and Crusade* (published by Dent/Dutton as an English
translation of *L'Église de la Cathédrale et de la Croisade*, 1957), the final chapter, Section
8: The Papacy at Avignon.

had never set foot in Italy, but had never ceased to declare that his sole desire was to return to Rome.

His successor, John XXII (1316–34), was a frail septuagenarian. He decided that no return to Rome was possible so long as the peninsula remained in its present state, and he confined himself to sending a legate there to wage on his behalf a lengthy and costly war that had no important results. An unexpected revival of the ancient quarrel between the Papacy and the Empire brought him into conflict with Louis of Bavaria, thereby convincing him that Divine Providence wished to see him established on the banks of the Rhône rather than upon those of the Tiber. John was a first-class organizer: he established the Papal Curia in the Provençal city, and strove to render the central government of the Church an efficient organization. Benedict XII (1334–42) and Clement VI (1342–52) had carried on his work. The impressive castle, built at their command high on the Rocher des Doms and covering some six thousand square yards, formed a bristling mass of towers and battlements, and demonstrated to the eyes of all the world the glory of Avignon, the provisional capital of the Church, and a highly inconvenient capital besides. Its streets and houses swarmed with cardinals and merchants, with officials and petitioners, with diplomats and courtiers, not to mention various less savoury forms of life. And the Italians, enraged to see Rome become the pontiff's widow, threw themselves wholeheartedly into the game of attacking what Petrarch dubbed 'the sink of iniquity, the cesspit of the world, the most noisome of cities'—a description which was highly exaggerated.

It must be remembered that not one of those French popes who had occupied the pontifical throne at Avignon ever abandoned the idea of returning to Rome. All of them laboured, with arms, silver and intrigue, to bring about the conditions which seemed to them essential for their restoration to the Eternal City. Although Avignon had been purchased from Queen Joan of Naples in 1348, a fact which appeared to confirm the final nature of the papal establishment there, Clement VI had in granting the jubilee year of 1350, specifically laid down that the graces attached to this year of pardon were to be gained at the Apostle Peter's tomb. The 'new Babylonian captivity,' as the situation was called at the time throughout almost the whole of Christendom, was therefore not intended to be permanent, despite assertion to the contrary by polemical writers.

The pontificate of Clement VI ended in 1352, leaving behind it memories of the most sumptuous times ever enjoyed by the Avignonese court, as well as of those appalling days during which the Black Death had swept down upon Christendom like the very symbol of divine wrath itself. The situation at that date appeared hopelessly confused, and unlikely to result in any lasting decision. Only one point had become clear: the question of relations between the Papacy and the Empire. When Charles of Moravia succeeded to the Empire as Charles IV [1] in 1346, he straightway fulfilled the undertakings he had made towards the Pope, abandoning the mischief-making descents into Italy, and showing a constant anxiety to respect the interests of the Holy See. When Petrarch called on him to become 'the saviour' of Italy, he replied, quite good-humouredly, in the words of Tiberius: 'You don't know what a monster the Empire is. . . .' And he appeared to be more interested in hard cash and tangible results than in lofty dreams of power. In 1355 indeed he went to Rome, but he journeyed as a pilgrim; and although he had himself crowned there, he left the city that same evening, in order to make it perfectly clear that he did not regard himself as its master. On the occasion of his next visit, during the brief residence of Urban V in 1368, the bystanders had been able to watch him leading the pontiff's steed by the bridle, and acting as a deacon at the Pope's side on the festival of All Saints. On this plane, therefore, all had worked out for the best.

Alas, however, other sections of the political map of Western Europe gave fewer grounds for optimism! West of the Alps the situation was extremely disturbing. The war which had broken out between the crowns of France and England in 1337 threatened to drag on for a long time; it was in fact to last one hundred years . . . and various papal attempts to mediate in this matter had failed utterly. Crushed first at Crécy and then, ten years later, at Poitiers, her sovereign John II dying in captivity, the France of Charles V and Duguesclin was indeed undergoing a revival of her strength; but the battle was raging in all four corners of her territory, and it was doubtful whether the Papacy could consider itself safe on French soil.

Even so it could hardly have felt any safer in Italy. The peninsula was in a state of complete chaos: political subdivisions had become accentuated, and factions were tearing one another to pieces in the cities, which were themselves a prey to ferocious wars. Not a single principle of authority or unity existed. The Angevin kingdom of Naples had foundered into impotence; the Viscontis of Milan were universally detested. In the states of the Church the local nobility were carving up the estates for their own benefit. At Rome the episode of Cola di Rienzo, in 1347, had shown how very ready the populace was to listen to agitators, no matter who they might be. The only point upon which all Italians seemed in almost total agreement, as symbolized by the League of Ferrara, was their common desire to prevent a foreigner from ruling the peninsula. Now the popes at Avignon were all Frenchmen. . . .

[1] Son of the blind King John of Bohemia, who died an heroic death in the French ranks at Crécy later in the same year.

And not merely the popes, but practically the whole of the Sacred College too! Out of twenty-five cardinals present at the conclave which opened on 16th December 1352, only three had no connection with the fleur-de-lis: two Italians and one Spaniard. Among the French cardinals, the close-knit, determined Limousin faction seemed bent on retaining control of the triple crown. For a time they considered electing the general of the Carthusians, Jean Birel, who hailed from Limousin; but they abandoned this idea for fear that this saintly individual, once set upon the pontifical throne, might prove a second Celestine V,[1] and that, in electing him, they would be making themselves a laughing-stock. At last agreement was reached upon the person of Cardinal Étienne Aubert, who also, needless to say, came from Limousin, and who took the name Innocent. Innocent VI (1352–62) was a learned jurist, and was well regarded by the French Court, but he was also gouty and prematurely aged, and was considered fickle and impressionable: an excellent tool, as the ambitious cardinals thought.

At the next conclave there were fresh manoeuvres by the Limousin clique, crowned by a further success. After hovering for a moment over the head of Clement VI's brother, the Holy Spirit alighted upon the highly respected abbot of St Victor's at Marseilles, Guillaume de Grimoard, yet another son of Limousin, but quite the reverse of a schemer. In the person of Urban V (1362–70) the Avignonese Papacy had given the lie to all those slanderers who saw it as a second Sodom and Gomorrah. This saintly monk, who never discarded his Benedictine habit, who always confessed before celebrating Mass, who never omitted to read the Office with his household, whose charity was endless, and whose sole relaxations consisted in busying himself with his labours on the canon law, with the wonderful library which he enriched and indexed, and with the 1,400 students whom he supported at Avignon, Montpellier and Manosque, well deserved the homage of all fair-minded men; and in 1870, five hundred years after his death, Holy Church herself rendered public homage to Urban in the ceremony of his Beatification.

One important fact, showing the injustice of those who represent the last Avignonese popes as playthings of France, was strikingly apparent in the truly Christian souls of both Innocent VI and Urban V, two sweet-natured and saintly men. That fact was the slow generation in their hearts, and subsequent declaration to the world, of a conviction that the Papacy must return to Rome at any cost. Despite the wishes of those who had elected them, it was the task of these two popes to prepare the way for such a return. In this arduous undertaking they

[1] For the extraordinary story of this hermit who became a pope see the first section of the final chapter of *Cathedral and Crusade*.

were most capably assisted by Cardinal Gil Albornoz, a former Arch-bishop of Toledo and a veteran of the Moorish wars, one who had been seen to hurl himself between the protagonists at Tarifa, and who had taken part in the sieges of Algeçiras and Gibraltar. A mighty figure he was, at one and the same time churchman, diplomat and warrior. Sent as Papal Legate to Italy he laboured to restore the Pope's authority there by reasserting the rights of the Holy See. In the Papal States themselves he undertook a campaign of reconquest, and the Patrimony of St Peter, the duchy of Spoleto, the Marches of Ancona and Romagna returned one by one beneath the crozier of the formidable cardinal. Control was regained over the mercenaries who were terrorizing the countryside; fortresses were built to control key positions, like the 'rocca' that can still be seen above Spoleto; and, legislating with the same firm authority, Albornoz gave to the Papal States the 'Egidian Constitutions' which remained in force almost without amendment until 1816. It seemed that only one obstacle to the Papacy's triumph in Italy now remained: the ambition of Bernabo Visconti. Albornoz made ready to destroy him; but the Milanese ruler's cunning diplomacy, abetted no doubt by certain judiciously distributed bribes which were all the more effective because the papal treasuries were considerably impaired at this juncture, succeeded in forming an alliance between the various interests whose jealousies were sustaining the legate's success, and in persuading the Pope to set him aside. In 1363 Albornoz was restricted to performing his legatine functions at Naples, and was thus unable to complete his great work.

It remained true, nevertheless, that certain definite results had been achieved; and these confirmed the popes in their intention of one day returning to Rome. Especially as various grave developments made it obvious to them that Avignon was far from offering those guarantees of security which alone could justify a prolongation of their stay on the Provençal hill-top. The war between France and England had resulted in a situation which might easily have been foreseen, but which was a formidable one none the less: the appearance of large numbers of bandits all over France. As soon as the 'great companies' of hardened mercenaries were no longer being paid by one side or the other, they would turn to making a living by pillage. Innocent VI had more than once seen them appear on all sides of his little Avignonese domain: on one occasion he had had to flee before them; on two others he had been forced to purchase their temporary withdrawal with hard cash, and he had had a strong battlemented wall, four miles long, constructed specially to protect his town from their attacks. The situation was no better under Urban V, who, in an effort to rid himself of this terrible menace, was obliged to pay Duguesclin an enormous sum to lead this redoubtable wandering soldiery against the Infidel.

But there was no guarantee that other similar hordes would not appear in the future, and around the year 1365 men had wondered aloud whether the battlemented wall of Avignon—a wall which can still be seen encircling the old town today—was not in fact rather like a prison wall, confining the Pope within its bounds.

It was in such conditions that Urban V announced to the Sacred College, to the Romans, and to all Christian princes, that he intended to return to Rome forthwith. Without waiting for their reply he had his palace in Rome repaired. Then, almost without further preparation, he set off on his journey. The cardinals had raised an outcry against this action. But the saintly Pope had turned a deaf ear to all their objections, and had merely answered their complaints by raising a young Franciscan, William of Aigrefeuille, to the purple. This was intended to make men understand that 'many other cardinals could spring from the fur of this hood.' Suddenly calmed, the Sacred College resigned itself to the situation and allowed the Pope to arrive in Rome on 16th October 1367.

However, this first attempt to return to the Eternal City proved a fiasco. No sooner had he set foot in Italy than Urban V felt uneasy and embarrassed. While passing through Viterbo the Pope and his little band of followers had been halted by a rioting mob. When he entered Rome he cut a sorry figure indeed in the eyes of all those fine folk, who, armed to the teeth, had come to escort him, and who appeared ready to slit one another's throats. The city authorities had shown a marked reluctance to help him re-establish himself there so that when the hot weather became intolerable he had taken refuge in one of the strong, thick-walled castles which Albornoz had built in many parts of the Papal States—at Montefiascone, above Lake Bolsena. This action had not pleased the Romans, and when Urban V subsequently awarded the red hat to six Frenchmen out of a total of eight cardinals created, the whole of Italy made its anger plain. Various revolts broke out, notably one at Perugia, where the rebels were assisted by John Hawkwood, one of the most notorious mercenary leaders of the age. While these were in progress, Bernabo Visconti invaded Tuscany. As a result, Urban V set out again for Avignon, giving as his excuse the possible role of arbiter which he hoped to play between France and England at some future date. Was this a mere excuse? The devout old man insisted that his present conviction that the Holy Spirit desired him to go back to France was just as strong as that other conviction, two years earlier, when he had felt the same Spirit urging him to depart for Italy. Neither warnings nor protests could deflect him from his purpose. All the appeals of Petrarch, the supplications of the Infante Pedro of Aragon, who had become a Franciscan, and even the powerful voice of St Bridget of Sweden had been unable to hold him back. Weary and sick of heart, but resolved in his purpose, the Pope had returned to Avignon.

It was then that the great controversy concerning the 'Babylonian captivity' reached its climax. National passions ran riot. In order to keep the pontiff within their tutelage the French had lauded the strength of their kingdom, the wisdom and goodness of their king, Charles V, the reputation of the University of Paris (which was in fact declining) and had even gone so far as to brag about the succulence of their national dishes and the fine bouquet of their wines: 'Rome is where the Pope is!' they had vehemently declared. The Italians, on the other hand, had invoked the witness of history, tradition and a thousand and one memories of glory and of loyalty, while Dante had provided them with several sublime poems with which they were able to proclaim the eclipse of the motherland of Western Christendom. It is in the atmosphere provoked by this national duel that the reader must interpret the indictments of Avignon, contained, for example, in the *Apologia* of Petrarch, published in 1373: Blessed Rome, city conse-crated by the blood of martyrs, and capital of the whole world, was waiting and yearning for her most important citizen! So ran the poet's appeal. But when Ancel Choquard, the representative of the King of France, came to speak before Urban V, he opened his harangue with this striking piece of dialogue: '*Quo vadis, domine?*'—'I am going back to Rome.'—'What, to be crucified there all over again?' And this argument too seemed well worth serious consideration. . . .

However, this mighty din of claim and counter-claim, biblical quotations and scurrility was heard only within the rather narrow circles of the intelligentsia. The common people, on the other hand, were sensitive to quite another type of propaganda, to the whole of that vast wave of sentiment whose source was Joachim of Flora,[1] a sentiment broadcast far and wide by the Franciscan 'Spirituals.' The age of the Holy Spirit was drawing nigh! The Church as now con-stituted, sullied as she was by abuses and scandals, was about to slide headlong into the abyss; a community of saints would be established in her place, composed of the elect who would be divinely singled out at the end of the world. For the end of the world was very close, and all the signs denoting it in Holy Scripture were now apparent. In this apocalyptic atmosphere, the 'Babylonian captivity' was bound to be interpreted as evidence of the wrath of God.

From an enormous mass of treatises, lampoons and prophecies, whose detail is of scant important but whose very existence and abundance have a symbolic value, one single work stands out. It is the

---

[1] The reader is directed to this name in the index to *Cathedral and Crusade* and, in particular, to the paragraphs devoted to this extraordinary character in the final chapter of that book (Section 2).

only work of its kind which is still readable today: the *Revelations* of St Bridget of Sweden (1302–73). Bridget was the daughter of the governor of Uppland. At seventeen she had married Ulf Gudmarsson, but had very soon been left a widow with eight young children. She had withdrawn from the world, and founded the Order of the Blessed Saviour, travelling to Rome to seek official recognition of her work. It took her twenty years of persistent struggle to obtain her end, for approval was not given until three years before her death. Over a period of some twenty-five years, her life of solitary contemplation had been punctuated by a series of visions, whose apocalyptic character is self-evident. The Swedish nun had seen the sign of blood—that self-same sign which St Catherine of Siena was to feel imprinted upon herself and upon the world with such visionary force—graven upon the tragic face of Christendom. To Bridget too Avignon had seemed the abomination of the Devil, the Satanic thorn in the Church's flesh. She declared that she had heard Christ Himself condemn the court of the French popes for its cupidity, its pride and its debaucheries, and that Our Lord had accused those same popes of populating Hell. In her terrible prophesying, she had said of Innocent VI that he was 'more abominable than the Jewish usurers, more treacherous than Judas, more cruel than Pilate,' and that she had seen him tumbling into the bottomless abyss 'like a heavy stone.' Bridget had been in Rome at the same time as Urban V. She had begged him to remain there, in spite of everything and everybody; and when the Pope had died very shortly after his return to Avignon, the prophetess had proclaimed, in tones louder and more confident than ever, that his death was striking proof indeed of the wrath of God.

This therefore was the climate of opinion in 1370, the year in which Urban V rendered up his gentle and saintly soul to God. In such a climate men who had the welfare of the Church at heart pondered the wisdom of the return to Avignon. A certain cardinal, Pierre Roger de Beaufort, had been present at the conversations between the Pope and the Swedish saint; and in fact it was this same cardinal who had been chosen by an exceptionally brief conclave to succeed Urban. Had Gregory XI been impressed by the words he had heard fall from Bridget's lips? At all events no sooner had he been crowned than he began to reconsider the idea of returning to Rome. The obstacles in his path were numerous; Visconti was once more attacking the Church's domains; the money with which to combat him was lacking; and Rome was in fresh turmoil. But at least—thanks to the pontiff—some sort of peace had been concluded between France and England by the Truce of Bruges. Over a period of several months Gregory had prepared for the great adventure, pawning his own jewels, taxing the bishops, and raising mercenary bands; even as he did so he was not ashamed to confess his fears, or to let men see his obvious hesitation.

At last everything seemed almost ready. Despite the pressure brought to bear on him by the King of France, the Avignonese and several of the cardinals, Gregory XI was openly referring to his departure for Rome as imminent, when a new development again jeopardized the project. Quite suddenly Florence precipitated herself into the struggle. She accused the papal authorities of wishing to invade Tuscany, and reproached them for having allowed its population to die of hunger while their own granaries were bursting. Emissaries of the red lily ranged far and wide throughout the Papal States, persuading the inhabitants to rebel against their French governors. They did not need much urging: in three months all Albornoz's work had been destroyed. The council of eight burgesses, the 'Eight Saints,' who ruled Florence with a rod of iron, seemed able to flout the Pope's authority.

Gregory XI was not the sort of man to allow himself to be held up to ridicule in this way. Florence was expelled from the Church's fold and laid under interdict; Christian princes were invited to expel all Florentine merchants from their kingdoms, and eagerly complied. One man of steel, Cardinal Robert of Geneva, had offered to go to Italy to restore order there, and the Pope had accepted his offer. As a result a dreadful war raged throughout the whole peninsula: mercenaries hired by the Papacy—Bretons under Malestroit, English under Hawkwood—had laid Tuscany waste, crushing all those who, near or far, were suspected of being Florentine sympathizers, recapturing the rebel fortresses belonging to the states of the Church, and, in addition, perpetrating innumerable acts of pillage and wanton cruelty. A devasted Florence, surrounded by hostile forces, gasped for life, and was ready to sue for peace; and Visconti was actually proposing to act as mediator when Gregory XI, risking all to gain all, decided to leave Avignon and return to Rome.

This chapter in the Church's history closed with an impressive and public appeal. It is easy to imagine the saintly pontiff, who had a most lofty conception of the duties of his office, sitting in the embrasure of one of those deep Gothic windows at Avignon, looking down on the yellow-roofed city and the purple countryside around it, pondering on what God really expected of him. The Duke of Anjou, representing the King of France, had come to tell him yet again that he was about to expose the triple crown to the direst outrages it had ever suffered; but on behalf of the Italians—and of Mother Church herself perhaps— Jacopo Orsini had replied: 'Has anyone ever seen a kingdom properly governed with its master absent?' And Gregory felt himself accountable to God for very much more than a mere kingdom. From month to month he put back the appointed date, still hesitating to take the final step, imposing 'perpetual silence' upon anyone who tried to remind him of the obstacles in the way of his journey, but unable to silence his own fears. . . . Would this well-intentioned man ever have had enough determination to crush all his misgivings and set off, despite everything, for that mystical Bride who awaited him at the Apostle's tomb, had not one inspired voice resounded in his ears like that of a herald of the Holy Spirit Himself?

THE MISSION OF ST CATHERINE OF SIENA

Towards the end of spring 1376 there appeared, in the midst of that excitable little world which was the Papal Court, a woman whom the Italians called 'la mantellata.' Dressed in plain black and white, she was, it had to be admitted, a disappointment. Legend had preceded this obscure religious. She had dared to send the Pope a letter couched in terms of reprimand; and her audacity might well seem justified, were it true, as was commonly asserted, that she had worked many miracles, that her slightest word was prophetic, and that she was coming in person to Avignon to bring Gregory XI a message entrusted to her by Christ Himself. It needed nothing less than this rumour to make the blasé, suspicious cardinals take some heed of the youthful visitor. But they saw only an insignificant little nun, whose charm and bearing impressed no one, who spoke neither French nor Latin, but only the Tuscan of the lower classes, and who, though she often said highly disagreeable things, neither healed the sick nor raised the dead to life.

Indeed, so far as outward appearances were concerned, there was nothing particularly attractive about Catherine of Siena. To those privileged souls who knew her well, she was a radiant and soul-stirring figure, possessed of that beauty which bears no relation to mortal standards, but which haloes the heads of those upon whom the Spirit has alighted with a supernatural brilliance all its own. She had an ineffable tenderness and a boundless generosity which made her love her fellow men just as she found them, despite their abjection and their misery; indeed one might go further and say that she loved them *because of* their imperfections. But it was on account of this abjection and this misery that she was forced to be stern, severe and pitiless; for the circumstances were of a kind in which love of men can be expressed by violence alone, and in which the gentlest of souls must gird itself with steel. The nun from Siena subsisted wholly on the charity of Christ, but she knew only too well how terrible this charity can be. Catherine's spiritual make-up contained none of the grace, the delicacy or the vivacity which Teresa of Avila was to possess in such abundance.

She gave an impression of unrelieved tension and turmoil, like a dedicated warrior. 'I want . . .!' These two words returned to her lips again and again. And yet, could this woman whom God was summoning to undertake such fierce battles in His Name, and upon whose shoulders the age was placing so heavy a burden, really have been any different?

Catherine had first heard God's call when she was still a very young child, at an age when most children are thinking only of the next game they want to play. When she was but six years old [1] her predestined eyes had seen the Heavens open and enjoyed a foretaste of Paradise; at the age of seven she had contracted a mystical marriage with the Child Jesus. From that day forward she had dedicated her whole life to Our Lord with a frenzied strength that nothing could overcome, her soul vowed to the arduous task of bringing the sinful world back to Christ. Very soon rumours concerning her had spread throughout fair Siena with its rose-red buildings lying on three hillsides like some lovely three-petalled flower; and those rumours not only became current in the tenements of the common people, but even percolated to the rich, dark rooms of the town houses owned by the wealthy merchants, with their slender turrets rearing up against the skyline. It was said that the young Catherine, the twenty-fifth child of the Benincasa family, had been blessed by a series of astonishing visions, and that she was living like a recluse in the most secluded part of her father's house, in the Oca quarter of the town. Folk in the most pleasant city in Tuscany were not much given to mysticism; but they had enough religious faith to feel no surprise that the Carpenter's Son had chosen the unknown daughter of a humble dyer to deliver His message to the world.

Moreover Catherine's visions had continued: in truth she lived her life in an astonishing intimacy with the greater mysteries of the divine. One night St Dominic appeared to her in a dream, showing her a religious habit which she instantly recognized: it was that worn by the Sisters of Mercy, a kind of Tertiary Order which sought its members from the women and girls of the town, and devoted itself to works of prayer and charity. At once the little Catherine had but one idea: that she herself should wear the white habit and black cloak of the 'mantellatas.' So strange did her destiny seem that she was forced to wait some time before this happiness was granted her. When she was finally admitted to the order she felt herself confirmed in the particular vocation which was hers: 'I was chosen and sent on to this earth in order to right a great scandal,' she declared; like her spiritual father,

[1] The date of Catherine's birth is a matter of some argument: many authors accept 1347. (E. Jourdan, 'La Date de naissance de Ste Catherine,' in *Analecta Bol*, 1922, p. 315, confirms 1347, in opposition to the date suggested by Fawtier.)

the founder, it was to be her task to proclaim God's truth and justice to mankind. She spent her whole life doing simply this.

Thus the outspoken young woman who toiled up the slope leading to the Palais des Doms in 1376 was herself the realization of one of God's mysteries—the coexistence in one human being of the purest of mystical experiences (the most irreconcilable with the accepted norms of reason) and of an incessant practical activity befitting a politician, a diplomat or a lawyer. Throughout the whole of her short life the living bond between Catherine and Him who had called her to Him by name was never once severed. This woman could read the hearts of men and lived for fifty-five days on no food but the sacramental species; she conversed with Christ so coherently that she could often recall His very words, and bequeathed them to posterity in one of the most valuable of spiritual treatises; above all, her body eventually received the terrible grace of the stigmata, as had that of St Francis before her. Yet she was the selfsame woman who forced her way into the city squares and the town halls, and at length into the heart of the Papal Curia itself, boldly proclaiming her formidable admonitions in God's Name. For, even in her ecstatic trances, Catherine saw the distress of Him whose Church was betraying Him, and she sensed the nearness of His wrath. Her mysticism was thus of a realistic and concrete kind, entirely orientated towards precept and example, and it was completely linked with her every action.

Catherine had not had to will this action herself: Another had willed it for her. She had but to leave her retreat, to mingle with her fellow citizens, to devote herself—and with what heroic simplicity!—to caring for the sick, in order to dazzle the eyes of every bystander with that 'soul of fire' which, as she confessed, was hers. When she was less than eighteen years of age her 'brave little brigade' had already formed itself around her, quite spontaneously. It contained quite a large number of men and women of every age and condition, who regarded her as their leader, as the one person who would lead them to the Father, and who, astonishing though it may seem, called her their 'dolcissima mamma,' their most gentle and sweet mother. This little group of fervent Christians read the *Divine Comedy*, meditated upon the mystics and combed the articles of St Thomas's *Summa* in an effort to discover what God expected from the men of that insecure and unhappy age.

It was thus that Catherine came to feel the entire weight of Christendom resting upon her shoulders. Her influence very soon spread beyond the Tuscan boundaries; the whole of Italy knew about her. In France and in the Empire, as well as at Avignon, folk learnt that it seemed possible that a virgin from Siena had been entrusted by God with a mysterious mission; and certain cardinals were uneasy on this account, and ready to suspect the saint's orthodoxy. But the more that Catherine learnt to know the world and the people in it, the more cruelly she felt their anguish and distress. Everything that she saw horrified her and plunged her deeper into despair. Italy was more abandoned to bloody internecine strife than ever; town fought against town, faction against faction, Guelph against Ghibelline. Every incident was marked by acts of atrocious cruelty, which laid bare the darkest recesses of the human soul; priests were flayed alive, prisoners thrown to the dogs, condemned persons buried while they still lived and breathed, and those enormous massacres which were perpetrated by the seasoned troopers of the mercenary companies were a commonplace everywhere. Morality could only stand to lose from these appalling disorders, and depravity gained a spreading stranglehold upon society, a depravity so shameless that it revelled in ostentation. There was worse to come, and it was on the subject of this grievous truth that Christ spoke with Catherine. In the Church itself, Christ's mystical Bride, the same symptoms of malaise were visible. The echoes which filtered through to Italy from the papal palace at Avignon, though of course borne by Italians who were hardly well disposed towards the French popes, were largely founded upon fact, and fully justified all Catherine's fears and strictures. It was while meditating upon this universal abjection that the staunch-hearted maid from Siena had uttered these terrible words: 'Alas, I am dying, and yet I cannot die!'

Who made her decide to take the road for France, and go there to talk to the Vicar of Christ in person? Serious reflection makes it clear that her mission was determined solely by her own conscience, in other words, by the voice of God. Catherine possessed such a lofty and noble conception of the Church, and such a profound love for 'him who is Christ upon this earth,' that she could never have admitted that he was unable to take the necessary steps and snatch Christendom from the abyss that gaped wide, ready to engulf it. If there is any truth in the suggestion advanced by several historians that she was sent by the Florentines as their ambassador, to try to reconcile them with the Pope, then her mission was abortive. For Gregory XI, who was only too conversant with the cunning manœuvres of the city of the red lily, declared soon afterwards: 'Either I shall destroy Florence or Florence will destroy the Church.' One thing, however, is quite clear: when Catherine reached Avignon she had been entrusted with a mission far more important than any diplomatic task; she was indeed the living voice of the whole Christian conscience, of that divided, sullied and crucified Church whom Christ had charged her to lead back to His fold.

So far as we know Catherine's message to Gregory can be summed up very simply: he must reform the Church and establish peace among warring Christians; to do this he must put an end to the Great Absence, to the Avignonese exile which was depriving Christendom of its rightful capital, the city consecrated by the Apostle Peter's blood; and finally, he must unite all the armies of the baptized world in the only legitimate enterprise open to them, the Crusade. As the true spiritual daughter of St Dominic, and, in many respects, as the last witness of the medieval Church, Catherine would have spoken exactly as St Bernard had done. It is of small consequence that, in the political sense —as historical criticism has been so anxious to prove—her labours were less effective than biographers, from Raymond of Capua onwards, have pretended, and that, even before she visited him, Gregory XI had already decided to leave Avignon. Catherine's role was something far greater than a politician's: she played the part of a prophet and a witness of the events that were unfolding. At the very moment when the Pope, a prey to conflicting influences and intrigues, was considering postponing his decision yet again, how vital must have been the pressure brought to bear upon him by the vehement pleading of the Tuscan mystic, who spoke to him in the name of the supreme authorities—God and the Church.

'I do not ask you to advise me, but to give me a sign of God's will!' said Gregory XI to the youthful prophetess at the end of their conversations. What was that sign? The chronicle does not tell us, but only one answer is possible. In that dread hour, when the armies of Robert of Geneva, the Breton bandits of Malestroit and the mercenaries of John Hawkwood were unleashing a fresh wave of slaughter upon Italy; when, in the depths of her soul, locked in prophetic frenzy, she glimpsed, beyond all the glory of the Pope's return, the terrible calamities that would fall upon the Church thereafter, surely there was only one sign which Catherine could possibly have given. She herself bore it upon her living, stigmatized flesh: the sign of the redeeming Passion, of the blood of Christ to which she refers in all her mystical writings, as the sole joy and giver of life. Nothing was more apt to show the world that it could achieve salvation only through suffering and sacrifice. Just as she had seen the grace of God penetrate the soul of a young condemned prisoner, whom she had accompanied to the block, at the very instant when the blood had gushed from his severed head, seeming to cleanse him of his guilt, so also, in the depths of her agony, Catherine hoped that all Christendom would be redeemed by the blood shed for it by Christ and, if it could but find a way to union with Him, by the blood of men as well. She had been sent by God to say this, and only this: her mission was to remind the world of the sign of Blood.

Appearances of Might and Prestige

If appearances alone are considered, that distress, of which the maid from Siena was regarded by her contemporaries as the living expression, was hardly justified. At the time when Gregory XI was re-establishing himself in Rome, the Church continued to offer a most imposing façade to the world, and the keenest eye was needed in order to detect those many fissures which heralded the collapse of her majestic edifice.

The geographical extent of Christendom included all northern, western, central and Mediterranean Europe. Islam retained only one small bridge-head on the continent, in the extreme south of the Iberian peninsula, around Granada. The danger implicit in the existence of the pagan principality of Lithuania, which jutted out like a wedge between Courland and Prussia as far as the Baltic, was about to disappear: the Gospel was beginning to penetrate that region, and very soon afterwards, on the occasion of his marriage to Hedwiga of Poland (1386), Duke Ladislas Jagellon officially proclaimed the victory of Christ in his domains. It was true that, in the east, Roman Catholicism had been obliged to abandon Serbia, Bulgaria and Russia, the Balkan highlands and the Russian plains, to the schismatic patriarchs of Byzantium. But faith in a reconciliation between East and West remained firmly rooted in the souls of all Christian folk, and the personal submission of the Emperor John Palaeologus V in 1369 was considered a prelude to the complete reunion of the two halves of Christ's Church.

To be sure, one danger undoubtedly existed. As viewed from Paris or Rome it might appear far enough away as yet, but it was sufficient to cause observant minds considerable anxiety. The Ottoman Turks [1] had recently overwhelmed Asia Minor, crossed the Bosphorus, gained a narrow foothold in Europe and skirted Constantinople, thus cutting her off from her Thracian granaries. Their pirates were now roving the Aegean Sea, while the Syriac-Egyptian Empire at Cairo had lately succeeded in wiping out the heroic little Christian community in Lesser Armenia. But the vast bulk of Christian opinion did not evaluate the Moslem peril accurately. A few generous-hearted spirits, of a somewhat fanciful type, waxed enthusiastic over various crusading projects. These were founded more on the idea of running the course of 'God's adventure,' in the sense understood by the Fathers, than on reasons of practical politics; no one considered it possible that Asia might conquer Christian Europe on the field of battle and eventually threaten her very existence.

Many circumstances also were believed to indicate an approaching

[1] See Chapter II, section: 'The Turkish Tidal Wave Attacks Christendom.'

victory of the Cross in that huge, mysterious continent which Western missionaries and traders had been penetrating for more than a century. In Palestine itself Friar Roger Guerin had succeeded in purchasing the Holy Places from the Sultan of Egypt, and had built there the religious houses of Sion and the Holy Sepulchre, the Bethlehem Grotto, and even an enormous hostelry, to which pilgrims flocked in thousands. Better still, in 1362 the Moslems had allowed Western craftsmen to enter Palestine and begin work on two churches, one marking the site of Our Lady's Dormition, the other that of Christ's Agony in Gethsemane. This implanting of Christianity in Asian soil was equally apparent in Persia. Notwithstanding an Islamic revival, missionaries had held their ground since 1318, when Pope John XXII had raised the new city of Sultanyeh to metropolitan rank with the Dominican archbishop Franco of Perugia at its head; and their influence was such that in 1402 one of them, Archbishop Jean Lycenes, a native of Bruges, was appointed ambassador to the French Court by Tamburlane. Even farther afield, in the heart of China, the prodigious results obtained at the beginning of the century by John of Montecorvino,[1] first Archbishop of Peking, seemed full of promise. In 1370, on the morrow of the revolution which had swept the Ming dynasty to power, the Holy See dispatched a new archbishop, William of Prato, with twelve companions, unaware, however, that the new rulers of China possessed none of the pro-Christian sympathies which had characterized the Mongol emperors.

While the evangelical impulse was continually expanding Christian territory, a singularly close-knit web of ecclesiastical institutions spread across those lands which the Church had won long before. Chapels, oratories, churches, monasteries, colleges, cathedrals: such marks of the Church's presence in the ancient European kingdoms were innumerable. Parishes, bishoprics and provinces inscribed upon the map the limits within which the faithful lived,[2] while ten centuries of monasticism had superimposed the map of its own foundations, so that England alone, to take but one example, counted no fewer than nine hundred religious houses of every type and of every Order—

[1] See the Index to the author's *Cathedral and Crusade*.
[2] This map is very variable in character, and the Church's impress differs according to the area concerned. Dioceses' dimensions varied a great deal; for example, that of Orange comprised some 190 square miles, while Bourges was about 10,000 square miles in area. Italy had 225 bishoprics, but England had only 21. The dioceses themselves contained a very unequal number of parishes: Amiens, for instance, had 763, Sens, which was roughly the same size, 580. Needless to say, the income derived from the different ecclesiastical benefices was just as variable: that of Paris was ten times greater than Vienne in Dauphine and thirty times greater than Die. Here we are concerned only with the external aspects of the imprint left by Christianity upon its ancient baptized territories: the question of religious practice is more difficult to assess. (It is treated in Chapter III, section: 'A Faith that was Still Very Much Alive.')

B

Benedictines, Cistercians, Augustinians, hermits, Franciscans, Dominicans, Carmelites and so on. It is difficult for us to imagine the power of the clergy at that time or their influence in every field of human activity. Their numbers far exceeded the effective strength necessary for parochial and analogous duties. Hence the vast army of tonsured clerks, whose status conferred valuable privileges, overflowed into the courts of kings, the castles of noblemen and the universities, as well as into the solitude of hermitages. The Church's power, in fact, rested upon a host of clerics, who may have comprised one-tenth of the adult population.

At the summit of this hierarchy of men and institutions stood their supreme head, the Pope, successor of St Peter and God's Anointed. His prestige remained enormous. Certain tendencies had been manifest ever since the eleventh-century reforms which Gregory VII had carefully defined in his *Dictatus papae*. These had been further elaborated, for example, by St Bernard who had recognized a 'plenitude of power' possessed by the Vicar of Christ. Innocent III and the jurists of the thirteenth century had finally erected them into a body of doctrine, and had thus created a veritable papal monarchy, one of the most powerful monarchies of the age to which the popes at Avignon had put the finishing touches.

The Apostle's successor was presented to the world as ruler and leader, as law-giver and judge. His legislative activity dated from the twelfth century, when the Canon Law had been founded upon bases furnished by the *Decretum* of Gratian.[1] Only the Pope could add to the existing body of ecclesiastical law. This had been done by Gregory IX in his Five Books, by Boniface VIII in his 'Sextus,' by Clement V in his 'Clementine Constitutions' and by John XXII in his 'Extravagantes.' As judge the Pope dealt with the more important cases in which prelates were implicated, received appeals from every sector of ecclesiastical jurisdiction and absolved the most heinous sins at the tribunal of penitence. As supreme disciplinarian he alone had the right to promote reform in the measure in which he judged it necessary, and whoever attempted to effect it without him was immediately chastized, as was done in the case of the Franciscan 'Spirituals.'

One of the objectives most tenaciously pursued by the Avignonese popes had been the capture of benefices, in other words, pontifical control of clerical nominations. Beginning in 1265, in the bull *Licet Ecclesiarum*, Clement IV had laid down the principle that the Pope, representing Christ Himself, possessed right to dispose of all ecclesiastical offices; but in practice the Holy See intervened in a limited number of instances, sometimes by acting as arbiter in a disputed

[1] See *Cathedral and Crusade*, Chapter XIV, section: 'Philip the Fair and the Outrage of Anagni.'

election, sometimes by using diplomacy or compulsion to replace a particular dignitary. In the fourteenth century the Pope had secured absolute control of nominations, not only in the cases laid down by John XXII's constitution *Ex Debito*; he could create this right of appointment whenever he pleased, by simply declaring any vacancy a 'reserve.' Thus we find Gregory XI retaining control of all episcopal churches and monasteries that fell vacant during his reign. Furthermore the 'expectative grace' enabled the Pope to name a successor to a benefice even when it was still occupied by another incumbent. In this way the temporal power lost much ground to the papal authority: even in France, whose monarch had taken advantage of his dramatic quarrel with Boniface VIII to protest against the system of reserves, papal intervention in matters concerning benefices had continued to develop steadily throughout the century, making the kings at Paris pay dearly for the various privileges they received from the pontiffs at Avignon.

Side by side with this control over the Catholic hierarchy, another phenomenon is observed: the extension and increasing complexity of the papal financial system. Ever since the first half of the thirteenth century the Papacy had been preoccupied with the development of its resources; it was no longer satisfied with the revenues it drew from the States of the Church, Peter's Pence, and those moneys contributed by the kingdoms and other societies under its protection. The tenth, originally levied to finance the crusades, had survived even though they had ceased. The 'general dues' of the prelates, the 'annates' paid by incumbents who were minors, the amounts levied upon benefices while they were vacant, the 'relief' demanded from the estates of deceased clerks, all these constituted a rich source of supply, to which, as must be recognized, the popes at Avignon devoted their most careful attention. Since their budget showed a permanent deficit, they strained their ingenuity to multiply the number of imposts and taxes, going so far as to arrogate to themselves the dues which the bishops and other dignitaries received on the occasion of the canonical visits which they made to the various institutions entrusted to their care. These excesses were to have the most unfortunate consequences.

In order to cope with their many tasks the popes had constructed a strongly centralized governmental machine and we are now far removed from that quasi-patriarchal power which had satisfied the medieval Papacy. No council had been held since that of Vienne (1311), which settled the question of the Templars. Instead the pontiffs had surrounded themselves with advisory bodies which they nominated, but which were never permitted to dominate them in any way. It was the popes who convoked consistories, consulting them only on questions of their own choosing; while some of them even refused to be bound by promises made in presence of the Sacred College before their election.

As possessors of a greatly extended authority, the Sovereign Pontiffs ruled by means of bureaucratic departments; and the Avignonese popes had brought these departments to a degree of perfection as yet unequalled anywhere else. The Chancellery drafted, engrossed and dispatched their edicts with stringent precautions to discourage forgery. The office of the Penitentiary took cognizance of cases requiring the exercise of the Pope's spiritual authority. The tribunal of the Sacred Rota gave judgment in cases reserved to the Holy See. The Apostolic Camera managed papal finances and controlled several associated departments which were continually on circuit. A system of this kind was well able to compete with those of the best-constituted secular government, such as that of France, which had actually been using Avignonese methods since the reign of Philip V.

All this, however, was but the outward expression of the enormous authority enjoyed by the Pope at that time. While exercising still more extensive powers over the Church, which he regarded as a perfect and completely independent society, he refused to abdicate a single one of his prerogatives over the secular world. Because the spiritual prevailed over the temporal 'as the soul dominates the body,' to quote Innocent III; because the Vicar of Christ held in his hand 'the two swords,' one of which he wielded directly to govern the Church, and the other which he delegated to temporal rulers in order that they might manage the affairs of the world, according to the doctrine expressed by Boniface VIII in *Unam Sanctam* (1302); because he was still, in his own eyes and in the eyes of the vast majority of men, the one and only rightful master of the monarchy of the baptized, for all these reasons the Pope had, in theory, abandoned none of the most categoric theological concepts of his predecessors. The world had seen him refuse the Empire to Louis of Bavaria in order to bestow it upon Charles of Moravia, and had heard him claim to mediate between France and England, Venice and Genoa, as well as in various feudal differences. Catherine of Siena, the perfect manifestation of the spirit of her age, could think only in terms of a world taken in hand by the Church, absorbed by her and ruled by her; she believed wholeheartedly in the principle of sacerdotal government, and in the omnipotence of the Pope, 'who is Christ upon this earth.' The Sienese mystic and the canon lawyers were united in proclaiming the unparalleled glory of this hierarchized, highly organized Church, invested by God with that omnipotence which the pontiff exercised in all its fullness; and this conviction was accepted by the generality of the faithful.

THE BURDEN OF THE WORLD

The chronicler Raymond of Capua describes how, in January 1380, exactly three weeks before her heavenly Bridegroom summoned her to join Him in Paradise, St Catherine was kneeling in prayer in one of the chapels of St Peter's at Rome. She raised her eyes to the mosaic which adorned the apse, and fell to the ground moaning. The mosaic depicted the 'navicella,' the vessel of the Church, tossing upon a raging sea which was about to engulf it. The apostolic steersman was at the helm, but he seemed incapable of bringing the frail craft safely into harbour. Christ alone was supporting it in His all-powerful arms. . . . Afterwards, when Catherine was asked the reason for her distress, she replied that she felt as though she were bearing the entire weight of this storm-tossed vessel upon her own shoulders—and the burden was oh! so intolerably great! In a moment of agonizing clarity she had wondered whether Our Lord Himself would be able to prevent it from foundering.

The mystic's vision corresponded all too completely with reality. It was quite true that, as the fourteenth century drew to its close, the winds of history were everywhere quickening to a tempest, and the Christian world, represented by that ship, seemed too heavily laden to survive the dangers confronting it. Some retouching was needed by the majestic picture of the mighty, well-ordered Church, conscious both of her power and her rights; and Christendom in all its aspects presented some highly disturbing symptoms.

Firstly let us deal with the material plane.[1] The prodigious vitality manifested by the West during the great centuries of the Middle Ages seemed spent; the demographic flood-tide, which had raised the level of the whole of medieval society since the year 1000, was slackening, and even beginning to ebb. In 1789 France would possess no more 'hearths' (i.e. families) than she had done in 1328. The Black Death, which laid waste nearly the whole of Europe between 1347 and 1349, wrought almost unbelievable havoc, wiping out entire villages, reducing towns to a tenth or even a twentieth of their former populations, exterminating, according to the most moderate estimates, one-third of the inhabitants of Europe, and leaving behind it a stench of the charnel-house and a terrible anguish. Lethal war soon followed, to assist in the task of destruction, and quickly learned to labour for long periods without respite, especially in France. The consequences of these catastrophies were numerous and grave in every sphere of activity: the economy gasped for life, trade was ruined, the religious houses were deserted, and their buildings allowed to fall into decay

[1] This sums up what has already been described in more detail in the final chapter of *Cathedral and Crusade*.

along with their spiritual life. Perhaps the lowering in quality of Europe's leading men should be attributed to this universal diminution of vitality, to a kind of physiological ageing of society. For their number had certainly grown smaller, and they were not of the calibre of those who did honour to the great epoch just ended. Save in regard to personal virtues, St Bernardino and St Vincent Ferrer were not the equals of St Bernard or St Francis; and in no respect can Martin V be weighed against Boniface VIII, or Eugenius IV against Innocent III, any more than can Charles V of France be compared with St Louis, or the Emperor Charles IV with his predecessor, Frederick II. All these facts are indisputable evidence of decline, but there was something even worse. This society, stricken in its very vitals, was controlled by secret and formidable forces. Engelbert of Admont, writing at the beginning of the fourteenth century, produced a work in which he established a similarity between the last days of the Roman Empire and his own. He prophesied that Antichrist would soon appear (a belief common enough at that time), and indicated the signs of his coming. Basing his argument upon a famous passage from St Paul's epistle to the Thessalonians, Engelbert picked out the three principal omens, which he called 'the three ruptures': the human soul would rebel against belief; Christians would rise in revolt against the legitimate authority of the Holy See; and their national states would shatter the ancient unity of the baptized peoples of Europe. This monk was an excellent prophet; these signs were not, as all men who live at turning-points of history tend to think, those of the end of *the* world, but they certainly heralded the end of *a* world, the end of one particular type of society.

The symptoms of this triple crisis had been numerous and easily discernible for some time past: the crisis of authority, the crisis of unity and, conditioning both, the crisis in men's souls, in their consciences and in their minds. The last-named involved not merely diminution of spiritual fervour or temporary relaxation of discipline. Such phenomena had been not infrequent in the course of the Church's history; it had been found possible to check them by moral reforms of the type effected in the eleventh century by Cluny, in the twelfth by St Bernard and St Norbert, and in the thirteenth by St Francis and St Dominic, all of whom restored the Christian soul to a true understanding of its loyalties and its needs. The present situation was far more serious. Those who censured the Church were now questioning her authority—her external authority, as well as that which she had for so long exerted over men's minds and souls. Human learning shifted from its traditional bases: faith was no longer discussed *per se*, but instead its relationships with reason and knowledge. So, whereas in earlier times those who had fought the Church had dreamed only of transforming her—the heretic is essentially a believer—a class of minds began to appear whose thoughts ranged altogether outside her limits. Literature, philosophy, science, art—all intellectual activities were on the verge of becoming secularized. The magnificent internal unity of the medieval mind, which regarded faith and submission to Christian teaching, not as fetters, but as the means of binding itself to absolute truth, was now threatened. The 'rebellion' foretold by the monk of Admont was drawing very near.

In this perilous hour the organic unity of the Middle Ages, moral, social and political, seemed under attack. Christendom, which was first and foremost an ideal which had been translated into living fact, could not survive the collapse of that ideal. From the end of the twelfth century onwards numerous signs had made clear how many new forces were working efficaciously against it. Political evolution was tending to the concentration of power in the hands of monarchs, and to a more urgent self-awareness among the national groupings which these same monarchs were transforming into autonomous units. Nation-states, each confronting the rest, were about to replace Christendom. Gone was the era of crusades, of those great collective enterprises waged by all Christians under papal leadership, regardless of their nationality. This does not mean that the danger to which Christendom had repeatedly reacted had become less imminent. Quite the contrary was the case. Resting on the Asian fringes, his greedy eyes turned towards Europe, the Turk was merely awaiting the chance to launch his decisive offensive against her, an offensive which would enable him to establish his rule over quite a sizable section of the continent.

But if Christian unity was being gravely undermined, the very authority of the Church, its guide and guarantor, was no less seriously threatened, her grandiose appearance notwithstanding. The dreadful conflict at the turn of the fourteenth century, when Philip the Fair of France resorted to violence in his dispute with Pope Boniface VIII, a dispute which ended in the famous 'Outrage of Anagni,' [1] showed all too clearly how precarious had become the power of the successors of Gregory VII and Innocent III. The establishment of the Holy See at Avignon had done nothing to restore an authority which secular governments could henceforth suspect of acting too willingly in the interests of France. Worse still, that authority was questioned not only in practice, on the political plane, but had begun to be disputed also upon legal grounds also. The revival of Roman jurisprudence resulted in a decline in the prestige of the canon law. The latter was founded upon divine institutions and ecclesiastical rules, whereas the new branch of learning regarded itself as self-sufficient. Within the bosom of the Church herself, moreover, ideological trends seemed to

[1] See the final chapter of *Cathedral and Crusade*, section: 'Philip the Fair and the Outrage of Anagni.'

call in question the traditional bases of her organization. Ockham, Marsilio of Padua and their pupils debated the very principle of papal authority, to which they opposed the principle of the Church as a whole, the collectivity of the faithful; and the first murmurs began to circulate suggesting that it might be necessary to impose the control of the Council, the expression of the universal Church, upon a failing Papacy. The advocates of these theories were only awaiting a chance to proclaim them from the house tops; and the opportunity was afforded in the shape of a disputed papal election resulting in schism, an incident not by any means uncommon in the Church's history, but which, on this occasion, was to lead to the most dramatic consequences.

The gravity of the situation was extreme. In the course of centuries Holy Church had survived many ordeals, but that which threatened her towards the middle of the fourteenth century seemed as if it must be the worst of all. Needless to say there were other more favourable signs which enabled the devout Christian to hope that this ordeal too would be surmounted. Spiritually minded men and women, and mystics, whose number was considerable, were working to renovate the Christian soul from within. The remarkable awakening apparent in certain fields of the mind, in the progress of the classics and in scientific discovery, might yet endow Christian intelligence and sensibility with some new weapons. But the vital question was this: could Christianity, exposed to this triple crisis, maintain the grip upon society which it had possessed in the preceding era ? And if the creaking audible on every side were really that of the sorely strained bark, swollen by the rising sap of spring, was the Church still capable of guiding this young and violent impulse? For a whole century, and with increasing urgency, events laboured to confront history with this problem. Much time elapsed before an answer was received.

THE GREAT SCHISM IN THE WEST

Of the three crises that concerning the Church's authority was the one which struck contemporaries most forcibly; moreover it was a shock to the Church, and presented her with a redoubtable problem. The dark forebodings which had filled Gregory XI with such anguish during the final months of his life were to be all too vividly confirmed in the events which followed his death. Gregory foresaw the explosive product that would result from a mixture of Avignonese intrigue and Roman 'combinazione,' and in an attempt to forestall the worst consequences he ordered that the conclave should meet immediately after his death, without waiting for the arrival of the cardinals from distant regions, and that the election of the new pope should be made by means of a simple majority. But it need hardly be said that the flimsy paper on which this bull was written was utterly inadequate to confront the storm that was about to break!

Gregory XI died on 27th March 1378. The sixteen cardinals who were then in Rome immediately assembled and spent ten days in informal talks. The conclave had not yet begun: the Princes of the Church were simply trying to come to an agreement among themselves, but they might as well have attempted to square the circle. The cardinals were split into three factions of unequal weight: four Italians, five from the 'French party' and seven 'Limousins,' who were deeply distrusted by their compatriots.[1] However, one unforeseen *de facto* elector had also to be reckoned with—the Roman mob, which was hammering at the walls of the Vatican, and whose shouts were to jar unpleasantly upon the ears of the conclave: 'We want a Roman—otherwise we'll kill the lot of you!' And the bells of the Eternal City were sounding the tocsin.

After a day of argument it was an Italian who, for want of a Roman, was chosen. The Limousin party were unable to impose one of their own group upon the conclave, and they therefore threw out as a suggestion the name of a prelate who did not belong to the Sacred College at all—Bartholomew Prignano, Archbishop of Bari. Only one abstention and three reservations were formulated against this choice. But would the Roman people accept it? The cardinals glanced down from the lofty palace walls at the seething, gesticulating crowd and felt uneasy. In order no doubt to be more certain that the Holy Spirit had indeed alighted upon their choice, they proceeded to vote all over again, and finally proclaimed that the Neapolitan prelate had indeed been elected pope. At this moment the mob invaded the chapel, demanding the enthronement of a Roman. How in the world were the cardinals to get themselves out of this difficult situation? Some sly rogue contrived to force the pontifical mitre and cope upon the cardinal of St Peter's, the aged Tibaldeschi, and to present him to the rabble seated upon a throne; he protested vehemently, but the acclamations drowned his wavering voice. The procession that filed past him lasted long enough for the most circumspect cardinals to make their exit. On the following day, 10th April, the Roman authorities, who had been advised of the fraud, made haste to round up the dozen *porporati* who still remained in the city, and invited them to enthrone the Archbishop of Bari with all speed. In this way *Urban VI* became the successor of St Peter, lawfully so, it must be admitted, since the intrusion of the mob did not occur until after his election, but in a manner which was dubious, to say the least, and which did not add much lustre to his dignity.

Once seated upon the pontifical throne this upright individual, who

[1] The Sacred College at this date consisted of twenty-three members.

* B

was austere in character, a competent jurist, and who had an excellent grasp of world affairs, unfortunately revealed himself as a sort of Fury, nay, almost a demoniac, who elevated the sledge-hammer to the status of a tool of government. He wanted to reform the Church as fast as possible, starting with the Curia and the episcopate. In all this he was perfectly right; his method alone was at fault. He declared war upon simony, misconduct and clerical extravagance with such vigour that all and sundry felt themselves to be under attack. His language, which one would certainly never have expected to hear issuing from such august lips, was well calculated to give general offence: the Cardinal of Amiens, who was an extremely influential figure in France, heard himself publicly branded as an idle scoundrel; Cardinal Orsini, who had crowned him, was rewarded by the Pope with the name of imbecile; and one worthy papal tax-collector, who had brought to Rome the fruits of some perfectly legitimate levies, had the money flung back full in his face, together with an apposite scriptural quotation comparing him with Simon the Magician. All in vain, a horrified St Catherine called on this formidable witness of Divine Love 'to moderate his impetuous temper in the name of Our Crucified Saviour.' When Urban VI announced before a gathering of the French cardinals that he was going to create such a batch of Italian cardinals that the rest of the Sacred College would have nothing to do save keep their mouths shut, he sealed his own fate. Robert of Geneva stalked out of the chamber, very pale. In addition, the irascible pontiff had become embroiled with the Queen of Naples and the powerful lord of Frondi: he was already at loggerheads with France.

The operation was planned swiftly; in secret, under pretext of taking a holiday, thirteen cardinals made for Anagni, where they went into deliberation under the protection of a troop of Gascon and Navarrese soldiery, commanded by Bernardon de la Salle, Duguesclin's comrade-in-arms. Realizing that they were in a place of safety the cardinals disdainfully rejected all Urban VI's unnaturally temperate gestures of conciliation. On 9th August 1373 they declared his election at Rome to have taken place under duress, and therefore to be null and void; after which, on 20th September, at Fondi, they elected a new pope, who took the name Clement VII.

The choice was an unhappy one, not because the man chosen was without merit, but because he was none other than Robert of Geneva who had prepared the way for Gregory XI's return to Italy by methods which were only too well known, and upon whom the blame for the terrible massacre of Cesena was generally placed. Canonically his election was entirely unacceptable. St Catherine of Siena judged it so; she supported Urban VI, despite his notorious failings, and dubbed the cardinals of Anagni 'devils in human form.' However, while the new antipope was taking the road back to Avignon, after trying in vain to establish his authority in Rome and Italy, the various states of Europe were backing one pontiff or the other, depending on their national interest. The Pope in Rome retained the obedience of England, almost all Germany, Scandinavia and northern and central Italy; while the antipope at Avignon was recognized by France, Scotland, Spain and the kingdom of Naples. The two rivals excommunicated one another, and each talked of nothing less than burning the other alive. The Schism, the *Great Schism in the West*, had begun. It was the most dreadful agony which Mother Church had yet had to endure within her very bosom; and it was to last for forty years.

Urban VI, being the man he was, clearly did nothing to settle matters. His agitation turned to frenzied rage. His own friends watched him despairingly. Moreover he was as courageous as he was tactless; during a day of rioting in Rome he actually stepped out before the hostile crowd, all alone, and looked it in the face saying: 'Here I am. What do you want?' St Catherine still found the strength, between two heart attacks, to plead with and advise him, but all in vain. On 29th April 1380 she died. Having learned that some of his own cardinals were trying to have him put under restraint as a lunatic, Urban VI had them arrested, tortured, tied up like so many bundles, paraded before him on the backs of mules and subsequently executed. The scandal was so enormous that the fiery pontiff was deserted by all his followers. He died in 1389, savage and alone, still as firmly convinced as ever that he was in the right. But for all that the Schism was not ended.

For no sooner had Urban VI gone down into the tomb than the cardinals owing him obedience proclaimed Boniface IX (1389–1404) pope in his stead. Boniface was an urbane Neapolitan about whom there is nothing particular to be said, save his admitted nepotism. After his death the Orsini and Colonna agreed to raise yet another Neapolitan to the papal throne, Innocent VII (1404–6); but this good and peace-loving man could not even maintain order in Rome, much less bring it back to the Church. And when Gregory XII (1406–15), the octo-genarian Venetian Angelo Correro, succeeded him, he too proved equally incapable of restoring Catholic unity. At Avignon the same uncertainty and weakness was apparent. The antipope Clement VII behaved less violently than Robert of Geneva, but also less effectively; and when he died the Cardinal of Aragon, Pedro da Luna, who had long aspired to the triple crown, managed at last to assume it as Benedict XIII. He reigned from 1394 until 1422, but without real authority; though austere and pious, sincerely convinced of the righteousness of his claim and determined to make it triumph, and a skilful yet firm diplomat besides, he was not altogether justly hated by half the Christian world. The French, who in theory (and after some hesitation) recognized his obedience, mockingly nicknamed him 'the moon pope'—a pretty phrase but one that failed to make the situation any less ugly.

It is hard for us to imagine the confusion wrought in souls by such anarchy. Schism had been brought about this time not by the ambitions of a German emperor but by the very men who were the repository of the Holy Spirit, and it caused havoc in the conscience of mankind. Its repercussions were felt throughout Christendom; in diocese upon diocese, parish upon parish, monastery upon monastery, bishop rose against bishop, priest against priest, abbot against abbot. No one could feel certain of his faith, or of the validity of his obedience. In the words of Froissart: 'Folk marvelled that the Church could have fallen into such dire troubles and remained in them so long.' The very saints were divided into two camps: on the side of the Roman popes there were ranged, after St Catherine of Siena, St Catherine of Sweden, Blessed Peter of Aragon, and even Gerard de Groot whom Thomas à Kempis called 'the light of the Church.' But the Avignonese popes had almost as many acolytes at Heaven's altar: the great Spaniard St Vincent Ferrer, who wrote a treatise to prove their legitimacy; St Colette, the celebrated reformer of the Poor Clares; and the charming little seventeen-year-old bishop, Blessed Peter of Luxemburg, who died at the age of nineteen and at whose tomb miracles multiplied in such profusion that many people regarded them as proof that Pedro da Luna was indeed the Vicar of Christ. Each camp therefore could, in perfect good faith, regard the other as heretical. In 1382, at the battle of Roosebeke, those who led the French army against the Flemings, wondered whether they had a right to bear the oriflamme, the standard which could be used only in a sacred cause. Their decision was affirmative, since the Flemish cities supported Urban, and to fight them was surely equivalent to serving God.

The spiritual anguish thus generated increased from day to day; desolation overwhelmed the souls of men, and it was widely believed that no one had gained entry to Paradise since the beginning of the Schism. The prophecies of Joachim of Flora acquired a new topicality, and a new edition by Telesphorus the Hermit in 1386 enjoyed great success. The rupture seemed to herald the end of the world, and many considered the year 1400 as a likely date. Troops of penitents appeared on the scene, clothed in the long white garments which caused them to be known as *Dealbati*. They came to claim the plenary indulgence for the jubilee year of 1400; but alas! the two popes, the one at Rome and the one at Avignon, had already granted it for the year 1390. The Flagellants made even more of an impression: they too talked of Antichrist and of the end of the world. Christendom so sorely rent was slowly foundering into chaos.

Various solutions were proposed. In 1394 the University of Paris, after much consultation concerning competences, drafted a memorandum which suggested three possible answers to the problem: joint surrender, compromise and a general council. In the first case the two popes would abdicate together; in the second a commission nominated by both sides would settle the question; in the third an oecumenical assembly of the Church would have to pronounce judgment. Gerson, the most eminent scholar at Paris, wanted each of these three methods tried. But how on earth could the pontiffs be persuaded to agree to the 'way of surrender,' which would set them both aside?

An extraordinary attempt was made in France to enforce agreement on this basis, one that reveals very clearly the mental and spiritual confusion of the period. In 1398, encouraged by the universities, the French clergy proclaimed the complete and immediate withdrawal of its obedience from Benedict XIII, hoping thereby to compel his immediate abdication; and Charles VI signed the decree in one of his rare moments of sanity. This was something quite unheard of: the Church of France was setting herself apart from the rest of the Catholic world, treating herself as exclusively Gallican. Benedict XIII, however, would not be intimidated by this procedure. Neither the desertion of seventeen of his cardinals, nor the counsel of his friends, nor even the siege of his palace, could overcome a determination worthy of a better cause: he absolutely refused to abdicate alone, or to be the first to do so. After four years of vacillation public opinion somersaulted and renewed its allegiance to him. The leaders of the Church of France also, realizing that the situation might give rise to the gravest political complications, and that the royal government was overwhelming them with irregular taxes, decided to return to his obedience. But the affair of the Schism was not so easily settled.

In 1406, on the death of Innocent VII, all the Roman cardinals swore to accept the principle of surrender; in other words, they promised that whichever of them was elected would renounce the tiara provided that the antipope declared that he would do likewise. Attempts were made to persuade Benedict XIII to give the same promise. As soon as he was elected, therefore, Gregory XII was invited to fulfil his undertaking, together with his rival; but neither pope had any intention of abandoning his title, each being passionately convinced that he was fully entitled to it. There followed an extremely complex diplomatic manœuvre. Both pontiffs were on the point of meeting one another at Savona, but halted when they were but a day's march apart. Each subsequently withdrew into his own territory, and both were promptly abandoned by many of their cardinals.

Thus the idea arose of convening a council which would depose both popes. This was the 'third way' which the University of Paris had recommended. In March 1409 twenty-four cardinals, of whom fourteen were 'Romans' and ten 'Avignonese,' accompanied by some three hundred leading prelates, held a meeting at Pisa, in the presence of envoys from all the Western nations. Since no pope had convened this council, their meeting was in fact illegal; but their discussions lasted a long time, from March until August. They deposed both rival pontiffs, holding each guilty of the double offence of schism and heresy, and chose in their stead a Greek, Petros Philarges (or Filargo), Cardinal of Milan, who became Alexander V (1409–10). 'Oh, happy choice! Peace has been restored! Oh, pacific union!' So declared the University of Paris. But something which no one had foreseen now occurred: both deposed popes refused to abdicate at the Council's order. Instead of two contested and questionable popes, there were henceforth three!

TABLE SHOWING THE VARIOUS POPES AT THE TIME OF THE GREAT SCHISM

POPES AT ROME	POPES AT AVIGNON	POPES AT PISA
Urban VI (1378–89)	Clement VII (1378–94)	
Boniface IX (1389–1404)	Benedict XIII (1394–1422, declared deposed 1417)	
Innocent VII (1404–6)		Alexander V (1409–10)
Gregory XII (1406–17, abdicated 1415)		John XXIII (1410–15, declared deposed 1415) d. 1419

COUNCIL AGAINST POPE: THE ATTEMPT OF CONSTANCE

This lamentable experience was not the result of chance, but the culmination of a mental climate which had been affecting the Church for some time past. The Council of Pisa was the work of a group of *avant-garde* intellectuals, who regarded it as an opportunity to legislate for all Christendom in the name of doctrines which they themselves had evolved. These doctrines were nothing less than revolutionary, intended to impose a new concept of the Church. But they derived additional force from the whole tendency of the age, were intimately linked with the nationalist theories which the emergence of modern states was bringing into fashion, and were also contaminated to some extent by certain completely heretical theses, such as would soon be advanced by Wyclif and John Huss.

What was the constitution of the Church, according to traditional doctrine as expressed by the greatest of thirteenth-century scholars? All of them, from Alexander of Hales to St Bonaventure, from St Albert the Great to St Thomas, were agreed upon four principles: the Church was a monarchy, governed by one leader, the Pope; the primacy of the Pope derived only from Christ through Peter, and not, in any sense whatsoever, from delegation by the faithful; the advice of the leaders of the Church meeting in council, should one be convened, could be effective only if accepted by the Pope, and conciliar decisions were valid only if confirmed by him; and finally, since the Pope was sovereign judge in all matters of faith and discipline, no one might appeal against his edicts to another tribunal, to wit, a council. It was against these four principles, which are still regarded as fundamental, that the revolutionaries rebelled.

The revolutionary movement had sprung into being during the last years of the thirteenth century and the first of the fourteenth, in the persons of *Marsilio of Padua* and *Ockham*,[1] whose subversive activity was not confined to this point alone. Marsilio, a secular scholar, had approached Louis of Bavaria when the latter was in conflict with John XXII, bringing him a treatise with the somewhat curious title *The Defender of the Peace* (1324), in order to provide him with arguments for use against the Pope. Taking up once more the ideas put forward by Nogaret and his followers at the time of Philip the Fair's struggle with Boniface VIII, Marsilio developed them and maintained that in the Church, as in the State, authority resided in the people, the majority of whom delegated it to, or withdrew it from, the Council; the true judge of faith and discipline was the mass of the faithful; and the elected leader was but an agent who executed their decisions. Furthermore the Bishop of Rome possessed no jurisdiction over his colleagues; at the most he enjoyed a primacy of honour. To sum up: the Church, regarded in this light, was no longer an institution, a society, but a body of teaching entrusted in common to all those who accepted it. These anarchical ideas were voiced by others too, notably by Michael of Cesena, general of the Franciscans, who declared: 'Any pope can err in faith or morals, but the Church as a whole never errs!' Another spiritual son of St Francis, William of Ockham, whose intellect and learning far outstripped those of earlier philosophers of this school, was the author of a *Dialogue*,[2] in which he revived

---

[1] On Marsilio and Ockham see the final chapter of *Cathedral and Crusade*. (Both names appear in its Index.)

[2] He chose this literary form as a matter of prudence.

Marsilio's themes, systematized them and carried them still further. It seemed clear to Ockham that a general council possessed an authority superior to the Pope, but that only the Church, the assembly of the faithful, which could be reduced to a mere handful of true believers, was infallible, even when the whole hierarchy was in error.

These rash theories had not become widely known when they were countered by a tradition of a thousand years and more, which viewed any schismatic tendency with horror. The Church attacked them as soon as she became aware of their existence, and in the University of Paris teachers were for some time obliged to swear on oath that they would not read *The Defender of the Peace*. The Great Schism, however, provided these subversive doctrines with an opportunity to spread, and in some cases to triumph. After all, since the Papacy was obviously disintegrating, were the conciliar theorists not correct in their conclusions? 'Who wants to found the stability of the Church upon Peter's infirmity?' inquired one Parisian schoolman, Pierre d'Ailly; and no one could gainsay him. Tragic though it was to hear it formulated, the whole question arose from the scandal.

Consequently Western Europe experienced a prolific growth of every type of treatise, pamphlet, argument and commentary, all of which came back, essentially, to proclaiming the superiority of a general council over the Pope. At Vienna Henry of Langenstein's *Peaceful Proposal for the Unity and Reform of the Church* asserted that the Schism had been willed by God in order to demonstrate that true power resided in the people, and that a council consisting of all the bishops could dispose of the Papacy. Conrad of Gelnhausen, another teacher who fled from Paris in 1391, went still further and declared that not only was the Pope subject to a council, but that the council itself was no more than a congress of the Church's representatives.

In Paris the schoolmen flung themselves heart and soul into these ideas. 'Dame University' there was extremely proud of her learning and prestige, which, she alleged, went back to the time of Charlemagne, and even further, to Rome and Athens! Jean Jouvenel modestly called her 'the venerable mother, sent by God from Paradise.' Temporal interests—those of the King of France, and others of an individual character—accorded fairly well with the spiritual interests of the Church, and, on the banks of the Seine, as is well known, people dislike nothing so much as lagging behind the very forefront of fashion and novelty. 'What does the number of popes matter? Why not have two, three, ten or twelve, or one for every kingdom?' cried the firebrands of the Sorbonne. Basing their argument upon the very nature of the Church, the most serious of them concluded that since she was intended to be a single entity, some other authority would have to be substituted for that of the Pope if he could no longer guarantee her

unity. A general council, they declared, meeting with or in opposition
to the Pope, would labour for the good of all. Pierre d'Ailly, a man
of no great intellectual eminence or strength of character, maintained
this thesis with vehemence: a far wiser man, John Gerson, chancellor
of Paris University, founded it, to the best of his ability, upon principle.
He demonstrated that if the canon law and the civil law, which were
both bases of unity, found themselves in conflict with divine law and
natural law, which were its other two pillars, the first two must yield to
the second; in other words, the collective conscience of the Church,
the repository of Christ's message, had the right to rebel against a
perjured or defective pope.

As can be seen, these were completely new ideas; had they been
adopted, they would have undermined the Church's order and over-
thrown her most basic institutions. But in the impassioned atmosphere
into which the Schism had plunged the whole of Christendom, few
paused to consider where such doctrines might lead, or to ask themselves whether anarchy would not be their logical conclusion. On the
eve of the conclave of Pisa, the Paduan scholar *Zabarella* (who ended
his days as a cardinal) assembled the whole collection of these arguments in one explosive treatise entitled *The Imperial Jurisdiction*, in
which he made an appeal to yet another personage. 'The plenitude of
powers resides originally in the mass of the faithful,' he wrote, 'and
in the Pope only in so far as he is the principal agent entrusted with its
execution'; therefore it was essential that a general council, the
expression of the will of the Church, must meet, whether this pleased
the Pope or not; and if the Pope refused to convene it, one man was
clearly designated to do so in his place: the emperor.

Now the emperor, Rupert of Bavaria, had recently died; and as three
claimants were struggling to succeed him, this mighty throne looked
as if it would be powerless to resolve the crisis for a long time to come.
Then, to everyone's surprise, one of these aspirants, Sigismund of
Luxemburg, King of Hungary, managed to enforce his claim and
become King of Germany. Sigismund was a handsome cool-headed
man, with a determined expression and neatly trimmed beard. He
straightway invaded Italy, announcing that he was going to settle the
question of the Schism. At the same time it was learnt that Alexander
V, the pope at Pisa, had just died—so suddenly that the circumstances
seemed suspicious—and that the cardinals recognizing his obedience
had elected, under the name of John XXIII, Balthazar Cossa, Cardinal-
Deacon of Ostia, who was the subject of some unsavoury rumours (it
was said that he had been a pirate), but who was the friend of the new
ruler of Germany. Therefore it seemed the opportune moment for 'the
'King of the Romans and Protector of the Church' to take the affair in
hand. John XXIII, who had been chased from Rome by a surprise

attack made by Neapolitan troops, could hardly object. During the year 1414 Christendom learned that a new council was about to meet for the purpose of restoring Christian unity.

The place chosen for the meeting was Constance. It was clearly hoped to remove the assembly from the sphere of Italian intrigue; but Sigismund must also have believed that the Holy Spirit would do him certain favours in this German town. The French, though little pleased to see the initiative slipping from them, held their peace. They were cunning enough to send their best men to the Council: Cardinals Guillaume Fillastre and Pierre d'Ailly, and the great schoolman John Gerson, all three of whom were famous for their writings and their doctrines. Zabarella, the Paduan canonist, who had just been elevated to the purple, shared their views; the mind of the Council would be largely French.

So, during the course of 1414, representatives of all sections of Christendom, and of all three rival obediences, streamed towards Constance, which had become the faith's provisional capital. John XXIII went there accompanied by a retinue of six hundred. The other two pontiffs did not attend in person, but both sent delegates. Crowded together in the town in the most incredible fashion were thirty-three cardinals, nearly five hundred bishops, two thousand representatives of the universities and some five thousand priests, not to mention ambassadors from every secular court, forty dukes, thirty-two princes and five hundred knights, every single one escorted by a train of servants, making a grand total, according to the chronicler Ulrich of Richethal, of some one hundred thousand souls! One painful detail throws a strange light upon the shadier side of this gathering: seven hundred prostitutes also came to Constance and took up residence there; it was doubtful if they had come to reform men's morals.

This illustrious assembly had a triple end in view: to put an end to the scandal of the Great Schism; to enact measures which would suppress the abuses whose extension was causing the best Christians much distress, abuses which the Church had been obliged to fight on several past occasions, and which had formerly gone under the names of simony and nicolaism; and finally, to crush certain heresies that were clearly gaining ground. Of these three aims, it must be admitted, only the first was seriously pursued; moral reform, which was the occasion of many long and frequent discourses, was far from being the over-riding concern of the Council of Constance; and as for heresy, while it is true that the hapless John Huss, who was imprudent enough to put himself into this canonical hornet's nest,[1] was burnt at the stake there, hardly any trouble was taken to make the doctrinal effort which alone could have cut the ground from beneath the erroneous doctrines. The

[1] See Chapter III, section devoted to John Huss.

Council of Constance cannot be compared in any respect whatsoever with that of Trent which was to save the Church and restore stable foundations to the Christian world one hundred and fifty years later.

But at least a solution was found to the actual question on whose account the Council had been convened. It was manifestly impossible to choose between the three existing popes. All three would have to be set aside and another elected; but this was easier said than done. One of these disastrous claimants, John XXIII, was present, so he was attacked first. The French had succeeded in forcing the acceptance of the system of voting by nations instead of by counting heads: France, England and Germany conspired against the Italians, and Sigismund promptly abandoned his protégé. Immediately a general assault, a whole flood of ignominy, was let loose against this bald-pate, this black sheep of Christendom. Disguised as an archer, John XXIII fled from the town, hoping that his departure would cause the Council to collapse. Nothing of the kind happened; his new protector, the Duke of Austria, had little influence compared with that exercised by the ruler of Germany. The wretched creature was taxed with simony, plurality, incest, sodomy, fornication and other niceties, and publicly accused of being his predecessor's murderer. He eventually broke down and agreed to sign his own condemnation, inscribing it with his Christian name alone: Balthazar. This mark of humility earned him a final scrap of consolation: five years later Martin V readmitted him to the Sacred College, and his wonderful tomb by Donatello in the baptistery at Florence is worthy of a Sovereign Pontiff.

It now remained to settle the fate of the two other popes, Benedict XIII and Gregory XII. The latter was weary of the disheartening role which he realized he was playing; he agreed to reconvoke the Council, whose legality had been in doubt ever since the flight of John XXIII. He negotiated his abdication, a gesture made seven years too late, but one which should be counted in his favour.

Benedict XIII still remained, austerely ensconced in his own rectitude, deserted by almost all his partisans in Aragon, Armagnac and Foix, but deriving a tragic greatness and a reinforced certainty of being in the right from this very abandonment. Sigismund went in person, beseeching him to accept an honourable solution, but all in vain. Taking refuge on the rocky pinnacle of Peniscola, between Tortosa and Vinaroz, a kind of Spanish Mont-St-Michel, Pedro da Luna continued to proclaim his profound faith in the justice of his cause; the whole of Christendom was with him on this mountain top, he alleged, just as all humanity had been with Noah in the Ark! It was finally necessary to proclaim his deposition (1417). This fact did not prevent Benedict from creating new cardinals who, after his death, actually elected another antipope, Clement VIII. Upon the abdication of this man only one rebel cardinal remained, but the spirit of Pedro da Luna lived on in the tiny, savage court of Valencia; and this was how Benedict XIV, the sacristan of Rodez, came to be elected pope by a single vote, an event, however, that caused little stir in the outside world.

The affair of the Schism having thus been terminated, there remained only the task of choosing a lawful pope. But this was not easy. Various factions were at work in the assembly at Constance, and many devout folk wondered whether the cardinals of the three obediences would again split up into groups when the time for voting arrived. It was Sigismund who, unintentionally, sealed their unity. This heavy-handed monarch, whose intervention in the assembly's affairs was becoming more and more indiscreet, had ended by antagonizing all the *porporati*, irrespective of origin or party. When he let slip his intention of continuing to control the Church, under pretext of ensuring the passage of reform before any election, the French cardinals had little difficulty in forming all their colleagues into one bloc, and Guillaume Fillastre talked of nothing less than martyrdom in order to resist the new tyrant. But there was no need to go to these lengths. The English court, which was at this time at the height of its fame, offered its services as mediator, and Sigismund hastened to accept. The conclave, which on this extraordinary occasion included thirty representatives of the five Christian nations as well as the cardinals, met at the Kaufhaus. After only eight days Otto Colonna, a scion of the illustrious Roman family and a cardinal formerly acknowledging obedience to Innocent VII, was elected under the name of *Martin V* (6th November 1417).

Thus peace was restored to the Church, but it did not follow that all her difficulties had been swept away. The Council, and the Council alone, had ended the scandal of the Schism; but that very fact might seem to lend a measure of support to the advocates of conciliar supremacy. Indeed, at Constance, decrees had been voted which, if recognized as valid, would place the Papacy in bondage. One declared that 'the General Council, representing the Catholic Church, and deriving its power directly from Christ, must be obeyed by everyone, whatever their condition or rank, even by the Pope.' Another, the decree *Frequens*, which was adopted shortly before Martin V's election, established the Council as the normal and regular authority in the Church, fixing the intervals at which it must be convened (five years initially, then seven and ten). In short, the Pope was allotted merely the role of a prime minister, elected by a Parliament which was intended to control him. Now were these decisions improvised to meet specific circumstances, or did they, as Gerson believed, lay down a rule for the future? What canonist could have given an answer? In the last resort everything hinged upon the strength and ability of the new pope.

Martin V was not the sort of man to allow himself to be put into leading-strings. This might have been suspected from a sermon he preached on the morrow of his election in which he studiously avoided naming Constance in the list of oecumenical councils to whose decrees he was committed. After which, though urged by Sigismund to settle in Germany, and by the French to return to Avignon, he courageously took the road back to Rome, preferring the pile of ruins which the Eternal City had now become, and the wolves which haunted the Roman countryside, to demands with which he was only too familiar. Martin, at the age of twenty-five, was an energetic man, in the prime of life, well educated, a shrewd judge of men and events, and irreproachable in his morals; he had also managed to keep himself free of intrigues, employing his retinue of nephews, on whose account he was later to be much reproached, to keep the powerful Italian families in order and to confront the anarchy existing in the peninsula. The steadfastness with which he reiterated his desire to undertake the indispensable task of reform [1] assured him the respect of the faithful, the prayers of his protégé St Frances of Rome [2] and the blessing of God. As for the vital problem, the Papacy's relations with the Council, he handled it with consummate skill.

It had not been possible to shake off the assembly's tutelage and tear up the decree *Frequens*. Martin therefore bided his time, letting it be understood that the very word 'council' made him shudder. At length, in 1423, he ordered the assembly to meet again, this time at Pisa. Embarrassed, however, by the close proximity of Filippo Maria Visconti, the tyrant of Milan, he took the opportunity afforded by an outbreak of plague and quietly transferred the sessions to Siena. Martin's delegates to the Council included a number of able men, competent to hold their own against the conciliar theorists; notable among them was the famous Dominican orator Jerome of Florence. The Pope's supporters cunningly laboured to set their enemies at loggerheads with one another, a task which it was particularly easy to accomplish so far as England and France were concerned. For the first time for very many years the spokesmen of Paris University felt less certain of their theses, which were nevertheless being taught at the Sorbonne as virtual articles of faith. After a year of fruitless discussion the Council of Siena disintegrated, but not before it had 'commanded' the assembly of another council, to be held seven years later at Basle. Martin V assented: he would not risk another clash between the throne of Peter and its enemies. Cardinal Cesarini, who was respected by both sides on account of his intellect, learning and exemplary virtues, was to preside over the forthcoming deliberations—a pledge that all would be well. The last antipope had just vanished from the scene,

---

[1] See Chapter III, section: 'Will the Church Reform Herself?'
[2] See Chapter III, *idem*.

leaving no appreciable traces and the Papacy seemed on the way to recovering its ancient authority. When 'the second founder of papal monarchy,' the restorer of Rome, died of apoplexy in February 1431, the most difficult stage of the battle appeared to have been won.

An Eventful Pontificate: Eugenius IV (1431–1447)

The victory was not in fact altogether complete; the slightest setback could place the result in jeopardy. The conclave met in the convent of the Minerva, and chose as Martin V's successor Gabriel Condulmero, a Venetian patrician and a nephew of Gregory XII; their choice seemed an excellent one. The new Pope, who took the name of *Eugenius IV*, was respectable in every way, and many aspects of his character were even to be admired. Pleasant and distinguished, reserved, yet utterly devoid of arrogance, he continued to pursue his monastic way of life (he was an Augustinian) after his elevation to the Apostolic See. Indeed he led the kind of life which all monks should have been leading, drinking nothing but water, eating only fruit and vegetables, and rising in the middle of the night in order to recite Matins. Furthermore Eugenius was resolutely hostile to all forms of nepotism and was interested only in governing in the best interests of the Church. Had he combined all these virtues with the flexibility and shrewdness of the diplomat he would have been perfect. But, being rigid in his decisions and imperiously curt in his commands, these were the qualities which he least possessed, qualities in fact which he would have regarded as frailty and laxity.

At the conclave Eugenius IV had been obliged, with his fellow cardinals, to sign a kind of capitulation which, if applied, would have subjected the pontiff to the Sacred College. It alone would have been entitled to receive the oath of loyalty from vassals and officials, to make alliances, to declare war, and even to control the reform of the Church, including that of the Papal Court and its leader. Did the cardinals mean thereby to show their deep distrust of the future pope or of the next council? Probably of both. A diplomatically minded pontiff would have turned the situation to his own advantage, first by ridding himself of the Council in reliance on the Sacred College, and then putting the over-ambitious *porporati* firmly back into their places. But if ever a chance was missed, it was certainly that which Eugenius IV allowed to slip by at the beginning of his pontificate.

The Council of Basle was about to open; nothing could prevent it. But conditions were scarcely favourable. The Hussite wars were raging all over Bohemia; at the very gates of Basle itself Philip the Good, Duke of Burgundy, was settling old scores with Frederick of Austria; France, where Joan of Arc would soon go to the stake, was in a state of total anarchy. The assembly which met in the Rhenish city was not a council at all, but a kind of conventicle, in which some forty abbots, about fifty clerics and a whole host of university professors loudly proclaimed that they represented the universal Church. Cardinal Cesarini was not even present, being engaged on a crusade against the Czech heretics. Martin V would have snuffed out the candle of Basle at one stroke, and all would have been settled.

Eugenius IV lost six months. He was, it must be admitted, extremely busy arguing with the Colonnas, his predecessor's heirs, concerning various ecclesiastical possessions which the latter had diverted to their own uses. The hard core of the conciliar party took advantage of the respite to recover and reorganize itself. A few bishops rallied to Basle. Cardinal Cesarini, whose crusaders had fled in disorder before the Hussites, rejoined the assembly, declaring that nothing short of the combined authority of the assembly and the Pope was needed to defeat the scourge of heresy. Suddenly this little pocket Council found an important *raison d'être*; for at this moment there arrived a bull in which Eugenius IV pronounced the Council's dissolution and decreed the convocation of another, at Bologna, in some eighteen months' time.

The effect of this was disastrous. Cardinal Cesarini wrote a pathetic letter, describing 'the explosion of anger and despair' which greeted the papal document. Why, asked the great legate, should Eugenius quarrel with a council which had in principle shown no hostility of any kind towards the Pope? Like Mirabeau at Versailles, the Fathers of Basle answered the papal threat by declaring that they would abandon the Council only if forced to do so. Sigismund, who intended offering to support the Holy Father if the latter would promise in return to crown and anoint him at Rome, secretly sustained the conciliar extremists. Even the wise and saintly Nicholas of Cusa, the apostle of unity and concord, asserted in his vast scheme of reform, *De concordantia catholica*, which had just appeared, that the support of the Council was indispensable. When Eugenius IV was elected people had compared his coming with the Archangel Gabriel's visit to the Blessed Virgin, but they were now less and less inclined to answer him: 'Be it done unto me according to thy Word.'

Thus conflict seemed inevitable. Reinforcements for the conciliar party reached Basle from far and wide. Charles VII, King of France, preparing the way for a manœuvre which later resulted in the Pragmatic Sanction of Bourges,[1] supported the movement. Burgundy, Scotland and Castile did likewise. One incident enabled the very legitimacy of the Sovereign Pontiff to be called into question. This was an appeal to the Council by Cardinal Capranica, whom Martin V had

[1] See the last section of this chapter.

raised to the purple, but upon whom he had had no time to bestow the red hat. Eugenius IV had committed the signal error of dubbing Capranica a rebel impostor; but if Capranica was indeed a member of the Sacred College, did not it mean that, since he had been barred from the conclave, Eugenius's election was therefore rendered null and void? The situation became so tense that the papal nuncios could no longer secure a hearing at the Council, and the Pope, who was summoned to appear before it, was declared contumacious. At Rome, in the Curia itself, the wind was changing: despite a papal ban the cardinals were slipping secretly away and heading for Basle. To what would the situation lead?

The year 1433 was a decisive one. In February Eugenius IV completely changed his tactics. He issued a bull which authorized the holding of the Council at Basle and commanded the largest possible number of priests to attend it. It was a clumsy manœuvre and could hardly succeed. Heeding only the section of the document containing the Pope's approval, the Council simply became more overweening on its account. Had not the secular princes, in particular Sigismund, whom Eugenius IV had just crowned as emperor in Rome, been there to exercise a restraining influence, the situation would have led straight to a fresh schism. In vain did Cardinal Cesarini propose a formula of conciliation: the exasperated Pope launched two new bulls which purported to annul all the conciliar decisions. This was too much. Christendom feared a rebirth of the Schism. The emperor, kings and princes, cardinals and canonists, even the Doge of Venice, representing the Pope's native city—everyone begged Eugenius to yield. At last he realized that herein lay his final hope, and a new bull, *Dudum sacrum*, proclaimed his submission. The import of this basic fact was not lessened by a slight reservation whereby the Pope declared his approval of the Council, but not of all its decrees, and when it was learnt in Basle on Christmas Day 1433 that the Sovereign Pontiff had capitulated, one German prelate, obviously given to hyperbole, asserted that 'the world had not received so great a benefit since the Incarnation.'

Shortly afterwards another event added to the tribulations of the luckless pontiff, who was now being threatened even in Rome itself. The Colonnas had been temporarily muzzled, but not disarmed. Now they discovered an ally who was more than willing to join them in embarrassing the Pope: Filippo Maria Visconti, Duke of Milan. Angered by the favours conferred upon Florence and Venice, the two republics he detested, Visconti invaded the Papal States. This touched off a ferment in Rome. In an effort to halt the invasion Eugenius IV took into his pay Francesco Sforza, a soldier of fortune whose alliance was not without its hazards. The situation deteriorated during the spring of 1434, until the Pope felt so unsafe in the Eternal City that he decided to flee. His escape reads like a chapter from an adventure story. Eugenius left the city on the night of 4th June, disguised as a Benedictine and accompanied by only one faithful servant. He intended to take ship secretly at Ripagranda. But the Romans detected his flight and went in hot pursuit. From the bank a hail of arrows and stones was directed at the little skiff, while a large boat tried to bar the passage of St Peter's steersman between the basilica of St Paul and Ostia. The Pope himself crouched in the bottom of the vessel, covered with a shield and anxiously following the bold manœuvre of Valentino, his boatman, who, not satisfied with having avoided an attempt to board him, endeavoured to ram and sink his adversary. At last, however, they reached Ostia, and the Pope was able to breathe freely once again. From there he travelled to Pisa, and thence to Florence. Not a wit disheartened, he made haste to order all his supporters to join him at the convent of Santa Maria Novella, where he had established himself.

This striking display of energy and courage restored a certain amount of Eugenius IV's authority. Several cardinals rallied round him in Florence and the republic of the red lily, extremely proud of her new position as the Church's capital, assured him of her protection. Eugenius then took the offensive: he ordered the closure of the Council of Basle, which was now in a state of utter chaos and had been abandoned by the legate, summoned a new Council at Ferrara, and almost at once realized the dream of so many Christians since 1054—the reconciliation of the Eastern Church with Rome, the union of the two sections of Christendom.

The project had been mooted for a long time past,[1] but the Turkish threat to Byzantium made its realization easier. In 1430 Salonica had fallen; and so it happened that the Basileus, together with the Patriarch, arrived in Ferrara with such an enormous retinue that the city seemed to have become quite Greek. Four sumptuous thrones were erected in the cathedral, the loftiest for the Pope, one slightly lower for the Patriarch, and two others, less elevated but exactly alike, for the two emperors. Innumerable difficulties between Greeks and Latins soon appeared, concerned as much with points of doctrine as with questions of precedence. Moreover an epidemic raging in the neighbourhood of Ferrara, forced the Council to adjourn to Florence, where its majesty may still be seen in Benozzo Gozzoli's picture on the walls of the Palazzo Riccardi. Finally, after many weary months of wrangling, the parties reached agreement, thanks mainly to the efforts of Bessarion, an Eastern prelate and future Roman cardinal. In June 1439 both sides agreed to a solemn declaration, which proclaimed 'the Roman Pontiff to be the authentic successor of the Blessed Peter, Prince of Apostles, the true Vicar of Christ, Father and Doctor of all Christians.'

[1] See Chapter II, section: 'Final Efforts for Unity.'

The act of union was signed a month later: it was a resounding victory for Eugenius IV, even though it quickly proved abortive.

Meanwhile the atmosphere at Basle was becoming both ponderous and frenzied. In order to give a lesson in morals to that Sodom, Gomorrah and hell-bent Babylon which Florence had become in the assembly's eyes, the placid pink town on the Rhine was subjected to a reign of puritanical terror, in which drinking, singing, joking and even resting became sins. As for the antipapal campaign, it was now under the direction of a fanatic, Cardinal Louis Aleman. The great powers reiterated warnings and reservations but all to no avail. In September 1439, while Cardinal Cesarini was leaving the banks of the Rhine for those of the Tiber, while Nicholas of Cusa was on the verge of winning a cardinal's hat in return for his skilful negotiation of the German princes' submission, the men of Basle consummated the rupture with Rome by electing an antipope in the person of Prince Amadeus of Savoy. Their choice was strange but reasonable in the circumstances: strange in that Amadeus was a layman, a widower and father of nine children; reasonable in that he was wealthy, well connected and (it was believed) morally irreproachable. The Savoyard accordingly left the shores of his retreat at Rapallo, where, it should be added, he was leading a life which hardly justified the reputation which the general public associated with his name. His ceremonial entry into Basle was a gorgeous affair: a dozen palfreys represented the twelve Apostles, Amadeus donned a wonderful golden cope, and took the name of Felix V. This done he very quickly realized that he had stepped into a hornets' nest. In fact, the Fathers of the Council intended to be the real masters of the situation. Thus Felix was obliged to witness the passage of several 'conciliar and pontifical' decrees—one of which instituted the Feast of the Visitation—without ever having been forewarned that they were on the agenda. Basle was fast degenerating into the kind of mess which is often the fate of democratic regimes which have no superior authority to organize them and no overriding sense of the general interest. Everything was an occasion for intrigue and personal rivalry.

An opportunity for revenge was now within the grasp of Eugenius IV, and he realized at last how to make use of it. Rome had become once more a widow; the absence of a mediator left her a prey to bloody feuds among the princely clans, and her distracted citizens were praying for the Pope's return. Eugenius therefore departed from Florence and re-entered the Eternal City amid scenes of wild acclaim. He straightway aroused popular enthusiasm to still higher pitch by preaching a crusade against the Turks. Scanderbeg, John Hunyadi and Ladislas of Hungary would lead it—to defeat, as was proved by the event. Finally, and most important of all, Eugenius realized that diplomatic skill was more in keeping with the times than brute force, and applied himself to the task of utilizing the general ill feeling towards the Council in order to win himself some friends. He received powerful aid in the most brilliant men of the age, his endeavours from one of *Aeneas Sylvius Piccolomini*, a talented humanist, whose morals can only be called austere, who had been secretary in turn to Cardinal Capranica and Felix V, and who was one day to become Pope Pius II. This wonderful diplomat, once he had realized that the true Pope's cause was the only righteous one, submitted to him and laboured strenuously to win over the secular princes, in particular, the new master of Germany, Frederick III. The Fathers of Basle and their wretched antipope thus found themselves universally abandoned, and prepared to capitulate. It was simply a question of saving their faces, and the astute Piccolomini threw himself into this task with enthusiasm. Men affected to believe that their submission was entirely voluntary, and that Felix V was becoming an ordinary cardinal and legate completely of his own free will, though in fact the Savoyard needed a good deal of coaxing. By the end of 1447 the settlement of the whole of this distressing affair was almost an accomplished fact. But Eugenius IV was no longer there to enjoy the sweets of victory; for Christ had closed his violent pontificate with the blessing of a peaceful death on 23rd February.

'He had a noble heart,' Aeneas Sylvius Piccolomini said of him, 'but no sense of moderation; and he was wont to follow as his rule of conduct not what he could do, but what he wished to do. . . .' Bossuet has taught us that there is a state of grave disorder inherent in such a condition, and events had shown the Pope that their lessons could not be disregarded with impunity. At least, this man whose character has been so much disputed had one unquestionable merit: he possessed the loftiest idea of his title and his rank, and even in dire misfortune he was determined to safeguard their prestige. It is said that the papal crown which Ghiberti chased for this ascetic Pope weighed fifteen pounds—fifteen pounds of gold, emeralds, sapphires and rubies. And the procession of artists that escorted his cortège adds a more human touch to the portrait of this blunt, desperate fighter, who was also Fra Angelico's friend.

Non Placet Spiritui Sancto

So the Papacy emerged victorious from the terrible crisis. It had prevailed over the Council, which had proved unable to impose its own tutelage upon it; it had prevailed also over the Sacred College, which had vainly attempted at every conclave to force capitulations on the pontiff and thereby to curb his authority. Even on the temporal plane the Papacy's triumph was remarkable: the Pope's subjects in central Italy appeared to have been reduced to obedience. In his *Outline of the Church*, written in 1448-9, John of Torquemada, one of the Papacy's most ardent flatterers, vigorously reasserted the Pope's prerogatives, his supreme power and his universal authority. Torquemada was certainly right, and yet . . .

Recalling one of the most eventful sessions of the Council of Basle where he had seen the two parties face to face in the cathedral, fists clenched, the one occupying the ambo, the other the notaries' benches, and each bawling out its own arguments, the excellent chronicler to whom we are indebted for the whole story dolefully concludes: '*Non placet Spiritui Sancto. . . .*' No, these discords, rebellions, schisms and intrigues were certainly no part of the Holy Spirit! Although triumphant, the Papacy had exhausted many of its resources in the struggle and had lost a great deal of prestige therein. The world was very far from being rid of the ideas that had been promoted by the conciliar theorists—ideas concerning the limitation of papal powers, the regulation of the weapons of excommunication and interdict, and, above all, the control of ecclesiastical finances by the faithful: this last point especially received a warm welcome everywhere. And in actual fact it was not merely the Holy See which emerged from the storm somewhat weakened. The Church herself had been badly shaken. The double crisis of the exile at Avignon and the Schism that followed it had achieved what all the subversive ideas emanating from Ockham and Marsilio had never been able to do: the masses cannot become accustomed to disputing what should be indisputable, and to calling into question the very legitimacy of their leaders, without dire consequences for the future.

The crisis of authority, the most heartrending example of which was provided by the Papacy, reverberated from top to bottom of the Catholic hierarchy. In many dioceses the bishops were no better obeyed than were the Pope and the antipope in the territories acknowledging their obedience. Several of them looked increasingly like tools in the hands of the secular powers. The crisis was equally serious in the religious Orders, which, at the time of the Great Schism, had almost all split into conflicting parties, each with its own general. The basic principle upon which the Church had organized the monastic institution, that of establishment upon a universal plane, was in process of disappearing altogether; the Orders were being broken up into national groupings, which were all virtually dependent upon the secular rulers. The great Benedictine abbeys and the houses of the Premonstratensians were practically independent of the central authority altogether. And for a period of thirty long years the General Chapter of the Cistercians was unable to hold a meeting!

It was not merely in the spheres of ecclesiastical organization and discipline that the crisis of authority had had such extremely distressing consequences. National groups had used it to take increasing liberties with the Holy See, and the various states had sought to impose their own restrictions upon the Pope's authority. Here we are dealing with a fact of crucial importance, one full of consequences for the future. The revival of the study of Roman law and the schoolmen's analysis of Aristotle's *Politics* had restored to favour the notion of the State as a power superior to all individuals, all particularisms and all privileges, whose sovereignty knew no limitations. From now on human society was considered fully mistress of its own destinies. In order to stamp out all ecclesiastical intervention in temporal affairs, French and English jurists had gone to the forgotten treasure-chests of their national traditions, there to bring to light again the customs of their respective monarchies, which were soon to be solemnly entitled their 'fundamental laws'; while the imperialist jurists, rejecting the consequences of the supposed 'Donation of the West to the Pope by Constantine,' and the theocratic thesis according to which the Vicar of Christ had granted the Empire to the Greeks, then to the Franks, and finally to the Germans, had exalted the universal authority of their own ruler. Ever since the violent crisis in which Philip the Fair did battle with Pope Boniface VIII in a struggle for the primacy,[1] William de Nogaret, a doctor of law at the University of Toulouse and adviser to the King of France, had not lacked emulators. A whole intellectual movement had been set in train, which had found in Marsilio of Padua the exponent of a secular state at whose service the Church should place herself. In the middle of the fourteenth century the growing influence of William of Ockham had helped to establish the theses of positive law, which was radically opposed to the juridical principles of the Church. And at the court of the wise French monarch, Charles V, there were numerous defenders of a government founded solely on experience and reason.

The Church's circumstances—the Avignon 'exile' and the Schism —had this serious result: instead of merely stirring up ideas they translated ideas into deeds. The principal Christian states threw off their sacerdotal tutelage. Often this was achieved without violence and with amazing ease. It is significant that the Emperor Charles IV, who owed his throne to the Papacy and who took the greatest pains to fulfil the written undertakings he had given it, was also the very person who fixed the method of choosing the 'king of the Romans,' the imperial candidate, in such a manner that the Pope should no longer play any part therein. The celebrated edict of 1356, known as the 'Golden Bull,' because its seal was encased in a gold casket, singled out the seven

[1] See the following sections in the final chapter of *Cathedral and Crusade*: 'The Struggle for Primacy: Boniface VIII' and 'Philip the Fair and the Outrage of Anagni.'

electors who were to make the choice, and provided for the vacancy of power without making the smallest allusion to the head of the Church. At one stroke the accession of a new sovereign was converted into a purely secular affair. In fact, this innovation was to bring the 'Holy Roman Empire' no happiness, since it preserved nothing of its bygone strength save its glamorous title, and was therefore plunged into a century of partition and anarchy. But it is no less impressive to note that the Avignonese Papacy failed to react vigorously against this obvious curtailment of its authority.

The process was even more marked in France and England. Since they were established on sounder bases than was the Empire, these two monarchies strove, with considerable success, to limit the competence of ecclesiastical jurisdiction, to get their hands on church livings and to tax the clergy to their own advantage. They set to work with quite remarkable flexibility, agreeing to accept clerks nominated by the Curia at Avignon, or taxes levied by it, on condition that they were allowed, in return, to offer their own candidates for benefices on a generous scale, and to demand substantial subsidies from their churches. In this game of tit for tat the Church was bound to be the loser. The kings of France profited richly from the system of reciprocal concessions; while the English monarchs, by dint of complaining loudly that the Avignonese pontiffs were showing a disgusting partiality towards Paris, obtained an analogous *modus vivendi*, such as that which was established by the negotiations at Bruges during the pontificate of Gregory XI.

These young and vigorous states directed all their efforts towards dominating and exploiting their national churches. One of the most effective ways of doing so was through the exercise of the *royal prerogative*. We·know what this comprised: during the vacancy of certain sees, which were either royal foundations or subject in some way to feudal dependence on the king, he did not merely collect the revenues (the temporal prerogative), but even nominated his own candidates for the benefices in the bishop's gift (the spiritual prerogative). A battle of wits was waged between the popes, who, as we have seen, were attempting to extend their 'reserves,' and the kings, who were equally determined to exploit the right of the royal prerogative to the maximum, and it must be admitted that victory fell to the latter. In France in particular all dioceses north of the Loire were made subject to the royal prerogative, in the name of the famous 'customs.' The last vehement protest on the subject had been that made by Benedict XII in 1337; from then onwards it was customary to see the French monarchs receiving petitions, dispatching the documents confirming appointments to various livings, and even distributing expectative graces in imitation of the papal chancellery, albeit with less method!

In 1351 the *Statute of Provisors*, enacted by Edward III of England, which claimed to confirm the traditional pattern of advowsons by recognizing the rights of electors and patrons, had resulted in sweeping aside all traces of papal intervention.

Likewise the Church was relentlessly attacked by the states on another front, namely, the privilege of 'benefit of clergy,' which exempted clerks from secular jurisdiction. This celebrated privilege had long been disputed; as early as 1329, in an assembly at Vincennes, Pierre de Cuignières, president of the Parlement of Paris, had maintained that the clergy had no right to a special court, that they should be subject to the ordinary courts of the realm. The French courts too had on many occasions used the 'appeal against abuse of power' to recall before them cases improperly taken to the ecclesiastical tribunals. In England matters had gone even further: the *Statute of Praemunire* threatened terrible penalties for any subject of the king who appealed to 'foreign' jurisdictions, namely, those of the Church! We are now far removed from the age when the Church's justice took precedence over all the rest, and drew appellants from every corner of Christendom.

If the states had made considerable gains before 1378, it goes without saying that their task became still easier when they had nothing opposing them save a divided Papacy, a Christendom split into two or even three obediences, and a number of councils which were themselves antagonistic to the pontiffs. It was all too simple a game to set one authority against another, to make accusations against the centralizing tendencies of Rome—which were, needless to say, held responsible for all this frightful disorder—and to impose royal control upon the national clergy under pretext of restoring their ancient liberties.

The most striking example of this kind of proceedings is the *Pragmatic Sanction*, the royal edict of 1438, in which Charles VII unilaterally determined the fate of the Church in France, after convening a meeting of its delegates at *Bourges*. This gave effect to the recommendations of the Fathers of the Council of Basle. Elections of bishops were entrusted to the cathedral chapters, those of abbots to the monks, the elections being confirmed by the archbishops and ordinaries. Papal reserves and expectative graces were prohibited. It need hardly be added that the annates collected by the Pope were abolished, and that henceforth the French clergy fixed its own contribution towards the expenses of Christendom as a whole. The wily men of the university, who had devised these measures, were far from being forgotten: one-third of the cathedral prebends were allotted to them. Eugenius IV and his successors steadfastly refused to sanction this edict, which had been drawn up without any reference to the Holy See, and which (after a first abortive attempt in 1472) was eventually to be replaced by a lasting Concordat; but they could not reduce it to a dead letter. In order to embarrass the Papacy, the assembly at Chartres in 1450 produced a spurious 'Pragmatic Sanction of Louis XI,' dated 1269, in an effort to endow the new policy with the authority of the saint-king. With the Pragmatic Sanction of Bourges *Gallicanism* was born, complete with its twofold claim: on the one hand, the French Church claimed freedom to administer itself; on the other, the French king, who from now on laid great stress upon the religious character conferred upon him by the coronation rite of anointing, and upon his thaumaturgical powers, claimed the right of controlling the national Church. Many serious problems were to stem from these two attitudes in the following period—and even in our own time.

Moreover the French Pragmatic Sanction had its replica in Germany the following year: at Mainz, in 1439, the imperial delegates adopted a series of analogous measures: ecclesiastical institutions, legislative power, and, to a large extent, financial rights also were removed from the authority of St Peter's successor. So we see that Rome was the loser on both the temporal and the political plane.

If only these losses had been compensated by spiritual gains! If only the king's tutelage had put an end to the favouritism, plurality of benefices and other scandals, of which the Church provided all too many examples! But nothing of the kind occurred. On the contrary, in Germany as well as in France, every election and every lawsuit in which the Church became involved was the occasion of wearisome quarrelling, and even of shameful fighting. In many instances the canons, unable to come to agreement among themselves, would elect two, three or even four bishops to the same see. The suffragans refused to recognize the authority of the metropolitans. Things went from bad to worse, even to the riot of 1492, when the canons of Paris beat up the Archbishop of Sens, their own metropolitan. This episode resulted in thirteen years of litigation and wrangling. At Pamiers there was a veritable diocesan schism; whilst at Uzès, Nevers, Poitiers, Rouen and Saint-Flour pitched battles were fought in the very choir of the cathedral! The king's tutelage, so far from bringing the crisis of authority to an end, merely aggravated it.

How could any devout Christian regard this debasement without unease—and without the fear of new tragedies yet to come? A weakened Papacy, a Church now less united around its leader, religious offices increasingly considered as objects of covetousness and political calculation, the Christian soul wracked by fundamental cleavages—these were the most apparent results of the tragic crisis through which the Christian world had just lived. But, worst of all, the means of surmounting these difficulties seemed to elude the very people who ought to have been directing the battle against them.

Throughout the whole of this crisis both popes and councils had been perfectly well aware that an even more deep-rooted crisis was raging right through the Church from top to bottom, in men's minds and in their souls; yet, despite their frequent good intentions, they had been unable to supply a remedy. Consequently the courageous efforts of a few saintly individuals had remained sporadic and largely ineffectual, because they lacked the organization of a single authority and will. A like situation existed on the intellectual plane, where the popes had had neither the time nor the inclination to undertake the indispensable work necessary to rejuvenate the ancient formulae, apply the principles of Christianity to the new situations of the Church, in brief, to do what was to be brought to a satisfactory conclusion by the Council of Trent.

The very conditions in which the Papacy was to exist from now onwards made it singularly difficult to carry out this twofold task of reform and adaptation. The pontiffs were re-established in Rome, but this fact had not removed all danger. The popes at Avignon had been accused of being French popes, devoted to the interests of the French crown. But from the time of Eugenius IV onwards men had to deal even more certainly with an Italian papacy, involved up to the hilt in the complicated intrigues of the peninsula, the stake in the battles between princes and cities, even between the various factions within Rome. There would also be the spectacle of a papacy succumbing to the simultaneously heady and perilous influences of that Italianate world—that epoch and atmosphere which witnessed such a marvellous flowering of art and learning, but in which morality received remarkably short shrift. It was this Italian character which was to weigh so heavily upon the Papacy's destinies throughout the whole of the 'Renaissance.'

The situation just described lasted in fact until the saving reaction emerged in the person of Paul III and triumphed in that of St Pius V. But that lay in the distant future, and might occur too late.

CHAPTER II

A CRISIS OF UNITY: CHRISTENDOM DISINTEGRATES AND LOSES THE EAST

WHILE ONE WORLD DIES, ANOTHER STRUGGLES FOR BIRTH

THE GREAT SCHISM, whose sorry spectacle the Church paraded before mankind for so many long and weary years, was but one aspect of the tragedy suffered by the West during the century which lasted from approximately 1350 until the fateful year 1453:[1] it was one of the most obscure and feverish periods in all our history. Other conflicts aligned themselves alongside those in which popes opposed antipopes, pontiffs fought councils and Rome was set against Constance and Basle. These secular issues had considerable influence upon the religious points in dispute, and their total effect was to make humanity exist in an atmosphere of anguish and distress. The final death struggles of feudalism, which was being ground under by the new monarchies; social troubles with a myriad different aspects; the first wars waged by nations against nations—all these are signs, in this tragic age, that large-scale violence, which had been largely held in check for the past three hundred years by the combined action of Church, kings and feudal lords, was being unleashed upon the world once more. And yet this period of murder, rapine and almost universal bloodshed was not just an age of destruction and dire settling of accounts: there are many indications of an effort to emerge from chaos, to endow the world with a new order. The epithet 'Middle Ages' is really better suited to this period of groping and transition than to the great epoch of Cathedral and Crusade. While one world was dying another was struggling to be born, and nature's law decrees that both birth and death shall be accomplished amid sorrow and suffering.

The dying world was called *Christendom*. This term, which gained general acceptance from the ninth century onwards, had, as generation succeeded generation, acquired an ever deeper and wider meaning; it had ended by defining an admirable concept of the world.[2] In the twelfth and thirteenth centuries Christendom did not simply mean

[1] As the reader will be aware, the date of the capture of Constantinople by the Turks is traditionally regarded as marking the end of the Middle Ages and the beginning of modern Europe. The last section of the present chapter will describe how true this idea really is.

[2] See the section 'Christendom' in the first chapter of *Cathedral and Crusade*.

those adhering to the Christian religion, any more than it meant the geographical territory inhabited by the baptized. It stood for the living, organically constituted community of all those who, because they shared the same spiritual beliefs, wanted to order the whole of human society according to their faith. Christendom was founded upon two great principles. The first of these was the sense of human brotherhood, which transcended all antagonisms founded upon self-interest, a brotherhood which followed naturally from the Divine Paternity, a brotherhood described by Rutebeuf in these moving lines:

> Tous sont un corps en Jésus-Christ
> Dont je vous montre par écrit
> Que li uns est membre de l'autre.[1]

The other principle concerned the orderly arrangement of the world, consequent upon the primacy of God. In Christendom each individual knew the whys and wherefores of his position in the hierarchies of society; in Christendom all human institutions were arranged within the framework of God's intentions, and according to a pattern which was accepted by everyone, from the Pope and the emperor down to the humblest of the faithful. The fact that a considerable gap existed between the theory of these great principles and their realization in practice does not detract in the least from either their beauty or their power. For nearly three centuries Western humanity based its way of life upon them.

But by about 1350 these bases were collapsing, and their ruin became more and more complete in succeeding decades. As early as the late thirteenth century the political and social organization of Christendom had begun to show cracks in its structure; the appearance of new forces, and their rapid development, was soon to shake the very foundations of the Christian world. Feudalism, one of the elements which Christianity had used in its effort to emerge from the chaos of the Dark Ages and to ensure an orderly society, was in complete decline. The nobility, whose actual services no longer justified its prerogatives and privileges, and which had, in addition, been financially ruined by the crusades, by the substitution of a trading economy for one based on the land, and by the constant depreciation of the coinage, saw its role in society becoming decreasingly important; but it still occupied a considerable position in that society. But from now onwards his position was one of showy appearance rather than of real leadership. The nobles became a class of sumptuously dressed, elegant folk, who were obsessed with tournaments, solemn vows, the orders of chivalry and duelling. It seemed that the whole force of political and

---

[1] 'All are one body in Jesus Christ, and as I will show you, each is related to his neighbour.'

social evolution was condemning them to an inevitable downfall: for example, the Hundred Years War, which was to decimate and ruin the nobility of France.

Other forces, however, which were in the full vigour of their youth, were asserting themselves against this power in decline. First and foremost there was the authority of the kings. Although stemming from feudalism itself, the monarchs had very rapidly sought and succeeded in shaking off its yoke; at first the Church had helped them to do so, since she saw in them a necessary element of hierarchical Christendom. In France and England in particular—the two realms which had preceded the rest of the European states along the path of national unity—the kings had laboured with admirable skill to centralize their power and organize the monarchical system. With an almost uninterrupted understanding of the opportuneness of the moment, they had grasped every occasion to extend their own authority, and to snatch this or that prerogative from the baronage. Everywhere they had realized how to impress themselves upon people's minds as the one and only element of stability and peace, as the ultimate arbiter whom the community needed. This sentiment, coloured by nostalgia, existed even in Germany and Italy, where the monarchical institution was unable to gain acceptance. The unequal worth of those who wore the crown did not stop this process from continuing. In France, for instance, John the Good (1350–64) was a ruler as weak as he was brave; the hapless, demented Charles VI (1390–1422) succeeded the wise Charles V (1364–80); and Charles VII took a long time to prove himself equal to the dramatic situation of which he was a vital part. Likewise in England, Richard II (1377–99) was an impulsive trifler whose cousin deposed him; Henry IV (1399–1413) doubted his own legitimacy; and Henry V (1413–22) died prematurely, leaving the throne to a babe in arms, Henry VI (1422–61). Yet none of the circumstances here described prevented the monarchical institution from gaining ground in either France or England. The trend of history was impelling it forward. Even the gravest of events were to work in its favour. The Hundred Years War prepared the way for the absolutism of Louis XI in France, and for that of the Tudors in England, just as the Castilian anarchy made possible the centralized rule of Ferdinand and Isabella in Spain. The Middle Ages were to close with the defeat of the feudal nobility and the triumph of the new monarchies. However, it was doubtful whether these youthful forces, which were now in the midst of their development, would regard themselves as contained within the rigid hierarchies in which the great Augustinian concept had placed the monarchs of bygone times. Even when the sovereigns were personally good Christians (and this was generally so), the whole mechanism of their development and growth worked against the system of medieval Christendom. In this respect the ancient order of things was to be irrevocably shattered.

It was also to be shattered, in an equally blatant fashion, by the appearance of an entirely new political and social element: the towns, the centres of the mercantile middle class, which was also undergoing a rapid growth at this time. The urban revival, which had begun c. 1150, had shown itself to be a fact of outstanding importance; and its impetus had not lessened with the passage of time. On the threshold of the fourteenth century the great cities, though never including the great numbers of the mighty urban conglomerations of the modern world (c. 1350 Paris had slightly more than 200,000 souls), constituted extremely stable and strong political elements, well aware of their own strength, and they were forces with whom it was most necessary to reckon seriously. In France and England the cities remained under the control of the sovereigns, with whom they had forged many bonds of common interest, and for whom they provided allies; in Germany and Italy, on the other hand, they had taken advantage—and were to take even greater advantage in the future—of the absence of all central authority to control their own affairs completely. The perfection of commercial techniques, which date, in the main, from the thirteenth century, notably those of book-keeping and accountancy; the creation of the great German, Florentine and Venetian banking-houses, whose bills and letters of exchange circulated from the Baltic to Cyprus; and the rise of the first large modern industries, particularly that concerned with cloth manufacture, enriched the towns in a quite incredible fashion. Italy is an admirable example of this process. Florence, where the cloth trade and banking aristocracy took over control of government in 1434 in the persons of the Medicis, Milan—where the Viscontis, and later the Sforzas, could rule only with the sanction of the great commercial interests—and Venice, where the merchant class actually held all the power, acting behind the glorious façade of the Doge, were but the three most striking of many instances of this ascendancy of bourgeois influence. In Germany there were numerous important cities: Aachen, Cologne, Ulm, Augsburg, Ratisbon, Nuremberg, Bremen, Hamburg and Lübeck—all bound to one another by a close-knit web of common interests, and sometimes even linked officially, as in the case of the towns belonging to the Hanseatic League, which was founded in 1343, on the shores of the Baltic, and whose banking-houses were to be found far and wide, even as far afield as Novgorod in Russia. As for Flanders, which had been the motherland of successful trade in the past, although Ghent and Ypres might now be declining, Bruges was rising in importance and was in the full flush of vigour: it was alongside the quays of Zwyn that the Nordic 'Kogge' encountered the galleys from the Mediterranean.

Did this urban expansion operate expressly against the Church? It certainly did so in part, and we already know that the Church had watched the prosperity of the communes with an anxious eye. But the burghers had not risen solely against the tyranny of certain prince-bishops. As they grew in importance the cities expected their magistrates to possess overriding authority in every sphere, and regarded clerics as bound by the common law in judicial and fiscal matters; many of them restricted or even prohibited the establishment of religious institutions within their walls. The point at issue here is not merely a question of laws and privileges: the new spirit, which gradually divorced men's souls from the simple, open faith which their fathers had possessed, gained its first real foothold in the great trading towns. The bourgeois concept of life rested increasingly upon the primacy of money and profit, to the detriment of moral values. Thus, as they increased in wealth, the great cities asserted their arrogant desire for autonomy in every sort of way. Urban Europe fitted into the pattern of Christendom no better than monarchical Europe.

Yet, in a sense, there was a factor even graver than the changes in the political and social bases upon which the old order had rested: the psychological bases were being overturned just as completely. The very sentiment which had set the seal upon Christian unity, the sentiment of the brotherhood of the faithful, was utterly discredited. Society had become a mosaic of monarchies, cities, baronies, corporations, orders, chapters and parishes, whose jurisdictions impinged upon one another's, but whose overriding interest was the defence of their separate, individual interests. No formula was used more often than that of the *iura et libertates*, which were claimed repeatedly and tirelessly. When the Council of Vienne met in 1311, purporting to study the problem of reform in the Church, one topic preoccupied the prelates from the start and to the exclusion of all others: the prohibition of encroachments which might tend to modify ecclesiastical boundaries. The fourteenth and fifteenth centuries were the heyday of jurists and quibblers, who were bitterly hostile to the whole idea of true unity. In addition, all these tiny organisms, which were labouring furiously to obtain fresh privileges for themselves, were beginning to run up against a new force that tended to subject them to itself, but which was working no less efficaciously against Christian unity. This was the force of national sentiment, which yielded before long to the worst kinds of deviation.

It was in fact from the middle of the fourteenth century onwards that the nations first became fully conscious of their own strength. The double thrust of political and social evolution forced them into this. The efforts of kings to centralize their own powers and to reinforce the authority of their states, were accompanied by a torrent of veritable propaganda—spontaneous or otherwise—which converted each individual sovereign into the symbol of national unity, the living bond which welded together all the folk living in the same country. Memories of the glorious past as well as the most material of self-interests played their part in this feeling; while the finest sentiments of love and loyalty rubbed shoulders with the most sordid jealousies, directed against foreigners who lived across the seas or beyond the mountains. Social progress, which followed upon the expansion of the towns, worked in the same direction; the more economically forward a country, the more subject it was to the fever of nationalism: in Italy province opposed province, and city city, in an effort to prove national individuality. The middle class was much more clearly marked by the specific characteristics of country and race than the nobility, which had been an international and strongly unified class. All this made for disintegration and divisions in European society.

One of the most obvious symptoms of this evolution is the development of national tongues. They had been formerly regarded as 'dialects,' but they were now being used increasingly in the fields of literature and scholarship. Latin declined: it remained the liturgical language, but apart from this it would soon be nothing more than the toy of a few specialists. Even those, like Dante, who deplored the effacement of the international idiom of Christendom, laboured to out-date it by their every action: the *Divine Comedy* is the first masterpiece of Italian literature. The same phenomenon occurred everywhere. In France French had taken the offensive as early as the twelfth century with the *Roman de Renart*, the *fabliaux* and Villehardouin's chronicles; it had developed in the thirteenth, with Joinville, the *Roman de la Rose* and Rutebeuf's miracle plays and pieces; in the fourteenth it had practically won the day with Froissart and the poems of Eustace Deschamps, to be followed in the fifteenth by the works of Charles of Orleans, Arnould Greban and Villon. In Germany the Great Saxon Chronicle (dating from *c.* 1250), the martial epics of the *Niebelungen* and the courtly poems about *Tristan and Iseult* and *Parsifal* had enabled the Germans to hope for a linguistic and moral unity which politics refused them. In Italy Petrarch (1304–74) completed the task, begun by Dante, of developing a literary language which was to be one of the most vivid in the world. National idioms were replacing Latin in every field: Nicolas Oresme, the scholar, wrote in French, while the historians Villani and Lopez de Ayala wrote in Italian and Spanish respectively; Suso, the mystic, used German, just as the wonderful Ruysbroeck used Dutch. The Castilian monarchs legislated in Castilian, while John Fortescue set out his political theories in English. The phenomenon was universal enough, but it was occurring at the expense of the feelings of universality.

This, however, is but one sign of the force of nationalism. National sentiment grew and asserted itself, creeping into every field of activity. It appeared in the economy. Here we have examples of kings, e.g. Charles VII of France, forbidding their subjects to travel to foreign fairs, and demanding that national manufactures be carried in national vessels. In many cases national feelings joined hands with religious aspirations, as was to be even more apparent during the period of the Protestant Reformation. The heretical rebellions of Wyclif in England and of John Huss in Bohemia [1] (the latter in particular was to result in a war of savage violence) were caused as much by explosions of national sentiment as by spiritual and intellectual movements. In an even subtler way nationalism tinged culture, which began to follow different paths. Until the fourteenth century cultural interdependence had been the rule, and men of the same intellectual standard and of similar interests constituted international castes which cared nothing for frontiers. Henceforth French, German, Italian and Flemish cultures were to assert themselves: the monk of Groenendael was quite obviously linked with Flemish painters, such as the Van Eycks, just as Petrarch, though a great traveller, was bound to those of the Italian peninsula. A Europe of multiple civilizations was replacing the civilization of Christendom.

Who was capable of opposing these forces of disintegration? The Church? Such indeed had been her role for centuries past, ever since the end of the Roman world when she saved Western society from falling to pieces and prevented the destruction of Western civilization. Even when violent tensions between the Church and certain elements of society were blatantly apparent—between Church and Emperor, for instance—these very tensions had operated within a unity whose existence they did not question. Could the Church still perform this role? From a political point of view, could the despised and slandered Papacy of Avignon, or that of the Great Schism, assume the functions of an arbiter? The contrary was in fact the case; it was the states who made use of the Papacy in their manœuvres. And was this clergy, whose weaknesses and failings were so well known to the humblest of the faithful, capable of serving as the moral bulwark of a society whose foundations were rocking? The whole of clerical authority was being questioned, from the Curia right down to the most insignificant priest. Above all, even had she wished to control the prodigious changes which were taking place, the Church would have needed men not only clear-sighted enough to be completely aware of what was happening, but also strong enough to break with a moribund past and stake everything upon the future. These men were simply not there. Another hierarchy might have replaced that which had founded Christendom, a more flexible hierarchy, in which each human group would have

[1] See the next chapter, sections on Wyclif and John Huss.

fulfilled its destinies without breaking the transcendent fraternity of the children of God; but the Church failed to realize how to construct such a hierarchy before it was too late, and, by clinging too closely to the ideal of feudal Christendom, it was to take her more than two hundred years to realize that history had passed that ideal by.

The other natural arbiter who, within the traditional concept of Christendom, might have prevented the forces of disintegration from doing their work, was the emperor. But it is scarcely necessary to state that there was no longer any question of him fulfilling this function. His universal authority, although never much more than a noble ideal, had managed to become an element of equilibrium. The development of separate monarchies in the West, the pressures of the urban economy, the anarchy resulting from the rival claims of various princes to the imperial crown, were all leading to an effacement of imperial authority which appeared total and final. Several emperors might indeed be observed solemnly convening diets with a view to settling all the problems of the day, but it was of these same pompous gatherings that Aeneas Sylvius Piccolomini was to comment so wittily: 'Not a single one was fruitless . . . since each engendered another.' The same far-sighted observer added, more sadly: 'Christendom no longer has a head; neither Pope nor Emperor are respected or obeyed; men treat them like myths. . . . Each state desires its own prince, each prince protects his own interests. What voice is strong enough to reunite so many antagonistic forces under the same banner?' The future Pope Pius II was right.

In addition, though it is painful for a Frenchman to have to admit it, the important role which France had played throughout the great epoch of the Middle Ages—often acting as Europe's arbiter, and almost always as its leader—was finally abandoned by her at the beginning of the fourteenth century; or rather it slipped from her hands. On the threshold of this period Dante had wondered, in one of his most famous lines, whether God Himself had not taken up arms on behalf of the fleur-de-lis; one hundred years later there was no longer any question of this being so. In fact, France was now in a state of decline. For a period of almost three hundred years she abandoned all thought of being in the vanguard of the West. The Hundred Years War had dealt her some terrible blows which were tragically apparent, despite a few noble, temporary efforts at recovery. In addition to the battle being waged against the foreigner, there were other conflicts taking place at the same time, in which Frenchmen fought Frenchmen, Armagnacs Burgundians. Besides all these, numerous revolutionary movements flared up sporadically in the great cities as well as in the countryside. A less obvious but equally serious phenomenon helped to accelerate the ruin; the axis of trade was shifting; it ceased to

* c

cross France; the roads from Florence and Venice leading to Bruges or Lübeck kept well clear of the ravaged, divided kingdom of the Valois. And the misery that flowed from all these sources was considerable; the country districts, which had been laid waste by the English, plundered by the mercenaries and subsequently terrorized by the extortioners, became depopulated. Banditry put a stop to trade even in such regions as Provence and the Alps, where the war against the English had never raged. Many towns were deserted by their inhabitants, who, like the peasants who had been hounded from their land, sought refuge in peaceful corners of the continent: in Brittany, along the banks of the Rhine and in Spain. It has been estimated that Lyons lost three-quarters of its citizens, and that the population of Saint-Gilles, in Languedoc, fell from ten thousand to four hundred souls. . . . How could a country possibly remain great, given circumstances like these? How could she continue to play the role of spiritual guide which the world had recognized as hers in the day when one observer had dubbed Paris 'the oven wherein the bread of the West is baked'? The Sorbonne was in a state of hopeless decay, its colleges impoverished, its buildings dilapidated, its professorial body still powerful but the subject of various unfortunate rumours. All these things contributed to the effacement of France; and as Michelet subsequently observed, whenever such an effacement occurs it invariably marks an era of 'world agony.' Christendom, now mortally wounded, possessed no guide, just as it possessed no arbiter; it no longer had any common purpose. Its future was one of darkness and chaos.

A Century of Chaos

To describe in detail all the crises marking the death agony of medieval Christendom is beyond the scope of an ecclesiastical history; but it is scarcely possible for such a history to ignore them. The men who were fighting with a violence and a lust for their opponents' utter destruction, which were quite new features, illustrating to what extent the ancient ideal of the brotherhood of God's children had been forgotten, were themselves Christians. The individuals taking part in these bloody conflicts were often churchmen, despite the fact that the Church herself gained nothing from such conflicts save ruination and grief. These struggles were in some degree repercussions of hammer-blows which, by their reverberations in the purely religious sphere, prolonged the Great Schism, weakened the popes and sapped the will for reform. This gasping world, caught fast in the grip of lethal forces, was the world in which the Cross had been planted. The Turks would soon uproot the Cross from the whole of one immense area of Christian

soil, and thereby show the faithful that by rending one another they
were dealing themselves a mortal wound.

The most famous of these crises, the most extensive and the most
prolonged, was the conflict between the French and English monarchies, each of whom strove with all its might and main to establish
its supremacy over its rival, a crisis known to history as the *Hundred
Years War*. In one sense this is an inaccurate title, since the war broke
out in 1337 and did not end officially until 1453; besides, military
operations were suspended several times by truces of many years'
duration. However, the name is fundamentally a good one, for,
roughly speaking, no less than a century of intermittent warfare was
necessary before a solution was found; above all, this period of time
had perforce to elapse in order that a new element, which enabled
problems to be posed differently, might become established. The
Hundred Years War was a war of transition, wholly characteristic of
an age in which the foundations of the world were altering. Was it the
last of the feudal conflicts or the first of the national wars? It was really
a combination of both, and in the most contradictory fashion. Its
outward origins appeared feudal enough. Edward III of England,
grandson of Philip the Fair through his mother, claimed the crown of
France; though his own sovereignty at home was absolute, he would
not do homage to the King of France for his domains on the Continent.
But there were some entirely different underlying causes: bitter Anglo-
French rivalry for the possession of Flanders with its port of Bruges,
and Guienne with that of Bordeaux; in other words, rivalry for control
of the sea, and of the corn, wine and wool trades. This was something
altogether new. Likewise, in its military techniques, this war marks a
transition from one age into another. Knights in armour, drawn up in
the ancient formations based on rank, and displaying a heroism that
was often no less than reckless, confronted the mobile and easily
manœuvrable infantry units supplied by the towns; and these units
were supported by artillery, which was then in its infancy but would
dominate all future wars. These very men who might lead one to think
that they understood the basic significance of the tragedy, enable us to
see quite clearly that they were fundamentally mistaken. In 1360 the
King of England, whose success had been due to his more modern
strategy, concluded the Treaty of Bretigny, whereby France was
obliged to cede six provinces. But this feudal operation of dismemberment ran counter to the current of history, which was tending to
exalt national sentiment among the peoples of Europe, a sentiment
which so many important figures, from Joan of Arc to Joan Hachette,
were to embody in their country's struggle against England. Yet when
Charles VII found this sentiment incarnate in the Maid of Lorraine,
and altering the situation in his favour in a way so prodigious as to be

almost unbelievable, instead of gathering all the forces in the land around her and driving the English into the sea, he hesitated and equivocated, caught fast in the toils of his prejudices, his *entourage* and his own feudal mind; it would take him another twenty years to learn the lessons of Orleans, Rheims and Rouen.

It is upon this shifting web that those bitter events, which were bought at the price of Christian charity as well as Christian unity, are woven. France under Philip VI was grievously stricken from the first at Sluys, Crécy, Calais, and almost overwhelmed under John II the Good at Poitiers (1356). She was revived by the staunch-hearted wisdom of Charles V and the cunning audacity of Bertrand du Guesclin; then she floundered a second time into defeat and discord, was mortally wounded at Agincourt and lay in the grip of alien occupation. Yet she rose again at the call of one inspired voice to save her ultimate loyalties, together with her young and new-found national honour. Confronting her stood England, straining every resource in her effort to conquer, exhausting her reserves of men and money in order to breathe life into a mighty project which, if successful, would make her the leading power in the West. Such is the simultaneously grandiose and depressing spectacle afforded by this long-drawn-out crisis, which, as all the evidence shows, was governed by historical determinism, and was as inevitable as it was disastrous for the two protagonists. It would need all the brutal discipline of Louis XI to enable a spent and devastated France to recover herself and revive her forces; while across the Channel the Wars of the Roses (1455–85) raged— the terrible and logical consequence of an over-ambitious enterprise.

Thus these two great nations, which, had they been in agreement, could have helped the West to weather a difficult period of transition, actually increased the chaos by tearing one another to pieces. Chaos, however, was everywhere, particularly in Italy, where all attempts at unification had failed, and where every province, and almost every town, stood alone, wrapped up in arrogant assurance of its own importance. The monarchical, even dictatorial, system of government, the living expression of this arrogance, was tending to impose itself throughout the country. Nationalism and commercial interests provoked endless conflict between these petty entities—city against city, republics against the states of the Church, North against South; and the inextricable tangle of hideous warfare was rich in horrible episodes. These wars were often fought to the death; an instance is provided by the conflict between Venice and Genoa, during which the Doge's fleet annihilated that of its enemy (1381). For more than a century Dante's phrase was to remain startlingly apt; at the very time when civilization was flowering within her bosom, Italy, Dante's 'hostelry of grief,' was slipping swiftly towards decline.

The Germanic world offered a scarcely less cruel picture, and anarchy was its lot also—anarchy in which the rule of law was abolished, and where *Faustrecht* was not seldom the *ultima ratio*. What remained of the old imperial authority? Some trappings and a few rites, but little besides. Although the Golden Bull of 1356 had swept away papal intervention in Germany, it had at the same time placed the imperial crown in the custody of the nobility, comprising notably the seven Electors, who made sure that it passed from one family to another—Nassau, Bavaria, Luxemburg, Hapsburg of Austria. Finally, in 1440, a member of the last-named family, Frederick III (1440–93), succeeded, despite his unprepossessing appearances and scant reputation, in firmly establishing his dynasty upon the throne in perpetuity, and practised that fruitful policy of marriage alliances with Burgundy, Spain and Bohemia which would enable his descendants to revive, with some semblance of truth, his haughty device: A.E.I.O.U. *Austriae est imperare orbi universo.* Meanwhile, however, the worst type of feudal anarchy reigned triumphant; barons fought counts, prince-bishops attacked dukes, town was against town; more than six hundred separate entities divided the soil of Germany between them. National passions clung tenaciously to a few walls, or to two or three acres.

In a situation of this kind, with its all-pervasive climate of violence, the bitterest of rivalries were bound to run riot. A settling of ancient and open banditry went hand in hand with antagonisms founded upon ambition. The dreadful Hussite War was only one among many frightful episodes in which brutality was allowed free rein. It can, even so, claim to have been waged in the interests of a superior principle in the shape of religious orthodoxy, whereas the majority of similar wars had no other cause save sordid questions of individual self-interest. A number of new groupings took advantage of the general anarchy to spring into existence and establish themselves on a permanent footing. Around the first three Swiss cantons, which had pledged themselves to mutual brotherhood in the meadow of Grütli in 1291, others soon gathered—Lucerne, Zürich, then Bern (1351–3). After the Austrian knights had been crushed by the sturdy mountaineers at Sempach (1386), the Swiss federation came into being, destined to a future of fruitful liberty. It was also due to this same anarchical situation, which was causing the break-up of the Germanic world, that a cadet branch of the Capetians attempted to breathe life into the ancient concept of a kingdom of Lotharingia, boldly established an intermediary realm between France and Germany, and succeeded in annexing elements ranging from Burgundy to Holland, and including Luxemburg, the native land of one of the imperial families: a great dream, shattered by Charles the Bold, who believed that he had brought it to fulfilment.

Thus, on all sides, anarchy and violence replaced the unity of yesterday; Christians fought Christians, and the blood of baptized souls was freely shed. Along the Baltic shores, where, in days gone by, a united Catholicism had forced paganism to recoil, and had contained the Slav advance, the Hanseatic League now attacked Denmark, utterly defeating her in 1369. Farther east this split among fellow Christians acquired an even more ungodly character in the struggle which Poland, controlled by the Jagellons since 1385, was forced to wage against the Teutonic Knights, those ex-crusaders who had, however, degenerated considerably and become mere agents of Prussian expansion. Poland settled this affair by inflicting the severe defeat of Tannenberg upon the knights (1410). But there were equally ungodly conflicts raging on the other side of Europe, in the shape of those fratricidal wars, arising from dynastic quarrels, whose theatre was the Iberian peninsula. They took place beneath the very eyes of the Moors, who still occupied the southernmost tip of Spain from which the Christians seemed to have abandoned all idea of expelling them.

It is therefore obvious that there is no single area of the West which does not reveal a pattern of disintegration and violence during this unhappy period. Even if we complete the picture by recalling the contemporary situation in the East, which was held fast in the grip of irresistible Turkish advance,[1] we have not accounted for all the consequences provided by this agony of Christendom. For it must be added that the disequilibrium resulting from the collapse of the old ideals, which was so deep-seated on the political plane, was no less so on the social, where indeed it was even more disturbing in some ways. Admittedly the lowliest members of the population had several good reasons for rebelling, for it was they in short who bore the brunt of the miseries of the age. In a sermon preached before the French Court, Gerson courageously declared that the poor were about to cry 'Down with hunger'; and Bishop Jean Jouvenel, the poet, Alan Chartier, and the chronicler Meschinot, echoed these complaints in similar words. The movements of social insurrection were only too fully justified by suffering and penury. Allied, however, with these instinctive urges were other forces, deriving from bourgeois ambitions. The class which had acquired wealth was increasingly reluctant to see itself prevented from playing any part in the administration of government and national finance, and was seeking to supplant or control the nobility. For this reason it did not hesitate to ally itself even with the mob. The chroniclers of the epoch were not so keenly aware of this movement as they were of the agitation of the poor. They were still preoccupied with the

---

[1] See section further on in this chapter: 'The Turkish Tidal Wave Attacks Christendom.'

ancient concept of society which place the nobility alone in the forefront of the picture; [1] but so far as history was concerned, this stirring
of the bourgeoisie proved far more important than the sporadic unrest
of the poor. As soon as the middle class became fully conscious of its
strength, the traditional social hierarchies, on which Christendom
rested, would be shattered into fragments.

There were countless symptoms of this social ferment. No epoch
that had gone before had produced so many demagogues, champions
of popular rights and revolutionary agitators. However, there was no
question of one co-ordinated movement, organized by one faction or
one doctrine; crises broke out spasmodically, short-lived in character
and dispersed over widely separated areas. In France 'Jacques Bon-
homme,' the ordinary peasant, took advantage of the lack of authority
during King John's captivity. Exasperated by squalor and famine, and
maddened by uncertainty, the peasantry rose in revolt, spontaneously,
almost everywhere. In the Île de France the 'Jacquerie' found a leader
in the handsome Guillaume Karle, who organized it along military lines,
and swept victorious through Soissons, Picardy and Valois. It was only
by chance that he was seized by a handful of noblemen outside Meaux;
after that a bloody sequence of reprisals sent some twenty thousand
peasants to the gallows. At the same time (1358) Paris experienced
a veritable political and social revolution; Etienne Marcel and his
followers attempted to impose bourgeois control over the public
authority there, but their attempt foundered in blood. Much later on
it was in Paris once again that the popular revolt of the Maillotins
(1382) took place. In Languedoc and Auvergne there was the rising
of the Tuchins, a collection of beggars and starving ne'er-do-wells,
which occasioned acts of dreadful violence, while that of the Cabo-
chiens, thirty years later (1413), was led by the Paris butchers.

France had no monopoly of these risings, which were invariably
followed by savage reprisals. In Flanders—where the career of Jacob
van Artevelde, at the beginning of the Hundred Years War, had already
revealed an extremely disturbing state of social affairs—the danger of
revolution was certainly apparent. On several occasions the large
cities were captured by veritable armies of rebel artisans, the most
famous episode of this type being the revolt led by Philip van Artevelde, Jacob's young and fanatical son, who subjected Ghent to a
thorough-going reign of terror. It was all very well for the French
cavalry to wipe out the infantry of Ghent at Roosebeke in 1382; their
subversive ideas were not suppressed for all that. These ideas, mingled

---

[1] In his *Temple de Boccace* Chastellain, the chronicler of Philip the Good, does not
allow a place for Jacques Cœur, the financier, who was a middle-class man of genius, but
he allots a place to Gilles de Rais, despite the latter's crimes, owing to his noble birth.

with religious considerations, came to the surface again in England, where a terrible peasants' revolt broke out simultaneously. This rebellion, which laid waste Essex and Kent, had affinities with a kind of pre-Marxian Communism. Under the leadership of Wat Tyler it set about the task of exterminating nobles, bishops and wealthy merchants, burning castles, opening prisons and looting towns. Tyler's frightful mob, with which the heretical sect of the Lollards was believed to have some obscure connection, got as far as London and forced its way into the Tower: the queen-mother was maltreated, the Archbishop of Canterbury's head was paraded on the end of a pike, and a dreadful wave of vandalism destroyed many works of art, archives and jewels. Fortunately the spirited action of the lord mayor in running Wat Tyler through with his sword put an end to this tragedy, which was one of the worst of the period.

But there were dozens more. In Germany town chroniclers are for ever recording the burning down of strong castles, the beheading of noblemen and widespread looting; but they also record equally atrocious acts of reprisal. Thus, in 1388, the Count Palatine, who had crushed a rising of this kind, had his prisoners roasted alive in a brick oven! The 'holy' Vehme, with its merciless courts, was created to wage war against the insecurity resulting from such crises, but how effective was it? Throughout the fifteenth century there were rumbles of peasant discontent, combined with claims for social justice: at Worms (1431), at Salzburg (1462) and in Alsace (1468), where the Bundschuh movement originated. In Italy the middle class, which was itself opposed to the aristocracy, often played the delicate game of using the mob even while controlling it, and this resulted in numerous tragedies. The same symptoms occur everywhere. In Bohemia the religious agitation set in train by John Huss rapidly turned to social revolt; and even in Serbia, long after the death of Stephen Dushan, the same troubles continued, sporadic in character, but none the less violent for all that. It was indeed a complete social ferment which was rocking the structure of moribund Christendom, a ferment aggravated by the mystical revivals of the Flagellants and the growth of heresy. On this plane, as on that of politics, the old order, logical and sound though it had once been, was crumbling away into violence and blood.

THE NOSTALGIA OF CHRISTENDOM

A number of contemporaries were well aware of this collapse— this 'Last Day'—of their world, and their mournful knowledge goes far towards explaining the general distress which manifested itself in several ways, obliterating spiritual life just as it destroyed art forms and literature.[1] There was a distinct feeling of nostalgia towards the past, which was not merely that regret for *temporis acti* with which the old constantly assail the ears of the young in every generation. To those who had pondered deeply upon the underlying causes of the many tragedies of the epoch, it was plain that Christendom had once constituted a perfectly logical and stable world order—even though it had always been more of an ideal than a reality—and that they could so far see nothing to set in its place. It is interesting to observe that the artistic work which is perhaps the most complete and profound expression of the whole spirit of the Middle Ages, the fresco depicting the 'Hounds of God' in Santa Maria Novella at Florence,[2] was actually painted in an epoch when it no longer corresponded to the true facts of the situation. Andrea da Firenze finished his masterpiece some time after 1350, and by then the majestic harmony which he had conceived was nothing more than a splendid dream—the harmony of a Christian society governed by pope and emperor, ordered by the sovereign domination of the Lamb, in which all conditions of men and all nations occupied their divinely appointed place.

As early as 1321, the year in which the mighty voice of Dante,[3] the last witness of medievalism, was silenced for ever, it was apparent that the arrangement with which he claimed kinship, the world which, in his fiery stanzas, he accused his contemporaries of betraying, was no more than a wonderful ideal on the point of disappearance. Had not Dante himself—for after all poets can scarcely be expected to be wholly logical—foretold the rise of secular societies and the separation of Church and State, in his dream of a world in which the Pope would reign supreme in the realm of faith, the philosopher in that of morals, while the emperor would govern the social hierarchies? In consigning Boniface VIII to Hell, had he not dispatched there, along with him, 'many Christian beliefs, and, in particular, the most splendid belief of all, that of a world in which temporal society would be organized into one of the supernatural ends of man'?[4] Although the great Italian genius was the last herald of the Church of Cathedral and Crusade, had not he marked, with equal emphasis, the transition to the age which was to follow and, possibly without being fully aware of it, tolled the knell of medieval Christendom?

[1] See the next chapter, section: 'Art's "Coat of Many Colours."'
[2] For the meaning of this fresco see the first few pages of *Cathedral and Crusade*.
[3] See the final chapter of *Cathedral and Crusade*.
[4] For this aspect of Dante, which corrects and completes the picture of him as the witness of Christendom, see E. Gilson, *Dante et la philosophie* (a series of lectures given at the Collège de France, 1934–5), and also the recent works of Renaudet, *Dante humaniste*, and Renucci, *Dante témoin du monde greco-latin*. It should be noted that certain contemporaries were perfectly aware of the danger which some of Dante's ideas held in store for the ancient order of things: it was because of this that Bertrand du Poujet, John XXII's legate, had the *De monarchia* burnt.

Nevertheless the splendid image which Dante had contemplated was to remain in the back of men's minds for a long time to come, and traces of it recurred in several literary works, even after the modern world had replaced the defunct Christendom of the past.

During the last quarter of the fourteenth century this outdated and generous loyalty was made incarnate in one man. His name was Philippe de Mézières. He possessed an inexhaustible imagination, tireless steadfastness and indomitable courage, and he devoted his entire life to the pursuit of a dream—the cream of imitating the Knights of the Round Table by drawing the baptized world back to its task of delivering the Holy Sepulchre from the Infidel. At the age of twenty de Mézières had fought beneath the walls of Smyrna. Next he had joined the *entourage* of Peter de Lusignan, had become the latter's chancellor and then his ambassador in Europe, and had subsequently departed to Egypt, to fight there a second time. Having won the confidence of Charles V of France, he had several conversations with the king,[1] in which he urged that there could be no better justification of Christendom reformed by a council than the reconquest of Jerusalem. It was de Mézières, also, who persuaded Pope Gregory XI to accept the Eastern festival of the Presentation of the Blessed Virgin, in order to further thereby the reconciliation of the churches of East and West; and an Order of the Passion, of which he dreamed, was to provide one hundred thousand warriors for the great crusade. These warriors, together with their wives, all of them subject to rigorous vows, would constitute a new race of Christians in the Holy Land. De Mézières was quite indefatigable. Around 1390 he described his plans to Charles VI of France, on whom so many hopes were still pinned, and later to Richard of England. He also conversed for many long hours with young Louis of Orleans.

But the cherishing of extravagant fancies such as these was not confined to imaginative dreamers like Philippe de Mézières. Traces of the same nostalgia are found also in the writings of Froissart, Monstrelet, Chastellain and several other authors. It can be detected likewise among those theologians who upheld the authority of a general council as superior to that of the Holy See—Pierre d'Ailly, for instance, and Gerson. Men debated whether supreme authority ought to belong to the Pope alone or to the assembly of the Church, but they still put forward as a principle what Gerson called 'the monarchical primacy instituted by Christ here on earth as well as in heaven,' and insisted that this should be exercised over the whole of human society.

One of the most obvious signs of the survival in men's minds of the idea of Christendom is provided by the continued desire for a crusade. In the golden days of medieval Europe, when Christendom was at the

[1] These talks were the origin of his book *The Dream of the Ancient Pilgrim*.

peak of its vigour, the crusade had been the most obvious political manifestation of its grandeur: by throwing themselves into the task of reconquering the Holy Sepulchre, the faithful had been made conscious of the fundamental unity which existed between man and man, beyond their sinful and futile quarrels; and their actions had provided proof of this. Even when the hard facts of the political situation prevented them from resuming the sublime adventure, they continued to see in it the complete expression of that unity whose loss they so deeply lamented.

In so far as it was a historic reality, the crusade had come to an end on that dark day in the year 1291 when the Moslems had captured St John d'Acre, the last surviving Frankish bastion in Palestine. After that there were only limited attempts at reconquest, and all these, though admirable in their individual episodes, were sporadic and ineffective. And yet, how many saintly souls, philosophers and theologians continued to nurse this splendid ideal, which, as history was henceforth to prove, was in fact quite dead! And, for centuries to come, how many soldiers and statesmen actually talked of putting it into practice! So real was the Christians' need of something which would give them back the old feeling of unity. . . . Throughout her turbulent life St Catherine of Siena worked constantly to promote 'the holy crossing' to the land of the Infidel, *il dolce mistero del santo passagio*. Moreover she regarded it less as an enterprise of extermination than as an immense enlargement of Christendom, to be brought about by the entry into its bosom of all the Moslems, who would thus be restored to the way of truth. In order to 'raise the banner of the Holy Cross,' to quote her own words, crowds could be seen arriving in Avignon on several occasions, reminiscent of the followers of Peter the Hermit, to beg the Pope to become the leader of the sacred adventure. Even in the very midst of the tragedy of the Great Schism, never a day passed without one or other of the pontiffs failing to announce that, as soon as he was victorious, he would launch the faithful along the highways of the Holy Land once more. In fact, it was one of these enterprises, conceived during a moment of extreme spiritual exaltation, without any serious calculations or patient preparation, that resulted in the catastrophe of Nicopolis.[1] For a very long time indeed this idea of a crusade turned up again and again in every land and in all strata of society. Philippe de Mézières viewed the crusade as the means of remedying all the ills of the age, by uniting in the same heroic enterprise not merely all nations, but all social classes too. When Henry V of England, the conqueror of Rouen and Paris, lay dying in 1422, he told his courtiers that 'if it had been the pleasure of God, his Creator, to permit him to live his full span' he would have led the crusade himself, as soon as peace in France had been restored. Much later still,

[1] See section further on in this chapter: 'The Turkish Tidal Wave Attacks Christendom.'

in 1451, Denys the Carthusian, the great mystic, was received in audience at Brussels by Philip the Good. He claimed to have learned in a vision that God was summoning the great Duke of Burgundy to don the crusader's mantle and liberate the Holy Sepulchre. This insistence upon the crusade seems doubly anachronistic to the modern observer. Firstly, events were clearly opposed to such daydreams; secondly, it had already dawned upon the Church that the future of Christianity no longer lay in conquest by force, but in victories achieved by apostleship and self-sacrifice.[1] But the idea was so firmly rooted in men's minds that even Raymond Lull, who spent his life studying Islam and finally sacrificed it in a heroic missionary enterprise, ended by developing his own plan for the reconquest of the Holy Land; and in the following century Cardinal Nicholas of Cusa, an expert on the Koran, finished by declaring that the crusade was an absolute necessity.

Meanwhile the idea of a crusade, though anachronistic as a proposition, was used by the most lucid thinkers to mask new historical realities. Proof of this is to be found in the *De recuperatione terrae sanctae* (On the Recovery of the Holy Land) by Pierre Dubois,[2] a notorious journalist of the early fourteenth century, who gave it the characteristic subtitle: *A Treatise on General Policy*. Thus, in the mind of Dubois, the notion of a crusade expressly covered and dominated all the elements of a political philosophy which, though rubbing shoulders with a host of curious and even crazy ideas, seems remarkably far-sighted, considering its date. Nationalistic, and violently in favour of the kings' autonomy, 'this pocket Richelieu, this potential Robespierre,' proposed that all sovereign states should be closely linked in a Christian federation, on which the crusade would set the final seal. This first project for a League of Nations or, more accurately, for a United States of Europe, had no immediate influence upon the actual policies of the various states; but it did exert an undeniable subconscious influence. In 1464 George Podebrad, King of Bohemia, a sort of Czech Napoleon, who was strongly influenced by one Antoine Marin, an eccentric French refugee at Prague, took it up again, almost word for word. He suggested that all the monarchs of Europe should unite in a league, thus forming a federation which would be governed by an elected assembly. The first object of this federation would be to halt the Turkish advance.[3] His scheme came to nothing,

---

[1] See *Cathedral and Crusade,* Chapter XII: 'The Holy War of the Missions.'

[2] He was a staunch supporter of Philip the Fair against the Papacy.

[3] It should be observed that, according to Podebrad's philosophy, these United States of Europe would be independent of the Pope, for the King of Bohemia was suspected of heresy (he was to be condemned by Paul II in 1466). Thus the idea of Christendom was being secularized. Moreover this is why the French Catholics brought about the project's collapse when envoys from the court at Prague took it to Paris.

but it remained in men's minds like a splendid dream; and it is interesting to note that among Henri IV's advisers, close beside Sully who cherished his own famous 'Grand Design,' [1] was the learned Calvinist Bongars, who, long before Renan's time, assessed the position held by Pierre Dubois and included the latter's *De recuperatione terrae sanctae* in his *Gesta Dei per Francos*.

The failure of these grandiose daydreams is of little importance: their interest lies in the fact that they show that, in this age of transition, when moribund Christendom was beginning to leave an increasingly apparent vacuum, a number of intelligent and clear-sighted men, even though they might be only dreamers, were already preoccupied with the problem of filling the void. The question they raised was a political one: was it possible in that critical hour, when the 'nation-states in process of formation were no longer held fast in the juridical concept of sovereignty,' to unite them, in order that their free association might replace the great mystery which was now in the act of vanishing? [2] In a deeper sense, however, the question was a religious one: Could this important historical fact, the emergence of national patriotism, be placed in a Christian setting? Could these young nation-states, which were all so conscious of what made them individual and irreplaceable, take their places in one fraternal whole, which would thus prove to be a rejuvenated Christendom? Many saintly souls longed for this to happen, and laboured to further such an ideal with all the strength at their command. Although she was an ardent patriot, St Catherine of Siena none the less defended the mighty idea in which her native Italy, nay even her tiny native town of Siena, might take its place in a loving harmony alongside all the other states of Europe. Much later on St Nicholas of Flüe (1417–87), the strange Swiss hermit who is famous for his prodigious fasting, left his cell at Ranft to go and advise the political leaders of his country and thus save the cantons from a disastrous war. He made no distinction between his compatriots and the generality of his brethren in Christ, and he consistently taught the former that it was their duty to maintain the living bond between all the Children of Light. Finally, this apparently contradictory twofold demand of national aspirations and the believer's loyalty to Christendom found its most perfect expression in Joan of Arc, to whom the service of her king and that of her God were inseparable, and whose youthful blood, while baptizing the newborn patriotism of France, was at the same time poured out for an ideal far greater than that of earthly motherland.

[1] See *The Catholic Reformation*, Chapter III, section 10.
[2] These ideas and projects are fully discussed in Bernard Voyenne's excellent little book, which is mentioned in the bibliography at the end of this work.

The Vocation of Joan of Arc

At the beginning of 1429 the French kingdom was in a sorry plight. For nearly a century the English had been laying waste the land of France, and this ordeal seemed to be drawing to a most melancholy close. Fourteen years earlier France had been defeated yet again, this time at Agincourt. The lawful crown had tumbled into the dust, only to be snatched thence by the English monarch. At the obsequies of the unfortunate and demented Charles VI, in 1422, the Duke of Bedford, regent of France in the name of the King of England, had led the mourners, walking alone, in solitary state, as if the hateful Peace of Troyes and all the intrigues of Isabeau of Bavaria had conclusively established England's right to the French throne. There was now no one left to defend the heritage of St Louis, save the slight young man with the long, timid, melancholy face, hiding in obscurity among the reeds of the Loire. Even his supporters hesitated to call him anything more than Dauphin; his enemies dubbed him King of Bourges. To crown all, in addition to the sufferings brought about by foreign invasion, there was the appalling misery of civil war, which reduced the common people to an even worse state of wretchedness. The Burgundians, forgetful of their French origins, seemed on the verge of realizing their duke's dream of making himself sovereign in his own territory by dismembering the kingdom; and to achieve this ambition they were collaborating with the enemy regime. All seemed lost, and indeed all would have been lost but for the grace of God.

Deep down in the hearts of this divided and exhausted people, in the ranks of the most lowly and most wretched, one feeling still survived, and was actually intensified by the stresses to which they were subjected. It was a sense of dynastic loyalty, as firmly rooted as their feeling of religious loyalty, with which it was indeed closely linked. Allegiance, such as it was, among the aristocracy and middle classes might be bound up with considerations of personal self-interest or high policy; but among the French peasantry it was almost instinctive, a pure and noble passion, of a simplicity that was at once naïve and wonderful. For the peasants there was but one lawful king—the man who, once anointed, would be Charles VII. He was the incarnation of this still young but already powerful idea of a nation united by glorious tradition as well as by a common spirit and a community of aims. How many humble villagers risked their lives for this idea, battling courageously against the English conquerors who burned their homesteads, hanged the menfolk and buried the women alive! God in no wise despises human instruments, and often makes use of natural means to further the accomplishment of His designs. Thus it came to pass that in a little 'Armagnac' village in the Barrois, hard hit by the war, like so many others, Divine Providence ordained the rise of the heroine who was to translate God's will into action, and whose advent was even then being silently prepared by all that vast wave of loyalty and need.[1]

Joan was the daughter of Jacques d'Arc and Isabelle Romée. Everything about her was typical of any ordinary daughter of France. She was a peasant girl who delighted in honest toil. To Joan the struggle against the English was a job of work like any other, except that it was the most difficult and arduous of tasks. From her forebears, all of whom had lived close to the soil, she inherited her robust common sense, sound judgment and placid candour, and also her completely natural foible of enjoying beautiful clothes, richly wrought armour and even her own sword, which she was always quick to use, 'rough and ready' though her blows might be. But besides these characteristics, and dominating them all, was her unswerving faith, which never deviated from the essential, and which was to leave the wily theologians who strove to catch her out in their interrogations utterly discomfited. Ever since infancy Joan had shared in the trials and tribulations of the French race from which she sprang—her birth-place, Domrémy, had been subject to the ravages both of mercenary bands and of Burgundians—but within her heart she carried the gift of hope. In her, and through her, Heaven echoed the fundamental longing of a Christian nation.

'The salvation of the kingdom of France.' In January 1429 such an eventuality seemed in the last degree improbable. The military result appeared already decided: five years earlier, at Carvant and Verneuil, the two remaining major armies in the Dauphin's service had been cut to pieces; and with the fall of Orléans, which Talbot had completely surrounded the previous autumn, the route to the Midi would be open to the English, who would then be able to effect a junction with their garrisons in Gascony. There was no hope of any human intervention on France's behalf: even the Pope had done nothing to save the crown of St Louis, most probably because there was nothing that he could have done. The Pope at that time was Martin V, who, though a man of courage, was completely immersed in the task of restoring at least a modicum of order to the Church which had been so ravaged by the Schism. Moreover he was fast approaching his death. But as in the case of nations, so in that of individuals, the moment of direst desolation is generally the hour which God makes His own. In that meadow where the Archangel Gabriel, accompanied

[1] One significant coincidence is worth noting. The Order of the Golden Fleece, the symbol of this Burgundian sovereignty, was instituted by Duke Philip the Good in the same year as that which marked the beginning of the rise of Joan of Arc.

by St Margaret and St Catherine, had talked for the first time to the little shepherdess, and in the fortress of Neufchâteau where he had repeated his order, the whole of France had received the summons of hope. Joan had been barely thirteen years old when the mysterious voices first echoed in her ears. She was seventeen or eighteen [1] when, despite her great humility, she agreed to obey them and to embark on her incredible adventure. Providence was using a child in order that the youthful spirit of a nation which desired to live in freedom might be made manifest, in historical time, in an upsurge of heroism and glory.

'Leave your village, daughter of God, and journey into France! Choose your standard and raise it boldly! You shall lead the Dauphin to Rheims, that he may there receive the crown and unction that are his by right! You shall deliver France from the English!' The astonishing aspect of Joan's career is not so much the fact that a young, divinely inspired peasant girl, who had been accustomed since childhood to living close to the supernatural in her prayers, should have heard these extraordinary commands, nor even that she should have carried them out. More surprising is the fact that her influence and authority should have been so great that she was able to convince, and that large numbers of men who were normally little inclined to mingle miracle with their politics or their strategy, should have yielded to her mysterious reasoning.

Indeed every aspect of this legend, which is also an historical fact, is quite extraordinary: Joan's recognition by the bluff Baudricourt, captain of the royal garrison at Vaucouleurs, who had begun by treating the shepherdess as a ridiculous joke, but who subsequently gave her a charger, a sword and an escort; the little party's uneventful journey from Barrois to Chinon, through territory infested with enemies, while the emotion of a whole nation was gathering momentum; the meeting of the humble peasant girl and the prince, the conversation whose secrets have never been pierced, but which resulted in the legitimate crown of France becoming a party to the apparently insane project of the Maid of Lorraine; and lastly the fabulous impulse which made troops who were all too used to defeat, and the very townsfolk who were virtually resigned to the worst, prove themselves equal to the task of liberating Orléans from the English—all the episodes in this heroic saga leave the historian disconcerted as he watches the supernatural stride so obviously athwart everyday actions.

[1] The date of Joan of Arc's birth is sometimes disputed. The years 1410 and 1412 have been suggested, and the second of these is most widely accepted.

Similarly the question as to whether Joan came from Champagne or Lorraine is still debated. A tiny stream which ran through her birth-place marked the border between the two provinces, and this stream has changed its course during the passage of the centuries. See Canon Gauroy, *Jeanne d'Arc champenoise*, Strasburg, 1946.

On 17th July 1429 the Dauphin Charles received the sacred unction which made him king in the flag-decked basilica at Rheims, and Joan of Arc's immediate mission, the task which she had declared she was undertaking in order to please God, was brought to a successful conclusion. Before the whole world she had asserted the need for both France and England to recognize each other as separate nations; she had proclaimed the right of every people to protect its own soul, together with its own freedom. The Lancastrian dream was an anachronism; it was the peasant girl of Domrémy who was in harmony with the current of history; and this is the reason why the English themselves now render her their own particular homage, for they realize full well that in setting them firmly along the course of their insular destiny, Joan was really doing them a great service. Yet even in her own day one or two contemporaries understood the fundamental significance of this astonishing achievement. Such, for example, was the Italian chronicler who wrote: 'Through the medium of this young, innocent, untainted virgin, God saved the finest part of Christendom; this was the most important thing that had happened for five hundred years.' He was right.

Joan of Arc's significance, however, is considerably lessened if her vocation is restricted to the fulfilment of this one enormous and essential task. She had been commanded to save France 'in the name of the King of Heaven,' in other words, for Christian purposes. Her motherland, the kingdom of France, and the king himself were certainly realities which the warrior-maid prized more dearly than her own life; but there was another reality which was more important than them all, because all the rest proceeded from it: God, Christ the Church. 'I serve God first!' It must be clearly understood that the heroine's motto embraced even the most extreme of her demands. For her everything, absolutely everything, was ordained according to the purpose of the justice which is love.

This is the meaning of Joan of Arc's patriotism. She loved France *in God*, just as other saints have loved the poor and the sinners in God; and she loved France simply because she saw her wretched, divided and sinful. Hers was a redemptive love. It held nothing arrogant nor aggressive: Joan never once spoke of conquering England, nor of imposing her rule upon anyone whomsoever. Likewise it never occurred to her that in doing what she did she would cover her native land with glory and that her feats of valour would give her the right to command others. All that she demanded for her country, her king and herself was a simple, humble life, in which each man would receive his just deserts. She sought to gain acceptance for the justice of God and for nothing else. 'So—does God hate the English?' she was to be asked, in a question designed to ensnare her. Not at all, she answered.

He loved the English just as much as He loved any other nation, but He loved them when they stayed on their own native soil, governing with justice, not when they attacked the liberties of others. It was not so much the English that Joan was fighting, but injustice. No other hero of the battlefield ever showed himself more tender, nor more filled with brotherly love towards his enemies.

Thus, beyond Joan's immediate aim of the liberation of France and the restoration of the kingdom in all its dignity, there was another, more fundamental goal. The little peasant girl, who knew nothing about the philosophy of history, distinguished it quite simply with the eyes of faith. She called attention to it on several occasions. For example, when she wrote her famous letter of Holy Tuesday 1429 to Bedford's army, inviting it to leave France voluntarily before it was driven out by force, or when she addressed herself to the Duke of Burgundy on 17th July of the same year, or even—and more astonishing—when she wrote her vehement letter, soundly scolding the Bohemian Hussites, because she had heard tell that their impious war, born of an exacerbated patriotic emotion, was tearing the Church asunder. In every case her conclusion was the same: there must be an end to strife among the baptized: all Christian forces must unite into one single entity in order to serve Christ; everyone must work with one heart for one enterprise alone. What was this enterprise? Joan suggested the crusade as the formal goal of reconstituted Christian unity, and in this she showed herself very much a child of her own time. But beyond the dream of the 'great crossing' what she really conceived was a new order of Christendom, in which each nation would have its own mission to fulfil, but in which all would be linked in one superior purpose—a purpose which was daily expressed in every Christian formula of prayer: the coming of the kingdom of God.

The historic importance of her mission explains the vicious relentlessness displayed by the English in ridding themselves of their youthful adversary. With the arrival of Joan on the scene the war had undergone a conclusive change of character. There was no longer any question of it being one of those feudal conflicts, of which there had been so many in the old pattern of Christendom and in which it scarcely mattered whether such and such a people found a new ruler, since that made no difference to the feeling it might have regarding its own destiny. Henceforth the struggle was one in which a nation strove to defend the life which God had given it, the *raison d'être* which Divine Providence recognized as its alone. And within these new perspectives of a Christian unity, bound together in fraternity and justice, Henry VI's troops became nothing more than brutal aggressors, seeking to destroy a sacred principle. Thus it was absolutely essential to discredit the woman who was the visible incarnation of France's right to be no longer a fief of the realm of England; and the sole way of destroying the prestige of the young heroine was to undermine the supernatural bases of that prestige which, in the common people's eyes, showed her vocation to rest upon the very will of God. This was an easy task, since the Church is always at first distrustful of extra-ordinary manifestations; and the mystery which surrounded the inspired peasant from Domrémy was so hard to pierce that the number of contemporary theologians [1] who dared to confirm the religious authenticity of her mission, was small indeed. In so complex a situation ecclesiastical judges, who were far from being all worthless men,[2] could, in the course of an appallingly inquisitorial trial, which was scrupulously fair in its outward appearances, but which was really conducted with the sole purpose of securing the prisoner's condem-nation, work in opposition to the Christian faith and contrary to the divine will, even without realizing it. All men are fallible, and it is not granted to us all to discern the paths by which Providence intends to achieve its aim.[3]

But having read the detailed records of those interminable interro-gations which lasted through the winter of 1430 and the spring of 1431, one is left with an inescapable feeling that the whole grandiose pattern of events possessed a meaning which bears no relation to any kind of historical determinism, and that a will transcending that of man was manifest in it. Here is a delicate and simple child who success-fully resisted the most crafty of theologians, and whose pure and discreet faith, conformable in all respects to the teaching of the Church, is constantly asserting itself. For this child to have been what she undoubtedly was, a supernatural power must of necessity have guided her; she must indeed have been a chosen instrument of God. And in the final hour, at the iniquitous stake on which she took her stand on 30th May 1431, in the old market-place of Rouen, Joan was actually to provide the compelling evidence of her divine mission by refusing to identify Mother Church with those evil priests who had condemned her, by proclaiming to the end her loyalty to the Pope to whom she made her final appeal, and by dying in a surge of faith so sublime that some of her executioners were themselves confounded.

[1] Among them Gerson, Archbishop Gélu of Embrun and the professors of Poitiers.

[2] It is likely that they were puppets in the hands of Cauchon, Archbishop of Beauvais, and a small group of other prelate-politicians.

[3] The author does not desire to approach the problem of the good or bad faith of Joan of Arc's judges (or rather, that of the judge and the experts) here. Cauchon does not lack his supporters, who plead extenuating circumstances in his favour. Without mentioning de Rigne, who has become Cauchon's advocate and almost his hagiographer, reference should be made to the extremely sound works of Pierre Tisset, who is both a historian and a lawyer (a combination which is absolutely indispensable to the complete under-standing of the affair): 'Le Tribunal de Rouen était-il competent?' and 'Quelques remarques à propos de Pierre Cauchon' (accounts contained in the Révue d'histoire de l'église de France, 1951, p. 100, and 1953, p. 277).

This is the fundamental meaning of the vocation of Joan of Arc, a woman who is a saint of the motherland of France, but a saint also of all Christendom. The immediate future would not heed the lesson of the great ideal which she had borne within her. Christian peoples became increasingly set in their narrow rights and egotisms, and national antagonisms soon substituted the balance of powers—in other words, chaos—for the brotherly unity for which the young saint had longed so fervently. Has justice at least been rendered to Joan herself? Twenty-five years after her death she was rehabilitated, in the course of proceedings conducted with more studious care than was formerly admitted, but in which political considerations undoubtedly played as large a part as religious ones, in the new climate created by Charles VII's victory over the English. In 1920 Holy Church offered her a still more striking tribute by canonizing her.[1] 'Saint Joan of Arc, Virgin,' says the liturgy; but though its validity is, theologically speaking, somewhat dubious, does not the title 'martyr' spring spontaneously to mind whenever we think of her? For the sins which Joan the Maid took upon her shoulders were not the sins of France alone: they were the sins of faithless Christendom, on the brink of self-betrayal. And her young blood was in fact to bear witness to the most profound of all Christian truths: that, above all the legitimate interests of individual nations, there exists one supreme interest, to which all the rest must bow: that even in politics God must be 'served first.'

The Turkish Tidal Wave Attacks Christendom

The concept of crusade, which still preserved in the mind of Joan its original sense of a sublime purpose, had already, even in her own day, acquired several other meanings. Here we are not concerned with those for whom ostensible preparation for the crusade served as a cloak for various military and business operations, or worse.[2] The title 'crusade' had also been used in a nobler sense, as a cover for one of the major political ideas which force of circumstances had imposed upon the rulers of the Christian West: the life-struggle against the Asiatic invader, whose progress was causing considerable anxiety to all who gave it a thought. There was no longer any question of leading an expedition of the flower of European chivalry for the purpose of

[1] This also took place in a setting in which political backgrounds are discernible—those of the French Republic's re-establishment of its embassy to the Vatican. The two reasons which prevented Joan from being declared a martyr are, moreover, completely valid ones: firstly, the English, through their judges, did not condemn her to death *because they hated the faith*; and secondly, the canonization of Joan the virgin meant the canonization of her whole life, and not just of her death, for that would have made her 'arrive in front of St Peter armed and helmeted,' in Cardinal Perrochi's phrase.

[2] During the trial of the Templars, for example, it was urged that the interests of the Holy Land itself required the abolition of the Order.

liberating the Holy Sepulchre. The issue now at stake concerned the defence of Europe's most vital interests. Here we have a strange contrast, characteristic of that age of transition, between the current idea of an indispensable military and political operation and the archaic, medieval formula which was used to describe it.

In fact, what we know as the 'Eastern Question' had now reared its ugly head, and it was posed in terms which were to remain virtually unchanged until the dawn of the twentieth century. At the end of the thirteenth century there had arisen, from the midst of that mosaic of somewhat ephemeral emirates which had succeeded the old empire of the Seljuks (recently broken up by the Mongols), the new, vigorous force of a tribe of Oghuz Turks, known as the Ottomans. From that time forward Asia had once again become a dangerous threat to Europe. Osman (or Othman), the founder of the ruling house, who gave his name to his people, had been succeeded by Orkhan I (1326–1360). Like Osman, Orkhan was a tireless fighter, who maintained constant pressure upon other emirates and upon the bastions of Byzantium. In 1326 he captured the charming pink-walled town of Brussa, which he made his capital; in 1330 he acquired Nicomedia and Nicaea. His army of professional soldiers, the janissaries, who were recruited from children seized from the peoples he conquered, seemed invincible. His systematic policy of 'Turkizing' the lands he conquered ensured him sound bases for his future offensives. In the middle of the fourteenth century Orkhan revived for himself the title of Sultan, which had fallen into disuse since the fall of the last Seljuk, and turned his arms against Europe. Claiming to be merely answering a call for help on the part of the usurping Basileus, John VI Cantacuzene (1341–55), who had just given the Turk his own daughter in marriage, he threw his resources into the task of helping the pretender in his struggle against the rightful emperor of Byzantium, John V Palaeologus (1341–96).

Thenceforward scarcely a single year had passed in which Christian Europe had not observed with distress some new Turkish advance. It was as if a vast, infinitely patient but irresistible tidal wave was surging forward to engulf the West, taking advantage of every breach in the latter's defences, and causing its dikes to crumble one by one. Where would it stop? In 1356 Solyman, one of Orkhan's sons, crossed the Dardanelles and occupied Gallipoli. Four years later Murad I (1360–1389), having finally subdued the petty emirs of Asia Minor, hurled his forces upon Thrace. He seized Adrianople and made it his capital, and took so many prisoners that he was obliged to sell them at bargain prices in order to get rid of them.

Who could resist this redoubtable attack? The answer of history should have been 'Byzantium,' whose role down the centuries had been to oppose an Asia on the warpath westwards; but alas, Byzantium was in a state of hopeless decline, undermined by the forces of death which were gaining an increasingly rapid hold. During the hundred years of its reign at the Blachernae Palace, the Palaeologus dynasty had striven hard to resist the edict of fate, but it had been able to do little more than slow down the inevitable march towards the abyss. The struggle between the two Johns—the lawful emperor and the usurper—had merely speeded up the dissolution of the sprawling, sick Empire. John V's reign, which lasted fifty years, had been nothing better than half a century of civil war. Ruined by the collapse of her maritime trade, competed for even in her own markets by the Genoese and Venetians, her customs yields reduced to nothing and her taxes non-existent, Constantinople was now no more than a motley, turbulent cosmopolitan city, abandoned to sophisticated luxury and doubtful animation. Her only surviving feature of real life was an intellectual impulse. Paradoxically this had regained its creative capacity in an age of catastrophe; the works of art left by the mosaic-workers of Karia-Djami and the fresco-painters of Mistra and Mount Athos enable us to feel its vigour even today.[1] The Basileus lived surrounded by the same ceremonial as his predecessors before him, and still played at being the Master of the World. But the jewels in his crown were only fakes, and when John V journeyed to the West to beg the Catholics there to save him, the Venetian bankers had him arrested and flung into prison for debt.

Failing Byzantium, there was no other great power left to oppose the Turkish tidal wave. What of 'Great Serbia,' which Stephen Dushan, its ephemeral founder, had believed he was raising so high in forming it into a state which rivalled the Empire? On his death, in

[1] After the disastrous establishment of the Latin kingdom in 1204, Byzantium had experienced a revival, and the arts had witnessed such a wonderful reawakening that it had been possible to speak of a 'new age.' This lasted throughout the fourteenth century during which period many churches and monasteries were built, often owing their inspiration to the influence of Western noblemen. In the capital itself the mosque of Karia-Djami, formerly St Saviour's Church, still contains mosaics whose fresh colouring and freedom of movement were something quite new. The metropolis of Arta, several of the churches of Trebizond, the 'little Byzantium of the thirteenth and fourteenth centuries,' and those which, among the ruins of Mistra, still evoke the past grandeur of the despots of the Morea, are splendid evidence of the artistic vitality of this epoch of decline. Crete possessed a very original school of painting. In addition to Mount Athos and the great monasteries built by the Macedonian emperors, six or seven new foundations were constructed, including Simopetra, Xeropotamou and St Gregorios. Although Byzantium's political influence had become so small, her artistic influence extended over the whole of the Balkans; in Serbia, where the fourteenth century was the great age of the arts, producing the masterpieces of Detchani, Markov and the Morava school; in Wallachia, where the buildings of Curtea de Arges, Voditsa and Cozia remain to this day; and in Bulgaria, where the numerous monuments in Mesembria and around Lake Ochrida still impress the modern observer. The art of the final Byzantine epoch affected regions even farther afield. It was to have a profound influence upon Russian art. (See further on in this chapter, note 2 on p. 103.)

1355, the realm of the Serbian Charlemagne had shivered into a myriad fragments, divided between North and South, and undermined too by one of those sporadic social crises of which there were so many in Europe at that time. Nor could anything be expected from the remnants of the Frankish kingdoms in the East. The pretty sword thrusts of Peter I de Lusignan, King of Cyprus, who succeeded in capturing Alexandria in 1365, but who was forced to evacuate it after three days, did little save exasperate the Turks, who exacted reprisals from the Italian banking houses. Moreover the hero of the last *chanson de geste* was soon to perish beneath the daggers of assassins armed by his own brother, dragging his kingdom down to destruction with him. The mountain dwellers of 'Little Armenia' were hard put to it to save their own increasingly precarious liberty; Leo VI, also a Lusignan, was to be their last king, and he managed to resist the Turks only for one year (1374–5).

In face of such an obvious menace the Christian West was at last stirred to action. It was Urban V (1362–70) who summoned Christendom to the crusade; but as Italy was in a state of chaos, France and England in the throes of the Hundred Years War and the Empire bereft of any real leader, none of these states responded to his appeal. The one and only ruler who set off on crusade at this time was *Amadeus of Savoy*. He left Venice in June 1366, and in August, as the result of a successful surprise attack on Gallipoli, won back from the Turks the key to the Dardanelles. Amadeus went on to sail up and down the Black Sea, engaging the Moslems in battle on several occasions before returning home, his vow fulfilled, thoroughly convinced that his solitary effort would not suffice to halt the Ottoman invasion of Europe.

However, the example of the gallant Savoyard was an encouraging sign. Gregory XI (1370–8) revived Urban V's idea of a crusade. The sovereigns of Eastern Europe, who were directly threatened by the Turk, grouped themselves together around the Angevin king of Hungary. Thus united the princes of Serbia, Bosnia, Bulgaria and Wallachia marched to battle against Murad; but in 1371, in a lightning counter-attack at Tchermen, on the Maritza, the Turk crushed them completely and advanced as far as Nish and Sofia. It seemed that absolutely no one could halt the conqueror from Asia. Torn asunder by the Schism, Christendom appeared quite incapable of uniting in order to make one final and supreme effort. But in 1389 a new coalition threw itself into the struggle, led by Lazarus, Tsar of Northern Serbia, and formed in answer to the appeal of those Serbs who were rebelling against their Moslem overlords. Murad hurried back westwards from Ankara. Christians and Turks confronted one another at *Kossovo*, on the 'Field of Blackbirds,' in a battle worthy of the greatest epics of the old *chansons de geste*. Murad himself perished, but his armies won a decisive victory. The whole of the Balkans fell beneath the sway of the Crescent, and henceforth Europe ended on the Hungarian frontier. When his Bulgarian flock inquired of Euthymius 'To whom are you abandoning us?' the Patriarch could only reply: 'To the Blessed Trinity.' But for centuries to come folk in Serbia and in all the other conquered Christian communities of Eastern Europe were to sing the glory of Lazarus, 'the golden-crowned,' who had died a martyr's death; of Milosh, the hero who had slain the Sultan; and of the countless gallant knights who had fallen on the 'Field of Blackbirds.' Right into modern times the Christian loyalties of the oppressed races of the Balkans were sustained by these great memories of their heroic past.

In consequence of these events the situation became increasingly fraught with tragedy for the whole of Western Europe. Murad was succeeded by Bajazet (1389–1402), nicknamed 'the Lightning.' One word from him was enough to reduce the Basileus, John V, to a state of abject terror. John agreed to pay tribute to Bajazet, and sent the Turk two of his own sons as hostages of his good faith. He even consented to join the Sultan in besieging Philadelphia, in Lydia, the last place in Asia Minor where a Christian garrison was still holding out against the Moslems. Bulgaria fell beneath the Turkish yoke, Wallachia paid Bajazet tribute and the Turk even intervened, with flagrant insolence, in the Morea. John's son, Manuel II (1391–1425), who succeeded in escaping from his Turkish jail, attempted to bring about a praiseworthy revival of Byzantium's strength and prestige: but the once great Byzantine Empire was now little more than one encircled city, awaiting the final death blow.

When it became known in the West that Bajazet had captured Salonica (1394), the shock was so great that a positive reaction to the danger occurred at last. With the somewhat surprising encouragement from both rival popes, a crusade was organized. It was summoned by Sigismund of Hungary, with the agreement of Charles VI of France, who was temporarily at peace with England. The majority of the crusaders came from France and Germany: John the Fearless led a strong contingent, accompanied by Boucicault, the marshal, and John of Vienne, admiral of France. But alas, this enormous operation was conducted with all the imprudence usually associated with adventures of medieval chivalry. Instead of lying in wait for the Turks at the Hungarian frontier, the impetuous Franco-Burgundian forces rushed forward to meet them. They had even laid siege to Nicopolis (1396) when Bajazet appeared over the horizon with an army of one hundred thousand men. The knightly jaunt turned to a terrible ordeal: it was another Crécy or Agincourt. Courageous to the point of foolhardiness, the Christian knights hurled themselves upon the stakes which protected the Turkish entrenchments, and quickly exhausted their strength. The janissaries' counter-attack found them disorganized, tired and abashed; they could do nothing save die, and this they did with wonderful heroism. 'No cornered boar ever gave himself up to the savage wolf more proudly,' says the chronicler. John of Vienne died a hero's death, brandishing the banner of Our Lady; Boucicault and John the Fearless were taken captive after performing countless feats of valour; only Sigismund managed to get away down the Danube. The enraged Bajazet had all his prisoners murdered, except for about forty important personages whom he released in return for a ransom of 200,000 florins. The disaster was complete.

The West seemed utterly lost. In any case, divided against itself as it was, Christendom appeared to be fast signing its own death-warrant. For this was the time when the election of Pedro da Luna (Benedict XIII) was exacerbating the question of the Schism, and the antipapal theologians were spreading far and wide the idea of a council superior to the Pope. It was the period in which the kingdom of France, weary of its mad monarch, Charles VI, was providing the world with the sorry sight of the royal princes wrangling for supreme power among themselves, whilst in England Richard II was soon to succumb to the assassin's blows directed by his own cousin, Henry of Lancaster. Many worthy souls read a divine warning into the frightful and sensational occurrence which had recently struck terror into the French Court— that 'Fiery Ball' at which all too many careless raptures had ended in a ghastly death. . . . Confronted by a decline of such universal character, Bajazet naturally exploited his victory to the full. He conquered Bosnia and the Danubian principalities of Wallachia and Moldavia, laid waste Styria, and threw his advance guards forward to the German frontiers. Then he suddenly changed his mind, and returned to the East in order to try to capture Byzantium in a surprise attack. Although almost isolated in the midst of all this chaos, the Emperor Manuel reacted with admirable spirit. He repulsed the Sultan's attack and refused to give up hope. In all this he was assisted by the gallant Boucicault, who had taken up the fight again immediately he was released from captivity, and who brought his own little contingent to harass the Turk.

However, the Christian world was really saved in the most unexpected fashion. The King of Transoxiana, a realm comprising the regions around Samarkand and Bokhara, was a certain Timur, surnamed Leng, or the Lame—a Turk, and not, as has sometimes been erroneously stated, a Mongol. Timur had carved out a vast kingdom for himself, stretching from Afghanistan to Cilicia, and he now intended to extend it still farther. All the petty emirs who had been defeated by Orkhan and Bajazet found a warm welcome at his court. In 1398 he

D

had seized Mesopotamia, Georgia, Armenia and part of India, all his conquests being accompanied by atrocious massacres. In 1401 he began the task of occupying Asia Minor. A decisive battle was waged between Timur and Bajazet upon the plateau near Ankara, whither the Sultan had ridden at full speed in a desperate attempt to save his empire. But Bajazet was betrayed by a section of his own followers and suffered an irreparable defeat. He was taken prisoner, and although humanely treated by his conqueror, he died of grief ten months later. All the Christian peoples whom he had terrorized breathed again. So the true saviour of Europe was a barbarian from Asia, the man whom history knows as 'Tamberlane.'

It is doubtful if the situation was basically much improved. Setting himself up as the arbiter of the Middle East, Tamberlane did indeed restore Salonica and the Ionian Islands to Manuel II, but only after forcing the emperor to accept a treaty which reduced him to the status of a quasi-vassal. At the same time he seized Smyrna from the Knights Hospitallers of Rhodes. In fact, Tamberlane was the real master of the whole of the Eastern world, and the Genoese merchants of Pera went so far as to fly his standard from the mastheads of their ships. Fortunately his nomadic temperament soon impelled him back to the Asian steppes. Byzantium breathed freely once more, and Mohammed I, Bajazet's successor, did not trouble her for several years to come.

Now was Christendom's unique chance to act. Anarchy held the Ottoman Empire firmly in its grip. The princes of the blood were in rebellion against their father, and the emirs were restive. A simultaneous rising of Serbs and Bulgars, a Hungarian attack combined with a Byzantine offensive, could have driven the Turks back to Asia. Moreover Salonica had slipped from their grasp, and they had lost control of the Dardanelles. But the futile quarrels between Greeks and Latins prevented this chance from being seized, and as soon as Mohammed I had put his kingdom in order the war was resumed. Once more, in 1422, the Turks hurled themselves against the walls of Constantinople. The defences fortunately held fast, the people fought back with savage fury and a vision of Our Lady, which was seen simultaneously by both sides, weakened the aggressor's resolve. However, the Ottoman Empire overflowed into and utterly devastated the Peloponnese, the last bastion of Christian resistance in Greece. By the time John VIII (1425-48) succeeded Manuel, nothing remained of the Empire save its capital.

Christendom seemed prepared to allow Byzantium to fall into Turkish hands. John VIII hurried westwards to make one final appeal for aid. He won the support of Pope Eugenius IV by personally accepting the union of the two churches. But the universal crusade for which the Basileus campaigned never materialized. France and

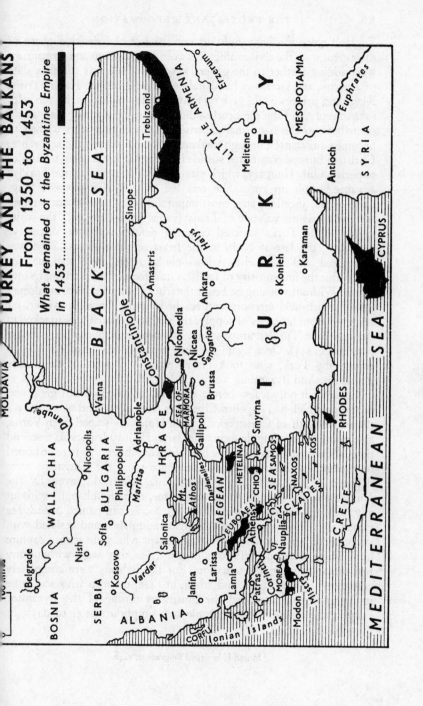

TURKEY AND THE BALKANS
From 1350 to 1453

What remained of the Byzantine Empire
in 1453 ....

MOLDAVIA

WALLACHIA

Belgrade

BOSNIA

SERBIA

Nish

Danube

Kossovo

Nicopolis

Philippopoli

Sofia

BULGARIA

Vardar

Maritsa

THRACE

Adrianople

Varna

BLACK SEA

Sinope

Amastris

Trebizond

LITTLE ARMENIA

Erzerum

MESOPOTAMIA

Euphrates

SYRIA

Antioch

Melitene

Karaman

Konieh

Ankara

Halys

Sangarios

Nicaea

Brussa

Nicomedia

Constantinople

SEA OF MARMORA

Gallipoli

Dardanelles

T U R K E Y

CYPRUS

MEDITERRANEAN SEA

CRETE

RHODES

KOS

SAMOS

CHIO

SEA

METELINA

Mt. Athos

Salonica

Janina

ALBANIA

CORFU

Ionian Islands

Modon

Mistra

MOREA

Patras

Corinth

Naupilia

CYCLADES

NAXOS

EUBOEA

Athens

Lamia

Larissa

AEGEAN

Smyrna

Nish

100 miles

England were too busy fighting out the last and decisive phase of their great war; the civil conflicts between Burgundians and Armagnacs were adding further to the general disorder; Italy was still in a state of anarchy, and Germany had barely emerged from the Hussite crisis. Kings and princes could give no answer to the pathetic cries for help, save to reply, as John the Fearless did, quite sincerely, that they would contribute to the baptismal expenses of any Turks who wished to become Christians! Through weakness, thoughtlessness and ignorance, Christian Europe committed suicide by allowing her Eastern territories to perish. Only Hungary, which was directly threatened by the Turkish advance,[1] took up arms. She was led by a sixteen-year-old king, Ladislas III, Jagellon, and, most important of all, by the outstanding man who was the vaivode of Transylvania, John Hunyadi, 'the white knight.' The Turks suffered crushing defeats on three successive occasions, the last at Nish, in the heart of the Balkans. Sofia was recaptured, and the road to Adrianople lay open; the Sultan sued for peace. But the impetuosity of Ladislas transformed these triumphs into defeat. Without warning he broke the truce and hurled his army deeper into Turkish-held territory and reached *Varna*. There, however, far removed from his bases of supply, the young monarch was attacked in the rear by a Turkish army which had been transported in Genoese warships (1444). Once again the only result of the 'crusade' was to enrage the Turk, who took his revenge in a series of large-scale massacres. And Byzantium was not delivered. . . .

Henceforth only a few heroic stirrings remained of that great and final urge which had impelled Christians from every land to try to save the eastern half of Christendom. John Hunyadi escaped from Varna, and resumed the struggle four years later. He invaded Serbia a second time, and advanced as far as the battlefield of Kossovo, where he hoped to avenge the disaster of 1389. But once more the Christians were defeated (1448), and all the prodigious valour displayed by the Hungarians was in vain. At the same time, though unhappily without any previous agreement with Hunyadi, a chieftain named *Scanderbeg* rallied the Christians in the Albanian mountains, and resisted with savage determination all the Turkish troops who were sent to capture him. These were splendid feats of arms, but they were without any real influence upon the situation. For the Balkans were completely conquered by the Turks, and when, in 1448, the man who was to be its last occupant ascended the illustrious throne of the Byzantine Empire, the fall of Constantinople was simply a matter of days, or even hours.

[1] Murad II besieged Belgrade in 1440.

FINAL EFFORTS FOR UNITY

It is hardly necessary to state that behind this political and military tragedy which was fast approaching its climax there lurked yet another element. This was a religious one, whose tragic character mingled with something that was sordid rather than pitifully comical. During the whole of this period the problem of reuniting the two sections of the Church, that is to say of ending the Greek Schism, was constantly raised. And yet, as had been the case upon so many past occasions, no final answer could be found. The Greek clergy continued to think as they had thought in the days when Innocent III launched his moving plea for reconciliation, before the unhappy diversion of the fourth crusade, and as they had thought in 1274, after the Council of Lyons. They would not understand that only the solution of this problem could save Byzantium.

The emperors had turned to the West on several occasions. In 1342, immediately he had established himself upon the throne, John VI Cantacuzene opened negotiations. John V did likewise in 1353, as soon as he had got rid of his enemy, and the Paleologus actually came to Italy in person to beg the Catholics there to intervene on his behalf. Much later on, when his throne was in grave danger, Manuel II had made a propaganda tour throughout Europe. His striking carriage, natural majesty and sad, handsome face, together with the sumptuous appearance of his escort, had had an enormous effect in Paris, London, Venice and Milan. He was in France when he heard of Bajazet's defeat at the hands of Tamberlane. Twenty years after this his son visited the West again to try to move Pope Martin V to some action; and while Mohammed II's Turks were preparing to deliver the final blows, John VIII Paleologus took the road westward once more, in a last attempt to obtain the military support that he believed would save him.

It may seem somewhat tasteless that in her answer to all these supplicants, who spoke in the name of a cause which was nothing less than that of the whole of Christendom, the Roman Church should have insisted upon one preliminary condition being satisfied: Union. But the Byzantines were regarded with such distrust that no pope could have acted otherwise. 'Let the Greeks first proclaim the Union, and we will go to their aid at once! If we start by helping them to defeat the Turks, they will want nothing more of us once they are stable and rich again, and they will turn their backs upon the Church of Rome!' These are the words of Benedict XII; but all the pontiffs who succeeded him spoke in very similar terms, and they certainly thought along the same lines. We can scarcely blame them for this apparent lack of generosity when we consider the attitude adopted by Byzantine emperors themselves. As he lay on his death-bed Manuel II gave his son the following piece of advice: 'If you are hard-pressed by the Infidel, go to the Latins, talk about Union, and start negotiations, but drag them out indefinitely; avoid the convening of a council, for this will be of no help to you. The vanity of the Latins and the stubbornness of the Greeks will prevent any agreement ever being made between them.' Consequently the efforts at reconciliation made by the two churches were more akin to a mendacious diplomatic game than to any real intention of putting an end to the scandal of the great division that existed between the baptized of East and West.

However, despite this fact, Byzantium did contain a few devout souls who were heartbroken by the Schism, and who were determined to fight to bring it to an end. Many of these were the disciples of *Patriarch Beccos* (or Veccos), who, at the end of the thirteenth century, had become an ardent advocate of unity, after years of resolute opposition to the idea, and whose change of heart resulted in his deposition and sixteen-year exile. Another exponent of unity was *Balaam*, a Calabrian monk of Greek origin, who spent his whole life acting as an intermediary between Rome and Byzantium. Certain of these sincere supporters of reconciliation were men of the first order. There was *Demetrios Cydones* (1320–1400), John VI Cantacuzene's former secretary, who, in the course of his studies of St Augustine, St Anselm and St Thomas Aquinas, realized the futility of the grudges which his compatriots bore against Rome. Even while he was busy translating the Latin masters he wrote many short treatises in his battle to make the truth triumphant. Above all, there was *Bessarion* (1395–1472), a monk from Trebizond, who was an outstanding orator and a kind of court chaplain. He was subsequently nominated to the metropolitan see of Nicaea, and he too derived the certain knowledge that Union was necessary from his studies of the Fathers. His public acknowledgment of his position led to the most damaging attacks being made upon him, and in 1439 he was forced to take refuge in Rome. He was made a cardinal, and his authority was so great that in 1455 he was nearly elected pope. In fact, therefore, there was a small intellectual and spiritual *élite* in existence in Byzantium which assessed the situation fairly, and which mourned the scandal of the Schism; this *élite* frequented the Latin monastic houses on the Asian border, which were real hotbeds of conversion, and read the *Summa* of St Thomas, which Cydones had translated into Greek.

This *élite*, however, was only a tiny nucleus in the midst of a mass of antipathy; it was virtually powerless against the fanaticism of the Greek clergy, which was, generally speaking, very ignorant, and whose members repeated the vilest accusations of heresy against the Latins without even understanding what they meant. For countless worthy

Greek Christians, the simple fact that priests in the West were often clean-shaven was an intolerable scandal! Preachers harked back again and again to the old argument of the *Filioque*; the Western custom of using unleavened bread for Holy Communion was criticized. Profound differences of mentality, rather than theological disagreements, were at the root of the Schism. The violent dispute which broke out inside the Greek Church at this period between the supporters of the 'mystical way' advocated by *Palamas*, and those of the 'logical way,' on the Thomist pattern, as taught by Balaam and his pupils, is an admirable demonstration of how two totally different ways of reasoning and thinking separated the two halves of the Church. Few Westerners could have agreed that the best way to reach God was to follow Palamas's instructions, and remain motionless for hours, chin on breast, contemplating one's navel, and repeating over and over again: 'Lord Jesus, Jesus Christ, have mercy upon us!' Yet it was this very doctrine which spread throughout the Greek Church during the fourteenth century! Palamas—'the trumpet of theology, the harmonious lyre of the Holy Ghost'—only narrowly missed canonization.

How could any efforts towards reconciliation possibly come to anything in such conditions? John V's decision to abjure the Schism, reached during his visit to the West, and the courageous way in which he subsequently strove to obtain real unity had no conclusive result whatsoever: at most his action merely ensured the continued establishment of a network of relations between Rome and Byzantium. Even various gestures of friendship, such as the Western Church's adoption of certain festivals which were customary in the East—the Presentation of the Virgin in the Temple, for example—had no repercussions at all within the Greek Church, where they were indeed scarcely noticed. Thus the only forces which were really working in favour of Union were political, and we know all too well that these were accompanied by the most equivocal of mental reservations; for one Isidore of Kiev, or one Bessarion, who, while desiring with all their hearts the armed support of the West, saw Union as something very far removed from a mere diplomatic manœuvre, there were scores of Greek metropolitans and prelates who were absolutely determined to make use of the Latins by appearing to play their game!

It was in this sort of atmosphere, at the end of March 1438, that there opened in Italy that council which, as the reader will remember, owed its origin to the initiative of Eugenius IV. The Pope rightly regarded Union as one of the mainsprings of his policy,[1] and John VIII agreed, realizing that herein lay his last card. It is impossible to remain unmoved when we read the pathetic pleas which one of the Greek delegates addressed to his compatriots, in order to describe the

[1] See Chapter I, section devoted to Eugenius IV.

appalling conditions of so many Greek Christians who were already subject to the Turkish yoke. Large numbers of them had been reduced to slavery and abjuration; and the speaker told too of the anguish of all those who, though still free, were awaiting the mortal blow. Yet, in face of this tragic situation, the Byzantines continued to quibble and equivocate. Ponderous arguments took place at Ferrara, and later at Florence, upon several points which seem utterly futile to the modern reader. Countless manœuvres were attempted, like that of Mark of Ephesus, who raised the following preliminary question: 'Is it permissible to add a single new word to the Creed?' Had a negative answer been forthcoming, all negotiations would have been broken off on account of the famous *Filioque*, which the Latins had added to the ancient draft. However, so pressing were events that, despite everything, an understanding was eventually arrived at. Various commissions studied the points of friction; the Dominican, John of Ragusa, Prior of Lombardy, expressed Rome's doctrine regarding the primacy of the Pope with serene assurance. Joseph, Patriarch of Byzantium, died while the Council was still at work, but he left his followers this explicit declaration: 'I recognize the Holy Father of the Latins and the Greeks, the supreme pontiff, the representative of Jesus Christ, the Pope of the old Rome.' Agreement was reached upon four delicate questions: the Procession of the Holy Ghost, the use of unleavened bread, the state of the souls in Purgatory, and the primacy of Rome. At last, on 6th July 1439, the Act of Union, was signed and drafted in Latin and Greek. Mark of Ephesus refused to add his signature: he was not the only cleric on the Greek side who thought that this decree amounted to an unacceptable capitulation, although he was the only one who actually said so.

For, when the conciliar delegates returned to Constantinople, the mob, which had been whipped to fanaticism by the monks, welcomed them with jeers and insults. Latins! Azymites! Apostates! Heretics! The unfortunate men were showered with niceties of this sort. They were accosted in the streets and asked how much gold they had received in return for their treachery. Mark of Ephesus became a national hero, while Bessarion was exiled to Rome. When the emperor nominated a patriach favourable to the cause of Union to the see of Byzantium, the incumbents of other sees refused to recognize him; and when Constantine XI succeeded John VIII he dared not even publish the decree of Union, though he knew very well how urgently he needed Western support.

In short, this final and over-tardy attempt to seal the alliance of East and West against the Turk proved a lamentable failure. Inside Byzantium, which was now completely surrounded by the Infidel and threatened with a ghastly fate, the mob was fundamentally interested only in such questions as whether it was lawful to communicate with unleavened bread; and interest in such matters went so far as street fighting and bloody rioting. . . . 'Byzantinism' never attained greater heights of madness than in these last days. In December 1452, in an effort to enlist the support of the Latin powers, the Emperor Constantine XI finally had the formula of Union, the *Henotikon*, proclaimed in St Sophia. But on the morrow various important Church dignitaries, led by George Scholarios and Luke Notaras, publicly declared, to the cheers of the crowd, 'We would rather see the turban of the Turks over Constantinople than the mitre of the Latins.'

Providence was soon to make their vow come true.

THE FALL OF BYZANTIUM

Murad II, the Sultan who had made all Europe tremble, died early in February 1451, but his successor, Mohammed II (1451–81), was to prove a still more formidable character. Mohammed was a mere boy of twenty-one, slightly built and pale-faced, with a hooked nose and fine black beard. His expression combined something of the sphinx and the dreamer; but beneath Mohammed's aesthetic appearances—he was a patron of European arts and a passionate lover of Italian painting—lurked an extraordinarily energetic man of action, the very type who is born to undertake great conquests. In addition he was utterly unscrupulous. Although he had great charm, he lied whenever it suited him, and he was coldly and calculatingly cruel.

Beside him Constantine XI Dragases (1448–53), the man who was to bring to their close both the dynasty of the Paleologi and the glorious line of the emperors of the East, was completely insignificant. Constantine was a good administrator, a prudent leader and a brave soldier, as he subsequently proved when he laid down his life for his country. He was the worthy heir of all those rulers who, for more than a century past, had by their wisdom, steadfastness, courage and patriotism, delayed the fatal day of reckoning. He might even have been distinguished from the rest of his dynasty by the noblest qualities of intellect and character, had he held in his hands something other than that useless instrument, the rotten stump of the Byzantium Empire. In practice all that remained for him to do was to give Byzantium an honourable end, worthy of her thousand years of fame and glory. This he did.

An ancient Turkish prophecy claimed that Byzantium would be delivered into the hands of Islam by a twenty-year-old conqueror; and this champion was promised a fame equal to that of the Prophet himself. No sooner was he on the throne than Mohammed II determined that he should be this champion. The capture of Constantinople was

* D

his one and only thought, and to the realization of his dream he brought
the implacable vigour and skill of one of the greatest conquerors that
history has ever known. The city still remained a difficult place to
seize, with its powerful ramparts, 200,000 inhabitants and ever-
present possibility of Western support. But a twofold strategic and
diplomatic manœuvre ensured its isolation. Mohammed set about
completing the task begun by Bajazet. The latter had built a line of
fortresses along the shore of Asia, in order to control the Bosphorus.
His descendant built more of these, to the north of the great city, on
the coast of Europe,[1] so that no aid could reach Constantinople from
the north: the first Venetian captain who tried to get through was
captured and impaled. Then a whole series of manœuvres and stratagems neutralized everyone who might have intervened: truces were
signed with Genoa, Venice, the Knights of Rhodes, Demetrios of
Morea, who was Constantine's own brother, and even with Hunyadi
and Scanderbeg. Not a single Western leader gave an effective answer
to the desperate appeals of the encircled Basileus. Only a few Venetian
sailors and Genoese pirates rallied to Byzantium; the remainder of the
Western world stood by, indifferent and bemused. Its blindness is
inexplicable; Christian patriotism seemed quite dead.

The siege proper began early in April 1453. Mohammed II had left
nothing to chance. With infinite care and patience he had brought
hundreds of ships into the Bosphorus, all small in tonnage, but so
numerous that the sea was covered with them; while the Christian
fleet, massed in the narrow creek of the Golden Horn and protected
by enormous chains which barred the entrance, was afraid to sail out.
He had transported immense numbers of troops to the battle area,
gathered from all four corners of his empire, and people in the beleaguered town whispered that their assailants outnumbered them by
a hundred to one. He had even had a gigantic bronze cannon, the most
enormous of the epoch, hauled to the scene. A special road had to be
constructed so that sixty pairs of oxen and two hundred men could
drag it forward until it was within range of the city walls. In the face
of forces like these the armed strength of the great capital's defenders
was negligible. At the most it consisted of five thousand men and
barely thirty ships. It was abundantly clear which way the scales of
fate were weighted. Yet at this time of crisis the Christians of Byzantium rose in rebellion because a Roman cardinal had celebrated Mass
in St Sophia, and their priests declared that they would never enter
the great church again, because it had been sullied by the presence of
the hated legate.

However—and this is really the reason why the historian can talk
of the suicide of Christendom—there is no doubt at all that, even at

[1] These enormous edifices can still be seen in the countryside around Istanbul.

this juncture, in this critical situation, a determined intervention by the fleets of the Western powers would still have saved everything. This is admirably demonstrated by the incident of 20th April. With a tiny squadron of only four large ships, a Genoese captain named Maurizio Cattaneo carved a trail of destruction through the middle of the Turkish fleet till he reached the Golden Horn, whose chains dipped before the prows of his boats; the puny Islamic ships were no match

The Siege of Constantinople

for the high-decked galleys of the West. In addition Mohammed II experienced disappointments of another kind. His famous cannon exploded after being fired a few times, blowing its engineer to pieces.

True leaders acknowledge the overwhelming sovereignty of efficacious decisions. The Grand Vizier, who was virtually in the pay of the Byzantines, advised the Sultan to raise the siege; but Mohammed II refused to listen to him. To gain the city he must neutralize its fleet and capture the Golden Horn. At this juncture, therefore, he attempted an operation which seemed the height of folly, but which was extraordinarily successful. As the result of the gigantic labour of thousands of men, a wooden road consisting of well-greased logs was constructed behind Pera, stretching from Dolmabagtche to Tershana. It was built within the space of twenty-four hours, and upon it the entire Turkish navy was hauled overland. On the morning of 23rd April the terror-stricken people in the beleaguered city woke up to see the enemy boats moored in front of the Blachernae Palace.

Mohammed II was in no hurry to strike the decisive blow. A weird atmosphere of negotiation and treachery hung over this war, in which a whole world was fighting for its life. The Genoese gave the Sultan warning of a surprise plan to burn his vessels, concocted by a valiant Italian sailor. On his side the aggressor offered the beleaguered emperor the chance to withdraw to the Morea, assuring him that he could reign there in peace under Ottoman suzerainty. Constantine nobly refused. Clearly the ancient capital could still make a great impression. It was only at the end of May, when Mohammed II learned that Paolo Lordano was preparing to launch a counter-attack with thirty or so Venetian ships, that he determined to make the final assault.

Byzantium's last days were worthy of her glorious past: they possessed a sombre, blood-stained grandeur. On 28th May while the mullahs in the Islamic camp were preaching the *jehad* or Holy War in an atmosphere of exacerbated fervour, the Christian population of Constantinople solemnly assembled in St Sophia. There, together with his whole court, and surrounded by all his clergy, both Greek and Latin, the emperor came to partake of the Body and Blood of Christ. This was the last Mass ever celebrated beneath the illustrious cupola, and the last Communion of the last Basileus.

The attack began on 29th May, at two o'clock in the morning. A first assault failed; the Greek and West European warriors, fired by the presence of their leaders, Constantine, Giustiniani and Trevisano, performed wonders in the field. A second failed likewise, but the Genoese leader was mortally wounded soon afterwards, and his death was an irreparable loss. Finally, just before dawn, Mohammed II sent in his janissaries, personally leading them in the final attack. The battle raged for twenty hours; the Turks overwhelmed the ramparts by sheer weight of numbers in ten places; the Circus gate was taken by surprise, and the defenders at the Adrianople gate were overwhelmed from the rear. However, even when the walls had been captured, the defenders fought on in the streets. When all was lost Constantine XI gave the world proof of the glory which still lived on in this once mighty Byzantium. He dismounted, stripped off all the imperial insignia, save his shoes, and hurled himself into the thick of the fighting, like an ordinary soldier. His body was found next day on top of a pile of corpses, recognizable only by the boots of imperial purple embroidered with gold eagles.[1]

---

[1] At least so tradition alleges. But Aeneas Sylvius Piccolomini gives a different version of this event. 'Instead of fighting as becomes a king the emperor fled, and was trampled

The looting and massacre were as expected: Mohammed II had promised his army the freedom of the city for three days and three nights. Only a handful of the vanquished managed to embark on a Genoese ship and flee to safety. Thousands of Christians who had sought refuge in St Sophia were slaughtered as they prayed. More than fifty thousand Greeks, men and women, young and old, were sold into slavery. All the important court dignitaries were executed, while Constantine's head was nailed to the top of the Augusteion column. Countless treasures of art and learning were pillaged and wantonly destroyed; statues, rare colonnades, religious ornaments, manuscripts and gospels. Plato was sold for a penny. At the end of it all the victor made his ceremonial entry into St Sophia, whose walls had been daubed with whitewash in order to obliterate the figures so reviled by the Koran. He recited the Moslem prayer and then, with a single word, stopped the massacre. Byzantium had suffered a change of rulers that was to endure for centuries: over a thousand years of Christian glory and greatness were at an end.

THE FINAL TREMORS

The fall of Constantinople was greeted with a vast upsurge of emotion throughout Christendom. Cardinal Isidore, that same Papal Legate whose presence in St Sophia had sparked off the religious disturbances, had a miraculous escape from the catastrophe. He returned to Rome and described the horrible deeds which he had witnessed with his own eyes. He predicted a gloomy future for the Christian world. Since the Turks no longer had any adversary capable of stopping their advance they would press on westwards; tomorrow it would be Italy's turn to suffer. One particular preacher, Robert of Lecce, made a speciality of commenting on this tragic episode, asserting that it was a certain proof of God's wrath, and on hearing him his congregations would fall to weeping and wailing. Ducas's written account of the last days of Byzantium was soon current throughout the West, and this succeeded in spreading the consternation still more. Christendom had no sooner allowed the demise of the centre which had been its protector and teacher for centuries past than it realized, too late, that its own ingratitude had placed it in terrible danger.

A tremor shook the whole fabric of Christendom. A vigorous effort was made to regain control of the situation and face it boldly. Pope Nicholas V sent his legates far and wide to summon Christians to the crusade: Capranica went to Naples, Carjaval to Florence, Venice and

---

underfoot when he stumbled: he was crushed to death by others who were running away.' The same Piccolomini declared, upon hearing that Constantinople had fallen: 'Homer and Plato have just died a second time!'

Milan. Appeals were addressed to Charles VII of France and to the English Court. At Lille, on 17th February 1454, Duke Philip the Good of Burgundy, who was filled with enthusiasm at the idea of posing as the saviour of the West, organized the famous 'vow of the pheasant.' A ceremonial banquet was held, in the course of which 'Holy Mother Church' appeared, dressed in mourning, seated upon an elephant, and recited a most touching metrical lament. Upon hearing this the prince and all his company promptly swore the crusader's oath upon the gold-collared pheasant. But these promises were nothing but fine-sounding words.

In such an obviously dangerous situation it is greatly to the Papacy's credit that it showed by far the most tenacious and clear-sighted vigour in rallying the Christian West, which lacked the will to defend itself. From the very day of the disaster every pope without exception—all those Renaissance popes who are almost always pictured as pre-occupied with very different matters—strove with all his might to preach the crusade and to assist anyone who still desired to fight for the Cross. Callixtus III (1455–8), the first of the Borgia popes, sold jewellery and Church property in order to raise levies to fight the Turks. Pius II (1458–64), the refined, erudite Sylvius Piccolomini, dreamed of converting the Sultan to Christianity, and even wrote to him personally with this in mind. When nothing came of the attempt the Pope convened a Congress of Christian Europe at Mantua, with the express intention of making ready for the battle against the Infidel, putting to shame those Christians who were allowing the Turks to drive them to their doom without lifting a finger to save themselves. In short, this vigour was to have its reward, for the Turkish advance was eventually slowed down, and in some places halted altogether.

In 1455, when Belgrade was besieged by the Turks, that great Christian champion, the Franciscan friar *St John of Capistrano*, acting in concert with Cardinal Carjaval, the Papal Legate, went to Hungary to offer comfort and encouragement to the terror-stricken Catholics there. The saint joined Hunyadi at the head of a crusade consisting of townsfolk, peasants, students and monks, supported by a few detachments of Polish aristocrats and German infantry. This motley army hurled itself upon Belgrade and forced the Turks to raise the siege (1456). This splendid victory, however, which Cardinal Nicholas of Cusa celebrated in a memorable sermon, proved indecisive. The death of the Hungarian hero, which was soon followed by that of the saint, prevented the counter-offensive from spreading farther into the Balkans. In Albania the indefatigable Scanderbeg, 'Captain-general of the Curia against the Turks,' continued to fight on alone, inflicting such crushing defeats upon the Moslems that when he learned of the Albanian's death, in 1468, the Sultan exclaimed: 'Christendom has lost

its sword!' On the sea too a papal fleet, commanded by the legate
Scarampo, defeated an Ottoman squadron at Metelina in 1457.
Finally, along the Danube, the Rumanian princes were also resisting
the enemy, though it must be admitted that Vlad of Wallachia and
Stephen the Great of Moldavia were somewhat strange crusaders, with
barbarian habits, who were accustomed to impale their Turkish
prisoners. But the Papacy could do little in the way of leading this
difficult enterprise, since it stood virtually alone amid the indifference
of all the great nations of the West. Pius II's plan for a crusade ended
in failure. Europe stood by and watched Mohammed II assemble his
forces, swallow up the Morea and go on to occupy Attica. In 1470 he
defeated the Venetian fleet before Negroponte, which enabled him to
occupy the island of Euboea, 'the pearl in His Most Serene Highness'
crown.' Europe watched him while he grabbed Crete and the Greek
islands; and worse was to follow. The Ottoman advance parties
actually appeared in the Venetian lagoons, snapping their fingers at
the Doge; they captured Otranto, on the coast of southern Italy,
where they put the archbishop and the governor to the sword. The
situation was indeed terrible, and the Christian apathy was quite
astounding. Only the papal squadrons set sail for Naples to halt the
Turkish advance. Mohammed II boasted sarcastically that his horse
would soon be eating its oats from the altar of St Peter's. Pope Sixtus
IV (1471–84) replied by addressing these desperate exhortations to his
fellow countrymen: 'Men of Italy! If you still want to be Christians,
come out and fight! This is your last chance!' All in vain. The epoch
of Machiavelli had arrived, and the crusade no longer possessed any
meaning. The merchants of Venice and Genoa were far keener on
making money than on defending the honour of Christ. In 1480 it
seemed quite likely that the whole of Western Europe was on the
point of falling into the hands of Islam: [1] a just reward for the blindness
which it had shown in allowing the destruction of the Christian East.

What became of those who had fallen beneath the Turkish yoke?
In this connection it is only fair to note that Mohammed II's record is
a surprisingly satisfactory one. In fact, once the three days of murder
and pillage already referred to were over, the terrible conqueror treated
the vanquished with extraordinary moderation. It is even possible to
say that he was amazingly tolerant, for he never sought to force the
faith, customs, language or laws of his nation upon the Christians. He

---

[1] In fact the West was saved by pure luck. When Mohammed II died in 1481, to
Christendom's overwhelming relief, his throne was disputed between his sons Bajazet and
Djem. The latter fled from Constantinople and took refuge in Rome. These internal
discords paralysed the Turkish Empire, and its expansion ceased. Negotiations were able
to take place between the head of the Church and the Sultan (1490). Shortly afterwards
(1492) the fall of Granada, which was captured by Ferdinand and Isabella, was a decisive
blow to Islam's prestige.

contented himself with making them pay a 'capitation tax,' which was levied by counting of heads, and in return he allowed them to practise their religion and to live according to the principles which had been theirs for centuries past. It is of course doubtful whether this was due to pure generosity on his part. More probably this astute politician believed that if he attempted to force the Turkish way of life upon the vanquished peoples he would merely succeed in infuriating them and in throwing them into the arms of Rome and the West. He therefore preferred to come to an understanding with the Greek clergy, and in particular with the leaders of the anti-union party, the men who had wanted to see the Sultan's turban rather than the legate's mitre over St Sophia. On 1st June 1453 George Scholarios, one of those who held this view, was elected Patriarch under the name of Ginnadios. Incredible and scandalous though it seems, the Sultan himself invested the new Patriarch, actually handing him the pastoral staff of gold. History shows that this policy, which was utterly contrary to all the traditions of the *jehad*, eventually led the Turks to disaster, since it enabled the subject peoples to make their great national revival in the eighteenth and nineteenth centuries. But that is another story. For the time being one of the obvious results of the fall of Byzantium was a further hardening of the Schism. Henceforth there was a deliberate refusal to discuss the Union, which was quite out of the question in regions held by Turkey. Christendom had suffered a permanent amputation in the spiritual field, as well as in the material.

RUSSIA EMERGES AS BYZANTIUM'S HEIR

Who would inherit this vast treasure-chest of civilization accumulated by Byzantium and now smashed to fragments by Mohammed II's terrible sabre thrust? There is no doubt that the West acquired something of its wealth, partly on account of the large numbers of refugees who made their homes there, bringing with them their literary and artistic cultures and scholarship of every conceivable type. Thus, in the field of Greek literature, the Renaissance was to owe much to exiles like Bessarion, Lascaris, Argyropolos, Chrysoloras and Plethon, the last-named actually becoming the leader of the Platonic school at Florence. But Eastern influence went far deeper than this. For centuries past Byzantium had taught the whole West, and Italy in particular, not only the art of making cupolas, mosaics, stained glass, manuscripts and miniatures, but also the principles of law, commerce and finance. When Western capitalism came into being, it was based on the maritime law established by the Phocaeans, which they in turn had culled from the Babylonians! And when the centralized monarchies of France, England and Spain imposed their own particular kind of government upon their peoples, they would seek their methods in the Roman state law deriving from the Late Empire and, farther back still, from the tradition of the Egyptian Pharaohs, which Byzantium had preserved. On the other hand, it is a regrettable fact that Byzantine influence upon the Western Church was so slight as to be virtually non-existent: the Schism had prevented any serious contacts between the two halves of Christendom, and the fruitless attempts at Union had not succeeded in enabling the powerful force of Greek spirituality to penetrate the West.

In the realms of the spirit the West was not Byzantium's heir. This portion of the Greek heritage passed to Russia, that vast, mysterious land of birch forests and rolling, limitless steppes which still remained lost in the impenetrable mists of history, but which was now beginning to be aware of her own soul. Very soon, despite the slow and arduous journey this entailed, the strongest tide of those who had escaped the Turkish yoke turned towards her. Monks, priests, scholars, princes and merchants came and settled in the wooden townships of Russia, with their churches topped by bulbous cupolas, in an environment which was undoubtedly very different from the one they had been used to in the past, but where the similarity of religion gave them the illusion that they were living in a familiar atmosphere.

Russia had been profoundly affected by Byzantine influences from the very start. Since the beginning of the eleventh century, when Kiev was the capital and the only real centre in the country, her rulers had sought their brides, their spiritual leaders, their architects and their artists from Constantinople. They had their own cathedral of St Sophia, an exact replica of the great original in Byzantium. The missionaries who had brought the Gospel—and the alphabet—to Russia had been Greeks, and the Russian monks owed most of their spiritual inspiration to Studion and its rule.[1] Greek Orthodoxy had provided the spiritual strength which had enabled Russia to resist the Latin West as represented by those Swedes, Poles and Teutonic Knights whose dangerous expansion had been checked by Alexander Nevski in a series of terrible battles during the thirteenth century. Finally, in the dark days of the 'tatarchina,' the period of subjection to the Mongols, it had once more been the Orthodox Church, Byzantium's spiritual daughter, which had kept Russia's national conscience alive and prevented her from abandoning hope.

The astonishing career of Genghiz Khan and his sons had marked the end of Kiev's age of glory.[2] In 1236–7 Batu, one of the Asian conqueror's heirs, had captured the holy city of the Slavs and razed it

[1] On the origins of Christianity in Russia see *Cathedral and Crusade*, references indicated under Kiev in the Index.
[2] Cf. *Cathedral and Crusade*, p. 466.

to the ground. He had swept across Volhynia and Galicia and established the rule of the *Golden Horde* from the Urals to the Danube. Only a handful of principalities on the Upper Volga and the Moskova, which were inhabited by Turks, Bulgars and Finns, as well as Slavs, remained theoretically independent; but even these were obliged to pay tribute to the powerful Khan of Kiptchak. Meanwhile Kiev's territories in the West passed to the dukes of Poland, or else into the hands of the Teutonic Knights; yet even during this period of tragic darkness contact with Byzantium had never been completely broken. Novgorod in particular, centre of one of the tiny 'free' principalities, continued to maintain commercial and spiritual relations with the capital on the Bosphorus.

Mongol domination was to endure for nearly two hundred years. But the leaders of the Horde were riddled with anarchical tendencies, and as they allowed their authority to weaken Mongol rule became less burdensome. There is no doubt at all that it had a profound effect upon Russia's destinies, influencing her methods of action and her ways of thought, and even her national soul; but it failed to eliminate the even more fundamental influence of Byzantine tradition with which it in fact eventually fused. When the new force which was to replace the Golden Horde in the days of the latter's decline sprang forth from the hardy soil of Russia, it depended for its will to conquer upon the religious tradition, in other words, upon that deriving from Greece and Byzantium.

Moscow is mentioned for the first time in 1147, but at that date it was still merely a summer residence in the heart of the forest. By 1170 it was a small township, controlled by a very modest ruler: Daniel (1260–1303), son of Alexander Nevski, conqueror of the West. He had made Vladimir his capital and had increased the importance of the straggling wooden village, and the history of his dynasty was henceforth linked with that of Moscow. It was not a particularly inspiring history; for by flattering their conquerors, by 'cringing to the Horde,' the *Grand Princes of Moscow*, who held their high-sounding title from the Mongols, were made tax-collectors in their name. Their zeal in this direction, which, as can easily be imagined, was far from disinterested, enabled them to build up a fortune and an army of sorts which was to be singularly useful to them as soon as the Khanate began to disintegrate and they were free to act on their own behalf. At the beginning of the fourteenth century George Danilovich (1319–25) began to annex territory on the Upper Volga and also maintained extensive contacts with the East. His son, Ivan Kalita (1328–41)—Ivan Full-Hands—increased his influence by a judicious policy of bribery, and resolute souls who longed to shake off the Mongol yoke began to foregather in Moscow. In 1326 a brilliant piece of diplomacy by Prince

George had ensured that the Metropolitan Maximus (a Greek) established his see in Moscow after his abandonment of Kiev, and Ivan determined to give his capital the character of a great religious metropolis. Was this the moment to crush the 'tatarchina'? Dmitri (1363–89) thought it was. Seeing the Mongols considerably weakened by the assaults of Tamberlane, the great ruler hurled himself into the attack. A first Mongol army was defeated in 1378; the Tatars of Kazan were forced to pay tribute—a just reversal of fortunes. Finally, in 1380, on the 'Field of Woodcocks' at Kulikovo, near the Don, Dmitri won such a striking victory that it seemed to many the signal of liberation. In actual fact this effort was premature. A new Khan appeared and raised an enormous army, enlisting Poles, Germans, and even Genoese and Navarrese mercenaries, against the Russians. Tamberlane lent him troops. Dmitri was incapable of resisting a force of this size, and could only stand by helplessly and watch Moscow burn. At this point it seemed virtually certain that the destiny of the Russian Grand Princes was drawing to its close. However, because they were too weak to reduce the whole country to submission, the Mongols preferred to let the principality vegetate, and under Vassili I and his successors it modestly and patiently rebuilt its forces. As Byzantium crumbled and fell, Moscow was rising again from the ruins. When Ivan III (1462–1505) beheld the increasing anarchy which was destroying the Golden Horde, he made ready to deal it its death-blow. The hour that heralded Russia's mighty future was about to sound.

Throughout the whole of this dark and tragic period, in which the humble principality of Great Russia was preparing the future of the entire Russian race, the Church had assumed exactly the same role which she had earlier filled in the West when confronted with the chaos of the Dark Ages. It was she who had saved the essential values of civilization. Together with the princes, and sometimes overshadowing their influence, she had been the incarnation of national unity, and had battled tenaciously against the forces of servitude. This Russian Church of the Dark Ages was entirely different from the Church of Kiev. She had had her martyrs, men who had been executed by the Asian invaders. She had sent her missionaries, such as St Macarius Jeltovodski and St Stephen of Perm, to work among the pagan tribes. Crucifix in hand, St Stephen had managed to instil the rudiments of civilization even into the extremely uncivilized Finns. Thanks to missionaries like these, the whole of North European Russia, extending as far as the shores of the Arctic Ocean, was evangelized in the space of three centuries, and the monastery of Solvetsk, on the White Sea, became the northernmost outpost of the Christian faith. There can be no doubt at all that these achievements constitute some of the most glorious pages in the Christian history of Russia. But in their making the faith there acquired that fanatically nationalist and profoundly mystical character which it was to retain into modern times, as the writings of Dostoyevsky so admirably demonstrate.

Likewise the Church was closely linked with the efforts of the Muscovite rulers to bring about a Russian revival. In so far as it had ever existed at all, the notion of the State had completely collapsed in the chaos following the Mongol invasion. Material conditions were so precarious that the people narrowly escaped reverting to barbarism. It was the Church who, through her rites, saved the Russian language and the rudiments of Russian art. It was she who maintained a minimum of morality and social life. It was she who, in the person of her bishops, provided society with its leaders. It was she who, by publicly choosing Moscow as the religious capital of Holy Russia, invited all patriotic Russians to unite around the Muscovite ruler. The Russian people preserved into modern times the memory of those great ecclesiastical leaders who laboured so hard to save the national conscience. There was *St Alexis*, counsellor of princes, healer, and friend of the poor, whose relics were to be venerated in the monastery of Chudov (the Miracle) right up to the time when the Bolsheviks profaned and destroyed its buildings. *St Sergius of Radonege (d. 1392)* revived monasticism in Russia. The Grand Princes themselves came to seek advice from this great forest hermit, and when the Russian army was setting out against the Mongols, on the expedition which was to end in the triumph of Kulikovo, Sergius sent two of his own monks to fight in the forefront of the battle, as a visible token of Heaven's presence and assistance.

It is abundantly clear that the Russian Church owed much to Byzantium. Her rites, vestments, art, icons, and the whole of the monastic system which had been rendered so active and powerful by the inspiration of St Sergius and his convent of the Trinity, followed the rule of Studion. This was the famous Byzantine foundation whose rule had been defined and expounded by St Theodore, 'the terrestrial angel,' at the beginning of the eighth century.[1] Hatred of the West, which was an integral part of the Byzantine tradition, had all too many reasons for taking root in this Church also. In her eyes the West was represented by those Teutonic Knights, Poles and Swedes who had attacked the Russians even while they were busy fighting for their lives against the Mongols. It meant *the folk who had stabbed her children in the back*. In fact, the very effort made by Catholics to penetrate Russia had worked against their faith. The Dominicans of St Hyacinthus had abandoned Kiev just as the Asian holocaust was about to break, and the fact that the popes had sent envoys to the Mongol Khans had certainly not created a good impression upon the Russian

[1] Cf. *The Church in the Dark Ages*, p. 366.

Christians.[1] Thus the Russian Church was to evolve in an increasingly anti-Western direction, and her attitude also contained a streak of distrust for the Church of Rome and for all that Rome appeared to represent.

However, on the eve of the tragedy in which Byzantium was to meet her doom, the last attempt to effect a union of East and West was made on the initiative of John VIII Paleologus and Pope Eugenius IV. Russia did at that time possess a few men sufficiently open-minded and fundamentally Christian in spirit to realize the frightfulness and the shame to Christians everywhere of the division of the Seamless Robe. The principal Russian witness in the cause of unity was *Isidore of Kiev*, a Greek by birth, and metropolitan of the ancient capital of Russia. Not only was he present at the Council of Florence but also took an active part in its proceedings. But alas, on his return to Russia he was met by a chorus of vociferous protests. No one really understood what he had said and done in the West: all that they knew was that something pertaining to their ancient traditional faith had been changed, and, above all, that the sacrosanct hand of the Eastern Church had been placed in that of the Pope of Rome. Isidore of Kiev was treated as a renegade, and threats and insults were heaped upon him. He was obliged to flee the country. And, when they heard of the fall of Constantinople, the simple-hearted people of Russia were certain that this was an obvious case of divine punishment.

Consequently Moscow, which had received so many excellent gifts as well as some of the basest of prejudices from Byzantium, stood thenceforward aloof in arrogant solitude. She, and she only, constituted the enlightened centre of undefiled faith. As the repository of the glorious past, she bore upon her the authentic sign of Christian loyalty. Her theocratic concept of the State was to be that which the regime of the Blachernae Palace had bequeathed to her rulers. They soon adopted the style of Caesar, or *Tsar*, and, like the Byzantines before them, were regarded as religious leaders as well as kings. The imperial heritage, which Byzantium claimed to have received from the dying Roman Empire of the West, was henceforth claimed by Moscow. The dream of world domination, which so many of the Basileis had cherished, and which had also been held by the great Mongol Khans, was revived by the Tsars. Mingled with it was an indefinable kind of Russian Messianism, which has survived all regimes and governments to linger on even today. When Ivan III married Sophia, the last Paleologus princess, he was thereby enabled to pose as the successor of Byzantium with all the most obvious appearances of legitimacy. A 'Third Rome' was arising to confront the Rome of the popes.[2]

[1] Cf. *Cathedral and Crusade*, p. 505 ff.
[2] Russia suffered severely from the Mongol invasion in the thirteenth century, but at the beginning of the fourteenth she experienced a most striking artistic revival. In

A Year of Destiny: 1453

The majority of historians accept the tradition which considers that the capture of Constantinople by the Turks marks the end of the glorious epoch still known as 'the Middle Ages.' Like all 'vital historical dates,' this one is somewhat removed from absolute truth; the evolution of human societies takes no account of such sudden ruptures. Changes from the past to the future are matters of gradual transformation rather than of abrupt mutation; many elements which are part of our modern civilization already existed, in embryonic form, in the epoch of the Cathedral and Crusade. It remains true, nevertheless, that 1453 was a year of destiny, one of those moments when it seems as though the very current of history is changing course. The years 405 and 406, when mankind stood poised upon the threshold of the Dark Ages, had been similarly crucial; and the future was to offer the turning-points of 1789 and 1917, the high-water marks of revolution, French and Russian. Within the space of the year 1453 Byzantium collapsed, and at Castillon [1] the West witnessed the end of the mighty Anglo-French conflict, the Hundred Years War. Upon the political plane these two events were decisive.

In the history of the Church this date was of really capital importance. Christendom emerged divided and maimed from the double tragedy. The Schism which had been a bleeding sore in its unity for centuries past, but which had never been regarded as final, was henceforth irreparable. Among the subjects of the Ottoman Empire, as well as in Russia, Eastern Christianity was to follow a path which separated it from the West more and more. In the West itself the complete disintegration of the hierarchies upon which medieval Christendom had rested, the weakening of papal authority, the secularization of the imperial ideal and the emergence of modern national states was about to force the Church to conceive her role in the world in quite new terms. In the end she did indeed effect this essential transformation. The old concept of a Christianity closely linked with the temporal pillars of society would be replaced by a more inward, spiritual concept, freer from the enslavements of politics and social life. Similarly,

---

particular Novgorod was an important centre of Christian art, and Theophanus the Greek embellished the Cathedral of the Transfiguration there with some imposing figures. Once the country had rid herself of the Mongol oppressors, churches sprang up everywhere. These were built to a square plan, with bulbous cupolas, and in all the iconostasis offered admirable scope for decoration. Inside the Kreml or Kremlin, Moscow's citadel, the Terem, or royal palace, was still extremely rustic in appearance; but it was soon to be rebuilt, complete with a whole bunch of cathedrals and basilicas, a task in which Italian architects were employed (c. 1475).

[1] Theoretically the Treaty of Picquigny, which hallowed Anglo-French reconciliation following a fresh war, dates from 1475, but in actual fact the military result was not in any doubt after the battle of Castillon, 1453.

when it became quite clear that the noble ideal of the crusade was irrevocably outdated, Holy Church realized, as St Francis of Assisi and Blessed Raymond Lull had told her long before, that her future expansion depended on the patient, heroic effort of the missions, and not on the outcome of military engagements. These multiple transformations, however, which were to give the Church of the Council of Trent such a fresh and splendid character, were not effected in a moment. Indeed they took place only after a long and painful ordeal, an ordeal far more terrible than all those of which the men of 1453 could have been aware.

For this half-way mark of the fifteenth century marks a turning-point not merely in the field of facts and institutions, but also in that of the mind and the spirit. At this very moment the invention of the printing-press was opening up whole new vistas to human culture; the creative dreams of Henry the Navigator, the Infante of Sagres and the early sallies of the Norman-born Jean de Betancourt were attuning men's minds to the discovery of the wide world. Literature and art too were shifting their bases and their principles, and the first generation of the Italian Renaissance, the generation of Ghiberti, Donatello, Brunelleschi and Alberti, had already committed aesthetic creation along entirely new lines. Lastly, and most important of all, the seeds sown by Wyclif and John Huss were germinating rapidly in men's souls, and preparing to bring forth a strange and formidable harvest. In 1453 Fra Angelico was within two years of his death (1455); Leonardo da Vinci and Savonarola had just been born (1452). A new era was dawning in which the great crisis was about to break. This was the crisis made ready by that vast fermentation of minds and spirits which moribund Christendom had been parading in such a disquieting fashion for more than a hundred years.

CHAPTER III

A CRISIS IN THE SOUL: CHRISTIAN FOUNDATIONS BEGIN TO TOTTER

THE REAL CRISIS IS IN MAN HIMSELF

THE CRISES which shake human societies are always, first and foremost, spiritual crises: political events and social unrest merely translate into deeds a disequilibrium whose real cause is something far more fundamental. The destiny of the world is shaped in the secret recesses of the mind, through the hidden dialectic of ideals and passions, and the new forces which make old empires crumble are the selfsame forces which each individual confronts in the depths of his own soul, making him the abettor of destruction. Those crises of authority and unity which attacked moribund Christendom during the decisive period spanned by the fourteenth and fifteenth centuries conformed to this rule more than most; everything points to the fact that a crisis of the soul explained and directed them; and this spiritual crisis provides the true explanation of their tragic history.

The crisis had been building up for several decades. Signs of the approaching decline could be observed even in the extremely sound and vigorous Christian world of the thirteenth century.[1] These signs multiplied from 1350 onwards. The crisis affected man's soul, mind and sensibility at one and the same time. That sluggishness which had so often dragged the faithful down during the course of Christian history now exerted itself once again, bringing with it the usual consequences. Unhappily, however, there was no longer a Gregory VII, a St Bernard, a St Dominic or a St Francis of Assisi to regain control over the dullard Christian soul and force it back towards the ideal. The human spirit, so long accustomed to living and flourishing within the atmosphere of the Church, now grew sick and tired of her tutelage, which, in addition, had signally failed to discover how to adapt itself to the new and changing conditions of the age. Little by little the observer can detect the disintegration of the principles upon which the scholars of the great epoch of medievalism had built their masterpieces; veritable philosophical and theological schisms occurred, which bordered on rebellion. Lastly, events themselves helped to accentuate this state of unbalance in a quite remarkable way. Epidemic, war, ruin

[1] See the final chapter of *Cathedral and Crusade*.

and devastation all played their part; suffice it to say that man's sensibility was just as stricken as his mind and his spirit. No power in the world could prevent the civilization of the Cathedral and Crusade from sliding down the fatal slope ahead of it.

The epoch which saw the culmination of this journey to the abyss was indeed a strange one. The clearest indication of its profound disequilibrium is its obvious lack of inner unity. Everything about it smacks of contrast and contradiction. This age of large-scale massacres is also one of great mystical impulses: the odour of blood and roses hangs over it, inextricably mingled. It is the age of macabre dances and of exquisitely delicate miniatures, of witchcraft trials and the *Imitation of Christ*. The thirst for pleasure goes hand in hand with the taste for excessive penance, and those very men whom we see possessed by such savage violence are also perfectly capable of astonishing flights towards sanctity. It is a morbid, feverish epoch, in which the noblest spiritual impulses turn all too easily to neurosis. Even the Christian is caught in the toils of the powerful emotions which he is straining after, and seems to waver. Everything everywhere is changing and falling apart; systems oppose systems, the new dogmatisms clash with the old; rigid formulae only half conceal all the uncertainty and anguish. The whole of human activity is held increasingly fast in the grip of an indefinable kind of agonizing fermentation.

The great panoramic scenes which history has preserved for us must be viewed against the back-cloth of these hidden tragedies of the mind and spirit. The puppet figures who campaign for one pope or the other during the Schism, or tear one another to pieces during the first of the national wars, are the same men for whom the essential of living has been put into jeopardy, and who now confront the powers of darkness with heavy hearts. It is impossible to make any sense of the trial of Joan of Arc unless the atmosphere of witchcraft which pervaded her epoch is taken into account. Nor should it be forgotten that the immediate *entourage* of that pure and radiant girl included a man like Gilles de Rais, whose abominable crimes put him in the same category as the legendary Bluebeard. And only by remembering that in taking sides for one or other obedience, for Pope or Council, men were, in a way, choosing a particular concept of Catholicism, can we understand what the great conflict and division within the Church really meant.

But it is precisely because these confused arguments really concern very much more than politics and its allied subjects, because they are in fact concerned with the very essential of life itself, that this period is more than just an age of decline. The century which covers approximately the years 1350–1450, marking the transition between the golden period of the Middle Ages and the Renaissance, is not merely politically creative. For even in the silent monasteries which shelter the mystics the future is being made ready, and Holy Church, which at present feels her grip slackening in affairs of the spirit, as well as in political and social fields, is, almost unconsciously, forging the weapons which will ensure her ultimate revival after a crisis she is now powerless to prevent. Amid all the chaos in which medieval Christendom lies dying, the Church of the Council of Trent is secretly sketching her first outlines.

A FAITH THAT WAS STILL VERY MUCH ALIVE

It would be quite wrong to represent this epoch of transition as an age of weakened faith and growing atheism. Its spiritual standard was a high one, equal to that of the age which had preceded it. There were undoubtedly very large numbers of saintly individuals in every land and every walk of life. This century of blood and filth produced many shining figures whose tenderness, charity and supernatural purity contrasted remarkably with the attitude of the bulk of their contemporaries, and these the Church very rapidly placed upon her altars. The reader has already been made familiar with the careers of St Catherine of Siena, St Bridget of Sweden and St Joan of Arc. Soon the world would witness the achievement of St Colette of Corbie, a courageous conventual reformer, and the example of St Frances of Rome, a model of piety. Nor were men such as St Vincent Ferrer, St Bernardino of Siena and St John Capistrano a whit inferior in virtue to their predecessors of the great medieval epoch. There was scarcely a single crowned family that did not present at least one of its members to Heaven: that of France, Blessed Charles of Blois, the perfect knight and great ascetic; that of Luxembourg, the pathetic little Blessed Peter, champion of expiation.

All the evidence demonstrates clearly that the faith remained very much alive in the souls of the men of that age, and vividly present in their lives: in this sense the epoch is really a continuation of the Middle Ages. Pious confraternities were everywhere, and had never so many members. Cases of impiety were rare. In almost every instance they were more an immediate reaction against certain practices and concepts imposed by the Church than a rejection of doctrine. For example, cases are quoted of certain bold spirits who queried the authenticity of the Scriptures, or Christ's Presence in the Sacrament of the Altar, and there were even a few who refused Extreme Unction. But this did not lessen their belief in God and in Jesus Christ; such people have nothing in common with the godless paganism and epicureanism of the Renaissance.

Conversely visible proof and expression of genuine faith are frequently found in men whose general conduct was as unchristian as it was possible to be. From the bottom of that pit into which his brutal instincts had thrown him, and sandwiched between two obscene refrains in honour of the wanton Margot, François Villon addressed a plea to Our Lady that is couched in words of exquisite tenderness, and proclaims in a cry of overwhelming sincerity:

> Notre-Seigneur, tel est, tel le confesse:
> En cette foi je veux vivre et mourir.[1]

Likewise when his horrible crimes finally brought him to the stake, Gilles de Rais went to his death with such sublime and supernatural faith, and with such an obvious desire for repentance and expiation, that those who watched him die were moved to tears, and talked of his 'sanctity.'[2]

Moreover faith was clearly very much alive among the less notorious individuals of the epoch too. It permeated the souls of the common people. The whole of men's everyday lives continued to be completely shaped by religious customs and observances; the liturgical calendar imposed its own rhythm upon the year, and determined the periods of work and rest; even the humblest daily tasks, such as warming the oven or milking a cow, each had their stock of prayers, and sometimes indulgences as well! Faith was linked with national politics also; a monarch going to war would seek divine support for his cause in the form of public prayers and processions, and would beg the advice of saintly souls like St Vincent Ferrer or Denys the Carthusian. International treaties often contained theological clauses. That made between France and Burgundy in 1435, for example, commences with a number of expiatory formulae in connection with Duke John's murder at Montereau.

Men's piety was unquestionably ardent. As we shall see, it ran almost to excess, for it reached the point where it slid dangerously near to superstition and pathological exaltation. Still, in many respects it was to be admired. The enormous success of various spiritual volumes addressed to the general public is proof of this. It is difficult nowadays to imagine the vogue enjoyed by Gerson's *Plain Man's A B C* and *Treatise on the Ten Commandments*, Raymond Lull's *Art of Contemplation*, Robert Ciboule's *Book of Sacred Meditation*, and the works of Tauler, Suso and, a little later on, of Ruysbroeck. This popularity is much easier to understand in the case of *The Imitation of Jesus Christ*, the 'best seller' of the age. The student is left with the definite impression that this was a time when men's souls were genuinely

---

[1] In other words 'I want to live and die in the Christian faith.'
[2] Needless to say, this faith also found expression among the finer spirits of the age. The case of Boucicault, the hero of Nicopolis, who wore a hair-shirt beneath his armour and prayed for three hours each day, was not an isolated one.

hungering for God, and, as Chancellor Gerson pointed out: 'You can love God and contemplate the divine without being a learned scholar.'

This devotion was apt to deviate a little, and, as in the preceding era, men sometimes bestowed more of their attention on the saints than on God. But this error was far from being universal, and certain of those forms of piety which we today still consider the most beautiful and significant, acquired their real force during the period in question. The cult of Jesus the Living Host, which was already in existence in the thirteenth century as a reaction against the heresy of Berenger,[1] assumed growing importance: it possessed its mystical herald in the person of Blessed Dorothea of Prussia, who expressed her longing to see the Host 'a hundred times a day.' The spread of the cult of the Sacred Heart was closely connected with the development of mysticism, and also with certain correlated trends of sensibility. Representations of the sacred organ which men recognized as the symbol of Christ's infinite love for mankind were seen everywhere, and at the end of the fourteenth century the *Herz Jesu Büchlein* had a most enthusiastic reception. Devotion to the Blessed Virgin was particularly popular. There were countless pilgrimages in her honour; her purity, virginity, obedience and faith were praised far and wide. The Franciscans became the enthusiastic protagonists of the theological doctrine of the Immaculate Conception; the Dominicans, led by Alain de la Roche, propagated the Rosary, and the 'Universal Brotherhood of the Psalter of Our Lady' was founded in order to promote its development. At this period the Virgin Mother possessed untold numbers of cantors, ranging from Petrarch—who coined the wonderful phrase 'the Virgin robed in sunshine'—Suso and St Bernardino, to Thomas à Kempis and Arnould Greban. On the instructions of Leo XIII, one of the thanksgiving prayers still enjoined upon the faithful today is that lovely simple fragment in Mary's honour which was composed by St Bernardino.

How much of this faith and piety was translated into practice? It is hard to answer exactly, for the necessary statistics are lacking; particulars are not sufficiently detailed until after the Council of Trent, and the student must needs fall back on the information of chroniclers, sermon writers (who are somewhat suspect in this matter) and, most important of all, on the reports of episcopal visitations. Nicholas de Clamanges, a prominent schoolman who was one of the leaders of the French clergy during the Great Schism, declares that attendance at mass was poor; the faithful, who were in the habit of bringing their hounds or falcons to church with them, did little save cross the threshold, dip their fingers in the holy water, genuflect before Our Lady,

[1] See the Index to *Cathedral and Crusade*.

kiss the foot of a sacred statue and then saunter out again, thoroughly pleased with themselves. Those who stayed until the Elevation would boast of it as though they had performed some feat of valour. It appears that the only religious forms observed by all and sundry were baptism, marriage and extreme unction—all these being obligatory simply from the point of view of the 'civil authority'—plus the Easter Communion, which was omitted only by a minority. Moreover until the middle of the fifteenth century even the devout were in the habit of communicating only four or five times a year at most.

In addition, Christians could put forward some fairly strong arguments in defence of their attitude. It was all very well to be summoned to church; but many places of worship were in a shocking condition, their roofs leaking, their walls unsound, their sacristies almost bare of ornaments and liturgical books. Above all, the clerical crisis,[1] whose importance will be discussed later in this chapter, makes the decline in religious practice almost forgivable. In France the Hundred Years War had driven the parochial clergy from the countryside and ruined the benefices. As a result the firm roots of faith which generations of French parish priests had driven deep into the soil, were utterly destroyed. Clerical absenteeism was rife. Numbers of incumbents regarded their benefices simply as a means of collecting revenues, and in many areas their insolent detachment from their clerical duties drove a wedge between the faithful and the Church. In England and Germany, where far too many benefices were bestowed upon foreigners, the distrust felt for this alien clergy found expression in violent reactions against it. Where the faithful still retained a living or exacting faith, they learned that to reach God they must dispense with this discredited or absent priesthood.[2]

On the other hand, although religious practice had declined, all those spectacular aspects of religion which possess an entertainment value enjoyed surprising popularity. Surprising is indeed the word to use here, for we should picture the sermons as kinds of theatrical performances, and realize that the men in the pulpits possessed a fame reasonably akin to that which surrounds the stars of the modern cinema. The churches were no longer big enough to hold the crowds who thronged to listen to the voice of the moment; sermons were also preached in the open, in the public squares. Often the preacher would break off to chide the children playing with their skittles, or the stall-holders crying their wares. Audiences of five thousand were not

---

[1] See the section later in this chapter: 'A Serious Decline in Clerical Standards.'
[2] It is interesting to note that fifteenth-century piety in general (the characteristics of which will be studied later in this chapter, on p. 144), and the 'devotio moderna' in particular, really owed nothing to the intervention of the priest between God and the individual soul. And it goes without saying, too, that this crisis helped to prepare the ground for the Protestant Reformation.

uncommon. The chronicle relates that on one occasion at Orleans so many people perched themselves on the roof tops to listen to a certain fashionable preacher that it took the tilers sixty-four days to replace all the tiles they had broken. And these heralds of God who drew such vast crowds were certainly outstanding personalities. *St Vincent Ferrer* (1357–1419) was a veritable popular orator, who toured the country on a donkey, with an enormous escort known as 'la bella brigata.' Whenever he spoke he was protected by an impressive body-guard, armed with cudgels and pious words; he sometimes preached as many as three or four sermons a day. *St Bernardino of Siena* (1380–1444), who was cast in a gentler mould, was almost equally successful, and his popularity was enormous. It is still amazing to think that St John Capistrano, who could speak only Latin, was able to attract audiences of several thousand in France. These were the leading preachers, but the Franciscan Brother Richard, and Oliver Maillard, who was also a Franciscan, were equally famous in their own lifetimes. The style of these eloquent speeches was deliberately rough and ready, almost vulgar in tone, designed to appeal to the emotions. Sensibilities were easily stirred by descriptions of the putrefaction of the tomb, the anguish of Divine Judgment and the hell-fire which lay in store for those who were listening. Sometimes there would be a great wave of collective exaltation in response to the orator's appeal. His audience would build a bonfire and stoke it with objects of luxury, the visible signs of their sins, and then let the purifying flames destroy them. Savonarola would kindle another such 'Bonfire of Vanities' in Florence at the end of the fifteenth century. In the extremely receptive atmosphere of the age there is no doubt at all that the preachers exercised considerable influence, so much so indeed that the secular authorities dealt severely with certain of their number who were over-ready with their criticisms. It is equally certain that these holy voices kept many souls upon the straight path of morality and brought countless others back to it: their type was to endure for a long time to come, and it is still encountered in the heyday of the Renaissance.

Any religious ceremony which constituted some kind of spectacle benefited from the same thirst for the flamboyant. The high masses which were celebrated on great Church festivals, on the feast-days of the guilds' patron saints, for the consecration of a bishop or, better still, of a king, drew such vast crowds that even the cathedral choir was packed out and the officiating clergy had scarcely room to turn around. On such occasions the decorations in the nave would send the spectators into raptures—the silken hangings and tapestries, the countless lights and the rolling clouds of incense. Their senses would be equally titillated by the new type of music, *ars nova*, recently codified by Philippe de Vitry (1291–1351). Its masterpiece, the famous Mass which for the first time made the divine office one harmonious whole, was soon to be composed by *Guillaume de Machaut* (1300–71).

But there was something else, something even better than all the solemn liturgies of the Church: the sumptuous processions which wound their way down the streets and through the squares, to the wild delight of the populace. There were certainly plenty of them. Every festival had its own procession, and *c.* 1400 the city of Cologne observed one hundred such festivals annually. In 1412 a daily procession was decreed in Paris, lasting from May to July. Day after day different corporations, Orders and relics were to be seen making their way along the streets amid demonstrations of piety which amply justified the enthusiasm of one chronicler for 'the most woeful processions ever seen.' The most famous and popular procession of all was that of Corpus Christi: the Blessed Sacrament was carried through the streets beneath a canopy, the Host being contained in a monstrance, which at this period was usually shaped like a perforated turret with a crystal seal.[1]

These facts do not imply that men sought from the great religious demonstrations only visual pleasure and distraction. Pilgrimage, another form of spectacular devotion which the Middle Ages had always held dear, and which often required a heroic effort, still remained in fashion. Jerusalem was now subject to the caliphs of Egypt, but Christian palmers could be found there in large numbers. The Moslems' cupidity had outrun their religious fanaticism, so that Christians could travel in the Holy Land with relative ease, now that the Franciscans were established there as guardians of the Holy Places. There are countless instances of pious folk making the ascent up the 'Via Dolorosa' on their knees. St James of Compostella remained extremely popular: both St Bridget of Sweden and St Vincent Ferrer carried the staff and scallop of his pilgrims. Numerous local pilgrimages, too, attracted large numbers of the faithful. In France there were Sainte-Baume, Mont Saint-Michel (which the English never managed to capture) and the Madeleine of Vezelay, while in Italy men visited all the places made famous by the Franciscan tradition, following in the footsteps of the Poverello. But the magnet which still drew the largest crowds of all was Rome, the capital of Christendom, 'whose streets are paved with gold and dyed crimson in the martyrs' blood,' as St Bridget described it after one of her ecstatic trances. Tens of thousands of the devout shared in this 'Roman ecstasy' which the Swedish mystic had experienced. The jubilee years attracted great multitudes to Rome: since Clement VI's decree, in

[1] The type of monstrance shaped like a radiant sun (as used today), which was first se en at Conques Abbey in the fourteenth century, became much more popular during t he fifteenth century, due to Italian influence.

1343, these were to occur, in theory, at fifty-year intervals from 1350 onwards. But this did not seem often enough, and so supplementary jubilees were added, first every thirty-third, and later every twenty-fifth, year. The custom of indulgences [1] was spreading very fast indeed at this time, and its most important occasion was the jubilee year. It contributed greatly to the popularity of the pilgrimage to Rome, and during 'Holy Years' it proved almost impossible to find accommodation in the city, so full were the inns; ceremonies and festivals would take place daily before immense gatherings of folk drawn from every corner of Christendom.

The most interesting of these manifestations of the piety characteristic of this transitional epoch between the fourteenth and fifteenth centuries is the *Miracle Play*. This had started as a liturgical performance in which sacred texts were read and mimed on the choir steps by a few officiants. However, from the thirteenth century onwards the spectacular aspect of the performance was accentuated: *c.* 1350 the play left the church and was performed in the public square outside. At the same time it acquired an entirely new character. Whenever a miracle play was being put on in the town, all the shops would shut and the houses empty; everyone came to watch, from new-born babes to gouty old grandfathers. Crowds of five or six thousand stood motionless for hours at a time—even for whole days—listening to the interminable streams of verse in which the authors narrated the entire history of humanity and of Christ, not to mention several other intermediaries. High above the crowd, on the long trestle platform, scene followed scene, all following the principle of simultaneous *décor*: here the spectator was in Paradise, there in Hell, here was the temple of Solomon, and there the bishop's palace. Needless to say all were duly indicated by appropriate notice-boards. The settings were sumptuous and the mechanical stage effects extremely resourceful: the audience saw Aaron's rod burst into bloom before its very eyes, and watched the water change to wine, the Devil fly to the topmost pinnacle of the temple in order to tempt Christ to do likewise, and many other wonders besides. This vast and prodigious spectacle was admirably suited to the psychology of the age: it was naïve and violent, cruel yet tender. Men saw Christ being beaten till the blood flowed, and the pagan executioners torturing the martyrs—it was of course really all an actor's sham—with graphic realism; but they also heard Our Lady and the angels uttering verses of exquisite tenderness. Vulgarity and even obscenity both had their part in the miracle play, as well as those enormous eating and drinking bouts without which no popular festival was conceivable. These scenes touched the deepest sensibilities

---

[1] Indulgences are studied in detail in Chapter V, first section: 'The Affair of the Indulgences.'

of the ordinary man in the street, and in them he recognized all the familiar themes of his faith, while the protagonists in the drama were often his nearest and dearest in real life. Watching them he experienced a religious emotion which might not have been of a particularly elevated nature, but which was assuredly both profound and genuine. The *Passion Play*, written in 1450 by Arnould Greban, a canon of Le Mans and formerly organist of Notre Dame in Paris, was to be the most outstanding French interpretation of this literary form. It is a form that is vividly characteristic of the contradictory, exaggerated, almost sick religion of this epoch in the no man's land between the medieval and the modern.[1]

A RELIGION LACKING ALL SENSE OF BALANCE

Anguish, exaltation and derangement: the historian who attempts to pinpoint the dominant characteristics of faith at the close of the Middle Ages finds himself forced to return to these words again and again. He is confronted with a state of religious agitation which manifests itself in various forms, and with an intense ferment of mysticism, both orthodox and heterodox in character. It is exceedingly hard to recognize here any of the stable, tranquil faith of the twelfth and thirteenth centuries, where the most striking flights towards holiness had something serene and reserved about them, and where even superstition retained some gleam of common sense and sanctity. By and large William James's phrase, 'a theopathic state,' is an apt description of this decadent society, a society in which the elements of a bygone greatness were in an advanced state of decomposition. The

---

[1] To these different manifestations of flamboyant religion should be added the enormous numbers of Orders of Chivalry which existed during this epoch. These new Orders were constantly being created, and their founders claimed that they were copies of the old military religious Orders formed during the crusades, and which were all now either disbanded, like the Templars, or in a state of decline. In fact, however, most of these new Orders were simply a means of furthering princely ambitions under the cloak of religion: there were the Orders of the Golden Buckle, the Tress, the Salamander and the Star in France, and the Order of the Garter (still flourishing) in England. About fifty such Orders can be cited: the object or badge worn by the knights was the tangible sign of their attachment to the ruler who had given it to them. Certain of these Orders had a distinctly religious character; the Order of the Sword, for example, created by the Lusignans in Cyprus, insisted on proper vows. The most famous of all, that of the Golden Fleece, founded in 1429 by Philip the Good, Duke of Burgundy, gave the great prelates and princes of the Church an important place in its hierarchy, and prescribed strict Christian observances for all its knights. Philippe de Mézières dreamed of founding an Order of the Passion. All these Orders possessed their own elaborate costumes, full of complicated symbolism. These costumes were vividly coloured; their insignia were very fine, and fashioned of gold and precious stones. On the collar of the Golden Fleece a tiny lamb, wrought in precious metal, tinkled upon the breast of the dukes of Burgundy: but it is doubtful if many even recognized it as the Lamb of God, symbol of the sacrificed Christ.

E

scene contains much that is undeniably picturesque, but it is none the less highly disturbing.

The Christian soul reflects the anguish of the times. This is an age in which the excessive taste for pleasure is linked with a kind of *taedium vitae*, a weariness of life in general, which had been completely unknown in the Golden Age of medieval Europe.

> Temps de doleur, et de temptation,
> Aages de pleur, d'envie et de tourment,
> Temps de langueur et de damnacion,
> Aages mcneur près du définiment.
> Temps pleins d'horreur qui tout fait faussement,
> Aages menteur, pleins d'orgeuil et d'envie.
> Temps sans honneur et sans vrai jugement,
> Aages en tristour qui abrège la vie.[1]

Countless contemporaries must have echoed the words of Eustache Deschamps's mournful ballad! They readily confessed that they regarded life as a distressing and grievous burden; and many portraits of the day are notable for their morose atmosphere, and for the quasi-romantic melancholy of their sitters' features. Sixty-six years after Deschamps, the chronicler Chastellain, prefaced his work with the following bitter description of himself: 'Unhappy man, born amid the shadowy darkness, in the drenching drizzle of lamentation.'

For many, of course, this feeling was inspired solely by the sufferings and hardships inflicted upon the living by the physical circumstances of the epoch, 'mighty wars, famine and the ever-present hand of Death.' The common people suffered acutely from cold and heat, from hunger and from thirst, not to mention various other trials which Jean Meschinot artlessly describes as 'fleas, mites and a multitude of other body parasites.' But for some this malaise stemmed from a deeper torment, from a tragic view of the whole of human existence.

The man of this period lived in a strange proximity to death: it held him fascinated, and at the same time he was on terms of astonishing familiarity with it. Preachers talked of it at great length, not only in order thereby to announce the glad tidings of everlasting life and the Resurrection, but so that the *Memento quia pulvis* of eternal wisdom might penetrate the souls of their listeners more surely. The theme which, when treated by Villon in his *Ballade des Dames du temps jadis*, has but an echo of gentle melancholy acquired quite horrifying

---

[1] 'Age of sorrow and temptation, tears, envy and torment;
  Age of languishment and damnation, leading close to the ultimate end;
  Age of horror, fashioning everything falsely;
  Filled with deceit and arrogance and lust;
  Age without honour or real judgment;
  Age shrouded in a gloom which cuts life short.'

accents when it became the subject of ecclesiastical eloquence. Pulpit orators would dwell in detail upon the putrefying flesh, the worms which multiplied in the entrails of what had been a pretty woman only yesterday and the hideous skeleton which burst forth from the living shell. And the public appears to have been much impressed. Yet in Paris the cemetery of the Innocents was the fashionable centre of the town, where people came to show off their fine clothes and to gossip, where the children played, and the harlots plied their trade but a stone's throw from the cells where the 'recluses' spent their whole lives in prayer. The passers-by strolled over human bones and could pick up human skulls there: the charnel-house stretched the whole length of the walls, and was open to the skies, exposing great piles of skeletons for all to see.

Art played an active part in this evocation of the horrific. Painters were no longer repelled by the theme of the decomposing corpse; on the contrary, it was to be said of them that they experienced a sadistic delight in multiplying the number of gruesome details. One would paint in the worms at their work, another would show toads eating their fill of human flesh. Even greater efforts were made to depict the bones stripped bare of the rotted tissue. Ligier Richier's famous skeleton holding its heart in its outstretched arms is of somewhat later date, but it was to be the height of artistic discretion compared with the things which this epoch enjoyed depicting. Sometimes Death was represented as one of the horsemen of the Apocalypse, on other occasions as a monstrous bat. Increasingly, however, it was given the artistic likeness of a counterfeit skeleton. Macabre dances, *Dances of Death*, multiplied. Although the etymology here is disputed, the word *macabre* possibly derives from a certain *Macabreus*, a distant descendant of the biblical Maccabees. He is said to have been the first to have had the idea of exploiting this undoubtedly enthralling theme of the dead enticing the living into a mad, irresistible dance, the dance of human destiny . . . unless of course the term comes instead from the Syriac *Maqabry*, meaning a grave-digger. The Dance of Death was first depicted in the famous fresco in the Campo Santo at Pisa. It was rapidly copied by artists at the Chaise-Dieu, Dôle, Basle and Strasbourg. From about 1380 onwards the theme became quite commonplace, and examples of it are found everywhere; it was to circulate in profusion in the form of the woodcuts made fashionable by printers. Social satire had a part in it, for the poor and the humble could console themselves with the cheering thought that the rich and well fed would rot all the better for their material wellbeing. Not that this prevented the high and mighty from deriving their own pleasure from this very sight. There was a performance at Bruges, in 1449, before Duke Philip the Good. In 1453, during a provincial chapter of the Franciscans at

Besançon, a Dance of Death was enacted in which the participants were dressed as skeletons. The audience applauded enthusiastically.

Man must die: this certainty was repeated again and again, in every conceivable way; but the world also must have an ending. It is true, of course, that apocalyptic anxiety occurs in every age, but it is always strongest in times of stress, and hangs like a pall over decades in which human suffering is particularly great. The old ideas of Joachim of Flora had been widely propagated by the Fraticelli, and although the latter had been suppressed (in theory), their ideas continued to circulate. They found new and more reflective modes of expression in the utterances of a number of important mystics. It was at this time that the famous sequence by Thomas of Celano, the *Dies Irae*, was adopted by the Church as part of her liturgy: it was no bad thing to remind a tottering world that even it must come to an inevitable end and submit to the judgment of God. In this connection the common people attached enormous weight to all strange or unexpected natural phenomena, be it the passage of a comet, landslides, volcanic eruptions or excessive rainfall.[1]

Even religion was inflamed by the general anguish of mankind. In all its manifestations it took its share of the passion which animated the whole life of the age, and which, on other planes, was translated into lust and violence. Buffeted this way and that by the brutal emotions which circumstances inflicted upon it, the Christian soul reacted with an exaltation which was all too often suspect. Piety became ostentatious, hysterical, easily given to excess. The episodes in Christ's life which aroused the most heartfelt devotion were those connected with His Passion. This was a constant topic of conversation, both in public sermons and in the privacy of the home. There is the example of a preacher who used to pause in his sermon for a space of fifteen minutes, and stand motionless, his arms outstretched like a cross, the living representation of the dying Jesus. As a child Gerson watched his father lean back against a wall to show him how Christ must have looked upon the Cross, and when she was but four years old St Colette would hear her mother's daily lamentations upon the Saviour's sufferings and death. The cult of the Five Wounds, and the ceremony of the 'Way of the Cross,' which is in effect a sort of 'spiritual pilgrimage,' date in their premises from this epoch, as does the representation of Mary 'of the Seven Sorrows,' with the seven swords piercing her heart. Henry Suso was completely obsessed with the Passion. Night after night he

---

[1] Quite serious men were addicted to the game of calculating the date of the end of the world: Nicholas of Cusa, for example, and Pierre d'Ailly. By a curious coincidence, in his *Concordia astronomiae cum historica veritate*, the latter predicts the following for the year 1789: 'A large number of important and prodigious divisions occurring in the world, and many changes affecting the future, concerning laws and factions in particular.' Which is an astonishingly accurate forecast. . .

would enact its principal scenes, bearing on his shoulders, next to his bare flesh, a leathern cross bristling with nails. Countless men and women recognized and adored that sign of blood, of whose reality the world had been so forcefully reminded by St Catherine of Siena. Both Angela de Foligno and the saintly mystic of Diepenveen felt themselves drenched in Christ's blood; and in one of his best-known prayers St Bonaventure describes it as a draught to slake man's spiritual thirst and feed his soul. This devotion to the suffering of Jesus was often accompanied by profuse floods of tears, themselves known as the 'daily baptism.' Indeed weeping was one of the habits of the age, and those listening to a good sermon would sob aloud like mourners at a funeral. Some idea of the extremes to which this emotional exaltation could lead can be obtained by recalling the example of Henry Suso, who had Christ's name tattooed across his heart.

This unbalanced mysticism and exacerbated symbolism mingled with a realism which was also part of the spirit of the times: the sublime brushed shoulders with the ridiculous. When eating an apple one pious individual would divide the fruit into four pieces, munching the first three in honour of the Trinity and the last in memory of the food which Mary had offered the Child Jesus. Since it was obvious that the tiny Jesus would not have peeled His own apples, the final quarter was duly eaten with the skin still attached. Another devout soul would drink a glass of wine in five gulps, in memory of the five wounds of Christ, first being sure to mix some water with it in order to commemorate that which had flowed from His blessed side when the lance pierced it. The manufactured representations of divine figures provided for popular devotion were incredibly crude. In Germany there were statuettes of the crucified Christ containing a bladder filled with blood, which was made to flow realistically through the five wounds; and several figures of the Virgin possessed a shutter in the stomach which, when opened, revealed the Holy Child in His mother's womb. At Chilly, in Franche-Comté, there was a contemporary representation of a *virgo parturiens*, and Gerson even describes one which contained the entire Trinity.

The same exaltation and, admittedly, the same readiness to go to extremes are apparent in the existence at this time of prodigious swarms of sects devoted to frenzied mystical practices. The *Flagellants* had sprung into being immediately after the Black Death. They roamed the length and breadth of Western Europe in large bands, everywhere making great show of their pious exercise of beating one another until the blood ran. Pope Clement VI's condemnation had not been successful in stopping their demonstrations, which in fact continued far into the fifteenth century.[1] Although the Flagellants could certainly be

[1] See *Cathedral and Crusade*, p. 595.

termed neurotics, they were dogmatically blameless; by contrast the multiple movements which are grouped under the common heading of *Brethren of the Free Spirit* were distinctly heretical. Among these were the successors of the Fraticelli and the apostolic fanatics of the preceding century, a section of the Begards,[1] those half-secular, half-monastic folk who were to be found in large numbers along the banks of the Rhine, both in Germany and Flanders. The Brethren asserted that by entrusting his whole self to the Spirit, and thus entirely abdicating his own free will, man was certain of achieving freedom from sin. His every action became unimportant, and this, needless to say, made many things incredibly easy. . . . In addition, all the Brethren were hostile to the established Church and the degenerate clergy, and in favour of a return to primitive morality.[2] These anarchical movements, which were extremely complex in character, and are little understood even today, had already been condemned by John XXII. They continued to flourish nevertheless, and even the rigorous persecution waged against them by the Emperor Charles IV from 1368 onwards did not succeed in stamping them out: traces of them are to be found as late as the middle of the sixteenth century.[3]

Coarseness went hand in hand with fanatical exaltation. The same people who wept loud and hard on hearing a preacher describe the agonies endured by Christ would spend the remainder of the religious holiday in drinking, gaming and debauchery. Dancing in churches and graveyards, to the accompaniment of highly indecorous singing, was a commonplace. This was the time when the notorious 'Feasts of Fools' and 'Feasts of Donkey' were all the rage, and even satirical masses in honour of Bacchus and the like. Gerson swore that he once encountered someone who maintained that the Feast of Fools, which was celebrated in December, and which was a veritable caricature of the liturgy, was just as sacred as Christmas. Even the clergy joined in these revels, and actually encouraged a type of humour which seems lewd and offensive to modern ears. The choir-stalls of many churches, and even certain cathedral porches, were the repositories of some really indelicate artistic detail. After all this it is hardly surprising to learn that the biblical scenes of Paradise on earth, which, in the big processions, came immediately after the reliquaries, were represented by living people who were most inadequately dressed. Episodes from pagan

[1] See *Cathedral and Crusade*, p. 557.

[2] The Dancers, or Turlupins, proclaimed themselves opposed to all authority: half naked and adorned with flowers, they gave themselves up to wild dances, interspersed with caterwaulings which were alleged to be litanies.

[3] It should be noted that many elements among the Begards remained free from heresy and were not condemned. But the suspect elements damaged the reputation of all the rest.

mythology were sometimes interpolated, the human participants in these being just as scantily attired. However, so powerful was the contradictory climate of the age that incidents of this sort did not prevent preachers from declaiming against human depravity and luxury with enormous success. Some went so far as to condemn marital relations between husbands and wives, and to demand the old classical penalty of death by stoning for the woman convicted of adultery.

Naturally in an atmosphere of this kind the most aberrant sorts of superstition abounded. Superstition was indeed rampant everywhere, eating its way into even the most rightful and soundly based devotions. The Church was soon forced to lay down rules concerning the public display of the Host, which was being abused by certain people. The occasions upon which the Blessed Sacrament could be carried in procession were henceforth strictly limited. At the end of his sermons St Bernardino of Siena would show his congregation a huge banner, displayed between two candles and depicting a sorrowful face, which bore the name of Jesus embroidered on an azure ground, and those watching would break into stifled sobbing. This custom, which spread far and wide, was so exaggerated that Pope Martin V put a stop to it. In their efforts to invite the faithful to Mass, the tonsured orators did not hesitate to assert that no one grew any older during the time lapse of the Holy Sacrifice—an obvious advantage—and also that no one who had been present at Mass could be afflicted by blindness or apoplexy during the remainder of that day.

The cult of the saints had for several centuries been accompanied by countless superstitions. Needless to say these now increased enormously. The ordinary man in the street was infatuated by the saints: he was familiar with their great deeds, their miracles and their frightful deaths, and everything about them fascinated him. He venerated them, but, being a practical individual, he also demanded their constant intervention on his behalf. Moreover the Church herself invited him to make this demand: the Bamberg and Utrecht Missals both state quite categorically that to reach God the intercession of the saints is quite indispensable. The famous 'Fourteen Holy Helpers' made their reputation at this period; the Council of Trent later abolished the special Office which had been allotted them. A saint's aid was requested in every conceivable human situation, serious or otherwise. The intercession of St Apollonia, whose teeth had been torn out by the executioners at her martyrdom, was sought after in cases of toothache; only St Roch could grant protection from the plague, but St Fiacre would do in the case of common pimples. The halt and the lame invoked St Pius; the gouty, St Antoninus. Even the individual desiring to urinate had his own celestial mediator, St Damian. It must be freely admitted that the Reformation was not wholly mistaken in its subsequent attack upon the cult of saints in its excesses.[1]

The cult of relics continued to provide innumerable instances of support for these ill-controlled devotions. It was as flourishing then as it had been in the heyday of medievalism, and until its fall Constantinople did a thriving trade in sacred relics. Saints' bones and holy souvenirs were bought and sold, and even stolen. A glass of water, said to be that given to the woman of Samaria by Jesus, or a morsel of bread allegedly from the Last Supper, would find a ready buyer. The record in this type of business really seems to belong to the cunning merchant who succeeded in selling the skeleton of one of the Holy Innocents! Should the famous 'shroud' of Turin be placed in this category of dubious relics? The argument is not yet closed, and it is impossible to give a definite answer here. It should, however, be observed that in 1390 the antipope Clement VII [2] sent a bull to the canons of Lirey, in Champagne, who were the proud possessors of the relic. In this bull he explicitly stated: 'Each time that the canons show the shroud to the people, they must take care to state, loudly and distinctly, that this is not Our Lord's actual winding-sheet, but a copy which represents Christ's.'

But we must go still further, as far as the extremity of psychical disturbance, if we really want to understand the spiritual atmosphere of this strange epoch. The most flagrantly erroneous beliefs enjoyed a success that is astonishing—astrology, for instance. In these troubled times people were so terrified of the morrow that they longed to find out what it held in store for them, by studying the conjunctions of the stars and other portents of the heavens. All great men had astrologers of some sort or other in their *entourage*, even the popes. Clement VI, for example, received guidance concerning the moment to undertake a crusade from one of these learned persons. Then there was alchemy, such as Blessed Raymond Lull practised in his search for the 'philosophers' stone,' and against which the popes reacted by repeating the warning strictures of John XXII. Worse than these existed too: demonology and witchcraft inflicted growing harm on Christian society. Belief in the devil was so general and so powerful that men saw his hand at work all around them; they did not scruple to establish

[1] One of the most astonishing examples of fetishism regarding the saints concerns the *Helper* (or Hulpe or Hilfe). In German *patois* these words indicated Christ dressed as He had been long ago. Gradually the qualitative word denoting sanctity was added: *heilig*. This led people to imagine a 'Sanctus Helpericus,' a 'Helperus' who was venerated at Plön in Schleswig-Holstein, Bremen and Lübeck (where the story of the saint's martyrdom was told!). In the same way the *Volto Santo* of Lucca, in Italy—the Holy Face which was so venerated by the pilgrims—gave rise to a St Viarius or Vicarius who was venerated at Tournai, and there was even a 'Confraternity of St Vicarius.'

[2] The real Pope Clement VII reigned from 1523 to 1534. Thus, in the eyes of faith, this bull has no validity.

relations with him, and even to seek his aid. The practice of sympathetic magic was rife, and the dukes of Burgundy, in particular, were quite convinced that their enemies all possessed wax statuettes fashioned in their likeness, which they pierced with bodkins. As for witchcraft, it was so widespread that one inquisitor confessed that one-third of Christendom was suspected of being implicated in it. Conciliar decrees sternly forbade women 'flying off into the night on broomsticks to go to celebrate the devil's feasts.' In the middle of the fifteenth century, Jacquier, the Dominican inquisitor, published a lengthy treatise on these practices, in which he offered weighty proof of the reality of the witches' nocturnal flights and the infernal ceremonies of their sabbath. This insane wave of sorcery spread far and wide, engulfing the whole of Western Europe. The crime of 'vauderie,' as it was called,[1] was punishable by burning at the stake; the 'Mirror of Saxony' and the 'Mirror of Swabia' say so categorically. From time to time an upsurge of terror-stricken wrath would shake the common people, who would rise against the witches, men and women, true or false, and burn them all. In 1428 two hundred such unfortunates perished at one fell swoop at Louèche, in Haut Valais; and for the next ten years the witches at Briançon were mercilessly persecuted.

Opposition to such acts of folly was extremely feeble. The Inquisition did indeed act severely against the practice of witchcraft, but it believed in its existence, and thus gave credence to every superstition. The bull of 1440, in which Pope Eugenius IV attacked the crime of 'vauderie,' ensured it an official consecration.[2] The common people believed in these things naturally enough when they heard it said that the Grand Inquisitor of Paris himself, Jacques Dubois, had gone mad because of all the horrors he had witnessed. Sensible men who tried to put such matters in their proper perspective and treat them for what they really were, as dangerous derangements of the mind and soul, were rare indeed. The most famous is Gerson,[3] who wrote a treatise against all superstitions, attacked aberrant mysticism, gibed at Begards and Turlupins, asserted that he distrusted even the visons of St Catherine of Siena and St Bridget of Sweden, and refused to believe in the powers of magicians, witches, astrologers and other workers of marvels. But he was quite exceptional.

---

[1] Owing to confusion with the Waldensian heresy, which originated in the Vaud but was quite free from all such aberrations.

[2] Moreover this shows clearly that faith in the devil, in his action in the world, and in the reality of witchcraft is indeed a part of the authentic Christian faith, despite all the exaggerations and wild fancies that are intermingled with it.

[3] Such an attitude makes all the more valuable the famous declarations made by Gerson during Joan of Arc's lifetime, in which he supported the veracity of her 'voices' and her vocation.

'LIFE'S BITTER TASTE'

Needless to say Christian morality had less and less effect upon society in an atmosphere such as this. Even during the most splendid epoch of medieval Christendom, the gospel principles had never been wholly accepted by mankind; their validity had always been admitted, but they had not been universally applied; humanity had never been truly Christian in the most literal sense of the word. From the fourteenth century onwards, however, moral degeneration went hand in hand with political and social decline. Men who had only narrowly escaped the numberless trials and tribulations of the age let themselves be borne along by a feverish thirst for pleasure. This was linked with a passionate abandon which the times encouraged all too well, and thus acquired that 'bitter taste' to which the most profound historian of this period has referred.[1] Moreover the law of contradiction, sign of the lack of inward unity, was at work in this as in every other field. 'Two concepts of life coexist in the human conscience, virtually side by side: the pious and ascetic, attracting all man's highest moral feelings, and, opposing this, a wholly unrestrained sensuality which wreaks a terrible revenge. Where one or other of these tendencies predominates, we find the saint or the sinner; but usually they succeed in maintaining some sort of unsteady balance between themselves, albeit with enormous fluctuations towards either heaven or hell.' The selfsame person would write both devotional poems, which reached almost mystical heights, and fragments of indescribable obscenity, and this with a kind of artless simplicity. Such contrasts play an important part in giving the epoch its distinguishing characteristics.

This was a society in which unrestrained violence was everywhere, taking every conceivable form; indeed it hardly merits the name of Christian. Its wars had a savage character. There was no place for the Peace of Christ in a France divided between French and English, Armagnacs and Burgundians; in the Low Countries, where aristocrats slaughtered burghers, and dispossessed Hoecks fought the wealthy Kabeljaus; or in Germany, where the anarchy resulting from tottering feudalism provoked the appalling reaction of the Courts of the Holy Vehme. Political assassination became a habit of the times: in the history of France the murders of the Rue Barbette and the Montereau Bridge stand out particularly, but countless similar incidents occurred in Italy, Burgundy, England and all over Western Europe. The 'dangerous classes' expanded in a most alarming fashion: truant students, former 'skinners,' bogus pilgrims, bandits or 'caimans,' and

[1] J. Huizinga. His work is referred to in the Select Bibliography at the end of this volume.

beggars of every possible shape and size committed hundreds of atrocities and depravities which were to be immortalized by the genius of one of their own number, a certain François Villon. There is a noxious, growing cruelty everywhere nowadays,' declared one preacher.[1] 'Where, may I ask, do compassion, mercy, clemency and righteousness hold sway? You find the father viciously and need-lessly persecuting his son, the son his father, brother fighting brother, neighbour slaughtering neighbour, Christian destroying Christian!' There was more than a mere flight of ecclesiastical eloquence here. Anyone who studies the contemporary life of this period in detail, as Pierre Champion has done, stands confounded by the enormous number of crimes, acts of violence, lawsuits and quarrels which it contains. A kind of open sadism prevailed on all sides, taking the place of the love of Christ; the most shocking evidence of this is the growing habit, despite all the efforts of popes and kings to the contrary, of refusing Holy Communion to those under sentence of death.

Flagrant sensuality was accompanied by unbridled violence, and all the preachers' fulminations against it were in vain. Over-indulgence at the table, on the subject of which the worthy bishop Jean de Cardaillac waxed so indignant— 'You stuff yourselves with fine victuals and drink the most rare wines!' he protested valiantly to his flock—was nothing compared with the behaviour which gave the moralists food for more legitimate grief. Sexual licence reached proportions which the twentieth century has barely attained. Adultery was general, and if Canon Machaut's *Hearsay* (whose author claims he is writing from personal experience) can be believed, the young women of the day enjoyed extraordinary independence. Marriage had little connection with love. In his attempts to educate his daughters, La Tour Landry narrates tales which would not be out of place in a modern gossip column. The nuptial theme, which enjoyed enormous literary popu-larity, bristled with erotic details of the most intimate kind. These found a parallel in equally astonishing customs that were in vogue during contemporary wedding celebrations, such as the public consummation of their union by the bride and groom. Feminine fashions were in keeping with the moral tone of the times. A synod held at Salzburg in 1418 prohibited priests from giving Communion to women who presented themselves at the altar-rails in gowns that were too *décolleté*; and though Gerson and others had already objected to the amoral digressions of the *Roman de la Rose*, the book's con-siderable success continued unchecked. Art followed suit. We know scarcely anything about the profane paintings of the period, since few examples have been preserved. For example, we have no idea what

[1] Jean de Cardaillac has been studied by G. Mollat in the *Revue d'histoire ecclésiastique* in the first two issues of 1953.

Van Eyck's *Women Bathing* looked like; but his naked Eves, like those of Cranach, have an erotic character entirely different from the serene innocence of medieval artists. In addition, if St Bernardino of Siena is to be believed, even sodomy was on the increase, especially in Italy: the famous preacher went so far as to say that there were certain schools in Tuscany to which no Christian should send his sons, for fear of seeing them corrupted.

This moral prostration was to continue for a long time to come. It lasted right through the Renaissance, and was linked with another form of rejection of Christian morality—the repudiation of social morality. Few periods in human history have shown such a scandalous gulf between the insolent ostentation of the wealthy and the misery of the poor. The French and Burgundian courts were places of unbelievable luxury and extravagance. This was the epoch of the 'hennins'— enormous head-dresses curved like a ship's keel, and supported by iron wires. Shoes had toes so long and tapering that the wearer could scarcely walk in them, and at the battle of Nicopolis the Western knights were obliged to cut the points off so that they might escape more precipitately. Decoration on clothing was not confined to sumptuous embroidery; precious stones, gold coins, and even little bells, were stitched on too. As for the luxury of the table, this went far beyond the limits of the absurd. From the gigantic pies that were borne ceremonially into the hall by dozens of pages, there sprang whole orchestras, ships fully rigged, fantastic beasts and scantily clad maidens: this sort of banquet was all the rage at the Burgundian Court and was the general topic of conversation. Yet, at the same time, the peasants were living in utter squalor, increasingly near to starvation, subsisting on lentils and roots, finding what shelter they could in the wretched hovels which mercenaries and brigands were vying with one another to destroy. It was the same story in the towns, and in the manor-houses of the bankrupt squirearchy: crushing poverty, and fear of the future. Such a contrast had nothing remotely Christian about it.

A Serious Decline in Clerical Standards

Nothing less than the united resources of a deeply respected Church were needed to grapple effectively with all these evil forces which were creating such havoc within the Christian soul. Alas! the Church was not merely disunited and divided against herself: the corruption of all too many of her own constituent organs meant that she actually played an active part in the moral degeneration of the period. Unquestionably one of the most serious elements in the multiple crisis which Western society was experiencing at this time was the decadence of the clergy.

The generality of the faithful was well aware of this decadence; it was in fact one of the commonest topics of conversation and a stock subject of merriment. The average Christian had a profound respect for the institution of the priesthood, but he distrusted a considerable number of those who wore its cloth. Even while he notes the good-humoured ridicule and anti-clerical jokes—several of which were subsequently collected by Rabelais—the student of the period gains a fleeting impression of latent hatred and a sense of betrayal, such as often follow hard upon a slighted love-affair. If a preacher really desired to stir his audience and arouse its enthusiasm he had only to introduce into his discourse a resounding diatribe on clerical morals and his success was assured. The same barbs were hurled quite indiscriminately at both seculars and regulars alike. All Paris delighted in repeating Molinet's mocking little prayer:

> Prions Dieu que les Jacobins
> Puissent manger les Augustins,
> Et que les Carmes soient pendus
> Des Cordes des Frères menus! [1]

However, this matter went much deeper than mere popular jesting. Many popes, bishops, theologians and saints expressed themselves in terms of terrible severity on the subject of the clergy of this epoch. Alvarez Pelayo's contention that 'the laity are saints in comparison with the priests and the monks' was undoubtedly intended as a witticism pure and simple, but he was right when he declared that the Church must be 'reformed from top to toe.' We know how vehemently St Catherine of Siena denounced clerical laxity; but she was surpassed by St Bridget, who spoke of the 'lupanar' which the Church had now become. In her recluse's cell at Corbie, St Colette spent many nights in frightful anguish, haunted by visions of the mystical Bride of Christ sullied by grievous wrongs, and, much later on, Denys the Carthusian was to emerge from an ecstatic trance with the assertion that he had seen 'a completely disfigured Church; she was corrupted from top to bottom; not a single vestige of purity remained to her.'

Of all the vices held against the clerics of the late Middle Ages, it seems that the one most frequently lamented, and that which scandalized the faithful most deeply, was the lust for money. The example for this emanated from above, from the Papal Curia itself. It was the Curia which increased the dues and rents which her 'collectors' gathered in

---

[1] 'Let us pray that the Franciscans
Will be able to make a meal of the Augustinians,
And that the Carmelites will be hanged
From the Brother Minors' cords!'

so zealously. The moneys so amassed were not used exclusively for Church administration, paying the armies of a hypothetical future crusade,[1] or financing the foreign missions: luxury and worldly amusements absorbed a great deal of it. Cardinals, important prelates and bishops all went hunting benefices, as though it were a kind of sport. It was common to see them collecting six or eight apiece, and the record number held by a single individual was as high as twenty-three. Even those who loudly advocated reform continued these disastrous practices so far as they themselves were concerned: Pierre d'Ailly possessed no less than fourteen benefices. On a lower level canonries were much sought after by younger sons; some twenty-year-olds held six or seven apiece. Below these rather disreputable beneficiaries the immense mass of the clergy lived in a state which often amounted to destitution. Around one single enfeoffed altar there would swarm a whole cluster of miserable clerks, whose pay was totally inadequate to support their basic needs, and who were obliged to share out the income derived from masses among themselves. In some parishes there were more than a hundred of these 'chantry priests,' mere beggars who naturally enough had but one idea in their heads: to get as much money as they could out of the faithful. Obviously clerical dignity could hardly expect to be enhanced by a situation of this kind.

Extreme caution should be exercised when dealing with the vexed question of the clergy's moral character. All priests were clearly not above reproach in this respect, and when St Catherine of Siena or Denys the Carthusian refer to clerks who spend their days in gaming, drinking and loose living, it must be assumed that they know what they are talking about. Dissolute monks and parish priests who maintained concubines did undoubtedly exist. But it is impossible to believe that such men constituted the majority. A bad priest invariably attracts far more gossip than a thousand who live blameless lives. A very careful inquiry made in the diocese of Rouen at the end of the thirteenth century had shown that out of a total of rather more than seven hundred clerks, eighty had been accused of incontinence, and twenty-three actually punished for it. In the middle of the fifteenth century the registers kept by Archdeacon de Josas, and referring to two hundred parishes, list only ten priests as guilty of loose living. Between 1315 and 1406 the register of the ecclesiastical court of Cerisy, in Normandy, contains fifteen accusations of clerical

---

[1] Many of the faithful complained of the fact that the moneys demanded by the Church were used to pay for the military expeditions in Italy. At the beginning of the fourteenth century Marsilio of Padua made a bitter and angry denunciation of a policy which was ruinous and wicked through and through. The echo of his words struck a permanent hatred into Christian hearts, and made invective rise easily to Christian lips ever afterwards.

immorality, and that for Grenoble, covering the period 1340–1419, seventeen.[1]

Absenteeism was a far graver problem than immorality; this evil was extremely widespread. The list of clerics who were interested in everything save their sacred duties was a long one, and it included both the most powerful prelates and the humblest parish priests. Despite conciliar decrees and papal instructions, many bishops did not reside in their own dioceses. The canons deserted their cathedral stalls: at York scarcely one-sixth of these pious dignitaries condescended to sing the Office, and when the archdeacons of Auch visited Lectoure, he found precisely two canons present out of a total of twelve. Priests abandoned their parishes, and war often forced others to leave their cures. About the year 1400 one priest in three was missing in the diocese of Rouen alone. In Upper Normandy ordinary peasants acquired the leases of some livings: needless to say they did not celebrate a single Office! The modern observer is faced with the astonishing picture of councils being constantly obliged to adjure priests (and even bishops) to say Mass at least four times a year!

Finally, there was another clerical shortcoming which scarcely troubled the average Christian, but which was to have the most serious consequences: ignorance. All the efforts made in the thirteenth century, notably by the Fourth Lateran Council,[2] to combat this deficiency gradually petered out. Priests were recruited indiscriminately and hurriedly trained, and far too many possessed a theological knowledge of such a rudimentary nature that it was virtually non-existent. There were no seminaries at this period, although Gerson, anticipating the work of St Vincent de Paul and Olier, dreamed of building colleges specially devoted to the education of priests. Priests simply did not know how to carry out their pastoral duties, particularly that of preaching. When the ministers of the Reformed Churches appeared on the scene, filled with missionary zeal and well versed in the Scriptures, the ignorance of the Catholic clergy was to make their task much easier than it would otherwise have been. As one observer remarked: 'How can the priests possibly combat these evil doctrines? Why, they don't even know which doctrines are sound and which heretical!'

Worst of all, the religious Orders, which had constituted the bulwarks of the Church during the great medieval epoch, were also in

[1] There were also some priests who were guilty of violence, and even of actual crimes, particularly in Germany, where the 'altar squireens' retained some extremely feudal habits. Their type increased in numbers in the fifteenth century. Moreover the parish priest of Mesvres, in Burgundy, who raised his own troop of bandits, was not alone in so doing, and Pope Gregory XI, who had known this unusual man, was powerless to correct him.

[2] See *Cathedral and Crusade*, p. 546.

the throes of a serious internal crisis. The number of new recruits had diminished considerably, and all too often the great monasteries and convents resembled empty cages from which the birds had flown. With the exception of the Mendicants, the various houses all regarded themselves as independent of the rest: there was no longer any principle of unity or authority. On the moral plane really scandalous abuses were rare, but it was impossible to apply the Rule properly in the half-empty abbeys where little handfuls of monks eked out a living as best they could, or in the select communities made up of the daughters of the nobility, who had taken the veil merely because they had failed to find husbands. The Mendicant Orders seem to have been particularly stricken by this crisis. They were now very far removed from the heroic poverty of St Francis and St Clare, and several examples are quoted of Mendicant 'superiors' who lived in well-appointed dwellings in great style, 'keeping an open table.' Among the Poor Clares the modified Rule of 1263 eventually resulted in extreme relaxation of discipline: there were sumptuous dinners, and lengthy visiting and parlour gossiping were common. Consequently the prestige of the regular clergy declined disastrously, and when Laurence Valla, the humanist, attacked the basic principle of monasticism in 1442, he found a ready audience throughout the entire Church. Luther and Calvin skilfully exploited the unpopularity of the religious Orders.

What were the causes of this appalling state of affairs? In the first place it is clearly attributable to that law of nature which can be seen at work time and time again throughout the Church's history. When left to its own devices the Christian soul sinks into the mire; the salt of the earth loses its savour; the yeast no longer leavens the dough. Confusion of temporal and spiritual interests, too, paralyses the best intentions. In one of his sermons St Bernardino of Siena declared: 'Even if you had a pope as saintly as your wildest dreams, he would not be able to get rid of all the evil priests and prelates. He would be forced to retain this one to please a king or baron, that one to suit the whim of some other influential noble. . . . It is quite impossible to reform the Church so long as the head remains in conflict with its members.' His assessment of the situation was extremely accurate.

Nothing illustrates more clearly the danger to which St Bernardino drew attention than the contemporary development of the system of *Commendam* and its disastrous results. The practice of commendam was a very ancient one: traces of it can be found as far back as the period of St Ambrose and St Gregory the Great. The original purpose behind the granting of a monastery *in commendam* was to entrust (Lat. *commendare*) its administration to a secular personage in the absence of the rightful titular, such trust being duly regularized by dispensation. However, with the progressive expansion of the system of ecclesiastical benefices, the commendam had become a most profitable operation for the holder, who was authorized to collect the revenues deriving from the office which he was temporarily exercising. Laymen at once became interested, and from the age of Charles Martel onwards there are examples of warrior-abbots laying their hands on the revenues of individual monasteries under pretext of becoming their protectors. Next, commendam, initially a temporary expedient, became a permanency: the 'commendatory' received the benefices on a life basis, and arranged for their ecclesiastical duties to be performed by a prior or other substitute who was canonically competent. This fatal practice had already gained much ground during the thirteenth century; regular benefices in particular, namely, abbeys and priories, had begun to be continually and systematically exploited.

As can be imagined, the crisis of the Great Schism and the rival bidding which resulted in the two opposing camps rendered this practice almost universal. In return for their oath of allegiance, secular rulers were loaded by one pope or the other with all the benefices that he had at his disposal—abbeys, monasteries, episcopal revenues and even humble parish livings; nothing escaped an appetite which became increasingly insatiable. Benefices *in commendam* became part of the recognized financial resources of the rich; we find them figuring in daughters' dowries, or being given to ragamuffins of twelve years old. The most astonishing aspect of the whole affair is the fact that not all these commendatory abbots were bad. Some of them actually battled valiantly for the reform of their communities. Generally speaking, however, they were interested solely in deriving the maximum return from their ecclesiastical possessions. They had no interest in matters of the soul, and allowed those in their charge to fall into spiritual jeopardy. In Germany, where confusion between the commendatory and the titular was both general and total, laymen frequently proclaimed themselves prince-bishops and count-abbots, but never dreamed of becoming priests. A much-quoted case of this sort concerns one of the bishops of Paderborn, who, in 1400, calmly and openly took a wife. Where conditions of this kind existed it is scarcely surprising that the whole clergy, from the highest to the lowest, lost much of its authority.

However dark though the picture is, it would be unfair to mention only those features which indicate clerical decadence. One extremely anti-clerical historian [1] admits that 'the complaints against the growing vices of the clergy, which were liberally heaped upon the priests of the period, were often inspired by the desire for edification, or by anger

[1] Felix Sartiaux, in *Foi et science au moyen âge*, Paris, 1926, a slight and anticlerical little book.

and envy rather than by an impartial appreciation of the facts'. The Church endured, and from her own bosom there subsequently sprang that mighty reforming impulse known as the Council of Trent. All this would have been impossible had there not existed, alongside all too many faithless shepherds, an immense mass of upright and serious-minded priests who tried to teach their flocks to the best of their ability, and to keep the faith alive among them. Even while the Protestant Reformation was causing the whole Church to shudder violently, Wimpfeling, the Alsatian humanist, rendered a well-deserved tribute to these humble and unknown witnesses of the Gospel. He speaks enthusiastically of 'these priests in our towns and villages who have the spiritual welfare of their parishioners at heart,' and adds significantly, 'Thanks to the grace of God, their number is not small.' As much can be said, he continues, 'of those religious houses which have remained true to the Rule of their Order, and have not acquired great wealth.' Holy Church was to lean hard upon these sound, healthy elements in order to effect her revival. But it has perforce to be admitted that those elements which were corrupting and wounding her were far too many.

WILL THE CHURCH REFORM HERSELF?—ST COLETTE

Would the Church react against this gravely disquieting situation? On so many occasions in the past her own deepest loyalties had produced the men and the means that could set her back on the straight and narrow way of truth. Would they do so now? Certainly the desire was there: many of her best and most devoted children were well aware that urgent remedial measures needed applying, and they made their views publicly known. As early as the dawn of the fourteenth century, Guillaume le Maire of Angers declared: 'The Church needs completely reforming, not merely as regards her constituent parts, but also at the top,' and Bishop Guillaume Durand of Mende commented: 'If reform is not carried out at once the situation will get steadily worse.' Throughout the period under consideration many powerful voices uttered the same warnings time and time again, loudly and tirelessly. Most vehement of all was St Catherine of Siena. It was she who wrote to Urban VI, with an acid frankness which compels our respect, that even if he could not restore the Church in all her beauty, he ought at least 'to wash her stomach.' St Bernardino of Siena said much the same thing, albeit in more moderate language; and behind him was ranged the whole enormous band of famous preachers of the day, such men as John Capistrano, Jacques de la Marche and Bernardino of Feltre. Moreover it was in order to work for the great project of reform that the contemplative St Colette deserted her recluse's cell and ventured forth into the wide world. And these appeals undoubtedly gained a sympathetic hearing in the highest places. Many of the pontiffs considered reform most seriously, even the popes of the Schism. There was probably not a single pope, in any camp, who failed to include the problem in his programme. Martin V was no sooner elected than he announced his intention of drawing up a detailed plan of reform; Eugenius IV confessed himself 'stricken to the heart by the Church's moral condition.' The councils were completely at one with the popes on this point: at Pisa, Constance and Basle reform figured largely in the order of the day.

The same aspiration existed on the local plane: the faithful themselves initiated a reaction. This was the period in which the first 'parochial councils,' in which ordinary laymen were linked with the day-to-day working of their church, were springing into being everywhere. The confraternities, too, with their apostleship and practical charity, can be regarded as a distant ancestor of our modern Catholic Action. These are revealing symptoms.

One thing only remained: to translate these undeniably excellent intentions into deeds. A number of saintly souls devoted themselves zealously to this task, and a distinct effort towards the correction of abuses is apparent from 1300 onwards, particularly in monastic circles. But, with certain rare exceptions, these efforts stemmed from below, from some monastery which had been reformed by a superior with sound ideas but who had not always sufficient power to persuade the Order as a whole to follow his example. For one St Colette, whose influence affected several Franciscan houses, there were countless reformers whose action was wasted in fruitless argument, polemics and rivalry. Although interesting as a symptom of something wider, this monastic reform was doomed to remain strictly limited in character.

It affected the oldest Orders first, and principally that of St Benedict, which was the most ancient of all. Benedict XII had already attempted to reorganize that Order in 1336. His 'Benedictine Bull' had divided it into thirty-five provinces, as well as strengthening the chapters; and the system of 'Congregations,' with centralized houses following the same customs, had yielded good results. The initiative of a number of energetic individuals breathed new life into several monasteries, and their influence spread: at St Giustina of Padua, Paul of Stra led a highly centralized congregation to which several houses were affiliated and where Luigi Barbo was soon to introduce the practice of systematic prayer. In Spain, thanks to the influence of the King of Castile himself, Juan I, this role was filled by the congregation of Valladolid, with which the famous monastery of Montserrat was linked. From Subiaco, where the memory of the Father of Western monasticism still lived on, reform spread to Germany. It extended northwards in the shape of the customs of Melk, and south with those of Bursfield; Johann Rode, Johann Dederoth and Johann Hagen are the leading names in this monastic renaissance. But in France, which was distracted by war, Benedictine reform was long delayed.

In the case of the Carmelites the reforming impulse came from *St Andrew Corsini*. This wealthy young man, who answered the Master's call and adopted the way of penitence and prayer, is an attractive figure, and his influence was altogether admirable. Under his direction the Carmelite houses of Tuscany, which he continued to control even after he had become Bishop of Fiesole, battled valiantly against all deviations from the Rule.

The Dominicans of course derived immense benefit from the prestige of their famous preacher, St Vincent Ferrer, and St Catherine of Siena. Raymond of Capua, who had been St Catherine's confessor, became the Order's Master-General, and he proved himself to be a leader bent on reform. Well aware that great collective measures were impossible to apply effectively, he reformed a number of individual houses to serve as models for the rest. This was done at Colmar, under Blessed Conrad, and at Venice, under Giovanni Dominici. The latter, in his turn, founded the monastery of Cortona, at Fièsole, which Fra Angelico and St Antoninus were to make famous, and St Antoninus subsequently founded Sain Marco, at Florence, which was to be Savonarola's monastery. In France the celebrated priory of Saint-Maximin sprang into existence at this period. All this activity was not without its dangers, for opposition between 'reformed' and 'unreformed' was often violent. The Master-General was not always obeyed in the different congregations where he was usually represented by a Vicar-General; but Generals such as Bartholomew Tixier and Auribelli made exemplary efforts to win over a majority of communities to the principles of reform.

The same problem existed among the Franciscans in an even more acute form. As early as 1330 a few souls faithful to the message of the Poverello had striven to realize the ideal of the 'Spirituals' without slipping into their errors; notable among them were John of Valla and Blessed Paoluccio of Trinci. The little convent of Brullino had remained the centre of these *Observance* movements, which were bitterly criticized by many of the other houses. With the appearance of John of Stroncona, and in particular of St Bernardino of Siena, whose personality dominated the Order, the movement gained a great deal of ground, but resistance was manifold, and considerable friction occurred. The French Observants, infuriated by the Order's tendencies in Italy, claimed the right to rule themselves, under the direction of a Vicar-General. The Spanish Observants immediately followed suit, and obtained the same privilege. St Bernardino of Siena and St John

Capistrano viewed with anxiety the disintegration which threatened the Order. They obtained from Martin V the 'Martinian Constitution' which was an attempt to restore Franciscan unity: it was a complete failure. There was often much more than simple rivalry between Observants and Conventuals: when the Observants acquired the sole right to elect the Minister-General, the Conventuals virtually seceded from the main body under the leadership of a Master General. Divisions occurred among the Observants themselves. There were ruptures between 'Cismontanes' and 'Transmontanes,' between 'Family Observants' and 'Community Observants.' On the fringe of the main Order, the Claretians, Amadeists and, at a later date, the Spanish 'Discalced' friars conducted their own affairs in the way which seemed best to them. This great Observance movement had, as Leo X later said, certainly 'revived an Order which was almost dead'; but it did not succeed in preserving the Order of St Francis as one whole.

While the ancient Orders were struggling hard to reform themselves, new Orders were being founded. There were the Alexeians, in the Low Countries, instituted in 1348, the Jesuati in Italy, created in 1360; the Hieronymites in Spain and Portugal, founded in 1390. Three foundations were particularly active. The first of these, the *Order of the Blessed Saviour*, was founded by St Bridget of Sweden in 1346. The severity of her Rule recalls Cîteaux, while the 'double' monasteries for both sexes are reminiscent of Fontevrault. Then there were the *Oblates of St Mary*, or rather of Tor de' Specchi, who, in 1436, grouped themselves around a pious widow, *St Frances of Rome*, and devoted themselves to good works, ministering to the poor, the sick and the destitute. Lastly there were the *Minims*, a curious Order, whose members were the direct successors of the hermits of ancient times. They owed their inspiration to St Francis of Paola,[1] a Calabrian anchorite whose example was contagious. None of these foundations enjoyed a success comparable with that of Cluny in the eleventh century, Cîteaux in the twelfth or the Minors in the thirteenth; there were so many other religious houses, and it must be remembered that the population of Western Europe was no longer on the increase. However, within about a century of their creation, the Brigittines had eighty houses, and the Minims four hundred and fifty, containing some fourteen hundred religious.

Although these reformers who battled so valiantly against the forces of decadence did not entirely succeed in snatching the Church from the slope down which she was slipping, they did at least save the spirit from extinction. The most radiant and attractive of them all was

---

[1] On St Francis of Paola see the next chapter, section: 'Forces that still Remained Intact, and the Anxiety for Reform.'

surely that great French virgin, who, though utterly overwhelmed by the agony of the universal betrayal that she saw all around her, refused to lose faith in the hope eternal, and fought a heroic, lifelong battle to bring the Christian soul back to its ancient loyalties. *St Colette* was almost the contemporary of Joan of Arc. She sprang from the same soil, and is in many respects not unlike La Pucelle. The Maid of Lorraine used her sound common sense and burning wisdom to restore a throne and rebuild her nation's religious faith. The nun from Picardy devoted the same mental resources to reawakening men's consciences, and giving back their ancient vigour to principles that had degenerated into clichés. Both these women were restorers, and because it possessed people of this calibre this dark and tragic epoch managed to retain a little grandeur.

As in the case of the Maid, the beginning of Colette's history exactly befits a page of the *Golden Legend*. When Dame Moyon, the wife of Robert Boellet, the carpenter of Corbie, gave birth to a daughter (13th January 1381), the happy event, if not entirely miraculous, must at least have been expressly wilied by God, for the Dame was well past her sixtieth year. In any case only the intervention of Divine Providence could have enabled such a frail, tiny girl, no bigger than a sprite, to reach adolescence without mishap. All the more so since, no sooner had she attained the age of reason than the carpenter's daughter began to practise the most rigorous asceticism. She 'ate very sparingly' and wore 'rough ropes, full of knots, next to her tender skin, and spent countless hours kneeling on the ground, deep in prayer.' It is true that Our Lord Himself visited her, counselling and instructing her: a group of extremely learned theologians divined this when they recognized 'a kind of knowledge of God' radiating from this still very young child. When she was but nine years old supernatural grace had granted her an understanding of the Church's wretched condition, and she realized that she would be called upon to be the bearer of its remedy. The whole of Corbie talked of this little Nicolette—she was nicknamed Colette—who slipped out to listen to the monks' Office at night, and spent her days visiting and comforting the poor and the destitute.

She knew that God would require her to perform important and arduous tasks, but she was still ignorant of the means ordained. To begin with, she groped blindly in the dark, hesitating on her road, changing direction several times, trying to be first a Benedictine, then a Poor Clare, then a Beguine, all without finding her true vocation. It was now that she attempted a terrible experiment: she had herself enclosed in a tiny cell, tucked away at the side of the Church of Notre Dame, in St Étienne. Here Colette lived the life of a real 'recluse'; her only link with the outside world was one narrow aperture through which a few kindly souls passed her the bare necessities of life. This was indeed a curious novitiate. A 'rough hair-shirt, unfit for humankind,' rubbed the skin from her breast; three 'cruel iron chains' dealt her back a barbarous punishment. But these sufferings were as nothing compared to the spiritual tortures which the saint experienced. She had to resist the devil's assaults; the Christ of the Passion appeared before her in visions, dripping with blood; and one idea never left her—the treason of the baptized, the ingratitude and apostasy of those men and women to whom Christ had confided His trust. Was this then her special task? Did Our Lord wish her to reform His Church, and, more especially, the Franciscans, whose spiritual child she felt herself to be? Must she leave her recluse's cell? Colette knew that such was the will of God: He had made it perfectly plain to her. There must be no hesitation, or the darkness of divine punishment would close in all around her. Finally, Christ's messenger paid her a visit, in the person of Henri de la Balme, the wise and saintly Franciscan. He had travelled from the other end of France, for he too had received divine enlightenment concerning Colette's mission. Henceforth Colette's doubts left her: the Voice which had commanded her to quit her cell, to throw herself into this gigantic enterprise, was certainly not the voice of the Evil One, and she obeyed it.

Now she was able to make straight for the goal which she believed God had set her. At the age of twenty-five her life had found its true direction, its *raison d'être*. The daughters of St Clare had mitigated their Rule time and time again, so that, when they followed it at all, its rigours had completely disappeared. Colette knew she must lead the Poor Clares back to the original demands of their Order, to the purity of the days at San Damiano. She might indeed have been content merely to found a convent where those who shared her views could join her. But no, right from the start she aimed at the heights. She was determined to influence the entire Order, and to do this she had to see the Pope. But which pope? The Schism was at its height, and two pontiffs claimed the Keys of St Peter. After deserting him for four years France had just accepted the obedience of Benedict XIII for the second time. Benedict was the Avignonese pontiff who was regarded by much of Christendom as a mere antipope, opposed to Gregory XII and the legitimate popes of Rome. He was the notorious Pedro da Luna, from Aragon, whom the French themselves mockingly nicknamed 'the moon pope.'[1] Yet, though Benedict was excessively haughty and excessively obstinate, he was nevertheless a deeply devout man, with genuine spiritual insight. He received the young mystic in audience at his residence in Nice. She stood modestly before him, a small, slight

---

[1] See earlier in this book, p. 30.

figure, her eyes cast down, so humble and yet so haloed in unseen brilliance that, so the chronicler assures us, the Pope 'dropped to the ground' when he saw her; he fell on his knees in prayer. The 'moon pope' had been blessed with a most marvellous understanding. The plague which was laying waste the land was surely a divine warning, and this young woman was the messenger whom God had sent to undertake the mighty works of mercy. On 14th October 1406 he granted her all that she asked: the privilege of complete poverty— that same privilege which Clare had claimed—the right to wear the habit of the Poor Clares. Finally, Benedict created her 'abbess for the duration of the whole reformation.'

For the next forty years she devoted herself selflessly and tirelessly to the task of reform. Under her direction the 'Second Order of St Francis' rid itself of everything cumbersome and corrupting, whatever the cost; and at the same time several male communities—for the Pope had granted her authority to inspect these also—were reprimanded and admonished by the saint. Nevertheless Colette said nothing novel or exceptional: true reforms within the Church invariably consist of a return to the original sources, and the greatest audacity must always be wedded to total humility.

So we see Colette hurrying up hill and down dale, traversing all France and half of Europe, in the Jura one day and Bavaria the next, then quitting the Languedoc to visit Flanders. Seated on her mule, accompanied only by a very modest retinue, she covered hundreds of leagues in her journeying across provinces laid waste by war and brigandage, crossing incessantly from the Armagnac zone into the Burgundian. Her intrepid, tireless figure was soon bathed in an immense radiance. Countless monasteries saw her arrive to beat upon their portals and utter the call to order which was that of Christ Himself: 'Transform yourselves!' Countless new houses were willed into being by her alone. Many important and powerful friends rallied to her assistance: Blanche of Geneva helped her to found La Baume and Besançon; Margaret of Bavaria, the pious wife of the formidable John the Fearless, paved the way for the creation of Auxonne and Poligny; Bonne d'Artois was responsible for Decize; then, in the kingdom of France itself, the Duchess of Bourbon founded Moulins and Aigueperse for her, and Claudine de Chatillon endowed the convent at Puy. One of her biographers asserts that Colette reformed no fewer than three hundred and eighty 'nuns' churches'; but this figure is probably somewhat exaggerated. .

Naturally enough her efforts ran up against a good deal of opposition, for her commands did not suit everyone; occasionally there were setbacks, as when an attempt was made to poison her. But Our Lord's protection enfolded her; sanctity was the passport with which she traversed the world. And being a good Frenchwoman, like Joan of Arc (whom she may once have met at Moulins), Colette took advantage of all her comings and goings to try to reconcile the two sides in the civil war, and rebuild the national unity of France. Claudel [1] has expressed this very charmingly:

> Sans cesse en route, comme une aiguille diligente à traversé, la France
> dechirée,
> Colette en recoud par-dessous les morceaux avec la charité.

In 1434, in order to safeguard the continuance of her reforms, she obtained approval for the *Constitutions* which she had established in all her religious houses. One section of the Order of St Clare, that practising rigorous observance of the Rule, was thus separated from the rest, and its members are still known as *Colettines*. Tireless to the last, Colette continued to rule her Order with a firm hand, although her health, which had never been good and which had been undermined by the many mortifications and asceticism which she had constantly practised, was failing slowly but surely. When the Council of Basle deserted Eugenius IV and offered the papal tiara to the aged Count of Savoy, Amadeus VIII,[2] Colette showed foresight in refusing to recognize the antipope, even though he was her old friend. New foundations were springing up everywhere all the time, reformed houses were flocking to join her movement: Heidelberg, Pont-à-Mousson, Hesdin, Ghent and Amiens. But her life was almost over: the hour of 'the last sleep' was drawing near. At Ghent her long journey ended at last. Her closest friends were already dead—Henri de la Balme and St John Capistrano, who had helped her so much. Once again the Saviour, who had been so near to His 'little child' throughout her life, came to her, forewarning her, helping her to clear the gates of death. And on 6th March 1447 a pious nun at prayer in the convent which the saint had founded at Orbe suddenly beheld an angel standing before her whispering: 'Your venerable sister Colette has just departed to God.' [3]

Shortly before her death St Colette is said to have uttered these bitter words: 'Alas, I have toiled so hard and long for religion, and all my work will wither away in a moment. . . .' This confession of disillusionment, which has a prophetic quality about it, must have been inspired by an accurate assessment of the current situation. This indomitable woman, who had traversed Christendom from end to end, and consorted with cardinals and important prelates as well as with

---

[1] *Feuilles de Saints*, 'Ste Colette.'
[2] See earlier in this book, p. 44.
[3] Colette was beatified in 1623, and canonized in 1807. The fifth centenary of her death, in 1947, was the occasion of some magnificent celebrations.

humble clerks, knew better than anyone the limited and inadequate character of all these reforming efforts, even her own, and she must have realized how incapable they were of saving the Church. Even in her native town of Corbie she had not succeeded in founding a community after her own heart. . . .

In short, this sporadic and fragmentary reform of the late Middle Ages was clearly ineffective. The lack of personalities endowed with universal prestige made itself cruelly felt. The epoch possessed neither a Gregory VII nor a St Bernard, neither a St Francis nor a St Dominic. And above all, as past experience had proved, reform could be fully effective in the Church only if the Papacy assumed direction of it, formulated the decisions, and enforced their application. Between 1350 and 1450 the Papacy was far too weak and subject to rivalries to be able to play any such role; while the councils opposing it were so concerned with asserting their own dubious authority, regulating their internal affairs and reaching an understanding with the secular heads of government, that reform was necessarily relegated to second place.

It was mentioned of course: indeed reform was a constant topic of conversation. Ten or fifteen times during the century questions like the reorganization of the Sacred College, episcopal nominations, the education of the clergy, the suppression of absenteeism and the improvement of clerical morals were brought up for consideration. There was no denying men's good intentions, but either the weapons were wanting or the methods were at fault. When Urban VI declared war on all abuses—simony, immorality and luxury—immediately after his election, with the claim that he was going to scourge the evil out of the Church's system, he antagonized the majority of the cardinals and officials of the Curia, whom he treated as fools or rogues, and the only result of all his effort was the outbreak of the Schism. Conversely whenever the popes of the Schism, in whichever camp they were, set out an extremely reasonable list of reforming precepts (as in the case of Pedro da Luna, Benedict XIII), it was only too obvious that these could not be enforced. In order to survive they needed the support of all those who acknowledged their obedience, even though such supporters might well be notoriously simoniacal or loose living. The Council of Constance probably gave the most serious study to the problems and methods of Church reform. But while its third session adopted certain measures, the fourth promptly abrogated the reforming clauses of its predecessors relating to conciliary primacy, obviously to avoid upsetting certain influential people. In 1418, as soon as Martin V regained control of the situation, he enacted certain excellent and sweeping decrees dealing with clerical morals, episcopal residence and the conferring of benefices. However, evidence that these were really ineffective can be seen in the fact that in 1425 he was forced to promulgate three more decrees, almost identical with the first. As for Eugenius IV, his efforts on behalf of reform were of the most limited nature. In all fairness he cannot be blamed; for in the circumstances in which he was placed it is clear that had he attempted to make the slightest move, his defeat would have been inevitable; he therefore confined himself to setting an example in the purity of his own life.

The question of reform thus remained on the table, and was destined to remain there for a long time to come. No sooner had he ascended the papal throne than Nicholas V dispatched his legates far and wide with the object of regenerating the Church. In France the cardinal-legate, William d'Estouteville, who was entrusted with the task of reforming monastic chapters, schools and universities (although he was the father of several bastards!), showed himself so preoccupied with luxury and wealth that no one took him seriously. In Germany the Pope's emissary was none other than *Cardinal Nicholas of Cusa* (1401–1464), a man who possessed goodness as well as great learning and sound judgment, a heroic spirit who had successively battled against the Hussites, presided over the Council of Basle and waged war against the Turks at the side of John Hunyadi. In the course of his (Grand Legation) he was extremely successful in persuading various provincial synods to recognize the necessity for putting a stop to disorder in the Church, for suppressing certain flagrant abuses, and for assisting the religious Orders, particularly the Benedictines, to undertake a number of exemplary reforms. Yet when all was said and done the results of his vast enterprise were to be far more modest. Nicholas himself ended by exhausting his energies in a dispute with the Duke of Tyrol concerning his rights and possessions as Bishop of Brixen.

These setbacks have a symbolic significance. All attempts at reform were as ineffectual as they were numerous, in so far as they were directed at the effects of the crisis and not at its causes. The real enemies were the state of society in general, the Church's entanglement in temporal affairs and the degradation of the Christian ideal by worldly appetites and interests.

MYSTICAL THEOLOGY COMES INTO ITS OWN, BUT DIVORCES ITSELF FROM THE WORLD

Nevertheless, confronted with a situation which was in many ways so distressing, the Christian spirit reacted in one respect altogether differently. Since everything was turning to dust, since man appeared to be slithering inevitably down the slippery slope of destruction, one refuge alone remained: God. The Christian's only hope of salvation lay in entrusting himself wholly and completely to the Almighty, living exclusively in Him and for Him; there alone resided 'the Inner Consolation.' [1]

In the second half of the fourteenth and first half of the fifteenth centuries, therefore, we see a development of mystical theology, so wonderfully vigorous that it constitutes the most splendid feature of the age. But mystical activity undergoes a change of character; it may be said to revert to its origins, to return to the days of the Dark Ages when souls who devoted their lives to God shut themselves away in the cloister and renounced all contact with the world. In the golden epoch of medievalism, mystical theology had taken the opposite course, and had been a part of day-to-day life and thinking. As we know, St Bernard lived a life of prodigious activity while maintaining daily contact with the ineffable divine. In the schools and universities, on the other hand, men had tried to create a unified theology, greedy for knowledge of God and aflame with desire to love Him, contemplate Him and possess Him; and as soon as the Mendicants, Franciscans and Dominicans alike, attained the professional chairs, they had striven with notable success to achieve such a synthesis as may be seen in the works of St Bonaventure and St Thomas Aquinas.

Mysticism still retained this theological character at the beginning of the fourteenth century. It preserved the vision of the universe bequeathed to mankind by the *Summa*; it never suggested that desire for knowledge was vain, and that contemplation and love were all-sufficient in themselves. As its impulse became more powerful, however, it increasingly divorced itself from all truly intellectual activity. That impulse stemmed from the seven Dominican houses at Strasbourg at the beginning of the century. Here *Master Eckhart* (1260–1327) had developed a burning, emotional doctrine which the Archbishop of Cologne had accused of pantheism and quietism, and the archbishop's condemnation had been confirmed by Pope John XXII. For example, in appearing to teach that man could really become God, that right could be equated with Christ, that part of the soul was uncreated, and also (with grave results in the field of morals) that God was present in all things, even in sin, the great mystic had laid himself open to criticism. But his followers—and they were many, for Master Eckhart was an inspired preacher, a writer of distinction, and a person of considerable charm—had been more responsive to the exaltation which he had aroused in them, to what the mystic himself liked to call 'the glitter of the soul.' His influence had been considerable the whole way along the Rhine, from Cologne to Constance, and had caused the whole district to be known as the 'mystical valley.'

Consequently the great Rhenish mystical theologians of the age followed in Eckhart's footsteps. Both were Dominicans; *Johann*

---

[1] *The Imitation of Jesus Christ* was first translated into French under this title.

Tauler was an Alsatian from Strasbourg, and Henry Suso derived from Swabia but had settled in Constance. Though following 'the well-beloved Master' with circumspection, they were undoubtedly his direct descendants. Johann Tauler (1290–1361) was a magnificent preacher, whose *Sermons* still possess the power to move us, and a remarkable spiritual director. Like Eckhart, he laid stress on that 'glitter of the soul' which went far beyond the faculties of the mind, and enabled the individual to reach God, on the 'Gemüt,' the 'essential will' or mysterious gift which permitted the soul to rejoin the divine, the faculty in which will and reason were united, and whose operation surpassed all other human attributes. As for Henry Suso (1295–1365), whom the Church afterwards beatified, his exquisite spirituality, permeated by godliness, is evident throughout his *Book of Eternal Wisdom*, his sermons and his letters. In all of them he exalts the Divine Wisdom in language of incredible beauty, speaking of it with an affection very similar to that which the Poverello bore towards Christ Himself. At all events we are now very far from the paths along which St Thomas had taught men to travel towards God.

Of course the trend of the times encouraged this divorce of mysticism and philosophy. We have already studied the tendency towards a religion which demanded much of human sensibility even while pandering to it, and this combined admirably with joyous exaltation and the desire to attain the divine. Since the essential goal was complete union with Christ, there could surely be no better way of achieving it than by linking oneself with His sufferings, His Passion and His Blood which had been shed for all mankind. Tauler derived astonishing effects from this theme. The *Herz Jesu Büchlein* (the first devotional treatise on the Sacred Heart) undoubtedly originated in Strasbourg, the centre of Eckhart and Tauler's influence, and the first representations of Mary Mother of Sorrows were Rhenish. All these symptoms combine to make one coherent pattern. And as they spread among the common people, these doctrines tended to become even more sentimental in character, and to accentuate the rupture with theological science.[1]

At the same time mysticism tended to divorce itself from life. For one Raymond Lull (1235–1316), who had combined the career of one of the first of the great African missionaries with the authorship of the *Book of the Friend and the Beloved*; for one Bernardino or Vincent

---

[1] Needless to say these tendencies combined with those studied earlier in this chapter —with all the spectacular manifestations, ecstasies and ostentatious mysticism. Entire communities of nuns experienced collective trances at Colmar, Toss, Medingen and Adelhausen. It was certainly no coincidence that the epoch produced so many visionaries: St Bridget, St Catherine of Siena, Dame Julian of Norwich and St Catherine of Bologna. The language of all these, but of Dame Julian in particular, is remarkably similar to that of Eckhart and Tauler.

Ferrer, sublime mystics who were nevertheless heavily involved in all the troubles of their age, and who travelled widely, there were tens of thousands of mystical souls who were satisfied with a far more leisurely existence. Tauler and Suso were purely and simply preachers and spiritual directors. Moreover the eremitical life became once again extraordinarily popular: Ireland and England swarmed with hermits and recluses, for whom Richard Rolle framed a rule in which he exalted 'the fire of love.' One of these English hermits was undoubtedly the author of the mysterious treatise entitled *The Cloud of Unknowing*. Here the believer is advised to concentrate all his spiritual effort upon the desire to attain God, but to throw a protective cloud of oblivion between himself and the world. Large numbers of hermits built their huts of branches outside the walls of Paris, some of them living close by the city gates. This rejection and abandonment of the world is highly significant.

There could be little room for objective theology in the new concept of spiritual life. Some considered it condemned to eventual disappearance, and it was this danger that *John Gerson* (1362–1428) strove to counteract. He desired contemplation to be based on the faculties of the mind; the mysticism he advocated was of a practical turn, soundly constructed upon the twin foundations of morality and asceticism, and allowing little rein to emotional outbursts. In this sense it is possible to call him the precursor of St Ignatius of Loyola. But his lofty spirituality and powerful intellect failed to rebuild the unity of the past. The mystics became increasingly hostile to a world which they regarded as irremediably sullied by sin, and they looked with suspicion upon a theology which had lost much of its real substance. As time went by their withdrawal from life became more and more complete. Hence the appearance of *devotio moderna*.

By *devotio moderna* we mean a warm, pulsating and profoundly human way of seeking perfection; a spiritual technique based entirely on the inner make-up of the individual; a modest kind of mysticism devoid of ostentation or exceptional phenomena, which subjected the whole soul to the imitation of Christ, the One Model. It was not totally new or 'modern'; for some of its elements, and even its formulae, can be traced back a long way to St Bonaventure, St Francis, St Bernard, the Victorines, pseudo-Denys the Areopagite and even to St Augustine himself. But the tone and orientation were entirely novel. We have but to open one of the works deriving from this school to judge how much separates it from its predecessors. These simple, arresting, easily remembered maxims, which are almost unconnected with one another and which seem to foreshadow La Rochefoucauld and Vauvenargues, are quite unlike the pious and scholarly writings of the spiritual thinkers of previous epochs. And while *devotio moderna* resulted in immense spiritual progress in the realms of emotional analysis and psychological knowledge, and led to a more acute sensibility, this was at the expense of intellectual study, scientific curiosity and even theology itself. The things which really counted, the things which touched the infinite mercy of God, were prayer, tears, meditation and supplication. What use then were questioning, learning and study?

This spiritual school established itself in the Low Countries towards the middle of the fourteenth century, in an atmosphere which undoubtedly owed a great deal to the movement represented by the *Begards* (together with their feminine branch, the *Beguines*).[1] France had little share in it: there pious souls tended to find refuge in existing Orders, or remained in the world, mingling with the mass of the faithful rather than forming separate groups. In Flanders, on the other hand, there developed a pious way of life, regular and strictly conventional. The new devotees among the laity could be recognized by their bowed heads, measured gait and sombre clothes; they were particularly favoured by the gift of tears, which was so common at that time. Their best and most zealous members retired from the world; they gathered together in communities where, helping and encouraging one another, they made a united effort to follow the difficult path which leads to Heaven.

Their first teacher was Blessed Jan van Ruysbroek (1293–1381), surnamed the *Admirable*. This former priest of St Gudule in Brussels was blessed with a soul of remarkable purity and simplicity. At the age of fifty he retired to the hermitage of Groenendaal—the 'Greenwood' (French: 'Vau-Vert')[2] of the Forest of Soignes—where he soon attracted a large group of hermits, and led a life of sublime sanctity, totally devoted to God, until his death at a very advanced age. His works, which include *The Adornment of the Spiritual Marriage*, *The Mirror of Eternal Salvation*, *The Tabernacle* and *The Kingdom of the Lovers of God*, bear a certain resemblance to the speculative mysticism of Eckhart, and thus caused him to be suspected in certain quarters. A profound metaphysician, he also attempted to discover and analyse the nature of mystical states. But his clear-sighted intelligence, wholly orientated to the divine, was impregnated with those grand ideals that were later manifested in *devotio moderna*. The Dutch mystic sought to identify his will with that of God, to understand the infinite abasement of his own human state, and to entrust himself wholly and completely to the Almighty. Countless pilgrims, among whom was

[1] This movement, which is little understood, is treated in the note on p. 557 of *Cathedral and Crusade*.

[2] This may well be the source of the French proverbial expressions 'aller au diable Vau-Vert.' In its original form 'aller au vau-vert' meant 'to go to seek enlightenment.' Popular usage, which slipped in the allusion to the devil, added an overtone of ridicule.

Tauler, flocked to seek the advice of the Prior of the Vau-Vert. When Gerard de Groote visited Ruysbroek he refused to be dazzled by the hermit's lofty speculations, but he was overwhelmed by the simplicity, faith and infinite goodness which made the love of Christ shine out so vividly around him. And it was this which he and his friends wished to imitate.

The religious groups which embraced these new tendencies and gave them their real significance were found in the Netherlands. The *Brethren of the Common Life* included both priests and laymen, who, without taking vows, devoted to the Lord a life of poverty, prayer and charity. They gathered together at Deventer around Gerard de Groot (1340–84), and then, after his premature death, around his friend Florentius Rodewijns. The movement rapidly gained ground. Its houses sprang up in large numbers, and it won thousands of recruits, particularly women. In 1387 the monastery of *Windesheim*, near Zwolle, which had been founded by six disciples of Gerard de Groote, formed itself into a community of canons regular. In theory it adopted the Rule of St Augustine, but in practice followed the spiritual methods of Ruysbroek, and even developed them. Throughout Flanders, the neighbouring Rhineland and part of northern France this new style of mysticism bloomed in wonderful profusion, and produced an abundant crop of marvellous offshoots. Among them were Gerard of Zütphen, author of *The Spiritual Ascents*; Gerlac Peters, who wrote an astonishing *Soliloquy* which rivalled the *Imitation*; Henry Maude; Jan van Schoonhoven, Ruysbroek's friend and disciple; and, most important of all, *Thomas à Kempis* (1380–1471). The last named may well have been a German, from Kempen, near Düsseldorf, but his fame centres upon the monastery of Mount St Agnes, near Zwolle, where he spent most of his life. He was the author of *The Soliloquy of the Soul*, the *Book of the Three Tabernacles* and (in Dutch) *Good Prayers to Speak and Read*. All these devout souls possessed the same distrust alike of speculative mysticism and unbridled asceticism; all shared the same desire for a humble, simple life, soundly based upon discipline and temperate habits. Their rule of life has been set down for the edification and admiration of all time in one little book whose value is never-failing, *The Imitation of Jesus Christ*.[1]

---

[1] It should be observed that, though there was no direct influence between the two, other religious centres had arrived at an almost analogous concept of the devout life. The trend of Windesheim was not far removed from the ancient, pure mystical theology of the Benedictines, which survived among the Carthusians alone of the more ancient Orders. Denys Ryckel, a Fleming better known as *Denys the Carthusian* (1402–71), philosopher, theologian, exegete and king's counsellor though he was, produced formulae nearly akin to those of Ruysbroek and Thomas à Kempis in his treatises on the *Source of Enlightenment* and the *Seed of Life* or the *Discretion of the Spirit*. In England Walter Hilton (d. 1396), an Augustinian canon, came so near to the *Imitation of Jesus Christ* in his *Ladder of Perfection* that the former has frequently been attributed to him.

This masterpiece is not merely one of the most wonderful achievements of the epoch which gave it birth, but also one of the most outstanding attainments in Christian history as a whole. It belongs to the type of sublime spiritual expression that would still bear witness to human greatness in the radiance of Light Eternal, even if the whole world were enveloped in shadow. The *Imitation* is not merely the perfect expression of that mystical current which completely enfolds it, of that *devotio moderna* which its success was to impose upon the whole of Christian piety—a 'spiritual revolution' as Michelet has called it: it is one of those great moments in the spiritual spiral which stems from the Gospel and will end only on the day of Judgment. It is also one of the world's major works of literature, one of the masterpieces in the treasury which is shared by all mankind.

Yet it is shrouded in mystery, which an entire library of commentaries has never been able to pierce. Its author is unknown, and has every chance of remaining so. Moreover his anonymity is entirely in conformity with his own precept: 'I delight in being unknown and counting for naught.' For many years the *Imitation* was attributed to Thomas à Kempis, but the prior of Mount St Agnes never mentions it in his list of works, which he himself kept meticulously up to date. St Ignatius, St Francis de Sales, Pierre Corneille and others considered that it could have been written by John Gerson; but the style has little in common with that of the scholarly chancellor of Paris University, and when his brother produced Gerson's bibliography, he made no reference whatsoever to the *Imitation*. As for a certain Gersen, a Benedictine from Vercelli, in Italy, whose name has been put forward by a number of critics, it seems highly probable that his name, and indeed his existence, is the result of a mere copyist's error. Thus the question remains open. Scholars have suggested many hypotheses, from Walter Hilton to Conrad Oberpeg, from Göttingen to Louis du Mont, and some have even attributed the masterpiece to St Bernard himself. No doubt still more names will be put forward in the future. The most probable solution attributes the book to one of the monastic groups at Windesheim or its environs. Here the maxims which we still read may have been used as themes of meditation by a whole community, and collected by one of its members simply in order to preserve for his brethren all the pearls from the treasury brought to light by their common effort.

We may well ask with Chateaubriand: 'How did a monk, shut up in his monastery, manage to attain this quality of expression? How did he acquire this extraordinary knowledge of mankind?' Here is another mystery. Anyone opening the *Imitation* immediately gains the remarkable impression, simultaneously painful and exciting, of being totally understood; he senses that the author has penetrated to the

F

darkest recesses of his mind. He cannot escape the serene light which
Eternal Wisdom shines readily on each one of us, and he has no desire
to do so. The inner life of the spirit at its most profound and authentic,
in all its ecstasy and exquisite delicacy, is contained herein, and is
analysed with a precision which the greatest moralists, even Descartes
and Pascal, have rarely displayed. Everything pertaining to man is
scrutinized and clarified, without any allusion to contemporary trials
and tribulations, but in the light of eternity. Man is treated for what he
really is, a creature made in the image of God, but stained by sin and
redeemed by Our Lord. Then, when he has been made to feel the full
measure of his baseness, to realize that he counts for nothing, and to
understand the pit of dereliction in which he lies, the anonymous
author takes him in his arms, turns him towards the light, and talks to
him of hope. This is not done didactically, with the demonstrations
beloved by the theologians, but with the utmost simplicity, merely by
evoking the Divine Presence. 'Here I am,' says Christ. 'I come to you
because you have called Me. Your tears and your soul's yearning, the
contrition of your humbled heart, have moved Me to pity, and brought
Me back to you.' After that there is nothing more to say: one needs
only to make God welcome, to pray and to love.

Thus the whole lesson of the *Imitation* can be summed up in a
practical mysticism which required man to reform himself, by imitating
the Ineffable Model as best he can, but which assures him at the same
time that his efforts are not in vain, that Christ is Mercy, and that, in
confiding himself to Christ, he will secure salvation. Intellect and
learning are left with little part to play. 'Of what use is it to you to
reason on the Trinity if you lack humility and thereby displease the
Trinity? In truth high-minded discourses make one neither holy nor
upright. A virtuous life alone makes one dear to God.' The only valid
knowledge is to do God's will and renounce one's own. Is this the
slogan of 'Grow stupid'? No, for the soul that follows this method and
devotes itself wholly to the one essential will possess the only knowledge which counts for anything, the one embracing all the rest.
'Happy is he whom Truth herself instructs, not by transitory words
and figures, but by what she is. . . .'

From the moment of publication—that is to say, *c.* 1400—the
influence of the *Imitation* was enormous. All Christendom was stirred
by this one little book, ten lines of which were enough to destroy the
fabric of lies so beloved by the epoch, and bring the world back to an
understanding of the one essential. It was translated into every language. The humanists and other prophets of the future were interested
in it, because it made the individual its focal point; but it held an equal
appeal for the traditionalists, who heard in it the echo of a more faithful
past. All over the Christian world, and even beyond, men followed in

its footsteps. The *Imitation* contributed both directly, and also through the agency of Jan Mombaer, who systematized its maxims into a method, towards the spiritual formation of those who were to be the leaders of the Catholic Reformation a century later. It had considerable influence on the greatest of them all, St Ignatius of Loyola. It was mainly through the *Imitation* that *devotio moderna* would shape the belief of the future, a less communal and more inward kind of belief than had prevailed during the Middle Ages, and which began to assert itself immediately after the Council of Trent.

Protestant historians have often considered that 'in plumbing the depths of piety, without retaining sufficient contact with the genuine evangelical faith, these mystics helped to add fuel to the anguish which filled so many souls at the end of the fifteenth century, notably that of Martin Luther.' [1] This is probably an exaggeration. It is true, however, that by causing a rift between theology and devotion,[2] they ensured the collapse of the ancient edifice which had been the glory of the Middle Ages, and even helped in a sense to prepare the divorce between religion and reason from which the modern world has suffered so severely. On the personal plane, the wonderful cry which rises towards Heaven from their pages moves us to the core; but it is no longer that of an entire society, clinging with all its fibres to its faith.

INTELLECTUAL BREACHES

There is yet another sign of this fundamental transformation. The development and isolation of mysticism had their counterpart (and also to some extent their explanation) in an intellectual evolution which was not without its dangers. In this field the Middle Ages had been characterized by an intimate union of faith and thought: literature, philosophy and the sciences all had religious bases. The breach was accomplished during the second half of the fourteenth century, when the intellect claimed autonomy, and a new atmosphere, which was to be that of 'modern' philosophy, began to establish itself.

The university, of course, remained in being, that great power-house which, in days gone by, had enabled the Church to control all learning and intellectual creation. But the university, while retaining its prestige and even possessing a measure of political power, had lost much of its youthful vigour. Paris, the most important of these intellectual centres, whose decisions had often been said to have the force of law, was in a state of decay, following a pattern of decline common to the whole of France. Large numbers of foreigners, including

[1] J. Courvoisier, *Brève histoire du protestantisme*.
[2] This is probably why taken as a whole, the Church has canonized so few of them.

such men as Eckhart, still went to study there, but Paris was no longer the torchbearer of philosophy, as she had been in days of old. During the age of the Schism and the councils she had made a determined attempt to impose her authority but in vain. Oxford, her principal rival, was also declining. Other universities were being founded all over Europe at this period: Prague, 1348; Vienna, 1365; Heidelberg, 1386; Cologne, 1389; Erfurt, 1392; fifteenth-century foundations included Caen, 1401; Leipzig, 1409; Rostock, 1419; Louvain, 1425; Freiburg, 1453. Even Poland had established her own vigorous centre of learning at Cracow in 1364. All these new universities had a markedly national character which limited their influence. Intellectual standards as a whole were on the wane and unfortunate customs made their appearance. At Paris the philosophy course was cut from six years to three; the four years' theology required for the doctorate were in practice much curtailed. The general corruption attacked the granting of university degrees: they could be bought at a high price, even—with papal permission—in towns where no university existed. The masters, who had formerly all been clerks, now came increasingly from the laity; and when Jean Buridan, who was neither a priest nor even in minor orders, succeeded in becoming rector of Paris, his example whetted the ambitions of several other seculars. Educated laymen began to write, and still more to read, books which no longer emanated from the teaching Church. At the beginning of the fifteenth century a number of completely new intellectual centres sprang up in Italy. These were the 'academies,' which had no relationship whatsoever with the universities, and whose influence was to be enormous.

Really outstanding personalities were rare, far rarer than in the great days of triumphant scholasticism; and even those who can be considered great rank far below St Thomas Aquinas and St Bonaventure, even below Duns Scotus and William of Ockham. Many men and women were remarkable in the religious field, but they were all mystics; and these, by definition, regarded speculative philosophy with deep suspicion.

Who were the leading intellectuals of this period? *Pierre d'Ailly* (1350–1420), a brilliant teacher at the Sorbonne, chancellor of the university, Archbishop of Cambrai and an influential member of the councils of Pisa and Constance, who was created cardinal by the antipope John XXIII, had nothing creative about him. His lengthy treatise *On the Reform of the Church* is a workmanlike exposition of the problem, peppered with judicious conclusions, but nothing more. D'Ailly's pupil, *John Gerson* (1362–1428), who succeeded him as chancellor of Paris, is far more important. Combining a lucid mind with an admirably upright conscience, Gerson was mainly preoccupied with safeguarding the ancient harmony of intellectual life, and in reconciling philosophical progress with faith. He envisaged a 'mystical theology' which would satisfy both the heart and the mind. But his extensive literary output was improvised for specific occasions only; it consists of treatises on reform, moral tracts, textbooks, biblical commentaries, poems and countless sermons (in French and Latin). The only book by Gerson which deserves to survive is his mystical dialogue on *Consolation through Theology*. Even this, however, is written in imitaion of Boethius. Cardinal *Nicholas of Cusa* is an equally remarkable and perspicacious figure. He combined an active role of great importance [1] in Church affairs with profound meditation on major intellectual problems. The essential of his ideas resulted in a theory of knowledge which he expressed in *Learned Ignorance*. But this very treatise reveals how far removed were men of his kind from the steadfast certainties of the Thomists. 'I know only that I know nothing,' it concludes. Truth cannot be attained by the rational operation of the mind, but only through intuition and mystical impulse; the influence of *devotio moderna* is clearly visible here. Thus, even men of great merit, entrusted by the Church with high office and important teaching responsibilities, seem more like passing figures, expressing all the doubts of their age, than spokesmen of eternal certainties. Though disturbed by the new tendencies, they accepted them, even those which owed their inspiration to humanism and the Renaissance. Nicholas of Cusa himself introduced such ideas into Germany, where they caused a widening breach between scholarship and religion.[2]

In the great medieval epoch theology had bound the two firmly together; but henceforward theology rapidly declined. Obviously the ancient systems continued to hold an important place in university teaching: Thomists, Bonaventurans and Scotists all attempted to prolong the work of the master of the past. But there was no longer any originality; men became lost in details and trifles, absorbed in clever but empty arguments, the most refined of which was the

---

[1] Nicholas of Cusa's part in ecclesiastical affairs is treated in Chapter I.

[2] A number of names in the literary field deserved to survive. *François Villon* (1431–6?), the turbulent and passionate author of the *Petit* and *Grand Testament*, is the most famous. But *Christina of Pisa* (1363–1430), a Venetian who came to France as a child of five, and is the first feminine name of note in literature, and *Charles d'Orléans* (1391–1465), son of the unfortunate Louis d'Orléans and victim of John the Fearless, who was himself a prisoner of the English for twenty-five years, both have infinite charm.

> 'Le temps a laissé son manteau
> De vent, de froidure et de pluie. . . .'

And *Alain Chartier* (1390–1450) is a prolific and fluent poet. But these can scarcely be called Christian writers. In Villon there are frequent glimpses of a faith mingled with remorse; Alain Chartier spoke extremely highly of Joan of Arc, and Christina of Pisa has left us two mystical works: *L'Épître de la prison de la vie humaine* and *Les Heures de contemplation sur la passion de Notre-Seigneur*. However, it can be said that not one of these four writers made any real contribution to prolonging the effort of Christian thought, in so far as it was a creative force.

quodlibet, or scholastic debate. Style too deteriorated: the Latin of the Sorbonne became utterly vulgarized. Not a single outstanding personality emerged from the mass of well-intentioned masters and rhetoricians: the leading Thomists, John Capreolus and John of Torquemada (uncle of the notorious inquisitor), and Peter d'Aquila, the principal Scotist, could only echo the teachings of their predecessors. The great Summas of Knowledge were still studied, and a few new ones were written, e.g. John of Torquemada's *Summa de Ecclesia.* They were more and more disparaged, however, notwithstanding the desperate efforts made on their behalf by one or other of the great Orders. It was clearly impossible for this enfeebled, stultified theology to retain its old position as the leading branch of knowledge, the key to all the rest. The mystics can be commended for abandoning it. In the old days all the different streams of learning—philosophy, rhetoric, grammar, history, scripture and the sciences—had flowed towards it; henceforth each tended to be an entity in itself and even to attack the mother that had once nurtured it. At the same time these branches of knowledge gradually introduced new methods of thought and proposed new solutions for the problem of the relationships which ought to exist between faith and reason.

Anyone reading the works of William of Ockham [1] is bound to have serious doubts as to whether any relationship at all still existed between these two. Ockham was a Franciscan scholar, at both Paris and Oxford. He died in 1349, but his powerful personality dominated the world of philosophy for a hundred and fifty years. An intellectual trend which goes back to Abelard, and which Pierre Auriol (*d.* 1322) and Durand de Saint-Pourçain (*d.* 1334) had previously expounded, reaches its culmination in Ockham. This was the *via moderna*, henceforth to be known as *Ockhamism*, or even as *Nominalism* or *Terminism*, because it maintained that general ideas have no reality, being merely words, names or terms. The only reality consists of what can be grasped by experience, i.e. individual beings. Everything else is *flatus vocis*! [2] As for man himself, he is certainly real, but only in so far as he is an individual actually existing at this point in time. Here we are dealing with a kind of premature Existentialism. It should be understood that where God was concerned, Ockham categorically refused to concede reason the power to prove and grasp God. However, in thus proclaiming himself a Christian, he found a palliative to his agnosticism in a radical and supernatural theology, in which faith was all sufficient. It was by faith and faith alone that man could understand the great truths of God's existence and attributes, of the spirituality and immortality

---

[1] See *Cathedral and Crusade*, p. 562 ff., which deals with William of Ockham and his ideas and disciples.
[2] The expression has remained proverbial.

of the soul. But this act of faith, this total submission to the will of God, had no connection with the processes of the mind enlightened by reason. Thus one aspect of Ockhamism proclaims a veritable rationalism, while the other preaches a doctrine advocating the supremacy of faith. Here we have a striking example of the collapse of inner unity, so characteristic of the men of that age.

Against such a background little remained of traditional Christianity. Metaphysic, whose real object was the universal, was utterly discredited. Its dogmas could no longer take root in reality, and faith was a totally gratuitous operation of the soul. The principles of morality also were undermined: everything on earth was willed by God; there was no distinction between good and evil; theft, crime, adultery, even hatred of God, were all a part of the divine scheme of things. It is easy to see that such a thesis would find no difficulty in winning adherents. Many years before Machiavelli, Ockham was already thinking that 'the end justifies the means. . . .'

Ockhamism, which had enjoyed considerable success even during its author's lifetime, made rapid advances after his death. Jean Buridan, rector of Paris, endeavoured hard to implant it in that university, as did his disciple, Marsilios of Inghem. Pierre d'Ailly was permeated with Ockhamism; Gerson was not free from its influence. *Gabriel Biel* (1425–1495), who liked to call himself 'the last of the schoolmen' and even 'the king of theologicians,' and whose *Commentary on the Sentences* won great renown during his lifetime, sowed the seeds of the system from the lofty heights of his professorial chair at Tübingen. He hoped indeed to make Nominalism the philosophy of the Church. It was primarily through Biel that Luther became acquainted with Ockhamism; he quotes him among the antecedents of his own views, boasting that he knows whole pages of Biel by heart. The Church in her official capacity reacted against Ockhamism strongly, but to no avail. On several occasions she condemned its theses and its protagonists, often with the active help of the secular authorities, who were disturbed by the scepticism which Ockhamism engendered. Little came of these efforts. In 1474 Louis XI hurled another edict of extraordinary violence against the Ockhamists, but they were sufficiently powerful to oblige him to revoke it the following year. At the beginning of the sixteenth century the Nominalist school was to possess yet another famous master, the Scottish John Major (1478–1540), a Parisian scholar against whom Rabelais subsequently let fly some of his most cruel barbs. Finally, humanism and Calvinism relegated Ockham and his theories to oblivion—somewhat ungratefully, for Ockham had done much to prepare the way for their success.[1]

[1] This movement was combined with the disgrace of Aristotle, who had dominated medieval thought. His natural philosophy was disparaged by all scholars; his logic seemed

However, it must not be thought that this complex intellectual movement at the end of the Middle Ages marked a regression in every sector of life and scholarship. Although it had done more than anything else to debase metaphysical and theological speculation, it had contributed to the progress of logic. Above all, it inspired a passion for experimental knowledge which was to be enormously important and which was manifested in many different ways in the extraordinary intellectual ferment which marked this epoch. Indeed new tendencies made themselves felt in every field of the mind. They existed even in the sacred domain of Holy Scripture, where revisions of the inspired texts resulted in the famous *Polyglot Bible* (printed between 1514 and 1517, and published in 1520), and where modern exegesis was foreshadowed in the studies of Nicholas of Lyra, Gerson and the scholarly Alphonsus Tostat. The growing interest in man as an individual explains the development of historiography. Its principal exponents were Froissart in France (*d.* 1404), Gobelin Persona and Thierry von Nieheim (who wrote a *History of the Great Schism*) in Germany. But it was the exact sciences—mathematics, physics, astronomy and so on —and the sciences concerned with observation and the individual that underwent the greatest development. Mathematics found their modern bases with Nicholas Oresme, Bishop of Lisieux and Descarte's precursor in the sphere of analytical geometry, with Nicholas of Cusa, and with Georg von Peurbach. The same Nicholas Oresme asserted that it was the earth and not the sun which revolved; Jean Buridan followed in Ockham's footsteps by pressing forward with the theory of gravity; Albert of Saxony and Marsilio of Inghem laid down principles of physics and mechanics; Jean de Linières measured the inclination of the earth's ecliptic so accurately that Le Verrier subsequently needed only to correct his calculation by seven seconds; while Georg von Peurbach and Johann Müller of Königsberg (surnamed Regiomontanus) constructed a planetary theory long before Tycho Brahe and Keppler. In the same period Thierry of Freiburg explained the rainbow and perfected the theory of the tides, and Albert of Saxony discovered the part played by erosion in the formation and destruction of continents. And it was from their reading of Pierre d'Ailly's *Imago mundi*, a book that first appeared in 1410, that Christopher Columbus and Amerigo Vespucci derived the idea that the earth was round and decided to reach the East by sailing westwards. . . . Great progress was also made in the field of medicine by Guy de Chauliac,

superfluous twaddle (which is what it had in fact often become); his metaphysic was rejected by the Ockhamists as absurd. Plato, his old adversary, regained ground, together with all the intuitive and mystical doctrines which were now developing. At the same time (see the next chapter) Renaissance Italy put him right in the forefront once again; in 1438, shortly before the fall of Byzantium, the first complete manuscript of Plato reached Western Europe from the East.

the teacher from Montpellier, author of the first important work on surgery. Advances were made even in the realms of economics and social science, but here again there was a divorce from Gospel principles. François de Mayronis found a large following when he declared that economic relations were subject to the law of interest, and not to morality.

This intellectual ferment had many admirable sides to it, but it was none the less disturbing. The structure which had once been the Christian intellectual order was fast falling into ruins, and it is easy to understand the anxiety openly confessed by such devout persons as Gerson, Pierre d'Ailly and Nicholas of Cusa. Where was the world going? And what would men think of next?

The First 'Protestant' Heresies: Wyclif

This intense ferment that was working men's souls and minds was virtually bound to break out even more violently in open rebellion. The climate favoured the growth of the poisonous plant of heresy in this decomposing soil only too well. Heresy accordingly appeared; it bore the mark of the age, being essentially different from the deviations of earlier centuries. Catharism had been a kind of aberrant ideological monster, deriving from the distant East, whose dualist dogma, despite its phraseology, had almost nothing Christian about it. The last remnants of the Waldenses lived in the Alpine valleys, but in their case intellectual demands had fallen short of moral exigences, with the result that these honest, decent folk possessed a theology so rudimentary that they scarcely understood their errors. As for the Fraticelli and other Brethren of the Free Spirit, who had made so much sound and fury, they were mostly fanatical hotheads in whom a sincere desire for purity went hand in hand with the most wildly extravagant speculations. The new heresies assumed a character of quite a different kind: on the one hand they sought to exploit the desire for reform, which undoubtedly existed among the devout, by deflecting it to their own advantage very much as the Waldenses and Fraticelli had done in the past; but, on the other, they added a number of dogmatic ideas borrowed from contemporary trends that were directly opposed to the traditional teaching of the Church. These were certainly to be the two characteristic features of both Lutheranism and Calvinism. The heretics who lived at the end of the Middle Ages were already claiming authority from the all-powerful Word of God, just as the leaders of the Protestant Reformation were to do later on. The sole point upon which they seem less advanced than their successors is the alleged exclusiveness of faith and the futility of good

* F

works in the task of salvation. But Voltaire was not far wrong when he wrote concerning one of them: 'What the Waldenses taught in private he preached in public, and his doctrine was almost identical with that of the Protestants who appeared on the scene more than a century later.'

Voltaire was referring to *John Wyclif*, whose career and ideas caused so much stir in England at the end of the fourteenth century, and whom many modern Protestants still claim as one of their spiritual forefathers. Wyclif was born *c.* 1328 in Yorkshire, and at Oxford distinguished himself successively as a student, philosopher and theologian. At the university he knew both Ockham and Thomas Bradwardine; and the latter's enthusiastic Augustinianism made a deep impression on him. Wyclif was a pure intellectual, a handler of ideas, rather than a teacher and leader of men; but he possessed a cold violence which much impressed certain people. None denied his eloquence, which was enriched with an imagery taken from the apocalyptic fancies of Joachim of Flora. Although, like Bradwardine, Wyclif's thought was Ockhamist in some respects, notably in its rationalist tendencies, he differed from the celebrated Franciscan in rejecting the latter's belief in free will and belonged primarily to the Realist School of philosophy. Wyclif declared that no free will existed, and that man was completely subject to the will of God.

Oxford always welcomed ideas, and Wyclif enjoyed great success there when he was still very young. His fame soon spread beyond the confines of the university. With consummate skill he played two winning cards. First, he violently attacked ecclesiastical abuses and clerical depravity, complaining that churchmen were far too fond of material possessions (although this did not prevent him from un-unashamedly indulging in pluralism himself). Anyone playing this tune was always sure of a ready audience. Second, he cleverly exploited the nationalist feeling which was particularly strong in England at that time, and which made his fellow countrymen generally hostile towards the Papacy, particularly after the popes had settled in Avignon. When, for instance, Urban V committed the extraordinary error of asking the King of England for the thirty-three years' arrears of payments which the latter theoretically owed in his capacity as the Holy See's 'vassal,' since he was John Lackland's heir, the Pope furnished Wyclif with an excellent opportunity of refuting this claim in a memorandum which was obviously to Edward III's liking.

Thus launched into public life, awarded the Mastership of Balliol College, Oxford, and employed by his government on various diplomatic missions, Wyclif felt encouraged to pursue his diatribes against the Church and to set himself up as the violent protagonist of reform.

Papal taxation, the traffic in benefices, the worldly possessions of the Church, the scandalous behaviour of priests and monks—the Mendicant Orders were Wyclif's *bête noire*—provided him with endless themes for sermons and lectures. The English hierarchy, considering itself under direct attack, reacted sharply, and William Courtenay, Bishop of London, cited Wyclif to appear before the Archbishop of Canterbury's court in 1377. Here the reformer was sworn to keep silent on several issues; but he was shielded by too many influential people, and the verdict served no useful purpose.

The Great Schism, which broke out in the following year, seemed to prove that the formidable scholar from Oxford was justified in his criticisms. When he began gibing publicly at the two popes who were quarrelling over the triple crown 'like two dogs scrapping over a bone' it was exceedingly hard to condemn him. His criticisms now became more radical, and not only in their mode of expression. 'What exactly is the Church?' Wyclif demanded in his treatise *De Ecclesia*, published in 1378. 'Is it the prelates and abbots, the monks and canons and religious mendicants and all the tonsured clerks, even if they live evil lives?' And his answer was a clear negative. The Church, he declared, was the assembly of the elect, the men whom God had saved, they and they alone. Against the established Church, with its fixed institutions and its visible hierarchy, Wyclif set an invisible transcendent society. Since no one could be sure of being saved, no one could be sure of his authority any longer, from the Pope down to the humblest parish priest. Those predestined to salvation, on the other hand, enjoyed a supernatural priesthood; they were in direct touch with God. In the name of these ideas, Wyclif poured scorn upon the priesthood, denounced indulgences, which were nothing but snares of the devil, and sifted out the saints whose canonization did not seem to him to be an adequate guarantee of virtue. And it was all done in language of almost unbelievable violence: the more moderate of the epithets he applied to the Pope were 'the man of sin,' 'Gog, the leader of the Caesarian clergy' and 'Lucifer's member.'

Although it offended many consciences, this propaganda was able to circulate quite freely for some three years, largely due to the fact that in his *De officio regis* Wyclif had, by means of scrupulously theological arguments, enunciated a theory of the divine right of kings independent of ecclesiastical sovereignty, which was far from unattractive to his government. But an unforeseen change of fortune put a stop to his activity. He had formed a kind of Order, or militia, which he called the *poor priests*, who journeyed through the land, clad in russet [1] homespun tunics and carrying staves, to teach the Gospel and the ideas of the Oxford scholar. Two of his disciples,

[1] This is the origin of their popular nickname: 'Redheads.'

Hereford and Purvey, had translated the Bible into English, and the preachers worked hard to disseminate this version, God being the one guide to whom the elect were obliged to listen. Although Wyclif's supporters did not really constitute an organized sect, they did form more or less compact groups to whom the Catholics gave the name 'Lollards.'[1] These groups, however, were rapidly joined by various suspect elements with anarchical tendencies, in which, as we have already seen, the epoch abounded. Such agitators found confirmation for their most extreme political ideas in Wyclif's theories: if a sinner had no right to own the things given by God, as the don from Oxford maintained, what justification had the landowner for retaining his manor and his fields? When the black and bloody revolt of Wat Tyler and his followers [2] broke out in 1381, in the course of which the Arch-bishop of Canterbury was murdered and all London ravaged by an appalling riot, Wyclif was seriously compromised despite the fact that he had not supported the rebels personally—indeed his own most important support came from the landowning classes.

At this juncture many of his adherents deserted him. It was now that men decided that his theses on the purely religious plane were reprehensible. In fact, he had published a treatise *On the Eucharist*, in which he attacked the doctrine of transubstantiation in his usual violent manner.[3] After the publication of this work, in 1380, the University of Oxford was less solid in its support of his theses. Shortly after the Peasants' Revolt, William Courtenay, who was now Archbishop of Canterbury, resolved to suppress them; in May 1382 the Council of London, without mentioning Wyclif by name—he still had important friends—condemned ten propositions derived from his writings, and the young king, Richard II, forbade unlicensed preachers to continue their mission. One by one the movement's principal leaders made their submission; one of them, Hereford, became a Carthusian. As for Wyclif, he withdrew to his pleasant living at Lutterworth, where he

---

[1] The origin of this word is disputed. In Germany a Dutchman named Lollard Walter had founded (c. 1322) a tiny sect which bore his name. Possibly this term passed into English and was applied to Wyclif's followers. Other critics have suggested that it may derive from the confraternities which accompanied the dead to their final resting-place, chanting—for 'lullen' means 'to sing solemnly and sadly.' Or the word may even mean 'sowers of tares,' since the Latin for 'tares' is *lolium*.

[2] See Chapter II, end of second section: 'A Century of Chaos.'

[3] Wyclif never openly denied the Real Presence, but only transubstantiation. To him the two were quite different. By the doctrine of 'realism' the present writer understands the 'metaphysical realism' of St Thomas Aquinas, which is directly opposed to the Nominalism of Ockham. Wyclif believed that after the Consecration the bread and wine retained their substance as well as their accidents, and that the communicant received the body of his Saviour in a merely figurative and sacramental sense, feeding on Him through the spirit. Consequently he interpreted Christ's words at the Last Supper symbolically, and he declared Christ's Presence in the Eucharist admissible in this same symbolic sense. To be specific, he rejected the Real Presence *identice et realiter*; thus it follows that he admitted the Real Presence *analogice et modo incorporeo*.

wrote his last work, *Trialogus*, a full but circumspect exposition of his theory in which he declared himself in communion with the Church. ... Less than two years later he died (31st December 1384), a peaceful, natural death, after having risked a heretic's end at the stake so often in the past.

His ideas survived him, though without giving rise to the formidable movement which those of Luther were to set in motion after the latter's condemnation by Rome. The Lollards continued to wage a campaign of violent anticlericalism, going so far as to nail placards which attacked the Church to the doors of Westminster Abbey and St Paul's. When Henry IV came to the throne in 1399 he dealt all the more severely with Wyclif's successors because their number included some adherents of his deposed rival, Richard II. A parliamentary decree unleashed a merciless persecution, in which several notorious Lollards perished in the flames. The movement, however, was not completely destroyed, and under Henry V Lord Cobham gave it a cohesion and organization it had never previously attained, before himself being condemned and executed in 1417. Something of Lollardry probably survived even this repression, but it was now only a feeble trickle which was to be totally engulfed in the mighty floodwaters of the Protestant Reformation.

Somewhat earlier, in 1415, the Council of Constance had examined and condemned forty-eight of Wyclif's propositions. It commanded that his remains be exhumed and burned, and this was done in 1424. This tardy ferocity was probably due to the fact that the Church was now more fully aware of the importance of the man and his ideas. The theses of the Oxford schoolman had spread beyond the shores of England and created a second and more serious hotbed of heresy: that kindled by John Huss in Bohemia. And men were beginning to suspect that such convulsions were the redoubtable manifestations of an entirely new spirit.

JOHN HUSS

From 1382 onwards, when Princess Anne of Bohemia had married the young Richard II, numerous relations had been established between England and Bohemia; in particular, many Prague students adopted the custom of coming to Oxford to take their degrees. Some of these were seduced by the Wyclifite theses which they heard propounded at the English university, and they carried these heretical notions back to their own homeland. There they found a singularly favourable climate for their growth. Without doubt the Bohemian Church was one of those most afflicted by the evils of the age: it was excessively wealthy (half the land in the country belonged to it) and its clergy provided far too many examples of scandalous living, typified by a mad rush for benefices, flagrant pluralism, endemic absenteeism and growing immorality. Consequently several reformers appeared, denouncing these miseries and infamies somewhat after the fashion of Old Testament prophets. Most outstanding among them were John Milicz, Conrad of Waldhausen and Mathias of Ianov, whom the authorities at Avignon had tried to suppress. Moreover, as the Bohemian kingdom was a part of the Holy Roman Empire, many Germans filled the most important posts, both in Church and State. To the Czechs, therefore, criticism of the higher clergy was a way of weakening the authority of the Germans whom they detested, and the demand for religious reform was thus inextricably linked with a powerful, politically inspired nationalist sentiment. 'Bohemia for the Bohemians' was a slogan that quickly rallied popular enthusiasm and enabled skilful liars to secure the triumph of their ideas.

One man grasped this fact: Jan Hussinecz, who is known to history under his abridged pseudonym—*John Huss*. Born in 1369, and soon left fatherless, his mother's devotion and self-sacrifice enabled him to pursue a brilliant university career. In his own words, the clerical state seemed to be the only one which would permit him 'to eat well, dress elegantly and possess popular esteem,' and he therefore adopted it. He had studied philosophy and theology at Prague, where he was appointed professor in 1398, although he had not yet been ordained. His learning, eloquence, piety and irreproachable morals soon won him great repute. By 1402 he was rector of the university, confessor to Queen Sophia and the most fashionable preacher at this popular university, where enormous crowds gathered at the Bethlehem Chapel to hear him talk in Czech.

Huss did not possess a particularly original mind; his ideas were borrowed from the common fund of the Waldenses (a few had existed in Bohemia, where fourteen of them were burned at the stake), reformers like Mathias of Ianov and, most important of all, Wyclif. Some of Huss's students returned from Oxford with Wyclif's theses and books; the *Trialogus* was Huss's bedside book, and he translated it into Czech. He was, however, a marvellous popular orator, with a vivid yet simple style, and he had the power to hold a whole audience spellbound. There was an exaggerated, uncontrolled side to his character, which could—and did—lead him as far as the supreme sacrifice. Wyclif had been unable to provoke a real religious revolution in England, but Huss managed to do so in Bohemia.

At the Bethlehem Chapel, where his congregations interspersed his sermons with the singing of lovely old Bohemian hymns, Huss set to work to disseminate Wyclif's ideas. Like the Englishman before him, he fulminated against the scandalous wealth of the clergy and papal taxation, and actually asserted the prince's right to secularize possessions which the clergy used improperly. Next, emboldened by his successes, he went on to teach that the Christian should base his faith upon the Word of God alone, namely, the Holy Scriptures; that Tradition was a meaningless word, the Roman primacy a lie of Antichrist—here the Great Schism seemed to bear him out—and that the whole ecclesiastical hierarchy, from the most important cardinal down to the humblest monk, were henchmen of Satan. On the dogmatic plane Huss rejected confession, confirmation and extreme unction, condemned the cult of saints, attacked indulgences and upheld the doctrine of predestination. The sole point on which he was somewhat more moderate than Wyclif concerned the dogma of the Real Presence; Huss seems to have doubted this, but did not reduce it to purely symbolical terms as Wyclif had done.

Such preaching could hardly fail to attract the Church's wrath. In 1403 the University of Prague confirmed the condemnation of Wyclif's propositions. For all that John Huss continued to teach them, and Innocent VII therefore ordered the Archbishop of Prague to relieve him of his duties as a synodal preacher (1407). About fifteen months later, however, Huss was afforded an opportunity of revenge. King Wenceslas, who was embroiled with the Germans, since they had deprived him of his imperial title, and on bad terms with Pope Gregory XII, initiated a policy of Bohemian nationalism, in order to gain the solid support of his people. Huss gave his wholehearted support; was not this his policy too? At Prague University the students were divided into four 'nations,' Bohemians, Saxons, Bavarians and Poles, a system which ensured that the Bohemians were always a minority vote. The king decreed that henceforth the Czech nation should have three voices and the rest only one, thus making the university into a purely national centre. The angry Germans abandoned Prague to found their own university at Leipzig.

This was a personal triumph for John Huss, or so he thought. He took advantage of the opportunity to repeat the most extreme of his heretical teachings. In fact, his excesses began to disturb even the Bohemian elements among the higher clergy, and also upset the merchant middle classes. His university colleagues deserted him. Alexander V had issued a bull against his theses and had forbidden all popular preaching, not excepting the Bethlehem Chapel, but Huss appealed against this to Alexander's successor, John XXIII of Pisa. When cited before the Curia, however, he made a secret escape, and in 1411 he was excommunicated. His violence now knew no bounds, and he seized the first opportunity to attack the Pope himself. This was the publication of the indulgences offered by John XXIII to all who would join the 'crusade' against his rival Gregory XII. John Huss and his colleague, Jerome of Prague, brought the students and then the townsfolk out in revolt. Violent incidents occurred. The papal bulls were burnt in the city squares. When three young men interrupted a preacher who was inviting the people to gain indulgences, with shouts of 'That's a pack of lies! Master Huss says so!' they were summarily arrested, sentenced and executed. Their funeral obsequies were consequently made the occasion for an enormous popular demonstration, and the Bethlehem Chapel was renamed 'the Chapel of the Three Saints.' The whole city was in revolt, and the university was on the verge of detaching itself from its terrifying rector when John XXIII, on the advice of a council convened in Prague, laid the capital under interdict so long as Huss remained in it. He therefore withdrew to his friends' castles (1412)—just as Luther was to do later on. There he wrote his *Treatise on the Church*, and continued to preach to the peasants in the fields and villages, while his followers, who had the support of King Wenceslas, kept the religious agitation alive throughout the rest of the country.[1]

It was now that John Huss attempted a manœuvre which leaves the historian quite confounded. The reader will remember that at this date the Emperor Sigismund was in process of convoking the Council of Constance which opened on 1st November 1414, and which would try to terminate the Schism. The exile appealed to the Council against the censure under which he lay. Did he hope to convince the assembly of the justice of his theses? Or did he really believe he ought to use the influential platform which the Council offered him in order to spread his ideas, even if he risked his own life in so doing? He was a great enough man to make this calculation and accept the sacrifice it implied. Whatever his reasons Huss set out for Constance, sending ahead of him a kind of provocative confession of faith, in which he offered to refute any adversary who might confront him. The Emperor Sigismund, Wenceslas's brother and heir, who was extremely anxious to restore order in Bohemia, had encouraged him to go to the Council by providing him with a guarantee of safe conduct.

There occurred the famous episode which, it must be admitted,

[1] Needless to say Wenceslas supported John Huss only for political reasons. Moral reform was scarcely among the preoccupations of this evil and perverted drunkard, who had his own cook roasted alive as a punishment for a few petty misdemeanours. Because he was unable to extort the secret of the queen's confession from St John Nepomucene, confessor to Joan, his first wife, Wenceslas is said to have had the saint thrown into the Moldava, with his wrists and ankles bound. His body was seen floating in the river, shining with an unearthly radiance, and gliding downstream. (However, a recent learned article, in the *Revue d'histoire ecclésiastique*, published at Louvain, seems to have proved that St John of Pomuk, whom we know as John Nepomucene, was not the queen's confessor, and that if he was indeed hurled into the Moldava, this was for a reason quite unconnected with her confession.)

reflects little credit upon the honour of Church or Emperor. Three weeks after he reached Constance, despite the imperial guarantee, John Huss was arrested on the order of Pierre d'Ailly and the commission of cardinals entrusted with investigating his affair. He was first confined to a monastery, and later thrown into prison, allegedly because he had continued to celebrate Mass, despite John XXIII's prohibition. The cardinals were all the more determined to show themselves doctrinally rigid, because the Council—which John XXIII had deserted—was wondering what authority it still possessed on the disciplinary plane. Wyclif's propositions were condemned yet again, and it was at this stage that it was decided that his remains should be exhumed and burned. After six months in prison Huss himself was brought before the judges. He divided the ideas which he was accused of holding into two groups, and objected that the majority of them were not his own. However, he admitted responsibility for the more important of them, and added that he was prepared to prove that they had their legitimate basis in the Gospel. It was obvious that these ideas too were heretical, and the Council, directed with more firmness than mercy by Pierre d'Ailly, duly condemned him to death.

John Huss's bearing in the face of death was a marvellous example of courage and faith. From his prison he had written his friends some extremely noble letters, in which he compared himself with the martyrs of the Early Church and offered his sacrifice for what he genuinely believed to be God's truth. He could almost certainly have saved his life by retracting his views, but he refused to do so. On 6th July 1415, after having been solemnly stripped of his liturgical vestments, he mounted the stake, reciting the *Miserere*.[1] A few months later his friend Jerome of Prague, who had come to Constance to plead his cause, suffered the same fate.

John Huss's condemnation, however, achieved something in Bohemia which that of Wyclif had been unable to accomplish in England: it unleashed a wave of popular emotion. Once he was dead the great Czech was hailed as the victim of both the Council—in other words, the Roman Church—and Sigismund, the Holy Roman Emperor and a German in Bohemian eyes. All the elements of religious and nationalist opposition in the country consequently formed an alliance. More than four hundred and fifty Czech noblemen sent an indignant protest against the execution of the man who was both 'an orthodox Catholic and a saint.' The Archbishop of Prague was besieged in his palace and forced to take flight. The town hall was occupied by the rebels, and seven Catholic counsellors defenestrated.

---

[1] Afterwards people told the story of an old woman who had brought a log for the stake because she had heard someone say that such an act would win her indulgences. On seeing her Huss murmured: 'Sancta simplicitas.'

This famous *Defenestration of Prague*, in 1419,[1] signalled the outbreak of a savage and terrible conflict, known as the *Hussite War*, in which the Emperor Sigismund, who had succeeded his brother as King of Bohemia, was to send vast expeditions, or 'crusades' as he called them, against the rebellious Bohemian nation. Bohemia was ravaged with fire and sword, not only by the imperial armies, but also by the quasi-anarchical fanatics who indulged in the most appalling atrocities in the name of the Hussite doctrines.

For while Huss's adherents confined themselves to following his doctrines and customs—particularly that concerning communion in two kinds, which Huss had instituted, and which gave them their name of *Utraquists*—a number of other fanatical zealots carried his theories to extremes. These sects abolished all churches, altars, liturgical ceremonies and religious ornaments, in order to practise a very primitive religion, consisting of preaching and the Eucharist. Since their religious centre was the 'holy city of Tabor,' where Huss had spent his final months on earth, they were known as *Taborites*. For a short time this religious and prophetic revolution seemed on the verge of success. The Taborites, who controlled much of the country, applied themselves to the task of establishing a patriarchal constitution, inspired by the Old Testament. A moral revolution was involved too, since the Taborites advocated the division of private property among the whole community, and the suppression of the wealthy classes and the aristocracy. Fanatical mystics, of which this epoch possessed so many, flocked to Bohemia from far and wide: the *Adamites*, for example, who had appeared on the scene as early as the thirteenth century, henceforth settled on an island in the Nezarka, where they claimed to be reverting to the customs of Paradise before the Fall, particularly in regard to matters of attire!

But after a while the moderate Hussites, the Utraquists, separated from the rest, and in 1433 the Council of Basle conceded them communion in both kinds. For fifteen years the Taborites with their primitive pitchforks and shovels resisted the lances of the imperial armies, and even those of Cardinal Nicholas of Cusa's crusaders. But they could not hold out against the terrible offensive which was launched against them in 1434 by a coalition of all their enemies, including the 'Utraquist' nobility, and at *Lipau* they suffered an appalling defeat. A somewhat precarious religious peace, based on the stipulations known as the *Compacta* of Gihlava, which had been drawn up by Eugenius IV, was imposed on Prague, and St John Capistrano was sent to convert the Taborites to Catholicism. But a strange, bloody and agonizing ferment continued to agitate the whole land. King George Podebrad

---

[1] This should not be confused with the Defenestration of 1618, which was the signal for the outbreak of the Thirty Years War.

was affected by it to some extent, while the more fanatical members of
the population, the 'Bohemian' or 'Moravian Brethren,' who were
ardent missionaries of their faith, very like precursors of the Quakers,
continued the fight. After much persecution they eventually settled
in Lusatia, in Germany; there are still about one hundred thousand of
their descendants in North America.

The Catholic Church emerged apparently triumphant from this
double crisis, which had been provoked by two heresiarchs of considerable importance; but was her victory really a total one? There were
still Lollards and Hussites c. 1450, just as there were still Waldenses,
and Brethren of the Free Spirit, and remnants of several other sects
which she had tried to destroy. These hotbeds of heresy were ready to
be fanned into flame again at the first opportunity. The frontispiece of
one Hussite hymnal, published at the time of the Protestant Reformation, has symbolic significance: Wyclif kindles a tinder-box, and
John Huss carries a load of fuel, but Luther brandishes the torch. The
truth could not have been better stated.

ART'S 'COAT OF MANY COLOURS'

'Art, and art alone, threw its coat of many colours'[1] over the
miseries and horrors of this uncertain epoch. The contrast between the
spectacle of a blood-stained society, twitching in its death throes, and
this delicate, ornate art, with its exuberant architecture, and pictures
a-glitter with the sparkle of gems and precious stones, is an arresting
one. It undoubtedly marks a decline, a regression, in relation to the art
of the great epoch of medievalism; but it is quite normal that an age of
prodigious fecundity should be followed by one in which the creative
urge becomes less vigorous. In many ways the art of this period, like
its literature, displays an excessive refinement, a banality and lack of
purpose which are sometimes not without their charm, but which are
all symptoms of decadence. At the same time, however, there are the
first traces—haphazard though they may be—of the modes of expression which are to be those of the future. Possibly it is in the realm
of art, more than in any other, that the transitional character of this
hundred years which begins in the middle of the fourteenth century
shows most clearly.

This art, which holds such an important place in men's lives, is no
longer wholly Christian in character. At all events it is not Christian
in the sense in which that of the painters and sculptors of previous
generations had been. There are several signs of that same
secularization which has already been observed in contemporary

[1] The phrase is that of Madame Lefrançois-Pillion in her excellent book, *L'Art en
France au XIV* siècle*, Paris, 1954.

politics and literature. Churches were still being built—particularly quite small country churches—but the human purpose behind them is only too apparent. Was it only to further the glory of God that the naves and choirs were almost too richly decorated? That the stalls were made more comfortable, and at the same time adorned with amusing carvings? That the pulpit and fonts were beautified—that every possible opportunity was seized to make the House of God more lovely? In Germany the practical-minded middle classes were responsible for the market churches known as 'Hallenkirchen,' which were comfortable rather than aesthetically pleasing. The *reredoses*, those wonderful painted and gilded panels which were set above the altars, did not fail to give pride of place to the representations of their donors, and *motifs* from profane inspiration were introduced into the great Christian themes. Secular rulers, who were often lovers of art and distinguished aesthetes, attracted flocks of painters and sculptors to their courts, and the dukes of Burgundy were the most lavish patrons of all. When such men distributed their largesse they certainly did not neglect God, and they often set their protégés to work on the building and embellishment of churches, but they made sure that their personal glory was enhanced thereby. Here is a characteristic but astonishing fact: France, which had been devastated by the Hundred Years War, constructed few religious buildings during this period, but erected many sumptuous houses for her great men. Many of these secular dwellings have disappeared—Charles V's Louvre, the Hôtel Saint-Pol, the castle of Mehun-sur-Yèvre, which is depicted in one of the famous miniatures in the Duke of Berry's *Très Riches Heures*, and which resembles an enchanted palace, a castle fit for a fairy-tale or a love-story. But the Hôtel Jacques Cœur at Bourges, the Palais de Justice at Rouen and the remains of Jean de Berry's castle at Poitiers enable us to obtain some idea of the beauty of these houses which were built solely for the world of men, not for the glory of God. All the arts were used to make life more beautiful and immortalize man. The painted canvas, intended to depict events of importance, underwent considerable development; the portrait, which flattered its sitters' arrogant feeling of being unique, became extremely fashionable. The wonderful development of monumental sculpture, which abounded in masterpieces, shows that, even when faced with the levelling force of death, the rich and the mighty were anxious to perpetuate their conceit for all eternity. In brief then we are dealing with 'an art-form created for the individual, and for him alone, which scarcely remembers that it once belonged to the whole community, that it was once truly national and wholly Christian.'[1]

A similar evolution is apparent among the artists themselves. The sole aim of the medieval artist had been the furtherance of God's glory.

[1] Ibid., p. 12.

The cathedral was a vast collective enterprise in which craftsmen and sculptors submerged their own personalities so completely that barely a dozen of their individual names have come down to us. If they sought to create beauty this was simply in order that the Lord might be better glorified thereby. From now on the picture changes. Increasingly artists seek perfection in order to vindicate their personal talents, and it becomes customary for the artist to sign his paintings or his statues. Thus the architect and sculptor Guy de Dammartin (*c.* 1385), who worked for the Duke of Berry, was famous throughout France, and thereafter the number of known artists quickly becomes large enough to fill the columns of an encyclopaedia. In 1391 the first Academy of Art was founded at Dijon by twenty-five painters and five sculptors. It was a quasi-syndical body, which, even at that early date, aimed at 'preventing the depreciation of art, guiding the preferences of the public, in short, legislating on beauty.' [1] The workshops of the preceding epoch certainly had no such intentions.

The religious architecture of the period must be seen against this background. In the first place it should be noted that in several areas its activity slackened considerably. In France, during the fourteenth and fifteenth centuries in particular, scarcely any new cathedral building yards were opened, with the exception of Bordeaux; the evil times, and also the abundance of building in the preceding epoch, go a long way towards explaining this lull. Existing structures were finished, repaired or added to (many additions were made); sometimes too the architects abandoned plans drawn up by their forefathers. At Chartres the transept towers were omitted; at Beauvais it was decided to make the cathedral itself out of the vast choir, which was repaired because it was in danger of falling down, without realizing the original design. In countries unaffected by the ravages of war, building activity was much greater: in England, Germany, Spain, Portugal and the Low Countries it was still considerable, and far from insignificant even in Hungary and Poland. But it was mainly a question of addition and completion. The wealthy and arrogant German towns distinguished themselves by the splendour of their churches. Ulm, for example, regarded it as a point of honour to have the highest belfry in the world. At Cologne, however, the cathedral building yard lay idle. In Italy Milan Cathedral, which aimed at being nothing less than the masterpiece of Gothic architecture, was slowly taking shape, unevenly, amid contradictions, mistakes and changes of architect: it was not to be completed until the nineteenth century.

The distinctive architectural style of the age now evolved: the builders, who possessed a perfect technique, which they tended to abuse, pushed the foibles and possibilities of Gothic to extremes. There

[1] Ibid., p. 114.

was a growing ambition for 'the design decked out in beauty.' Verticals became more and more slender: enormous windows took the space of whole walls, reaching right down to ground level (in Saint-Urbain at Troyes, and in Saint-Nazaire at Carcassonne, for example); the feeling of height was accentuated by the suppression of horizontal lines, so much so that it gave a sense of barrenness and emptiness; columns became slimmer and the capitals were reduced to mere rings, while groining burst into decorative bloom like marvellous bouquets. The French masterpiece of this fourteenth-century Gothic is the abbey church of St Ouen, at Rouen. Here there is a wonderful impression of lightness and airiness, of a triumph over gravity; but there is also a slight tendency towards abstraction and theorism to which other less gifted artists succumbed completely: Saint-Urbain at Troyes is also an almost perfect architectural gem, and, in the Midi, Carcassonne, Albi and Narbonne are other interesting examples of this art of ultimate achievement. In other respects pure Gothic had lost none of its attraction. It inspired the architects of the Low Countries, at Saint-Pierre, Lille, or Saint-Saviour's at Bruges. It inspired those of Alsace and north Germany, who mingled stone and brick quite freely in their building, as at Lübeck and Danzig. It inspired those of Italy too; for even while the Renaissance was conducting its offensive, Gothic structures were still being erected all over the peninsula—at Milan, Venice, Florence, Como, Pistoia, Naples and Palermo. In England, where architecture invariably evolved an original style, 'Perpendicular' —the term is somewhat inadequate—was all the rule. It became the English style *par excellence*, with its criss-crossed lines, forming the pattern of grills, and its depressed arches whose curve approached the horizontal; this was the style of Gloucester, of the abbey churches at Sherborne and Peterborough, and it had countless imitators.

These forms, however, remained a part of the inner logic of traditional Gothic. At the dawn of the fifteenth century, in circumstances which still remain something of a mystery, a wonderful flight of fancy burst upon the world, the grand finale of medieval art, so strange and original that it is hard to relate it to what had gone before. This was the *Flamboyant* style, known in England as the '*flowing Decorated.*' It was as if the builders and architects had been seized by a kind of aesthetic delirium, and were seeking to utilize all the resources of their technique in a fantastic, exuberant virtuosity. The basic plan scarcely altered, but the nave changed its appearance: the traditional crossing of the pointed arch was elaborated with 'liernes' and 'tiercerons,' and their interlacing formed the most extraordinary tracery; sometimes the basic arch actually disappeared altogether. . . . Fillets sprang from pillars without capitals, like delicate branches from the trunk of a tree. Windows, spandrels and façades were decorated with scores of different *motifs*—'pendants,' crockets, curves and countercurves, 'frills' and 'furbelows.' It seemed as if the very stone had germinated, bloomed and multiplied, and sculpture was invited to join in this lavish spectacle more fully than ever in the past. Saint-Madou at Rouen, Notre-Dame at Caudebec, Sainte-Foy at Conches, the choir at Mont-Saint-Michel, Saint-Fiacre at Faouet, Notre-Dame at Folgoët, Saint-Wilfram at Abbeville, Saint-Saviour's at Aachen, Saint-Nicolas at Port, in Lorraine, and many other lesser buildings besides, provide, in their multiple differences, fine examples of this simultaneously disturbing and fascinating art. Flamboyant is the Gothic baroque, which is to Chartres and Amiens what Bernini is to Michelangelo; its masterpiece is unquestionably the exquisite church of Notre-Dame at l'Épine, which rises up, movingly fragile, among the solitudes of Champagne, like a hymn of hope in a spiritual wilderness.

The success of the Flamboyant style was enormous; in France it delayed the triumph of Renaissance architecture by a hundred years; it spread far and wide, exerting its influence in Germany, Bohemia and even Italy. In the Iberian peninsula, e.g. at Seville, it became fused with strange Arabic elements. And the last shoot from this mysterious tree was to spring up in Portugal, in the middle of the fifteenth century. This was the *Manueline* style which produced combination after combination of rope moulding and arcades, *motifs* inspired by the sea and exotic flowers, all of which can be seen in fantastic profusion at Batalha, the Hieronymite monastery of Belem, and, best of all, at Tomar.

Sculpture, which architecture had served so well, proved itself ungrateful, tending to become more and more autonomous, divorcing itself from the art-form which had once been its mentor and its guide. This epoch marks the fulfilment of a process of evolution noticeable in places as far apart as Chartres and Rheims: the old statue column is on the point of detaching itself from its means of support. In Rouen Cathedral statues are no longer set flat against the walls and pillars: they are sculptured in the round and placed in niches. Moreover the artist uses them to mitigate the excessive verticality of the buildings, or to play their part in the flamboyant scheme by placing them on a column or a bracket. Soon it became customary—and has remained so ever since—to have isolated statues, which were set in the chapels where the confraternities wished to represent their patron saints. Our Lady provided the most frequent themes for this new art-form, and statues of her appeared in such large numbers that in the second half of the fourteenth century more than eight hundred could be located in France alone. Monumental art, the fruit of the rich man's overweening arrogance, also gave the sculptors ample opportunity to practise a talent which remained Christian to a certain extent, but which was in practice divorced from the Church; every church floor was strewn with innumerable flat tombs on which the dead man's effigy was outlined in deep, sweeping strokes, and filled in with lead. Monuments to kings, princes and wealthy citizens rose up more majestically, filling the aisles and lurking in the shadows of the side chapels. Here the dead man was represented lying full length on his sarcophagus, in the peace of death, surrounded by angels and 'weepers.' The final touches of decoration were provided by scenes from his life or from the Scriptures. This monumental sculpture produced such masterpieces as the tombs of Saint-Denis, and also those of Philip the Bold and other dukes of Burgundy. The most striking example is in the Louvre, at Paris. Here Philippe Pot lies on a simple marble slab borne on the shoulders of eight officers, all pathetically enshrouded in mourners' mantles. Many of the figures represented on these tombs are undoubtedly true portraits. The art of portraiture was spreading and its technique was being perfected. Donors too were often depicted in the guise of saints; and certain of these portraits are wonderfully true to life, such as the famous bust of Charles V of France, which used to be in the Hospital for the Blind in Paris, and is now in the Louvre.

One name stands out from all the sculptors of this period—a man whose undeniable genius characterized all the tendencies of the age: *Claus Sluter* (1360–1406). Sluter was a Dutchman from Haarlem, whom the mighty Duke of Burgundy invited to his court at Dijon, and who became the leader of the groups of international artists who were assembled there. It is to Sluter that we owe the admirable 'weepers' on the tomb of Philip the Bold; his masterpiece was the famous Calvary in the Charterhouse at Champmol, wrongly called 'The Well of Moses.' With its six prophets this group still conveys such a strong impression of greatness, despite its mutilation, that no one can look at it and remain unmoved. But Claus Sluter is not really a wholly medieval sculptor. His St John the Baptist undoubtedly reminds one of that on the La Grange buttress at Amiens, and his style conveys much of the serenity and wisdom of the old Burgundian craftsmen; but the epic grandeur of his faces, figures and draperies foreshadows the sculptors of the Italian Renaissance, even Michelangelo himself. Several influences were at work at the cosmopolitan court at Dijon, deriving not from Italy alone, and these gradually replaced the Gothic tradition all over France. Even during the lifetimes of Michel Colombe and Ligier Richier (*b.* 1500), both of whom were in many respects medieval artists, Renaissance art was to force the general acceptance of its own rigid rules. As for Flamboyant sculpture, which was carried along by its own dizzy impetus, it was to end in the delightful, lissom—if slightly worldly—figurines that can be seen in the Burgundian basilica at Brou.

But of all the arts of this transitional epoch, that which asserted itself most forcibly, and which experienced such a triumphant development, was the art of painting. Indeed this age marks the beginning of the primacy of painting, a primacy characteristic both of the Renaissance and of modern Europe, and which has continued into our own day. A history of medieval art gives pride of place to the cathedral, the architectural creation, to which all other art-forms are subject; a history of modern art necessarily starts with painting. This predominance of the pictorial over architecture and sculpture was conclusively asserted during the fourteenth century; it is abundantly clear that Sluter and his fellow sculptors owed a great deal to the Flemish painters, their contemporaries. And this replacement of one technique by another in the hierarchy of the arts corresponds to a similar process which has already been observed in other fields. For painting tended to divorce itself from the Church; it no longer considered itself linked to the general plan of one united effort, made for the greater glory of God; it too became an entity in itself.

It is significant that mural painting, the colouring of vast surfaces of wall, declined almost everywhere. It found its last chance for large-scale realization in the Papal Palace at Avignon, where the murals in the celebrated 'Stag Chamber' and in several of the oratories remind us of the dignity and charm of this type of decoration. Elsewhere the standard fell. This was not simply because it was excluded by the prevailing architectural style, which concentrated upon the play of light through the enormous stained-glass windows that were springing up everywhere at this time—though without corresponding improvement in quality. Examples in the Petit-Quévilly and the Palace of Jacques Cœur at Bourges show that young artists could find plenty of scope for their talent in the segments of the vaults. The taste for murals was declining, but there were still a few great panoramic paintings, such as the scenes from the life of St Louis in the Carmelite house in the Place Maubert and in the Saint-Chapelle, now all unfortunately lost to us; those of Brancion, Tournus, Saint-Geniès and the Dominican house in Toulouse are all that remain to preserve the memory of this medieval art—the Christian art-form *par excellence*—which now adorned secular buildings rather than churches.

Having been almost completely banished from wall surfaces painting found its revenge elsewhere, in reredoses, miniatures and easel-pictures. And what a revenge! It first became apparent in the tiny but exquisite illustrations which embellished the pages of manuscripts. This kind of art was extraordinarily fashionable in the fourteenth century. When King John of France was taken prisoner at Poitiers, he was found to be carrying a precious manuscript on his person. The ornamented book soon deserted the abbeys and chapter-houses to become the pride of princely collections: it too was secularized. Themes remained religious: Books of Hours (manuals of private devotion), Gospel-books, Legends of the Saints; but very often the calendar pages, with their background paintings of castles and hunting scenes, were far more beautiful than the sacred subjects. There are endless marvels to wonder at in these small, detailed compositions, which range from the *Belleville Breviary* (1342) to the *Très Riches Heures* and the eighteen other manuscripts which the Duke of Berry commissioned between 1400 and 1420. Here the artists gave free rein both to their gifts of observation and their imagination, to their love of delicate colour and elegant line, to their taste for a somewhat unreal, poetic, fairy world—a world which is, in short, not altogether Christian. The heir to all this countless effort, in whom the miniature achieved its ultimate triumph, was Jean Fouquet.

Large-scale painting found expression in the reredos, the decorative altar panel. Miniatures had pointed the way, and the first reredoses, like the first easel-pictures, were clearly descended from them. But an important stage had been reached whose significance must not be underestimated; for a vast composition cannot be created simply by enlarging a miniature. Triptychs and polyptychs provided painters with new opportunities to display their talent. These enormous, highly formal compositions flattered the sensibility of the masses and intensified the piety of the devout, as well as satisfying the donors' vanity. Consequently their number multiplied, and almost every church of the slightest importance possessed one. Flanders swarmed with them: the famous reredos of the *Lamb of God*, painted by Jan and Hubert Van Eyck for the church of Saint–Bavon in Ghent, is the finest work of its kind; but those of their compatriot Roger Van der Weyden, of Enguerrand Quarton from Laon, painter of the sublime *Pieta* at Avignon, of Nicholas Froment or the Provençal Bréa are also among the most beautiful artistic creations of the age.

One element now separated itself from the reredos: the artist devoted himself to a single subject; and so began the glorious career of the painted canvas, which dealt with one scene only, and was content with more limited surfaces. Henceforth art had found a new field. The picture was easily placed on a church wall, although it never became an integral part of its surroundings, but always retained a rather remote air; on the other hand it was perfectly at home in the private oratories of the rich and influential, and looked even better in their state apartments. A purely decorative function, the embellishment of everyday living, replaced the religious role played by painting in the past. Thus the picture became extremely fashionable, and once the Flemings had discovered the still rudimentary but none the less attractive technique of oil-painting, most artists were drawn towards this particular art-form.

Several men of genius played an important part in this evolution, which once again involved the 'secularization' of art. *Jan Van Eyck* (1386–1440), for example, and the anonymous artist known as 'the Master of Flemalle,' painted some wonderful Annunciations and other scenes from the Gospels (in which, moreover, the *entourage* and profane details were often more prominent than the religious subject), but they also painted the middle classes and scenes from everyday life. When all is said and done, the triumph of the picture marks the final severance of painting from that Church which had sheltered its infancy.

Thus, in its most fundamental attributes, art matched the age, being at the same time the latter's most agreeable expression. Moreover in every respect it bore the stamp of that age. It loved magnificence as reflected in the splendour of Flamboyant churches and glittering triptychs, in the pomp of lavishly decorated buildings and over-sumptuous tombs and also in the products of those minor but highly decorative arts—carving, cabinet-making, jewellery, ivory work, tapestry—that were immensely fashionable. Art became increasingly accurate and realistic. It was the art of the individual, the single living being, just as Ockhamism evolved into the philosophy of Being. In depicting a man, an animal or a plant, it paid far higher regard to truth than its predecessors had done. From the spirit of the age, too, art derived its emotional, brooding character. This was carried to extremes in the Dance of Death, whose representation became increasingly common at this time, and expresses all too faithfully the obsession with death which preyed so heavily on men's minds. Yet this emotion is just as apparent in the equally numerous reminders of Christ's Passion or of His Mother's Sorrows—the *Pietas*. The perfect and terrible synthesis of these two elements—the worldly and the Christian tragedy —was belatedly realized at the end of the fifteenth century by a brilliant Teutonic artist named *Mathias Nithard*, better known under the traditional name of *Grünewald* (1470?–1528?). His famous altar-piece at Colmar seems to embody all the anguish and faith of moribund Christendom; but the effect is achieved by techniques that are entirely modern. *Grünewald*'s work no longer belongs to the past.

This art which expresses the mood of a rapidly changing society, and which brings to a close the art of the Golden Age of medievalism, is to a large extent an art of conclusion, even of decline, despite the masterpieces which it still produces. Yet it is this art, rather than the literature, religious thought or politics of the period which conveys the strongest impression of a travail that would give birth to the future. Obviously a new art is about to be born; indeed it has already seen the light of day. Italy, on this plane, had always pursued her destinies quite independently of the rest of Europe. Long ago, in the peninsula which seemed eternally doomed to partition and anarchy,[1] various artists had not merely prepared the way for future development, but had even discovered new sources of inspiration. The Pisanos, contemporaries of the sculptors of Rheims, had given stone a fluidity and feeling that no longer had anything Romanesque or Gothic about it. While Pietro Cavallini and his successors still hesitated between the formalism inherited from Byzantium and the realism which they sensed the future held, the genius of *Giotto*, a medieval artist in respect of his chronology (1267–1337) and in many of his characteristics, had already taught the world—long before the appearance of Michelangelo—that painting could create a dramatic poem just as solid as sculpture, and could give life and substance to the most fundamental symbols.[2] Brunelleschi, Ghiberti, Donatello, and even the pure and simple Fra Angelico—in a sense the last of the Gothic artists[3]—no longer belonged to a past whose days were numbered, but turned their creative talents to the future. Few of the lessons of the past would remain when the new art reached its full maturity. But would that art still be Christian? This was the basic question, and it was a question addressed not to the artists alone.[4]

FACING THE FUTURE

In 1448, displaying his usual commendable grasp of the situation, Cardinal Aeneas Sylvius wrote to Pope Nicholas V in the following terms: 'Dangerous days await us: storms are gathering all around: the sailors will soon be called upon to show their ability to ride out the heavy weather.' These were prophetic and highly significant words. . . . At this point in the middle of the fifteenth century a clear-sighted individual like Piccolomini could survey the world around him and feel more afraid of the future than saddened by the spectacle of the immediate past. And every far-sighted person was bound to ask himself the question implicit in his sentence: would the sailors whose duty

[1] This dissociation of political primacy and artistic primacy is yet another sign of the collapse of the fabric of Christendom. At the height of the Middle Ages, France, the dominant political power, was also the leader in the field of art. Henceforth Italy, a peninsula with no political stability whatever, was to play this role.

[2] On Giotto and his contemporaries see *Cathedral and Crusade*, p. 391 et seq.

[3] See Chapter IV, section: 'The Glorious Sunrise Breaks Over Italy.'

[4] Music evolved in a fashion entirely analogous to the plastic arts. With Philippe de Vitry (1291–1361) it escaped from the tyranny of ecclesiastical conventions: the modern scale came into being, with all the harmonies that derived from it. The perfect cadence and the discipline of the measured bar became obligatory. Thus the whole trend was away from the Church's plain-song. In his famous *Mass*, Guillaume de Machaut (1300–77) utilized these new features to the full, and the boldness of his polyphony is outstanding. For the first time the mass is seen as a complete musical entity, a *genre* that was to rival the symphony, concerto and sonata. Through Machaut, the French *Ars nova* influenced much of Europe before the appearance of the rival *Ars Italiana*.

it was to man the barque of Peter show the skill that the rough seas would demand of them?

The medieval structure of the world, like the cultural and spiritual attitudes which constituted its bases, was fast disintegrating. The Church could no longer claim to be identified with the West; the idea of Christendom was out of date; the very principle which had ensured the fundamental unity of human existence was discredited, and spiritual authority looked more and more like a chain of bondage, from which mankind ought to break free. Everything which, for three hundred glorious years, had enabled Western man to feel himself the master of his own destinies—and, at the same time, everything which had made man himself into a creative force—was sinking into ruins.

But Christianity is a far larger thing than medieval civilization; Christianity and Christendom are not synonyms. The history of the Church had certainly not begun with the glory of the Middle Ages. Long before this type of civilization sprang into being and produced what was indeed the richest harvest ever reaped from Christian soil, other Latin, Teutonic and Celtic civilizations had existed too, and they also had been animated by the Breath of Christ. It is abundantly clear that the creative forces of mankind were now in the midst of an agonizing labour, and that a new form of civilization was about to emerge from the mists of history. Would this new civilization be a Christian one? This was the fundamental question.

Will the sailors manage to ride out the storm? inquired the humanist cardinal. And this brings us back to the question: would the Church know how to face the future? Would she possess minds intelligent enough to understand this nascent world, and to effect a fresh synthesis between the permanent values of Christianity and the new components of the epoch? Would she possess men steadfast and pure enough in heart to dominate the forces of anarchy and subject them to the law of Christ, as had been the case four or five centuries earlier, when she had assumed control of feudal chaos and organized it according to her own principles?

There were several symptoms which might well justify Piccolomini's pessimism and anxiety. The Papacy had emerged victorious from the conciliar crisis, though with diminished authority, but the feeling of a common Christian responsibility for the general welfare of the Church had virtually vanished, giving way to disputes between the Roman Curia and nation-states who were increasingly certain of their rights and their strength. Genuine religious philosophy seemed to have become stultified, and devotion, by shutting itself away in an exclusively mystical effort, lost its grip on the world. Finally, the moral conduct of those in authority over the Christian flock scarcely entitled them to pose as its undisputed guides.

In this troubled world Christianity could have filled the part she had erstwhile played only upon condition that the Church made one really energetic attempt, with all the collective forces at her disposal, to effect her own *Reformation*. By this is meant a reformation in the fullest sense, a reformation at the intellectual, moral, political, administrative, and above all at the spiritual level. Later on, too late, Holy Church did emerge from such an effort, purified. But she emerged weakened and sorrowful, bereft—perhaps permanently—of some of her dearest members.

In the decisive hour she was found wanting; instead of retrieving the inexhaustible vigour of the Word from the most deep-rooted of her loyalties, she allowed herself to be deflected far too long by the manifold temptations of the World, those alluring and almost irresistible temptations that history dangled before her eyes just as the mighty impulse of the Renaissance was about to burst on the Italian scene.

CHAPTER IV

THE RENAISSANCE POPES

THE RENAISSANCE

THE RENAISSANCE! The mere echo of these syllables fills the mind with a score of images, all very different in design, but all endowed with the same remarkable brilliance. High on the scaffolding erected in the Sistine Chapel, Michelangelo spends his days lying stretched flat on his back, busily painting, making a whole new world rise from out his anguish, and when the brush wavers in his tired fingers an imperious pope commands him to go on. In the gardens of his villa at Careggi, Lorenzo the Magnificent, prince of patrons, listens to the academy founded by his father discussing the learned dialogues of Plato; then, as evening falls, he wanders along its shaded avenues reciting to himself the poems of Angelo Poliziano. Elsewhere, after painting his enigmatically smiling beauties, as if in fun, Leonardo probes other secrets, trying to penetrate the mathematical meaning of the world, dreaming of enabling man to fly like a bird and of substituting machines for men. All over the peninsula the human mind is seething with genius and intelligence; in the smallest towns, and even in the humblest villages, the immeasurable talent of three generations of artists is preparing a limitless treasury of riches for the future. Along the roads there wind the glittering cavalcades whose magnificence is depicted by Benozzo Gozzoli. All Italy is enveloped in a golden haze of luxury and glory, of creative passion and sheer beauty.

This is not, however, the complete picture. This brilliant scene contains great areas of shadow, so dark that one scarcely dares examine them closely. The voice of Savonarola, successor of the inspired prophets of Old Testament times, made no mistake when it proclaimed the certainty of inevitable punishment to the ears of a horrified Florence. This exuberant society, with its abject sins, depravities and violence, deserved such a punishment only too well. For vice lurked everywhere, and blood lust too, and crime. The policy advocated with such cold detachment by Machiavelli was cruel; but the despots were not alone in pursuing it, for a militant Papacy practised it also. The assassin's dagger struck down the Medicis at the height of their power, just as it slaughtered so many others, whose very names are long forgotten. Horror mingled so intimately with beauty that it eventually came to seem perfectly natural. The same princes who bankrupted themselves in embellishing churches, would have their victims stabbed to death, prolong an execution for a whole month, bury people alive and keep their enemies' heads in urns, pickled in salt. Popular opinion scarcely exaggerated when it denounced the intrigue, debauchery, poisoning and incest which was taking place on the fringes of the Holy See itself. But let the critics only wait a little! As Savonarola predicted, the horsemen of the Apocalypse would shortly appear over the Alpine horizon: Florence was to burn her prophet in her principal square; and the plain of Marignano would echo to the clatter of lances and the flap of the victorious banners of France, billowing in the wind.

These are contradictory yet inseparable images. In short, this epoch bore such prolific fruit simply because it was both voluptuous and ascetic, delicate and terrible, scholarly and barbarian. The tragedy which came to the surface in violent wars and massacres betrayed another tragedy, which was being played out in the secret recesses of men's souls. Indeed the one abetted the other. Why should one not go to the extremes of self-gratification when life was so short and tenuous, when the traitor's poison and the executioner's axe threatened at every moment to halt the mind on the edge of its own abyss? The real reason why the century abounded in unusual people who were never humdrum in anything (talent, virtue, or vice) was because it was a century of prodigious ferment, in which a new conception of man and the universe was struggling for birth, and in which all the old certitudes were being called in question. Possibly no other period in Western history has experienced such prodigious creative animation, simply because no other has felt so intensely or trembled so sincerely. Moreover all that is greatest in man invariably seems to emerge from a travail of contradiction and combat.

Thus to define the Renaissance as a straightforward return to the study of classical literature and a rediscovery of Graeco-Roman art is to limit its historical content very significantly. There is no doubt that the fashion which encouraged so many men to wax enthusiastic over the treasures which the ancients had bequeathed to the world did exert a marked influence upon man's behaviour, and upon the basic values of the new civilization. The lessons of antiquity—or rather Renaissance man's interpretation of them—affected the field of morality as much as that of artistic creation. But interest in the classical heritage had not been lacking in medieval times. The schoolmen had been infatuated with the Greek philosophers whom they encountered in their studies; so that if the Renaissance were nothing more than a movement of scholastic curiosity, it would have to be traced back to the learned men at Charlemagne's court. But this earlier study of the pagan past had never led to consequences such as the fifteenth century produced; for the appeal of classical art and literature was but one element (important, but not uniquely so) in that historical complexity —social, moral, aesthetic and philosophic—which made up the phenomenon which we call the Renaissance.

Did this phenomenon mark a progress so decisive that it in fact constituted a definite break with all that had gone before? Etymologically the word 'Renaissance' implies this to be the case, and admirers of this dazzling epoch have all understood it in this sense.[1] For Michelet —who, in his *History of France* (1855), was the first to use the word to designate a chapter in the history of civilization—for Burckhardt in particular, and even for Taine, there was indeed a definite break in the even passage of time: humanity made a sudden decision to change its course. This idea became linked with a completely unjust view of the civilization immediately preceding the 'break,' and gave rise to a myth which far too many people still regard as the truth. It is said that after the sepulchral darkness of the Middle Ages humanity broke from the tomb and underwent a glorious revival. This is an attractive picture, and one not easy to destroy, but during the last fifty years or so several historians have laboured to demonstrate its falsity. Nördstrom in particular has questioned the very concept of the Renaissance, and has maintained that it was the cumulative scholarship of the revival of the classics. In a field like this all valid opinions appear subjective and gratuitous. The period in which Michelangelo, Leonardo, Raphael and so many other men of genius produced such a wealth of eternal masterpieces was certainly a great one, but our legitimate admiration for it does not entitle us to despise the preceding age, which, to a very large extent, explains it—the age of Chartres and Rheims, of Dante and St Thomas Aquinas.

This does not imply that there was no broadening of human horizons at the time of the Renaissance, which is traditionally associated with a number of inventions and discoveries. The day when Gutenberg conceived the idea of representing each letter on a small piece of embossed wood, and later metal, thus permitting the manufacture of considerable numbers of copies of the written word, it is indeed fair to say that he enabled human thought to take a considerable step forward. And when at about the same time Henry the Navigator sent his sailors out from his palace at Sagres, to begin the conquest of a world that was now supposed to have no final boundaries, it is certainly true that he and his successors—Christopher Columbus, Bartholomew

---

[1] Contemporaries took a long time to come round to this idea. In his *Lives of the Most Eminent Painters*, written at the beginning of the sixteenth century, Vasari used the word 'Renaissance' for the first time. However, he applied it only to the return to the forms and ideas of Greek and Roman antiquity. Quite rightly, as we shall see, he regarded it as a specifically Italian phenomenon.

G

Diaz, Vasco da Gama and the rest—threw open whole new perspectives to stimulate the intellect of creative man.[1]

However, it would be an exaggeration to attribute the responsibility for the psychological evolution to these inventions and discoveries alone. In the first place their immediate influence was far smaller than is usually imagined. The printing-press was invented *c.* 1450, in other words, at a time when the Italian Renaissance was already well under way. It did not spread like a train of gunpowder. Although it was in use at Venice almost at the same time as at Strasbourg, it was not introduced at Bologna and Florence before 1471, or at Palermo until shortly before 1490. The process long remained the monopoly of the rich, for the first printed books were extremely costly; Mentel's Bible, for instance, printed at Strasbourg in 1466, cost as much as three bullocks! [2] Moreover many distinguished men despised the printing-press, preferring beautiful manuscripts: the Alsatian humanist Wimpfeling was still making this point in 1507. . . . As for geographical discoveries, they continued to be treated with indifference for a long time to come. Savonarola's Florence was poking fun at the idea that the world was round at the very moment when Christopher Columbus was setting foot on American soil; and in 1539 neither Jacques Signot's *Description of the World* nor Boemus's *Compilation of the Various Histories of the Three Continents of the World* made any reference to the new continent. Above all, there was no reason why technical advances and progress in scholarship should alter the moral structure of civilization at this point. The book, and even the manuscript, had been carrying men's thoughts far afield for a long time past, and the embossed wooden letter, the tool of mechanical reproduction of the written word, was in current use. Contrary to accepted belief, the Middle Ages had not lived shut in on itself: its people had certainly read numerous accounts of prodigiously adventurous voyages, such as those of Marco Polo. In order that the Renaissance might acquire the characteristics which were essentially its own something more than this was needed. The rejuvenation of the intellect and the arts must occur in a very particular kind of environment, resulting from an evolution which had already filled a very long period of time, wherein humanity had been slowly preparing the way for a fundamental change. In its important capacity as a prime factor in the spiritual history of the Western world, the Renaissance was born of the meeting between a particular climate of belief and a particular state of mind.

The climate was Italian; for it is most important to note that the

---

[1] On the great discoveries see *The Catholic Reformation*, Chapter IV, section 2.

[2] It should also be noted that the earliest printed works were Bibles and manuals of piety. The invention was just as capable of supporting traditional ideas as it was of aiding the diffusion of new ones.

Renaissance was, substantially as well as chronologically, an Italian phenomenon. The movement was born in the Italian peninsula, and received its most powerful impulse from there. While the remainder of the West was still the scene of the death struggle of medieval civilization, a new culture had already come into being at Florence, Siena, Venice and Rome. There is a striking time lag between the Italian Renaissance and the phenomena similarly named in France or Germany. West of the Alps men were thinking and building in Gothic while Brunelleschi was designing the cupola of Florence Cathedral; on the banks of the Loire and the Seine artists and writers were only just starting to develop their own kind of classicism, at a time when those on the Arno and the Tiber were already well committed to Baroque. How did it come about that Italy, which had been relegated to the background for several centuries past, now assumed the leadership of Western civilization? It is not enough simply to evoke the existence of countless marble classical monuments on her soil, the beauty of her sunlight and her landscapes, and the ambition of her despots to become lavish patrons of the arts. The truth is that for two hundred years this fortunate land experienced one of those upsurges of creative vigour, one of those prolific developments of genius and talent which can be observed in Periclean Athens, twelfth-century France or the age of Louis XIV. Such an occurrence defies all logical explanation, and gives man a guarantee of his own greatness. Because it took place in Italy, however, this marvellous phenomenon was marked with the seal of that country, with the stamp fashioned from several centuries of anarchy and violence. The total absence of unity, a constant state of rivalry between different rulers and different towns, the enormous value put upon money, in short, the whole social and political situation, conditioned a psychological and moral climate in which a number of powerful personalities were indeed enabled to assert themselves, but which also rendered the most appalling deviations only too understandable.

Such a climate was singularly favourable for bringing to a head the forces which had long been at work upon the Western world. Here it is essential to think back to all those symptoms of decadence and disintegration which had been so apparent during the final one hundred and fifty years of the Middle Ages. Gradually, as has been seen, a new state of mind emerged: philosophy tended towards emancipation; the human personality grew tired of the moral and social rules to which it was subject, and the basic disciplines crumbled; the very meaning of life itself seemed about to be called in question. When it reached Italy this state of mind discovered circumstances most conducive to its full development. If ever a land understood the meaning of 'life's bitter taste,' it was certainly the Italian peninsula. The sense of personal destiny, formed by fifteen hundred years of Christianity, but which

Christianity alone had placed at the service of the whole community, had flung off all its restraints; and this resulted sometimes in an explosion of genius, which tended to become the norm of value, and sometimes in ruthless self-assertion by an individual guided solely by his own interests, his love of glory or his passions. Social bonds in the anarchical peninsula had been weakened or actually broken; they could not prevent the individual from being propelled by his own egotism along the slippery slope of damnation. The shift in ideas, principles and morals was not therefore the consequence of the revival of classical culture, as has been too often suggested; the 'pagan' fashion merely gave this phenomenon some picturesque characteristics and a semblance of justification. But Italy, cradle of the 'Renaissance,' was really the land best prepared to bring the process to fruition.

This phenomenon was to set in motion the most serious revolution yet known in the history of ideas. How would the Church react? In the first place, would she know the right path to follow in a world of ambiguity where all contradictions were possible? Would she try to oppose current trends of thought, the upsurge of creative vigour, or would she attempt to impress the stamp of Christ upon this nascent civilization? Would she hallow a divorce or effect a synthesis between the immutable truths entrusted to her care and the new elements in the world? If the evolutionary process were not to operate against her and against her dogmas she would have to retain considerable authority over men's minds and hearts. But how could she do so when even her leaders, the Sovereign Pontiffs, were permeated, and perhaps contaminated, by the frenzied and pernicious atmosphere of the place and of the age? The Bride of Christ would endure many years of crisis and suffering before she found the strength to answer all these questions.

A Decisive Pontificate: Nicholas V (1447–1455)

The year 1450 was noteworthy in the annals of Rome. The jubilee, whose ceremonies had lasted for twelve long months, would remain in men's minds as the most brilliant that had been seen for many years. To find another so splendid it was necessary to go back a century and a half to that of 1300, whose praises had been sung so sweetly by Dante,[1] one of its pilgrims. This was the jubilee celebrated by the hapless Boniface VIII shortly before the Outrage of Anagni. During the intervening century and a half several more attacks, equally sacrilegious, had been launched against the Holy See. Fortunately, however, they had all come to grief, and the Apostle's successor was once more really and truly sole and rightful leader of the faithful. Hence the rush to see him and acclaim him. Although countless

[1] See *Cathedral and Crusade*, pp. 68 and 604.

temporary hostelries had been improvised, and many private individuals induced to let rooms in their own houses, so many pilgrims found themselves without lodgings that the churches had to be thrown open to shelter them. Even the plague, which usually invited itself to festivals of this kind, did not diminish the fervour of these tens of thousands of pious folk. St Bernardino of Siena's canonization was proclaimed in 1450, and this attracted enormous crowds: the great preacher had been very popular, and the entire Franciscan Order was determined to fan public opinion in order to give the desired splendour to the glorification of one of its own members. There were actually so many people in Rome that on one occasion an enormous crush on the bridge of Sant' Angelo resulted in two or three hundred pilgrims being thrown into the Tiber. There could be no more striking proof of the jubilee's success.

The Pope who presided over this triumph was *Nicholas V* (1447–1455), one of those small, skinny, rather ugly Italians, but with eyes sparkling with intelligence, and a tongue quick to subtle repartee. Nicholas came from a middle-class background—he was the son of a doctor from Sarzana, on the Ligurian coast, and he owed his career solely to his brilliant intellect. He began as a Carthusian, and then studied at Bologna. Shortage of money obliged him to become a tutor to the sons of the rich, and this experience made him extremely sympathetic to poverty-stricken scholars during the remainder of his life. He became a priest, and entered the service of the pious Cardinal Nicholas Albergati, whose name he decided to adopt, out of gratitude, when he became pope. The Council of Florence had established his reputation, for his knowledge of theology, scriptural exegesis and ecclesiastical history had enabled him to stand up to the Greeks in the lengthy debates. An outstanding scholar, he was supported by influential groups of writers who were beginning to play a substantial part in Church affairs. Consequently when Eugenius IV died, and it became clear that neither the Orsinis nor the Colonnas would be able to impose one of their own relations upon the Sacred College, it was quickly agreed to elect Thomas Parentucelli.

Nicholas found the Holy See in an unquestionably favourable position, better placed than it had been for a long time past. Papal authority, which had been shaken by the crisis of the Great Schism, and disputed by the theorists who advocated conciliar primacy, was again much stronger. Martin V and Eugenius IV had laboured long and hard in order that their successors might be powerful. Nicholas V's adaptability too had played no small part in bringing the Church's ordeal to an end. Won over by his adroit concessions, the principal leaders of the Council of Basle [1] had made their submission. The

---
[1] See Chapter I, p. 40 et seq.

antipope, Felix V himself, threw in his lot with Nicholas; in any case
he was dying, as was the lone Cardinal of Arles, Louis Aleman, who
had combined with him to resist the legitimate pontiff. The France of
Charles VIII had returned to the bosom of the Church, amid the
splendour of solemn processions and festal bonfires. The conciliar
ideas were now propagated only by obscure hacks upon whom the
theorists of absolute power, John Torquemada, Pietro del Monte, St
Antoninus and Roderigo Sanchez de Arevalo, poured a rain of learned
treatises which brought them easy victories. The 'grand legations' of
Nicholas of Cusa in Germany, St John Capistrano in Central Europe
and Cardinal d'Estouteville in France, spread the papal instructions
far and wide, albeit with unequal success. Thus the battle was won, and
in the glory of the jubilee year Nicholas V might well have fancied
himself back in the age of Gregory VII or Innocent III. Scarcely
fifteen months after the festivities had ended, the Emperor Frederick
III came to Rome to celebrate amid scenes of dazzling splendour the
double event of his marriage to Eleanor of Portugal and his coronation.
'It used to be the emperor who chose the Pope,' observed the sagacious
Piccolomini; 'But now the Pope is master.' In crowning a German
emperor, Nicholas V bore open witness to the victory of the Papacy.

This victory was real enough, but there is reason to doubt whether it
was as significant as the honest bystanders were inclined to think, as they
lined the streets of Rome to acclaim the procession led by the two
heads of the Western world. The medieval idea which suggested the
dream of a unity between Emperor and Pope, of a reconstituted
Christendom harmoniously governed by the authority of the two
swords, was an anachronism, gone for ever. Increasingly each of the
great states of Europe was to manage its own destinies, with no concern
for anything outside the scope of its national interests. In Germany,
where national sentiment barely survived, the mediocre Frederick
III (1435–93), a Hapsburg without lustre or prestige, nevertheless
paved the way for his family's power and glory by marrying his son,
Maximilian (1477), to the wealthy Mary of Burgundy, sole heiress to
Charles the Bold's vast domains. France, which had emerged sorely
wounded from the Hundred Years War, rapidly rebuilt her forces,
thanks to the steadfast wisdom of *Charles VII* (1422–61). Soon, under
Louis XI (1465–83), she was to shatter the ambition of the mighty
dukes of Burgundy and succeed in binding their lands to that Capetian
crown which seemed daily more national, absolute and incontrovertible.
In England the same result was to be obtained by a different route: the
bitterness resultant from a ruinous, profitless war and the weakness of
Henry VI and his advisers were to provoke a crisis which found its
most dreadful manifestation in the atrocious *Wars of the Roses* (1455–
1485). So long as these lasted the country could concern itself with

nothing but its own tragic affairs, until the day when absolutism ascended the throne in the person of *Henry Tudor* (1485). As for Spain, she was divided into four kingdoms—not to mention the Moorish kingdom of Granada—which were frequently at war with one another, and often in the grip of complete anarchy. Her ruling classes were split between 'Portuguese' and 'Aragonese,' in the same way that the French nobility had formerly been divided into 'Armagnacs' and 'Burgundians.' She continued to pursue her humble and lonely course, until the love-match of two young people, who were predestined to do great things, snatched her from obscurity.

Nicholas V was far too shrewd a man not to be perfectly aware of the realities of the situation. Although his position as pope was henceforth undisputed, he could no longer claim, as his twelfth- and thirteenth-century predecessors had done, to be the supra-national ruler of all secular states, and to impose his law upon them. The theocratic ideal was out of date; from now on it was only raised for diplomatic reasons, without being regarded very seriously. It was far better to come to terms with the new forces in the world. In France the Papacy turned a blind eye to the strange manner in which her kings had unilaterally proclaimed the *Pragmatic Sanction of Bourges*,[1] their motive being to make the clergy an instrument of absolutism. In Germany the *Concordat of Vienna*, which was signed in 1448, might serve as a model for the kind of agreements which the Papacy henceforth sought to reach with secular states. The right of the Holy See to annates and reserves was recognized; but election of bishops was permitted to the secular authority, the Papacy merely reserving to itself the right to sanction the choice.

Force of circumstances thus led Nicholas V to become at least as much an Italian as a universal pope. In the days of Avignon the Sacred College had had an overwhelming French majority. This was now replaced by one in which Italian cardinals held the lion's share of the votes, along with Germans and Spaniards. And since the role of leader of Christendom and arbiter of the West was daily slipping further from his grasp, Nicholas V decided—and his successors were to follow his example—to assume this role within the more limited framework of the Italian peninsula, where moreover the immediate interests of the Apostolic See and the Papal States were at stake.

At this period Italy was more divided than ever; split up into a mosaic of kingdoms, duchies, cities and republics, each element being entirely preoccupied with its own interests. In the north lay the mighty and Most Serene Republic of Venice and the Duchy of Milan, Genoa on the Ligurian coast, and, straddling the Alps, stretching westwards as far as the Saône, the Duchy of Savoy. In the south was

[1] See Chapter I, p. 49.

HOLY ROMAN
EMPIRE

KINGDOM OF
HUNGARY

SWITZERLAND
TYROL

Lyons
Geneva
SAVOY

VENETIA

Brescia
Verona
Padua
Venice

Trieste
ISTRIA

OTTOMAN
EMPIRE

Milan
Mantua
Pavia
Po

Modena
Ferrara

DALMATIA

Genoa
Bologna
Ravenna

Lucca
Pisa
Nice
Florence
Siena
TUSCANY
Forli
Urbino
MARCHES
Perugia
Spoleto
Orvieto

Ancona

ADRIATIC

CORSICA
ELBA

Civitavecchia
Rome

KINGDOM OF NAPLES

SEA

Lucera
Pontecorvo
BENEVENTO

Gaeta
Naples
Salerno

Taranto

KINGDOM OF
SARDINIA
(to Spain)

TYRRHENIAN

SEA

CALABRIA

ITALY
At the end of the
15th Century

Papal States
Republic of Genoa
Republic of Venice
Duchy of Milan
Principality of Piedmont

Palermo

KINGDOM
OF SICILY
(to Spain)

Syracuse

the kingdom of Naples, which was large if not powerful, and that of Sicily, which the Spaniards held, together with Sardinia. The Papal States were in central Italy, between these two blocs, sprawling obliquely across the peninsula from Gaeta to Mantua. They were an ill-assorted jumble of territories, and their position was a somewhat perilous one, rendered no easier by the fact that Florence and her ambitions were poised dangerously on their flank. These domains had been indispensable at the time when a papacy without land or arms might have been a plaything in the hands of politicians. But their possession in the future might prove to be a cannon-ball which the Vicar of Christ would find remarkably cumbersome to carry.

For more than a century, ever since the futile attempts of Robert of Anjou and Charles of Bohemia, no one had cherished further dreams of unifying Italy. Such an undertaking seemed completely out of the question. The rivalry of these petty states, which was to be so fruitful on the artistic plane, had the political result of producing a permanent state of anarchy, war and revolution. Alliances were made, then broken, then made again in various new combinations, and this perpetual political game kept going a seemingly incurable fever. The *condottieri*, mercenaries who were ready to serve whomsoever paid them best—and also to betray any cause which ceased to be profitable —helped to maintain a state of disorder which constituted their livelihood. Within each state anarchy had engendered tyranny, as it always does. There was dynastic tyranny at Naples, and the despotism of the aristocracy at Mantua, under the Gonzagas, at Ferrara under the Estes and at Verona under the della Scalas. The tyranny at Milan was of military origin, the Sforzas having established their authority there in 1450. At Venice and Genoa the regime was supposedly democratic, but in fact plutocratic; in Florence, which had been controlled by the Medicis since 1434, it was oddly middle class. A far-sighted pope might therefore consider it one of his first duties to safeguard the independence of his city and his states in such a disturbing situation.

Nicholas V seems to have been the first pontiff to conceive the idea that the Papacy might constitute the guiding element which the peninsula so sorely lacked. He was aware also that the prevailing disorder might well offer foreigners, particularly the French and imperialists, a pretext for intervening in Italy. Secret negotiations were entered into by Simonetto de Camerino, an Augustinian monk, with a view to establishing an alliance between Venice and Milan, and Florence was subsequently invited to join the bloc. Under the papal aegis the Peace of Lodi (1454) gave rise to the 'Italic League,' the first attempt to weld the mosaic of states into one federal whole. Thirty months of relative tranquillity followed the realization of this plan. Much later Alexander VI and Julius II adopted the same policy, using different methods. The

* G

idea was undoubtedly a judicious and fruitful one, though not without danger for the Papacy. In his capacity as ruler of the 'Papal States' the Pope was a temporal sovereign. Moreover by virtue of this title he was beset with all the difficulties surrounding the Italian governments of the day, continually in conflict with the petty despots who challenged his rights at Perugia, Urbino, Rimini and Bologna, and also perpetually threatened by popular riots, baronial plots and middle-class conspiracies. By deliberately involving himself in Italian politics, the Pope ran the risk of becoming an increasingly temporal sovereign. Like his partners in alliance, he had interests to defend, and he might well employ those same unedifying weapons of which they made use. The fact is indisputable: quite unconsciously the wise and well-intentioned Nicholas V prepared the way for the intrigues of Alexander VI and the militant policy of Julius II.

But there is another even more important way in which this worthy man's pontificate marks a decisive turning-point. At Florence, where he had lived, Nicholas had been closely connected with the *élite* of the literary and artistic movement, which he supported with boundless enthusiasm. In his youth he was often heard to say that if he ever became rich he would spend all his wealth on books and artistic treasures. On becoming pope he was able to realize his ambition. He developed a grandiose scheme: Rome, capital of the faith and illuminated by the Holy Spirit, was also to be the capital of the spirit which guides art and intellect. This city which he had found in ruins would become the most beautiful in the world and the most lively cultural centre of the age.

Nicholas therefore applied himself to the task of summoning artists to Rome; and thither they joyfully hurried, not only from every corner of Italy, but also from France, Germany and Spain. There was more than enough work for all—architects, sculptors, painters, jewellers and embroiderers. The whole face of the Eternal City was transformed; contemporaries were lost in admiration at the scope of the plans conceived for her. The four churches where the Pope celebrated Mass on specific days as indicated in the Missal, were replaced by nine. Nor was the practical side neglected: ramparts, aqueducts, fountains, rose on all sides. With the help of *Leo Battista Alberti* (1402–72), whose ten volumes on the *Art of Building* had sent him into raptures, Nicholas V conceived the idea of making the Vatican, the Leonine Citadel and St Peter's into one architectural whole which would have no rival anywhere. The papal city was to be surrounded by impregnable walls, and would be both military strongpoint and palace. Led by Fra Angelico, the finest painters in Europe were to cover the walls with masterpieces. As for the basilica beneath which the Prince of Apostles slept, its magnificence would surpass anything else in the world. To make room for this it was resolved without hesitation to destroy the venerable Constantinian Church, an act of vandalism that was afterwards severely criticized.

Nicholas V was a patron of literature as well as of the arts, and scholars, no less than painters and architects, were summoned to his court. His confidence in them was so great that numbers of pen-pushers, who scarcely merited any respect, could be observed among his *entourage*. He ordered them to translate Homer, Strabo, Herodotus, Thucydides, Xenophon, Diodorus and, needless to say, Plato and Aristotle. Above all—and this is undoubtedly his highest claim to renown—he started the collection of precious manuscripts and rare books which were to constitute the *Vatican Library*. The moneys received during the jubilee of 1450 were mostly used for this purpose. Almost nothing remained of the ancient library which had been amassed by scholarly popes since the days of Pepin the Short and Charlemagne: the best things in it had been left at Avignon or carried off to Paris. Like the prudent bibliophile he was, Nicholas V patiently hunted down beautiful copies, and numerous messengers were sent far and wide to obtain them. At his death the Vatican Library boasted nearly fifteen hundred books, of which eight hundred and eighty were Latin manuscripts.

Thus Nicholas V was the first 'Renaissance Pope,' the first successor of Peter who had the idea of making the creative impulse, which was then arousing all Italy, serve to further the glory of God and of His Church. It was a splendid notion, but it was also fraught with peril. The introduction to the Papal Court, and even into the highest counsels of the Church, of men whose morality was often highly suspect tended to throw open the gates to evil influences. A pope so pre-occupied with architecture and learning ran the risk of neglecting his graver interests. The essential matter on which vigorous action by the Church was necessary was that of her own reform; yet Nicholas V seems to have done little more than utter a few fair words at a time when the word 'reform' was on the lips of all men. This brilliant pontificate was not the one to translate words into deeds. . . .

In the course of 1453, however, Providence gave Nicholas V two tragic warnings, as if to remind him that Italian politics and the development of art and literature ought not to be the Pope's only preoccupations. Stefano Porcaro, one of the type of intellectuals whom the Pope loved so dearly, and on whom he bestowed his confidence so lavishly, became dangerously inflamed by his reading of the classical historians, and sought to re-establish the Roman Republic with himself in the role of a new Gracchus. A careful plot was laid which involved nothing less than setting fire to the Vatican during High Mass and arresting the Pope. The plan was discovered and Porcaro was hanged. But it was a very bad sign, and the fall of Constantinople a few months later provided an even more tragic augury. At the time of his death in 1455, after prolonged suffering courageously endured, it is doubtful whether Nicholas V had understood the full meaning of this twofold warning from Heaven. The Romans mourned him sincerely, grateful to him for having brought back such splendour to their city: he had 'embellished it with all the resources of art, enriched it with books and tapestries, adorned it with magnificence.' So says the beautifully cadenced epitaph which we can read upon his tomb in St Peter's, an epitaph written as a last tribute by another outstanding scholar: the future Pope, Aeneas Sylvius Piccolomini.

THE GLORIOUS SUNRISE BREAKS OVER ITALY

This powerful artistic and intellectual movement, whose fruits Nicholas V had sought to use for the Church's benefit, had been strikingly apparent for several years. It was as if Italy had been blessed by a luxurious spring time, in which a myriad stupendous flowers bloomed in riotous profusion. A glorious sunrise, which was soon to burst into the dazzling brilliance of a glittering noon, was fast spreading over this fortunate land.

Until now the Italian peninsula had been much less fruitful and creative than France. To find the origins of the phenomenon which was to transform it into the leader of the Western world, it is necessary to go back as far as the middle of the thirteenth century.[1] Even then the architects building the double Franciscan basilica at Assisi, or the cathedrals of Siena and Orvieto, had intermingled a number of extremely personal elements with the lessons taught them by their Gothic masters. The Pisan sculptors had turned away from the craftsmen of Chartres and Rheims, and, taking their inspiration from the tombs and ivory statuary of the classical age, had given their art a passion and wealth of expression hitherto unknown. Cavallini, a Roman, and the Florentine Cimabue had sought to rescue painting from the hieratic conventions which the 'Bizantineggianti' had made obligatory for far too long; Duccio and Simone Martini had imparted a sweetness which the Sienese school never subsequently forgot; and above all the outstanding genius of Giotto, whose emotional inspiration was as important as his technical influence, threw open whole new vistas to the art of painting. About 1350 Andrea's paintings in the chapter-house of Santa Maria Novella at Florence,[2] and the frescoes in

[1] See *Cathedral and Crusade*, p. 388, section 11, 'The Italian Exception and the Glory of Giotto,' and p. 67 of this book.
[2] Andrea da Firenze or Andrea Bonaiutti. The first few pages of *Cathedral and Crusade* describe one of the scenes from this work.

the Campo Santo at Pisa, where the honours are shared by Francesco da Volterra and Traini, provided examples of an art which was still far from complete fulfilment, but whose solid achievements had already gone beyond the stage of mere promise.

Little by little this artistic revival became an irresistible force, and it was soon plain for all to see. Several trends and influences played their part in its growth, but these, though readily noticeable, are less easy to interpret. The mighty ruins scattered up and down the length and breadth of the peninsula were abruptly roused from a sleep which resembled death, and regarded with new eyes; but we do not know why this suddenly happened. For them it was undoubtedly a matter of 'renaissance' in the fullest sense of the word. Men suddenly tried to understand the sculptural techniques which the great masters of Greece and Rome had used so well: in the perfection of capitals and columns they had discovered maxims which applied to the human body, and long-forgotten principles of construction had emerged from a careful re-reading of Vitruvius's treatise on building. Thus this return to the most distant past had constituted a real rejuvenation. Ideas and methods underwent a fundamental change, and the artist no longer considered that the masters of the recent past could teach him anything.

Other factors also intervened, and although these had no immediate relationship with the return to classicism, they moved in the same direction. The love of nature, and an increasingly marked taste for truth and reality (which were actually heritages from the final epoch of the Middle Ages), helped to emancipate the arts at least as much as the imitation of classical statues and monuments had done. The artist's subjects henceforth consisted principally of landscapes, flowering trees, animals and, above all, people. He set himself to studying them in minute detail, and this rapt attention opened up unbounded fields of experience to the creative mind.

Technical advances also contributed to the revival. This is particularly true in the case of the painters, who learned almost nothing from the artists of classical times. Flanders had given them the technique of working in oils, and Italy was soon to bring this to the height of ultimate perfection. Working upon the vast areas allowed them by the architect, the fresco-painters took only two generations to perfect an art-form in which a sharp eye and a steady hand were all important. Giotto, the first master of perspective, had enabled them to escape from the tyranny of the luxurious but lifeless Byzantine style, by resolutely cramming their space with animated material, and creating a whole world on one wall.

By the beginning of the 'Quattrocento'—our fifteenth century—all these acquisitions had been made, and all these elements were in process of becoming flesh and blood. And it was now, when they were all matured, that their providential fusion determined the phenomenon which alone provides the mysterious and all-important key to the Italian Renaissance: the eruption, proliferation and accumulation of genius and talent. For some two hundred years the peninsula was to produce more outstanding artists than have ever been found anywhere else, either before or since. They were many-sided geniuses: nearly all were capable of expressing themselves in each of the plastic arts, and a few—Alberti and Leonardo, for example—went even beyond their limits. With their boundless intelligence, so quick to grasp every aspect of the inexhaustible current that was influencing their age, they were to make such a deep impression upon the society in which they lived that we still see it through them, in superhuman dimensions. These artists were freed from everyday cares by those many rulers and despots who considered patronage of the arts to be a way of endowing their authority with a prestige it could not always derive either from their origins or from their behaviour—the Sforzas of Milan, the Malatestas of Rimini, the Gonzagas of Mantua, the Estes of Ferrara, and last but not least the popes. Six generations of them were to be allotted more than two centuries in which to impart their message to mankind, and the history of their creative endeavour constitutes one of the most magnificent pages in European history.[1]

It is usual to divide this history into three parts. The first ended with the death of Nicholas V. During it the Primitives of the 'Trecento' had gradually evolved a conception and a method which had been brought to admirable fruition by the first generation of the fifteenth century. There quickly followed the age of incomparable triumphs, the age of real glory, which glittered with the names of a unique triad—Leonardo da Vinci, Raphael and Michelangelo. Finally, in the sixteenth century, even before the deaths of Titian and the lonely old artist of the Sistine Chapel, genius was to give way to talent—talent that was still enormous and able to serve as teacher for the rest of the world, but which did not equal the brilliance of the masters of the Golden Age.

It is not easy to describe the beauty of that first Italian Renaissance which ended in 1455. It had a soft, delicate charm, freshness and endless variety. It is still in some respects clumsy and unfinished, a fact which lends its masterpieces a certain charm that may be found lacking in more highly accomplished works.

[1] The one art-form in which Italy remained largely dependent on France for a long time to come was music. Fourteenth-century Italian composers followed the example of the French composers, notably of Guillaume de Machaut, but they modified this teaching in obedience to the fundamental instincts of their own race, notably its love of singing. *Francesco Landino* (1320–97) is among the outstanding Italian musicians of this epoch; his talents for melodic invention were remarkable. But his successors slipped all too often into over-intellectual compositions, which lacked real feeling. Not until the sixteenth century did Palestrina restore emotional force to music, and, at the same time, make it into a wonderful means of religious expression.

In this early period one city undoubtedly took the lead: Florence, where Thomas Parentucelli, the future Pope, had first become acquainted with intellectual life. While Venice still reclined on her money-bags, seeking a way to express her mystery in which cupidity and fever, idealism and sensuality, were curiously interwoven; while Rome, only recently reoccupied by the popes, still licked her wounds; while Naples continued to sleep in peace amid her picturesque squalor, the City of the Red Lily, the pride of the Medicis, the motherland of Giotto and Dante, had produced so many artists and so many wonderful works from her cramped little squares that the mind stands bewildered before such a prolific outpouring of talent.

Every single art-form had already produced its masterpieces there, and the future of each seemed irrevocably decided. In Venice, Bergamo and Milan architecture was feeling its way forward in the pointed Gothic of the Lombard cathedral, in the paradoxical style of the Doge's Palace and in the over-elaborate structure of the Certosa at Pavia. In Florence, however, *Brunelleschi* (1377–1446) was reviving the dream of Arnolfo di Cambio. His cupola, comprising a perfect double octagonal sphere, solidly planted upon black-and-white marble bases, crowned the church of Santa Maria del Fiore, and supported the cross of Christ four hundred and fifty feet above the town. It was at once accepted as the model, and the word 'duomo' came to be used for the whole cathedral. Brunelleschi was not satisfied with the erection of this exquisite jewel, which taught his epoch what added majesty such aerial masses could give to church buildings. At San Lorenzo and San Spirito his inexhaustible genius demonstrated also how the cylindrical column could replace the pillar without loss of beauty, and the semicircular Roman arch be substituted for the pointed Gothic. Thus he restored the Christian nave to its most venerable traditions, to the simplicity of the ancient basilica. Countless architects immediately followed in Brunelleschi's footsteps. His example may be said to have been exceeded rather than copied. In the Florentine convent of San Marco and the Milanese Chapel of the Portinari, the serene Michelozzo was to continue along the same course, while the theory behind the whole of this immense contribution was set out in the form of a treatise by the youthful genius of Alberti.

Florentine sculpture was even more outstanding, the art-form in which the prolific genius of the city discovered its most perfect medium. Year after year artists in stone and bronze lived in a strange creative fever continually competing to produce the absolute masterpiece, men of different ages and varying temperaments working at the same themes. It was as though all the genius of their race had been waiting for this moment from the beginning of time, in order to immortalize itself in the figures of St John the Baptist and Bartolommeo

Colleoni, or in the bronze gates, where Florence recognized herself. All the heritage of the past had been turned to good account. The lessons of the ancient masters of Orvieto, and beyond them those of the unappreciated craftsmen of France; the lessons of the marble antiquities which their native soil was yielding up in such abundance; the lessons of the Pisans and the virile genius of Jacopo della Quercia, who rediscovered sculptured perspective, and created that bas-relief in San Petronio at Bologna, before which the youthful Buonarotti whiled away so many hours—all these had been meditated on and most thoroughly studied. Added to them, however, was that indescribable flash of brilliance which, by suddenly breaking through the normal course of an aesthetic evolution, produces the masterpiece which stamps its particular impress upon the age, and which is something entirely new, despite all the anterior influences in its make-up.

Thus *Lorenzo Ghiberti* (1378–1455), who had defeated Brunelleschi in an open competition for the design of bronze doors for the baptistery at Florence, had shown that sculptured bas-relief had the same gifts as painting for evoking life and giving scenes containing human figures their depth and scope. Breaking firmly away, however, from this marvellous imagery—which Michelangelo was to declare worthy of Paradise—*Donatello* (1386–1466), in his figures of saints and prophets, and in the contorted torsos visible beneath the gentle folds of drapery, had splendidly depicted that human drama whose tragedy he later represented to perfection in 'The Slaves.' This master of form was so audacious that he dared to challenge antiquity and accomplish something which had not been done for centuries—the bronze equestrian statue of Gattamelata, more perfect even than that of Marcus Aurelius at Rome. About 1450 a boy of fifteen stood day-dreaming in the piazza where stood this figure of Gattamelata. He was *Verrocchio* (1435–88), who applied Donatello's lessons fifty years after they had first been taught, and produced a still more epic ring in another bronze horseman, the Colleoni at Venice. Verrocchio was the sculptor of psychological undertones, of delicately moulded flesh, of a hardly perceptible system of planes which betrayed the soul beneath the statue. So rich was the creative genius of Florence at this period that *Lucca della Robbia* (1399–1422) was at the selfsame moment competing with Donatello for the cathedral pulpit. Della Robbia, who was soon to be followed by a whole dynasty of artists, no longer used the sculptor's art to proclaim life's pathos, but to give thanks for the face of a child, the purity of inviolate souls, the heavenly innocence of the little singers of God.

In painting, as in the other fields of art, Florence had not previously held the quasi-monopoly. Here too, however, she had begun to impose that primacy we have earlier observed in Flanders and France, and which is the factor dominating modern art. Here artists were at work everywhere, decorating walls, erecting splendid retables above the altars, and, most important of all, producing a whole mass of painted canvases which were completely self-sufficient. Borrowing from sculpture the precision of line and sense of depth, from architecture and mathematics the henceforward constant use of lineal perspective, and from contemporary society its love of colour, the painters of the early Renaissance achieved a harmonious whole that was both sophisticated and naïve, realistic and yet poetic. They had already produced numerous great works, so different from one another that they might well have been considered an ill-matched assortment had they not manifested an indefinable, mysterious inner unity. *Fra Angelico* (1378–1455), an artist whose purity of heart shines out for all to see, had created his masterpieces on the walls of the cells in San Marco at Florence, in devotional pictures, and in diptych panels. The message of his very simple scenes, rather after the style of the illustrations in a missal, and with colouring deliberately flat, is both moving and supernatural in quality. *Masaccio* (1401–28) was Fra Angelico's friend, although thirty years his junior. This dazzling genius, whose fire was snuffed out at the early age of twenty-seven years, was more directly loyal to the lessons of Giotto. In the frescoes in the Brancacci chapel he stands revealed as the initiator of that combined psychological and decorative art which Michelangelo later carried to perfection. At Florence, Viterbo, Orvieto and Montefalco *Benozzo Gozzoli* (1420–77) covered vast areas of wall with frescoes which joyously proclaim the sumptuous beauty of the age. *Filippo Lippi* (1406–69) was a bad friar, but a good painter. His art enabled him to recapture his lost innocence, and he taught his countless disciples that the human beauty of a Madonna could go hand in hand with spiritual meaning. The art of the brush and pallet multiplied its discoveries in all directions: Paolo Uccello's battles, in their quasi-metallic rigidity, afforded prodigious lessons on the simplification of massed material; the powerful faces of Andrea del Castagno showed what fields of speculative exploration existed in one man's expression; while in Umbria *Piero della Francesca* (1416–93), the wise and brilliant decorator of the church of Santa Croce at Arezzo, taught his admiring compatriots how large-scale mural painting could convey the very feeling of light and air. As the pontificate of Nicholas V drew to its close, two young northerners of twenty were making ready to employ these manifold lessons taught them by their predecessors in the production of paintings more accomplished in execution, if not more sensitive in feeling. Their names were *Andrea Mantegna* and *Giovanni Bellini*.

What had the Church gained from this magnificent expansion of the arts? And what truth was there in the idea that by patronizing the

arts the popes could make them serve the glory of God? Since the great
artistic impulse began, men had certainly done much to beautify the
house of God; large numbers of churches, cathedrals and monasteries
had been, and still were, being built. Even more church decoration was
going on. All the resources which sculpture and painting could offer
were devoted to producing exquisite and brilliant ecclesiastical interiors.
Holy pictures, statues for private devotion—in particular, gentle
Madonnas with exquisitely delicate features—were produced in
increasing numbers, a consequence of the current trend of the age
towards personal devotion. Often they were the standardized products
of large studio workshops. The Church had found none of this
displeasing; but some other obvious aspects of the artistic renaissance
were far less favourable to the Christian cause.

Several symptoms made it clear that Renaissance Italy was suffering
from that same process which had already been affecting the rest of the
Western world for many years past—the divorce of art from its ancient
Christian loyalties. Men built a great deal for God, but, unlike the past,
they were no longer building for Him alone. The sumptuous palace
oratories, which princes, despots and popes embellished with works of
art, were not always genuine places of prayer, but mere pretexts for
rich decoration. As many palaces as churches were built during this
epoch, and possibly even more. They were constructed in that handsome Florentine style which was to improve in delicacy throughout
the fifteenth century. They included the Pitti, Ricardi, Rucellai and
Strozzi palaces, and many others, and Italy remains justly proud of
them. The growing habit of erecting over-large, over-sumptuous
tombs, which filled the side aisles of the churches or stood ostenta-
tiously in the public squares, was inspired more by the desire to exalt
the vanity of human vanities, even beyond the grave, rather than from
motives of disinterested Christian devotion. Among such imposing
monuments were those which Donatello made for John XXII and
Martin V. But the custom spread far beyond Rome. At Naples
Camaiano adorned the magnificent tombs of the princes of Anjou, and
the haughty Campionesi erected others for the della Scalas at Verona.
The enormous fashion for framed pictures, which were intended to
hang as decorations in state apartments and galleries, was equally
characteristic of this evolution; even more so was the growing liking
for portraits. We value the latter because, like so many masterpieces,
they afford us the rare chance to see into the characters of the men and
women of that age; but their purpose is obvious: art aimed at flattering
man's egoism and pride at least as much as at praising God.

Did its inspiration remain Christian? Certainly the great majority
of artists remained Catholic in both observance and belief; actual
unbelief was still uncommon at this time. Even those whose obedience

to the Ten Commandments was somewhat half-hearted obviously regarded themselves as Christians. A much-quoted example is that of Filippo Lippi who, friar though he was, led an extremely dissolute life, acknowledging no rule save that of his own personal satisfaction. He even had his mistress sit as the model for one of his Madonnas, albeit without the slightest intention of committing sacrilege. However, we should also recall the example of another humble and radiant religious, whose purity and chastity were exemplary. The Church beatified him, and his name *Fra Angelico*—the angelic brother— perfectly expresses his great spiritual qualities. Between these two extremes there was the general mass of well-meaning Christians, all of whom sinned on occasion, but practised their religion after the fashion of their age, which was very different from our own. Among them Donatello and Masaccio both give the impression of possessing a profound understanding of Christian experience, and of wishing to express its tragic side.

However, although the artists of this period were personally devout, possessing a faith that had many admirable facets, it is questionable whether religion had the same meaning for them that it had had for their predecessors during the best centuries of the Middle Ages. In the past collective work, representing the faith of a whole people, had been the artist's main preoccupation. Hundreds of nameless craftsmen had laboured on it, with no hope of recompense save that of the Lord's silent approbation of their effort. Was this the aim of those generations of Renaissance artists, who were so conscious of their own personal merits, and whose names were bywords from town to town, even beyond the borders of Italy? It is abundantly clear that when such men produced a masterpiece, they were often thinking far more of their own glory than of God's. Like the whole epoch Renaissance art was highly individualistic. It was to divorce itself more and more from the fundamental feeling of belonging to the whole Christian community; and it was because he was aware of this separation that Michelangelo suffered such mental torment.

Above all, the law of contradiction which, as has been seen, affected the whole century, applied in the field of art, as in all the rest. Why did these artists, who worked for churches and convents, deriving from the Scriptures so many lofty themes which they treated with obvious respect, often devote an even more considerable part of their life and talent to treating subjects in which Christianity had no place whatsoever, subjects from pagan mythology? With the sole exception of Fra Angelico, whose entire work is confined within the bounds of Christianity, and whose genius is so obviously linked with heavenly inspiration that it is quite impossible to imagine him painting the nude deities of Olympus, there was probably at this time not a single artist who, along with the Christian side of his work, did not possess a second and completely different one, diametrically opposed to the first. The old craftsmen of Rheims and Chartres would have been appalled to see Donatello sculpting a Cupid with the same chisel which he had used to create his wonderful prophets. And his case was legion.

The influence of this contradiction extended even to works of a religious nature. A certain ambiguity was apparent in them, and this became increasingly marked as the artists grew surer of their technical skill, and aimed rather at producing works of art capable of attracting the public than of translating fundamental religious feeling. In the crowded paintings of Benozzo Gozzoli and Piero della Francesca, the importance accorded to picturesque and sumptuous details is somewhat excessive in relation to the basically religious subject which provides the theme. 'The Procession of the Three Kings' seems primarily intended to exalt the glory of the Medicis, while that of the 'Queen of Sheba' provides an excellent opportunity for displaying the beauty of the noble ladies of Umbria. This was the beginning of a process which resulted in the Venetians, led by Bellini, deserting sacred subjects altogether in favour of great ceremonial scenes, and which led to Carpaccio painting dazzling processions under pretext of exalting the martyrdom of St Ursula.

At the end of the first period of the Renaissance this danger was apparent, but not yet acute. In the main secular preoccupations had not yet damaged religious inspiration. Even though they treated them in a different way from the past, sculptors and painters remained so abundantly loyal to the ancient themes of Christianity that a man like Nicholas V, who was sincerely devout and at the same time an enlightened patron of the arts, could believe it perfectly possible to use this marvellous impulse to benefit the Church. But what would happen if pagan inspirations overwhelmed Christian ones, or if art allowed itself to be deflected from its ancient loyalties by its own pride, tending thereby to become an end in itself? Would Christianity itself not risk contamination?

FROM THE 'HUMANITIES' TO 'HUMANISM'

The same question posed itself even more urgently in the realm of ideas; for, admirable though the artistic development was, it alone did not constitute the 'Renaissance.' Another eruption of creative vigour was occurring in the intellectual sphere, and the consequences of this were to affect the future of civilization in an even more decisive manner.

This intellectual movement is known as *Humanism*, and the reason for the name is still a matter of dispute. The starting-point of humanism can be found in the enthusiastic trend towards classical literature

which had its counterpart in that which attracted the artists to the
masterpieces of ancient Greece and Rome. Its origins go back to the
thirteenth century, when Dante chose Virgil, as the epitome of reason,
to guide him on his mysterious journey. *Petrarch* (1304–74) had stated
that he attached more importance to the discovery of an ancient manuscript than to the capture of a town; and his epic, *Africa*, as well as his
treatises on the disreputable state of the world were written in Latin,
albeit of a rather rough-and-ready kind. The attractive and salacious
Decameron had earned *Boccaccio* (1313–75) the title of founder of
modern Italian prose; but he also made several scholarly copies of
Latin classics, and boasted of being the first Italian to have had read
the whole of Homer.

By the beginning of the Quattrocento this interest in classical
literature had become an irresistible passion. Scarcely anyone with any
interest in culture was free from it. In 1438 Cardinal Nicholas of Cusa
was already referring to it as a revolution. The same fever which sent
artists hurrying to excavation sites, where the tiniest fragment of
classical sculpture was regarded as a treasure, drove scholars in pursuit
of ancient manuscripts. And what a frenzied pursuit it was! Poggio,
who accompanied the Pope to the Council of Constance, took advantage of the opportunity to scour several German castles and monasteries,
and brought back forgotten fragments of Cicero, Plautus and Tacitus.
One wicked Sicilian, Aurispo, whom some called a clever rogue, made
a fortune by filching precious stuffs from Byzantium and selling them
in Venice. When he brought the first complete edition of Plato to the
West, in 1438, he was acclaimed as a great man. On leaving the East to
settle in Italy, the future Cardinal Bessarion brought six hundred
manuscripts among his luggage, a fact which sent all the intellectuals
into transports of joy. And the Rome of Nicholas V, with its wonderful
Vatican Library, was not the only city which prided itself on its store
of classical rarities; at Florence and Venice, rulers, governments, and
even ordinary citizens, spent colossal sums in order to acquire these
treasures of the mind.[1]

Men became passionately fond of the languages of Virgil and
Homer. The capacity for writing good, pure Latin, free of the vulgarisms with which scholasticism had tainted it, became the hallmark
of an educated person. Latin poetry regained a perfection worthy of
the Augustan Age. Greek was perhaps even more popular still: gone
were the days when this marvellous tongue had slept almost a sleep of
death, hidden away in scrolls that were relegated to the depths of

---

[1] As soon as printing had been invented, it was used to disseminate the classical masters.
The earliest Italian editors devoted themselves to publishing the works of Virgil, Caesar,
Tacitus and Livy. The most famous of them all was Aldo Manuzio (1449–1515), the
Venetian printer and scholar, whose editions of the Greek classics are still renowned for
their flawless texts and splendid typography.

rat-infested cellars. At Florence Marsilio Ficino's pupils were forbidden to use any tongue other than that of Plato for the space of a whole day; and a little later on, at Venice, Aldo made his students speak nothing but Greek for a week. Women too joined in the current craze for learning. At the age of eight Cecilia Gonzaga could conjugate all the Greek verbs, while at fifteen Beatrice d'Este excelled in both Latin and Greek poetry. This knowledge of classical literature was henceforth regarded as the norm of all human culture. In referring to the Hellenic heritage, Cicero had once used the word *humanitas*, and Leonardo Bruni applied it to that of Rome as well.[1] Thus the adjective *humanus*, which in Latin meant 'well educated' and 'courteous' and many other things besides, came to designate the entire movement which this return to the tongues of the ancients appeared to have set in motion.

This passion for Latin and Greek was only one sign among many of a fever which was agitating intellectual circles at this period. Men hungered after knowledge: they were aflame with ideas. Academies were established in imitation of the institutions which had been seen, in days gone by, on the banks of the Ilissos. They had no official approbation or status, but men of culture and taste flocked to them to discuss art and literature. Princes and great noblemen mingled with them on terms of delightful familiarity. Did they not all share one state of mind? And were they not united by their most ardent cult, that of the 'divine Plato'? Today, when intellectualism so often goes hand in hand with a certain amount of pedantry, it is difficult to imagine the stirring, rapturous nature of these gatherings. Here, in an atmosphere of *camaraderie*, admiration and criticism, all the talented, knowledgeable and even outstanding individuals of the day tussled together with the most important problems of the universe. The Platonic Academy at Florence, founded at the instigation of Cosimo de' Medici, was the first such institution. It was soon followed by others at Rome and Naples. Rather later on (thanks to the influence of the learned master-printer) the 'Aldine' Academy at Venice became a leading school of Greek. Fruitful exchanges took place between one centre and another all the time. Moreover every occasion was good for an intellectual discussion. At the councils—at those of Constance and Basle, for example—the apostolic secretaries who accompanied the cardinals argued among themselves about Plautus and Terence at least as much as about theology and canon law.

Like art humanism was served by scores of men, with many varied titles to fame. They were of all sorts and conditions: Popes Nicholas V, Pius II and, later on, Leo X; Cardinals Bessarion, Bembo, Capranica, Bibbiena; clerks, monks, and even the superiors of religious

---

[1] It is in this sense that we speak of 'the classical humanities' and of 'receiving a good education in the classical humanities.'

Orders such as Traversari, Spagnoli, Canisio of Viterbo and Jerome Aleandro. But they included laymen such as the great aristocrat Pico della Mirandola, the politician Salutati, the diplomats Laurence Valla and Machiavelli, and even Manetti, the banker, as well as many less famous professors and scholars. These men, who can be seen so hard at work, exploring every avenue of the mind, were indeed an amazing band. At the beginning of the Quattrocento there was *Salutati*, chancellor of Florence, who had official documents drafted after the style of Seneca, and Leonardo Bruni, his successor, who was the first man to write his city's history. *Poggio* (1380–1459) was a scholarly discoverer of manuscripts, a sceptic philosopher and a master of the art of letter-writing. In his own lifetime Alberti was considered as much a humanist as an architect. The group included a number of Greek refugees from Byzantium, headed by *Cardinal Bessarion*— Chrysoloras, Lascaris, Argyropoulos and Gemistius—who had chosen the virtual synonym 'Plethon' in order to make his name as similar as possible to that of his idol, Plato. Following in the footsteps of these early humanists was *Marsilio Ficino* (1433–99), the favourite physician of Lorenzo the Magnificent, who made Plato the official teaching of the Florentine Academy. Among his contemporaries were two attractive aristocrats, both extremely intelligent, their minds seething with ideas: *Aeneas Sylvius Piccolomini*, a future pope, and the amazing *Pico della Mirandola* (1463–94), who, like a star, was to travel his short course bathed in a halo of beauty, genius and the reputation of universal wisdom. With Laurence Valla humanism became dialectic and critical, foreshadowing the qualities of Voltaire, but in the hands of Angelo Poliziano and Sannazar it went into raptures over the play of poetic cadences. In Rome another academy, which had been founded to rival that of Florence, was full of extravagant praise for Pomponius Leto, Perotto and *Platina* (1421–81). Here men's love of the classical carried them to the lengths of calling themselves by Latin or Greek names, decking themselves out in togas, and celebrating holidays according to the Roman, and not the Church, calendar. Obviously, in a group of such vast dimensions, both excellent and dubious elements were bound to exist. There was much to admire, much also to question, and even, as will be seen, a certain amount of scandalous licence.

What was to emerge from this enormous hotchpotch of theses, tracts and interwoven ideas? Unquestionably much that was good, and it is possible to agree that Marsilio Ficino's phrase, 'a Golden Century,' aptly describes that in which grammar, eloquence, poetry and history held such a place of honour, in which the classical languages were so frequently spoken, and in which the ancient masterpieces were purified of all the dross beneath which generations of medieval copyists had buried them. The thirst for knowledge which possessed these intellectual circles found its greatest encouragements in the humanism of Greece and Rome. Terence's famous precept is an example of this, and its influence was quite remarkable: 'I am a man, and nothing that is human seems alien to me.' The tasks of penetrating to the heart of the mystery that is man, and of seeking to find the meaning of the world and of life itself, were all equally necessary and excellent. Large numbers of these scholars and artists were passionately interested in science. Leonardo da Vinci obtained permission to dissect human corpses. Maurolycus of Messina, the founder of optical science, reproduced a rainbow with a prism and showed the nature of the crystalline lens of the eye; and Giambattista Posta, a Neapolitan, picked the first principles of natural science from amid a welter of useless material. At Brescia, Nicholas Tartaglia, a mathematical genius, succeeded in solving equations to the third degree, and his pupil, Jerome Cardano, was to go still further. There was manifest progress in every field of learning.

But this very progress raised serious problems in itself, for it was swinging forward on axes very different from those of former times. The change in studies resulted in an increasing change in methods too. What counted most henceforth, the faculty on which the humanist prided himself, was his capacity to observe, test and study the nature of things. Criticism acquired growing importance. Laurence Valla applied the methods of philological examination to the sacred texts, which quickly stripped them of their prestige. According to one Socratic maxim, truth must be sought in the free collision of ideas. At this juncture medieval scholasticism, which was founded on Divine Revelation and had constant recourse to scriptural and traditional arguments, was bound to be outmoded. Most unjustly it was relegated to the dusty debris of the past which the new society intended to destroy. Such a divorce from tradition would have its dangers for Christianity and the Church. As for the now fashionable critical methods, these probably had their uses when applied to sacred texts and traditional documents; vulgarisms were banished and legends resolutely swept away (Laurence Valla specialized in this kind of work). When they were applied to the fundamentals of faith, however, there was a danger that they might do great harm. It was all very well to ridicule the apocryphas which had been so dear to the folk of the Middle Ages, and to prove that the notorious 'Donation of Constantine' had never existed; but would this not inevitably lead to men questioning the authenticity of the Gospels or the authority of the Pope? The example of the Roman Academy was to show that this danger was all too real.

There was an even graver side to the problem. Classical humanism contained something besides cultural resources and means of expression, something more than 'the humanities': it implied a certain concept of the world, a particular attitude to life. 'O Asclepiades, what a wondrous thing is man!' These words of Hermes Trimegistus were on everyone's lips; indeed men were intoxicated with it. Beginning as the object of study—'Know thyself,' as Socrates had said—man tended to become something more: the unique centre of interest, the norm of everything, the measure of the whole world. The further the century progressed the more humanism tended to become a doctrine founded upon man alone, on his 'wondrous' nature and boundless possibilities.

There was a clear danger here of complete subversion. In the Christian perspective God, not man, was the dominant factor. It was time that Christianity itself became fundamentally humanist, since it recognized the unique character of man, and made him the recipient of revelation. Terence's maxim, of course, was Christian in spirit: it defined the love of Christ. And it was possible to detect aspects of Christianity even in the attributes which this neo-classical humanism proclaimed essential to man. Reason, for example: the Church had never denied it its place, quite the reverse. We have only to open the works of St Thomas to be convinced of this. Nature: sacred texts had exalted it for a long time past, and the Church had always rejected as heretics those who tried to condemn it, from Docetists and Gnostics down to the Cathars of recent times. But while Christianity praised nature, it made it subject to Divine Grace; although it used reason, it was a reason ordered by faith; and it exalted man only in so far as it recognized in him a divine image. The danger now was that pride would win the day, and that unique man—natural, reasonable man— would decide to do without God.

A number of the Italian humanists foresaw this and, as Christians, they strove to maintain the alliance between the new doctrines and the Christian faith to which they remained subject. Marsilio Ficino, author of a treatise *On the True Religion*, sought to indicate the fundamental connection between Christianity and the spirit of humanism by conferring a Christian meaning upon classical texts. He regarded the Platonic love of all the beauty scattered throughout the world as a kind of foretaste of revelation, and attempted a sort of apologia, in which he tried to show Christianity's relationship with the best human emotions. He even envisaged an embryonic kind of Christian-humanist spirituality. Notwithstanding several deviations, in which magic and paganism mingle with dogmas in the most bizarre fashion, and which caused him some trouble with the religious authorities, Pico della Mirandola had an even stronger conception of a humanism in which nature was exalted in all its beauty, intelligence and genius, but in which it found its fulfilment only by virtue of Divine Grace. Very wisely he was on his guard against those very excesses into which nature could so easily carry man, and he recommended asceticism; he even rebelled against the excessive cult of the humanities, which he would have liked to turn towards God. Had such minds been able to make their point of view prevail a synthesis would have been effected between humanism and the Christian religion, analogous to that which was to occur, much later, during the lifetime of St Francis de Sales. But alas, they were too few in number, and their dream—shared elsewhere by Lefèvre d'Étaples, Erasmus and Thomas More—never became a reality.

This does not mean that the great majority of humanists were divorced from Christianity; most of them were believers, or at any rate respected Christian dogmas and customs. Petrarch, the first of their line, had once said: 'The more I hear against religion, the more I love Christ, and the stronger my own faith becomes.' The somewhat unkind sarcasms which so many of them, even clerics, directed against the monks and higher clergy must not be taken too seriously; they are a part of the folklore of the age, and implied no deep convictions. Though we shall quite soon encounter a handful of bold and impious spirits among the motley band of humanists, the devout, who never had the slightest suspicion that their enthusiasm for Plato and Virgil might remotely endanger the faith, are very much more numerous. Traversari, the Camaldolese editor of St John Chrysostom, Manetti, his pupil, who spent his whole life collating the text of the Bible, Matteo Vegio, St Bernardino's biographer,[1] and the admirable *Vittorino da Feltre*, founder of the 'casa giocosa,' whose pupils were the young nobility of Mantua, who was the precursor of modern Christian pedagogy—the list of these devout humanists is a long one, particularly at the beginning of the period; but even at the end of the Quattrocento, Savonarola's sermons in Florence effected many remarkable conversions among the Platonists and other intellectuals in the city.

However—and herein lay the real peril—most humanists, sincere Christians though they were, allowed an element of paganism to linger in the centre of their thoughts, not perceiving it to be irreconcilable with their faith. Sharing the contradictory nature of their age, they found it perfectly normal to go to Mass, yet to keep a candle lit in front of Plato's bust—as did Marsilio Ficino. They preached the love of nature, but never determined at what point it could become dangerous unless rigid moral barriers were imposed upon it. Nor did they realize that this exaltation of man which they professed so loudly—and which, in the prevailing atmosphere, fell on all too many willing ears—would end by setting up man as the rival of God.

What was the Church's attitude to such a situation? We must understand that it was singularly difficult for her to obtain a clear view

---

[1] We also owe to him a description of the basilica of St Peter's which enables us to gain some impression of what the ancient Constantinian structure looked like.

of the facts and to parry the threat. She heard the new style of intellectualism and the classical themes put forward by her own men. And the
Latin that roused such keen enthusiasm was her own sacred language,
used in her liturgy and by the Fathers of the Church. Besides, St
Augustine, St Jerome and the Greeks as well—St John Chrysostom
and St Gregory Nazianzus—seemed likely to benefit from the trend
which was impelling scholars towards the treasures of the past.
Religious teaching might well be rejuvenated and revitalized by these
new methods. After all, she herself, *Ecclesia mater*, had been the
protector of all pedagogy in the dark days when her monasteries and
cathedrals were the scholars' only refuge. In addition, advanced
teaching remained in her hands at Pavia, Milan and Padua; also at
Rome, where the College of the Sapienza was regaining all its old
importance, and where Cardinal Capranica in 1460 founded a theological college that was soon to become famous. The Church could
even imagine that the doctrinal position of the humanists contained
something of her own views. Platonism might be winning the day, but,
thanks to the mediation of St Augustine and the other Early Fathers,
and of pseudo-Denys the Areopagite in particular, not to mention
Boethius, 'the father of scholasticism,' its influence had always affected
Christianity to some extent. Plato proclaimed the existence of God,
creator of all things, and also the expression of the supreme beauty
which man recognized in the created world of which he was a part;
it was probably an exaggeration to call him 'the Greek Moses,' but this
excess did not seem particularly blameworthy. In turning away from
Aristotle and his disciple St Thomas, were not the humanists merely
finding a different way of attaining the Truth, achieved by substituting
Plato's mysticism and sensibility for Aristotle's rational logic? None
of this seemed remotely dangerous.

Modern historians who have examined the Church's attitude to
humanism are divided into two schools of thought. The first,[1] while
admitting that both popes and cardinals showed 'excessive indulgence,'
considers that the Church acted wisely 'in linking herself with the
movement which was overwhelming the human mind,' and which was
moreover irresistible. The second,[2] though not denying that the
Renaissance and humanism eventually contributed a great deal to
Christianity, observes that the Church should not always associate
herself purely and simply with the trends of the age however irresistible they may be, and that in this instance she ought to have fought
more energetically against the formidable tendencies which were
apparent therein. Obviously the best course would have been for the
Church to welcome those attributes of humanism which could assist

[1] Baudrillart, for instance.
[2] Jean Giraud.

her own rejuvenation, while inspiring them with her principles. Long ago she had taken, or tried to take, this course on another plane, when faced with the Roman Empire, the chaos of the Dark Ages and the violence of feudalism. In this kind of situation, however, it has always been hard to keep Christian society free of contamination, for it is a society composed of human beings who do not always see clearly, and who are creatures of ordinary flesh and blood. The solving of the grave problem which confronted the Church amid the brilliant complexity of the Quattrocento needed a genius able to grasp all the fundamentals of the age and of co-ordinating them with the Christian revelation. But another St Thomas was lacking, and the Church advanced across the shifting sands amid confusion and uncertainty.

THREE POPES, HUMANISM AND THE TURKS

The pontificate of Nicholas V had been a Golden Age for the humanists. There had certainly been a number of popes favourable to learning and the arts before his time: Innocent VII, who had concerned himself with the restoration of the Roman University even at the height of the Great Schism; Martin V, who, with Capranica's help, had filled the college of apostolic secretaries with intellectuals; and Eugenius IV, to whom the College of Sapienza owed its lustre, and who had discovered and shielded Traversari, the great Christian humanist. However, matters had been put on quite a different footing with Nicholas V. Young Thomas Parentucelli had considered all humanists his friends, and on becoming pope he had immediately summoned as many of them as possible to Rome. The trouble was that he had not chosen very well; there was little the matter with Filelfio, who was merely a conceited fop, but Poggio and, from a moral point of view, Panormitus were totally unsuitable. Nor was it exactly opportune to flatter Laurence Valla, as Nicholas V had done, while the Neapolitan's anticlericalism was causing so much scandal—although this was an age when men were not easily shocked by this particular theme. But the humanist Pope was an indulgent man. He had been interested only in the lustre he imagined would accrue to the papal throne from the presence around it of so many brilliant minds.

Would his successors follow his example? In fact circumstances were such that they seemed to be utterly absorbed in matters of a very different order. This was indeed the period when the West at long last became aware of the Turkish menace. The fall of Constantinople had not marked the end of the Moslem attack; on the contrary it might even be asked if it were not their intention to annex the whole of Europe. The reader will remember [1] that, no sooner was he victorious

[1] See Chapter II, section, 'The Final Tremors.'

over Byzantium than Mohammed II hurled his forces against Wallachia, Serbia and Hungary. . . . Despite the heroic resistance offered
by John Hunyadi and Scanderbeg, the advance of the Crescent now
seemed irresistible; each year signalled some new triumph for the
aggressor. In 1458 the Morea fell, and the Prophet's banner waved
above the Acropolis; Serbia was conquered in 1459, and was soon
followed by Bosnia and Herzegovina; the Aegean islands succumbed,
one by one; in 1470 Venice allowed Negroponte, the fortress of
Euboea, to be swept from her hands. Ten years later the terrible flood-
tide reached Italy; in 1480 Otranto was stormed by a Turkish raiding
party, and a cry of horror and despair resounded throughout the
peninsula.

In a situation of this kind it is understandable that Nicholas V's
successor considered it his first, nay, his sole duty to confront the
menace of Islam. Yet the new Pope was an old and somewhat un-
obtrusive figure, of high moral probity. His principal titles to the triple
crown were his advanced age of seventy-seven years—in other words,
the general hope that he would not long occupy the See of Peter—and
also the fact that he was a foreigner, which meant that the Orsinis and
Colonnas could agree to accept him as a candidate suitable to both
camps. *Alonso Borja* (in Italian *Borgia*) was a Spaniard of humble
origins, and his name would never have acquired much fame had his
family not later contrived to give it a bizarre notoriety. Nevertheless
during his three years at the Vatican (1455–8), *Callixtus* III was very
far from inactive. It was in answer to his appeal that John Hunyadi and
St John Capistrano launched their counter offensive against the Turks,
which resulted in the saving of Belgrade in 1456; and during the
following year the fleet he had created seized twenty-five Turkish
vessels. Anxious to undertake a regular crusade, he approached the
sovereigns of the great states, even going so far as to sound the King
of France upon the matter and rehabilitating Joan of Arc. But although
he did his utmost to prepare the way for this mighty enterprise all his
efforts were fruitless; the time for such things was now long past.

A pope so preoccupied with political affairs could devote little time
to intellectual pleasures. Unlike Nicholas V, he was no 'father' to the
humanists; but so far from turning his back on them, he continued to
employ the services of Valla, for he remained a medieval Spaniard all
his life, and never dreamed that humanism might raise a serious
problem for the Church. This well-intentioned and devout Christian
can be held largely responsible for the degradation which the climate
of the Renaissance was to inflict upon her. Spaniards are generally
considered to possess a highly developed sense of family, and in the
mind of Callixtus III this very natural sense was strengthened by
political considerations. In Rome he was regarded as 'the foreigner';

and he was well aware that the Sacred College, with a view to dominating the papal throne, was wont before each conclave to attempt the imposition of a statute upon the future pontiff, limiting his authority. In order therefore to strengthen his position Borgia summoned other members of the family to his court. The laymen among them were granted a *condotta*, a licence permitting them to enlist mercenaries for the defence of the Papal States, and one of these was the Gonfalonier of the Church. Worse was to follow: the Curia and Vatican offices were entrusted to other Borgias who were either clerics already or who were admitted to holy orders for this purpose. *Nepotism* was of course no new thing: Eugenius IV had showered gifts on his nephews. The circumstances make it easily explicable, but it was one of the major causes of the Church's lamentable decline. The least that can be said of the three young nephews whom Callixtus III elevated to the purple is that none of them was personally worthy of the honour. One of them was a cynical libertine—'*il più carnal uomo*' the Romans called him—brilliant, courageous and artistic, but with few moral virtues. His name was Roderigo Borgia—the future Pope Alexander VI.

On the death of the Spanish Pope a majority of the cardinals quickly agreed to elect an Italian. Their intended choice was Cardinal Capranica, who would certainly have made a great pope had he not followed Callixtus to the grave only a few days after the latter's death. One other individual in the Sacred College occupied a position which, if not undisputed, was at all events considerable; and despite some opposition, notably from Cardinal d'Estouteville, he was elected. The new pontiff was none other than the astonishing Aeneas Sylvius Piccolomini, whom we have observed picking his way through the thorny thickets of the immediate past with an impudent charm and quite unusual luck. Piccolomini was a man of considerable guile. He had served a succession of important ecclesiastics, ranging from Capranica to the antipope Felix V, and had proved himself adept at leaving a sinking ship at the first sign of impending disaster. In the days when the Council had seemed to triumph at Basle, he had been an ardent supporter of conciliar supremacy, but once Eugenius IV had firmly grasped the helm of the 'navicella' he had proved himself more papalist than the Pope. Moreover he was a complex character, typical of his age, switching his mood and his behaviour as freely as his convictions. He began life as an impetuous, aggressive type of person, of somewhat loose morals, and was the author of a number of romantic novels which can justly be called the ancestors of the modern love-story. Then, having taken Holy Orders without much enthusiasm—'*timeo continentiam*,' as he himself admitted—he completely mastered his frailties of the flesh. He became pious and ascetic, so devout that he went on pilgrimage barefooted. Moreover he had a scintillating intellect, an extremely erudite mind and the ability to judge men and situations with considerable shrewdness. When he became *Pius II* he was fifty-three years old.

Unhappily Providence did not give him time to show the full extent of his capacities. The six years of his pontificate (1458–64) scarcely allowed him time to introduce a policy that would have been quite outstanding if brought to fruition. Pius himself was a humanist, and had connections with all the great intellectuals of the age. He invited many of his own stamp to the Vatican, but, unlike Nicholas V, never reposed excessive confidence in any of them. A lover of the arts, he encouraged artists, and Pinturicchio's wonderful frescoes in the library at Siena, which were commissioned by his nephew (subsequently the ephemeral Pius III) are a worthy tribute to his good taste, as is that exquisite little town which he had built on the site of his birth-place and which still bears his name—Pienza. The Roman Academy of Leto and Platina received much support from him, even though he considered it to be excessively enamoured of pagan ideas. The Pope continued his own literary endeavours. He produced those unforgettable *Commentàries* which are a mine of information for the historian. He also dreamed of making Dante take another journey to Hell under the guidance of St Bernardino of Siena; and when the pamphleteers reminded him that his literature had not always been so exemplary he answered them courageously, repudiating the sins of his youth: '*Aeneam rejicite, Pium accipite!*'

In fact this scholar who was now Pope assumed full charge of the Church, devoting to his task all the energy and intelligence he possessed. He was alive to every one of the major problems of the age. Naples, where Ferdinand of Aragon had succeeded to the Anjou inheritance, must be prevented from setting all southern Italy ablaze; order must be maintained in Rome, where a certain Tiburzio was hatching a fruitless conspiracy; Sigismund Malatesta's ambition must be held in check. Germany too needed closely watching, and efforts must be made to restore peace to Bohemia, where the Hussite War had laid bare so many open wounds. Finally, a settlement must be reached with Louis XI, lest the Pragmatic Sanction render the King of France absolute head of the French clergy. Pius II performed marvels on this vast keyboard. However, one grandiose and remarkable idea dominated everything he did, demonstrating a belated medievalism in his characteristically Renaissance personality: he sought to revive the idea of a crusade, to unite the whole of Christendom against the Turk. The fiasco of the Congress of Mantua, to which he had vainly summoned the emperor and all the secular heads of Europe, probably made him realize that his dream was a delusion. Christendom was dead, and modern Europe not yet born. Nevertheless he resolved to wage the struggle alone, or almost alone, as if to save his own honour;[1] and a fleet, to which Venice condescended to contribute a few ships, was assembled at Ancona. But pestilence now took a hand in the affair. Pius II died of the epidemic, far-sighted, anxious and, at the end, probably in a state of utter despair.

The humanist Nicholas V had been succeeded by a man who had almost totally ignored the intellectual movement of the day, and Pius II had restored humanism to favour. Would this almost constant law of alternation, according to which one pontiff was succeeded by another of completely different tendencies and temperament, operate yet again? Unexpectedly enough *Paul II* (1464–71) was sufficiently wise to understand what was the Church's most serious problem— the increasingly far-reaching effect which the insidious influence of Renaissance was exerting upon society, and the consequent dangers that threatened the Christian faith. Such wisdom was unexpected; for this handsome, attractive man was not outstandingly intelligent. As a Venetian too, delighting in all the luxury associated with those born and bred on the banks of the Grand Canal, he possessed no element of asceticism, even though he declined the extravagant gifts offered him by foreign ambassadors immediately after his election. The palace he built at Venice, occupied in recent times by Mussolini, still bears witness to his judgment of what a papal residence should be; and it was during his pontificate that the Roman festivals, carnivals and triumphs acquired the ostentatious though scarcely edifying character which they henceforth possessed. Paul II was less actively concerned than his predecessor with the Church's major interests. He confined his struggle against the Turks to a few fair words, which did nothing to prevent the fall of Negroponte; his discussions with Louis XI ended in failure; and in awarding the cardinal's hat to Jean de la Balue he cannot be said to have enriched the Sacred College. With this exception he tried to nominate men of merit to high ecclesiastical office, but he did little to prevent such dignitaries as Cardinal Roderigo Borgia from leading a life that was the reverse of exemplary.

All the same it was this rather frivolous and languid aristocrat who was the first to raise the crucial question. Not that he was a barbarian, as the Roman humanists suggested after his death. He loved the arts, supported scholars and schools, and restored a number of classical monuments, e.g. the arches of Titus and Septimius Severus, and the equestrian statue of Marcus Aurelius. With the help of Cardinal Juan Torquemada and Bussi, the 'corrector' and editor of the classics, he encouraged printers to establish themselves in Rome. But the tendencies

---

[1] At this juncture he took the curious step of writing a friendly and detailed letter to Mohammed II, suggesting that the latter be converted to Christianity, and thus become Emperor of the East. But the conquering Sultan did not feel the vocation of Clovis. . . .

of certain humanists disturbed him greatly. He began by dismissing over-advanced intellectuals from the 'College of Abbreviators'—a kind of Vatican secretariat-general—and when Platina objected to this in impudent language, he interrogated him very severely, and then threw him into prison. Next, the members of the Roman Academy, the institution of which Leto claimed to be 'Pontifex Maximus,' concocted a conspiracy of intellectuals at the Procaro—rather after the style of Gracchus or Catiline—and held secret meetings in the Catacombs. Leto and his fellow conspirators were imprisoned in the castle of Sant' Angelo, and were not released until they had made a full apology the humility of which had nothing in common with the proud bearing of their classical ancestors. 'If God spares me for the task,' exclaimed the Pope, after the discovery of this plot, 'I shall forbid the study of absurd histories and foolish poems, for they are full of heresy and evil spells.' This was a very wise decision. Was it not high time that the Church resisted certain tendencies inherent in the Renaissance and humanist movements? It is to Paul II's credit that he thought in such terms.

THE ERA OF MACHIAVELLI

As humanism developed, those features which suggested a threat to the Catholic faith became more marked, and among its leaders were some for whom Christianity had less and less meaning. The coexistence of pagan tendencies and traditional beliefs, which are apparent to some extent in all the humanists, led in some cases to a definite predominance of the former over the latter. Christian scholars sincerely regarded Graeco-Roman culture as a means of enlarging the bases of their faith, and saw in the classical ideal an ally of gospel morality. But another type of intellectual now sprang into importance alongside them. This, though it undoubtedly included a number of distinguished minds, also swarmed with vain and servile hacks, acknowledging no religion and no law, who pandered to the despots and were quick to flatter man's basest instincts. Christian humanism was increasingly opposed by a pagan humanism which, from now on, was of a very determined kind. In men like Poggio, Valla, Panormizio and Filelfio, whose influence had been allowed to grow too excessive by a few over-indulgent popes, the Church ought to have recognized her enemies.

Nevertheless a number of far-sighted people, including Petrarch, had already grasped the danger. As early as 1404 the saintly and learned Dominican, *Giovanni Dominici*, wrote a booklet entitled *Lucula Noctis* ('a small beam in the darkness'), warning Salutati, the Florentine chancellor, against the pagan deviations which he could see developing in the intellectualist trend. 'It is more profitable for

H

Christians to till the soil, than to devote their time to reading pagan books,' he declared. But his words had been considered as no more than an example of ecclesiastical eloquence. Nevertheless there was a very real danger that scholars and artists would be tempted to find in classical paganism justification for a concept of life which was radically opposed to that of Christianity; and as the Quattrocento advanced this peril became increasingly obvious.

It began as a vociferous campaign against the Church and her authority; a campaign rendered so much the easier to conduct in that she had laid herself wide open to criticism. Nothing was respected. Poggio, the precursor of Voltaire, regarded priests as mere knaves and idlers, who, 'under the cloak of faith, were interested only in acquiring wealth without working for it.' Besides, it was common knowledge that their conduct was a permanent source of scandal. The bad example emanated from above, from the Curia itself, 'where the vices of the world abound to such an extent that it mirrors them all.' They were vices which Lapo de Castiglionchio gladly enumerated: 'arrogance, avarice, mendacity, boastfulness, greed, luxury, perfidy and immorality. . . .' The regulars were considered no more sacrosanct, rather the reverse: their alleged monastic vocation was said to be a sham façade, erected to trap the innocent customer of their wares! Monks were the target of pamphlets by Poggio, Leonardo Bruni and Filelfio. As for nuns, 'the lights o' love benefit humanity more than they do,' asserted Laurence Valla. It is hard not to wonder why men who proposed such views were employed as papal officials; Poggio held such a position for fifty years!

Needless to say the Church's methods were attacked, as well as her personnel. Scholasticism was the particular object of general sarcasm; men ridiculed its fruitless rambling, unnecessary arguments and intellectual gymnastics. In fact, it was not simply the method which was under fire; the very basis was being attacked, and piece by piece the whole of Catholic theology was being reduced to ruins. An intellectual attitude, utterly unknown to the Middle Ages, now began to make its appearance in the form of religious scepticism. This was a fact of capital importance, perhaps the most important in the whole spiritual history of the Christian West; it marks the birth of the 'modern world,' the beginning of its errors and betrayals. From now onwards this scepticism is apparent in the minds of certain intellectuals. At first it was only half conscious and ill defined, but it slowly gained ground. We can discount the scepticism of writers like Boccaccio, Bembo, or even Angelo Poliziano. Boccaccio continued to observe the forms of Christianity and treated the Church with respect, at the same time letting it be understood in his famous novel, *The Three Rings*, that all religions were equally meritorious. Bembo asserted that he had no desire to read the breviary, lest its deplorable Latin might spoil his taste for the language. Such a pronouncement, coming from the lips of a cardinal, was remarkable, to say the least. Angelo Poliziano confessed that he preferred Pindar's odes to David's psalms, and had only opened the Gospels once in his life; it is abundantly clear that the poet was a canon only in name and income! Others, however, entertained a far more resolute and deep-seated scepticism, involving the denial of dogmas, and a more or less complete rejection of faith. Laurence Valla systematically undermined all the bases of Christian morality by asserting that the ethics of Epicurus were far more meritorious. Marsupini, Bruni's successor as chancellor of Florence, refused the Sacraments on his deathbed (which did not prevent his fellows citizens from erecting a magnificent tomb for him in the Church of Santa Croce). The leading members of the Roman Academy, Platina and Leto, behaved—to use an anachronistic comparison—like veritable Freethinkers, worthy of M. Homais. Pomponnazzi denied the immortality of the soul, and as he drew his last breath reasserted his conviction that death was total and final. As for Pontana, the Neapolitan poet and founder of the Pontanian Academy, which rivalled that of Rome, he spared not one Christian dogma, mercilessly criticizing them all in a style reminiscent of Lucian, and under pretext of putting an end to old superstitions. These many representatives of the irreligious mind, however, were always on their guard, quick to excuse themselves and to proclaim their obedience to Holy Mother Church whenever the Inquisition got wind of their views. But in Italy, at all events, the Holy Office seemed a little hard of hearing when blasphemy called for their attention, and showed extraordinary indulgence towards humanists of all shades of opinion.

For these sceptics the Christian faith was hardly more than an empty shell. What did they put in its place? A pagan ideal which they claimed to have adopted from their classical idols, and which no longer had anything in common with religious truths and the norms of traditional morality. The Christian concept of life rested on the belief that human nature was corrupted by sin and needed God's help to recover its integrity; that man could participate supernaturally in the divine life on condition that he led a good life and received the Grace of God. Such Christian humanists as Marsilio Ficino and Pico della Mirandola were loyal to this concept. Paganism was based on the radically different theory that nature itself was the sole condition of everything that existed in the world, the goal of all knowledge and action, the criterion which enabled man to appreciate what was right, healthy and perfect. Pagan humanism established itself firmly on these bases.

Thus *sequere naturam* became the axiom, the rule of conduct. In

France Rabelais expressed it most completely in his fictitious Liberty
Hall, whose motto was: 'Do exactly what you please, because all free,
well-born, well-educated people have a natural instinct and stimulus
which invariably encourages them towards virtue.' Men who professed
these beliefs had few illusions. Following nature meant for them a
total obedience to natural instincts; the question of their moral value
was altogether irrelevant. In such perspectives the Christian revelation
became nothing but a useless impediment. The true revelation was that
of man himself, fulfilling the whole of his nature, going to the furthest
limits in his quest for self-satisfaction, 'living his life' to the full.

Here we touch the heart of this new civilization, and find its fundamental explanation. The proclaimed ideal was that of *virtù*. This word,
which is almost impossible to translate into French or English, implies
that quality of soul possessed by the individual whose self-assertion is
total, and who is determined to derive his ultimate end and ultimate
perfection from his own personality and efforts. The fact that some of
the individual qualities which he intends to develop to the full may
include attributes which morality regards as defects and vices is not of
the slightest consequence. *Virtù*, real greatness, was just as present in
crime as in the work of art. Those magnificent and awe-inspiring
figures, the contemporary despots who achieved the whole of their
particular 'virtuality' through cruelty and treachery, were models of
virtù; but the great financier who triumphed by gambling his florins
was another example of the same pattern. The importance acquired by
the concept of 'genius,' a concept entirely unknown to the Middle
Ages, is typical of this period. The ideal was now the man who was
master of his own destiny, who built his life just as he created his own
work; he was, quite literally, a 'superman.' [1] When Nietzsche wrote
that 'man is a creature who wishes to be surpassed' he was merely
giving concrete expression to the Renaissance dream.

There was even a kind of Satanic grandeur in this concept, a kind
of grandeur that is found in the most evil rulers. But for lesser men,
who were not so concerned with *virtù*, following nature meant nothing
more or less than yielding to their least elevated instincts. In trying to
fulfil himself man was in fact being degraded. This is the origin of
the sensuality, and even of the gross debauchery, which are characteristic of the age. Some pagan humanists delighted in describing and
justifying it in their writings. Boccaccio had opened the way for this
type of literature with his relatively discreet erotic tales. Laurence
Valla wrote an entire treatise on *Sensual Pleasure*, which he described
as 'the true goodness.' Poggio, Filelfio, Platina and several others

---

[1] To be accurate, a classical demi-god, Poggio, wrote: 'Heaven belongs by right to
vigorous men who have maintained great struggles and accomplished mighty works on
earth.' The human archetype was no longer the saint, but Hercules.

shared his view. The modern reader stands abashed before the openly pornographic character of so many of the novels, poems and comedies of the age, whether their author be a prince like Lorenzo the Magnificent, or a future pope like Aeneas Sylvius Piccolomini. The record in this direction is held by Beccadelli, known as Panormizio, who describes the traditional Greek vice of sodomy with a crudity and enthusiasm which even no twentieth-century writer has yet been able to approach.

This sensualization of literature, which had its more restrained parallel in the field of art, corresponded all too closely with the kind of behaviour common in men's daily lives. The chronicles of the times are full of these debaucheries, and there is little point in listing them here. Anyone can guess what the results of 'follow nature' might be when applied without restraints, and indeed the Quattrocento had its full share of atrocious deeds of revenge, assassination and treacherous poisoning. We are bound to take Machiavelli seriously when he writes, as if it were the most ordinary thing in the world: 'As for us Italians, we are thoroughly irreligious and depraved!'

Machiavelli! The very name of this all-seeing witness of his era has symbolic significance. This calm, cool individual, sauntering through the squares and offices of Florence just as the Quattrocento was acquiring its peculiar stamp, was an observer and nothing more; but he was probably the shrewdest observer that any age has ever known. There was a perpetual smile on his thin lips, and nothing escaped the sharp eyes beneath the hooded lids. Machiavelli watched the life of his contemporaries rather as a scientist studies the habits of birds or insects. He analysed their behaviour and movements with the strict accuracy of an entomologist; he formulated laws whereby it seemed to be governed, laws akin to those of mathematics or sociology, wholly unrelated to moral principles. He saw vice and virtue as mere natural phenomena and nothing else. He regarded his compatriots' depravity and irreligion as a simple fact: it was not a subject on which one should wax indignant.[1]

Machiavelli founded his dominant theory upon this radical amorality, but he wisely and deliberately avoided making too obvious a break with official customs and principles. His political treatise, *The Prince*, was the perfect expression of his mind. While the term *Machiavellianism* is inaccurate when it suggests that the author himself possessed these cunning intentions and underhand methods, it is just in so far as it

[1] He was right when he harshly criticized the temporal policy of the popes. They were incapable of unifying Italy, and their policy merely succeeded in maintaining its divisions and inviting foreign intervention. The one occasion on which Machiavelli really felt in full agreement with the Church was when the militant Papacy, under Julius II, took up the sword to chase the French out of Italy, in other words, on the very occasion when the Church played a completely unchristian role!

characterizes a political system entirely devoid of principles, the very system which Niccolò Machiavelli could see with his own eyes. In divided, unstable Italy the technique of power appeared to demand the employment of trickery intermingled with brute force, and a combination of intrigue and cruelty. The end justified the means, and anything was right and proper in the name of *virtù*. What was the good of Christianity, with its precepts of gentleness, humility and loving kindness, in the face of demands like these. Such qualities were absurd in the realm of politics. By the time this man had finished his heartless observations, the divorce between the religion which had been Western society's basis for centuries past and the world which was in process of being born was absolute. The rupture was complete.

When Pope Paul II reacted so violently against the pagan tendencies of humanism and the Renaissance it is probable that he did not fully understand their potentialities. But the vision of Christian society tainted by neo-paganism was far from illusory. A day might come when the Papacy itself would be interested solely in the arts, or, even worse, might yield to 'nature' in its most degrading form. The history of the popes who succeeded the aged Patriarch of Venice was one of increasing surrender to this triple temptation.

THE DOWNWARD SLOPE: SIXTUS IV AND INNOCENT VIII

'The historian of the Church will be the better able to bring out the meaning of her divine origin, which is superior to any purely terrestrial and natural order, since he is loyal enough not to conceal the terrible ordeals which the sins of her children and, on occasion, of her own ministers, have inflicted upon the Bride of Christ during the course of centuries.' These words of Leo XIII [1] spring immediately to mind as we enter upon this painful period, which is the most melancholy in the whole history of Christianity; and they serve to encourage and console us. The spectacle provided by the Bride of Christ over a period of fifty years is so distressing that filial respect instinctively prevents its description, and one would like to be able to turn quickly from the stained and sullied page. It is possible, however, to offer some excuse for those popes who often proved themselves most unworthy repositories of the sacred treasure entrusted to their charge. They must be judged against the background of their own times. Its customs were not ours, and, in particular, it was dominated by a sexual licence which is hard to imagine even today. It must also be remembered that after the failure of the final attempt towards a Christian universalism, which had been made by Pius II, the dangers confronting both Italy and the papal throne were such that the popes may be considered justified in

[1] In a letter to the French clergy, 8th September 1899.

regarding as their prime duty a political line of action which our
notions render quite out of place in a successor of St Peter. Nevertheless no Catholic can but blush with shame at the memory of pontificates like those of Sixtus IV, Innocent VIII and, above all, of the
Borgia pope, Alexander VI. It may be fair to suspend final judgment on
such men, but righteous indignation is inevitable; any other sentiment
could be supported only by apologetics of a most unworthy kind.

Yet Francesco della Rovere, who became pope on the death of
Paul II, was not a wicked man. The candidature of the austere Cardinal
Bessarion had been rejected, and the new pontiff, who was elected
through the concerted action of Cardinal Borgia and the Orsini
faction, adopted the name of *Sixtus IV* (1471–84). Sixtus came of an
impoverished branch of a noble Ligurian family. It was thanks to the
Franciscans that he was able to pursue a brilliant scholastic career at
Padua, and his ability had won him the generalship of his Order. He
was a simple, virtuous religious, whose morals have never been
criticized, and who undoubtedly continued to lead an upright life after
his election to the papal throne; had he been otherwise his austere
confessor, Blessed Amadeus of Portugal, would not have remained at
his side. His poor beginnings and Franciscan upbringing, however,
had clearly not prepared him to handle the enormous sums of money
which henceforth came into his hands, and certain people knew exactly
how to take advantage of this weakness.

In Callixtus III's time the Spaniards at the Roman Court had carried
family loyalty too far, but the example of Sixtus IV showed that the
Italians were more than a match in this field. The new Pope had two
brothers and four sisters, and their offspring provided him with no
fewer than fifteen nephews and nieces. He loved them all so dearly
that he was incapable of refusing them anything. Violating the undertakings which he had signed before his election, Sixtus hastened to
make two of his nephews cardinals. While one of them—Giulio,
subsequently Pope Julius II—had various talents which could, to
some extent, justify his choice, the other, Pietro Riario, a young
blood of twenty-nine, abandoned himself to such riotous living
that all Rome was shocked—a very rare occurrence! His debaucheries
were such that he was dead within three years: the Vatican was
besmirched by his scandalous escapades. As for the other nephews,
one became prefect of Rome and the other a governor in the papal
cities; the nieces were provided with wealthy husbands. An Italian
prince of the period would have acted no differently.

However, Sixtus IV did not lack good intentions, and it cannot
fairly be said in his case, as it can in others, that the pope in him was
effaced by the prince. It is not true that he despised the interests of the
Church. When the Turks, whose sallies were becoming increasingly

bold, reached Italy and sacked Otranto, where they committed countless atrocities, Sixtus refused to flee to Avignon. Instead he managed
to send out a fleet which recaptured Otranto from the Moslems, for
Mohammed II was now dead. He tried to continue his predecessor's
policy towards Louis XI of France, and the ephemeral Concordat of
1472 was intended to put an end to the abuses which had resulted from
the Pragmatic Sanction. He encouraged the Spanish monarchs to
undertake the final stage of the *Reconquista*, and also attempted to
establish relations with Russia.[1] Even the question of ecclesiastical
reform was not neglected; Sixtus had the vision to realize that troops
must be enlisted before battle could be joined, and his bull *Mare
Magnum*, reorganizing the Mendicant Orders, was a very useful
measure. But the same weakness which led him to the practice of
nepotism deterred him from the consistent pursuit of a sound ecclesiastical policy. After the recapture of Otranto he abandoned operations
against the Turks; his relations with Louis XI were lethargic,
the wily French monarch trifling with him as he pleased; and finally,
even while he was talking about reform of the Church, he was appoint-
ing to the Sacred College far too many men devoid of all moral worth.

Needless to say under such a pope the humanists had little difficulty
in reoccupying the positions from which Paul II had dismissed them.
There was a return to the traditions of Nicholas V. The groups of
intellectuals summoned to Rome at this period undoubtedly contained
some distinguished names: the Greek scholar Argyropoulos, the great
German astronomer Regiomontanus, and the attractive, devout
Sigismondo del Conti, author of an enormous *Contemporary History*
in seventeen volumes. Meanwhile, however, the clique at the Roman
Academy gained the upper hand. The Vatican Library, with its count-
less precious manuscripts, was put in the charge of none other than
Platina, who at once started work on his *History of the Popes*. This
was dedicated to Sixtus IV, whom it praised as lavishly as it denigrated
Paul II. On the librarian's death Rome was astonished to see his friend
Pomponius Leto, a notorious pagan, mount the pulpit of Santa Maria
Maggiore to pronounce the funeral oration. The wheel had turned full
circle. Sixtus IV was indeed a perfect 'Pope of the Renaissance' in the
worst sense of the phrase. In the Vatican itself the glorious Sistine
Chapel, which bears his name, and the hall of the library still remind
us that this knowledgeable lover of art had the good taste to employ
Botticelli, Ghirlandaijo, Perugino, Signorelli and other famous artists.
But his splendid achievements as a generous patron of the arts are small
compensation for the indisputable decadence that beset the Church
during his reign and which marked the beginning of her downward
path.

[1] See *The Catholic Reformation*, Chapter IV.

In 1478 a terrible tragedy shocked the whole of Italy. Giulio de' Medici was assassinated in the cathedral of Santa Maria del Fiore during High Mass. His brother Lorenzo escaped, and, having established himself in power, butchered every conspirator he could lay hands on, together with their friends. It very soon became known that a nephew of the Pope, who was married to a Sforza, had organized the plot; that another Rovere, an eighteen-year-old cardinal, was also implicated; and that the Pope himself, aware of what was going on, had confined himself to counselling feebly the avoidance of any bloodshed. . . . This was the kind of situation to which the Holy See's entanglement in Renaissance politics could lead. In the war which followed this crime it was all very well for Sixtus IV to throw the weight of his spiritual power, enforced by excommunication, into one of the scales. What authority would the ordinary run of mankind allow a pope who lent himself to the familiar stratagems of contemporary despots?

Unfortunately, on the death of Sixtus IV, the law of alternation failed to operate as usual, and the pontificate of Innocent VIII (1484–1492) was no better. The circumstances of Innocent's election made any improvement virtually impossible. The new Pope, a wealthy Genoese, owed the triple crown solely to two factors: the schemes of Giulio della Rovere, whose creature he was and remained, and the anxiety of the cardinals to escape from the mob which went howling through the city and pillaged the mansion of the prefect Riario, the dead man's nephew. In order to make his choice more certain the astute candidate made a written promise to his future electors, agreeing to grant each of them whatever he might ask, an undertaking which clearly constituted the crime of simony. The man himself, moreover, was affable and pleasant, but of a sickly appearance. He was abominably weak: compared with him Sixtus IV seemed like a rock. Innocent was known to have two natural children. Under such a pontiff the decline of the Church was bound to be accelerated.

Consequently the balance-sheet of the eight years of this pontificate shows heavy liabilities. What can be put on the credit side? Defence of the faith against the adventurous theories of Pico della Mirandola; the promulgation of the bull *Summis desiderantes* against the follies resulting from belief in witchcraft;[1] papal support for the enterprise of the Spanish sovereigns; the continuance of Rome's position as the capital of poetry and the arts, which was ensured by the Pope's success in attracting to his court Angelo Poliziano, Mantegna, Filipino Lippi and other famous men. The debit column heavily outweighs this mediocre credit. All the states, from Venice to France, and from

---

[1] This, however, was a two-edged sword, and repression in its turn gave rise to even worse follies.

* H

Portugal to Hungary, openly flouted papal authority and disposed of their benefices exactly as they pleased. The struggle against the Turks was abandoned.[1] Owing to the venal system of preferment the Vatican administration was increasingly controlled by unworthy men, and was rocked to its foundations by the scandal of false bulls, which were drafted in some thieves' kitchen and authorized all manner of things, even permitting priests to maintain concubines. The Sacred College was filled with worldly cardinals, who were passionately fond of building luxurious palaces and indulging in licentious pastimes. Among them was a thirteen-year-old boy, Giovanni de' Medici, who had received the purple in token of the Pope's gratitude to his father, the great Lorenzo. The latter had given his daughter in marriage to the pontiff's own bastard, a marriage solemnized by Innocent VIII himself in his own palace. . . .[2] It is easy to understand why the Church resounded with indignant protests at the sight of such occurrences. Above this clamour rose one terrible voice, echoing against the towers of San Gimignano and across the Florentine squares, announcing that divine chastisement was imminent. But even if the pronouncements of one insignificant Dominican friar had penetrated to the Vatican, they would have been regarded as nothing more than pulpit oratory and malicious gossip.[3]

THE TEMPTATION OF THE FLESH: ALEXANDER VI, BORGIA

Two years after Innocent VIII had given up the ghost, however, the tragedy predicted by the Dominican Savonarola actually came to pass. The armies of this new Gog and Magog, the instruments of divine justice, were none other than those of the King of France. The prudent Louis XI had been succeeded by the mediocre Charles VIII (1491–1498), a neurotic weakling, with thick, pendulous lips, the worthy scion of a diseased stock which had produced one mad and several sickly monarchs. This twenty-two-year-old king, whose head was stuffed with tales of chivalry, was nevertheless endowed with a strength of purpose out of all proportion to his feeble body. He dreamed of unifying Italy, making it the spring-board for a new crusade, recapturing Constantinople from the Turk, and assuming the sacred Crown of Jerusalem. The extremely dubious rights which he held from the Anjous—his cousins twenty times removed—provided him with the excuse to claim possession of Naples, which was then in the hands of

---

[1] Innocent VIII scored a point against Bajazet II quite by chance. The Sultan quarrelled with his brother, Djem, who fled to Rome and was received with great honour.

[2] Later on the marriage of the Pope's grand-daughter to an Aragonese prince from Naples was celebrated in the same way.

[3] See p. 227.

the Aragonese. Lodovico 'the Moor,' the Sforza despot of Milan, encouraged him. After entering into three disastrous treaties, whereby a section of good French soil was sacrificed to what Commines rightly called 'this pipe-dream,' Charles hurled his armies into his daring adventure. While the Duke of Orleans occupied Genoa, the king himself swept down into the valley of the Po. Its inhabitants trembled before his artillery, which was the best of the age. Cities which resisted him, such as Lucca, were severely punished. Florence had just revolted against the Medici, and expelled them. In November 1494 the foreign conqueror entered her gates, amid the glare of hundreds of torches, riding beneath a sumptuous canopy, clad in a golden cloak, amid the flash of naked swords, collars and cuirasses. This was no longer just one of those countless internecine wars with which the peninsula was so familiar: this was a foreign invasion, which possibly foreshadowed servitude.

The Papacy's position was serious, for the French army surrounded Rome. What would the conqueror do next? Most alarming rumours concerning his intentions were current everywhere. Had he not actually talked of expelling the Pope, whom he accused of simony, and of convening a council to replace him? For a few weeks Innocent VIII's successor barricaded himself in the Castle of Sant' Angelo; but once he had come face to face with the puny little king from Paris, on 31st December, he rapidly recovered his courage. Even before the French attack the Pope had prepared an alliance between Venice, Ferrara, Mantua and his own domains. Once the Frenchman was far away in Naples, it would be easy to form a coalition against him from among all those who found his presence in Italy an embarrassment. For the time being then the pontiff was careful to treat the victor of the moment with extreme friendliness and admiration, amounting to virtual subservience. Of course Charles might have free passage across the Church's territories. As for hostages the king's wish was his command. Charles VIII was well content, and solemnly acknowledged this charming fellow as the legitimate pope. But as soon as the splendid knights of France had made their fabulous entry into Naples, almost without a blow, the pontiff added to his league the Emperor Maximilian, the King of Spain, and even Lodovico the Moor. Under pretext of organizing a crusade he had forged an alliance between all the states who distrusted the ambition of France. Isolated, and far from his bases, Charles VIII had no alternative but to fight his way back to France; at Fornova it needed the full weight of the *furia Francese* to open up the Alpine passage for him. Surely the Pope who had carried out this successful manœuvre was a politician worthy of the highest praises?— Alas, he was a skilful politician but nothing more. . . .

The cunning conqueror of the French was none other than that

Roderigo Borgia whose career had had such a propitious start some thirty-five years earlier, thanks to his uncle Callixtus III. Created cardinal-deacon at the age of twenty-five, and subsequently vice-chancellor of the Church, the Borgia had managed to pursue his brilliant future under the succeeding pontificate. Sixtus IV had even conferred on him the venerable bishopric of Porto. His personal conduct rendered him quite unworthy of the honour; it had been constantly disgraceful since he reached manhood, and during the reign of Pius II a notorious ball which he had held in a private garden at Siena had earned him a reprimand—though an excessively mild one—from the Sovereign Pontiff. Shortly after this incident Roderigo had flaunted his liaison with a certain Roman beauty, Vanozza Cattanei, one of Titian's Venuses, by whom he had four children in addition to the two he already possessed and whose mother is unknown. Moreover he was an excellent father, ever concerned for the future of his progeny, whom he had duly made legitimate; he had obtained the bishopric of Pampeluna from the feeble Innocent VIII for little Cesare, his favourite son, who was then seven years old. In contemporary Rome such a parade of immortality was not really considered surprising. At all events it did not compromise the future of the guilty individual in the slightest degree. Cardinal Roderigo had skilfully prepared the way for his own eventual elevation, first assisting Sixtus IV to don the triple crown, then letting the Roveres set their own creature from Genoa upon the apostolic throne. He was biding his time. The enormous fortune which he had amassed enabled him to soften the hearts of many cardinals. Having distributed titles, prebends and offices to the most influential electors, Roderigo calmly awaited the result of a conclave whose connection with the workings of the Holy Spirit is singularly difficult to imagine. He adopted the name Alexander, letting it be known that this was in memory of the Greek conqueror of the world. His eleven-year pontificate was to be the most deplorable in the whole history of Christianity: with *Alexander VI*, Borgia, the Church sank to her lowest depths of degradation.

Borgia—the very name of this family awakens such scandalous echoes in men's minds that it makes temperate discussion exceedingly difficult. A literary legend has added a whole host of crimes to the already over-numerous misdeeds which must perforce be laid at his door. The famous 'Borgia poison' with which, it is said, the Pope ridded himself of various cardinals and other lesser lords who proved an embarrassment to him, was possibly not wholly an invention of a few ill-disposed chroniclers. At this period the poisoning of letters, handkerchiefs, shirts, rings and sword-hilts was quite commonplace, but the fact remains that there is not a vestige of proof that Alexander

VI had recourse to this weapon of government on any occasion whatsoever. As for the rather too notorious accusation of the Pope's incestuous relation with his daughter Lucrezia, this is pure and simple calumny: anyone believing it must also accept as fact that written history consists exclusively of social gossip columns and the kind of pamphlets that pass clandestinely from hand to hand.

Romantic literature has popularized the picture of this diabolical Borgia trio, united in crime—Alexander, the worthless Pope; his dreadful son, Cesare; and Lucrezia, his shameless, scheming daughter. Their true portraits, however, are not so wholly black. Alexander was a tall, handsome man, of noble bearing, and possessing a rare sort of charm. He had real ability: he was haughty to the rich, and accessible to the humble, a skilful politician, a shrewd diplomat, and a man of highly cultivated tastes. But he also had a hedonistic temperament which was incapable of resisting temptation of any kind, be they of the flesh or of the table; he was one of those thorough-going sensualists who arrange everything to suit their own pleasure, but who, when satisfied, are agreeable and pleasant to live with. These are clearly not the aspects of character most admired in a pope, all the more so since Alexander VI was as sceptical about morality as he was about men, and gave no indication at all that his sins lay heavily on his conscience. As for his two favourite children, both of them differed from him very considerably. Cesare, a gaunt young man consumed by his passions, had one of those turbulent and complex natures in which zest for life and desire to give the fullest expression to himself were mingled with anxiety and hidden doubts. Arrogant, scintillating, possessing such outstanding lucidity and energy that Machiavelli afterwards used him as the model for his *Prince*, Cesare Borgia seems to have been just as savage and wicked as this type of energetic creature generally was in his day—no more and no less than the average. His vices, however, were far too pronounced for a leader who commanded in the name of the Pope; and as head of the 'army of the Keys' he clearly tended to use the force at his disposal for his own personal interests rather than for the glory of the Church. Finally, Lucrezia, the daughter who was betrothed again and again, who was married and then divorced to suit the requirements of political alliances, was, it seems, the pitiable victim rather than the culpable criminal; at all events not a single ambassador or chronicler points to any instance of personal misconduct on her part. Fragile but energetic, intelligent and well educated besides, she was an admittedly conscious part of the systematic plan elaborated by her brother, whose ambitions she shared. Later on, when she was left to rule the duchy of Ferrara single-handed, she proved a perfect sovereign. Lucrezia Borgia was in fact very different from the hell-cat painted by Victor Hugo. But there is no doubt at all that the influence which these two young people exerted over Alexander VI was partially responsible for involving him so deeply in temporal politics, and for keeping him from the duties properly attached to his office.

The Borgia, however, was not a totally bad pope. He had a most exalted idea of the authority that should belong to the head of the Church; and though he was so sinful as to forget that this authority must be based in the first place upon spiritual prestige, he did at least labour to make it respected upon the temporal plane. His reorganization of the Vatican finances, which had suffered badly from the extravagances of Sixtus IV; his re-establishment of a more rigorous justice in the Papal States; his struggle against tyranny, both great and small, which he pursued far too resolutely for the liking of the individuals concerned—these were no mean achievements. The material interests of the Papacy were better defended by Alexander than by any of his predecessors, at any rate since the pontificate of Eugenius IV. Nor can it be said that he completely failed to understand the meaning of the Church. In the sphere of pure religion he never did anything, or published any document, which could lay him open to the slightest reproach: he might behave badly, but his thinking was sound. When the Turks resumed their incursions into Hungary and Poland, and even seized Navarino and a number of other Mediterranean bases which were still Christian, Alexander worked tenaciously to raise an expeditionary force which could undertake a counter-attack. The fleet he formed had already begun to threaten the Turkish coasts when the practical Venetians decided that it was preferable to come to an understanding with the Infidel on commercial grounds—a decision which the Pope strongly challenged. Moreover his far-sighted mind was equally alive to the problem of Christian expansion, hope of which was offered by the great Spanish and Portuguese voyages of exploration which were taking place. After Christopher Columbus's second expedition Alexander suggested that missionaries be sent to the newly discovered lands; Bernard Boyl and his companions set out, and were later followed by teams of Franciscans. Next, in 1493, in order to avoid a colonial war between the two great nations then engaged in the discovery of the world, Alexander VI wisely traced the famous dividing-line to mark the boundary between the territories claimed by Spain and Portugal.[1]

No, the Borgia Pope is most culpable in the field of morals, and chiefly in that of private morality. His election to the Papacy brought no improvement whatsoever in his behaviour. Although he had passed his sixtieth year he actually deserted Vanozza Cattanei for the rather more youthful Julia Farnese, by whom he had two more sons; but this liaison did not detain him from love-affairs with several other

[1] See *The Catholic Reformation*, Chapter IV, section 2.

women. Although the Renaissance looked upon such weakness with an indulgent eye, the presence of this large family, all the offspring of illicit passion, around St Peter's successor gave rise to considerable scandal. The scandal was all the greater because, instead of trying to push his children into the background, Alexander paraded them openly, lavishing honours and offices on his son, and personally conducting Lucrezia's splendid marriage service in the Vatican. Her divorce, some two years later, was equally scandalous. So was the defrocking of his son Cesare; the young Borgia discarded his cardinal's cloak in order once again to wield the sword, which was much more to his liking. The banquets and parties, whose echoes resounded through the papal palace, were no less scandalous; likewise the stables filled with champion steeds, and the stud farm, where, it was said, the Pope liked to watch his stallions at work.

The counterpart of this misplaced love of luxury and ostentation was clearly Alexander VI's taste for artistic and intellectual masterpieces. A generous patron, he beautified Rome, and transformed the Leonine citadel by separating the Castle of Sant' Angelo and turning it into the fortress as we know it today. Pinturicchio painted some exquisite frescoes in his private apartments. All the works begun by his predecessors were energetically continued, and the money spent so freely by the pilgrims who came to Rome for the jubilee of 1500 was largely devoted to the rebuilding of St Peter's. But Alexander VI carried his enlightened love of the arts and desire to make Rome the intellectual capital of the world rather too far. The notorious bull of 1499, which permitted the faithful to gain plenary indulgences for themselves and for the souls in Purgatory by donating money towards the restoration of St Peter's (the amount to be fixed by the priest awarding the penance), ran the risk of encouraging all kinds of abuses and of becoming a real scandal, even though it might well be canonically defensible. The world knows only too well what happened to it in Germany, and how a certain Augustinian monk who opposed it thereby provoked a revolution. . . .[1]

Just once, however, in the course of his unedifying life, Alexander VI felt an inward shudder which may have been a qualm of conscience. One morning news came that his eldest son, Juan, Duke of Gandia, had been assassinated. By whom? Gandia's Spanish bodyguard could give the distracted father no answer. Perhaps the culprit was Giovanni Sforza, the victim's brother-in-law, or the Orsini clan, or some cuckolded husband. The body was recovered from the Tiber, pierced by nine dagger wounds, but it kept its tragic secret. Popular rumour had it that the criminal might easily be the murdered man's own brother, Cesare, Gonfalonier of the Church. Be that as it might be,

[1] See Chapter V of the present volume.

for a brief moment Alexander saw this tragedy as a warning from Heaven. He declared that he was going to change his way of life, suppress clerical simony and moral laxity and reform the Church. A plan was actually drawn up and duly drafted as a bull, which ranged from recruitment to the Sacred College to the control of papal taxes. If ever good intentions paved the way to hell those listed in this decree of reform did so. The body of the unfortunate Juan had not even returned to dust before matters at the Vatican resumed their old familiar course. Cesare, who had been under suspicion for a while, and who had taken advantage of the situation to go to live in France, charm its court, marry Charlotte d'Albret and obtain the duchy of Valentinois, was restored to favour, and returned to take his customary place at his father's side. So nothing was changed, and there was even a recrudescence of scandal; while the hangers-on, cardinals and the like, or simply men upon whom fortune smiled, set to work to retrieve their alarming spiritual complacency. There were indeed a few protesting murmurs here and there, but most Italians considered that, from the moment they protected the Church's interests, Alexander and Cesare were no longer so guilty, and that their conduct could actually be ignored. Poison and the assassin's dagger were thus justified by the deeds performed.

Once again politics dominated all other considerations. Charles VIII, the last of the Valois in the direct line, had been succeeded by his cousin, the Duke of Orleans. Through his Visconti grandmother *Louis XII* (1498–1515) had a claim to the duchy of Milan, and he intended to use that claim against Lodovico the Moor, the Sforza usurper. Alexander was beginning to be disturbed by the policy of the ruler of Germany, Maximilian, who seemed bent on posing as a second Barbarossa; and in order to counter this danger he resolved to employ the ambitions of the King of France, whom he hoped to dominate. By decree which however well founded canonically caused considerable scandal, the Pope annulled Louis's marriage with the wretched Joan,[1] daughter of Louis XI, so that the French monarch could marry Charles VIII's widow, Anne of Brittany, and set about claiming the kingdom of Naples for himself. The result was the outbreak of the second Italian war. Although Louis XII was more sensible and clear-headed than his cousin, he too allowed himself to be drawn into this insane adventure. After defeating Lodovico the Moor at Novara, and taking him prisoner, the King of France advanced on Naples, in alliance with a Spanish army; Ferdinand and Louis were to divide the spoils between themselves. But while these two allies, who were soon at loggerheads,

---

[1] *St Joan of France*, who was canonized in 1950. After her divorce she became a nun, and led a life of exemplary piety at the head of the Order of the Annunciation, which she had founded.

wrangled over their prize and fought confused skirmishes in which the knight Bayard covered himself with glory, Alexander VI was skilfully playing his own game. Who knows? Possibly he was aiming at nothing less than the unification of all Italy under papal domination, a goal which Nicholas V had dimly perceived and which Julius II later pursued with all the strength at his command. Cesare swept through the Romagna, crushing those aristocrats who might prove an embarrassment to the Pope—Colonnas, Savellis, Gaetanis and the rest—and made the banner of the Church respected everywhere. The fact that the Pope's French ally was subsequently expelled from the peninsula was of no consequence at all. The wily Alexander had played his cards brilliantly.

But Alexander VI was not to enjoy his victory long. In the middle of August 1503, on one of those hot, humid evenings which were quite commonplace in Rome at that period, when the marshes in the countryside around Rome swarmed with malarial mosquitoes, the Pope and his beloved Cesare went to sup beneath the vines in Cardinal Corneto's garden. Next day both father and son were attacked by a violent fever. Cesare, being younger, recovered, but the old Pope succumbed. Naturally there were immediate rumours of a poison plot; but later on an even stranger version of the affair became the talk of Rome. This alleged that the Borgias were victims of the poison which they had prepared for their own host, and that some absent-minded or disloyal servant had administered it to them instead. The fact that men readily believed this story shows that the legend created by the Borgia scandals was already well established. 'The soul of the glorious Alexander was now borne among the choir of the blessed,' declared Machiavelli dryly. 'Dancing attendance on him were his three devoted, favourite handmaidens: Cruelty, Simony and Lechery.' Alas, there was considerable justification for a funeral oration of this kind. . . .

THE CRY OF RIGHTEOUS INDIGNATION: SAVONAROLA

The Church had certainly not deserved such a pope, and a chorus of voices rose from her midst, protesting against this manifold wickedness. One was more vehement and moving than all the rest, but unhappily its vehemence and emotion were carried to excess.

'Come, infamous Church, listen to the words of your Lord: "I have given you splendid robes, but you have made them cover idols; I have given you precious vessels, but you have used them to exalt your false pride. Your simony has profaned my sacraments; lechery has made of you a pock-marked harlot. And you no longer even blush for your sins! Whore that you are! You sit on Solomon's throne, and beckon to all who pass you by. Those who have money you bid a welcome to, and have your pleasure of them; but the man of goodwill is cast outside your doors!'"

These dreadful words had echoed through the nave of Santa Maria del Fiore during the Lenten season of 1497, and had been heard by countless throngs of people, pressed one against the other, filling the great cathedral to capacity. The man who had uttered them from the height of its pulpit was a small, spare, shrivelled figure, with heavily lined features and the full, expressive lips of the prophet, created for invective and imprecation. While he spoke an unearthly glow illuminated his pale face; his green eyes became darts of fire, and the sleeves of his black-and-white Dominican habit seemed to circle around him like the wings of some strange night-bird. This little friar alone could fill the immense cathedral with his listeners, magnetizing all who heard him, turning this human mass into a single mind, with himself as its living voice. And no one who heard his indictment doubted for a moment the righteousness of his words.

He was so persuasive. Now sweetly gentle, quivering, vibrating with love, like the plaint of a flute or violin; but more often harsh as a tocsin, crashing down on his listeners like a peal of thunder. In the pulpit he seemed utterly transfigured, quite different from the monk who walked the cloisters every day, and who might be considered a somewhat colourless individual. As soon as he mounted the steps of the rostrum a new spirit animated his whole being: he was seized by a mysterious trance. It was as if he had inherited the very fire and style from those Old Testament prophets—Isaiah, Amos and Jeremiah—whose message he so loved to interpret. And every one of the people standing there listening, trembling, echoing his own panting emotion, fully understood his message, whether great or small, rich or poor, scholars absorbed in the pleasures of the intellect or humble artisans. Among those lost in the crowd, as spellbound as the rest, were such men as Botticelli, Della Robbia, Michelangelo and even Pico della Mirandola, Giucciardini, Machiavelli, John Colet and Commines. Few of his hearers escaped the domination of this awe-inspiring man, in whom the fire of the Holy Spirit seemed to burn so brightly. The phenomenon of his hold upon Florence had already lasted seven years.

The friar's name was *Girolamo Savonarola*. He had been born in Ferrara, of good, solid middle-class stock. At first there seemed nothing at all to indicate his future calling as the herald of the Lord, the vocation which he later assumed in Florence. He was a shy young man, much addicted to the guitar, and at the age of twenty or so (he was born in 1452) it did not seem that he would enjoy a particularly distinguished future. But then God had called him—or at least so Savonarola thought. In visions that were to continue throughout his life he had felt himself summoned to a clear-cut task, whose demands he clumsily expressed in some of his own youthful poems. He was to proclaim the *ruinous state of the Church*, and work to provide a remedy for it. When he was twenty-three years old Savonarola entered the Order of St Dominic at Bologna. He proved an exemplary novice, outstanding in his attendance at the divine office, a brilliant scholar, and by far the most rigorous in his fasting and asceticism. But he noticed that even in this spiritual family, where he had hoped to find the fervour and discipline of bygone days, the contamination of the century had wrought its damage. It seemed as if everything in the Father's house was in sorry need of repair, and Savonarola believed that he was the man to do it.

His initial efforts resulted in almost total failure. So long as he confined himself to being an ordinary 'lecturer,' and commenting on the Bible to the students of San Marco, he gained a ready hearing. But when he tried to preach from the pulpit to large congregations, his rough-and-ready speech and over-ponderous, academic constructions drove his audiences away. The Florence of Cosimo and Lorenzo de' Medici was much too accustomed to fine oratory to be impressed by this second-rate Thomism. However, Friar Girolamo himself was more than ever convinced that Christ had chosen him to be the repository of His divine message: had he not actually been assured of this in an ecstatic trance? Though he had not yet found a way of reaching these souls so riddled with paganism and its monstrous allies, God would surely give him the key one day. Had not St Paul suffered a similar defeat at Athens? At San Gimignano he had suddenly let his sentences stream forth in an unrestrained flood, straight from his heart, and had discovered that this was the way to overwhelm men's souls. Savonarola's threefold cry of doom resounded round the feet of the lofty towers whose jagged battlements enclosed the little town, with such force that it was heard throughout the whole of Tuscany: 'The Church will be reformed, but Italy will first be scourged, and her chastisement is imminent!' From Brescia to Genoa his call had aroused the same echoes of fear and fury. By the time he returned to Florence Savonarola had learned that truth finds entry into hardened hearts not through reason, but through the blessed folly of the Cross.

Henceforth Savonarola was the centre of one of those popular emotional movements which occur from time to time, and which suddenly lift a man to the crest of fame, only to desert him and cast him out of favour shortly afterwards. He became well known. The sermons which had recently been ridiculed now attracted huge crowds. One after another his enemies gave way before him. Savonarola had been made prior of San Marco, where so many young men were now offering themselves as postulants, that the monastery's numbers rose to over two hundred, and matters reached the stage when it was difficult to find accommodation for any more new entrants. The friar had publicly castigated the Medici for their luxury and their general way of life, but to everyone's astonishment Lorenzo the Magnificent bore these rebukes in silence, and refrained from punishing their author. Even better, it was Friar Girolamo whom he summoned to his bedside as he lay dying, and it was said that the implacable religious had taken advantage of this occasion to demand the restoration of Florence's ancient liberties.

What magnetic force gave this slight, shrivelled and unprepossessing man such power over his fellow citizens? He himself supplied the answer: his power was supernatural. Savonarola was convinced that he had been invested with that gift of prophecy which God had promised the most faithful of His witnesses; and since he was speaking in the name of the Almighty, no being on earth had the right to silence him. Moreover he had flashes of extraordinary insight, which unquestionably enabled him to predict correctly the course of several future events. These successes made an enormous impression on the mob, which was far more impressed by them than by erroneous predictions which he also made, and which force the historian to regard his prophetic capacity with some scepticism. When he evoked what he had seen in the course of his extraordinary ecstasies, it seemed indeed that the mantle of the Old Testament prophets had fallen upon his shoulders: on earth the Sword of Fire which the Archangel brandished on the threshold of Paradise lost was ready to strike; a black cross, the symbol of divine wrath which hovered in the sky above sinful Rome, would soon be replaced by the golden cross of the celestial Jerusalem; and once the Virgin Mary actually appeared to him, expressing her disgust for the faithless Church, and telling him that the hand of the Lord was about to mete out punishment.

This was the theme of all Savonarola's sermons: the Bride of Christ was tainted with sin and must be purified. She must regain her faith. Reform had probably never before had so vehement an advocate. There had been no one more resolutely determined to bring to light all the abuses and denounce every breach of faith. Alexander VI's conduct brought this righteous indignation to its climax: with their cliques of voracious nephews and courtier-cardinals, Sixtus IV and Innocent VIII had seemed unworthy enough, but the Borgia on St Peter's throne must surely be the 'abomination of desolation' foretold by the Scriptures. Was this simoniacal and profligate Pope, who flaunted his mistresses and his bastards, still the rightful head of the Church, the Apostle's successor, entrusted with Peter's keys? But punishment could not be long delayed; the forces of heavenly wrath were already on the warpath. A new Nebuchadnezzar, a new Cyrus, was about to intervene in history. Stretching his arms towards the Alpine horizon, Friar Girolamo appeared to summon this mysterious instrument of God to come forth at his command.

It was now that the drama came to a head, and that Savonarola's mistakes began. While he confined himself to trying to make Florence, 'set in the centre of Italy, like the heart in the body,' a model Christian city, whose reformation would permeate the rest of the peninsula, he remained on safe and familiar ground. But his influence became so enormous that it acquired political significance; and, as it happened, this suited him only too well. By a remarkable aberration of his prophetic foresight, Savonarola recognized the puny Charles VIII as the long-awaited messenger of God, and by linking his cause with that of the French he was henceforth involved in the complex web of intrigue which the Roman diplomats were successfully weaving around the invaders. Pietro de' Medici, Lorenzo's son, was expelled from Florence by a popular uprising, and the Dominican played a direct part in establishing a new, democratic constitution, in which authority was in the hands of a grand council, elected by the middle class, and where military service was compulsory for all male citizens. Such matters appear to have little connection with the Word of God and the message of salvation.

Step by step Savonarola imposed a dictatorship upon Florence, which was his version of Paradise. It was in fact a regime consisting of a singular fusion of elements from the city of God and the city of man, of temporal politics and spiritual apologetics, of bureaucratic rules and the strictures of the Ten Commandments. For years he succeeded in instilling such terror of divine wrath into the entire city that its easy-going inhabitants, so accustomed to worldly pleasure, adopted the way of renunciation with panic-stricken fervour. Despots had governed Florence in the old days; the new despot was to be Christ Himself. He would rule through the mediation of His prophet Savonarola, and anyone who resisted would be judged a heretic. Theocracy never put forward such claims elsewhere, save in Calvin's Geneva during the following century.

These were strange years indeed in the history of Florence. Women gave up their jewels and other finery, and rakes no longer frequented inns and brothels. The bankers returned all the money they had wrongly acquired, and debtors and creditors embraced one another as brothers. In the main square blazed the 'Bonfire of Vanities'; and everyone hastened to throw into the flames all that might recall their shameful past, while some artists even destroyed their masterpieces upon pagan themes. But this idyllic reversion to primitive sanctity was also accompanied by less pleasant aspects. Savonarola was carried away by his enthusiasm and allowed his followers to commit excesses of zeal. Everything had to be sacrificed to what was alleged to be God's will. Even if a wife entered a convent against her husband's will, this was considered right and proper; and the son who denounced his father as a blasphemer was showered with praise. Quite minor faults, such as playing with dice, were severely punished. Bands of young men were formed to persecute public sinners, and these would waylay women with painted faces, and over-richly dressed merchants in the street, and beat them up. 'Having a fling for the love of Christ' was their watchword. 'There is a reign of terror in Florence,' wrote one ambassador from Mantua. Surely this was not the desire of the God of love!

On the throne of St Peter Alexander VI was keeping a close watch on events. He had two reasons for bearing the Dominican ill will. First, Savonarola's pro-French policy was a betrayal of Italy's interests, which were part and parcel of those of the Holy See. His second complaint was less explicit, but ultimately more decisive. In his repeated attacks upon Rome, the Dominican was distinguishing less and less between Alexander the man and Alexander the Pope, and his assault on the Borgia was thus becoming an assault on the Vicar of Christ Himself. Yet Alexander VI treated the prophet with astonishing lenience. This attitude may not have been determined solely by the Pope's desire not to quarrel openly with so turbulent an ally as the King of France. Possibly, despite everything, the still small voice of conscience was telling him that the friar's attacks were justified. Month after month he temporized, and it is certain that had Savonarola allowed a cardinal's hat to buy his silence, the Pope would have been very happy to make the necessary arrangements. But the Bible had said: 'When God has spoken who can remain silent?' Only death would silence Friar Girolamo.

In 1495 Savonarola was invited to go to Rome to prove the divine origin of his prophecies. He refused to go. Alexander forbade him to preach; he continued just the same, and during Lent 1496 declared from the pulpit that no Christian is obliged to obey an order which infringes justice and charity. This was followed by a spate of furious diatribes against Rome, the new Babylon, and the vices which were flaunted there. Alas, these were only too well founded. Alexander VI's reply came six months later, when he summoned the Florentine envoys and protested against their terrible preacher. The latter's answer to this was not long delayed: it comprised the indictments whose most moderate clauses have already been quoted earlier in this chapter.

But Savonarola's star was beginning to fade. The French, who had been hounded out of Naples, seemed to have dropped the sword of Divine Justice. In Florence, the former city of plenty, things were going badly. Unemployment was rising; people began to consider the penances and interminable sermons rather too austere; and the public festivals, where monks sang and danced, garlanded with roses, no longer entertained anyone. They longed for the carnival of former times. Factions sprang up which were opposed to Savonarola's 'Piagnoni,'•or 'weepers,' and a riot broke out in the cathedral during one of his sermons.

The Pope seized his chance and struck. Now that he had been excommunicated and summoned to appear in Rome, what would the friar do next? He proclaimed the divine character of his mission more strongly than ever, and rebelled against the papal decision in words of unparalleled violence. The 'simoniacal, heretical, faithless' Alexander VI was not really pope, he was merely a 'broken rod' whose blows could be universally ignored. 'Soon I shall turn the Key!' he cried in his usual mysterious way. Mounting a pulpit erected in the middle of the piazza in front of the cathedral he raised the Blessed Sacrament on high and shrieked: 'Lord, if my words are not yours, destroy me as I stand here now!' His fury, excusable to some extent when the worthlessness of his enemy is remembered, drove him to terrible extremes. He demanded the immediate assembly of a general council to depose the Pope. This would have meant a revival of the crisis of the Great Schism, and no sensible Christian dared follow Savonarola into deep waters of this kind.

Savonarola's fall was as rapid as his rise had been. In February 1498 Alexander VI warned the Florentines that unless they surrendered the preacher he would place their city under interdict. They assessed the danger implicit in his threat. Interdict would involve not merely blockade and economic ruin, but also an attack by all the enemies of Florence, who would be only too happy to obey the Pope's voice in this respect. Medici supporters, advocates of Italian unity, and all those who believed in freedom of thought and good living united to destroy the troublesome friar. The Franciscans, who were obviously not very fond of him, provided the weapon. Savonarola had talked on several occasions of personally submitting to the ordeal of fire in order to prove the divine origin of his mission. A Franciscan now took him at his word and challenged him to risk the ordeal. He declined, and this dealt his prestige a mortal blow. One of his fellow Dominicans agreed to undergo the ordeal in his place, but interminable arguments ensued as to whether the champion had the right to take the Crucifix or the Blessed Sacrament into the flames with him. Finally, before the ordeal started, it began to pour with rain. The crowd melted away, angry and disappointed, its attitude towards its prophet having undergone a complete reversal in the space of a few minutes. Next day, Palm Sunday, the convent of San Marco was invaded by the mob. Savonarola was arrested and thrown into prison along with two of his brethren; all the rest disowned him with an alacrity which tells us a good deal about their real feelings in the matter.

The trial began. The Florentine Government was determined to conduct this itself, refusing to extradite the friar as the Pope desired, and merely allowing two Roman judges to be present throughout the proceedings. When interrogated the 'defenceless prophet,' as Machiavelli described him, confessed that he was neither God's messenger nor divinely inspired. But such words, dragged from a man by torture, were of little value; the essential fact was that the Christian folk of Florence had deserted him. They were incapable of maintaining the standard he had claimed to set them, and were probably vaguely conscious of the excesses which had vitiated the whole enterprise. On 23rd May Savonarola and his two companions in misfortune were burnt at the stake in the Florentine piazza where he had so often been acclaimed in the past. His ashes were consigned to the Arno, so that his last loyal supporters could not preserve them as relics.

How should this bizarre and tragic episode be judged? This chaste, austere religious, with his message of divine vengeance, strikes such an extreme contrast to the Pope who excommunicated him that the observer is sorely tempted to admit the validity of his case, and regard him as an authentic witness of the Word. Some of the saints and faithful children of the Church thought so, among them St Francis of Paula, St Philip Neri, St Maria-Magdalena dei Pazzi, St Catherine de Ricci, and the chronicler Commines.[1] But although his principles were right and his intentions good, Savonarola committed so many grave errors that it is impossible to accept his message without serious reservations. St Catherine of Siena had already made it clear that however worthless a pope might be as an individual, it was a Christian's prime duty, despite everything, to recognize and venerate in him the Vicar of the Incarnate Word. By the excesses which he allowed to colour his religious despotism, and the political motives which crept in to contaminate his ideal, Savonarola compromised a cause which his virtues and his oratory alone might have served well. Like so many others, he was a typical figure of the Renaissance, a perfect example of the *virtù* which impelled men to go to the utmost limits in their urge for self-fulfilment. Above all, however, he showed to what violent emotional outbursts the anxiety for reform which was agitating the Christian soul at this period could lead. He himself was incapable of being anything more than a discordant herald of that sober, temperate

---

[1] However, it should also be observed that their sentiments were not shared by other saints. In 1583 the future Pope Leo XI wrote: 'I am certain that Pius V, of blessed memory, would have corrected all those who cherish a devotion to Savonarola, for he regarded him with horror and even had some doubts concerning the authenticity of his faith.'

movement towards reform which was to take place within the traditional framework of the Church some fifty years after his death.[1]

THE SPANISH BASTION: THE CONQUEST OF GRANADA

We can now turn for a while from these tragedies and miseries, and look towards a part of Christendom where the memory of ancient loyalties was still very much alive. By a striking contradiction the very land which had produced the deplorable Borgias was at the same time bearing moving witness of its deep religious faith. Spain, which had written one of the most glorious pages in the history of Christianity during the great medieval period,[2] was now opening a new chapter in her existence. In 1469 *Isabella*, the heiress of Castile, had chosen from among her many suitors *Ferdinand*, who was heir to the throne of Aragon. Ten years later the two crowns were reunited and the royal couple decided to rule all their domains conjointly—Sicily, Sardinia and the Balearic Islands as well as Spain proper. This idyll between a blonde, blue-eyed princess and a swarthy 'caballero' was worthy of the pages of a courtly romance, but it was to have far-reaching consequences. Henceforth the bloody feuds which had rent the Iberian peninsula for two hundred years past, paralysing its development, were at an end. A new Spain was about to arise—a Spain fully conscious of her own greatness—and this young love was about to receive a crown of youthful glory.

No sooner were they established on their thrones than Ferdinand and Isabella determined to revive the Spanish task *par excellence*, the task which their ancestors had considered their prime duty for the past eight hundred years, the task of chasing the Moslem invaders from the Christian soil of Spain. Ever since the capture of Seville (1248), the last and most splendid action of Ferdinand III, the work of 'Reconquista' had been at a standstill. Rulers of the petty Spanish kingdoms had been so preoccupied with internecine warfare that they had had no time to draw their swords against the Infidel. Indeed the little realm of Granada, which constituted the last remnant of Moorish domination in Spain, was not particularly troublesome to the Christians; it was situated at the very tip of the peninsula, clinging to the side of the Sierra Nevada, like some fairy-tale province. The poets called it 'a piece of heaven which had fallen down to earth.' Under its hard blue

---

[1] Contrary to the views of certain historians who have placed him alongside Huss, Luther and Calvin, this does not imply that he can be regarded in any way as a herald of the Protestant Reformation. His doctrine has never been questioned, and his treatise, *The Triumph of Christ*, was fashionable in seminaries for many years to come, even after the Council of Trent. 'He who denies the Church,' wrote Savonarola, 'denies Christ too.' But surely he who denies the Pope denies the Church as well.

[2] See *Cathedral and Crusade*, p. 485, section 2: 'The Reconquista.'

skies the 'huertas' flaunted their vines, their orchards full of figs and almonds, and their fields of lavender and roses. Among the splendours of the Alhambra and the Generalifa the last Moslem kings of Granada seemed to live a life befitting a legend from the Arabian Nights, but the atmosphere of their dream palace was disturbed by countless intrigues. About 1480 the situation was favourable to the Christians, for a dynastic crisis, aggravated by a women's quarrel, had just shaken the little kingdom to its foundations. Aicha, the repudiated queen, had recaptured Granada at the point of the sword and put her sickly son Boabdil on the throne of the mighty Abencerages. He was to be its last occupant.

The Spanish attack was unleashed in 1481, and required more than ten years of concentrated effort. One hundred thousand resolute believers were hurled across the Sierra, assured by Pope Sixtus IV, through his nuncio, that they were engaging in the holy task of a genuine crusade. The peripheral towns fell rapidly into Christian hands, one by one: Malaga, Almeria and Guadix. But Granada still held firm. The enemies of yesterday had joined forces against the aggressors: Abencerages and Zengirs were now reconciled. The siege of Granada began in 1491. Isabella had accompanied her husband on the march, sharing with him the discomforts of camp life and the hazards of war, and inspiring the army with her indomitable energy. Her chaplain was the celebrated Archbishop of Toledo, Ximenes de Cisneros, who ventured into the thick of the fray. When fire destroyed the crusaders' tents, the queen commanded that a real city be built, of permanent materials, to make it quite plain that nothing whatsoever would drive her from the spot. This warrior town, which she named 'Santa Fé,' was so near the enemy fortress that Moors and Christians were able to hurl abuse at one another from their respective walls. Single combats frequently took place on the nearby plain, lance opposing scimitar, and the champions of the Cross were sustained by feats of valour worthy of the age of Geoffrey de Bouillon. For instance, Perez del Pulgar rode out one dark night to nail a copy of the *Ave Maria* to the door of a mosque with the point of his dagger. But these splendid deeds were not the only means employed; the Christian generals had made secret contact with the vizier of Granada, who realized that the situation was hopeless. A treaty of capitulation was agreed upon, and in this Ferdinand and Isabella showed truly Christian clemency. Not only were the vanquished granted their lives, but their religion, mosques and property also were guaranteed to them; those who wished to emigrate to Africa would be helped to do so, but the conversion of any who desired to become Catholics would also be permissible. At dawn on 2nd January 1492 the last act in this drama took place under a cloudless sky. Among the standards fluttering in the wind were those bearing the arrows and Gordian knot, badges of Aragon and Castile. Boabdil rode out to meet the victorious couple, dismounted and presented them with the key of the Alcazar. Then he set off into exile with his little band of followers, accompanied by the taunts of his awe-inspiring mother: 'Why weep like a woman for a kingdom you could not defend like a man?' Meanwhile, from the tower of Vela, a herald proclaimed that Granada now belonged to 'the Catholic sovereigns,' using the title recently bestowed by Alexander VI upon the two young rulers who had served Christendom so magnificently. In a sense the capture of Granada seemed to compensate for the loss of Constantinople, and Spain was now one of the leading nations of the world.

Ferdinand and Isabella had accomplished this work of territorial unification in a truly masterly fashion. Both, however, were aware that they would have to devote themselves to another task, on the internal plane, as much administrative and political as spiritual and ethnic. This was the other side of their achievement, and one perhaps even more decisive than the first. Two hundred years of feeble government and disorder had left Spain in the grip of appalling anarchy. Nobles, burgesses and clerics did exactly as they liked, and scoundrels of every type and class abounded everywhere. The victors' immediate aim was to put a stop to this. A royal police force, the Holy Brotherhood, was empowered to act expeditiously and inflict terrible penalties, and the young criminals were quickly tamed. The 'ricos hombres' were forced to return to their rightful place in the social scale and give up their ill-gotten gains. Henceforth the great military religious Orders of Alcantara, Calatrava and St James, formerly so powerful, would have the king as their Grand Master. The towns were stripped of most of their 'fueros'—sacrosanct privileges—and from now on were governed by royal 'corregidors.' Government counsellors, many of whom were chosen from the legal profession, which was strongly in favour of centralized authority, discarded the administrative system of the old feudal monarchy and substituted methods of their own. Next, the army was reorganized according to a pattern that appeared so remarkable to the rest of Europe that the Spanish word for 'infantry'—from *infante* —passed into almost every other tongue. As for the clergy, the Crown had made certain of its control by obtaining from Alexander VI the right of 'supplication.' Henceforward, in effect, the king chose all the bishops. Ferdinand and Isabella foreshadowed the royal absolutism of the future quite as much as Louis XI of France or Henry VII of England.

But for the rulers of Spain the problem was not solely political: they were not concerned simply with institutions. There was a much more delicate issue, affecting the very structure of their people. This was nothing less than the celebrated question of ethnic minorities, which has confronted so many states in recent times with tragic and dramatic consequences. Spain in fact contained a number of elements which had not been properly assimilated by her indigenous population. First of all there were vast numbers of Jews, 'one-third of the townsfolk and merchants of Castile' according to Vincenzo Quirini, the Venetian ambassador. They were extremely wealthy, for they made enormous fortunes by lending money at interest rates which went as high as 40 per cent, and they flaunted their wealth in an insolent fashion. Several of them had been converted to Catholicism, especially since the great apostolic missions of St Vincent Ferrer.[1] Some of these men were a credit to the faith, but not all such conversions were sincere. Far too many Jews had sought baptism for business reasons only, or because they were afraid to do otherwise; they remained Jews at heart and often practised Judaism in secret. These people were popularly known as 'Marranos' from a word-play which recalled both the Hebrew 'Maran atha' ('the Lord cometh') and the Castilian-Portuguese 'marrano,' meaning 'little pig.' The infiltration of the Marranos into the Christian ranks led to the most astonishing results; even the higher clergy was contaminated, and made little attempt to hide the fact. A story (doubtless apocryphal) was told of a certain Bishop of Calahorra on a visit to Rome. While there he ate meat on Friday, prayed in Hebrew according to the Jewish rite, demanded kosher meat, refused to utter the name of Christ, and afterwards thrashed the priests of his diocese when they dared to remonstrate with him. There was a real threat to the faith here, which, if allowed to continue, might lead to the rise of some strange, unimaginable Judeo-Christian syncretism.

But alongside the Jewish threat was another: the presence in Spain of persons of Arab origin. This problem had arisen in the recovered territories at each stage of the Reconquista; one example is afforded by the Moslems of Barcelona and the Balearic Islands, whom Blessed Raymond Lull had made such courageous efforts to convert. The final stage, the conquest of Granada, still further increased the number of Arabs in Spain. Besides those remnants of Moorish occupation who officially retained their religion, there were many Arabs who had been

---

[1] The numerous conversions of Jews had enabled the Spanish Church to improve her knowledge of the Holy Scripture considerably. The first Catholic edition of the Hebrew text of the Bible, which appeared in 1522, was revised by three learned Jewish converts. A number of eminent rabbis became Christians during the fifteenth century, and they contributed to their new faith a long Jewish tradition of familiarity with the Old Testament. Solomon Halevi, a converted rabbi, became Bishop of Burgos under the name of Paolo de Santa Maria between 1415 and 1435. He was a member of the Royal Council and Papal Legate. His son, Alfonso, who succeeded him in the see of Burgos (1435–56) was an important figure, who wrote on behalf of converted Jews. (Cf. Guy Sauvard, 'St Jean de la Croix et la Bible,' in *Cahiers Sioniens*, 1952, p. 133.)

partially converted, and who proclaimed themselves Christians while secretly remaining faithful to the Koran. They were known as 'Moriscos.'

The Catholic sovereigns could not allow such an equivocal situation to continue for very long. When it became necessary for them to take action, Ferdinand and Isabella sought the assistance of the Church. The weapon already existed: the *Inquisition*. This had been established in the Middle Ages to deal with all the forces hostile to the faith and especially with the menace of Catharism. The Inquisition had since fallen more or less into abeyance; but in 1478, during Holy Week, a conspiracy of Marranos was discovered in Seville, and its antichristian purpose aroused great popular indignation. Ferdinand took advantage of this incident to ask the Pope to revive the ancient institution, and to entrust it to him with a view to its more effective employment. Sixtus IV weakly agreed, and issued the bull of 1st November 1478. It was a grave mistake, for it sealed the confusion between temporal and spiritual authority, although the Holy See later attempted to rectify the matter. During the siege of Granada the two monarchs strengthened their control over the institution, no doubt through fear of a stab in the back at so critical a juncture. The supreme Council of the Inquisition was created, presided over by the Grand Inquisitors; 'Instructions,' forming a kind of Inquisitorial code, were sent out to all the local tribunals, and the institution thus became a regular organ of State.

The work of the Spanish Inquisition is a subject which must be treated with extreme caution, for popular imagination has heavily embroidered it. *Thomas of Torquemada*, the first Grand Inquisitor, has been depicted as a sadistic torturer with blood-stained hands, who instituted a reign of terror throughout Spain; he was in fact a very austere religious, convinced of the usefulness of his function, but completely devoid of cruelty. On several occasions he used his influence to moderate the excesses of other ecclesiastical judges. Moreover the Dominicans who provided the personnel of the Inquisition were far from being 'Torquemadas' in the traditional sense of the word. Many of them sought to redeem rather than chastise the sinners brought before them. As for the methods of this notorious tribunal— the 'Iron Law' which actually compelled a suspect's own family to denounce him, and the questioning of the accused under torture in order to obtain their confessions—these, it must be remembered, were customary practices of the age; and the twentieth century has precious little ground for reproaching the fifteenth in this particular field. There remains the problem of the number of actual victims—of those who were imprisoned for life, or burnt or strangled alive, following the famous 'acts of faith' (*autodafé*) at which their condemnation was publicly proclaimed. The historian is hard put to it to propose an accurate figure, for there is much discrepancy among the sources; some suggest a few hundred, and others tens of thousands. In proportion to the number of cases dealt with by the tribunals, capital and life sentences were undoubtedly very few. Naturally they were still far too many to satisfy anyone who believes that the religion of love should on no account be imposed by force; but that is another matter altogether. One thing is certain: the Inquisition cast an atmosphere of fear and gloom, and almost of terror, over the whole of Spain, something akin to that which the Revolutionary Tribunal, instituted for different reasons, cast over France in 1793. It is equally certain that the Spanish people not only accepted it, but even welcomed it willingly and thankfully,[1] as a manifestation of that fervent, sacrificial faith which had enabled their country to forge its destiny.

The double apparatus of State and Inquisition, therefore, swung into action as soon as the sovereigns realized that the presence on their soil of these large foreign minorities seriously threatened to contaminate the faith and unity of Spain. The first to be attacked were the Jews. In 1492 a radical decision was taken, whereby all Jews who had not been converted to Catholicism were expelled from the kingdom. Through the long, sultry summer all the roads leading to the frontiers were packed with some two hundred thousand proscribed Jews, their rabbis at their head, making their tragic way towards Portugal (where their presence raised serious problems), southern France, the Balkans and North Africa. Next, it was the turn of the Moslems. A number of saintly priests, such as Hernando de Talavera, the new Archbishop of Granada, tried to convert them by kindness, but without much success. A more brutal policy, conducted by Ximenes de Cisneros, who had been made cardinal and Grand Inquisitor, led to a few hundred conversions, but also sparked off a rebellion which established its strongholds in the scrub country of the Apujarra and the hilly district of Albaïcin. Now severe measures were adopted: in flagrant violation of the terms of the treaty of capitulation, the Spanish rulers began persecuting the Moslems, confiscating their sacred books, and finally converted the great mosque at Granada into a church. In their turn many Moslems took to flight and made for Africa. As for those Jews and Moslems who had accepted baptism but seemed indifferent Christians, the Inquisition went into action against them. It directed its fiercest attacks at the Marranos, so much so that the Holy See became disturbed, and counselled the Inquisitors to use more moderation. In short, these were violent measures which no Christian conscience can now sanction, but they seemed necessary enough at the time.

[1] Even such impartial foreigners as the Venetian ambassador Quirini, who wrote: 'The Inquisition alone makes King Ferdinand and Queen Isabella worthy of eternal praise from both God and man.'

If proof of the value of this work were needed it can be found in the following observation. None of the pernicious tendencies of the age was able to infiltrate and menace this austere and zealously guarded kingdom. Spanish humanism was to provide the movement with one of its outstanding leaders, *Luis Vives* (1491–1540), a professor at Louvain, a scholarly commentator on St Augustine, and one of those who inspired the celebrated Polyglot Bible; but it never abandoned its Christian bases. Protestantism failed almost completely in the peninsula. Spanish art too, notwithstanding the Italian influences apparent in Ferrer Bassa and the Flemish traits that have been detected in Borasso or Dalman, retained in its best exponents—Bago, Huguet, the Catalan Bermejo and the Andalusian Hispalensis [1]—a very striking originality, which is visibly related to the religious fervour to which they all bore such devoted witness. In the following century Spain reached her apogee, and this she owed to the fact that, at the very moment when Christopher Columbus and the Conquistadores were giving her a whole new world, the courage and faith of her sovereigns had transformed her into a bastion of the Christian faith.

The Temptation of Politics: Julius II

Would the death of Alexander VI mark a turning-point for the Church? Was the Papacy about to effect the necessary moral and spiritual regeneration? For a brief moment it seemed as if this might be so, for the Sacred College chose as the Borgia's successor a man of eminent holiness, Cardinal Piccolomini, Pius II's nephew, who adopted the name Pius III in memory of his famous uncle. Cesare Borgia's candidate had been defeated, and Giulio della Rovere, who had returned from a ten-year exile, and whose status as an enemy of the Borgias made him extremely popular, put the whole weight of his authority on the side of the new Pope. 'I shall be the Pope of peace, and I shall reform the Church,' Pius III publicly declared; and he was one who might well have translated his plans into action. But alas, the rheumatism from which he suffered so cruelly killed him less than a month after his election. 'This is a great misfortune for Rome and for us all,' wrote one Sienese chronicler; 'but our sins are so grievous that perhaps we deserved nothing better.'

The next pontificate, on the other hand, was far less unedifying than that of Alexander VI. Although the new Pope had not led an altogether irreproachable life before his election, once established in St Peter's chair he managed to behave with dignity and continence, and was very severe in his criticism of Alexander VI, whom he dubbed a 'Jew' and

[1] In addition it should be noted that the leading Iberian painter at this period was the Portuguese Nuno Gonçalves, who was also a most devout Christian.

a 'renegade.' Moreover he was so deeply engrossed in his passion for politics that he had little or no time for frivolous delights. Politics was this man's prime concern, to the exclusion of almost everything else, and the circumstances of the time made politics a singularly turbulent and complex game. There were certainly many ways in which the Papacy might yield to the climate of the age and betray its divine vocation. It might, for example, yield to that hedonist paganism which was formulated by all too many of the humanists, as Alexander VI had done; or it might become so completely involved in temporal affairs as to end by being little more than another Italian state, defending its interests by methods whose rules were even then being written down by Machiavelli. The conduct of Julius II (1503–13) had this last result.

Raphael's famous portrait of *Julius II* is so wonderfully lifelike that Vasari declared that when he looked at it he felt as frightened as if he were in the presence of the living man himself. Even so it does not reflect the full force of a personality which was one of the most remarkable in an age which produced so many men of his calibre. Anyone who studies the picture of this venerable, grey-bearded man, with his deep-set eyes, thin, tight lips and sad meditative expression, which conveys an overwhelming feeling of implacable determination and will-power, is immediately reminded that his contemporaries called him 'homo terribile.' Julius himself applied the same epithet to Michelangelo, and it is equally true of both men. There he sits, his hands resting on the arms of his chair. Any moment, it seems, he will spring to his feet, seize the cane which never left his side and whose tap-tap was enough to turn the faces of his secretaries pale with apprehension, and hurry down the Vatican corridors, where, entering one of the offices, he will bang violently on the table, or even belabour the shoulders or shins of some unfortunate protonotary whose work he has found unsatisfactory. Or perhaps he is about to make one of his whirlwind visits to the Sistine Chapel, to inspect the work of Michelangelo. If a single square inch of the painting is not to his taste he will not hesitate to hurl insults worthy of the slums of Rome at this other giant of the age. But to complete the portrait of this extraordinary pontiff, we must imagine him in helmet and breastplate, leading his armies to battle in person against the 'Barbarians' even when he was well past sixty-five; or visualize him at his most supple and cunning, 'Machiavellian' in the worst sense of the word, feigning modesty, amiability and conciliation in order to ensnare Louis XII of France or Ferdinand of Spain in his toils. In short, Julius II was an exceptional man, who merits our real admiration, though it is not the kind of admiration which one willingly offers a Vicar of Christ.

His election was a triumph, for he was summoned to succeed

Pius III at the first ballot, by thirty-seven out of a total of thirty-eight votes. All that the Sacred College knew was that the Church was in dire need of a strong man, and that since Cardinal Giulio della Rovere had been in disgrace under Alexander VI, his choice would seem to imply a radical change. All who might have opposed a nephew of Sixtus IV had been skilfully neutralized with promises; thus in return for continuation in his post at the head of the army of the Keys, Cesare Borgia had persuaded all his friends among the *porporati* to vote for Rovere, a gesture he would soon bitterly regret. Consequently, though it was not strictly simoniacal, the election was suspect, and the new Pope's first act was to promulgate a bull condemning simony at whatever level of the ecclesiastical hierarchy, and rendering those who practised it liable to the most severe punishments. Julius had absolved himself very cheaply.

As soon as he was installed in the Vatican, Julius II let it be understood that he had his own well-laid plans, and that he intended to realize them notwithstanding any resistance there might be. The first stage comprised the restoration of the temporal power of the Holy See and this he quickly accomplished. Far too many greedy mouths had taken advantage of his predecessors' weakness to swallow up estates and properties which belonged by right to the Papacy. Julius II set about his task in a systematic way, first of all settling accounts with the lesser fry, and saving the more important, notably the Republic of Venice, until later. Machiavelli describes it thus: 'Boldly displaying the sacred banners, and full of all his natural fury, the Pope first vented his spleen upon all those who had possessed themselves of cities in his domain.' In all fairness it is difficult to reproach him on this score. The petty nobility, who were virtually brigands, were brought to their senses; the Roman factions that had turned the city streets into cut-throats' alleys were quieted; and the Orsinis and Colonnas were actually reconciled. Order was restored to papal finances by dint of rigorous administration. But the most striking episode in the whole of this reassertion of papal authority was the fall of Cesare Borgia. When called upon to hand over the places he occupied illegally the Duke of Romagna attempted to prevaricate; the terrible Pope had no hesitation in imprisoning him and keeping him in the Castle of Sant' Angelo long enough to ensure that his prestige was severely affected. When the young *condottiere* eventually managed to escape, there was no longer any future for him in Italy; choosing to seek his fortune in Spain, he was killed and left the Pope free to claim his heritage. 'In short, Cesare served the grandeur of the Church extremely well,' comments Machiavelli with his usual irony.

However, Julius II had cleared only the first rung in the ladder of that laborious ascent to power upon which he had determined. He

I

made no secret of his plan. 'I should like to see the Roman pontiff the one and only permanent master of Italy, our common mother,' he said; 'but I am distressed to think that time may prevent me from bringing my schemes to fruition. No, I shall not be able to do for Italy all that my heart desires. Ah, if only I were twenty years younger.' This dream of a unified Italy under papal authority, with Rome as its artistic, spiritual and intellectual capital, had been dimly foreseen by Nicholas V, and moulded into concrete shape by Alexander VI. Julius II strove to give it reality in the few years at his disposal. The sands of time were running out but he brought to his task all the energy and determination of which he was capable, together with the wisdom of a seasoned and wily politician.

The principal obstacle was Venice, whose aggressive policy aimed at nothing less than making the whole of northern Italy into a kind of vast protectorate. She had just seized Ravenna from the Papal States. Julius II could not hope to defeat the mighty republic single-handed. Needing allies, he appealed to the French and the Spaniards, whom he termed 'Barbarians,' having already made up his mind to rid himself of them later on. The affair was not difficult to manage, for everyone hated the Venetians, who were 'insatiably greedy for blood, land and wealth,' according to one French chronicler. Papal diplomacy was applied with consummate skill. It was suggested to Louis XII that to take the place of Naples, which was lost for ever, he might seize from Venice those towns which she had torn from his Milanese fief— Brescia, Cremona, Bergamo and so on. The Emperor Maximilian received hints that Padua, Vicenza, Treviso and Friuli were really Germanic areas. Even the kings of England and Spain entered the lists, and the League of Cambrai, formed in 1508, constituted a most formidable coalition against Venice, even more formidable than the interdict which Julius II applied as his crowning touch. Any Italian towns that showed themselves unwilling to join the league, such as Perugia and Bologna, were attacked by the terrible pontiff in person. In the spring of 1509, absolutely convinced that he was brilliantly avenging his Neapolitan failures thereby, Louis XII led his army to the attack, and routed the Venetian forces at Agnadello. Julius II had won the first set in the game.

Louis XII very quickly realized that he had been hoaxed. It was soon clear that the Machiavellian pontiff sought to expel him from that very Milanese duchy whose possession had meant so much to him that he had been foolish enough to abandon Burgundy, Brittany and Blois for its sake. '*Fuori barbari!*' This was the watchword which sped like wildfire across Italy. For the present 'Barbarians' meant the French, who, although they had just been fighting to restore Ravenna to the Pope, were still rulers of Genoa and Milan, allies of Florence and

Ferrara, and as such represented the strongest force in the peninsula. A separate peace was signed with Venice. Ferdinand and his troops were cunningly prevailed upon to change sides, against the promise of the kingdom of Naples. Henry VIII of England was offered the French province of Guienne, and the Swiss, who found Louis XII's remuneration too low, were easily bought. 'I am not the French king's chaplain!' sneered the Pope, and donning his helmet again he set off to capture Mirandola from one of the Barbarians' allies. Under his guidance the Holy League would sweep every Frenchman from the peninsula.

In fact things were not quite so simple. Although the opposing coalition comprised nearly all the rest of Europe, the French held firm. The fantastic feats of Gaston de Foix, Louis XII's nephew, a young Napoleon of twenty-two, completely shattered the attacks of the Swiss, Spanish and papal armies. Men began to wonder where this formidable young warrior would stop. He even talked of swooping on Rome, ejecting the Pope and having another elected, when he was killed before Ravenna, pierced by twenty sword-thrusts. Gaston's army won the day, but his death made the victory more tragic than a defeat. Julius II, who had been barricaded in his palace, gnashing his teeth, ready for the Barbarian attack, breathed again.

In addition Louis XII had committed a serious tactical blunder: he had believed it possible to transpose the affair on to the religious plane and thereby weaken the very principle of papal authority. A section of the French clergy, meeting at Tours, proclaimed that the state which had declared war on a Christian king was scandalous and utterly depraved. Then, supported by a few cardinals (including a Borgia) who bore a grudge against Julius II, Louis convened a so-called oecumenical Council at Pisa (1511), in order to reform the Church, starting with the Papacy. But the ancient war-machine of Constance and Basle was a spent force. 'This is not a council, but a conventicle,' declared Julius II, noticing how few delegates came to the assembly. These accusations and suspended decisions were pure comedy. The Fathers of the council were expelled from Pisa by the angry inhabitants, and their reception at Milan was so cold that they quickly left for Asti. Finally, they took refuge in Lyons, having become the laughing-stock of Europe. Louis XII had lost face, and even the Sorbonne refused to join his campaign against the Pope. Moreover the tide of battle was now running against him. La Palisse, Gaston de Foix's indifferent successor, had evacuated the duchy of Milan; in the following year La Trémouille was beaten at Novara, and the victorious Swiss hurled their advance guard into Burgundy, aiming to capture Dijon. The terrible battering-ram which the warrior Pope had set in motion seemed certain to crush France; the emperor prepared to attack the kingdom from the north and east, while the English made ready to land on the Normandy coast. But

Julius II was wondering if this success was not perhaps excessive and likely to prove a Pyrrhic victory. He asked himself whether his policy of sweeping the French out of Italy in order to deliver it into Spanish hands had really been so clever after all. The marriages between Don Juan of Spain, son of the Catholic sovereign, and Margaret of Austria, on the one hand, and between Philip the Fair, Maximilian's son, and Joanna of Castile (Joanna the Mad) on the other, had united the Spanish and Hapsburg crowns, and made the danger much more obvious. The policy of 'the balance of power,' which England was just beginning to envisage at this time, also struck Julius II as the wisest course to pursue. 'If God will but grant me a few more years,' he said, 'I will deliver Naples also from the yoke of Spain.' But the Lord would not allow him to put his final plans into practice: in February 1513 He forced an everlasting peace upon this indefatigable warrior.

'There was once a time when the humblest baron thought himself entitled to flout the authority of the Pope,' observed Machiavelli; 'today that authority commands the respect of the King of France.' The prestige of the Apostolic See emerged from this militant pontificate immensely enhanced. Moreover Julius undoubtedly possessed a real understanding of the Church's greatness; it was not solely on the military and political plane that he worked for her glory and also, as must be admitted, for the defence of the Catholic faith. He realized the importance of the Spanish and Portuguese conquests across the seas, and he arranged for several missionaries to be sent to these areas. For example, it was he who nominated an archbishop and two bishops for Haiti. The intelligent steps he took to facilitate the conversion of the Bohemian Hussites, to deal with the Marranos in Spain, and to help the reforming movement which was taking place in certain monasteries —among the Benedictines of Vallombrosa and Monte Oliveto, for instance—are sufficient to show that, although he was so deeply involved in politics, he did not allow them to absorb him completely.

Before his greatness can be awarded the crown of interpretation in the truly Christian sense, it must be shown that Julius II had at heart the general question of reform, which was being proclaimed as indispensable by so many great minds of the age. We cannot be certain that this was the case. It is true that a few months before his death he decided to convene an oecumenical council, the eighteenth or *Fifth Lateran Council* (1512–17), and that he included ecclesiastical reform among its agenda, alongside the crusade against the Turks and the extirpation of the French Schism. The early sessions of this assembly consisted solely of striking manifestations of the current strength of papal prestige. The Pope's authority was solemnly and repeatedly proclaimed. But there is little doubt that such measures were essential in the circumstances. This politically minded Pope probably considered that the restoration of the Holy See's authority, and the reassertion of its independence in the face of the pretensions of secular powers, was his genuine duty, and in this field his success was enormous. Yet by delaying the hour of reform still further, and by allowing venality and corruption to flourish among his followers, just as it flourished in several sectors of the Church, he may well have aggravated the internal crisis which was soon to break out in such violent form. It was not enough to have compelled kings to recognize his authority, to have covered Rome with new glory, and to have set in train those vast artistic enterprises in which the genius of Raphael, Michelangelo and Bramante expanded in a profusion of masterpieces. The amazing fragment of what was to have been the most gigantic tomb of all, the one which Michelangelo envisaged for Julius II himself, has an unequivocal symbolism of its own. This unfinished masterpiece corresponds most admirably with the man whose memory it preserves; for his work too was great, but none the less fragmentary and incomplete.

THE TEMPTATION OF ART: LEO X

For Julius II, as for Nicholas V long ago, art had been just one means of increasing Rome's prestige and of manifesting the glory of the Apostolic See. For his successor it was something entirely different: it was a ruling passion, an activity which must needs dominate all the rest, a kind of reason for living. The new Pope did not yield to the temptations of the flesh, like Alexander VI, nor to those of politics, as Julius II had done. His pontificate, however, demonstrates very clearly that when the cult of intelligence and beauty loses its sense of proportion and makes intellectual and artistic creations an end in themselves, it too constitutes a formidable spiritual temptation. The Pope who builds the most splendid basilica in the world over the Apostle's tomb, but loses a quarter of his entire flock in the process, is surely carrying foolishness to the point of treachery.

Leo X (1513–21) was a Medici, Giovanni by name. He was the youngest of Lorenzo's sons, and the only one to have inherited his father's rare talents. He was only thirty-eight years old at the time of his election, but he was a heavily built, florid man, with protruding eyes, and he looked considerably older. He had been loaded with benefices from his earliest years, and was already a cardinal at the age of fourteen. He had a distinguished mind, and had been educated by the greatest scholars of the age, Angelo Poliziano and Marsilio Ficino being among his teachers. From childhood onwards he had breathed the air of that brilliant worldliness and intellectual refinement which gave Florence such an atmosphere of charged excitement. Possibly this was not the type of education best suited to a future pontiff. His election was easily accomplished: presents and promises had been distributed to good intent. Next he was hastily ordained priest and consecrated bishop, for he was still only a deacon, and finally he was crowned as pope on the steps of the ancient basilica of St Peter, which was in process of being demolished to make room for the new cathedral. The exceptional pomp and pageantry of the 'cavalcade' in which he showed himself to the Romans was generally assumed to herald a sumptuous and magnificent reign. Nothing was missing: there were endless processions, distributions of largesse, parades of chariots depicting pagan allegories, fireworks and illuminations. Leo X was the first Medici to become pope, and his family spared no expense to mark the event.

Leo X was an ardent believer in peace. In the first place he was pacific by nature, and secondly war has never been favourable to artistic and literary expansion. Consequently he entered with enthusiasm into the policy of truce-making which his bellicose predecessor had come to desire at the end of his reign, and helped to negotiate the marriage between Louis XII, an elderly widower, and the young sister of Henry VIII, which brought the war to an end. At the same time he obtained the French king's adhesion to the Lateran Council, which seemed to set the seal on the general reconciliation. Unhappily, however, Louis XII died very soon afterwards and was succeeded by his cousin and son-in-law, *Francis I* (1515–47). The latter, a great-grandson of Valentina Visconti, was a handsome young blade of twenty, a great believer in brilliant escapades, and devoted to everything Italian. No sooner was he on the throne than he laid claim to his Milanese inheritance, and set to work to reconquer it. He bought the emperor's benevolent neutrality for a considerable sum, made an alliance with Venice and took the field. The Swiss who guarded the Alpine passes were taken by surprise and fell back beneath the walls of Milan. Finally, after two days of bitter fighting, the French cavalry charge brought their resistance to an end at *Marignano* (1515).

When he received this news Leo X was filled with consternation. Was this a return to the days when Charles VIII and his army wandered across Italy as though it were a tournament field? The Swiss negotiated the famous *Perpetual Peace* (1516) with the King of France; Maximilian was on the threshold of the grave, the conqueror seemed on the point of invading the Papal States. It looked as though the Pope would have to defend himself by force of arms. But Leo X was not a Florentine for nothing; he had all the flexibility so generally associated with his native city. Proceeding with considerable skill, he flattered the young monarch's pride, pretending to make him protector of the Holy See and of all the Medicis into the bargain, and thus established with him the most cordial relations. What could be juster than a French duchy of Milan?—providing of course that the republic of Florence remained in the hands of the Pope's family. Parma and Piacenza were to be ceded as an act of grace; and when it was suggested that these independent principalities would need a ruler, the name of the pontiff's brother Giulio was at once put forward.

Leo X now conceived the idea of taking advantage of the king's favourable state of mind to settle a question which remained unresolved between France and the Holy See; that of the Pragmatic Sanction. Rome had never accepted the unilateral decision which claimed to regulate the position of the Church in France; it had been the source of countless disputes, first under Louis XI, whose Concordat with the Papacy had been purely verbal, and then in turn under Charles VIII and Louis XII. Clerical supporters of the Pragmatic Sanction had actually been the object of papal warnings, and at the bottom of their hearts neither kings nor popes had been satisfied with the way it worked. Surely it would be better to replace it by a properly drafted concordat, something after the style of that which existed between the Empire and the Papacy. King and pope met at Bologna, towards the end of 1515, amid all the pomp and ceremony which they both loved so well; a year later the concordat was signed and promulgated, despite the opposition of the French Parlement and clergy. The concordat acknowledged the king's right of nomination to the more important benefices—ten archbishoprics, eighty-three bishoprics, and five hundred and twenty-seven abbacies—but these nominations were subject to certain conditions of age and competence being properly satisfied, and the Pope alone possessed the right of canonical investiture. The role of the Tribunal of the Holy See as a court of appeal was confirmed, and the Papacy obtained the restoration of annates. In fact, the king remained the protector and controller of the Church in France, but the Sovereign Pontiff's authority was clearly asserted, and France officially abandoned all conciliar theories. This concordat was to remain in force until 1790, and was to have most profound consequences upon French religious history as a whole. It was to be accused of having prepared the climate for the Gallicanism of the future, and also of having helped to divide the clergy into two sections—the higher clergy, which tended to be wealthy and well born and chosen from the royal *entourage*, and the ordinary priesthood, which was recruited from the common people and severely underpaid. But it was to have another and much happier result. Since the 'Most Christian' king was now the official adoptive head of the Church, he had a major interest in preserving his links with the Pope and in ensuring that no doubts were cast upon his own orthodoxy. This fact was to be of capital importance in the troubled days of the Reformation, and to some extent the conversion of Henry IV was the direct result of the concordat.

Thus the diplomatic skill of the Medici Pope, and his desire to establish a lasting peace in Italy, had served the Church well. Such a peace seemed ensured by the Treaty of Noyon, which guaranteed the duchy of Milan to Francis I and Naples to Charles of Spain. Unhappily Leo X appears in a much less favourable light in a number of more serious matters. Unlike Julius II, who had worked solely for the glory of the states of the Church and for Italy, and not for his own family, Leo X reverted to the nepotism which Callixtus III, Sixtus IV and Alexander VI had practised, regarding the Papacy as a personal possession which he had the right to dispose of exactly as he pleased. Working on this principle, he detached the duchy of Urbino from the Papal States in order to bestow it as a fief on one of his relations. Here he showed a lack of standards which cannot be excused by his illustrious antecedents. And there were other weaknesses besides this slipshod type of behaviour. There was his love of pleasures—principally those of the table, for Leo X conducted himself quite properly in other respects—his thoughtless prodigality which encouraged venality and corruption, his flagrant incapacity to appreciate the grave dangers of the times. 'Since God has given us the Papacy, let us use it to our advantage,' Leo X had exclaimed at the time of his election; at least so the Venetian Giorgi alleges. And he practised this principle all too assiduously. Although his pontificate was less scandalous than that of Alexander VI, it helped to degrade the Church at a time when her recovery was more than ever necessary.

And what of Church reform? The Lateran Council was actually in session at the moment when Leo X ascended the throne of St Peter, and reform was a constant topic on its agenda. But there is some doubt as to whether its views on this subject were really sincere. Various eminent figures in the assembly expressed alarm at the current situation. In fact, however, the Council dared not go to the roots of the problem and cauterize corruption as it should have done. A number of decisions were reached and votes taken condemning certain abuses pertaining to ecclesiastical nominations and the holding of benefices in plurality; regulating the lives of cardinals and bishops; exhorting priests to chastity; and censuring all who indulged in simony or despoiled the Church. After several disputes the religious Orders were subjected to episcopal authority so far as their powers of ministration were concerned, and certain rules regarding preaching were drawn up. All these decisions are undoubted evidence of good intentions, but the strength to pursue reform to the bitter end, and above all to see that it was put into practice, was sadly lacking. Who had the power to impose these half-measures on the Church? 'You cants, bigots and hypocrites!' cried the satirist Pierre Gringoire in his pamphlet *Fools' Enterprises*. 'You claim to correct abuses in others, and yet you are a perfect example of them yourselves.' His derision was only too well founded.

'The present demands audacious, uncommon and unusual decisions. . . .' observed Machiavelli. Leo X was not the man to make them. In 1517 he brought the Council to its close, and showed virtually no interest in executing its decrees. His main preoccupation was the life of the intellect and the senses. He considered himself far more fitted for this than for stern struggles to preserve the world's faith and morality. 'Great authors are the rule of life, and our consolation in misfortune,' he wrote enthusiastically in the licence he granted for the printing of Tacitus. He went on to add that the protection of scholars and the acquisition of books seemed to him a leader's most important duties and thanked Heaven for allowing him to devote himself to them. In consequence intellectuals and artists of every description flocked to his court. Bembo, Sadolet and Dovizi were his friends, and he made two of them cardinals. Wherever he went—in his palace, at the theatre, even in church—he was besieged by crowds of poets and writers. To express his thanks for their eulogies and panegyrics he would dive into the red velvet purse which he always carried with him, and throw them handfuls of gold coins without the slightest thought of the alarm which this distribution of largesse caused his treasurers. Carnivals and comedies of the most unedifying kind had no more enthusiastic spectator than the Pope; all the arts knew him as a connoisseur of discerning taste, and a patron whose generosity was quite inexhaustible. When he made his way down the corridors of the Vatican, he was invariably escorted by a chamber orchestra, and spectators could watch him joining the violins in the refrain. He showered such largesse on Raphael, his favourite painter, that the artist was able to maintain quite a little court of admirers and pupils. The new St Peter's was rising from the ground, and the site teemed with craftsmen, architects and artists who had been summoned from the four corners of Europe to share in the work. This was the kind of glory which Leo X coveted so dearly; this was the kind of glory with which he did indeed halo Rome. Undoubtedly the price paid for it was very great. But the papal administration strained its ingenuity to discover fresh resources: new indulgences were granted to provide funds for the rebuilding of the basilica, and far too many zealous propagandists exploited these after the style of a commercial operation. The money had to be found somehow.

Did the sumptuous pontiff realize the danger into which his thoughtless attitude was leading the Church? He lived and was to die (1521) in a state of sublime artistic intoxication. Did he understand the importance of the trouble provoked four years earlier by an obscure German monk, which specifically concerned the question of indulgences? Had he even bothered to read the letter which this violent

* I

agitator had sent him, modelled on St Bernard's *De Consideratione*, in order to remind him of the duties of his office? While he was stag-hunting at Magliana, one spring day in 1520, surrounded by his brilliant retinue, someone had brought him a bull which pronounced the ex-communication of the monk from Wittenberg. He had signed it, and then resumed the chase. Had he assessed the full significance of this irre-parable act? As he had intended, the pontificate of the Medici pope would indeed mark the glorious apogee of the Renaissance. But it would also be remembered, not merely by history, but before the tribunal of God as well, as the pontificate during which the Seamless Robe was most tragically rent asunder.

ROME, CAPITAL OF THE ARTS

Nevertheless it would be unfair to belittle the splendour and the consequent influence which enlightened love of the arts, as practised by Leo X, undoubtedly brought to Rome, capital of the Church. As has been seen, however, he was not the first nor the only pontiff to strive for the goal to which Nicholas V had long ago pointed the way, and which all Nicholas's successor had sought more or less consciously to attain. That phrase 'the age of Leo X,' which bathes the name of the Medici Pope in the glamour of the most brilliant period of artistic creation that the world has ever known, is obviously an exaggeration. On this plane Julius II and Alexander VI were no less active and decisive. But by making patronage of the arts one of the basic principles of his pontificate, Leo linked the throne of St Peter with the glory shed by those immortal masterpieces; and in this respect he helped to fashion the new look of the Church, and his role was thus conclusive, for both good and ill.

The salient fact about the seventy-five years which span the period between the pontificates of Nicholas V and Leo X is that Rome then became in a very real sense the capital of beauty, the meeting-point of all creative energies, the sun which radiated the fruitful heat of artistic inspiration.[1] These Renaissance popes considered that everything of artistic merit should be diverted to the Vicar of Christ, and used to further his prestige. All the classical marble sculptures revealed by

[1] Curiously enough this was not the case on the purely intellectual plane. Humanism certainly did not disappear altogether from the Eternal City. The Vatican Library con-tinued to accumulate precious manuscripts; men like Cardinal Bembo continued the tradition of the Roman Academy; and another Christian Virgil, *Marco Vita*, Sannazar's rival and author of the ambitious *Christiad*, lived there. But the masters of political philosophy and history remained faithful to Florence. *Machiavelli* (1469–1527), *Guicciar-dini* (1483–1540), and *Balthasar Castiglione* (1478–1529). When *Ariosto* (1474–1533) came to write his great work, *Orlando Furioso*, he too made his home on the banks of the Arno.

recent excavations must go to augment the papal collections. Apollo, Laocoön, the Nile—all provided striking decoration for the famous 'Belvedere' in the Vatican Palace. An artist had but to prove his genius and he was straightway claimed by Rome; he was summoned to the Papal Court and liberally rewarded for his talents. As soon as the Florentine Michaelangelo made a name for himself with his *Pieta*, Julius II commanded him to erect a tomb worthy of the emperors of ancient Rome. No sooner had *Bramante* (1444–1514) revealed the vast range of his architectural ability, against the background of his native Urbino, than the Papacy offered him the chance to aim still higher and show the full extent of his capacity. From 1499 in particular —the crucial year in which the creator of the new St Peter's was summoned to direct the building works—a prodigious animation possessed the entire city. The whole place seemed wholly given over to the pick and shovel, the mason's trowel and the painter's brush. Such grandiose plans were conceived that their realization was to take several centuries. Craftsmen were ordered to finish in four years works which would appear to demand the effort of a lifetime. And the wonderful thing was that this sublime improvisation was neither slapdash nor ephemeral, and that time was to honour the creations it produced. These were marvellous and exciting decades,[1] when a thousand craftsmen were fashioning the marble of the largest basilica in the world, when Michelangelo lay flat on his back, facing the ceiling, painting the vast surfaces of the Sistine Chapel for twelve hours at a time, and when Raphael was embellishing the Pope's private apartments. . . . The pontiffs who had willed such artistry into being had some reason to be proud.

This sudden apogee of Rome was all the more impressive because it coincided with her rivals' relative eclipse. Florence was now in decline. She had undoubtedly fulfilled her function as the initiator of the Renaissance, and perhaps she was too sophisticated and too obsessed by problems to be capable of solving them all. Other artistic centres certainly continued to thrive in every corner of the fortunate peninsula, and some of them produced undeniable masterpieces; but their influence was very limited in character. Venice was the only place which could have vied with the Eternal City in this field, but her rivalry was an incomplete one, for her sensual genius was almost wholly expressed in pictorial art, and the techniques of building and sculpture were virtually neglected. In Rome, however, all the arts, without exception, attained complete fulfilment. The pontiffs' ambitions, their 'Roman patriotism' with its roots in the classical revival, their taste for splendour, and even in some cases their sensuality, all

[1] Six years after Leo X's death the sack of Rome by the Imperialists was to shatter this artistic impulse.

combined to provide the capital of the Church with the artistic adorn-
ments of which she is still justly proud. This implantation of genius
in the heart of the Seven Hills, in a place so charged with history, at the
centre of a plain whose austere horizons encompassed the nostalgic
splendour of her ancient ruins, may well have provided the opportunity
for the complete realization of all the potentialities accumulated by the
generations that had gone before. And it must have been Roman
orderliness which enabled the art of the Renaissance to operate this
prodigious synthesis of gentleness and violence, sensuality and asceticism, licence and discipline, which makes the works of this epoch such
unsurpassably perfect masterpieces.

The glory and greatness of Papal Rome—the Rome of Julius II and
Leo X—corresponded exactly with the moment in which all the discoveries and contributions of a prodigiously creative century were
blending together and becoming stabilized into one powerful and
majestic style, which was to remain known everywhere as the *classical*.
By 1450 the first period of the Renaissance was over,[1] and the second
had begun. Even greater hosts of brilliant talent seemed, in almost
every case, to be striving after absolute perfection in their own field.
The transition from the first stage to the second was virtually imper-
ceptible; artists from the earlier period—Verrocchio, Piero della
Francesca and the della Robbias—overlapped into the second, but
without acquiring its spirit. In the course of his long life *Giovanni
Bellini* (1430–1516), the pliant Venetian, progressed from an art-form
that was still 'primitive' towards an inspiration and technique of a
quite modern kind. His brother-in-law, the scholarly and sober
Mantegna (1431–1506), learned from the ancients the secret of drawing
the human body in accurate proportions, by scrupulously careful
anatomical observation, and of producing detail that was genuinely
lifelike. These were things which Michelangelo was to remember in the
future. Even the more unusual personalities, who pursued their talents
in directions where posterity would not follow, marked a decisive stage
in artistic progression. *Botticelli* (1444–1510), for example, with his
tormented soul and rare talent, wavering between the evocation of an
equivocal Paradise and the illustration of Dante's *Inferno*, was a kind
of erratic disciple of Fra Angelico—albeit an Angelico who found the
smile of bad angels rather too attractive. His painting enables us to
understand the link between the pious of artist of San Marco and
Raphael.

At this period, before Rome emptied them to her own advantage,
Italy was full of schools and other intellectual centres. These produced
a series of masters whose providential role seems to have been that of
preparing art to take the decisive step, beyond which lay the field of

[1] On its division into three periods see p. 192.

genius. Although Pietro Vanucci's (generally known as *Perugino*, 1445–1523) superabundant production of Madonnas would lead to a depreciation of his own talent, he nevertheless bequeathed to his pupil Raphael his sense of overall colours, iridescent atmosphere and perfectly balanced composition, while his moving 'Crucifixion,' at Florence, was not unworthy of a corner of the Sistine Chapel. *Signorelli* (1441–1523) served as Michelangelo's teacher. He was yet another Umbrian, and to the strength and fondness for space, which he derived from Piero della Francesca, he added his own discovery of movement, in order to create those astonishing scenes at Orvieto—the 'Last Judgment,' for example—where the savage rendering of human form and muscle in the nude representations of the damned being flayed alive foreshadows the awe-inspiring figures of Michaelangelo's frescoes. The heirs of *Ghirlandajo* (1449–94) would retain his passion for accurate draughtsmanship, which he himself carried to extremes, but which would be studied and then modified by Leonardo da Vinci. As for *Pinturicchio* (1454–1513), 'the dauber,' his diffuse talent as it appears in the Piccolomini Library at Siena and the Borgia rooms at the Vatican possesses an almost too facile element, attractive though it is. He undoubtedly bequeathed to his successors his love of knowledgably illustrated decorations in which he could use his taste for story-telling and colour to the full.

As Julius II called Bramante to his side, just as the Quattrocento ended, the age of the highly talented drew to its close. The one now opening was an era of outstanding genius. The time of pursuit and conquest was over; that of sovereign ease and incomparable perfection of execution was now at its height. The greatest fifteenth-century artists show a kind of stiff, hard and almost clumsy quality in the exploitation of their gifts, and their ambitions were clearly limited. Henceforth the mighty aimed at infinity, and so perfect was their artistry that everything they attempted, no matter how difficult or dangerous, became simplicity itself in their hands.

Three names mark this peak of unequalled glory: *Leonardo da Vinci, Michelangelo* and *Raphael*. They have often been compared with one another, but are in fact incomparable, so different is the soil whence each derives his fundamental gifts. Although their ages were rather different, they can be regarded as contemporaries by virtue of the common date at which their talents matured, and because of the position they occupy in the historical evolution of art. A quarter of a century separates the painter of the 'Mona Lisa' (1452–1519) from the creator of 'Moses' (1475–1564); and while *Raphael* (1483–1520) was Michelangelo's junior by only eight years, the brevity of his life seems to displace him in relation to his mighty rival, who survived him by forty-four years. But on the glorious threshold of the sixteenth century, in whose great book each was to write so sublime a page, all three were in full possession of their talents and at the height of their creative powers.

Leonardo da Vinci is a lone, isolated figure. He remained apart from everyone—from his age, his compatriots (he died in France) and from Rome, which he was almost alone in disdaining, and where he is scarcely represented save by his wonderful St Jerome. His was a universal genius. He possessed to the full that fever which fired all the greatest souls of the epoch, the fever to know and understand everything. For Leonardo painting and sculpture were but two occupations among many. He was just as passionately interested in studying physics or mechanics, as in imagining men in flight or bridges yet unbuilt. Yet, though he treated art as a mere pastime, regarding it with a kind of regal negligence, his contributions enabled it to take some decisive steps forward. His draughtsmanship was well worthy of a pupil of Verrocchio, and he made it express human feelings. Painting owed to him the discovery of *chiaroscuro* and *sfumato*, the portrayal of transparencies veiled in shadow—secrets which have not always since been used to the best advantage. Leonardo, however, considered technical advances mere means to obtaining a better knowledge of the spiritual mystery of things and people. Anyone who studies his fascinating and charming portraits, or those rare composite pictures in which he tore traditional themes from their normal imagery and made them expound spiritual truths—his 'Last Supper,' 'St John the Baptist' or 'St Anne and the Virgin'—is overwhelmed by a feeling of profound awe, almost bewilderment, a sense that he is very close indeed to an ineffable secret. Certainly no painter has ever gone so far as Leonardo in this effort towards an understanding which, were it possible to take it to its absolute conclusion, would give art a hold on the divine.

Michelangelo Buonarotti possessed the same intention, but he regarded it from a different angle; and heaven alone knows what spiritual torments it caused him! He appeared to seek his goal through that semi-divine element in his genius. From the moment he was born he seemed to possess all the gifts which enable man to express himself by the co-operation of tireless hands and a perpetually creative brain. Though less interested in science than Leonardo da Vinci, his was a universal genius. He was an outstanding engineer and stirring poet, as well as a painter, sculptor and architect. From marble he fashioned his perfect and disturbing representations of David, Moses and the Slaves, and the mysterious figures on the Medici tombs. He became a fresco painter quite by chance, at the whim of a pope, re-inventing by himself this art-form, of which he had been hitherto completely ignorant, by covering the ceiling of the Sistine Chapel, the vastest decorative surface in the world, with his magnificent groups. All the knowledge acquired by the past reached its perfect fulfilment in Michelangelo. The lessons learned by his compatriots, the earlier Florentine sculptors, and by so many painters from Giotto to Signorelli, from Ghirlandajo to Piero della Francesca, were all used to the best advantage; but he transcended and transfigured everything contained in this inheritance by his feeling for form, brilliant composition and spiritual power, which have never since been equalled. He sought to give expression to a kind of man far removed from the realities of this world, a man more splendid and perfect than had been possible since the Fall. Because Christianity was a fundamental part of his being, Michelangelo was constantly torn between his desire to exalt the beauty of the human body and his realization of the tragedy inherent in the drama of the human soul. All his life he remained a withdrawn figure rejecting the base and tawdry world around him, refusing to have any contact with it and standing steadfastly face to face with his God. Imprisoned in his feeble body, his mighty soul often seemed on the verge of plunging into the abyss of despair. Yet he survived all his contemporaries and witnessed the deaths of six successive popes. Until the hour of his death he continued to accept the sublime challenge, where the creative artist seems to pass the bounds of nature. He flung the terrifying chaos of his 'Last Judgment' on to the wall of the Sistine Chapel, and at the age of seventy-two he became an impromptu architect, thrusting the most tranquil and solemn of Hosannas high into the Roman sky, for the glory of Christ and His Church.[1]

All the currents of the past converged and united in *Raphael* also, but here there was no torment and no tragic drama. In that brief, full life honours, glory and wealth seem to have been awarded in exact proportion to the brilliant, easy fluency of the most receptive of temperaments. Raphael was a pupil of Perugino, and responded to every influence with which he came in contact. At Florence he was a Florentine, in Rome, where he had to compete with Michelangelo, a Roman. He progressed and changed from year to year, pursuing a constant apprenticeship. Raphael began with small decorative pictures, and ended with enormous and brilliantly constructed compositions, such as the 'School of Athens' and the 'Dispute of the Sacrament.' He is the really typical 'Renaissance' painter, marking the point of extreme perfection beyond which lies only empty facility and the capacity to copy, not learn, from what has gone before. But something is lacking. Raphael was a perfect draughtsman, a wonderful colourist and a brilliant constructor of great crowd scenes—his 'Mass of Bolsena' and the 'Heliodorus' are unsurpassable—and he showed infallible psychological insight in his portraits of Julius II, Leo X and Balthasar

---

[1] St Peter's and its celebrated cupola were not completed until much later; they are studied in the first section of Chapter V of *The Catholic Reformation*.

Castiglione; moreover, so far as historical and religious painting are concerned, he was the creator of modern iconography. Why then does his work fail to touch the soul at its vital core? The answer is provided by those little pictures which are sometimes called his 'Bible,' and by his overpretty Madonnas: he lacked the seal of suffering, the secret trembling of the spirit.

The whole of the High Renaissance seems to be expressed in this astonishing triad. However, this is not a completely accurate picture. Within less ambitious limits a number of other centres in Italy also produced artists of considerable stature, who came very near to genius. Florence scarcely counted any more. Nevertheless Andrea del Sarto carried on the great tradition of fresco-painting there, and Bronzino, despite the chill of his colours, was a penetrating portrait painter. At Parma, however, the supple *Corregio* (1489–1534), in spite of his rather poor draughtsmanship, made skilful use of chiaroscuro to produce the exciting female figures which eighteenth-century art was to admire so passionately. The boldness of his vast painted ceilings—which were often rather muddled and real 'riots of angels'—foreshadowed Tiepolo. But sensualist, realist Venice, whose reign as queen of the Sea and of the East continued some while longer, was the principal artistic centre outside Rome. Thus *Carpaccio* (1455–1526) delighted in observing the play of light on spectacles of legendary splendour; *Giorgione* (1478–1510) blended his love of accuracy with a quality of poetic translucency; and *Titian* (1477–1576), the greatest Venetian painter of them all, was at the height of his astonishingly full and lengthy career. Titian endowed oil-painting with many assets which the future was able to realize: he rejuvenated the rules governing the composition of large and crowded canvases and he executed countless portraits, altar paintings and mythological scenes suitable for drawing-room decoration. Although the master of the exquisite 'Presentation of Mary in the Temple' and 'The Man with the Glove' did not attain the same penetration as Leonardo or the sublimity of Michelangelo, he produced an alliance between the most liberal taste for colour and an extremely accurate feeling for truth that was little short of miraculous.

This epoch then marked an apogee, an unsurpassable crest on which Bramante, Leonardo da Vinci, Michelangelo, Raphael and Titian created and uprooted whole worlds. It was not to last: human achievements cannot long retain such heights. Each of these great men would leave his imprint in the realms of art, but none was to better them. Michelangelo had lived rather like a wild boar, hiding in his lair, and it is hardly accurate to speak of him having pupils. But his imitators retained his least happy features (excess of movement and of muscle), and rapidly foundered into turgidity. Leonardo's disciples tended to borrow his taste for *sfumato* rather than the austere discipline of his draughtsmanship. The best of them actually displayed notable talents, but none of them bore the stamp of genius. They included *Sodoma* (1477–1549), who managed to safeguard his own voluptuous individuality beside the Raphaelite masterpieces, and *Luini* (1480–1530), whose sense of order and charm verged on affectation. As for Raphael, his numerous band of assistants produced many skilful technicians and excellent draughtsmen, but not a single good painter. The best was *Giulio Romagna* (1449–1540), whose occasional gems excuse his usual appalling taste; but the creator of the admirable *Virgin of the Grand Duke* was to be responsible for untold numbers of insipid Madonnas, objects of sickly sweet piety, and Guido was his successor.

The Italian art of the High Renaissance did not remain confined to the peninsula for very long. It soon broke bounds and radiated far beyond. The two Italian wars which coincided with the culminating points of the first and second epochs of the Renaissance gave the French a glimpse of artistic creations which were entirely different from those they were accustomed to see at home. They brought back from Italy various works of art, both ancient and modern, as well as memories and experiences; they even managed to fetch back some of the actual artists, such as Leonardo da Vinci. This Renaissance influence was to make itself felt far and wide, to a greater or lesser extent. It reached as far afield as Moscow, where Fioraventi and Solario worked to rebuild the burnt-out Kremlin and where the Friazines erected the churches of the Dormition and Annunciation. It was to bear fruit throughout Europe and elsewhere. Its impulses still exercise some effect upon the world, even today.

The close and constant association of the Renaissance popes with this admirable movement undoubtedly entitles them to a measure of fame. In constituting herself protector of literature and the arts, the Church was unquestionably remaining loyal to her most authentic tradition, which went back as far as those Dark Ages when she alone had saved culture and learning in a world that was foundering in bloody chaos. She was fully in her element when engaging artists to work on her behalf. Moreover she gained much from the creative fever of the age. Builders' yards continued to increase in number throughout the length and breadth of Italy; more and more new churches were erected, or restoration carried out on old ones. The grandiose basilical style became the rule at St Mary Major, and also of St Paul-without-the-Walls with its severe lines of marble colonnades and sumptuous ceilings. Statues were everywhere: on façades, behind altars and in chapels, used for internal decoration as well as for exterior ornament; and painters worked furiously to cover the vast mural surfaces offered them by ceilings, vaults and cupolas. Far below, the great altar painting took the place of the stone reredos; it was the object of many an artist's finest efforts, and often provided the occasion for a master-piece. During this period there was not a single architect, sculptor or painter who did not devote some of his talents to religious themes.

But not to them alone. During this later period those symptoms which had been clearly visible ever since the beginning of the Renaissance became increasingly apparent. Artists worked for men at least as much as for God, and probably rather more. Palaces sprang from the ground faster than churches: at Rome the Farnese and Medici establishments rivalled the Vatican in their splendour. The art of creating beautiful gardens, one that is perhaps the most flattering to human sensibility, produced some brilliant results. It is characteristic that, while the Church spread Gothic beyond the limits of France, the Italian Renaissance first influenced areas outside the land of its birth through its profane works, long before it had any effect upon their religious art. Again, the colossal dimensions adopted by the sculptors chosen to work on the tombs of the great were undoubtedly indicative of a state of mind which was nothing new, but which the pride of Julius II brought to its climax. And the truthful portrait painters, from the savage Antonello de Messina to the calm, unyielding Titian, from the lucid Raphael to the bitter Bronzino, all immortalized man's basest passions—violence, cynicism, pride and sensuality.

The position was indeed one of absolute contradiction. Paganism was suggesting its own themes more and more insistently, and the same brushes and chisels that were used to evoke Christ, the Blessed Virgin and the saints were no less happily employed in representing the nudes of Greek and Roman mythology. Michelangelo began his career as a sculptor with 'Love Dormant'; he also created a Bacchus, an Apollo and several similar figures. Raphael, without the least qualm of conscience, divided his talents between scenes from sacred history on the walls of the Vatican and the sensual representations in the Farnese Palace. And do we find the real Botticelli in the pious 'Annunciation' or in the 'Birth of Venus' and 'Spring'—both perfect manifestations of pagan joy? On the other hand, Titian, the most profane of painters, the one best able to express Dionysiac joy on the grand scale in the material abandon of his figures, was also the artist who evoked the depths of Christian suffering in his agonizing 'Christ Crowned with Thorns' and his overwhelming 'Pieta.'

The same contradiction was present in the souls of these artists, who were increasingly torn between two antagonistic forces. It was not resolved by the elegant scepticism of Leonardo, by the agnosticism of Vasari, or by the pleasant hedonism of Raphael; and as for the alternative solution, that of a work totally ordered by faith, Fra Angelico was no longer there to point the way. For many this contradiction had to find its solution in and through art, and genius or mere talent managed to discover sufficiently lively sources of religious emotion to make it sincere.[1] In others there was a sense of terrible division, a schizophrenia which, in the case of Botticelli, found expression in the tears which he shed at Savonarola's feet and in his destruction of some of his pagan masterpieces. In Michelangelo, however, the greatest artist of them all and another convert of the prophet of Florence, this feeling manifested itself in a creative way, finding its outlet in a Pascalian quest for truth and a tragically moving succession of forms and figures.

This great classical art of the High Italian Renaissance raises a difficult problem for the devout believer. Its loyalty to Christian tradition is self-evident in some of its characteristics; and when we remember that generations have looked upon Raphael's Madonnas as the height of perfection so far as concerns works executed solely to evoke piety, we can scarcely condemn it as utterly lacking religious inspiration. Art need not be crude in order to bring men nearer to God. The great biblical lessons of the Sistine Chapel, as well as countless moving Christs and mystical Virgins, are there to prove that the age of genius was also an age of Christian fidelity. Yet the witness of faith which this art affords possesses a somewhat disturbing element. These prolific painters are increasingly apt to overlay fundamentally religious sentiments with others of a very different kind. Anyone studying a Madonna by Leonardo, Raphael or Luini is moved not only by piety, but also by other emotions which the artist knew all too well how to awaken. Despite its Christian themes, Raphael's work in the Vatican yields to a somewhat equivocal ingenuousness, which is most apparent in his 'Creation of Woman' and the 'Expulsion from Paradise.' Even in a masterpiece such as the ceiling of the Sistine Chapel, where there is not the slightest doubt of Christian inspiration, it is surely the splendour of man that is exalted, and not the ineffable splendour of the Almighty; and when Michelangelo evokes suffering he is in fact representing the suffering of mortal man, in whom he recognizes the ephemeral nature of his own agonized being, rather than of God's eternal Son who came on earth to redeem him.

This shift of interest from God to man is undoubtedly the characteristic feature of the epoch; Raphael, during his brief career in Rome, was treated as a prince, fauned upon and flattered by all and sundry, even by Pope Leo X who talked of making him a cardinal. This glamorous entry of the artist into high society marks the end of a process which had begun long before in the anonymity of the medieval craftsmen and which now culminated in the exaltation of genius. In

---

[1] This marks the beginning of the divorce between the artist's fundamental convictions and his work, a divorce hallowed in our own day, when notorious atheists are invited to make representations of the Blessed Virgin or Christ. There can surely be precious little religious emotion left here.

point of fact God held only a very minor place in the field of art; the conceited artist, yielding to the trend of the times, ventured to usurp His place. He no longer gave spontaneous thanks to the Creator for his success, but rather paid tribute to his own faculties. Whereas in the Age of Faith beauty proceeded from God alone and reflected His ineffable image, the most Christian artists of the High Renaissance considered beauty as showing the way to God and enabling man to know Him.[1] This notion, Platonic in origin, is not irreconcilable with Christianity, but its affirmation marks a singular progression in relation to traditional faith.

Consequently the wonderful period of artistic creation over which the patron Popes presided has a Christian look, but only in an incomplete sense; it is subject to various reservations, and its Christian quality is no longer that of the past. What the artists are exalting now is the authority of the pontiffs, the majesty of the Church and the temporal image of the Most High. The Passion and Death of Christ are not wholly absent from their thoughts, but His figure is somehow obscured by the radiance of power and splendour. Likewise in the solemn basilicas, and particularly in St Peter's, the most majestic of them all, the worshipper is drawn to the theology of Glory rather than to the suffering of Calvary.

This new vision undeniably helped to separate many devout souls from Rome. Even more certainly the brilliant aura surrounding the Vicar of Christ prevented him from seeing the cancer that gnawed the Church's vitals in the shape of a menace that was growing daily greater. From the depths of the Christian conscience the protracted complaint which had been demanding reform for so long past was becoming more and more imperious. But amid the merry din of cathedral workshops, festivals and music no one really heard it.

THE REVERSE SIDE OF THE SPLENDOUR

Rome, however, was not the Church, nor was Italy the entire Christian world. How would the ordinary mass of the faithful regard this glorious but disturbing spectacle of the Papacy? Would their conscience be made uneasy by such examples; would not the sins of the leaders exercise an unfortunate influence on their own behaviour?

One thing is clear. These unedifying pontificates threw grave discredit upon the See of St Peter and its *entourage*. The Italians

[1] 'The radiance of a beautiful face urges me heavenwards,' said Michelangelo. Or again in a letter to Vittoria Colonna: "Nothing is more noble or more pious than a good piece of painting, for nothing is more fitted to arouse piety in enlightened souls.' And Savonarola himself once declared: 'Artistic masterpieces attract the soul to the extent that when we contemplate them we experience a kind of vertigo: sometimes we think ourselves in a state of trance, and forget our own personalities. This is the same impression which the love of Jesus Christ produces in the soul.'

themselves, even those who lived very close indeed to the Curia, did not hesitate to criticize it violently. The historian Guicciardini, who was certainly no innocent, confessed that during the whole time he had been in papal service 'no one was more disgusted than he by the ambition, cupidity and debauchery of churchmen'; and he added, with a touch of cynicism, that had it not been for his exact understanding of where his own interests lay, 'he would have liked Martin Luther to put this band of rogues in its place.' When Cardinal Giovanni Dominici declared that 'everything here is squalor nowadays' his words were doubtless intended to convey something more than their literal meaning. Savonarola may be thought to have exaggerated when he prophesied that 'the coffin will soon be opened, and when that time comes the stench will be such that the whole of Christendom will hold its nose'; but Michelangelo was hardly less stern in the famous sonnet in which he adjures Our Lord not to revisit a city where all betray Him: 'Helmets and swords are fashioned here from chalices, the blood of Jesus Christ is sold dirt cheap.' It is easy to imagine the reaction of foreign pilgrims visiting the capital of Christendom, when they heard tell of scandals to which popular malice added a wealth of detail. We have already noted the interval between the Italian Renaissance and the corresponding 'revivals' elsewhere. It rendered the character of the humanist popes even more astonishing and shocking in the eyes of a German or a Frenchman who was used to seeing Christianity in a very different setting. Crotus Rubianus, one of Luther's earliest supporters, wrote to him in 1519: 'I have seen two things in Rome: the monuments of the ancients and the seat of pestilence. How joyful the first made me, and how ashamed the second!' But many other visitors, who never embraced heresy, were equally severe in their criticism—the pious Canon Morung of Bamberg, for example, or the German knight Arnold von Hartt. 'I have spent several months in Rome,' wrote one of them, 'and I have seen prelates and important personages behaving in such a way that if I were to remain here I would be afraid of losing my faith.' In strict equity of course the distinction ought to have been made between the *function* of the Vicar of Christ, which deserved the absolute respect of the faithful, and the *defects of individuals* who exercised it for the time being. But such a distinction is always very hard to draw; Savonarola had failed to do so, and Luther would not even try. Thus criticism of the popes and their *entourage* amounted to an attack upon the Papacy itself and, in a sense, upon Holy Church as well.

Michelangelo's verses accurately express the content of such criticism. The age regarded moral laxity with indulgence; conscientious Christians were far more troubled at the sight of ecclesiastical leaders behaving like army officers, and the disciples of the Poorest of the Poor indulging such flagrant cupidity. Marsilio Ficino had already protested to Sixtus IV: 'The kingdom which Christ has given you is a divine kingdom, composed of souls, not weapons.   He has entrusted you with the Keys, not with helmet and sword.' One wonders what he might have said to Julius II. But churchmen's preoccupation with money was an even greater source of irritation. As the reader will remember,[1] accusations of greed had been levied against the clergy for many years, and this topic was one of the strongest causes of anti-clericalism. While the centralization of papal administration had un-doubtedly put an end to intrigue at the local level, it had resulted in making many nominations (and payments connected with benefices) dependent on bureaucrats in Rome. These levied taxes in their official capacity, and unofficially engaged in shameless trafficking in eccle-siastical offices. The structure of the papal finances had been perfected by the popes of Avignon, and its demands were constantly on the increase. Buying and selling of offices had become systematic practice, particularly since the reign of Sixtus IV. There were apostolic peti-tioners, secretaries and *plumbatores* galore—every conceivable title was invented for putting on the market. 'The Lord does not desire the death of the sinner,' remarked Innocent VIII's Cardinal Camer-lengo mockingly, 'but rather that he may live and pay.' Naturally enough a man who had acquired his office at considerable cost was determined to profit therefrom; and this was ultimately achieved at the expense of the ordinary humble Catholic—the penitent, the pilgrim and the litigant.

It may be asked whether the moral abasement of the Papacy, and the discredit which surrounded it, had any real effect on the main body of the faithful. Such repercussions were probably less serious than one might be tempted to think; for looked at against the background of their age the political prestige acquired by Alexander VI or Julius II compensated to some extent for their moral degeneracy. Machiavelli is clearly exaggerating when he declares that 'the guilty examples provided by the court of Rome have extinguished all religion and devotion in this country.' What is certain, however, is that the crisis, whose symptoms had long been apparent,[2] now increased in gravity and took on an extremely disturbing character, not in Italy alone, but throughout the Church.

'I have never been able to find out whether certain German bishops model themselves on the Pope or vice versa,' Erasmus used to say sarcastically. It was a fact that the behaviour of many members of the higher clergy was very similar to that of the incumbents of the Vatican. This was not true in every case; it would be unfair to generalize and attribute to the whole episcopate vices of which only some were guilty.

[1] See Chapter III, p. 126.
[2] See Chapter III, fifth section: 'A Serious Decline in Clerical Standards.'

On the other hand, natural as it was that bad prelates should invite more comment than did those whose lives were blameless, the number belonging to the first category was far too large.

At the end of the fifteenth century the type of prelate who was 'puffed up with pride' was fairly commonplace. Johann Butzbach describes such men in these terms: 'They are decked out in the best English cloth; their hands loaded with jewelled rings rest proudly on their hips. They prance about on sumptuous steeds, followed by a vast *entourage* in brilliant livery. Their palaces are splendid places; they sit at their heavily laden banqueting tables and give themselves up to an orgy of revelry. The offerings of the pious go to provide them with baths, horses, hounds and hawks.' The German bishops who were the targets of this indictment had countless imitators in both Italy and France; the hunt for benefices was so general that few people thought anything of it, and the higher aristocracy practised it quite openly. 'We ourselves want episcopal dignities as dowries for our children,' admitted one duke of Saxony. A certain duke of Bavaria and Count Palatine was simultaneously dean of the chapter at Mainz, canon of Cologne and Trèves, provost of the collegiate church of St Donatian at Bruges, parish priest of Lorsch and Mochlein, and, to crown all, Bishop of Spires into the bargain. The Curia could hardly object, considering its own conduct was no better. Furthermore by its financial demands it forced the bishops to indulge in some very peculiar monetary operations. Thus when Albert of Brandenburg secured his election to the archbishopric of Mainz by promising to pay Rome the twenty thousand ducats which should theoretically have been disbursed by the chapter, he was obliged to borrow this enormous sum from the famous banking-house of Fugger, and to traffic in indulgences in the most unsavoury fashion in order to obtain the money for his repayments. And what happened in Germany was just as commonplace elsewhere; many nefarious dealings relating to ecclesiastical sees went on in France, and Rome permitted them in return for suitable financial recompense.

The disastrous features of the system of commendam [1] became more marked. Fewer and fewer bishops resided in their own dioceses. Some of them did not even trouble to take orders, and several were so ignorant of Latin that they could not translate the articles of the Creed. It is futile to speak of piety in connection with this type of personage; one oft-quoted example is Rupprecht von Simmern, who, though Bishop of Strasbourg for thirty-eight years, never once said Mass during that time. The nepotism of Rome, where boys of fourteen were created cardinals, was copied on all sides; incapable adolescents, and even children of six, were provided with episcopal titles. Little could be

[1] See p. 130.

expected of an episcopate chosen in this way, and it is indeed astonishing to find that its ranks yet included a high proportion of decent people. We must not be surprised to discover that a great many men, even after their elevation to the episcopate, remained nothing better, roistering, greedy, violent noblemen, for this was all they really were. One such specimen, by no means unique, was Dieter von Isemberg, Archbishop of Mainz; he was constantly at war with his neighbours, and even attacked the papal envoys who had come to demand his arrears of tax. Another was Tristan de Salazar, Archbishop of Sens, who presented himself before Louis XII, armed cap-à-pie and grasping an enormous javelin, as the king was setting off to the wars. As for those numerous bishops throughout Christendom who were employed by their sovereigns in governmental tasks where their aptitude for diplomacy or administration might be used to the best advantage, they were certainly not shepherds of souls.

These deplorable practices were rife from top to bottom of the hierarchy. While the bishops hunted benefices their canons fished assiduously for fat parishes or comfortable prebends and, at their own level, lived in the same style as the prelates. As for the lower clergy, separated from its superiors by a social barrier which was increasingly difficult to surmount, its decline continued. Parish priests were too often designated by lay 'patrons' and offered virtually no pledges of good conduct, religious zeal or scholarship. Almost all lived in a state of near destitution, and evidence from Italy, France and Germany concurs in showing these unfortunate men 'hanging on to the devil's tail,' to quote the phrase popularized by legend. Since the lay patrons appropriated the tithes from their livings, the priests were obliged to live on their bare stipend, and led a wretched existence. There is a good deal of excuse, therefore, for their keenness to extract some return from their religious duties, but it is none the less appalling to find men of God spending their time demanding pittances for baptisms, funerals, anniversary masses, marriages, saints' days, and even confessions.[1] The moral behaviour of the clergy had lapsed even further. Since the Pope's bastards held the limelight at Rome humble parish priests could scarcely be prevented from keeping their mistresses. As early as 1410 the preacher Olivier Maillard had delivered a condemnation in a racy mixture of French and Latin, rudely calling to task 'sacerdotes fornicarii tenentes concubinas à pain et pot.' The indignant protests of

---

[1] Many clerks were concerned in shady financial deals. The Italian and German bankers were on exceedingly good terms with certain ecclesiastics. In order to find a way round the prohibition against usury, which was still in force, one theologian, named Angelo de Clavero, devised a subtle system whereby interest was regarded as a premium against risk and a simple matter of profit-sharing. It was to combat clerical usury that the pious Franciscan, Barnabo of Terni, founded his institution for borrowing on pledged securities. This started at Perugia, later moved to Orvieto, and was afterwards extended by Blessed Bernardino da Feltre. It was the origin of the modern pawnshop.

St Antoninus, St Lawrence Giustiniani, the Castilian Tostat and the
Alsatian Wimpfeling are sufficient indication that the evil was a general
one. There were certain priests who lived quite openly as fathers of
large families, as did Alexander VI, and statistics prove that in fifteenth-
century Burgundy half the natural children seeking legitimation were
the offspring of priests [1]. And even those priests who did not obviously
offend against morality were generally earthy, hard-living men, who
nevertheless enjoyed the affection of their flocks; they would join in
their parishioners' feasting and revelries, and be present at the most
unedifying spectacles. Naturally enough such a clergy was almost
always notoriously ignorant. This is revealed by the parish registers
and the accounts of pastoral visitations. In theory a candidate for holy
orders had to study theology for three years before being ordained, but
in fact this requirement was purely formal. When confronted with the
preachers of the Protestant Reformation, the Catholic clergy almost
invariably showed itself sadly wanting.

As for the religious Orders, the crisis which had been affecting them
ever since the fourteenth century was to grow still worse, despite
numerous countermeasures some of which were partially successful.
Here more than anywhere else the observer must beware of exaggeration. Preachers like Maillard and Geiler von Kayserberg depicted the
religious houses as hotbeds of every conceivable vice and, as is well
known, the monks were constant targets for the gibes of intellectuals
ranging from Laurence Valla to Rabelais. But it remains true that
several of these criticisms were justified; the decadence of the regular
clergy gave rise to all the more indignation because people had the
right to expect of it greater austerity, fervour and learning. In too many
cases men became monks in order to obtain security, and truly ardent
spirits felt ill at ease among companions whose main preoccupations
were eating and drinking, even when they were nothing worse. The
system of commendam was a catastrophe for the religious houses. It
meant that the prior was robbed of all authority, and all too often the
monastery's income was deflected by the commendatory, while the
monks were forced to indulge in every kind of expedient. In these
badly supervised communities moral standards approached those of the
parish priests. Even the Mendicant Orders had lost some of their vigour
and integrity. They were perpetually fighting one another (Franciscans
against Dominicans) or disputing within the same family (Conventuals
against Observants), but all would unite to embarrass the secular clergy.
In 1472 the Minors had established their right to accept legacies;
in 1502 the Parisian Franciscans demanded financial endowments.

---

[1] Consequently a number of people, such as Cardinal Zabarella of Florence and
Guillaume de Saignet, proposed the legalization of clerical marriage as the only way of
checking the evil.

The vehement criticisms which Luther levelled at the Dominicans concerning the matter of indulgences were probably not justified, but there were so many other features to convince ordinary people of the venality and rapacity of the monks that the most heinous accusations found a ready hearing. Rome had set the example for a scandal whose repercussions were felt in the most distant corners of the Church. These in turn aggravated the crisis, and left the Church wide open to the attacks of her enemies.

Forces that Still Remained Intact, and the Anguish of Reform

Such a situation looked very serious, but it was not quite desperate.. For, as is always the case in the darkest moments of Christian history, it had another side to it. This degraded, criticized Church, which presented to mankind the sullied countenance of an Alexander VI, nevertheless remained the Holy Church, heir to the Saviour's Promise, against whom the Gates of Hell shall not prevail.

One observation comes immediately to mind : the doctrinal bases remained sound, and the Church's fundamental principles were un-affected. It is significant that not a single heresy made its appearance during the whole of the Renaissance period until the arrival on the scene of Luther, and also that Italy, by no means an exemplary region, turned out to be one of those areas of the Christian world which Protestantism had most difficulty in penetrating. Although the personal behaviour of all these popes may be called in question, not one of them issued a bull whose dogmatic purity can be faulted : even Alexander VI himself thought along sound lines, although he behaved so abomin-ably. When the French bishops drew up plans for reform in 1485 and 1493, Sixtus IV, and subsequently Alexander VI, encouraged them vigorously and sincerely. Pius II, Callixtus III and Paul II had all tried to combat the forces threatening the faith's integrity. Even Leo X, who seems to embody those features of the age which are furthest removed from Christianity, obtained from the Lateran Council some stern decrees condemning various theses advanced by certain humanists upon the nature and immortality of the soul. In the main it was not clear-sightedness which the popes lacked, but energy.

This doctrinal integrity, therefore, constituted one element on which the future would be able to build anew. But there was something even better : the Christian mass itself, that immense flock of humble, un-known souls, contained a number of inviolate and powerful forces which were only awaiting the chance to swing into action.[1] This fact must always be emphasized : the forefront of the stage might well be

[1] See Chapter I of *The Catholic Reformation*.

occupied by sensual prelates, scheming and self-interested cardinals, or such fearsome brutes as Sigismund Malatesta and Cesare Borgia; but in the background were all those far less conspicuous people who seemed to be unworthy of notice precisely because they caused no scandal of any kind. All cardinals were not Riarios, Borgias or Bembos. Not every bishop was preoccupied with hunting and money-making; countless prelates were ardent supporters of ecclesiastical reform, and could be seen trying to put their ideas into practice on the local plane, in the midst of fantastic difficulties.[1] Even among the ordinary parish clergy, which left so much to be desired, books and diaries and chronicles allow glimpses of many worthy priests who, with the limited means at their disposal, strove to maintain their little flock's faith as best they could. Even the religious houses, which are so harshly criticized, were certainly not all dens of iniquity. The most striking proof of this assertion is the testimony of no less a witness than Luther, who praises the Carthusians of Erfurt and his own community of Augustinians for the spirit of total renunciation which he himself has witnessed in their lives. Innumerable pure and noble souls continued to find the cloister a fruitful ground for spiritual development. Although by the beginning of the sixteenth century the living stream of *devotio moderna*[2] scarcely possessed the force and vigour which it had had in the days of the *Imitation*, it still watered the verdant pastures of piety, and produced yet another outstanding witness in *Jan Mombaer* of Brussels, a monk of Mount St Agnes, who was Abbot of Livry at the time of his death in 1501. His *Rosary of Spiritual Exercises*, an attempt to systematize the theme of the *Imitation*, taught generation upon generation of Catholics the practice of self-examination, mental prayer and communion with God.

Above all, however, the crisis of humanism and the Renaissance was made less disastrous by the fact that, it took place, so to speak, on the surface of a society which remained basically Christian and which had not yet disintegrated under the continuous pressure of rationalism and materialism. Faith was still its framework. Agnosticism had undoubtedly made certain advances, but outside humanist circles these were extremely limited. The Italian chronicler Beniveni is often quoted in this context; but he must not be taken literally, for there is abundant evidence against him. 'The country has lost faith in Christ,' he says; 'most people think that all things, and human affairs in particular, are the outcome of mere chance, though some admit the influence of the stars. Life after death is rejected, religion derided. All Italy has turned sceptic, and nowhere more so than in Florence.' Such

---

[1] On the bishops who were precursors of Catholic reform see the beginning of Chapter I of *The Catholic Reformation*, section 2.

[2] See Chapter III, p. 144.

a description is hardly applicable to the crowds who thronged Santa Maria del Fiore to hear Savonarola preach, and to weep when the Dominican proclaimed the sinfulness of the whole world. Moreover, although the humanists themselves might gibe at religion and popular belief—'Let's go and conform to popular error,' said one of them as he walked to church—very few of their number remained impenitently atheist to the end: even Machiavelli received the Last Sacraments before his death.

True this popular religion contained some highly questionable features, and in some respects showed signs of deterioration. All those symptoms of religious unbalance which have been noted in the preceding era were now far more obvious. Superstition was quite as widespread as it had been at the end of the Middle Ages, and perhaps even more so. The cult of the saints tended to occupy such a large place in Christian piety that it sometimes bordered on idolatry, or at least gave rise to scandal. No one dared to do anything without the help of the saints. Yet no one showed much fear of the punishment the saints they treated with disrespect might inflict, and it is difficult to explain why Italians painted St Anthony with a fiery sword on walls which they sought to protect from the defilement due to natural urges! The quest for relics acquired a character of collective insanity; all kinds of powers, however improbable they might seem, were attributed to such objects. As we shall see, the Elector of Saxony possessed nine thousand treasures of this kind, including forty-two complete corpses, not to mention some drops of the Blessed Virgin's milk! Belief in witchcraft too exercised a pernicious influence on Christian faith. The number of trials of those accused of sorcery increased considerably; witches were seen at work everywhere, and when one of Luther's sisters died at a ripe old age, the event was attributed to wicked spells. It is essential to consider the purchase of indulgences in this peculiar setting, in order to understand what a very real danger it might constitute: people who found it so easy to make satisfaction for their misdemeanours were all too likely to repeat the selfsame sins.

Popular faith, however, though undoubtedly open to criticism in some respects and powerless to enforce obedience to the moral law, was nevertheless still firmly implanted in men's souls. A people whose whole existence was ordered by the liturgical calendar and the regulations of the Church remained unquestionably Christian, a fact clearly demonstrated in the jubilee years of 1475 and 1500. Rome was then the scene of unrelaxed fervour; and crowds continued to throng the great centres of pilgrimage, old and new—Loretto, for example, after 1507, when the Pope officially proclaimed that Our Lady's house had been miraculously carried thither by angels. Again the vast numbers of men, women and children, in almost every corner of

Europe, who set out in the dark by candlelight and packed the cathedral naves, in order to hear the words of some famous preacher were most certainly Christian. Proofs of this fundamental faith are innumerable. Italy, for all the violence of the Quattrocento, witnessed at the same time those great charitable foundations and works of piety to which countless men and women offered tireless devotion—men and women whose model was St Catherine of Genoa, 'rector' of the hospital in her native city. Our knowledge of the kinds of penance voluntarily practised by Christian men and women in this pleasure-loving age gives a fair idea of the spiritual demands to which they were ready to submit. Catherine herself may have exceeded the normal in sleeping on a bed of thistles and brambles, mixing wormwood and aloes with her food and fasting for two months at a time; but the practice of wearing a hair-shirt and the daily discipline were fairly widespread. At every level of society souls without number endeavoured with all sincerity to live their lives in God; such were the two Tornabuoni princesses, who were the leaders of Florentine fashion and whose archbishop, St Antoninus, wrote for them a work that foreshadows the 'Introduction to the Devout Life.' Towards the end of the fifteenth century 'Fraternities of Divine Love' sprang up all over Italy, particularly at Vicenza, Venice and Genoa. These consisted of laymen who aimed at nothing less than implanting true Christianity in the souls of their fellow men; and in 1517, the very year in which Luther began his conflict with Rome, Gajetan of Thiene and Giovanni Pietro Carafa established an 'oratory' which became one of Italy's principal centres of ecclesiastical reform. No, faith was certainly not dead among a people which in many lands dedicated its cities to the Blessed Virgin or to Christ Himself. The Council of Trent had but to rid it of its blemishes, and the sound, healthy flesh and clean pure blood would once more be revealed.

In this age, as in any other, the most striking indication of continuing religious vitality is the presence of holiness. The history of the Church is first and foremost the history of her saints. It is they who give that history its true significance; through them the human soul is raised above itself and faith endowed with its full meaning. Now this period abounded in saints. If we confine our study for the time being to Italy alone, land of the Renaissance, pagan humanism and civil strife, we shall find an amazing contrast between the world of tyrants or *condottieri* and the galaxy of saints with which it co-existed. There were saints in every class and in every province. They included humble members of the proletariat, merchants, scholars and artists, monks and bishops, priests and soldiers. Even more remarkable is the fact that among them were sons and daughters of aristocratic families some of which were guilty of crimes and deeds of violence that fill the history books. It was as if these pure souls were determined to expiate the sins of their relations. St Catherine of Bologna was the daughter of an ambassador. St Laurence Giustiniani, Archbishop of Venice, for whom the Pope created the title of Patriarch, belonged to one of the most noble families of the republic, just as the other St Catherine of Genoa was related to the leading aristocracy of her native city. Blessed Battista Varani's mother was a Malatesta, niece not only of the terrible Sigismund, but also of Blessed Roberto Galeas, the husband of Margaret d'Este; while Blessed Sueva was the wretchedly unhappy wife of the brigand lord of Montefeltre. Christ chose His own even from the reigning houses. Thus the ducal family of Savoy could claim both Blessed Amadeus IX (1435–72), famous for his charity, and also his daughter, Blessed Luisa (1462–1503), who became one of the heads of the Franciscan Order after the death of her husband.

Apart from the reformers of the older Orders, we shall soon see [1] the founders of many new Orders disposing their troops in readiness for the Church's triumphant counter-offensive: St Gajetan, St Anthony Mary Zaccaria, St Angela Merici, St Jerome Emilian and St Philip Neri. There are so many of these noble figures that the Renaissance epoch is perhaps entitled to be known as the era of saints, as well as of artistic geniuses. Several of them made such a profound impression on their times that a halo of glory surrounds them, as is amply testified by those many artists in whose works they so frequently occur.

St John Capistrano (1393–1456) has already been mentioned several times in the course of this volume. We have seen him leading the crusade against the Turk, or heading important delegations on behalf of the Pope; but his whole life had been exemplary since his student days at Perugia, when, as an unofficial political agent acting on the town's behalf in its conflict with the Malatestas, he had seen a vision of the Poverello bidding him set out on a new career. He performed many feats on the Saviour's behalf, including some long missionary tours, during which the whole of Italy was roused by his preaching—grave or gay as occasion demanded—and the Holy Name of Jesus praised wherever he went.[2]

The charitable work of *St Catherine of Genoa* (1447–1510) and her extraordinary asceticism have already been noted; but other features of her life are no less remarkable. Her joyful acceptance of an intolerable

---

[1] See Chapter I of *The Catholic Reformation*.

[2] It was also in the Name of Jesus that St John Capistrano's friend and companion, St Jacopo della Marozza (1394–1476), performed so many miracles. He was born of a poor family and became a Franciscan at the age of twenty. An enthusiastic disciple of St Bernardino of Siena, he was sent by the Holy See to both Hungary and Bohemia (where he worked among the Hussites); he also played an important part in resisting the tendencies of the 'Fraticelli.' St Jacopo was one of the great preachers of the age. He was also one of the precursors of Blessed Barnabo and Blessed Bernardino da Feltre in the creation of 'pawn-shops.' (See note on p. 266.)

husband is as surprising as the fact that she managed to combine constant practical activity with a truly spiritual existence, and her mysterious consoling *Treatise on Purgatory* still bears witness of her closeness to the Ineffable.

St Antoninus (1389–1459), called 'Anthony the Little' because of his short stature, seems to redeem all the sinfulness of Florence. This learned Dominican, who was prior of numerous religious houses as well as author of a *Summa moralis* and some precious *Chronicles*, founded the monastery of San Marco which was afterwards made famous by Fra Angelico and Savonarola in their very different ways. Appointed Archbishop of Florence, he at once placed himself at the service of every member of his flock. Goodness and kindness radiated from him. He would visit the poor, humbly seated on his little grey ass, but he was also ready to undertake the spiritual direction of wealthy women. The celebrated 'Confraternity of St Martin' which he founded, and which still flourishes, foreshadowed in many ways the modern continental 'Catholic Relief'; and he was quite fearless in visiting victims of the plague, among them Pope Eugenius IV who refused to receive extreme unction from any hand save his.

Of all these saints, possibly the one most famous in his own life-time was the 'holy man from Calabria,' *St Francis of Paola* (1416–1507), whom Louis XI, feeling the approach of death and thoroughly alarmed, summoned to Plessis-les-Tours to comfort him and, who knows, perhaps prolong his days. For the reputation of Francis as a miracle worker was such that he was believed to walk upon the waters, heal the sick and raise the dead, as Christ, his model, had done. This erstwhile hermit had lived for several years in a cave, eating only the bare minimum of fruit and vegetables; he had renounced everything for his Saviour, practised continual mortification and was poor even among the very poorest. He is in striking contrast with another Franciscan who at that time occupied St Peter's throne—the ambitious Sixtus IV. Christians were able to distinguish between the humble hermit and the arrogant conventual; the fame and glory of the apostle far outshone that of the pontiff.

These are indeed noble figures and they compare very favourably with the popes of their day. Not a single one of them, however, was any more equal to events than their fourteenth-century predecessors had been. Not one of them was capable of shouldering the heavy burden of Church reform. None of these saints was a Gregory VII, a Bernard of Clairvaux or a Francis of Assisi. The ways of God are inscrutable, and no doubt Divine Providence desired mankind to wait still longer for the appearance of such men as St Ignatius of Loyola and St Pius V, perhaps because some sins necessarily call for punishment. But for the Church this was a tragedy.

It remains true, nevertheless, that these saintly men and women were the embodiment of genuine Christianity, which had been entrusted to their care. It is therefore pertinent to ask why such upright souls did not react when faced with the appalling spectacle all too often provided by the official Church. There had been talk of reform in the past two hundred years, but no one had dared to tackle it seriously. Why did sincere Christians not urge in stronger language that a start be made? Not one of these saints ventured either to bid or to implore the Holy See to grasp the realities of the situation and take some positive action. Of course mere warnings were not lacking. They had been heard time and time again since the beginning of the fourteenth century. During one session of the Lateran Council Giovanni Francesco Pico della Mirandola, nephew of the great humanist and a most generous and saintly individual (he was Savonarola's first biographer), had shown Leo X where his responsibilities lay with terrifying frankness: 'Supreme shepherd of souls, if you once let go the reins which you hold so loosely, I fear that under your pontificate Christendom will crumble, sensuality will conquer modesty, insolence will overwhelm fear and folly dominate reason. Will you be taken unaware by the attack of the enemies of our faith?'

By the beginning of the sixteenth century the desire for reform had become a veritable anguish in many devout souls. Some were so disheartened and discouraged that they no longer dared to hope. After years of effort and argument the preacher Johann Geiler had come to the melancholy conclusion that 'the best thing to do is to hide in one's corner, head in hands, and practise virtue with one's own eternal salvation in mind.' And Michelangelo's wonderful, despairing verses are well known: 'To sleep is pleasant, but it were better still, while misery and shame persist, to be made of stone. How fortunate he who sees nothing and knows nothing! Talk in whispers, lest you wake me!'

But the voices raised in fiery indignation were far more numerous. The reform which all true Christians demanded was twofold. First through a revival of fervour, charity, asceticism and discipline it must work upon that point at which each individual knew himself to be inwardly threatened, and rouse every living being to wage war against his own sinful heart. '*Metanoeite!*' The gospel precept was at the root of all the teaching which the prophets of this epoch lavished so generously, from the mystics of *devotio moderna* to Savonarola and, later on, St Philip Neri. Transformation of the individual was always the first and foremost obligation; but this alone was not enough, as the saints again pointed out. The scandals which besmirched and disfigured the glorious face of the Church must be brought to an end, and it was this conviction that preachers expressed most vehemently. Sometimes their language was such that one cannot help wondering whether, in branding the evil which they saw around them, they were not in danger of bringing the Church herself into disrepute. Men were becoming increasingly aware that in order to be really effective reform must also be institutional, that it was necessary to remedy those structural defects which prevented the Church from fulfilling her real task. Cardinal Aleandro, the Pope's legate in Germany, summarized the opinion held by a great many people when he wrote the following words of wisdom to Leo X: 'I, and all Catholics with me, beseech you for the love of God to put an end to all these reservations, annates, dispensations, provisions and expectative graces. No one here wishes to reject God, but everyone seeks revenge for these flagrant abuses.' Failing the popes, however, there was no one to undertake this structural reform, combined with moral and spiritual rejuvenation, and bring it to a successful conclusion.

On 3rd May 1491 the Blessed Virgin appeared to a group of men on a hill top in the Vosges, which was subsequently to be known as 'The Three Ears of Corn.' It was her first appearance on the threshold of the modern world, and it is significant that it took place on the fringe of that Germanic society in which the tragedy was to break out twenty-five years later. Her words were heavy with warning. The wrath of God, she declared, was about to descend like a hailstorm. She predicted the imminent destruction of many of Christianity's most ancient crops. And today on that high Alsatian hill we still venerate a Virgin of Sorrows whose tears are perhaps shed more for the sins of the world than in mourning for the Child seated on her lap. Some years later the Pope promulgated a bull recognizing the authenticity of the vision and making the place which the Virgin Mother had 'made resplendent with portents and miracles' into a centre of pilgrimage. But it seems doubtful if he himself had understood the meaning of the miracle, for his name was Alexander Borgia.

Christianity would at length emerge from its unhappy situation. This picture of an unedifying Papacy, a dubious hierarchy, and the faith threatened by evils of the worst kind would soon be replaced by one of a Church rejuvenated and renovated, ready to grapple with all the new problems that awaited her. But before this redemptive tremor could take effect a dramatic tragedy was to take place, whose prologue had just been enacted in a small German town in the Holy Roman Empire. The Roman Catholic Church had not known how to undertake the necessary religious revolution. Now it was to be carried through on individual initiatives beyond her control, outside her bounds, despite her and against her. And this, as Bossuet said, would be 'her manifest punishment.'

K

CHAPTER V

THE TRAGEDY OF MARTIN LUTHER

THE AFFAIR OF THE INDULGENCES

IT WAS 31st October 1517. In the little town of Wittenberg, a part of the Elector of Saxony's possessions, the crush and animation were at their height. Every year the Feast of All Saints attracted countless pious folk, who came to see the precious relics which His Highness the Elector, Frederick the Wise, had collected at great expense, and which were brought out for the occasion from the storerooms of the Schloss-kirche. There were plenty of them—several thousand—and they were of the most varied kind: they included not only the complete corpses of various saints, nails from the Passion and rods from the Flagellation, but part of the Child Jesus' swaddling-clothes and some wood from His crib, and even a few drops of His Blessed Mother's milk! Large numbers of most valuable indulgences were attached to the veneration of these distinguished treasures.

That same morning a manifesto, written in scholastic Latin and consisting of ninety-five theses, was found nailed to the door of the castle's chapel. Its author was an Augustinian monk who was extremely well known in the town, and he declared his intention of defending its contents against any opponent prepared to stand up and argue with him. In fact, the document concerned those very indulgences which honest folk were even then showing such eagerness to obtain by praying before the relics and slipping their guilders into the offertory boxes. The pilgrims assembled outside the church heard the more knowledgeable among them translate its words: 'Those preaching in favour of indulgences err when they say such indulgences can deliver man and grant him salvation. The man who gives to the poor performs a better action than the one who buys indulgences.' There were three hundred yet more bitter lines in this strain. And the worthy pilgrims wondered what could be the purpose of this monk in thus shaking one of the pillars of the Church.

For this was what indulgences seemed to have become: a pillar of the faith. Palz, Master of Erfurt, actually taught that they were 'the modern way of preaching the Gospel.' Was there anything intrinsically reprehensible about them? A rereading of the treatise which the learned Johann Pfeffer had devoted to the subject a quarter of a century earlier, in that same town of Wittenberg, or a glance at the sermons of the celebrated Johann Geiler of Kayserberg, makes the real meaning of indulgences clear beyond any shadow of a doubt. What the Church understood by *indulgence* was the total or partial remission of the penalties of sin—to which everyone was liable, either on earth or in Purgatory—after the Sacrament of Penance had afforded him absolution from his fault and remission of eternal punishment. But the state of grace was indispensable for the obtaining of such temporal remission; good works, in the shape of prayers, fasting, pilgrimages, visits to churches and almsgiving, were only an incidental, or, to put it another way, a contributory factor. Where there was no firm resolve or inward glow there was no remission. In strict doctrine an indulgence was certainly not an automatic means of gaining a cheap discharge from penalties that were justly deserved. In 1476 a bull of Sixtus IV had recognized that indulgences could be applied to the souls of the departed, whose sufferings in the next world would be alleviated thereby; and the declaration of this principle had contributed to the success of the jubilee of 1500.

It was not of recent origin. As early as the eleventh century crusaders had reaped the benefits of the plenary indulgence. Since then it had been awarded more generally and bestowed on less heroic occasions. It had had a number of happy results, and countless works of religious or social utility had been financed by the money collected in this way; churches too, hospitals, pawnshops, even dikes and bridges. Thanks to indulgences the Church in France had been materially restored on the morrow of the Hundred Years War. Nor had the spiritual results been insignificant: when proclaimed by special preachers the grant of an indulgence provided a spiritual jolt rather like the 'missions' of modern times, and was the means of bringing numerous penitents to the confessional.

But it was not these excellent reasons alone which caused the institution to become so widespread, particularly from the fourteenth century onwards. For close on two centuries years of indulgence had been granted with unrestrained liberality in return for the briefest visit to a church, or the least meritorious of pilgrimages. In a period of twelve months the pious Elector Frederick the Wise laid up no fewer than 127,799 years, sufficient to empty a whole province of Purgatory and ensure himself more than one heaven. It is not difficult to imagine the kind of excesses which found their way into this practice, and they had already been condemned in 1312 by the decretal *Abusionibus*. Simony discovered some splendid material here and it is open to doubt whether preachers of indulgences, with their attendant collectors stationed at the foot of the pulpit, were primarily interested in saving souls or in collecting ducats. All too often the grant of an indulgence was part and parcel of some shady deal, and sometimes the right to collect for it was actually sold at auction. Pope Leo X himself once empowered the Fuggers, a celebrated firm of bankers at Augsburg, to preach an indulgence by way of security for a loan. The climate of the age was only too favourable to this type of proceedings. In 1514, when the Hohenzollern Albert of Brandenburg secured his election as Arch-bishop of Mainz, the heavy chancellery dues of 14,000 ducats, plus a 'voluntary settlement' of a further 10,000 intended to ease the scruples of the Curia, were financed by the Fuggers, who were guaranteed in return one-third of the revenues from the great papal indulgence.

Misconduct such as this was not the only menace to the institution; the doctrine itself was affected by something even worse. Far too many preachers taught that an indulgence possessed a kind of magical quality, and that by spending money to obtain it men were taking out a mortgage on Heaven. One popular jingle ran:

> Sobald das Geld im Kasten klingt
> Die Seele aus dem Fegfeuer springt! [1]

Moreover Germany was not the only country where such rubbish was taught. In 1482 the Sorbonne had condemned one preacher who recited it from the pulpit; at Besançon, in 1486, a certain Franciscan swore that provided a man wore the habit of his Order, St Francis would come in person to collect him from Purgatory. Naturally enough there were lively reactions to these specious claims. As early as 1484 a priest named Lallier had publicly rejected the view that the Pope had the power to remit the pains of another world by means of indulgence, and despite objections from the theological faculty, the Bishop of Paris had absolved him. In 1498 the Franciscan Vitrier had been hauled before the Sorbonne for having declared that 'money must not be given in order to obtain forgiveness.' His disciple Erasmus had lately written: 'Any trader, mercenary soldier or judge has but to put down his money, however nefariously acquired, and he imagines that he has purged the whole Lernean Marsh of his life.' Views of this sort were taught in the University of Wittenberg, which considered itself the rival of Leipzig and Erfurt; and trenchancy of tone helped to further the renown of that centre, where, during 1516, statements such as the following had been heard: 'It is an absurdity to preach that the souls in Purgatory are ransomed by indulgences.'

In 1517 the most important indulgence preached in Germany was that which the popes had twice accorded to generous Christians donating money for the new basilica of St Peter's: Julius II in 1506, in order that building might begin, and Leo X in 1514, to enable it to continue. It was the fruits of this indulgence which had been the object

[1] As fast as the money rattles in the box, the soul [on whose behalf it is given] leaps out of Purgatory.

of that extraordinary share-out which we have already noticed on the occasion of the Mainz election. The archbishop had entrusted the task of preaching the indulgence to the Dominicans, and this had provoked a fraternal but somewhat bitter jealousy among the Augustinians.

At the head of these preachers was a certain Brother Tetzel, a burly, voluble fellow, who pleaded his case with extreme enthusiasm. He was a well-intentioned man, whose own moral conduct was perfectly honourable, and he did not deserve the calumnies with which his opponents were to befoul him; but his theology was highly questionable. His method of procedure merely increased the public belief that an indulgence was a mere financial transaction. He visited the whole area dependent on Mainz, and would arrive with a vast retinue, preceded by the bull which was carried on a velvet cushion embroidered with gold. The people would come out in procession to meet him, accompanied by the ringing of bells and waving of banners; and Tetzel would then mount the pulpit, or stand in the town square, offering 'passports to cross the sea of wrath and go direct to Paradise.' This was indeed a splendid opportunity to make certain of escaping the seven years of suffering—which, as all agreed, any forgiven sin still required in the Beyond—by obtaining the plenary indulgence accorded by a confessor of Tetzel's choice. Besides, here also was an opportunity to snatch some friend or loved one from the fires of Purgatory. Nor was the price extortionate. The penitent must go to confession, visit seven churches, recite five *Paters* and five *Aves*, and place an offering in the indulgence box. The offering demanded was a modest one, scaled to the resources of each individual believer: for the poorest a quarter of a florin was sufficient.

It was against such practices and such teaching that the manifesto nailed to the door of the Schlosskirche protested so strongly. Tetzel had not preached in Wittenberg, which was Saxon territory, but all recognized the target of this attack. It was all very well for the author to maintain discretion by advising his readers to receive 'the Apostolic Commissioners with respect'; his theses rejected not only the Dominican's interpretation of the indulgence, but also the institution itself. He denounced its financial side: 'The indulgences so extolled by preachers have only one merit, that of bringing in money.' Or again: 'Nowadays the Pope's money-bag is fatter than those of the richest capitalists; why does he not build this basilica with his own resources rather than with the offerings of the poor?' These somewhat clumsy arguments made a deep impression among the common people. He also criticized the theological bases of the institution, suggesting that the indulgence caused men to lose their sense of penitence. 'True contrition gladly accepts the penalties and seeks them out; the indulgence remits them and inspires us with aversion for them. When a

Christian is truly penitent he has the right to plenary remission, even without an ecclesiastical indulgence. The grace of Jesus Christ remits the penalties of sin, not the Pope. Man can hope to receive this grace by experiencing a hatred of self and of his sin, and not by the accomplishment of a few acts or the sacrifice of a little money.' Although, in so far as they contain authentic Catholic doctrine, these theses are acceptable in many respects, they deviate from orthodoxy to the extent that they deny the Pope's power to remit penalties and refer implicitly to a theory of grace according to which man's merits are almost worthless.

What motive had impelled the author of this document to defy the official teaching of the Church? Indignation against traffickers in sacred things? Undoubtedly. Hatred of the Pope and contempt for the simoniacal Roman Curia? No. There was something deeper, more decisive, and it is revealed in the very last sentence of his ninety-five theses. Tetzel was trying to persuade the faithful that salvation was easily effected through works; he was concealing from his hapless listeners that it is necessary 'to enter Heaven by way of many tribulations,' as the Acts of the Apostles makes quite clear; he was encouraging them to 'rest in false security.' Here was the crux of the matter. It was against 'this appalling error' that the professor of Wittenberg entered the lists; and he entered them with all the violence of a man for whom this theological dispute represented a drama played out in his own life, and whom false security had brought very close indeed to total despair and unbelief. His name was *Martin Luther*.

A Brilliant Young Monk

At this date Luther was a tall, lean, bony man with powerful expressive hands. They were never still: they were for ever pointing an enemy or punctuating an argument. Everything about him indicated a passion, unease and a latent violence that was always on the verge of erupting to produce total destruction. The eyes in the rough-hewn face, with its high cheekbones, square chin and lined cheeks, often sparkled with anger or intelligence, but no less frequently they allowed a glimpse of uncontrollable anguish. It is difficult to escape the fascination which this monk in his simple Augustinian robe exerted on everyone who saw him. In 1517 he was thirty-four years old.

What had Luther's life been like up to this time? What events and reasoning had led him to quarrel openly with official conformity and make the gesture which, by setting him in the forefront of world affairs, was to turn him into the living symbol of contradiction? The *Rückblick*, that rapid and superficial glance which he threw back to his youth in 1545, a year before his death, is hardly an adequate answer to these questions; when old people evoke their memories they very often amend both truth and falsehood.

As for the traditional account, still widely believed, it seems best to retain here only the bare outline of the facts and not their substance. The explanation of Martin Luther's attitude must not be sought in his allegedly unhappy childhood and adolescence, nor, as the psycho-analysts [1] would have it, in the crises of a monk beset by temptations of the flesh, nor even in the scandalized indignation he is supposed to have felt during a brief visit to Rome. It is to be found rather in an inner conflict, something like those experienced by St Paul, St Augustine and Pascal—a conflict through which Luther lived in keen spiritual agony and uncertainty, and from which he unhappily emerged along a path which was no longer that approved by Mother Church. [2]

Martin Luther was born on 10th November 1483, at Eisleben in Saxony, the second of eight children. He was brought up at Mansfeld, where Hans, his father, had settled six months after the boy's birth. His early years were no more and no less happy than that of many sons of ordinary folk. The harsh realities of life brutalized this class of person, and in a large family there was no time for emotional refinement. Hans was a devout, stern man whose morals were irreproachable but who was easily roused to anger. He was striving with all his might to rise from artisan to foreman, and finally to become a small foundry owner on his own account, and his sole desire was that his entire household should behave with absolute propriety. Hans Luther's hard-working wife, Margaret, née Ziegler, was a stolid Franconian. She did not find it difficult to share her husband's ideas, and she directed her family with a firm hand which her children occasionally found too heavy.

Martin's parents sent him to school at Mansfeld when he was six years old. There he received the customary education of the age, consisting of the old *trivium* and the catechism, instilled by the peda-gogic methods which were then in current use and in which the cane played a large part. When it became apparent that he was an excep-tionally gifted boy, his father decided that he should continue his studies with a view to the law. He spent a year in the Cathedral School at Magdeburg, which was excellently conducted by the Brethren of the Common Life, and there he acquired an unhappily all too brief experience of genuine spirituality: it was most probably here that he made his first real contact with the Bible. Then, because his great-uncle was sacristan of St Nicholas's, Luther was drawn back to Eisenach, and there he developed his innate talents for music. Finally, at the age of

---

[1] And others, such as Father Denifle, who was writing long before Freud.
[2] At the beginning of his remarkable work (quoted in the Select Bibliography at the end of this book) Lucien Febvre has given a pertinent and spirited exposition of the inadequacy of the traditional scheme.

eighteen, he entered Erfurt University—his father, who was now more comfortably off, was henceforth able to pay him an allowance—where he obtained an outstanding degree and greatly improved his powers of self-expression and reasoning. His teachers, Fathers Usingen and Palz, trained him in their methods, which were those of Ockhamist scholasticism. His fellow students regarded him as an honourable, devout, but merry companion. So far everything about Luther's life had been utterly normal and ordinary. Then, just as he had begun his legal studies, an unforeseen event completely altered his destiny.

On 2nd July 1505, while he was returning alone from Mansfeld to Erfurt, a thunderstorm of unusual violence suddenly broke upon him. The lightning flashed so close that he believed himself lost. In the midst of this danger he invoked St Anne according to custom, and promised: 'If you come to my aid I will become a monk.' This was perhaps a rash vow, but it was certainly not spontaneous. Various other incidents had preceded this spiritual decision. Legend has embroidered upon them so much that their detail has become obscured, but their meaning is abundantly plain. A serious illness during adolescence, the sudden death of a friend, a sword wound acquired in a student's duel and which had bled for a long time—all these had brought Luther face to face with the one great fact that youth tends to ignore—the fact of death. The episode of the thunderstorm set the seal on this revelation. Luther's impressionable nature and naturally vivid sensibility responded urgently to that mortal fear which the thunderclap had inspired in his soul. He remembered the good Brethren of the Common Life, the Anhalt ruler in the Franciscan habit whom he had known at Magdeburg, the dedicated young Carthusians he often saw at Erfurt. He thought of all the people he knew who seemed to have found peace of heart, and the answer to the most dreadful of all questions beneath the homespun of the monastic robe. This vow of his was undoubtedly forced from his soul by terror, but the terror was not caused by the thunderstorm alone. Neither his family nor his friends could prevent him from remaining faithful to his promise. Fifteen days after the incident on the Erfurt road he set off to knock on the door of the Augustinian monastery there.

In 1517 then, when he nailed his theses on the door of the Schloss-kirche in Wittenberg, he was a monk—and a monk of some importance in his Order—and he was moreover a monk who had not the slightest desire to renounce his vows. 'I have been a pious monk for twenty years,' he was to say; 'I have said a Mass every day; I have worn myself out in prayer and fasting.' Witnesses have described him as a good monk, 'certainly not without sin, but above serious reproach.' In 1507 he was ordained priest. Luther mounted the altar steps for the first time with an ardour mingled with fear, as befitted one who was about to hold the living God in his own hands. Theology had made him increasingly fervent; Duns Scotus and St Thomas, Pierre d'Ailly and Gerson, William of Ockham and others in the same tradition, notably Gabriel Biel, had been the object of his voracious reading, together with the Bible, and St Augustine, and all the mystics from St Bernard to Master Eckhart. In 1508, by order of Staupitz, the wise Vicar-General for Germany, who was much interested in this brilliant young man, Luther was transferred to Wittenberg, there to teach philosophy and acquire the title of Bachelor of Arts. He enjoyed a high reputation in his Order.

This was made very clear when, during the winter of 1510–11, he was chosen to go to Rome to submit the dispute between the Augustinians of the strict and conventual observances to the superiors of the Order. Legend has it that what he saw in the Eternal City so upset the young monk that he resolved to undertake the reform of the Church. This is a convenient story, but all the evidence is against it. Luther stayed in Rome for four short weeks, behaving like any other pious pilgrim. He was most anxious to see as many churches as possible, to win the indulgences attached to these visits and to climb the 'scala sancta' on his knees; in short, as he himself recalled, he was filled with 'holy madness.' All he saw of the Papal Court were the usual glimpses that any humble visiting German cleric might expect to obtain. He obviously heard a good deal of gossip, but this did not have much immediate effect upon him. It was not until much later on, when he had been condemned by the Catholic Church, that he sought to justify his own attitude by reviving his memories of Rome. So great was men's ignorance in the capital of Christendom, he recalled, that he had been unable to find a confessor there; in St Sebastian's he had seen seven priests hurry through the Mass within the hour at a single altar; and he himself had witnessed the shameless behaviour of women in church. Perhaps; but he did not pronounce these strictures until twenty-five years after the incidents concerned—very much *a posteriori*.

On his return to Germany Luther was assigned to the Augustinian house in Wittenberg; in the following year, having been made doctor of theology, he was awarded the chair of Holy Scripture at the university. His lectures were outstandingly successful: he spoke on the Psalms and the Pauline Epistles; he was also a celebrated preacher, highly regarded by his congregations. Staupitz, his immediate superior, had a very exalted opinion of him; he made him 'district vicar,' in other words, provincial, with jurisdiction over eleven of the Order's houses; and he even went so far as to tell Luther: 'God speaks through your mouth.' Thus Luther's importance and prestige added considerable weight to his stand against the preachers of indulgences on All Saints' Eve 1517.

* K

THE DRAMA OF A SOUL

In order to understand Luther's reasons for acting as he did we must penetrate his soul and reach into those dark and dangerous recesses of the mind wherein each man worthy of the name seeks, amid suffering and contradiction, to give a meaning to his own destiny. Because the light which he himself sheds upon the drama of his youth was given long after the period concerned, a number of critics have treated it all as legend.[1] The aged Luther, they allege, invented the background of a Pascalian debate in order to provide his rebellion with fundamentally lofty and mystical origins. But an impartial study of the documents covering the decisive years—for example, his commentary on the Epistle to the Romans—is sufficient to convince the reader that their author could have adopted certain attitudes at the end of a secret and painful effort to find the answer to the gravest of man's problems. Anyone who refuses to believe that Luther was fundamentally one of those individuals for whom life and belief are serious matters is guilty of traducing historical and psychological truth. He was essentially a protagonist in great spiritual battles. The Augustinian monk who seemed to be making for himself such a brilliant career was inwardly tormented by that peculiarly religious anxiety which it is easier to feel than to define.

Luther had entered the monastery hoping to discover peace of mind, but he had not found it. He was very much a son of his age and of his native land—of Germany, where man's struggle against the powers of darkness was translated into a multitude of terrible or sublime legends; of Christianity at the crossroads, where morbid sermons and dances of death caused the faithful to be haunted with thoughts of their ultimate destiny. He had not been able to get rid of these phantoms merely by donning the monastic robe. 'I know a man,' he wrote in 1518, 'who declares he has experienced such mortal terror that no words can describe it; he who has not suffered the like would never believe him. But it is a fact that if anyone were obliged to endure for long, for half an hour or even the tenth part of an hour, he would perish utterly, and his very bones would be reduced to ashes.' Luther was in the grip of terrible anguish, and his friend Melanchthon relates that during the whole of his monastic life he was never able to throw it off. 'My heart bled when I said the Canon of the Mass,' Luther confesses, in reference to his years as a young priest. These are words that no one can read without emotion.

Whence came this anguish? Certain authors [2] have suggested that it was caused by hereditary neurosis, but there is no real proof of this. It is perfectly clear to anyone reading many of his own confessions

---

[1] Father Denifle in particular.

[2] Notably Father Grisar (his work is listed in the Select Bibliography).

that Luther was not so much a sick man as one burdened with the tragic sense of sin in all its intensity. But of what sin? It is futile to pretend to find an answer in the stirrings of his flesh. Some have seen Luther as a monk in the grip of secret lusts, a familiar of the *delectatio morosa*, unable to quell the beast within him and revolting against the discipline of the Church in order to satisfy his craving. Yet if this were a true picture,[1] if he had acted on the strength of such contemptible motives, his influence would scarcely have been so far-reaching, and would scarcely have inflicted so much suffering upon the Church. Besides, Luther himself frequently emphasized that the worst temptations were not carnal: 'evil thoughts, hatred of God, blasphemy, despair and unbelief—these are the main temptations.' The concupiscence which he had to conquer was not primarily that which draws male to female, but an irresistible craving of both body and soul that urges man to embrace all that is terrestrial and manifest—in a word, human—deflecting him from the invisible and divine.

In the monastery he had hoped to be delivered from these monsters. He was a mystical personality in many ways, and he dreamed of a warm, consoling presence which would shield him from evil and from himself, but he had discovered nothing in the monastic routine to provide such comfort. Was this because he lacked true humility, or because he had not the spirit of prayer? Only God, who has already judged the soul of Martin Luther, can supply an answer. One obstacle, however, certainly, prevented him from running like the Prodigal Son to the arms of his Father, for whenever the least flicker of impurity, violence or doubt crossed his mind he believed himself damned. He tried prayer, asceticism, and even daily confession, but none of them could rid him of this ever-present obsession with hell, which continually threatened to overwhelm him. 'I did penance,' Luther says, 'but despair did not leave me.'

The obstacle which barred Luther's way to the path of peace and love was his concept of God. He insists that this was the picture shown him in religious life. 'We paled at the mere mention of Christ's Name, for He was always depicted as a stern judge who was angry with us.' Was it necessary to work oneself to death in prayer, fasting and mortifications from fear of a Master wielding the rod of chastisement, a Divine Executioner? What was the good of it all, since one could not even be sure of melting His wrath? 'When will you do enough to obtain God's mercy?' he asked himself in anguish. In that age of misery the message of Christ's love seemed sterile; there remained only the atrocious doctrine of inevitable punishment meted out by an inexorable judge.

It has not been difficult for Catholic critics to show that this doctrine

[1] Unfortunately Luther's marriage gives this view a semblance of truth.

has never been that of Holy Church. In a book of no fewer than 378 pages, Father Denifle has conclusively demonstrated that the 'justice of God' mentioned in a famous passage of the Epistle to the Romans (i. 17), and which Luther took to be the supreme spiritual reality, was intended to signify something far more than *justitia puniens*, divine wrath punishing the sins of men; the words were used rather of sanctifying grace, of the omnipotent mercy lavished by God on all who believe in Him and submit to His ordinances.[1] Luther's interpretation of the phrase reveals a surprising failure to understand the philosophy of such writers as St Augustine and St Bernard, with whose works he was undoubtedly well acquainted. To explain the spiritual drama of the young Augustinian monk, however, it is sufficient to acknowledge that he himself regarded this erroneous doctrine as valid, and as that which his own professors had taught him.

The fact may have been due to the imperfect theological training offered by the representatives of decadent scholasticism who filled all the university chairs. Moreover the teaching then in fashion contained one feature calculated to impel a restless soul along the downward slope. To such a man as Luther, obsessed with the desire to appease his terrible God, and deriving not the slightest comfort from his prayers and mortifications, one system in particular provided a kind of answer: Ockhamist Nominalism, in which, as we have seen, he had been brought up.[2] Luther had discovered from the writings of this school not only that man could overcome sin by will alone, but also that no human action became meritorious unless God acknowledged it and willed it to be so. But if man's will failed it had no means of recovery, for reason was unavailing and grace was not conceived as a supernatural principle raising man's spiritual forces to the level of Divine Justice. Thus nothing was left save a capricious God, granting or withholding His grace and forgiveness for motives that defied all the rules of logic. Before Him stood a defenceless man, inert and passive in relation to the work of salvation. Destiny appeared to be regulated by the cold mechanics of a despot in whose eyes nothing had any merit. Luther strove hard to find confirmation of these theories in certain passages of St Paul and St Augustine, for they corresponded all too well with his fundamental and powerful belief in the futility of all human effort. In several respects he remained an Ockhamist all his life; but he rejected the voluntarism taught by Ockham's disciples, he denied the human liberty which they recognized, and he gave it a ring of predestinationism which was absent from the master's philosophy. None of this did anything to grant him peace of mind.

---

[1] Translator's Note.—Monsignor Knox's recent translation of St Paul's phrase, i.e. 'God's way of justifying us,' makes this very clear.
[2] On Ockham see Chapter III, p. 152.

But a number of more peaceful influences were at work. Luther had read all the mystics, especially the German writers of the late Middle Ages, notably Tauler.[1] Here too he had found elements that tended to deny the importance of external works, to discard free will and to exalt the part played by faith in Christ the Redeemer. Man must lay himself open to God's action, submit to it and do nothing to resist it. This was one of the fundamental ideas of the *Theologica Germanica*. Furthermore Staupitz, anxious to heal this ravaged soul, had gone a long way in the same direction by showing Luther the gentleness of God's love and the need for supreme surrender to Providence. Neither the subtleties of the schools nor ritual practices would give him the divine life to which he aspired, but only the impulse of a believing soul, and the piety which sprang from the most secret recesses of the heart. 'True repentance begins with love of justice and of God.' At once the young monk felt that part of his burden had been lifted, that he was on the way to a new enlightenment; and it seemed that ideas, arguments and biblical references poured in from all sides to confirm this doctrine 'and dance a jig around it.'

It was now that there happened the 'discovery of mercy,' a wholly spiritual event to which Luther's disciples afterwards traced the origins of the Reformation. The date and place of this occurrence are the subject of some dispute. He may have had had his first glimpse of it in Rome, while making the pious pilgrimage on his knees up the 'Scala sancta.' It may, on the other hand, be necessary to advance the date to 1518 or 1519; if so he can have had only a kind of presentiment of his doctrine on the day when he nailed his theses to the chapel door.[2] Its main features, however, are already apparent in the university lectures which he gave between 1514 and 1517. The most probable truth is that the 'discovery' took place in his mind by gradual stages, before imposing itself on his soul with such force that all arguments and reservations became as nothing in the blinding clarity of what seemed to him to be incontrovertible evidence.

In the preface to the 1545 edition of his *Works* Luther describes in detail this 'sudden illumination of the Holy Spirit.' He was pondering once again the terrible seventeenth verse in the first chapter of the Epistle to the Romans when the true meaning—that is to say, the meaning he henceforth considered to be true—was revealed to him. 'While I pursued my meditations day and night, examining the import

[1] See Chapter III, p. 143.

[2] Luther himself, when far advanced in years, claimed to have received enlightenment in a secret and solitary place, which he calls the *cloaca*, in a tower of the monastery at Wittenberg. Many were revolted by this detail, but Luther answered with a reference to St John's statement that 'the wind breathes where it will' (iii. 8). Some Catholic writers have sneered at his extraordinary account, which ought perhaps rather to be treated as evidence of pathetic candour.

of these words, "The justice of God is revealed in the Gospel, as it is written, the just live by faith," [1] I began to understand that the justice of God signifies that justice whereby the just live through the gift of God, namely, through faith. Therefore the meaning of the sentence is as follows: the Gospel shows us the justice of God, but it is a passive justice, through which, by means of faith, the God of mercy justifies us.' To the young monk, tortured by fear and anguish, this was indeed a prodigious discovery! The hangman God, armed with His whip, faded away, yielding place to Him towards whom the soul could turn with perfect trust and confidence. . . .

At this juncture, as always happens where great minds are concerned, all kinds of reflections and arguments crystallized around this one apparently quite straightforward idea. It became the basis of a system. 'System' is perhaps the wrong word here; for Luther there was no question of dry doctrine or paper thesis, but of a vital experience, the answer to all his own terrible problems. But he saw the answer so clearly that he was able to express it in the form of categorical principles. Man is a sinner, incapable of making himself just (i.e. righteous) and condemned to impotence by the enemy he bears within himself. Even though he conforms outwardly to the law, he remains in a state of sin. Even though he tries to behave righteously and hopes to acquire merit, he is unable to do so, for at the root of his very being there is a deadly germ. There must therefore be, and indeed there is, a justice exterior to man, which alone will save him. Through the grace of Jesus Christ all the soul's blemishes are, as it were, covered by a cloak of light. Thus the one means and only hope of salvation is to entrust oneself to Christ, as it were to cling to Him. 'The faith that justifies is that which seizes Jesus Christ.' Compared with this saving reality all man's miserable efforts towards repentance and self-improvement were ridiculous and worthless. 'The just live by faith.'

It must be admitted that this view was perfectly adapted to set an anguished soul at rest. Where did it deviate from the orthodox? The Church teaches that God is 'just' in the simplest sense of the term, that is to say, He distributes His graces to us all in an equitable manner, and not by virtue of a kind of incomprehensible caprice. She teaches that salvation and eternal bliss are earned in the world through positive effort and good works. She affirms the importance of sin, but she refuses to admit that man can do nothing to combat it. She does indeed proclaim the indispensability of the love of God and union with Christ, but she asserts that they demand from man a positive effort to acquire a supernatural resemblance. Faith is but the beginning of justification.

[1] Translator's Note.—Monsignor Knox's translation reads: 'It reveals God's way of justifying us, faith first and last; and, as the Scripture says, it is faith that brings life to the just man.'

It is completed by reception of the sacraments, in the act of contrition or the act of charity. Salvation demands much more than mere belief.

Luther, however, was so intoxicated by his discovery, so exalted by the joy of escaping at last from the vice which had held him in its grip, that he would consider no argument advanced against his theory. 'I felt suddenly born anew,' he said, 'and it seemed that the doors of Paradise itself were flung wide open to me, and I entered in.' He was saved! He knew he was a sinner, but Christ had taken upon His shoulders the sins of the whole world. It was distasteful to realize that all the pious exercises and all the theological reasoning to which he had recourse were of no effect, but in the blinding light of the Redemption all human things were nothing but dry dust. The dialectic of sin and grace contained the answer to everything. The exultant professor of Wittenberg announced his discovery at all his lectures even before his own philosophy had been fully defined, before it had been crowned with the maxim (not formulated until after 1518) that in order to be saved all that one needed was the inner certainty of one's own salvation. He set out his thesis at Easter 1517, at the beginning of a series of lectures on the Epistle to the Hebrews. 'Man is incapable of obtaining relief from any sin by his own efforts alone. In the sight of God all human virtues are sin.' He also directed one of his pupils, Bernhardi, to take 'Grace and Free Will' as the subject of his thesis for the doctorate; it was to conform in all respects with the principles of Luther, who later admitted that at this period he felt 'divinely possessed.'

The preaching of indulgences offered Luther a splendid opportunity to make the truth blindingly clear to everyone. He was disgusted most of all by this computation of so-called merits shamefully acquired, in order to escape the just pains of the after-life. He himself enjoyed true security in that prodigious wager upon Christ which he intended to maintain from now onwards. The false, pitiable thing which these wretched folk believed that they acquired, by kneeling in front of some relics and throwing their money into a box provided by someone like Tetzel, was no true security. As for the authority of the Pope, who guaranteed the value of such practices, the Ockhamist in Luther recalled what the leaders of that school had had to say, their reservations on papal infallibility and indeed on the function of the Papacy in general. He remembered Gabriel Biel's declaration that every Catholic was competent to reform the Church. He had, of course, not the slightest idea that in adopting positions of this kind he was going to set in motion the gravest crisis which Christianity had ever experienced. He was, in his own words, 'a blind wretch who set off without knowing where he was going.' Spiritual argument did not really interest him. He was fundamentally interested only in making the world hear and understand Heaven's response to his *De Profundis*; but 'the voice of

Germany, restless and secretly trembling with unrestrained passion,[1] was not slow to answer his cry, and the drama of one soul unleashed a revolution.

GERMANY IN THE TIME OF LUTHER

The whole Germanic world was at this time in a state of utter contradiction. Thanks to her fertile soil, her cities at the crossroads of Europe and her people's capacity for hard work, she seemed the very picture of prosperity; but she was also a scene of anarchy perhaps more serious than that which reigned in the Italian peninsula. There were four hundred states, great and small, interlocking like pieces of a jigsaw. They comprised a political aggregate without the least semblance of cohesion. There were Germans in plenty—stolid, active people, all speaking analogous dialects and all thinking along roughly the same lines, but there was no such thing as Germany.

This anarchy embraced two rival elements: the rulers and the cities. In Germanic territory the higher ranks of the nobility had made a success of the operation which had been tried unsuccessfully in France: they had to all intents and purposes freed themselves from central authority. Some ten or so families had left the emperors to seek their fortunes south of the Alps, and had each set to work on its own account to increase its own power and possessions. Saxony, the Palatinate, Hesse, Württemberg, Bavaria, Brandenburg and Mecklenburg were all regions where the local leaders were kings in all but name, exercising more or less control over a crowd of lesser nobles of all ranks, who remained nevertheless turbulent and dangerous.

But there were holes in this feudal fabric: the cities, which were increasing both in number and in strength, less and less subject to their theoretical overlords. Their wealth was enormous: besides trade and banking, they had developed timber and iron industries, and engaged in mining. Though the maritime towns of the Hansa were now in decline, those in the German interior were growing fast: Cologne, one of the most important cities in Europe, Augsburg, Ulm, Nuremberg, Basle, Frankfurt, Strasbourg and a score of others. Modern capitalism was being born in these cities, with all its arrogance and audacity, in the persons of the Fuggers and their many rivals. These sumptuous places possessed no common bond, no sense of common interest; each clustered around its town hall, symbol of its liberty, ready to defend itself not only against the marauding squirearchy, but against its business competitiors as well. Many good ducats were frittered away in battlements, armies and embassies. Machiavelli called these urban entities 'the sinews of the Empire'; but they aggravated the anarchy of the German world still further.

[1] Lucien Febvre.

The Empire still existed, but it was no more than a hollow shell, and the emperor merely a name. Ever since the Golden Bull of 1356 the 'pillars and torches,' that is to say, the seven Electors—the three archbishops of Mainz, Trier and Cologne, and the secular rulers of Bohemia, the Rhine Palatinate, Saxony and Brandenburg—had met at Frankfurt after the death of each emperor in order to choose his successor. The elective system made the imperial crown dependent on the complicated intrigues of lesser rulers, all of whom were anxious not to choose anyone whose authority might be real. This illustrious but cumbersome crown was unable to derive from Germany the resources which an efficient governmental organization would have demanded, 'no more than a hazel-nut,' as Cardinal Granvelle said; and it was virtually powerless against the armies of princes and the gold of bankers. The Imperial Diet, with its three colleges of Electors, nobles and merchants, limited its prerogatives still further; it too, however, was incapable of achieving unity, for it was rent by countless different interests and jealousies.

The emperor's real power, therefore, rested on his personal authority and intelligence. At the moment when Luther came on to the stage of history, the reign of *Maximilian* (1493–1519) still had two years to run. He was an affable, courteous ruler, a scholar and musician who possessed some rather wild ideas (in 1512 he had dreamed of being elected pope) but who, instead of interesting himself solely in his hereditary domains in Austria, wisely attempted to organize the Empire by administering a preliminary dose of centralization. The creation of the Circles, the Council of the Empire and the Imperial Chamber of Justice showed that his plans were good; unfortunately most of them never left the drawing-board. He was most successful in his matrimonial policy. By his own marriage to Mary of Burgundy, Maximilian had acquired the bulk of Charles the Bold's inheritance; and he had married his son, Philip the Fair, to Joanna the Mad, daughter and heiress to the 'Catholic Sovereigns' of Spain. On becoming a widower the emperor took as his second wife Blanche Sforza, and thus obtained a claim to the duchy of Milan; in 1515 he had just arranged the betrothal of the younger of his grandsons, Ferdinand of Austria, and Anne Jagellon, who inherited Bohemia and Hungary eleven years later. Altogether this was a long stride towards concentration of power.

The elder of his grandsons, whom Maximilian designated as his successor to the imperial crown, was named Charles, and is known to history as the *Emperor Charles V*. Charles was born in 1500 and became King of Spain in 1516 on the death of his grandfather, Ferdinand of Aragon. He was then a robust, alert young man, whose long, prominent chin made him appear more wise than handsome. While he lacked the sparkle of true brilliance, he possessed sound qualities of application and a slow but meticulous sense of judgment. He was a voracious eater, an intrepid drinker and a capable sportsman; he was also fond of sexual adventures, but he knew how to pursue them with discretion and did not allow them to dominate his life. At the same time he was pious to the point of being sanctimonious, and his mysticism verged on anguish. He was in fact a somewhat contradictory figure. When this boy of nineteen became emperor on Maximilian's death, he seemed from a distance to be the most powerful sovereign of the age. He controlled the Austrian estates of the Hapsburgs, the splendid ruins of Burgundian ambition, the reunited and reconstituted Spain of the Catholic monarchs, together with its Italian appendages, and last of all those prodigious lands which the Conquistadores had just conquered in America: 'The sun never sets on my dominions,' he could fairly claim. This was all very fine in appearance, but the reality was somewhat different. How could Charles exercise his authority with equal force over the whole mosaic of realms, principalities and cities? Where was the centre of gravity in so vast a collection of territories? The very immensity of his inheritance was a source of weakness, for it obliged him to make incessant journeys from one far-flung possession to another. Although he was regarded as the national monarch in Burgundy, things were likely to be very different in Spain, where only the rough hand of Isabella and Ferdinand had been able to salvage unity, and where, but for his mother's memory, he was virtually a foreigner. In Germany he would have to deal tactfully with the princes who had elected him, and with the capitalists who had provided the funds to smooth the way for his accession. Then, along the Hungarian frontier, he would have to resist the thrust of Turkey; and wherever he turned he would have to take account of the highly organized and powerful kingdom of France, who could not allow herself to be thus encircled. Charles V was not the man to snatch the Germanic world from its anarchy and to give it a heart and a soul.

The Germans suffered grievously from this lack of unity, even though they did nothing to cure it. Compared with the many realms, notably France and England, where centralization proceeded apace, they were only too well aware that their divided state was a sign of weakness. 'Poor Germany!' the Emperor Maximilian had declared. And Luther would one day write: 'No nation is so despised as we Germans. Italy calls us *bestias*; we are the laughing-stock of France and England, and all the rest ridicule us as well!' Germany was sick and tired of being exploited, divided and held in tutelage. She was waiting in a confused kind of way for a voice to arouse her to full national consciousness.

A number of other causes, social in origin, were also fomenting muffled groans of anger. At the bottom of their hearts, rightly or wrongly, all classes other than the very limited category of great feudatories, longed for change. The middle class, from the artisan to the high financier, detested both princes, priests and all who could impede its own autonomy. Other classes had more legitimate grievances. The petty nobility, which had been ruined by the division of hereditary property, the depreciation of land values and its predilection for luxury and pleasure, hated its overlords—dukes, electors, counts and bishops—whose good fortune set at naught its own discomfort. An 'aristocratic proletariat' came into being, an 'iron-gloved knighthood,' personified in such men as Götz von Berlichingen and Franz von Sickingen; these rebels were never without helmet and crossbow, were constantly at war with princes, cities and priests. Their 'ultima ratio' was the 'Faustrecht,' the right of force; and around them gladly gathered all the professional swordsmen, all the *Reiter*, whose motto was 'Strong today, dead tomorrow.'

As for the common people, theirs was an unhappy lot. Everyone suffered: workmen were underpaid, small traders ruined by large combines, the peasants weighed down by taxes and constantly pillaged by rebellious squireens. In order to pay their rents and tithes they were forced to resort to Jewish money-lenders who charged exorbitant rates of interest. Many had relapsed into serfdom. This wretched proletariat longed ardently for some improvement in its condition. Men recalled the slogans of John Huss and the struggles waged by the Taborites. A preacher like Geiler, who invited the poor 'to chase the monopolists like ravening wolves,' was wildly acclaimed. People remembered the courageous Swiss who had triumphed over the Austrian oppressor: 'We too desire to be like the Swiss' echoed throughout western Germany. Ever since the beginning of the fifteenth century disturbances had constantly flared up in every corner of the Germanic world; the rebellions of 1461, 1470, 1476 and 1492 had been in the nature of sharp warnings, heralds of the Anabaptist revolution. Nicholas of Cusa had already prophesied that 'today the German princes devour the people, but one day the people will devour them.' By 1517 the appetite of the German nation was becoming more acute.

The Germanic world was still in many ways medieval; but the forces of the modern age also were at work, and these accentuated the unrest still further. It was being permeated by the influences of the Renaissance and of humanism, supported by the printing-press, which spread here more quickly than anywhere else, so that in 1500 there were more than a thousand German printing houses. During its development in this climate, however, the intellectual and artistic movement had acquired a number of highly individual characteristics.

In Germany the study of antiquity was not pursued with the same filial devotion that the Italians had shown. German customs did not easily lend themselves to the often savage but nevertheless creative individualistic impulse which has been observed in the peninsula. In Germany also there were fewer geniuses and fewer patrons. The past still exerted an extremely powerful influence upon the future that was struggling to be born. This fact is particularly noticeable in the field of art, where *Martin Schongauer* (1430–91), the contemporary of Giovanni Bellini, and *Matthias Grünewald* (?1460–?1528), who was Leonardo da Vinci's junior by eight years, retain several semi-Gothic features in works which all possess the same mystical quality, be they terrifying or naïve. Peculiarly German characteristics became apparent in the development of the new tendencies; they provoked a number of violent reactions, to one of which Reuchlin fell victim, and occasionally threw up such bizarre personalities as *Paracelsus* (1493–1541), a physician endowed with either genius or wizardry, and who, though a fanatical believer in esoterism, was granted a Chair of Physics and Medicine at Basle.

In Germany, thanks to the existence of many excellent universities, scholarship was a considerably stronger force than art. There were many active groups of humanists and literary figures—at that time regarded as 'poets': Rudolf Agricola (1442–95), the spiritual heir of Nicholas of Cusa; Jacob Wimpfeling (1450–1528), an able pedagogue who taught notably at Strasbourg; Johann von Dalberg, the somewhat unedifying Bishop of Worms; Johann Trithemius (1462–1516), who was considered to possess universal knowledge; and *Johann Reuchlin* (1455–1522), the doyen of Hebrew studies and professor at Tübingen, who unleashed a storm of controversy by seeking to protect the Old Testament, as source of the New, from the blind orthodoxy of the learned.[1] The most celebrated and influential scholar of them all was *Erasmus* (1466–1536). This 'prince of humanists' was a Dutchman, born in the imperial city of Rotterdam; but he had studied first at Paris, then at Oxford, and his thirst for knowledge and information had taken him on journeys through Italy, France, Germany and England. He eventually settled at Freiburg-im-Breisgau. His wonderfully lucid mind ranged, with equally happy results, from exegesis to

[1] The affair of Reuchlin foreshadowed Luther's in many ways, although it affected the more limited field of biblical criticism. It contained features characteristic of the disputes later provoked by the monk from Wittenberg. The two sides fought tenaciously, the Dominicans and the theologians of Cologne and Paris against the humanists and Ulrich von Hutten. Leo X displayed the same weakness and the same hesitant delaying tactics which he showed at the start of the Lutheran tragedy. As on the later occasion, the Curia was divided by contradictory influences; and lastly, nationalist passion was already shifting the focus of the dispute. The Reuchlin affair thus helps us to understand why, in posing the fundamental problem, Luther was to unleash all these forces in their full violence.

philosophy, from psychological analysis to political criticism. In 1517 educated Germany, and indeed all western intellectuals, was still laughing over *In Praise of Folly* (1511), which had fired its darts at many privileged skins. But his *New Testament* (1516) had inspired some very serious thought; sweeping aside all traces of scholasticism, and even of medieval mysticism, Erasmus was laying the foundations of what might prove to be a new type of Christianity.[1]

For in the main, and far more so than in Italy, German humanism remained Christian. Save for a few very rare exceptions—Mutian, for example, a dissolute canon and notorious Epicurean—there is scarcely a trace in Germany of that current of scepticism which, as we have seen, made such deep inroads into Italy. Rudolf Agricola maintained that 'the study of the ancients should, above all, help us to a better understanding of the Scriptures,' and Johann Trithemius stated that, so far from applying himself to this kind of study 'in a worldly spirit,' he was following the example of the Early Fathers and 'gathering in its ripe fruits in order to add to Christian knowledge.' But all these humanists were enthusiastic supporters of reform in the Church; they were sickened by the prevailing errors, obscurantism and deceit. Without always appreciating the full strength of their blows, they directed their vigorous criticism against those practices which they considered superstitious, and against the ecclesiastical habits which they believed to be dissolute and decadent. It is questionable, however, whether they invariably distinguished accurately between what really deserved condemnation and institutions which should remain permanently unshakable. To a certain extent their passion for freedom of thought paved the way for free-thinking, and even free inquiry. In calling upon the Church to reform herself they were inadvertently encouraging deviations of the worst kind.

Was the Church in Germany in need of reform? The need here was no greater and no less than elsewhere in Christendom. Faith was very much alive in Germany. In 1494 a worthy merchant wrote in his diary: 'My country abounds in Bibles, works on salvation, editions of the Fathers, and other books of a like sort.' Pilgrimages were extremely popular, and sermons attracted huge congregations. The Brethren of the Common Life had influenced virtually the whole of Germany, causing a general intensification of piety and practice. This faith clearly possessed the same faults which existed elsewhere: the common people displayed appalling ignorance of the most elementary Christian truths; superstition, whose roots went far back into the subsoil of ancient Germanic paganism, was rife; cult of the saints too often verged on idolatry, and as for relics we need only remember the vast numbers collected by the Elector of Saxony in order to realize their

[1] On Erasmus's religious ideas see p. 328.

popular attraction. Sorcerers and witches were imagined to be every-where. It should be added that in Germany, more than in most coun-tries, the fundamental ideas of a mercantile middle class were growing further and further removed from the ideal of the Gospels, thanks to the rising power of capitalism. No one yet dared openly to attack religion, but its representatives were freely castigated.

They undoubtedly invited criticism. The German Church presented the same spectacle as the Italian and the French. In other words, though the water itself was still kept pure and sweet by a vast quantity of good and pious souls, it was topped by a scum which was far more visible and offensive to the nostrils—the putrid scum of a sensual and simoni-acal upper clergy and of a priesthood that was grasping in the extreme. There is no point here in returning to the unhappy scene provided by all too many dissolute bishops, surrounded by their jesters and their men-at-arms. Many of them were younger sons who had been loaded with benefices at the age of thirteen and who spent their time adding to the number of their benefices held in *commendam*. The scandalous career of Albert of Brandenburg, Archbishop of Mainz, is example enough. The enormous wealth of the Church in the Empire—she owned one-third of the soil of Germany—was bound to excite the greedy glances of a bankrupt squirearchy, of covetous knights and of the downtrodden commonalty, to whom such ostentatious wealth seemed a flagrant insult. There was a superabundance of the lower clergy. At Cologne, 'the German Rome,' where the total population was certainly not more than 50,000, there were said to be 5,000 priests. This ill-paid body, too often obliged to earn its daily bread in ways very far from ecclesiastical, constituted a proletariat which regarded the aristocratic bishops with considerable jealousy, and which longed for a chance in the established order of things. From this class emerged Luther, Bucer, Karlstadt, Munzer and Oeclampadius, all leaders of the German Reformation; they were sons of the people, who had become priests only to remain beggars.

One characteristic has still to be noted: German Catholicism was very different from its Italian counterpart. The latter was a cult of externals, much given to exuberant demonstration; the former was a more intimate, idealistic religion, full of dreams. Racial hatred, which dated from the conflicts between Papacy and Empire, was fed by differences of temperament. 'Uncouth beasts!' exclaimed the Italians. 'Vicious pagans, liars and rogues!' retorted the Germans. In Luther's religious revolution there was a latent Ghibellinism, which was easily roused by those who claimed to show the German people that they were being fleeced, exploited and robbed by the Curia and its collectors. Luther's clarion call 'Germany, awake!' was bound to fall on ready ears, and indeed it did.

Thus when he embarked on his campaign, the monk of Wittenberg, though quite unaware of the fact, was faced with a situation more than favourable to revolutionary proceedings. Here was a nation devoid of unity, troubled by dark and secret forces, suffering in its anarchy. Its local potentates were intensely jealous of their privileges, preferring to do anything rather than lose them. The emperor was quite incapable of imposing unity of administration—and *a fortiori* of doctrine—on the land. Social conditions were unstable. Ideas of liberty, particularly if erroneously interpreted, might unleash a hurricane of elemental lusts. An intellectual movement was in full development, and was working almost unconsciously to undermine the foundations of the traditional edifice. Beneath the surface too there lay an element of nationalism, which readily crystallized into hatred of Rome, a hatred that seemed to be justified by numerous excesses. The ground had been well prepared for Luther; but it would be wrong to underestimate the vital influence of the man who was going to take upon his shoulders the confused expectancy of a whole nation. He benefited from circumstances only at the cost of several ambiguities, and on many occasions courageously attempted to put an end to those very compromises of principle which would have helped to bring him success. Briefly, in becoming the spokesman of Germany, Luther allowed himself to be deflected from his true path. It is not the political, social and religious conditions of Germany which explain Luther. The answer lies in Luther himself. He did not rise, in all good faith, against the institutions of the Church, with a view to uniting the Germanic world and making it conscious of its own potential strength. Nor did he make his protest in order to reform ecclesiastical morals.[1] Luther himself roundly asserted that such had never been his aim. 'Someone said to me: "What a sin and scandal all these clerical vices are, the fornication, the drunkenness, the unbridled passion for sport!" Yes, I must confess that these are dreadful scandals, indeed, and they should be denounced and corrected. But the vices to which you refer are plain for all to see; they are grossly material, everyone perceives them, and so everyone is stirred to anger by them. Alas, the real evil, the incomparably more baneful and cruel canker, is the deliberate silence regarding the word of Truth, or else its adulteration. Yet who feels the horror of this?' His words make it quite clear that the problem of reform, in the sense understood by so many men of the age, was of secondary importance to Luther. The invectives which he subsequently hurled at the dissolute clergy were dictated by polemic considerations. The revolution he desired to effect was neither social nor political nor ecclesiastical, but theological. He

---

[1] Moreover, in Germany as elsewhere, several useful measures of reform had already been taken, in both the religious Orders and the dioceses, which he could have followed up and supported.

was trying to wage war against the tyranny of error and sin on behalf of what he understood by 'the Truth.' But the juxtaposition of forces turned his campaign into something very different, and gave his message a destructive power which he had scarcely dreamed existed.

LUTHER VERSUS ROME

By nailing his theses to the door of the Schlosskirche, Martin Luther had, according to the academic customs of the age, offered to debate them publicly. No one came forward to do battle with him, but his message had not tumbled into the void. It was disseminated in printed form throughout Germany and even beyond, provoking some lively reaction both for and against. At that time Luther's assertions, which seem to us so clearly marked 'Protestant,' were regarded simply as criticizing excesses on the part of those who preached indulgences, and as fixing the limits of a dogma which was still imperfectly defined. It was in this light that Staupitz presented them to the Elector of Saxony; but public response convinced Luther more firmly than ever that he possessed the truth, or, as he said later, 'that he held the Gospel not of men but of Heaven, through the good offices of Jesus Christ alone.' In October 1517 the students of Wittenberg acclaimed their professor's name, and made a bonfire of Tetzel's *Antitheses* which had just been published against him.

By this time the dispute had become more than a mere monkish squabble, more even than a theological debate. The indignant Archbishop of Mainz had forwarded the Lutheran theses to Rome, and the entire Dominican Order was about to rise up against them. At first Leo X did not consider the affair as particularly serious; he probably never understood its fundamental gravity. In December, however, Cardinal Tomaso de Vio of Gaeta, known as *Cajetan*, studied the file and clearly perceived therein what came to be described as 'the material and formal principle of the Reformation.' On the one hand it propounded the doctrine of justification by faith and the attack on the notion of merit; on the other it called in question the infallible supremacy of the Church. Thinking such a step quite sufficient, Rome directed Staupitz to make his subordinate recant. Luther explained his position at a meeting of the Chapter in 1518, but would not withdraw an inch and sent his final memorandum to Rome. This was the *Resolution on the virtue of indulgences*, which was quite the reverse of recantation. The Vatican now reacted sharply. The Dominican Prieras, Master of the Sacred Palace, was ordered to draw up an indictment summoning Luther to submit or to appear before the Roman Curia. Prieras did his work clumsily and without tact, accentuating only the revolt against the Church, not the error of doctrine, and exalting papal omnipotence in such exaggerated terms that Luther found no difficulty in refuting the charge; he also gave vent to insults of which the least offensive described the Dominician as 'son of a bitch.'

The Elector of Saxony, forewarned of the danger threatening the professors at his university, obtained from Rome the concession that instead of having to visit the Eternal City, Luther should be cited to appear before Cardinal Cajetan, who was then at Augsburg, where the Diet was considering the Turkish menace. A meeting duly took place between the prince of the Church and the monk; it was a cautious exchange of views, but entirely without result. Cajetan spoke to Luther like a father, asking the young Augustinian to retract his errors and cease teaching them. The only reply was a memorandum or *Explanations* in which the Lutheran theses were restated and further defined, and in which Cajetan could see nothing but rebellion. Luther returned to Wittenberg, and the Prince Elector refused to extradite him as Rome would have liked. On 21st October he issued an appeal 'from the ill-informed Pope to the well-informed Pope.' Five weeks later, having read the recently published bull on indulgences, he appealed once again, this time to a council which would rectify the Pope's errors.

Had the breaking-point been reached? Luther hoped not; he believed himself a thoroughly good Catholic, and actually increased his protestations of respect, but not of surrender. When submitting his *Resolutions* to Leo X he had written: 'Approve or disapprove: for me your voice will be that of Christ, and if I have deserved death I will not hesitate to die.' Even in the following year, in March 1519, he asserted that 'before God and man, I have never wished to attack either the Roman Church or Your Holiness, and today I have even less intention of doing so.' However, a number of persons anxious to use him for their own ends were already gathering around the young prophet. One man in particular had seen the right manœuvre—*Ulrich von Hutten*. This strange and mysterious individual, at once humanist and virtually lawless knight, was the living expression of German nationalism which united scholars, merchants, soldiers and aristocrats in one muddled aspiration, and which led inevitably to hatred of Rome. Supported thus by public opinion, and indeed protected thereby against all Rome's condemnations, Luther was able to follow his own course, develop and spread his views and grow increasingly bold. It is a fundamental law of heresy to go further and further along its road, to harden its positions proportionately with the threats uttered against it and to proclaim antagonisms where at first there was probably no more than verbal error or secret intentions.

The Church, however, seemed in no desperate hurry to strike him down. It is possible that the Pope, being ill informed, believed that the matter could be settled amicably; or perhaps Luther's respectful protestations had their effect. So far many worthy folk could see no danger of schism: Erasmus, for instance, wrote that, so far as doctrine was concerned, Luther was not cutting himself off from the Church, and that his only serious error lay in the aggressive exposition of his ideas. Moreover Rome was driven to temporize by a number of grave political motives. In order to overthrow the rebel recourse to authority was essential. But which authority? Frederick of Saxony? The Pope did indeed send him a kindly chamberlain, Charles von Miltitz, under pretext of presenting him with the proud distinction of the Golden Rose; but the Elector cunningly avoided making any reply when the question of arresting Luther was raised. This makeshift diplomat thought he would be able to bring the accused to Rome, or persuade him to retract; but he failed completely. Who then might be able to execute the sentence? The Emperor Maximilian would probably have tried; but he was already on his death bed, and died on 12th January 1519. The question of who should succeed him resulted in an absurd diplomatic contest, in which Francis I, King of France, and Charles, the grandson of the dead 'Weisskönig,' employed the weapons of barefaced bribery. There was a market in votes for six months, one Elector allowing himself to be bought six times—thrice by each bidder. Fugger, the great financier whose fortune depended partly on imports of Styrian iron-ore through the port of Antwerp, offered the use of unlimited credits to support the candidature of the ruler of Austria and Flanders. This was no time for Rome to unloose a religious conflict, more especially as the Pope, who was hostile to both Hapsburg and Valois, looked upon Frederick of Saxony as a useful card to hold up his sleeve. He was mistaken: on 28th June the gold of Augsburg was victorious over French largesse, and Charles was elected.

The affair of Luther, which had been dormant for a while, now broke out afresh. It had in fact remained an issue in the universities, where the Lutheran position was passionately debated. In his talks with Cardinal Cajetan, Luther had declared his willingness to submit to the judgment 'of the eminent doctors of the imperial universities of Basle, Freiburg and Louvain, or, if these are not enough, those of Paris also.' As it happened, however, the professors of Louvain had severely censured his theses during the winter of 1518–19. Those of Cologne were on the alert, and were preparing to take similar steps. Among the Catholic theologians who almost everywhere showed themselves eager for battle were Emser, Cochloeüs, the satirist, Thomas Murner, one of Luther's own colleagues at Wittenberg, the Franciscan Alfeld and, needless to say, innumerable sons of St Dominic. The most ardent of these Catholic apologists was *Johann Eck*, vice-chancellor of the university of Ingolstadt. One of his pamphlets, which first appeared in December 1518, was circulating throughout Germany; it was entitled *Obelesci*, from the word applied to the typographical sign with which passages suspected of heresy were marked in the margins of books.

Luther was in great danger. Had Frederick the Wise not acceded to Erasmus's request and protected the rebel from the fury of theologians, he might well have suffered the fate of John Huss. But he took no notice; contradiction spurred him to greater efforts. When he read the arguments of his opponents he not only felt his position strengthened, but his views became even more extreme. From now on he was the leader of a school of thought, and as such he could hardly avoid doing battle with those who contradicted him. His friend Karlstadt and Melanchthon supported him. It was therefore decided to hold a public debate, according to custom, at which Lutherans and antiLutherans would confront one another. This took place in the town hall at Leipzig, at the end of June 1519, before an immense gathering of professors, students and representatives of German and foreign universities. Luther was not happy about the course of the debate. Eck, an outstanding dialectician and powerful orator, endowed with an astonishing memory, subjected him to attacks which he had difficulty in sustaining. His back to the wall, the reformer was led by his opponent to express ideas which were probably still quite vague in the depths of his heart. In particular he adopted a categorical position on the decisive issue of papal primacy: the Church had only one real head—Christ. 'I do not know whether the Christian religion can suffer another head on earth.' With reference to the doctrinal value of conciliar decisions, Luther went so far as to say that the propositions condemned at Constance had contained some that were 'entirely Christian and worthy of the Gospel.' But if neither Pope nor Council were infallible, his appeals were meaningless. Likewise, on the question of free will and justification by faith, Luther committed himself even further than before. Thus the Leipzig debate marked a serious hardening in the evolution of his thought.

Henceforward he could not withdraw. All Germany was divided into two camps, for or against him. The humanists, who had at first regarded this monkish quarrel with some sarcasm, now represented Luther as the victim of avaricious prelates and ignorant theologians. Melanchthon, who had become his close friend, threw himself wholeheartedly into his cause. Hutten wrote to him, saying that if he rose against Rome the squirearchy, led by Franz von Sickingen, would come to his aid; Sylvester von Schaumberg offered him a hundred *Reiter* for his personal protection. A number of towns joined the movement, notably Nuremberg, where priests were booed in the streets. Luther grasped the importance of these allies who were coming forward to join him. 'The die is cast,' he declared. 'I no longer wish for reconciliation with Rome.'

The year 1520 was decisive. Luther produced three revolutionary books: *An Address to the Nobility of the German Nation*, *On the Babylonian Captivity of the Church of God* and *On the Liberty of a Christian Man*. While the last named was primarily a theological treatise in which the reformer developed his views on the primacy of faith over good works, the two others were indictments against Rome, who held the Church in bondage, and a kind of agenda for a future council. This, according to Luther, would proclaim the universal ministry of all Christians, the individual's right to interpret the Scriptures in the way in which the Spirit guided him (free inquiry), and the abolition of disciplinary rules made by the Church in the past, e.g. clerical celibacy, and of such pious practices as pilgrimage. Finally (a clever touch), this projected council would pronounce the civil authority's right to prohibit all financial collections by Rome and to control the episcopate. Even the Sacraments did not escape his criticism; claiming to base his views on the Gospel, Luther now acknowledged only three of them to be valid.

The year 1520, however, was decisive in yet another respect. After his triumph in Leipzig Johann Eck had left for Rome,[1] determined to have his opponent condemned. Miltitz, who was considered too much of a nuisance, was disowned. A commission presided over by Cajetan examined forty-one propositions taken from Luther's works, and pronounced them heretical. A bull was submitted for the Pope's signature (15th June 1520), beginning with the words *Exsurge Domine*, 'Arise, O Lord, defend Thy cause!' (Psalm lxxiv. 22). The heresiarch's writings were to be destroyed, he was forbidden to preach and teach his theology, and he was given two months in which to retract his views under pain of excommunication.

The news of his condemnation found Luther beset by violent but conflicting emotions. He undoubtedly felt deep sorrow: 'I am in grievous pain,' he wrote, 'like a child abandoned by its mother.' But at the same time he struck back, and it was anger that dictated his invectives. 'Now I know that the Pope is Antichrist,' he declared; and this was among the more moderate of the insults that sprang to his lips. No doubt he was regretting the letter which he had just written the Pope on the advice of Miltitz. It was a dignified letter and respectful in tone, reminiscent of St Bernard's *De Consideratione*; and although it contained some violent attacks on Rome and the Curia, its author had none the less assured the pontiff that 'my heart has not turned against Your Holiness.' Shortly afterwards Luther produced his violent

---

[1] Meanwhile, in order to reply to him after the event, Luther was brooding over his treatise on *The Papacy*.

pamphlet *Against the Bull of Antichrist*, an outright declaration of war. Elsewhere, throughout Germany, the papal legates Caracciolo and Aleandro, who were accompanied by Johann Eck, were running into fierce opposition. There were disorders at Leipzig, Erfurt and Magdeburg; at Vienna the rector of the university had to be forced to receive the Pope's envoys by express command of the emperor. Finally, on 10th December, having learned that Aleandro was coming to Cologne to burn his books, Luther assembled his friends near one of the gates of Wittenberg and consigned to the flames a copy of the bull, together with a volume of the Canon Law. 'Since you have corrupted the divine truth, may the fire consume you!' he cried. In his lecture on the following day he declared that this act was purely symbolic: in reality it was the Pope himself who should have been burned.

The rupture was complete. On 3rd January 1521 a new bull, *Decet Romanum pontificem*, declared Luther excommunicated, and threatened with interdict any city which afforded him asylum. The first act in the tragedy was drawing to its close. What did the future hold? 'I see that many people consider that severity is the main remedy for this evil,' wrote Erasmus, 'but I fear that the outcome of events will one day show that it was ill advised. I fear that this affair will end in atrocious carnage.' Luther was carried away by the fatality inherent in all heresies, and was also impelled by political forces whose motives partially escaped him. He had brought down the thunder upon his head by the violence of his language as much as by his doctrinal declarations; but the Church was not entirely free from blame. 'Luther's initial outbursts were casually treated by Leo X. Then followed sudden and unexpected severity, where one would like to think that the haste to condemn was nothing but the fruit of an ardent love for the Catholic faith.'[1] The Papacy's choice of men to attempt a settlement was questionable to say the least. Cajetan, though full of good intentions, was hardly one to understand the psychological complexity of the German monk; Prieras was rigid and insulting; Miltitz was much too superficial. Above all, there was in many ecclesiastical quarters a deplorable ignorance of the most elementary Christian needs. Luther's genuine piety was not enough to make him a Catholic, for it did not guarantee his orthodoxy; but his adversaries' correct grasp of the faith was too often linked with total indifference to the demands of the spiritual life. The 'atrocious carnage' foreseen by Erasmus did indeed come to pass; and all the children of Christ were to suffer thereby, as though Providence had determined to exact terrible expiation from one and all.

[1] Fr. Vicaire, *Histoire illustrée de l'Église*, ii. 26.

Worms, the Wartburg and the Bible

It was now the emperor's turn to speak. He had just been crowned (23rd October 1520) at Aix-la-Chapelle, and it remained to be seen whether he would place his sword at the disposition of the Church. Aleandro hoped to persuade the young man to do so; at Rome the imperial edict putting the bull into effect had actually been prepared. There is no doubt that Charles V was profoundly Catholic in his personal convictions; as King of Spain he could hardly fail to defend the faith. He had the papal orders carried out in the Low Countries, at Louvain and Liège, and then at Mainz and Cologne on the Rhine. But everything was not so simple and straightforward as might have appeared from the legate's letter to Rome. Charles had received irritating news from Spain: there had been outbreaks of rebellion, and these had been fostered by the clergy whom the Vatican refused to call to order. As he made his progress into the Empire he realized that the situation was dangerously tense and that rigorous measures might cause a violent explosion. This was no time to make enemies of half the German nobility. Conflict appeared inevitable with Francis I, who was even then trying to win the alliance of England on the Field of the Cloth of Gold; [1] and Charles suspected Rome of seeking to make common cause with the French in Italy. He therefore decided to do nothing precipitate, and to leave the task of settling the Lutheran affair to a Diet which was about to open at Worms.

The delegates thus considered the question of Luther as one topic among many, and that by no means the most important, for the administrative reorganization of the Empire aroused much more heat. For three hours they listened to the Papal Legate Aleandro demanding that the bull be enforced and the heretic placed under the imperial ban. Charles was about to strike when the Elector of Saxony objected. The nuncios protested vehemently against further debate on a decision reached by Rome; but the emperor agreed to have the monk appear before the Diet and explain his position, and his own herald-at-arms carried a safe conduct to his 'honoured, well-beloved and devoted Martin Luther.'

Though fully aware of the danger Luther agreed to come to Worms. The memory of John Huss was in everyone's mind; he too had been given a safe conduct. 'I will not flee,' he declared; 'I will not abandon the Word. I am sure that these bloodthirsty men will not scruple to

---

[1] Another coincidence of date should be noted here: Ignatius of Loyola, who had been wounded before Pampeluna, decided in his solitude at Manresa to devote his whole life to God.

take my life, but I want the Papists alone to be blamed for my death.' He was uplifted by a fever of joy, an almost morbid exaltation, and this was brought to its highest pitch by the triumphal demonstrations which marked his journey from Wittenberg to Worms. He was cheered wherever he went. At Erfurt the crowd promptly looted the houses of the canons after hearing him preach, and as he approached the city of Worms he found that an enormous procession had come out to welcome and congratulate him.

Luther was thrice interrogated by Johann von Ecke,[1] judge of the ecclesiastical court of Trier, and thus had a threefold opportunity to clear himself. On the first occasion, perhaps because he was abashed by the presence of the emperor and so many important dignitaries, he was unimpressive, almost hesitant. 'This monkling won't make a heretic out of me!' laughed Charles V. Next day, however, Luther recovered his self-possession. He declared that his doctrine was in conformity with the Scriptures, reiterated his attacks upon papal authority and boldly demanded that, instead of condemning him without discussion of his theses, his accusers should demonstrate in what respects they were pernicious. 'There is to be no discussion,' interjected the examiner. 'Will you or will you not retract?' And Luther replied: 'In so much as you have failed to convince me by scriptural proofs of one shred of evidence—for I believe in neither pope nor councils, which have so often been mistaken—I am bound by my own texts. My conscience is a prisoner of the Divine Word. Whatever "retract" may mean, I cannot and will not do so. May God help me!' Ecke made one final attempt to convince him before a much smaller gathering: 'Your conscience, Brother Martin? Do not trouble about that! The only certain answer is to make your submission to the established authority.' [2] Judgment was given. The emperor ordered Luther to leave Worms as quickly as possible; his safe conduct would cover him for a further twenty-four hours.

Luther was now officially under the ban of the Empire, but who would execute the sentence? The duty belonged to Frederick the Wise as Luther's temporal superior, but he was not much inclined to act. It was necessary to have recourse to stratagem. On 4th May, while Luther was making his way back to Wittenberg along the Gotha road, in company with Amsdorf, his colleague in the university, and another Augustinian monk, a party of horsemen suddenly appeared, seized their carriage and dragged it into the nearby forest. The Thuringian nobility, with the Elector of Saxony's consent, had just saved the

---

[1] He must not be confused with Johann Eck.

[2] This sentence is frequently quoted by those who claim to see Luther as a champion of 'liberty of conscience.' He was a man who hungered and thirsted for bondage in God all his life. . . .

reformer's life. During the night his kidnappers led him by devious ways to the fortress of *the Wartburg*, a regular eyrie above Eisenach. There Luther was to remain for ten months, calling himself 'Sir George' and living like a Junker with a sword in his belt and a gold chain round his neck; he let his beard and hair grow long in order to avoid recognition.

All Germany believed him dead. Ferment was increasing; Luther's writings and those of his ally, Ulrich von Hutten, were being circulated everywhere. 'Is he still alive? Have they murdered him? I do not know. But if he has been killed he has suffered in the cause of Christian truth'—so wrote Dürer, the great painter, in his diary. No, Luther was not dead, but those who valued his life forced him to maintain absolute secrecy. His adversary, Leo X, had just died; but from the difficult conclave which followed there emerged a more rigorous Pope in the person of Charles V's former tutor, the Dutchman Adrian of Utrecht —*Adrian VI*. The new Pope was a harsh man, and he was also a warm supporter of the imperial policy.

Strict confinement saved the heresiarch's life, but it weighed very heavily upon him. Those ten months caused Luther measureless anguish. His health was bad and he was tortured by intestinal pains; but his moral sufferings were even worse. Now that he had been cast out from the Church, he was haunted by doubts and feelings of remorse. 'My heart trembled,' he confessed. 'I said to myself: Are you alone right? Are all the rest wrong? Suppose you are the one who is in error? Suppose you are dragging all these souls into error and damnation along with you?' And then, in a sudden rush of spirit, he rebelled against himself; he reproached himself for not having dared enough and said enough. 'At Worms I let the spirit grow weak within me, instead of rising up as a new Eli against the idols. Ah, if only I could appear before them again! They would hear some very different things.' This conflict of conscience reached the stage of pathological crisis; hallucinations filled his solitude; in the silence of the vast rooms and the black darkness of night the old temptations and spiritual doubts returned, together with 'the hot desires of the untamed flesh.' He afterwards said that he had been obliged to use his feet and fists in order to defend himself against the furious assaults of the enemy; legend states that he actually threw his ink-pot in the devil's face.

However, in the midst of this crisis he found enough moral strength to continue his work. A treatise on *Auricular Confession* and another on the *Abrogation of Private Mass* were both written at the Wartburg. Above all, it was here that Luther began his *German Translation of the Bible*. Within three months he had successfully completed the New Testament, relying upon some of his humanist friends, Melanchthon,

Mutian and Spalatinus,[1] for help with a few difficult passages. Then he started work on the Old. This was a far longer task, and, despite the collaboration of such Hebrew scholars as Aurogallus, was not finished until 1534. Luther considered this work of translation as absolutely fundamental. God Himself spoke through the Bible, yet the sacred volume 'which ought to have been found in the hands of all pious men, day and night, was lying hidden under the benches, between the seats and the dust, fallen into universal oblivion.' This was not true. Between the invention of the printing-press and 1520, one hundred and fifty-six Latin editions of the Bible had been published, together with seventeen German translations, not to mention manuscript copies which have been estimated at more than a hundred. What is true, however, is that the literary merit of Luther's style, which possessed a vigour and clarity that have made it one of the models of the German language, caused the Scriptures to be widely read all over the country. 'In my translation I have done my utmost to speak in pure, clear German,' he said. 'My teachers were the housewife in her home, the children at their games, the merchants in the city squares; I tried to learn from them how to express and explain myself.' Generally speaking, his translation is a faithful one, although in several instances the text is distorted in a sense which is not difficult to guess. 'Just' is replaced by 'pious' and 'church' by 'community.' The word 'alone' is added to the end of the sentence in the Epistle to the Romans: 'We proclaim that a man is justified by faith' (iii. 28). There are even a few questionable glosses. For example, in connection with Mary Magdalene's action in pouring ointment over the feet of Christ, Luther asserts that this proves 'that faith alone makes a work good.' At all events the success of his enterprise was considerable: the first edition of the New Testament, which was illustrated by Cranach and comprised three thousand copies, was sold out in three months. More than three hundred editions were published during Luther's lifetime.[2] Thanks to him 'Hochdeutsch'—High German—became prevalent throughout Germany, and his book played a decisive role in a great many fields.

[1] A number of authors have insisted that his followers and collaborators also included some rabbis: but the question remains in doubt. In any case it does not give Bernard Lazare, in his book L'Antisemitisme, authority to write: 'The Jewish spirit triumphed with Protestantism. A large proportion of the Protestant sects were half Jewish.'

[2] It was during his residence in the Wartburg, too, that Luther wrote the work which, of all his many writings, is the one most capable of touching Catholic hearts—his Translations and Commentary on the Magnificat. This treatise on the Blessed Virgin reveals a deep piety. The intercession of the Mother of Christ is besought twice, at the beginning and the end. Mary's virtues are considered with fervour and accuracy, notably her humility and total submission to the will of God. However, Luther warns his readers against the excesses of certain people who turn to her rather than to God Himself: 'She gives nothing. God is the only giver.'

L

OPPORTUNITIES AND DANGERS OF REVOLUTION

Luther brought this painful but fruitful period of solitude to an abrupt end. On 1st March 1522 he left his refuge, having notified the Elector of Saxony in a long and somewhat haughty letter. He declared that he intended to place himself no longer under the protection of an earthly prince, but was determined to put his trust in a very much more powerful Master. Enough of this cowardice, and this too convenient asylum! 'Christ has certainly not taught me to be a Christian at another's risk.'

This was the underlying motive which drove Luther on to the roads of Germany at this bitter winter's end. He was still dressed as a knight. Two Swiss girls saw him one evening at the Black Bear Inn at Jena, in his purplish doublet and cerise-coloured hat, with his sword in his belt, hastening towards Wittenberg. In actual fact the risks he was running were not particularly great. Looked at objectively, they amounted to very little. Certainly they were nothing compared with those braved by young Calvin twelve years later. The situation was really quite favourable to him, and would remain so for some years. Circumstances kept the emperor far from Germany, to which he did not return until 1530. War with Francis I had just broken out and there was prolonged fighting in France and Italy. Even Pavia (1525) and his captivity in Madrid did not prevent the fiery Valois from continuing the struggle, forcing the Hapsburg to divert his attention from German affairs. Besides the French danger there was the threat from Turkey. For the past two years *Solyman the Magnificent* (1520–66) had controlled the Ottoman destinies. Leaving his palace with its sumptuous vestibules, guarded by eighteen panthers and a dozen lions, he had launched his peoples once again into the holy war, and in 1521 had captured Belgrade by direct assault. As for the Church, she was virtually power-less. Pope Adrian VI, who was said to be determined to join battle and, by carrying out reform from above, to cut the ground from under the Lutherans' feet, was in failing health. He died a year later, in September 1523, leaving the Apostolic See to the irresolute Medici, *Clement VII*, who was more concerned with Italian and dynastic affairs than with the heresy from Wittenberg.

These were Luther's negative opportunities; the positive were no less certain. That trend of thought which had been set in motion two years earlier, and which in short had enabled Luther to snap his fingers at the authorities with impunity, had become more and more powerful. The humanists supported him, some of them—e.g. Mel-anchthon and Justus Jonas—with sincere fervour. Others, such as Johann Faber, the future Bishop of Vienna, were not fully aware that their alliance rested on a misunderstanding and that deep down Luther had nothing in common with them. Even Erasmus was still his fellow traveller, somewhat anxious at heart but resolved to march in step with him as far as possible. Luther himself was quite happy to take advantage of the misconception. Perhaps this was deliberate, or possibly he had not yet fully realized its existence.

The situation with regard to the petty nobility was much clearer: they regarded Luther as their man, and Hutten, their spokesman, borrowed many of the monk's ideas to mingle with his own in a series of violent pamphlets. German nationalism recognized itself in that typical son of his country, in that strange mixture of rugged coarseness and mystical sentimentality, in that ardent longing and intimate religion, and above all in that furious hatred of Rome which Luther henceforth exhaled. Luther himself was too much a child of German soil not to be moved when he received appeals such as those addressed to him by Crotus Rubianus: 'Martin, I am accustomed to call you Father of the Fatherland. You deserve to have a statue of gold raised in your honour, for you are the first to have stood forth boldly as the avenger of a people steeped in criminal errors.' The reply was to come from his heart: 'I was born for my Germans, it is they whom I wish to serve.' But this alliance was going to prove embarrassing. The squireens and the nationalists were not dreaming of internal reform, but of the erection of a German Church, freed of Roman tutelage. Their assistance was valuable, but it had dangerous implications for the future.

Thus Luther's ideas had gained the support of both intellectuals and politicians; but they benefited also from influences of a more obscure kind. They spread far and wide, sown in countless different ways in a soil which was fully prepared to receive them. Here a pedlar in casual conversation would discover someone's religious anxiety, and would leave a Lutheran pamphlet on the table. There an orator, perhaps a mendicant friar, might preach without contradiction the doctrine of justification by faith and the sole authority of the Bible. Elsewhere, in some school, a teacher would read one of the writings from Witten-berg, and would teach his pupils that every Christian was his own priest. Bookshops did an under-the-counter trade in proscribed books; the printing-press poured out the heretic's ironies and popularized his arguments. Reaction on the part of the ecclesiastical authorities, who were not always well informed, was often feeble; the distinction between what was legal and what had been condemned was often not at all clear. Besides, the preachers of this 'free' Christianity were animated by such tremendous enthusiasm! The men of the sixteenth century were fired with an ardent longing for change, and the old Church no longer seemed capable of satisfying their dreams and aspirations. 'Luther has become the most celebrated man in Germany,' wrote a Nuremberg notary in 1518. His friends sang his praises, adored him, fought for him and were ready to endure anything for him. His most trivial writings were covered with kisses, he was described as the Herald of Truth, the Clarion of the Gospel; St Paul, as they believed, spoke by the mouth of Martin Luther. Myconius, one of the first Lutherans, went so far as to declare that the theses emanating from Wittenberg had spread through the whole of Christendom in the space of four weeks.

Not throughout Christendom perhaps; but they had very rapidly become known all over Germany and its immediate surroundings. There were Lutherans at places as far apart as Hamburg and Stras- bourg, Bremen and Breslau, and even in distant Antwerp and Riga. All classes were affected, from the highest ranks of the aristocracy to the humblest strata of society. Most captivated by the new ideas was the clerical proletariat, disgusted with its lot. Augustinians and Bene- dictines threw off the habit, as did the Dominican Bucer, the Fran- ciscans Eberlin and Pellican, as well as many secular priests among whom were Capito, Osiander, Justus Jonas and Amsdorf. Large num- bers of them married, following the example provided by Bernhardi, who had been one of Luther's favourite pupils at the time of the famous theses in 1517, and had become parish priest at Kempen. He was soon followed by the former Archdeacon Karlstadt, who wished thereby 'to free so many unfortunate priests from the devil's bondage.' When he learned of these clerical marriages the reformer was distinctly embarrassed; [1] but they were the natural consequence of the attitude he had adopted towards monastic vows, and he ended by justifying them.

These matrimonial incidents, however, were not the most serious. While Luther was meditating in the Wartburg and translating his Bible, others occurred to show him that when pure speculation finds a hearing it runs up against the demands and difficulties of practical action. The immediate reason for his sudden descent from his refuge was the outbreak of trouble at various points of Germany, occasioned by his doctrine. Stirred up by the agitation of unfrocked priests and by nuns who had violated their enclosure, the mob seemed on the verge of starting a revolution against the entire clergy. At Erfurt marauding bands had attacked and pillaged ecclesiastical dwellings. At Wittenberg itself the impetus was given by Karlstadt: at Christmas 1521 he had celebrated in the Schlosskirche a strange form of the Mass, using the German language, dispensing with liturgical vestments,

---

[1] He had written jokingly to Spalatinus on the subject of Karlstadt's marriage: 'By God, we Wittenbergers even provide wives for monks—but never for me!' He would change his mind four years later.

omitting a number of essential ceremonies, and finally distributing Holy Communion in both kinds to anyone who wished, even if they had neither confessed nor fasted. He became the idol of the mob, and organized expeditions against churches, in which crosses were pulled down and the statues of the saints mutilated. Luther was faced with a serious problem: should he agree to this violence? Would these riots help or betray the spiritual revolution which he sought to carry through? As invariably happens in the case of those who initiate a revolution, he found himself swept aside by extremists and fanatics. This was the real danger he hoped to parry when he came down from the Wartburg.

The seed he had sown was germinating well, but here and there it was doing so in an extraordinary fashion. In Switzerland a new prophet was about to arise, more explicit than Luther, and preaching a doctrine that the German reformer was unable to accept. His name was *Zwingli*. Since May 1520 one *Thomas Münzer*, a misguided Franciscan, heir to the Fraticelli and the Hussites, had proclaimed 'the kingdom of God,' with himself as ruler, in the little Saxon town of Zwickau. Assisted, like Jesus, by twelve apostles and seventy-two disciples, he had preached dozens of open-air sermons, generously larded with anathemas and prophecies, in which he announced the destruction of the Roman Church, the right of every believer to speak in the name of the Spirit, universal brotherhood, the common ownership of wealth and property and the expropriation of the rich. These zealots declared the baptism of infants null and void, and demanded a second adult baptism. Consequently they were known as *Anabaptists*, though they called themselves the *Regenerate* or the *Saints*. The sect had made fairly rapid progress, swarming over Switzerland, eastern Italy and Saxony. Expelled from Zwickau by the city magistrate, Münzer and two of his followers fled for refuge to Wittenberg. Their message made some impression on a number of Luther's supporters, including Amsdorf, Melanchthon and Karlstadt; and it was under their influence that the last-named encouraged destructive expeditions against the churches, under pretext that the Bible commanded it: 'Thou shalt not make to thyself any graven thing.' Luther could hardly consent to recognize himself in this distorted mirror, or allow people to believe for a single moment that he approved of all this fanaticism and excess.

The Anabaptist affair was quickly settled, at least provisionally: Luther's ascendancy was so great that in eight days of restrained but decisive preaching he demolished the doctrines of the sect. Subjugated by his personality, the crowds submitted to his word, not only at Wittenberg, but also at Erfurt, Weimar and even Zwickau, although they reverted to many of Münzer's errors once Luther was gone. The majority of the former rites of the Mass were re-established—the elevation of the Host, the use of liturgical vestments, the placing of the consecrated morsel on the lips and not in the hand. The prophet of universal brotherhood was obliged to flee to Swabia, thence to Thuringia, and finally to Alsace. Karlstadt settled as a minister at Orlemund, still preaching his terrible social asceticism, walking with head uncovered, refusing the style of 'Herr Doktor' and modestly referring to himself as 'neighbour Andrew.' Anabaptism was conquered but not destroyed, and it would resume its progress.

The affair of the Anabaptists had been an awful warning to Luther. He received another shortly afterwards; a second dangerous plant seemed to be germinating from his seed. His friends the petty nobility interpreted denunciation of simoniacal prelates in their own particular way, and an army commanded by Franz von Sickingen and Ulrich von Hutten invaded the territory of the Archbishop of Trier and laid siege to the city. The great feudatories saw the danger, and the Elector Palatine with the Landgrave of Hesse hurried to the archbishop's aid. Sickingen was surrounded in his own castle and captured. Hutten sought refuge with Erasmus at Basle; but Erasmus was not at all pleased and hurriedly betook himself to a little island in Lake Zürich, where he died. By order of the princes more than twenty strongholds of the brigand lords were razed to the ground. Luther had been extremely careful not to become involved in this adventure, and had even formally expressed his disapproval. He had lost some allies on its account, but his prestige had suffered no other injury thereby.

At the two Nuremberg Diets (1522 and 1524) he could see how enormous his authority had become. It was all very well for the papal envoys to demand enforcement of the decisions taken at Worms; the majority of the assembly refused. Charles V wrote a letter full of reproaches, but all in vain. Only the Archduke Ferdinand of Austria, the Duke of Bavaria, the Archbishop of Salzburg and the Bishop of Trent signed an agreement at Ratisbon to maintain their loyalty to the Pope. On 2nd October 1524 Luther performed his final act of rupture by discarding the Augustinian habit which he had donned so piously nineteen years earlier.

THE PEASANTS' WAR AND THE ALLIANCE WITH THE PRINCES

Some months later an appalling occurrence reminded him more sternly of his responsibilities. The German peasants, the poverty-stricken class with 'neither bread nor salt nor fat,' whose lot was so pitiable, broke out in open revolt. This in itself was nothing new. Popular uprisings had been commonplace for the past two hundred years; that of Hans Böheim in 1476 had been followed by Hans

Ullman's in Alsace (1493) and the Styrian revolt in 1515, while another (1517), led by Joss Fritz, had affected the whole Rhine valley. But the rising of 1524 was to be a more serious affair, on account of its extent as well as because of the ideological ideas involved. The poor folk who took up arms to obtain more social justice were of course imperfectly acquainted with Luther's theses; but they had heard tell that he proclaimed liberty, that he denounced the exactions of the wealthy and that he wished to see the gospel principles put into practice. This was reason enough for them to acknowledge his authority. Moreover the whole of this affair was indescribably confused. The remnants of Sickingen's army, and even a duke of Württemberg who had been deposed from his throne, found the opportunity to intervene, not to mention the Anabaptists, to whom it afforded a splendid opportunity. Under the banner of the 'Bundschuh'—the hobnailed boot—all kinds of passions, most of them legitimate, were allied together. But when they were unleashed they made the whole land tremble.

The rebellion began at Stühlingen, near Schaffhausen, where the peasants rose against the countess, who claimed the right to make them gather mushrooms during sowing time and snails in the harvest season. It spread to Swabia, where one preacher urged his congregation to refuse payment of tithes and taxes. Next it was the turn of those living on the shores of Lake Constance, who rallied to the cry: 'Let's go to work bravely with the sword!' Their leaders even drafted the *Twelve Articles*, a programme of combined political, social and religious reform. The conflagration quickly gained a hold in several places elsewhere—the Tyrol, Franconia, Hesse and Saxony. Acts of violence began, and religious houses were pillaged; in Alsace the library at Marmoutier went up in flames. Götz von Berlichingen, the Knight with the Iron Hand, put himself at the head of some rebel bands, and all the nobles and priests at Weinsberg were murdered on Easter Day. This 'Peasants' War' was turning into a real revolution, in which the violent spirit of the Taborites lived again. Münzer, the Anabaptist pope, joyfully entered the lists: 'Forward, forward, without mercy,' he cried. 'Let your swords be constantly tempered in warm blood.'

The authorities reacted promptly, and all the more terribly on account of their fear. The rebellion ended in appalling catastrophe for the peasants. All the forces which represented the threatened order united against them. Münzer was defeated at Frankenhausen, and was captured and beheaded. Berlichingen too was beaten. The Duke of Lorraine crushed the last remnants at Saverne in May. When twenty thousand unfortunate wretches surrendered he ordered them to be butchered.

Luther's attitude to this horror has been strongly criticized, for in his condemnation of the unfortunate rebels he used some expressions of extreme severity, and exhorted the princes to the massacre: 'Go to, beloved lords, save us! Exterminate, slaughter, let anyone act who can! We are living in such extraordinary times that a prince can become worthy of Heaven much more easily by spilling blood than the rest can by praying!' Moreover Münzer was nothing but a 'mad dog,' and the folk of the Bundschuh 'fiends of the devil.' Here is the fury of a man exasperated by the taunts of those who reproached him as ultimately responsible for this folly. Above all, it is the wrath of a doctrinaire who saw his theories in process of distortion. In reply to the peasants' *Twelve Articles* Luther composed his *Exhortation to Peace*, which defined his doctrinal position. He roundly condemned the rebels' claim to be fighting in the name of the Gospel, and their use of force to obtain justice. The liberty which he preached was an inner liberty, whose other name was servitude in God. 'Authority has been instituted by God. He alone can destroy it.' But such theology was too elevated for bands of half-crazed wretches who were stupefied to find themselves without the backing of Holy Scripture. Believing themselves betrayed by Luther, many relapsed into a sorrowful indifference, which goes some way towards explaining the ease with which the principle *cuius regio, huius religio* was enforced. The princes decided their people's faith. Luther was to suffer from this terrible tragedy all his life. 'The devil has assailed me countless times, almost suffocating me to death,' he said, 'telling me that the peasants' revolt was the result of my preaching!' He never forgot the bitter words of Erasmus: 'You would not recognize the rioters, but they recognized you.'

The Peasants' War had important consequences regarding the future of the whole Lutheran movement. Whether he desired it or not, the reformer found himself bound in alliance with the princes. Not that he shirked his duty of criticizing the excesses of the repression, condemning those 'savage and insensate tyrants who cannot assuage their thirst for blood, even when the battle is over and done with.' But he realized that he was obliged to side with them. 'My own feelings are clear,' he wrote to Amsdorf. 'It is better to have all the peasants dead than any of the princes.' 'Revolution is worse than murder!' he had cried: Goethe's famous comment that he preferred 'injustice to disorder' was in the best traditions of Lutheranism. In these circumstances, however, the religious movement became political and nationalist, and the heads of State placed their strength at the service of principles which in effect served their own interests.

These interests were wholly temporal; for by adhering to Lutheranism the great lords received doctrinal authority to confiscate the possessions of the Church, at which they had looked with such greedy eyes. The impetus was given by *Albert of Brandenburg, Grand Master of the Teutonic Knights*. Having consulted Luther about his conscientious scruples, he received advice to break his vows and secularize the estates of his Order to his own advantage. Albert found little or no difficulty in following such judicious counsels; in 1526 he married, thus founding simultaneously the dynasty of the Hohenzollerns and the duchy of Prussia. The bishops of Pomerania and Samland took their cue from him. In the same year *Philip of Hesse* went over to Protestantism, bringing to the service of his new cause a will of steel, together with considerable political talents totally devoid of scruples. Once launched upon this road, the movement rapidly gathered force. Church lands were confiscated all over Germany, bishops secularized their dioceses and the Duke and Elector of Saxony quickly followed these examples. The importance of this phenomenon should not be underestimated, but it had precious little connection with Luther's earliest intentions! [1]

A second result of the tragedy of 1525 was to turn Luther conclusively towards a 'German conception' of his mission. He had now exchanged his earlier relationship with Hutten, Sickingen and the nationalist squires for an alliance with the princes. Besides, in order to combat Anabaptist sectarianism, he had to make himself understood by *Herr Omnes*, by the ordinary mass of his countrymen. Both these factors led him to think in German, talk in German and act as a German. Hitherto he had written three-quarters of his work in Latin, the universal language of scholarship, but henceforward all his books were published in German. Here is proof that he was no longer addressing the whole of Christendom: 'After 1530 it is no surprise to see Lutheranism marking time in Europe, and even drawing back.' [2] In short, the tragedy of the Peasants' War paved the way for the success of Calvin's universalism.

Finally, and most important of all, this episode led Luther to modify fundamentally his own conception of the Church. Until then, faithful to his own scholastic theories,[3] he had defined it as a spiritual reality—

[1] H. Strohl, the Protestant historian, makes the following optimistic comment on this process: 'Though it is true that the rulers augmented their power by secularizing the wealth of the Church, this was not their prime motive, as has so often been held against them. For they generally used this wealth, not to increase their own prestige, but in conformity with its original purpose—to benefit the common good, by ensuring the existence of a Protestant clergy and the provision of charitable and educational establishments.'

[2] Lucien Febvre. The date 1530 is a little premature; the situation described was more strictly true five or six years later.

[3] Insufficiently based on theology. This is one of the points where Luther's theological grounding seems particularly fragile, and it is also the aspect which underwent the most change in Protestantism's later 'variations.'

* L

the Christian spiritual reality. The Church was essentially invisible, being formed by faith within the individual, and a man became a member of the Church when the Word deposited the Christian revelation in his soul. The members of this invisible Church would be visibly recognizable in the world by two signs: Baptism and the Gospel. These signs, however, were not in themselves sufficient to determine true spiritual reality; for among the baptized and those who claimed kinship with the Gospel there were some who possessed no faith at all. It was abundantly clear that such as these did not belong to the Mystical Body of Christ, a concept which led Luther to reject any kind of established, institutionalized and hierarchized Church, without understanding the authentically spiritual meaning which the visible organism of the Church possesses as the means of grace and guardian of the sacred repository. His doctrine was nothing less than anarchism, allegedly founded on the example of the first Christian communities. He even went so far as to write: 'It would be contrary to the whole essence and nature of the Church to possess any leaders.'

The tragedy of 1525 made him change his positions. In his heart he never abandoned his early notion of the Church as a mobile entity, like the tabernacle in the days of Israel's wandering; but he was forced to accept another kind of Church, fixed, established, organized and subject to a hierarchy. 'If we governed according to the Gospel, would we not be setting wild beasts at liberty and giving them a free hand to wound and kill?' Thus recourse to the State was obligatory. In order that excesses may be prevented and the people educated, 'it is necessary to impose external piety by means of justice and the sword.' Any restlessness on the part of *Herr Omnes* demands recourse 'to the rod and Master Hans'—the public executioner. The duty of those whom Providence had placed upon the thrones was quite clear: 'The prince should not tolerate division or disorder; he must impose the practice of one doctrine alone.' In the rulers Luther recognized the agents of divine will and the guarantors of Truth.

The first prince to understand this lesson was the Elector John, brother and successor of Frederick the Wise. From October 1525 John took steps to impose Lutheranism on all his territories, and in 1527 the Church of Saxony was organized along the lines laid down in the *Pastoral Institution*, which had a preface written by Luther. This example was quickly followed by all states whose rulers had adopted the Lutheran faith. The authority of secular sovereigns replaced that of the Pope, and at the same time the Church of princes, the State Church, superseded the invisible Church of saints. 'The Reformation ended in a contradiction,' comments Harnack.[1]

---

[1] *Dogmengeschichte*, 1897, III, 788.

The 'Protestants'

It was in this anarchical situation, which was nevertheless highly advantageous to the princes, that the Diet of Spires (1526) held its meetings. When Charles V convened it he seemed at the height of his power: Francis I was his prisoner, and had been compelled to sign the disastrous treaty which gave the emperor Burgundy, suzerainty over Flanders and Artois, and all the French rights in Italy. The question was whether Charles would use his authority on behalf of the ancient faith. On 22nd May, the very day upon which the Diet opened, a piece of news spread rapidly through Germany. On regaining his freedom the King of France had denounced the treaty and immediately set up the 'Holy League of Cognac,' which had been joined by all states (including the Papacy) which were apprehensive about the extent of Hapsburg power. England was lending Francis her moral support, and the Turks were negotiating with him.

Luther's supporters at once took new heart. Ferdinand of Austria, who presided over the Diet, was not anxious to secure enforcement of the instructions which had been sent by his brother from Madrid and which required that the decisions of Worms be carried out. His enthusiasm was still further reduced by the consideration that he would have to appeal to the princes and the cities for help against the Turks, whose offensive was now reaching its climax. He therefore agreed that until such time as a council should meet each ruler should settle the religious affairs in his own territories 'in such a fashion as he believes will enable him to answer satisfactorily before God and His Imperial Majesty.'

Lutheranism had practically a clear field, and events assisted its expansion. The Diet had scarcely closed its doors when news arrived of the appalling disaster of Mohacs (19th August 1526), in which Hungary had collapsed beneath the blows of Solyman, at the same time losing her king, Louis II, the last of the Jagellons. Summoned to succeed his brother-in-law as King of Bohemia and Hungary, Ferdinand was more interested in securing his thrones than in crushing heresy. Finally, in May 1527, the whole of Christian Europe stood aghast at a most horrible and sacrilegious spectacle: the grandson of the Catholic Sovereigns was so incensed against Clement VII that he allowed his troopers to sack Rome, the holy city of the Christian faith.[1] The Pope himself was held captive. The Lutherans, led by Philip of Hesse, took advantage of these circumstances to impose their doctrines and establish institutions based upon them. They had just formed a defensive league against their opponents at Torgau, when the situation was once more reversed.

[1] On the sack of Rome see *The Catholic Reformation*, Chapter II, section 1.

The emperor, who, but a short time before had been threatened by Lautrec's brilliant campaigns in Italy and by the Turkish assault, succeeded in extricating himself from his difficulties. He was reconciled to the King of France by the Treaty of Cambrai, and he made the Treaty of Barcelona with the Pope, who resigned himself, not without some anxiety, to placing the crown of the Holy Roman Empire upon Charles's head. Consequently the second Diet of Spires (1529) might well have been dangerous for Luther's followers had Charles been really determined to re-establish religious unity in Germany. In fact he hesitated. Several of his advisers, notably Cardinal Osma, his confessor, were of the opinion that matters should not be rushed. It was necessary 'to listen to the thoughts and opinions of each man with charity.' Since a council was becoming increasingly certain, it seemed more convenient to wait for its decisions before taking any action. Therefore the emperor confined himself to deciding that the Edict of Worms should be enforced in all the Catholic states, so that Lutheranism might not be allowed to penetrate those areas which still remained uncontaminated. Wherever it existed it would be tolerated subject only to the reservation that there should be no further preaching against the Eucharist, that Catholics should be allowed to celebrate Mass in their own way and that they should not be disturbed. Now this was a decision which maintained the *status quo*, and it should have been perfectly acceptable. But the extent of the authority already acquired by the supporters of the new doctrine is shown by the fact that this compromise was rejected. The Lutherans declined to tolerate in their midst the papist Mass, which they declared idolatrous, nor were they prepared to confine their preachers to a straightforward exposition of their theology. Supported by fourteen cities, Philip of Hesse and various other influential nobles sent the emperor a vehement protest, and it was thus that the supporters of the Reformation became described as *Protestants*.[1]

MARRIAGE AND MATURITY

Luther had now reached that point of his career which Dante calls 'the half-way stage in life.' He had attained full maturity. The febrile monk of earlier days no longer existed. In his place stood the man depicted in Cranach's paintings at Brunswick and Florence—a heavily built individual, with the body of a fighter and the high colour of a beer-drinker, with soft hands, and grizzled curls straggling from beneath a black cap—a cross, one might think, between a canon and a notary. Nothing remains of the sharp features of the young prophet

[1] The word has a negative character which has often been deplored by adherents of the 'Reformed' faiths, but its use has nevertheless become customary.

save the deeply lined temples and, despite the roundness of the double chin, the strong, almost savage jaw. But the expression is still strangely sad and distant, as if the bitter wisdom of the adult has joined with the anguish of forgotten youth.

Marriage had contributed to this consolidation and weightiness; for Luther had married a few months earlier, in April 1525. Five months earlier still he had been telling his friend Spalatinus that 'his heart was little inclined to the conjugal union'; but in the former (now secularized) Augustinian monastery where he lived, he had offered hospitality to a group of nuns who had deserted their convents, and this cohabitation had caused him to alter his views. He had taken to wife an ex-Cistercian, *Catherine von Bora*, a daughter of the lesser nobility. Why? Certainly not as the result of passion. 'I am neither enamoured nor impassioned,' he confessed. Perhaps he hoped to find in those marital relations of which he was so fond of talking a means of quietening the tempest raging within him. 'This cools my blood.' Or it may be that he was driven to take the step by his need to carry things to their furthest extremes, to be totally true to his principles, to demolish an ecclesiastical rule which he regarded as a human invention, to free the priestly vocation from the yoke of celibacy. Or again he may have acted as he did partly in the certainty of causing a scandal, and out of arrogant delight in so doing. But Luther's main reason for plunging into matrimony was 'to set the devil at defiance.' In his view carnal love remained a sin, which God forgives out of pure mercy; but had he not once uttered this profound paradox, which sums up all his doctrine: 'Be a sinner, and sin hard, but believe even harder, and rejoice in God'? In accepting his sin completely he undoubtedly considered he was finding grace. All these reasons combined may well have been responsible for his decision. To them all must be added one last and very human factor—that fear of loneliness which man experiences as he sees the shadows lengthening. . . . What an admission is implied in this marriage of an apostate priest! [1]

Outwardly marriage seemed to bring Luther peace. From now on he lived a typically middle-class life, surrounded by the cries of children and festoons of washing, hugging his 'better half' without the least discretion. He gardened, and tried his hand at wood-turning and clock-making, always surrounded by a whole cluster of somewhat second-rate disciples, who paid him board and lodging. In their company he would indulge in his endless and astonishing *Table Talk* where mysticism mingled with idle gossip, and the sublime rubbed

[1] For a Catholic of course. For the Protestant viewpoint is exactly the opposite: a celibate minister is an incomplete minister; he invites defiance and is under a real handicap at elections. Consequently, in Protestant eyes, Luther did not betray himself, nor his own spirituality when he married: on the contrary, he completed it by an essential experience, in other words, he fulfilled himself.

shoulders with the vulgar. Only the strenuous work which he set himself in writing his books and keeping up his monumental correspondence really restored him to his true self. For all the rest was superficial; beneath the surface the troubled, vehement Luther still remained. He had wanted this marriage, yet for the remainder of his life it never ceased to embarrass him. Now he exalted it in deep sagacious sentences concerning the union of man and woman. Now he attempted to justify it: marriage was the basis of society, of the economy of religion; but then he added crudely: 'It is one of man's natural needs, like drinking, eating or spitting,' and so on. Sometimes he gave vent to his irritation against the numerous ties of the matrimonial bond, sneering that 'the law creates rebellion' and that this is why men 'like women and not their wives.' During one sermon he even let fly the following quip, which is too cruel to be taken seriously: 'If your wife is not willing take your servant-wench.' All this betrays the hidden tragedy, the unappeased anxiety, and perhaps the remorse —albeit remorse of a topsyturvy kind, which was searching for assurance. The sarcastic Erasmus was utterly mistaken in referring jokingly to Luther's marriage as 'a tragedy that has ended in farce!' A much more real understanding can be gained of the unfrocked monk who became the husband of the 'tüchtige Käthe' by reading the following sincere confession: 'I have humbled and debased myself so far by this marriage that the angels must be smiling—or at least I hope so—and all the demons weeping.'[1]

His character was accentuated. He was still amazingly complex, perhaps more so now than in his thirties. There was mysticism in him. He was uplifted by many admirable bursts of faith, and yet in so many other aspects he was singularly earthy. His ardent nature was carried away by any idea which attracted him, quite illogically, and yet at the same time his dogged brain was capable of developing his theories with reasoned deliberation. In a certain sense Luther was an arrogant man, somewhat coarse and almost naïve; but these failings are counteracted by his fundamental need to humiliate himself before God. Throughout all the events of his life the themes of boldness and meditation, of action and of dreams, are bound together by a kind of polyphonic link, and this is why all those who have attempted to paint him have done so in such very different ways. Three factors, however, are common to every one of these portraits. First there is the authority which emanated from him, a magnetism which drew crowds whenever he spoke, his eyes flashing and his clenched fists beating his breast; and when he was arguing with men of his own stature he would seem to crackle with ideas. In the second place he possessed that faculty described by the German word *Gemütlichkeit*, which has no real parallel

[1] Quoted by H. Grisar, *Luther*, i. 471.

in French or English—an inner radiance, humane generosity, sensibility and even sentimentality, which in Luther's case was translated into loyal friendships and family affections (the death of his daughter Magdalene afflicted him sorely), and into delicate love of animals and flowers. But contradiction retained its hold on him, for all eye-witnesses agree on his terrible propensity to violence, which carried him to lengths of unbelievable coarseness. There was not a single one of his adversaries whom Luther did not publicly wish dead, and whom he did not load with insults—Karlstadt, Münzer, or Zwingli, or Henry VIII,[1] 'the vilest of swine and asses,' or the Pope. For the last named such expressions as 'devil's henchman,' 'Antichrist' or 'mouth of lies' seemed to him far too moderate. It is in this triple make-up—authority, sensitive charm and violence—that we must seek the fundamental reasons for his influence. Luther was typically German in his best as well as in his worst features.[2]

Bossuet himself recognized Luther's 'force of genius,' which found expression both in his speaking and in his writing. Luther was one of those born orators who are inspired the moment they make contact with their audience, spontaneously seizing on images which will impress the mind, and expressions that reach deep into the heart. He was more than ever convinced that 'what he preached came not from him, but from Christ alone,' and he was carried away like a torrent in full spate. He was an indefatigable writer; despite all the disturbances in his life he found time to write more than one hundred books, not to mention the six volumes of his *Correspondence*, and the *Table Talk* which others collected from his own lips.[3] His gifts were considerable; there was something of the poet in him—not one of his thirty-seven hymns leaves the listener unmoved—and his flights of language were often magnificent. Yet at the same time he knew how to turn scholar, dialectician or philosopher as occasion demanded. Few men have had at their disposal such power to convince their fellows, and the pity is that it was placed at the service of heresy.

[1] Henry was guilty of having written a refutation of Luther's theses. (See Chapter VII, fourth section: 'England on the Eve of the Reformation.')

[2] On this point the reader is recommended to L. Cristiani's accurate comments in the article 'Réforme,' in the *Dictionnaire d'Apologétique d'Alès*.

[3] Luther's principal works can be divided into the following categories: (1) Commentaries on the Scriptures and his translation of the Bible. (2) Polemic works (e.g. *On the Babylonian Captivity of the Church of God*). (3) Political works (e.g. *An Address to the Nobility of the German Nation*). (4) Dogmatic treatises, in which the polemic element nevertheless plays a large part (*Treatise on Free Will* or *On Monastic Vows* or *Private Mass*). (5) The two *Catechisms*, several oratorical pieces and the hymns. Although the 7,075 pieces of *Table Talk* provide most interesting information about Luther's life, they are unquestionably only an incomplete translation of his thinking: it is essential to make allowances for his known love of paradox and the errors of interpretation made by those reporting his conversation.

LUTHERANISM: THE CONFESSION OF AUGSBURG

Such was the mature Luther—the man whom one half of Germany regarded as a symbol, and the other as a sign of contradiction. At this moment his doctrine was obliged by force of circumstances to become fixed; and in expressing itself in concrete terms it lost that characteristic of constant spiritual debate, of answering the contradictory questions of the soul, which it had possessed at the beginning and which, to a large extent, it was to retain, so far as Luther himself was concerned, until the day of his death. Something even more serious occurred. As had happened in the case of Luther's original conception of the Church, his doctrine, by virtue of its success, deviated considerably from his own fundamental intentions. The distance between Luther and Lutheranism became obvious; it was to become even more so after his disappearance from the scene.

When Charles V returned to Germany, at the beginning of 1530, he found a situation very different from the one he had left. It was impossible to go back on the concessions already made to the Lutheran rulers. Germany constituted the imperial bastion, the reserve against the Turkish menace, and it was therefore essential to re-establish religious peace; but there was no longer any question of doing so by force. It was therefore agreed that the 'Protestants' should express their views at the Diet then meeting at Augsburg, and that these views should be fully discussed. It was in these conditions that Melanchthon drafted the document known as the *Confession of Augsburg*, which was later recognized as the basic formula of Lutheran Protestantism. Circumstances encouraged its author to smooth the edges; besides, his temperament was infinitely more moderate than that of his friend and teacher. He went so far as to write to Cardinal Campeggio, the Papal Legate attending the Diet: 'In doctrine we are at one with the Roman Church. Even today we continue to respect the Papacy.' Consequently several of Luther's essential theses—those on transubstantiation, papal authority, Purgatory and the cult of saints—were toned down, or even passed over in silence, as were those on Predestination. And when the Catholic theologians, led by Johann Eck, answered the *Confession* with a vigorous *Confutation*, Melanchthon was anxious to make even more concessions. It was Luther who, from the heights of Coburg Castle where he was following the Diet's proceedings, imperiously prevented him from doing so.

Thus Luther's complete philosophy, the very essence of Lutheranism, is not to be found in the twenty-eight articles of the Confession of Augsburg. This declaration, which is in a sense as much a political as a theological document, must be supplemented by the information provided in his treatises—those on free will, the Mass and monastic vows—and by the two catechisms which he compiled in 1529—the *Small Catechism* for the ordinary laity, the *Great Catechism* for the clergy and educated laymen. Nor should the observer forget the margin of uncertainty and approximation relating to each position, in view of the fact that we are dealing with the direct expression of a singularly unstable philosophy.

What is the essential of the Lutheran *credo*? And in what respects does it deviate from that of the Catholic Church? The Lutheran faith contains nothing heretical so far as the persons of God and Christ are concerned. It proclaims the unity of substance and the Trinity of persons, as stated by the Council of Nicaea. Following the Apostles' Creed and the Council of Chalcedon, it asserts the unity of Person and the duality of Natures in Jesus. But as soon as the problem of man's destiny and relationship with God is touched upon, the rift becomes apparent. It was in fact on this very point that Luther, in attempting to solve his own inner conflict, strayed from the Catholic Church. The logical exactitude with which he was capable (despite several repetitions and contradictions) of carrying his ideas right through to the bitter end, led him, in all fields, to draw from his theory conclusions that were increasingly far removed from the dogmas of Rome.

Since the fall of Adam all men have been born in a state of sin, that is to say, lacking both fear of God and trust in God, bearing concupiscence in their being; and this original sin would be sufficient to merit their eternal death had the grace of baptism not been given them by the Holy Spirit. But man is so corrupted by sin, so vitiated in his faculties, that his reason can no longer recognize the gift which is to save him; and even if he discerns the truth his will is radically incapable of doing good by itself alone. Luther therefore rejects man's *free will*.[1] Although, as the Confession of Augsburg admits, the will has some latitude to realize 'civil justice' and to make up its mind 'reasonably' in the usual sense of the word, it is radically incapable of realizing 'justice according to the Spirit,' in other words, of leading to salvation. How then can man be saved?

Catholicism also asserts that man is incapable of living without sinning, and incapable also of reaching God by his own efforts alone; but it adds that he remains free to obey or reject grace, and that by his efforts on this earth, by his *works*, he acquires merit which, when united with those of Christ, enable him to be saved. It was on the problem of works that Lutheranism and Catholicism first parted ways

---

[1] This was the decisive point in Luther's spiritual evolution, even while he was still a monk—his discovery of the total corruption of human nature and his rejection of free will. From this moment he became, unconsciously, a heretic in the bottom of his heart.

most clearly. Not that it is necessary to confine ourselves to the celebrated formula 'salvation through faith without works,' in which historians have too often claimed to sum up the Lutheran faith; it is false. On this point the reformer's thought varied a good deal. Sometimes he presented good works as a basis of faith, and sometimes asserted that they were consequent upon it ('if everyone had perfect faith the moral law would be superfluous'), a position adopted by the Confession of Augsburg; more often he taught that an action in itself was neither good nor bad, that its sole value depended upon the faith which accompanied it (this is the meaning of the famous phrase 'Sin hard!' a doctrine which, if interpreted too broadly, obviously resulted in certain immorality. The basis of Luther's thinking is that, when set against the burden of sin, all little human merits are absurd; something else is needed in order that the power of death may be overcome. But what?

Grace, clearly. Grace alone can lead man to goodness. Moreover it leads him there irresistibly. The righteous man is no more free than the sinner; both are prisoners of 'servile will.' If the original Pelagian heresy [1] had belittled the fundamental role of grace, the Lutherans tended to overestimate it. But how is it to be obtained, since everything man does to 'merit' it is worthless? In the strict sense of the word man does not *obtain* either grace or salvation. In the most profound of all mysteries God grants it or refuses it, for reasons which are fundamentally impossible for man to understand. This is the doctrine of *predestination*. Unlike Calvin, Luther did not make this the almost complete basis of his philosophy; but he nevertheless believed in it, albeit reluctantly, for as he said: 'The thought of predestination is like fire that cannot be put out: the more we turn it over and over the more desperate it makes us.'

Here is the crux of the matter. It brings us to that spiritual crisis during which Luther had believed himself lost in despair, and in which he had discovered the foundation of his doctrine. Was there no hope left for him? Yes, indeed. 'God, who is Perfect Holiness, envelops with His love a humanity irreparably subject to the state of sin, and incapable, even with the help of grace, of acquiring sufficient merit to make it worthy in the sight of God' (Strohl). It is to this love alone that man must make appeal, to this love which God has freely and gratuitously given. Man is *justified* not because he undergoes an inner transformation, but because the love of God covers him like a cloak of forgiveness by virtue of the infinite merits of Christ. All his religious effort must strive to cause the merits of the Son of God be imputed unto him, and this imputation is obtainable by *faith*. Now what

[1] See the author's *The Church in the Dark Ages*, and its Index references to Pelagius and Pelagianism.

exactly did Luther understand by faith? The question is extremely difficult to answer, for his thinking on this point was in a state of constant flux; it was at all events quite different from Catholic teaching, which interprets faith as the individual's submission to the teaching of the Church and his total acceptance of the truths which she pronounces as revealed. Luther's idea of faith is one of steadfast trust in God, the certainty that He will pardon all his sins in the Name of Christ, a kind of total abdication into the hands of the Almighty, and, to go even further, the conviction that the simple fact of possessing this faith is in itself a guarantee of salvation. 'Justifying faith' thus complements and indeed takes the place of all man's vain efforts; 'only believe and do what you will' can be regarded as its formula. Through this faith the Christian, existing in the midst of that frightful servitude imposed on him by sin, rediscovers a liberty sovereign to all others.[1]

Whence does this faith proceed, and on what must man base his life in order to possess it? To quote a phrase of the early Christians, where is 'the rule of faith'? Catholics would reply that the teaching Church is its repository, that she is the judge of revealed truth, which has been transmitted to her in two ways, through Holy Scripture and Tradition. The Lutherans certainly recognize one of these two sources of truth—Holy Scripture—but they deny the Church any right to intervene in order to extract from it principles of application, on the ground that her intervention obstructs the direct relationship between man and God. Each Christian conscience must refer itself to the sacred text, to the Bible,[2] and derive its rules of conduct from this one source of faith; the Holy Spirit will be its guide. This is in fact the theory of *free inquiry*. In brief, the Lutheran concept of faith derives from a quasi-mystical impulse, from an appeal to Him who illumines all intelligence, and whose mercy will open the way to forgiveness.

Christianity's centre of balance is thus completely shifted; while traditional Catholicism centres its faith on the Revelation of the living God in His Incarnate Son, to whom the Church renders perpetual and sure witness, Lutheranism is based on the subjective certainty, which must be deeply felt by each individual believer, of being personally redeemed by Christ. Away with external principles, unchallengeable

---

[1] Here we have the formidable contradiction which so impressed Bossuet. Luther had criticized indulgences for engendering a false security, and his own doctrine consisted of believing himself saved by faith alone, therefore possessing a total security by a totally gratuitous process.

[2] However, Luther removed from the canon of the Scriptures all the 'Deuterocanonical' books of the Old Testament (cf. the author's *Histoire Sainte*, p. 356), while from the New he rejected the Epistle to the Hebrews, those of St James and St Jude, and the Apocalypse.

dogmas and disciplines; this is an inner experience of spiritual liberation.

In such a perspective there could no longer be room for all those intercessors between God and man, those mediators to whom the individual Christian, in his weakness, turns for help and support. All those consoling and profoundly human features of the Catholic cult of the saints no longer have any meaning at all; the saints might continue to be upheld as examples, but one must not invoke them or implore their aid. The difference between Catholics and Lutherans on this point is particularly marked in connection with the Blessed Virgin Mary. Luther undoubtedly venerated her; but he refused to admit that, in accepting the angel's proposal that she should become the Mother of the Saviour, Mary had in some way worked in intimate co-operation with the grace of God, and that this made her, though a humble creature separated by an immeasurable abyss from the Divine Majesty, the recipient of particular privileges, and able to intercede before her Son on behalf of every sinner.

Since faith alone justifies, the sacraments cannot be the means, the vehicles of grace. Luther did not reject them altogether. He differed from the ancient Donatist heretics [1] by asserting that they were efficacious in themselves, by reason of their institution by Jesus Christ, in other words, that their validity did not depend on the minister who conferred them. But he maintained that they were only symbols: they showed that the individual receiving them had faith and that he hoped to be justified by the merits of Christ, but they themselves produced no effect of grace. Moreover Luther retained only those *three sacraments* whose origins he considered directly ascribable to the Scriptures. First, *Baptism*, which the Confession of Augsburg proclaims as essential, even for infants. Here Luther seems somewhat illogical, for there is little point in conferring a sacrament which has no efficacy of its own upon someone who is not yet capable of possessing faith; the Anabaptists, who baptized none but adults, showed more logic in this respect. Second, *Penance*, which is, however, reduced to an act of appeal to God and of profound humility. The enumeration of sins is unnecessary, since all human actions are tainted with sin; contrition does not depend on the man; [2] and any attempt at satisfaction constitutes only a kind of insult to the merits of Christ which alone are capable of satisfying the Divine Justice. Moreover any Christian can give absolution, since all are witnesses of the Holy Spirit. Finally, the *Eucharist*. It too was fundamentally distorted from its Catholic sense,

---

[1] Cf. *The Church in the Dark Ages* and its Index references to Donatism.
[2] The meaning of true contrition is defined in the Articles of Smalkald: 'not by *activa contritio*, repentance made by the penitent himself, but by *contritio passiva*, the real repentance of the heart and the fear of death.' Further on it states that penitence comprises two elements, repentance and faith.

even though, on this particular point, Luther went infinitely less far than several other Protestant reformers.[1] According to him there is no real Sacrifice of the Mass, any more than there is any transubstantiation. Christ, however, is certainly present in the Host, *with* the bread and the wine, but the bread does not change into His Body. This is the theory of *impanation* and *consubstantiation*. As for the other sacraments, they were either abandoned or robbed of their genuinely religious value: marriage, for instance, ceased to have any sacramental meaning, a theory which implied the authorization of divorce.

All this doctrine obeyed a strict inner logic, once its basic principle was accepted. It was, as has been seen, as a result of these same premises that Luther formulated a conception of the Church which was totally different from Catholic doctrine. Even though events had already forced the movement to modify fundamentally its point of view, the Confession of Augsburg still proclaimed that the Church was the society of saints, adding, however, that 'the society of saints' was that in which the Gospel was correctly taught and the sacraments correctly administered. Who then was to be the judge of what was correct? The hierarchical principle of the Catholic Church was rejected in favour of direct relationship with God; but because of the necessities of apostleship and administration of the sacraments, the Confession of Augsburg accepted the institution of a clergy, and actually specified that this clergy should be *rite vocatus*, officially called. But the *pastors* or *ministers* were to be elected by the community.

At the end of it all what remained of the traditional cult? On this point Luther showed himself rather inexplicit, far more so than many of his rivals and successors. In his heart he considered rites and formulas to be unimportant; they could be admitted on condition that they did not contradict the Gospel or the very essential of his doctrine. Vows, for example, were swept away because they impinged on the total liberty of the spiritual impulse towards God. On the other hand many liturgical festivals might as well remain. They were conducive to good order, and could help to elevate men's souls. As for the Mass, it was retained, but reduced to two elements: the teaching of the Word and the celebration of the Lord's Supper; its mysterious sacrificial character vanished. Naturally there was no longer any question of all those forms of devotion so dear to Catholic piety: penitential exercises, pilgrimages, veneration of relics and the like.

Such are the essential attributes of Lutheranism. They defined a completely new type of Christianity which claimed to be the true one, the Christianity of Primitive times and of Christ the Redeemer Himself. Even in points of detail Lutheranism asserted its determination to make a positive return to first beginnings. In the last seven articles of

[1] See p. 337, and also the following chapter on Calvin.

the Confession of Augsburg it demanded the suppression of clerical celibacy, communion in two kinds and the abolition of auricular confession. In short it swept away everything which fifteen hundred years of faith had implanted in Christian tradition. But the Catholic Church was not rebelling against this return to primitive origins, nor was she necessarily fighting to maintain all these customs whose meaning she understood so completely. No, she was defending something far more essential. Luther and Lutheranism had lapsed into heresy on four fundamental points: in their conception of the omnipotence of sin, in their exaggeration and distortion of the role of faith, in their misunderstanding of the function of the sacraments, and, last of all, in their rejection of the authority of the Church. There could be no basis for agreement on these four issues.

LUTHER VERSUS THE HUMANISM OF ERASMUS

Luther had very soon to defend his doctrines against opponents other than the Catholics. By preaching free inquiry he seemed to admit that each individual could interpret the Scriptures to suit himself, and consequently make his own dogmas. But Luther himself was the very opposite of liberal; he was strictly concerned about orthodoxy, and throughout his life he was on the look-out to prevent any deviation from his doctrine. This accounts for several of the violent quarrels which were a part of his existence; his temperament naturally lent itself to bitter wrangling.

The most famous and most noisy was undoubtedly his pen-and-ink duel with *Erasmus*. At the beginning, as we have seen, the two men appeared to be allies. Both had the same enemies: the theologians, the Dominicans—all those ignorant and fanatical monks! Erasmus had considered that it was in the best interests of Christianity that Luther's voice should not be smothered. Melanchthon had assured the Dutchman of the great admiration which Luther cherished towards him, and there had been a most friendly exchange of letters. Even when Luther's rebellion had begun to cause scandal, Erasmus, while attempting to calm him, had defended him before both the princes and the Church. When invited to attack the reformer publicly he had replied: 'I derive more profit from glancing at a page of his than from reading the whole of St Thomas.' But this was unquestionably no more than a witticism; he had added, somewhat drolly: 'Luther has committed only two wrongs: he has hit the Pope over the head, and kicked the monks in the belly.'

In fact, nothing was more uncertain than this alliance. Although outwardly good friends, the two men knew that they had nothing in common. The shrewd humanist told Melanchthon that Luther knew nothing about real culture, that he was basically only a scholastic—and a scholastic of the worst kind. For his part Luther confessed in 1517: 'I read our Erasmus, and I feel his attraction for me diminishing daily.' Their characters were so different. One has only to look at Holbein's famous portrait of Erasmus, and study that lean, ageless face with its pointed profile, wrinkled from the nose to the corners of the lips, and the smile holding back the malicious witticism, to guess that he would be separated from the solemn, impassioned monk by everything that was most fundamental in his nature. 'A studious leisure and tranquillity are all I want,' Erasmus used to declare. They were not enough for Martin Luther, to whose rigid mind the humanist's admirable play on all the instruments of the intellect were nothing but suspect pleasures and virtually sinful vanities. As for Erasmus's semi-scepticism, it could not but fill with horror a soul of such profound faith as was Luther's. Learning of all the trouble stirred up by Luther in the name of truth, the great scholar murmured: 'Truth? . . . Is it worth turning the world upside-down for the sake of truth? Sometimes silence is the better course. Jesus was silent before Herod.' Prudence of this kind merely incited Luther's fury.

The two men were diametrically opposed to one another on the doctrinal plane, and even more so where their attitude towards life was concerned. Erasmus was a Christian humanist, in the direct line of his Italian predecessors [1] who dreamed of realizing the synthesis between the new attributes of learning and the eternal truths of the Gospel. He was the heir of Marsilio Ficino and Pico della Mirandola, and the friend of those outstanding English Christian humanists, Thomas More and John Colet. Despite several passing whims and a number of positive errors, Erasmus's philosophy was deliberately woven within the framework of Christianity. He placed his confidence in human nature, which was created by God in His own image and which, according to him, bore within itself a natural inclination towards beauty and goodness, though it needed grace in order to blossom to the full. Man's nature must open its very heart to grace in order to be transfigured. In the eyes of Erasmus God was no angry and capricious master, nor was his Christ only a negative, peaceful, sorrowful figure. His Christianity was a tranquil, confident faith: all man's attributes should find their place therein, natural virtues as well as qualities of the mind, knowledge as well as sanctity. Supported by reason, the spiritual life should be something calm, established and solid, in which prayer had its appointed place, in which decent practices helped man in his weakness, and in which the highest peaks of mysticism were reached by a daily progress. In short, this was a doctrine which has often been likened to that subsequently put forward by St Francis de Sales. Had Erasmus had the opportunity to die a martyr's death, like Thomas

More and John Fisher, he might today be included in our Calendar of Saints.[1]

It suffices, however, merely to summarize his principal ideas to see that they were exactly the opposite of Luther's teaching. The reformer's reaction is not difficult to imagine. 'Have confidence in man! in his sinful nature!' 'Admit that grace wells up from within the soul which merits it!' 'Rely on reason!' These Erasmian theses were, to Luther's understanding, gross insults to the Truth. 'There is not a single article of faith which Erasmus cannot find some way of ridiculing,' he cried. And then of course it was obvious that Erasmus was a mere moralist who reduced the Gospel to a manual of good behaviour. The real significance of religion—its mystical meaning—escaped him completely. As for Erasmus's anxiety to connect Christianity with all the great sources of antiquity, it is an understatement to say that it was meaningless to the ill-educated monk from Wittenberg, who regarded it as pure and simple nonsense.

In fact, when these two men came to blows, two quite different expressions of Christianity were in conflict. At this time an Erasmian concept of religion was shared by numerous intellectuals, as well as by many prelates and politicians. It was a very humane concept—perhaps rather too humane—which was to have its adherents everywhere, in France as well as Spain, and even in Rome itself, where it attracted Pope Paul III. It went beyond the personality of its initiator, and outlived him. In short, it might well have been the concept of the Catholic Reformation, had it not been rejected by a number of more rigid and strictly orthodox elements. Luther himself was probably not fully aware of what was at stake in this conflict, although he often had strong intuitions. He felt instinctively that Erasmus and himself were total opposites, and that there could no longer be any question of agreement or collaboration between them.

The original alliance gave way to antagonism. The two men were very soon divided by a hatred which only theologians are capable of maintaining at fever heat for so long, each cherishing the conviction that by grappling with his adversary he was striking down the sin incarnate in him. However, the wrangle did not begin straightaway; each feared that in helping to crush the other he might be preparing rods for his own back. There was even one rather amusing letter in which Luther warned Erasmus: 'Do not join forces with my enemies; provided you publish nothing against me I will take care to publish nothing against you.' But the humanist knew that he was suspected of friendship with the rebel. The bull Exsurge had just appeared, and

---

[1] It is true that in any canonization proceedings the devil's advocate would derive plenty of material from In Praise of Folly or the Colloquia (which contain a number of pages, intended for the young, which are frankly shocking).

although Erasmus regarded its promulgation as a blunder, it did away with all ambiguities. With flattering insistence Pope Adrian IV praised 'his extremely great intelligence,' and besought him 'to use his gifts for the glory of Christ and the defence of Holy Church.' Erasmus therefore made up his mind to provide some evidence of his allegiance. 'I have always hitherto given proof of an orthodox spirit,' he replied to the Pope, 'and I shall maintain this position until my dying day.'

In 1524 his *Dialogue on Free Will* appeared. He defined free will as 'the power of the will which enables man to apply himself to what concerns his salvation, or to turn deliberately aside from it.' Erasmus proved its existence with the aid of the Scriptures. The tone of his treatise was extremely moderate, and many scholars saw it as a basis for discussion which might afford Luther the opportunity to correct his theses. But this was not at all the sense in which the vehement reformer interpreted it. He was touched to the quick. 'Your quibbling details about the Papacy, indulgences, Purgatory and all this other nonsense don't worry me!' he screamed. 'You alone have pulled the knot tight, you alone have bitten me in the throat!' Back came his answer. This was the treatise on *Servile Will* (1529), perhaps the most complete work which ever came from Luther's pen. He reaffirmed his principles. Free will? There was only one—God's. Man was impotent, corrupted, linked perhaps with evil, perhaps with grace, a horseman set on a dark road with an invisible companion in the saddle behind him, who might be either God or Satan. These ideas were far too closely bound up with his own harrowing, essential belief for him to allow the half-sceptical Erasmus to lay his frivolous hand upon them. There was certainly no element of humanism in Luther's approach to Christianity. He let fly some steely barbs, aiming no longer at his adversary's ideas, but at the adversary himself. What was he, when all was said and done? Some sort of Sophist, a cynical Lucian, ignorant of Holy Scripture into the bargain and incapable of genuine piety.

The break was now absolutely final. Contemporary witnesses were not deceived: this din of clashing pens marked the end of the alliance between humanism and Lutheranism. Some applauded, others deplored the fact. When attacked Erasmus answered back in kind, giving Luther's fat cheeks some cruel slaps, pointing to his many errors and textual alterations, gibing at his vanity and even at his personal conduct. Such behaviour is not uncommon among the very wise when anger takes possession of them.

'I hate Erasmus!' Luther repeated these words over and over again during the remainder of his life. 'I hate him from the bottom of my heart. Listen to me and be my witnesses,' he commanded the disciples who were piously making notes of his *Table Talk*. 'I consider Erasmus to be the greatest enemy Christ has had these thousand years past.'

Some Reformers Outside Luther's Influence: Zwingli, Bucer, Oeclampadius

The defence of his ideas against the assaults of a former ally was not the only polemic effort which was forced upon the champion of the Reformation. Luther observed an increasing manifestation of tendencies which he regarded as heretical among those who, like himself, were outside the Catholic Church. 'The Reformation,' says one Protestant historian,[1] 'was not an organized movement born in the mind of one man or one group of men in close relationship with one another, which was to be developed according to a plan established in advance, with one leader holding all the levers of command. It was a movement in which men followed rather than led. . . .'

Anabaptism, which had been halted for a time by the defeat of Münzer, had resumed its progress more strongly than before. Various new prophets filled the scene; one came across them everywhere. Adherents of the second baptism were numerous in Switzerland, in the Augsburg district of south Germany, in Alsace and Moravia, but they were also penetrating northern Germany and the Low Countries. They had found a new leader, a former craftsman furrier named *Melchior Hoffman*, a fanatic whose words were often obscure in meaning, but who possessed powerful magnetic gifts. Their doctrine had absorbed the old apocalyptic and millenary dream which so many of the Joachimites and Spirituali had cherished. They proclaimed a reversal of social values, the perfect equality of possessions, and 'the kingdom of God on earth.' When they were hounded from Moravia, where Hubmaier, one of their ministers, was burned, and from the Upper Rhine, where Eusisheim was the scene of 'the butchery of Alsace,' they reappeared elsewhere, apparently indestructible. The City Magistrate of Strasbourg tolerated them. Hoffman predicted that the town on the Ill would be the 'new Jerusalem,' and that in the year 1533 the one hundred and forty-four thousand elect mentioned in the *Apocalypse* would gather together there to inaugurate the new Golden Age. On all sides the Anabaptists came into collision with other reformers who, whenever they were the masters, treated them exactly as the Catholics did elsewhere. In Switzerland Zwingli had those he captured thrown from the Limmat, and the gentle Melanchthon had loudly approved the measures taken against them in Saxony.

Anabaptism could still be regarded as a movement of fanatics on the fringes of the true Reformation, but several unacceptable tendencies were visible within its own bosom. Even worse, the master detected them in the very heart of Lutheranism itself. His friend *John Agricola*,

[1] Courvoisier.

a professor at Wittenberg, who had been one of his earliest followers, had rebelled against the measures taken to assure state control of the Church. At the same time he put forward a proposition which was in short quite a logical consequence of his leader's own theology. He proclaimed that faith had nothing in common with the Law, even with that expressed in the Ten Commandments, a doctrine which allowed his disciples to take various moral liberties. Luther had been obliged to develop some categorical theses against Agricola. At Torgau, in 1527, the *enfant terrible* of the Reformation had agreed, in response to Melanchthon's mediatory efforts, to take a more prudent attitude; but he was ready to relapse into his errors at any time.

More serious were the differences of opinion which divided Luther from other reformers who had sprung up in large numbers here, there and everywhere. Whether fundamentally inspired by the ideas of Wittenberg or acting on their own initiative, all—thanks to the discovery of 'free inquiry'—fashioned their own doctrine to suit themselves. In practice these various forms of 'Protestantism' combined with one another, and many people did not distinguish between them. But their leaders, who had become hardened to theological jousting, applied themselves to the task of distinguishing their own theses from those of all the rest,[1] a habit which was not very favourable to the cause of unity.

The most important of these reformers was *Ulrich Zwingli* (1484–1531). He was a Swiss priest, a heavily built man with a pink, bearded face, whose fiery spirit belied his placid appearance. Zwingli was born in the Toggenburg, where his father was a well-to-do peasant farmer and mayor of his commune. He was Luther's exact contemporary. He received his earliest education from his uncle, the parish priest of Wesen, and afterwards studied at Berne and Basle. In 1506 he was ordained priest, and had been attached in turn to the parish of Glaris, and then to Our Lady's at Einsiedeln. Much of what he saw around him filled him with anger and indignation. The Church in Switzerland was no better than elsewhere, and Zwingli's wrath was aroused by such examples as the soldier-abbot of St Gall, who repressed a rising among his subjects by a generous use of the pike, and the superstitious devotion exhaled by the crowds who took part in the famous pilgrimage to his parish. Furthermore, being no less interested in politics than in religion, he abhorred the detestable custom of 'capitulations' whereby the Swiss hired themselves out as soldiers in the service of foreign powers. For a time he had even served as chaplain to a band of mercenaries, taking part in the victory of Novara and the defeat of

---

[1] It is not possible here to describe in detail the doctrinal differences between the various reformers. There is a careful study of the question in Henry Strohl's *La Pensée de la Réforme*.

Marignano. Zwingli was consequently a reformer on two different planes: the religious, where he regarded himself as a pupil of Erasmus, as a Christian humanist, even though his ideas went far beyond those of the prudent scholar, and the political, where he sought to restore the liberty of his people.

In 1518 the office of principal preacher at the Grossmünster in Zürich was vacant, and Zwingli obtained it; from now on he had a platform for his views. His ideas were already fixed; they had been formed quite independently of Luther, of whom Zwingli alleged that he had scarcely heard at this time, and whom he was to underestimate all his life. The voice of the new preacher tore Zürich from its prosperous tranquillity; he thundered against abuses, capitulations, monastic vows, the cult of saints—in fact against everything. When a Milanese Franciscan named Sanson came to Zürich to preach indulgences, with the same clumsiness which Tetzel displayed elsewhere, Zwingli followed Luther's example, and in a sermon of exceptional violence voiced his determined opposition to the system. Now follows a curious detail: instead of punishing the insolent priest Leo X, who badly needed Swiss help to pursue his Italian policy, tried to flatter him by making him a papal chaplain. Zwingli continued on his way, behaving more violently than ever and attacking on all fronts simultaneously. During Lent, in 1522, the question of abstinence enabled him to win a decisive victory. Zürich did not fast, and the Bishop of Constance's protest to the Helvetic Diet had no result. Henceforth Zwingli was the master of both his city and his canton. During two public disputations in 1523 he crushed his enemies, had his theses accepted by the Council of the Canton, and drafted his own reforming code. Churches were stripped of their ornaments and statues, and the religious houses were converted into schools or hospitals. Zwinglianism was declared the official religion of the canton of Zürich; the prophet's *De vera et falsa religione* provided its catechism and its law.[1] In 1524 Zwingli married. 'This is his way of mortifying himself,' quipped his friend Erasmus.

Zwinglianism was an extremely radical religion, in which ideas akin to those of Luther were carried to extremes. Holy Scripture, interpreted by each individual according as the Holy Spirit enlightened him, was the sole authority; Tradition was rejected, and every believer was

---

[1] It would, however, be unfair to represent Zwingli's message and activity as wholly destructive. We possess very few of his texts, but it is known that on his arrival in Zürich he undertook a commentary, paragraph by paragraph, on the Gospel of St Matthew, in which he quoted St John Chrysostom and St Augustine, and then continued through the Acts of the Apostles. By 1525 he had completed the New Testament. In the same way it would hardly be fair to regard this middle-class doctrine as merely an empty shell. The *De vera et falsa religione* possesses a sincere faith and a profound understanding of human wretchedness and the love of Christ, which renders Zwingli in some respects more human in outlook than Luther. 'Come to me, all you that labour and are burdened' (Matt. xi. 28) was his favourite sentence from the Gospel.

able to invent his own theology. True religion consisted simply of the Scriptures, and nothing must be added or taken away from them. Consequently anything which was not expressly mentioned in the Bible, as well as anything condemned in it, had to be discarded. War was declared on crucifixes, statues, pictures, stained-glass windows and altars. Zwingli declared that he could find only two sacraments mentioned in the New Testament: Baptism and the Lord's Supper; and even these were but symbols, acts of commemoration; there was no Real Presence. As for those many grave problems which Luther had argued out so painfully in his own conscience, Zwingli, who was not at all the type of man likely to question himself in such dramatic terms, found the solutions in philosophy. As the emanation of God, man was not free; God was the author of evil as well as of good; and evil was not a sin, since it was part of the divine plan; sin was in short the animal part of man, against which no effort was possible. None of this philosophy lacked logic, but it was to have far-reaching results.

Needless to say the Zwinglian concept of the Church no longer has anything in common with Catholicism. The hierarchy was rejected; it had no longer the right to make decisions on dogma, morality or religious practice. Being a practical Swiss, however, and the enemy of all disorder, Zwingli did not make Luther's mistake of dissociating himself from ecclesiastical organization. He was a true son of those fine free cities, whose wealth was founded on trade and which were extremely jealous of the independence they had won by their own efforts. They were certainly anxious to shake off the tutelage of the abbots and bishops who had made them a part of civilization, but they would tolerate neither anarchy nor the intervention of the princes, as in Germany. Zwingli therefore built them a State Church, whose leaders were to be the prosperous citizens themselves, and which would be controlled by the Council of the Canton, itself a democratic body. This was the earliest realization of a State Church anywhere. In this respect Zwingli was a real initiator; his theology was a part of his political ideas, and Calvin later on remembered his example at Geneva.

From their starting-point in Zürich, Zwingli's ideas spread rapidly throughout the rest of Switzerland—partly by fair means, partly by foul—winning over Berne, Lausanne, Geneva, and then percolating to the cities of the Rhine valley. Strasbourg gave them a welcome, as also did Basle, Glaris, Saint-Gall and Mulhausen. Moreover their progress was marked by the destruction of churches and the burning of monasteries. The bishops of Constance, Basle, Lausanne and Geneva were forced to abandon their sees. Seven of the Swiss cantons, however, remained loyal to Catholicism: Schwyz, Uri and Unterwalden (the three founders of the Helvetic Union) as well as Lucerne, Zug, Freiburg and Soleure. These formed a coalition known as the 'League

of Valais,' in order to defend their faith; Ferdinand of Austria assisted
them. The consequence of this religious division was civil war. In 1531
the Catholics took up arms to avenge the abbot of Saint-Gall, who had
been expelled by the Zwinglians; and the Protestants suffered a cruel
defeat at Kappel, near Zürich, in which Zwingli and twenty-four of his
pastors lost their lives. Henceforth the Swiss were split between
Catholic and Protestant cantons. The two 'Helvetic Confessions' of
1536 and 1564 were to constitute the official expression of the latters'
principles of faith; but owing to the influence of Calvin (who settled
in Geneva in 1536) these documents were no more than partially
Zwinglian in content, particularly in the case of the later text.

A second city which, although acknowledging imperial suzerainty,
was also situated in Switzerland, had undergone its own Reformation
parallel with that of Zürich. The developments in *Basle* differed in
some respects from those in Zürich, even though the two centres were
in constant communication. Basle was at this period one of Europe's
most flourishing cities; its university was famous; and among many
famous scholars who taught there were Wittenbach de Bienne, the
Alsatian Köpflein, better known as Capito, Pellican and Glareanus.
Froben, the printer, who had published Luther's works, was the pole
star of many great minds such as Beatus Rhenanus, Amerbach and
Oeclampadius, an unfrocked monk. Erasmus also had been living in
Basle since 1521, supervising the printing of his books and posing for
Holbein. The Reformation at Basle was a doctrinal compromise
between Lutheranism and the more radical Zwinglianism, with a
number of humanist features. It was a religion of intellectuals who had
no desire to go to extremes. Under their influence the senate allowed
the Catholic Mass and Protestant cult to subsist side by side for some
time, but once Bienne had introduced Zwinglianism, fanatics obtained
control. All the Catholic town counsellors were forced to resign. The
mob hurled itself upon the churches and monasteries with iconoclastic
fury. Oeclampadius proclaimed his delight: 'What a sorry sight for
superstition!' he wrote to Capito. 'The Papists will be weeping tears
of blood over this. . . .' Meanwhile Erasmus, filled with disgust, took
himself off to live at Freiburg-im-Breisgau.

At *Strasbourg*, where yet another form of Protestantism had established itself, events passed off in a less violent fashion. The leader there
was a former Dominican, *Martin Bucer*, 'the Bishop of Strasbourg,' as
Calvin afterwards called him. He was a moderate, lucid, level-headed
man, painfully aware of the dangers with which disunity and division
threatened his cause, and doctrinally more flexible than any of his
fellow Protestants. Bucer aimed at bringing the different Protestant
elements closer together, and even at maintaining contact with the
Catholics, an attempt which earned him Bossuet's rather unkind

description as the 'architect of subtle equivocation.' Of his closest followers, Matthew Zell was more ardent, while Capito, who was constantly on the move between Basle and the banks of the Ill, represented the humanist element. At Strasbourg too Lutheran and Zwinglian ideas intermingled, not to mention a few whiffs of Anabaptism; for in the main this city showed itself remarkably tolerant and receptive towards both ideas and individuals, which was rather unusual in the climate of the epoch. Thus it became a centre from which Protestant ideas radiated throughout the rest of north-western Europe. The final break with Catholicism was not consummated there until 1529, amid the havoc and destruction which was henceforth a customary part of these proceedings. As for the actual doctrine proclaimed by the Strasbourg brand of Protestantism, it too betrayed Bucer's readiness for compromise. For instance, it rejected the Lutheran insistence on absolute justification by faith, and, like the Catholics, admitted the preliminary necessity of internal regeneration, of the effort of self upon self.

Luther looked with the deepest suspicion on all these reformers who, notwithstanding the fact that they were to some extent his descendants, were so obviously deviating from his views. The least that can be said is that he was very far indeed from reposing any trust in them. After all Luther, the supreme anti-rationalist, could scarcely have much in common with a practical Swiss like Zwingli, who had virtually nothing mystical about him, and whose humanism was so pronounced that he had once been so bold as to state that he very much hoped to meet Seneca and Socrates in Paradise. Nor was he at all drawn to the scheming Bucer, who was lending himself to all kinds of ambiguities under the pretext of furthering Protestant unity. Luther spewed them all out as half-hearted and lukewarm. Nowadays we refer to deviationists of the Right and the Left, and this political language would have suited Luther perfectly, for the ally and friends of princes looked upon these city democrats with withering contempt.

The seed of discord between them was the question of the Eucharist, the Sacrament of the Lord's Supper, and this is why the name 'Sacramentaries' is frequently given to the continental Protestant sects who did not adhere to Lutheranism. Luther had already been in conflict with Karlstadt on this point. Zwingli and Oeclampadius rejected the Real Presence, and confined themselves to interpreting Christ's words 'This is my body, this is my blood' in a symbolic sense. For them the Eucharist was nothing but a kind of commemoration of Our Lord's last meal on earth. Here Luther's attitude was both exalted and courageous. In a treatise which Father Moreau has not hesitated to call 'quite remarkable' he adopted a stand violently opposed to all those who denied the Real Presence; the reader will recall that, although he did not accept transubstantiation, he believed in consubstantiation and impanation. Moreover he himself honestly confessed, in reply to those who reproached him for supporting a thesis so out of keeping with his doctrine of justification by faith, that he had tried to find a way out of the dilemma, in order to give the Papists 'a really hard slap in the face,' but that he had been 'imprisoned by the text' of the Gospel and obliged to accept the Real Presence. This is one of the most touching proofs of the conflict within this extraordinary man.

The sacramental dispute thus set all the different reformers one against the other. From 1524 until 1527 a minor pen-and-ink war took place between them, in which the blows administered took the shape of lampoons and treaties. Oeclampadius criticized Luther's theses, and the latter made reply with his usual vigour. But as political events tended increasingly to split Germany into two opposing camps, the secular leaders, as well as some of the religious leaders, such as Bucer, struggled to come to some understanding. So on 1st October 1529 Philip of Hesse managed to persuade Luther and Melanchthon on the one hand, and Zwingli and Oeclampadius on the other, to come to the castle of *Marburg* and discuss their theses amongst themselves in a fraternal spirit. Some idea of the fraternity which actually reigned at this pious colloquy can be obtained from the fact that when Zwingli held out his hand to Luther at the moment of parting the latter declined it with the comment 'Your spirit is not ours!' However, except on the fundamental issue, agreement was reached on a large number of points. All had subscribed to one extremely vague formula: 'The Eucharist is the Sacrament of the actual Body and the actual Blood of Jesus Christ, and it is the bounden duty of every Christian to participate in it'— which really meant very little. But on the question of the Real Presence disagreement remained serious and complete. At the Diet of Augsburg, in the following year, the non-Lutheran Protestants refused to be associated with the famous 'Confession,' and sent the emperor a separate declaration, the *Tetrapolitan*, formulated by the four cities of Strasbourg, Constance, Lendau and Memmingen. Protestantism had split asunder.

Thus by 1530, when Luther could consider the object of his struggle attained (in so far as he had ever really had one), he saw his doctrine threatened by deviations of the worst kind. His mixed feelings of despair and fury were betrayed by many of the phrases which slipped from his pen or his lips. 'It would be better to announce eternal damnation than salvation after the style of Zwingli or Oeclampadius.' He regarded his adversaries as raving madmen and slaves of Satan, and considered them even greater enemies of Christ than the Pope himself. When he heard of Zwingli's death on the field of battle, he remarked by way of a spoken epitaph that he had 'met an assassin's end.' And when Oeclampadius followed the reformer of Zürich into the grave, the terrifying prophet of Wittenberg concluded that 'the devil's blows have killed him.' Melanchthon, who was wiser, murmured: 'I am extremely afflicted by the universal trouble of the Church. Had Christ not promised to be with us until the end of the world, I should fear lest religion be totally destroyed by these dissensions.' And Calvin, the more shrewd politician, was to write: 'It is of great importance that no suspicion of the divisions between us be passed on to future generations; for it is ridiculous beyond measure that, having broken with everyone, we should from the very beginning of our own reform agree so little among ourselves.'[1] But this wise and prudent language found scarcely an echo.

Luther, of course, was impervious to such arguments. He pursued his own course, like a man chasing after a dream: 'I have the Pope in mind,' he said; 'I am on the heels of the Sacramentaries and the Anabaptists; but I shall march alone among them all; I shall challenge them to fight; and I shall trample them all underfoot.'

MELANCHTHON AT WORK

Crises, contradictions, divergences of view, opposition—nothing seemed able to halt the progress of Lutheranism in Germany. Elsewhere, beyond the boundaries of the Germanic world, the pace of the Reformation slackened a good deal from 1535 onwards. Within its native framework, however, the doctrine of Wittenberg continued to expand. Princes, bishops and abbots all embraced the new religion, and had it preached in their territories, usually for the economic reasons observed earlier in the present chapter. The play of politics encouraged this trend. When Duke Ulrich of Württemberg, who had been stripped of his domains by Ferdinand of Austria on account of his maladministration, had them returned to him by the Landgrave Philip of Hesse, a notorious Protestant, he hastily brought them over to the Reformed faith. Other rulers, without themselves adhering to the Reformation, allowed the preaching of its doctrines in their territories. Such, for example, was the Prince-Abbot of Fulda; and it is even known that some bishops actually sold to their flocks the right of adhering to the new faith.

Moreover every social class found various advantages in leaving the Catholic Church. Rulers, whether laymen or clerics, obtained substantial material benefits thereby; the lower clergy obtained a better share of ecclesiastical revenues; clerics of all degrees were freed from

---

[1] This is no doubt why Strohl writes of the arguments between the different Protestant factions: 'The heat of their controversies is primarily attributable to their intense desire to serve the truth. They mostly endeavoured to help one another quite amicably.'

M

their obligations; and in most cases (not, for instance, in Anglican England) the people profited from the abolition of tithes. In a much deeper sense, in so far as it marked a return to primitive religious conceptions, Lutheranism corresponded to a reaction of the ancient nationalist and tribal Germanic mentality against Romano-Christian universalism. Religion was integrated into the national community, thus flattering national pride. By sweeping aside the idea of the equality of men, which was professed by all Catholics and which was soon to be put forward by the Calvinists also, Lutheranism fused with the primitive solidarity of the least advanced of the Germanic peoples. In consequence the only Catholic bastions which resisted it successfully were the two areas where civilization was most advanced: Bavaria and the Rhineland.[1]

Moreover the Catholic Church herself, the main adversary of Lutheranism, seemed to be making only feeble efforts to halt its progress. She certainly possessed her share of polemists, theologians or humanists, who did all in their power to refute the heresy; and the writings of Cochloeus, Emser, Johann Eck, Nausea and Dietenberger were widely circulated. Her adherents also included a number of loyal princes, typified by George of Saxony; and this is the reason why considerable areas of Germany remained subject to her obedience. But she lacked determined war leaders and capable battle formations, nor did any such appear until the second half of the sixteenth century. The wretched Clement VII was no fit man to wage this struggle: he has been called 'the most unhappy of popes.' Held fast in the toils of inescapable political complexities, he had seen Rome laid waste by German *Reiter* echoing the call 'Long live our Pope Martin Luther!' Nor, by and large, were the Catholic clergy, ill disciplined and ignorant, a match for the ministers preaching the new doctrine. All this was to change after 1550, when the initial measures of the Catholic Reformation began to take effect, and a series of vigorous pontiffs succeeded one another on the papal throne just as the impetus of Lutheranism was failing and its founder's contempt for intellectual studies was bearing fruit in the lowered standards of its pastors. Meanwhile the reverse was true, and the movement emanating from Wittenberg went from strength to strength.

From this point of view, then, the last fifteen years of Luther's life were happy ones. He saw his doctrine spreading and, in a sense, taking root in the soil of the Germany that he loved so dearly. But the achievement itself raised several new problems. All successful movements require organization, discipline and an administrative staff. It is rare

[1] These remarks have been developed by Jacques Pirenne in *Les Grande Courants de l'histoire universelle*, vol. ii. They convey an excellent understanding of Lutheranism's connections with Pan Germanism and even with National Socialism.

for a spiritual initiator also to possess the more humble but necessary gifts of organization and administration, and in many instances he feels himself torn between these contradictory demands. This had been so in the case of St Francis of Assisi. Luther was a prisoner of himself, a man wholly preoccupied with his own problems and fundamentally uninterested in temporal success. He was quite incapable of imposing his own strong mark on a vigorously organized Church, as Calvin managed to do at Geneva soon afterwards. He was obliged, therefore, to have at his side a man who could perform this essential task. That man was *Melanchthon.*

Melanchthon was one of Luther's most faithful followers, one of those who had believed in him from the very beginning. *Philip Schwarzerd* (1497–1560), Reuchlin's great-nephew, was originally a humanist— hence the Greek rendering of his name—and at the bottom of his heart he remained one all his life. In his youth he had taught first at Tübingen, then at Wittenberg University. When scarcely twenty years of age he had discovered in Luther's teaching the answers to questions just as grave as those which the Augustinian himself had had to solve, although in Melanchthon's case the questions had been less violently formulated. Luther's vehement language had seemed to this Greek-bound scholar genuinely prophetic. He was a good-hearted fellow, 'moderate and naturally sincere,' as Bossuet said, meditative and of the highest principles. Though he followed the path of heresy, he did so out of deep conviction and not without many a detour and agonizing spiritual debate.[1]

For this *alter ego*, this man who discreetly played St Paul to the new messiah, strayed rapidly and very far from the ideas of his master. At first he was dominated by Luther, and gave himself body and soul to the new doctrine. In 1521 (at the age of twenty-four) he published *Loci communes rerum theologicarum,* a treatise expounding the theology of the new faith, and his leader had thereupon decided that the work should become part of the Protestant Canon. Very soon, however, the author of this first official doctrinal summary freed himself from external influences. The crisis of 1525, the Peasants' War, showed him the danger of allowing so many souls, who were now cut adrift from all the old disciplines, to run loose in unfamiliar surroundings, without offering them anything to which they might cling. Thus even in his

[1] One of the most curious features of Melanchthon's character, which proves how very different these Renaissance humanists were from their modern counterparts, was his morbid tendency to superstition. For example, at the time of the Diet of Augsburg he wrote that several prodigious portents seemed to favour the success of Lutheranism: the bursting of the Tiber's banks, the prolonged labour of a mule, the birth of a two-headed calf were all signs which suggested Rome's ruin. By contrast, when his daughter fell ill, Melanchthon was filled with terror by the unfavourable aspect of Mars. He never did anything without consulting astrologers.

concept of practical action Melanchthon had moved far away from Luther. But it was not only Luther's theology of the Church which he called in question; terrified by the growing moral disorder, he had reacted against the doctrine of *justification by faith*, which, to over-simple minds, appeared to authorize every sort of licence. In a new edition of the *Loci communes* (1535) Melanchthon corrected his position in this respect and gave human co-operation a share in the work of salvation, whereas Luther had proclaimed that 'God saves anyone who wishes to be saved.' [1] Consequently Melanchthon was infinitely nearer the Catholic Church than his master on a number of essential points. Indeed his peace-loving nature felt no desire to be separated from her, and as the author of the *Confession of Augsburg* he had done his utmost to discover formulas which seemed acceptable to both sides. 'Better that the earth should open beneath my feet,' he said, 'than I should find myself divorced from the understanding of the Church where Christ Jesus reigns.' Or again: 'I submit myself to the Catholic Church.' It is true, of course, that he qualified this latter assertion with the words: 'I mean to men of goodwill and to the learned'—which enabled him to recognize only the authority of those who suited him. But he was undoubtedly pained by the frightful gash inflicted by the Reformation upon the Mystical Body of Christ.

Such, paradoxically, was the man to whom Luther entrusted all practical responsibility in the movement he had inaugurated. The older man was not ignorant of the differences which existed between him and Melanchthon, and which were to increase still further after his death, converting Lutheranism into veritable 'Melanchthonism.' On the contrary, he was well aware of them. He was no doubt partly influenced by deep affection for this shrewd, subtle man whose out-standing spiritual and mental qualities he so greatly admired; but his main reason for making the decision was most probably his feeling that Melanchthon's talents fully complemented his own. 'I am the rough wood-cutter who has to clear the paths,' he said. 'Clever Master Philip makes progress gently and serenely; he cultivates and sows, he plants and waters most felicitously.'

Ever since the great peasant crisis Lutheranism had been the prisoner of a serious contradiction. On the one hand its fundamental principle, which defined faith as a completely personal creation—the blossoming of a spiritual experience in the realm of each man's con-science—obliged it to leave the religious individuality of every believer to expand freely, without any restriction from hierarchical ranks or formal discipline. On the other hand Luther had been ultimately compelled by the necessity of erecting a barrier against anarchy to accept the concentration of power in the hands of

---

[1] This doctrine is known in theology as 'Synergism.'

secular rulers; moreover he had justified his doctrine by proclaiming the divine origin of all authority. For him this contradiction was no great embarrassment; his essentially dialectical genius was easily adapted to such illogicalities in so many fields. But to make a great new religious movement survive and expand less equivocal formulas had to be found. The history of Lutheranism is one continuous effort to reconcile the sensitive spiritual anarchism of its founder with the need for order and organization which its development made essential.

Melanchthon, who was used to handling ideas, understood the dilemma completely: either growth must be accompanied by organization, or the spiritual anarchism left to turn into political and social anarchy. 'Master Philip,' whom Luther gently reproached for being so much concerned with the fate of empires and the problems of politics, was far more clear-sighted than he was. Melanchthon therefore concentrated upon the notion of the Church. In *Loci communes* (1535 edition), he stated quite categorically that the invisible Church was not the only one—in 1543 he actually referred to it as the 'Platonic Idea'!—and that the visible Church must also be taken into account. An entire chapter of the book was devoted to the *politica ecclesiastica*,[1] which he pronounced to be 'worthy of our love and respect,' and in which the ministry ordained by God is exercised by men chosen by their fellow men. Thus, side by side with the unorganized Church of the saints, he recognized an organized society whose adherents might be far removed from sanctity; and the 'signs' of the existence of the invisible Church became the criteria of the visible. This 'congregation of men who profess the Holy Gospel and use the sacraments correctly' surely had many theoretical affinities with the much-criticized visible Catholic Church. After all, it was necessary for Christians to unite together in order to obtain salvation, and its leaders and orders were expected to be obeyed!

Further, in order to preserve the integrity of Lutheran doctrine and enable it to permeate men's minds, the 'preceptor of Germany,' which Melanchthon had become, eventually admitted that it was not possible to entrust its interpretation to the unfettered disposition of each individual believer. Pastors were to be instructed in sound doctrine, so that they might subsequently impart their knowledge to the faithful 'as to a class of pupils.' And the faithful were to receive this teaching with respect and submit to its precepts.

During the last fifteen years of Luther's life his movement was increasingly based on these new principles, although Melanchthon did not formulate them completely until six years after the founder's death. This organization dealt with four principal points.

[1] From 1543 onwards he favoured the use of the word *coetus*, meaning 'class,' instead of *politica*, meaning 'society.'

The authority of secular rulers in Church matters was erected into a formal system. In default of bishops, whom Melanchthon would have liked to retain, the princes were entrusted with the virtual control of religious affairs in their states; the *visitors*, who were charged with the task of exerting this control, and for whom Melanchthon had drafted detailed instructions, were for all practical purposes their delegates. This system, which was first perfected in Saxony, was gradually established throughout Lutheran Germany, so much so that the Peace of Augsburg in 1555 afforded it official recognition.

Parochial organization varied according to whether rural or urban areas were involved. The first of these, the 'Haufen,' showed small interest in making any effort to establish regular assemblies, and remained an inert mass in serious need of evangelization. Rural parishes therefore were organized in accordance with hierarchic tradition, being grouped around a pastor who was entrusted with the cure of souls and the maintenance of discipline; even in such areas as Hesse, where it seemed possible to associate the faithful in this kind of organization, the rulers opposed any such action. In the towns, on the other hand, parishes were constituted in a much more democratic fashion. Leading citizens joined in the work of reformation and administration by means of elected elders; at least this was the theory, for there was grave danger that the secular authority would interfere in every field, including the spiritual.[1]

The third important aspect of Lutheran organization was the creation of the *Consistory*. This occurred first in Saxony, in 1542, then in most other Lutheran states. Here was a permanent body composed of ecclesiastics and laymen nominated by the ruler, and entrusted with the general control of the reformed communities. It had to choose or confirm pastors, settle disputes between the faithful and their clergy and supervise the purity of the faith. 'Superintendents' served as intermediaries between the Consistory and the local clergy. Later on, after Luther's death, the Consistory arrogated to itself even the right of settling matters of doctrine, like a minor council.

Finally, a fourth fundamental was the institution of an official dogma, whose teaching was made obligatory. Luther, who had so often said that the Word must remain free to act as it might on individual souls, allowed Melanchthon to establish a university syllabus

---

[1] Bucer went much farther at Strasbourg. He aimed to make the Church educate the city; in the sense that it was a religious structure, the parish controlled the secular municipal community. Bucer encountered the opposition of the magistrate, and was finally expelled from Strasbourg, in 1548, because he refused to accept the Interim of Augsburg. He then sought refuge in England, where he played a fairly important part in that country's religious evolution. But his ideas were resumed by Calvin, who first of all applied them in his French parish at Strasbourg itself, in a relatively independent way, but practised them most whole-heartedly in Geneva in the dictatorial fashion which is described in the next chapter of this book.

dealing with dogmatic instruction. No theological teaching was permitted outside its boundaries. In practice this meant the imposition of
a new canon and a new orthodoxy. Anything not included in its
scope, whether Protestant or not, deviated from the official 'Credo.'

Cardinal Baudrillart has rightly observed that Lutheranism was able
to establish itself and become an enduring force 'by imitating Rome,
against which it had rebelled, in other words, by instituting regular and
sovereign Churches, inspiring set formulas of faith, and, through
education and preaching, transmitting to its children ready-made
doctrines which were imposed from above in exactly the same way as
Catholic doctrine.' It is not easy to assess how far Luther himself
agreed with this evolution. Henry Strohl considers that he remained
permanently in disagreement on the fundamental issue, 'that he
recognized as the Church only the invisible Church, of which the
Word, God's ineffable gift, recruits the members.' Although on
several occasions he approved measures which tended to emphasize the
existence of a visible Church (e.g. in 1539, when he publicly rejoiced
at the new organization of parishes), on others he protested against the
secular authorities' excessive interference and their claim to legislate in
ecclesiastical affairs. It seems that in this case, as in so many others, the
law of contradiction, which was so powerful a factor in Luther's
character, was in full operation. In 1541, in his treatise *Wider Hans
Worst*, Luther exalted the Church as an institution—'our pure, well-
organized Church'—but a few pages later he wrote that 'the Church
is something so hidden that no one can see it. . . .'

Perhaps this is one of the most heartrending aspects of Martin
Luther's tragedy, if not the most striking. In order to live and expand,
his creation was obliged to grow away from him and his fundamental
aspirations, even to the point of coming into actual conflict with them.

LUTHERANISM BECOMES A POLITICAL FORCE

The evolution of Lutheranism into a visible Church possessing a
formal doctrine and a concrete organization had its counterpart on the
purely political plane, due to the pressure of national and international
events. When brought into conflict with the emperor, the Protestant
princes of Germany passed from a state of mere religious agreement
into a veritable political and military alliance.

By 1530 Charles V was becoming increasingly aware of his universal
vocation as the temporal head of Christendom, but he did not consider
that the Reformation should be brutally repressed. Being a sincerely
religious man he realized that its progress had been facilitated by
several fundamental deficiences in the Catholic Church herself. He
believed in a policy which owed its inspiration to the ideas of Erasmus,

a policy which aimed at correcting abuses and procuring a dogmatic reconciliation between the different confessions. This was why he had permitted Lutherans and Sacramentaries to express their respective doctrines before the Diet of Augsburg. In 1540 and 1541 he even encouraged the conferences of Haguenau, Worms and Ratisbon. But though inclined towards religious conciliation—an inclination rendered even more pronounced by the general difficulties of his situation —he could not allow Lutheranism to become a political faction, which was what it in fact now was.

In November 1530 the Diet of Augsburg had ended in a rupture between the two sides. An imperial ordinance had restored the Edict of Worms in all its vigour; episcopal authority was to be re-established with all its former rights, heretical books suppressed and ecclesiastical possessions handed back to their rightful owners. It is open to doubt whether Charles V really wished to see these measures applied; they were probably intended as nothing more than a declaration of principle. Alarmed, however, by the threat of finding themselves deprived once more of their one-time ecclesiastical domains, the Lutheran rulers responded by setting up a political organization known as the *Schmalkaldic League* (1531). Luther proclaimed that rebellion against a master as unjust as the Hapsburg emperor was perfectly right and proper. At a meeting near Gotha, called by Philip of Hesse and John of Saxony, the leading Lutheran nobles and cities decided to combine in order to protect any Protestant state which might be attacked by the emperor: 'air and space' would be given him. Thus a Protestant, anti-imperialist Germany sprang into being, which negotiated quite unscrupulously with all the enemies of Charles V. Soon all the Lutheran states had joined it, including even Denmark.

Conflict, however, did not break out immediately. Though encouraged by Francis I, who sent his brilliant ambassador Guillaume du Bellay, and by Henry VIII of England, who afforded it some financial aid, the league took no action at all. Had it dared to do so it would have crushed the emperor; but it hung back afraid, no doubt restrained by long-standing respect for the imperial institution, and probably impressed by the severe defeat sustained by Zwingli's Protestants at Kappel. For his part Charles V had no desire to rush things: the Turkish danger was just then causing him far more anxiety. Turkish corsairs were sweeping the Mediterranean, halting traffic even in the Straits of Messina, while their land forces were massing on the Hungarian frontiers. Ferdinand of Austria appealed for help. Philip of Hesse answered by demanding the suspension of the Augsburg clauses, and this he obtained in the *Peace of Nuremberg* (1532). 'The Landgrave,' wrote one enthusiastic supporter, 'has done more for Protestantism than a hundred of Luther's books.'

For twelve years Germany was the scene of a prodigiously complex political game, in which all the elements of European politics were deeply involved. The Schmalkaldic League had become a major pawn in the political chess-board. Charles V, combining holy war with his ultimate material object of Mediterranean hegemony, launched a massive attack against Tunis, liberating twenty thousand Christian slaves. Disturbed to see his traditional adversary thus completing the encirclement of France, Francis I at once hastened to conclude an astonishing alliance with Solyman II. At the same time the king offered his services as mediator in order to bring about religious reconciliation in Germany without imperial intervention; but when this gesture ended in nothing save fruitless discussions, he entered into an even closer alliance with the Protestant rulers.[1] In this way everything tended to strengthen the power of the league, while Luther actually drafted the *Articles of Schmalkald*, in readiness for a German Protestant council which Philip of Hesse was talking of convening. This was a document in which his Romanophobia was given free rein.

The old duel between Francis I and Charles V had broken out again at a time when (1526) international conditions were causing the emperor a great deal of anxiety. The Most Christian King signed a fresh offensive and defensive alliance with the Sultan, which was completed by a commercial treaty, the whole being known as the *Capitulations*. Historians are in the habit of acclaiming this alliance as an extremely skilful move on the part of France. It certainly re-established the balance of power in the Mediterranean, but from the Christian point of view there can be no doubt whatsoever of its scandalous character. It is true that scandal was everywhere in this highly confused epoch. The Catholic Christianity of the Bavarian Wittelsbachs, like the Lutheran Christianity of Schmalkald or the brand of religion practised by Henry VIII of England, latest of the schismatics, were all at one in regarding the Moslem as a most valuable ally against the ambitions of the Hapsburg. Luther declared that the Turks were 'Gog and Magog,' the righteous emanations of divine wrath; and the Pope himself, Paul III, who looked upon Charles V with the deepest distrust, was the friend of Francis I. This was a strange coalition. In taking their stand upon it, however, the Protestant rulers of Germany continued to see their power increase.

A surprise attack by the imperialists on Marseilles (1538) ended in disaster. A double offensive against the Sublime Porte terminated in twofold defeat: Ferdinand was overwhelmed before Budapest, and Charles V's fleet was vanquished before Algiers. Francis I invaded the

---

[1] This did not prevent him from repressing Protestant agitation in France at the same time and in the most sanguinary fashion (for the Placard Affair of October 1534 see Chapter VI, p. 380). 'He rides in two saddles,' commented Bucer.

* M

duchy of Milan, while the Turks threatened the Spanish coasts. The very foundations of the Empire trembled. Had Henry VIII listened to the advice of Thomas Cromwell, and thrown himself whole-heartedly into the fight, Charles V would have been crushed. He made haste to arrange a peace with the German Protestants which was at least provisional; the *Interim of Ratisbon* (1541) theoretically maintained the *status quo*, but one informal clause gave Lutheran rulers authority to secularize any Church possessions situated in their territories.

From now on the Schmalkaldic League regarded itself as mistress of Germany. Fighting broke out afresh between Francis I and Charles V; but the latter was henceforth supported by Henry VIII, because of Henry's desire to restore the balance of power. This was a confused war, in which the French were victorious at Cerisola, but saw the imperial advance guards push forward as far as Meaux, while the English seized Boulogne. Meanwhile the members of the league completely disregarded the stipulations of Ratisbon. They forcibly imposed Protestantism on many dioceses, invaded the duchy of Brunswick-Wolfenbuttel while Duke Henry was dispatching his troops against the Turks, snapped their fingers at the emperor's representatives at the Diets of Spires and Nuremberg, and converted the Count Palatine Henry von Neuberg to their cause. In 1544 Hermann von Wied, Archbishop of Cologne, who had become friendly with Bucer, seemed on the point of going over to Protestantism. This would have given the members of the Reformed faith a majority of the Electoral College of the Empire.

Could this situation continue? Would Charles V do nothing to prevent the whole of Germany becoming Protestant? 'He has one rather uncommendable characteristic,' his confessor remarked to a Venetian ambassador. 'He remembers offences and does not easily forget them.' In 1544 Charles V signed the peace of Crépy-en-Laonnais, which temporarily freed him from the French threat. Finally, in 1545, Paul III decided that the famous Council which had been talked of for so long should meet at Trent; but this Council was going to open under the influence of the intransigent faction in the Curia, a faction of which Charles V disapproved. So confining his efforts to Germany, and reassembling all his forces—in particular the celebrated Spanish 'Infanteria'—he planned to put paid to the Protestant princes and compel them into submission. In January 1546 yet another conference was held at Ratisbon, to try—or appear to try—to reconcile the different religious theses. The arrogant League of Princes realized that it would soon have to face the whole might of the emperor, and shortly before Luther's death war seemed inevitable.

New Difficulties and New Tragedies

Fear of seeing Germany shortly delivered to fire and slaughter was not Luther's only anxiety at this time. Difficulties and even tragedies came thick and fast during the second half of his public life.

The most serious of these occurred between 1531 and 1535. It consisted of a further episode in the Anabaptist affair. Despite the imperial edict which ordered that any member of the sect 'no matter what their sex or age, be conducted from life to death, either by the sword or by the stake, or by any other suitable method, without need of previous inquisitorial trial and sentence,' its members had continued to increase. The years 1532-4 had been marked by a grave economic crisis in Germany, and a sudden sharp rise in the cost of living. Such conditions were extremely favourable to a religious propaganda which made so much of social justice. After his expulsion from Strasbourg, Melchior Hoffman, Münzer's successor, had sown his message throughout the northern confines of the Empire—in Sweden, Denmark and especially Holland—where the Messianic and apocalyptic faith had acquired the shape of a formidable and revolutionary Adventism, under the influence of a Haarlem baker named *Jan Mathuys*. But the most terrible tragedy of all took place at *Münster*, in Westphalia.

In this opulent town on the banks of the Aa, sheltering safely behind a city wall constructed in the shape of a merchant vessel, the religious crisis began with a Lutheran attack, led by Bernard Rothmann, one of Melanchthon's disciples, against a disreputable bishop named Franz von Waldeck and his clergy who were little better than himself. The usual kind of disorders occurred; churches were looted and statues broken. Anabaptism had been brought to the town by Knitterdolinck, a cloth merchant, a sanguinary demagogue who had encountered Melchior Hoffman in Sweden and fallen beneath his spell. Very soon shoals of miserable, psalm-singing Anabaptists descended upon Münster, some arriving from Alsace, others from Holland. The Dutch contingent was particularly strong; for a young friend of Jan Mathuys, *Jan Bockelsoon* (usually known as *John of Leyden*), whose mother was a Westphalian, had persuaded a number of Anabaptists that 'the new Zion where there will be neither rich nor poor, masters nor slaves,' was not to be Strasbourg, as Hoffman had prophesied, but Münster. Rothmann was converted to Anabaptism, and some weeks after John of Leyden's arrival there the city expelled its bishop and established itself as a kind of Anabaptist Rome, the capital of the 'saints.'

They were strange saints indeed! For the space of some eighteen months Münster was the scene of one of the most bizarre episodes ever recorded in history, an episode that, was simultaneously farcical and horrible. Calling itself 'Mount Zion' or even 'the Jerusalem of the new Israelites,' the town turned itself into a communist republic, where all wealth and property had to be shared in common, where the principles of Holy Scripture were claimed to be literally applied, and where a disordered prophetism inflamed the fanaticism of the masses. There has scarcely ever been a more arresting example of collective aberration. After Mathuys's death young John of Leyden became leader of the sect, exercising absolute authority, although he was only twenty-five years old. He forthwith proclaimed himself 'King of Zion,' the living Christ, the returned Messiah. Needless to say he surrounded himself with twelve apostles. The reign of God in the house of fools! But it was also some kind of foretaste and caricature of that politico-religious dictatorship which Calvin was to establish in Geneva a year after the fall of Münster. The height of this pious indecency was reached when John of Leyden, noticing that his kingdom was short of males, and determined to assure posterity of a plentiful supply of new Israelites, forbade any woman to remain a virgin, and made polygamy compulsory. He himself took sixteen wives, and his lusty example was quickly followed.

The modern observer contemplates with amazement that such insanity should have been carried to these lengths. At Amsterdam, under the leadership of the tailor Van Geelen, as well as in Friesland, an Anabaptism, mingled with nudist Adamism, had gained much ground. Lübeck, controlled by Wullenweber, had shown itself more restrained, but had also become addicted to the Second Baptism. Social unrest among the common people was so great that at the beginning of 1535 there were genuine fears that the whole of Germany might be set ablaze. The reaction came, implacable as ever. The princes came to the aid of Bishop von Waldeck, who was besieging his city. Münster held out in agony for some months, completely blockaded by an unbreakable line of fortifications. Her citizens starved, and there were many frightful scenes of cannibalism and coprophagy. The indomitable John of Leyden maintained discipline to the bitter end, himself beheading his favourite wife because she was guilty of defeatism. Finally 'Mount Zion' was captured, thanks to a traitor. John of Leyden and two of his associates were done to death in a most atrocious fashion, being slowly torn to pieces with red-hot tongs. Their bodies were then placed in iron cages, and hoisted to the top of the cathedral belfry, where they remained for more than three hundred years. Bloody repression had crushed the 'saints' wherever they had been found.

Luther had followed the whole of this terrible affair with close attention. He did not regard John of Leyden as a serious adversary, considering him far less important than Münzer. But he was disturbed by the moral, social and religious state of which this crisis was the symptom. 'If a mere schoolboy devil could do such things as this, what can the real devil do? He after all is a good theologian!' He also very rightly asked himself whether the Catholics would not hold him responsible for this incident: had he not sown the wind from which this stormy whirlwind had arisen? Indeed Francis I used this very argument to justify his persecution of their French co-religionists to his allies, the Princes of Schmalkald. It was easy to claim that all his Protestants were Anabaptists. The tragedy of Münster caused the originator of religious rebellion to suffer even more cruelly than the Peasants' War had done.

Shortly after this there occurred the less tragic and even rather comical affair of the *Bigamy of Philip of Hesse*, or, as it was known at the time, his 'Turkish marriage.' Under pretext that his lawful wife filled him with repulsion, that in any case his constant comings and goings in the service of the cause often kept him away from her, and that his temperament did not suffer sexual abstinence, the celebrated landgrave had asked the Protestant leaders whether, like Abraham, Jacob, David and Solomon, he might be permitted to marry another woman. In truth there is something rather touching about this conscientious scruple; just at this time Henry VIII of England was having nothing like so much difficulty in ridding himself of successive wives; whilst Francis I and Charles V, Catholics though they were, treated the sixth and ninth commandments with the most scandalous indifference. These facts, however, did not relieve the pious reformers of their acute embarrassment in face of the applicant's request for a licence to commit bigamy. After meditating long and hard on this painful case they composed a reply [1] signed by their eight principal members. While rejecting the principle of polygamy, the heritage of the Old Testament but condemned by the New, the reformers authorized the prince to marry the object of his desires 'for the salvation of his body and his soul, and likewise for the glory of God.' One condition was attached, however: 'let him do it secretly!' The marriage was celebrated without fuss by the chaplain to the court of Hesse, but the secret was ill kept. Several strict Protestants were aghast; Joachim of Brandenburg and John of Saxony refused to meet the bigamist again (which severely prejudiced the Schmalkaldic League). Angered beyond measure by the criticisms of those who reproached him for his excessive indulgence, Luther was impelled to write: 'Falsehood is truth when it is used against the fury of the devil for the benefit of one's neighbour.' Melanchthon, however, was unconvinced by this argument, and spoke some bitter words: 'I notice that you righteous folk very

---

[1] Bossuet gives the text of it in the Appendix to his *L'Histoire des variations*.

readily take the woman who pleases you. Why won't you let us poor sinners do the same?'

The incident of the Turkish marriage, in fact, was only one symptom, among many others, of a moral crisis which the whole of Lutheranism was undergoing, and whose gravity was accurately assessed by its founder. In spreading among the masses his Reformation had certainly not managed to accomplish that inner transformation which he had proposed as its ultimate aim. In 1525 he had made this defeatist observation: 'There is not one of our evangelists who is not worse today than he was yesterday.' Year by year Luther seemed to see the situation growing blacker. 'Our peasants no longer fear either hell or Purgatory. Consequently they are proud, coarse, insolent and lustful. "We have faith," they say, and that is quite enough.' He even went so far as to declare: 'Just imagine a universal law imposing the exact opposite of the Ten Commandments, and you will understand exactly what appears to govern the way of the world.' These were not simply the paradoxes and exaggerations of a man carried away by fury. Amsdorf too recognized that 'Germany seems to be sunk deep in gluttony, drunkenness, avarice and lechery, and the faithful no longer take any real notice of the Gospel.' And the moderate Melanchthon made some equally painful observations: 'Just look at this evangelical society; see how many adulterers, drunkards and gamblers it contains, see how many vicious and ignoble folk there are! Take a peep into our homes. Are they any more chaste than those you regard as pagan? You know quite well the sort of tales I could tell if I wished.' And he concluded in these melancholy terms: 'All the waters of the Elbe would not suffice to weep for the misfortune that has stricken the Reformation.'

Luther felt himself more and more responsible for this moral decadence. He could ponder bitterly over the cruel barbs which his enemy Erasmus had let fly at him—the warning that from his theses there would emerge 'an impudent, anarchical, insolent race whose responsibility would be his.' Those to whom he preached morality did not scruple to fling his own words back in his face, interpreted to suit themselves: 'Have you not taught us that man is incapable of doing good and of justifying himself before God?' Consequently his wrath grew ever greater. 'Long live invincible concupiscence!' he jeered, when someone told him of fresh scandals. What did he think of German women? 'Profligate sows.' And of students? 'Out of two thousand there are scarcely two or three who are worth anything at all.' What of the peasants and the merchants? 'A pack of drunkards, addicted to every sort of vice.' And Wittenberg, that Tabor of divine illumination, was 'a Sodom and Gomorrah,' worthy of all the punishments God might devise.

Doctrinal anarchy was as serious as moral anarchy. The deviations against which Luther had battled in days gone by had not disappeared. The death of 'that assassin' Zwingli had not terminated the expansion of Zwinglianism, and in 1544 Luther fulminated against one of its theological pamphlets, the *Short Confession on the Blessed Sacrament*. With Agricola the situation was even worse: 'this lost soul, this perfidious creature,' had now become the intimate of Joachim of Brandenburg. He flouted Luther and mocked him openly in his treatise *Against the Antinomists*, so that when his former friend returned to Wittenberg the vindictive reformer refused to shake hands with him. This was not all. Karg, one of Luther's former colleagues at Wittenberg, began to teach a brand of Arianism mingled with Docetism on the subject of the nature of Christ. He alleged that, in so far as He was a man, Our Lord was subject to the Law and that He would have been able to sin; and also that the Passion was not imputable to men. Luther was obliged to fight him. *Osiander*, one of his oldest friends, who was also horrified by the moral crisis he saw around him, had conceived a theology of justification which was radically different from Luther's and which came fairly close to that of Catholicism; he was only awaiting the chance to profess it publicly as soon as 'the Pope of Wittenberg,' as Luther was currently known, disappeared from the scene.

The anguish which seized the initiator of the Reformation as he contemplated this sorry spectacle is easy to understand. One day, when his beloved Philip Melanchthon came to see him at the 'Black Monastery' of Wittenberg, he let fall the following bitter prophecy: 'How many different masters will men be following in a hundred years' time? Confusion will then be at its height. No one will submit to government by anyone else's ideas or authority. Everyone will be trying to make himself his own Rabbi. Look what Osiander and Agricola are like even now. . . . What enormous scandals are in the making!' And he even went so far as to wish that a council might be convened to parry this anarchy, but he immediately added angrily: 'The Papists will evade it; they are so scared of the light.'

At the end even the attitude of his beloved Melanchthon came to torment him. Their views were diverging further and further apart in the doctrinal field. The wise Master Philip was too prudent to rush things: once his leader was dead he would reveal the whole of his philosophy, even going so far as to describe Luther's theses as 'Manichaean.' But Luther was under no illusion about their apparent agreement. The older man blamed the disciple much more for his inclination to try to come to an understanding with everyone, his impenitent wish to gamble on the most unlikely odds. Melanchthon, with his conciliatory views, never abandoned hope of reaching agreement with other

Protestants, and even with the Catholics. At the conferences of Haguenau, Worms and Ratisbon, in 1540–1, he got on far too well with Bucer and with the young French pastor, *John Calvin*, whose blinding intellect henceforth exerted an important influence upon him. Even with the friendly legates chosen by the Pope, Melanchthon was sorely tempted to begin a *rapprochement*; and his manifesto, *The Reformation of Wittenberg*, was couched in terms so prudent that they could well be considered ambiguous. These dangerous weaknesses must be nipped in the bud! Some months before his death, a sick, exhausted man, Luther sat down to write the most terrible of all his pamphlets, *Against the Papacy founded in Rome by the Devil*, which was directed as much against his own over-accommodating supporters as against his arch-enemy. He even chose the illustrations which were to add zest to his argument: the Pope being dragged by the devil into the gaping jaws of hell, the Pope riding a sow, the Pope in the form of a donkey. Death did not permit the heresiarch to finish this book; it is scarcely to his credit that he ever started it.

THE DEATH OF A PROPHET

Luther's last years were sombre indeed. He suffered from the stone from 1538 onwards, and at times it caused him intolerable pain. He had become the man whom Cranach painted on his death-bed: corpulent, pasty-faced and bloated. His swollen features no longer recalled that gaunt young monk, who, thirty years before, with a gesture of desperate defiance, had hurled himself into a single-handed attack on the ancient bastion of the Church.

The bastion had not fallen. At the Council of Trent, which was now just beginning, and which Luther could not find words strong enough to revile, Holy Church would carry out her own complete rejuvenation. Troops were lining up in her defence: the Society of Jesus had now been in action for nine years. And, when all was said and done, what was Luther himself? He who had dreamed of bringing the message of salvation to the whole of Christendom was merely the leader of one sect, and even there his authority was not unquestioned. He was plagued with doubts concerning the legitimacy of his mission: on what was it founded? Terrible outbursts sprang from his lips: 'If I wanted I could lead everyone back to his old errors, in just three sermons!' And he burst into a peal of atrocious laughter. He was filled with remorse for all the ruptures he had had to make, all the condemnations he had been forced to utter, and all this sound and fury which had been part and parcel of his whole life—the quarrel with Erasmus, the rejection of Karlstadt, the execution of Münzer ('It weighs on my conscience,' he said), the slaughter in Westphalia, the duel with

Zwingli. He had been quite sincere when he declared: 'Why has the Lord not accepted the offering of my earthly life, made with such a pure heart? Why has He held fast the hands of the wicked?' These words were spoken in 1525, when Luther seemed to be rising rapidly to heights of glory. And now that he was going to die he experienced a sensation felt by so many men who appear to have made a success of their lives. He saw a vehement, unsullied boy from the days of his youth considering him, in silence, and he knew he was condemned in his own eyes.

Luther had never been a mild man, and his character now became quite terrifying. This was not always so, for he had moments of ease and joy, when he still composed his hymns and looked with tenderness upon flowers, animals and children. But most of the time, wracked by disease and overwhelmed by work and worry, he gave way to an irascibility which spared no one, neither his wife, his friends nor his nearest and dearest. Melanchthon admitted that life with Luther seemed like 'an unbearable imprisonment,' and this beloved disciple had only one ambition—'to rest his weary head on Calvin's bosom.' The old man's fury had several targets: the Pope, 'that swine of Satan'; the priesthood, 'which imprints all priests with the sign of the Beast'; the Mass, which he regretted having celebrated for the space of fifteen years. 'I would have done better to have been a pimp!' and the masters of the universities—'those temples of Moloch'—in particular those of Louvain and Paris, at whom he hurled interminable abuse, regarding them as 'filthy swine, lecherous Epicurean pigs, cesspits bubbling with hell-fire.' For some obscure reason the Jews had become one of his *bêtes noires*: the last thing Luther ever wrote, which was published in 1546, invited the Turks to expel them from all their territories.

During the winter of 1545–6, although he was spent, exhausted and eventually seriously ill, Luther twice dragged himself to Mansfeld in order to settle a dispute between the two counts of that name, regarding their rights in the copper mines. Tribute should be paid to this splendid devotion.[1] In February he had to take the road home in cold, icy weather, but as he passed through Halle he preached a sermon sharply criticizing monks who refused to cast off their habits. By the time he reached his native soil at Eisleben he was feeling very weak and ill, and talked of his approaching end. During the night of the 17th–18th February he awoke his friend Jonas, who was sleeping in his room. He was in the throes of a sudden attack of either apoplexy or pulmonary congestion. The doctors who hurried to his side were powerless to help him. At three in the morning Luther gave up the ghost, having assured his disciples who questioned him that he persevered in his

---

[1] The following quotation does Luther credit: 'If I manage to reconcile my beloved lords I shall go to my grave quite happily.'

doctrine. His last words were this verse from St John's Gospel, which he repeated, lovingly and tenderly, three times: 'God so loved the world, that He gave up His only begotten Son, so that those who believe in Him may not perish, but have eternal life.' [1] On the wall near his bed, however, one of his doctors discovered the following inscription, scrawled by the dying man: '*Pestis eram vivus, moriens ero mors tua, papa.*' ('I was your plague while I lived; when I die I shall be your death, O Pope!') This was the heresiarch's final insult, his last gesture of supreme defiance.

The whole of Luther is contained in this twofold attribute, with his ardours, his faith, his contradictions and his ungovernable violence. His was a deep, demanding soul, to whom no Catholic can in charity deny fraternal pity; but his mind contained also something of the devil, which made his arrogant desire to trace his own path alone turn to rebellion of the worst kind. His turbulent, tormented life, so characteristic of the upheavals and anxieties of his age, provides two of the greatest and most moving themes of meditation: the drama of a conscience engaged in spiritual conflict, 'as brutal as the battles fought by men,' as the poet says; and the drama of a man of genius, who reaches the heights alone and is obliged by social pressures to permit the betrayal of his fundamental ideal. Luther certainly emerged battered, bruised and bleeding from the struggle with the Angel, but he failed to carry off real victory. He never obtained true peace of heart. And in the tragic battle which he fought during the whole of his life, almost everything at length slipped from his grasp. Like so many ambitious men, he was 'punished by success.' [2] What proof of immanent condemnation!

Luther's role in the history of the Church was in many respects considerable; it can almost be called providential. Blame for the hideous rent suffered by the Seamless Robe of Christ does not lie at his door alone. Many in the Catholic camp share some of the responsibility. Nevertheless it remains true to say that the greatest guilt was Luther's. He was the initiator, the leader, without whose action none of the events we can observe would have happened in quite the way they did. In making the Church so brutally and tragically aware of her problems, however, he also forced her to emerge at last from that muddy slough of complaisance and collusion which was bogging down the best of Christian spirituality. Without Martin Luther and the fear which he inspired Holy Church might never have undertaken that genuine reformation, effected within the bounds of her own loyalties

---

[1] The most absurd and odious rumours circulated concerning Luther's death. It was said that he had committed suicide out of remorse and despair. Others claimed that he had expired blaspheming. Father Grisar has warned Catholics against these degrading legends, which are completely without foundation.

[2] This expression was used by Georges Sand in reference to Talleyrand.

and disciplines—a reformation whose need was recognized by so many, but which so few dared attempt. Dialectically, to a large extent, the Church of the Council of Trent sprang from the Church of Wittenberg and the Confession of Augsburg—Martin Luther, you who read St Paul so assiduously, did you ever take to heart the terrible meaning of the Apostle's remark to the Christians of Corinth: '*Oportet haereses esse*'? [1]

[1] 'Parties [i.e. heretics] there must be among you, so that those who are of true metal may be distinguished from the rest.' (1 Cor. xi. 19.)

CHAPTER VI

THE SUCCESS OF JOHN CALVIN

WILL PROTESTANTISM CONQUER THE WHOLE OF FRANCE?

THE JOLT given by Luther had shaken the whole of Western Europe. As the first quarter of the sixteenth century drew to its close there was not a single Christian nation which was not to some extent wondering whether the new ideas emanating from Wittenberg did not contain the answer to questions which so many people were asking, and whether or not it might be necessary to seek salvation outside the rotting framework of the Roman Church. Himself the living embodiment of contradiction, the heresiarch was going to force a categorical option on anyone giving serious attention to the drama of the age. He would have to choose, either for or against.

Of all Christian countries the one whose choice could be the most decisive was unquestionably France. The kingdom of the fleur-de-lys covered an unbroken area of about 240,000 square miles, containing twenty million inhabitants at a time when the population of Europe was no more than one hundred million. She was well organized under an efficient ruler, and occupied what was the leading position from a material point of view. She had been for many years shielded from the depredations of war; for every conflict in which she was involved had taken place either on her frontiers or beyond. Consequently France was prosperous. She had sufficient grain and wine to sell abroad, as well as exporting cloth, furniture, metallurgical products and books. Her fairs did a thriving trade, while her bankers rivalled the great German and Italian financiers. Washed by three different seas, she was on the point of diverting traffic from the Mediterranean to the Atlantic. If such a kingdom were to place both her material strength and all the vigour of her intellectual genius at the service of heresy, the outlook for Catholicism in Europe would be black indeed. As in days of old, the fate of Truth was to be decided on the ancient territory of Clovis.

Conditions in France were in some respects not so favourable to the success of the new doctrines as they had been in Germany. In the first place one fact of capital importance should be observed: there was absolutely nothing in France reminiscent of the anarchical and piecemeal divisions which existed in the Empire. Quite the reverse. Discipline had been restored first by the iron hand of Louis XI, and then by the prudent lenience of Charles VIII and Louis XII, the 'Father of the People.' The Valois kingdom seemed at this period the very epitome of that 'absolute monarchy' towards which all states were tending more or less, in which the prince, surrounded by impressive majesty and served by a highly centralized administration, ruled over a nation whose every class was strictly subject to his authority. Brought up by his mother, Louise of Savoy, to share her belief in her inborn omnipotence—he referred to her as 'my Caesar'—*Francis I* (1515–47) was a good-humoured despot who worked hard and enthusiastically to strengthen the authority of his crown. In France the Reformation would not have the benefit of an elective and therefore virtually ineffective emperor, whose authority was questioned on all sides.

However, it was not altogether unlikely that France would surrender to Protestantism. Although she was in many respects so stable and sound, she was none the less searching for certain assurances in other directions. She had risen from the ruins of the Hundred Years War, but she had not retrieved—and would not do so for another century to come—the position she had held in days gone by. Then she had been the guide of the nations, the 'oven wherein the bread of the West is baked,' as the Middle Ages had so nicely expressed it. And, in a confused kind of way, this realization made her suffer. Once she had been the centre of influences, now she was the crossroads. Each of the two important movements of the age began outside her frontiers: the Renaissance in Italy and the Reformation in Germany. Just as her policy hesitated between the undertaking of chivalrous escapades beyond the Alps and the more realistic method of slow, patient territorial expansion, so her spiritual and moral life seemed torn between the sturdy forces of national tradition and those fruitful influences which were penetrating her from outside. She felt that new answers were required to the eternal problem of relationship between life and the individual, but she could not as yet express them in her own tongue. This picturesque, fascinating land of Francis I, with all its intellectual excitement, was also seething with strange ferments. Everything seemed possible, because nothing had yet been properly defined.

At the end of the fifteenth century the phenomenon known as 'the Renaissance' had just reached France, fifty years later than its appearance in Italy, the country of its origin. Although they were not the sole cause of the transformation affecting France, the wars in the peninsula had made it inevitable. Charles VIII and Louis XII had returned from their splendid expeditions bringing with them wonderful examples of Renaissance work, and even teachers such as Fra Giocondo and Boccador. Their effect was immediate: austere, fortified castles were converted into smiling dwellings; at Chaumont, Loches, Blois, Lude and Azay-le-Rideau elements of military architecture were turned into ornamental motifs; Chambord became a glorious monstrosity, whose feudal framework was covered with florid decoration copied from the Carthusian house at Pavia. Under Francis I a second wave of the Renaissance had swept France. In the train of the conqueror of Marignano came *Rosso*, Michelangelo's disciple; *Primatizio*, a pupil of Giulio Romagna; *Vignola*, the famous architect; and *Leonardo da Vinci* himself—although the last named, who settled on the banks of the Loire, was interested in little else than scientific research. The Palace of Fontainebleau, with its strangely mysterious sumptuousness, was the perfect framework in which these still rudimentary and contradictory talents could achieve some sort of unity. During the 1530's the classicism of the French Renaissance was still trying to find its feet; those who were to realize its masterpieces were still young men of only twenty: *Jean Goujon* (1510–68) and *Pierre Lescot* (1510–70), the future builder of Anet. National influences remained extremely powerful: the ancient French style of building is recognizable beneath the Corinthian piers of Saint-Eustache in Paris; at Troyes Martin Chambiges was putting the finishing touches to the cathedral in pure Gothic. Other architects were building in the same style, as witness the famous tower of Saint-Jacques in Paris and the Tour de Beurre at Rouen, while the Flamboyant style continued to blossom in countless decorative motifs in the Palais de Justice at Rouen as well as in the basilica at Brou, in Bresse. This conflict of styles would last for a long time to come. It disclosed a deeper and more spiritual struggle: Jean Goujon achieved great success with the enchanting pagan figures of his nymphs and graces at a time when *Germain Pilou* (1535–90), his junior by twenty-five years, still remained loyal to the lessons of the fifteenth-century painters. This art of the first French Renaissance was characteristic of a nation that quivered with life but was still seeking her true self.

The same creative fever is apparent in the realm of literature and philosophy. *Humanism* had reached France at the same time as the artistic Renaissance. It too derived from Italy. As in the peninsula its original aim was to 'draw from the fertile source of Greek and Latin genius'—to quote from Guillaume Fichet's *Rhetoric*, one of the first printed books. Enraptured with this idea the finest minds had discovered their kinship with the classical masterpieces. Men threw themselves at Greek, devouring Xenophon, Diodorus Siculus, Homer and Thucydides with joyous abandon. By about 1500 Paris had become one of the centres of humanism, but groups of enthusiastic intellectuals had also sprung into being at Lyons, Le Mans, Poitiers, Orleans, Grenoble, and even as far afield as Fontenay-le-Comte, Cognac,

Noyon and Coutances.[1] The movement found its followers in every class of society; it claimed magistrates, professors, clerks and newly rich merchants. The printing-press, which had first been tried out in a rudimentary form at Avignon, ten years before Gutenberg's invention, quickly came into general use. In 1458 Nicholas Jenson had brought the new technique from Mainz by order of Charles VII; in 1469 the Sorbonne had summoned Michael Freiburger from Colmar, Ulrich Gering from Constance and Martin Krantz from Basle, in order that these experts might establish a printing-house within its very walls. Shortly afterwards Pierre la Rouge had founded his own, and this produced the admirable edition of the *Mer des Histoires* in 1487. In 1500 Lyons already contained fifty publishing houses working at full capacity; and not long after this the *Estiennes*, a dynasty of printers, started their celebrated business in Paris. In the first quarter of the sixteenth century the book—and also the numerous booklets, consisting of a few pages only, the ancestors of the modern magazine—was spreading information and ideas far and wide. As early as 1533 Rabelais could write: 'Nowadays all branches of learning have been revived, and every language has its established place: Greek, without which no one dare claim himself educated, as well as Hebrew, Chaldean and Latin.' In this sparkling world the influence of *Erasmus* was enormous: his *Adages*,[2] his *In Praise of Folly* and his *Enchiridion Militis Cristiani* were read avidly everywhere. The only French scholar who seemed in the same class was *Guillaume Budé* (1467–1540), an eminent hellenist, historian and scholar, as well as a theologian and philosopher. A number of writers of a new tone were about to conquer the public: the lovable, sensitive *Clément Marot* (1496–1544) and the truculent, knowledgeable and often profound *Rabelais* (1495–1553), whose first *Chroniques de Gargantua* were published at Lyons in 1532. Both these men were still writers of transition, not yet fixed in the framework of classical humanism, preceding the Ronsards and Du Bellays of the Pléiade by a quarter of a century, and Montaigne by forty years. Francis I, 'the Father of Literature,' accorded generous protection to all this lively competitive effort, although he himself was entirely ignorant of Greek, and perhaps also of Latin and much else besides. Striking evidence of the royal interest is seen in the prodigious expansion of the royal library during his reign, and particularly in his foundation of the *Collège des Lecteurs Royaux* (afterwards known as the *Collège de France*), an institution whose curriculum and methods of teaching were quite unrestricted.

[1] From 1522 to 1537 Bishop Jean de Pins made his palace at Rieux an influential centre of humanism. All the great minds of the day made a kind of pilgrimage there. (Cf. G. Cormary, *Jean de Pins*, Castres, 1933.) Bishop Geoffroy Herbert filled an analogous role at Coutances. (Cf. C. Laplatte, *Le Diocèse de Coutances à la fin du moyen âge*, Coutances, 1950.)

[2] On Erasmus see Chapter V, p. 329.

To what extent did this ferment prepare the ground for the Reformation? French humanism, like that of Germany and England, differed distinctly from the Italian by its interest in moral and religious problems. There was hardly a single writer of the day (even court poets such as Marot, and great literary noblewomen such as Marguerite of Navarre) who did not state his views on these questions. But did the spirit of their approach favour the eventual development of heresy? The 'spirit of the Collège de France' inclined to literature, philosophy and the sciences without any other preoccupation than that of free, unrestricted research. It deliberately went beyond the rigid limits of medieval teaching, and in this sense the year 1530, when this celebrated institution opened its doors, really marks the breaking-point with the Middle Ages. It can even be said that this spirit had affinities with certain aspects of Lutheranism. But from the moment that Protestantism was led to erect itself into a dogmatic system, the essential of humanism was in conflict with it. A glance at Master Rabelais will soon convince the reader of this fact. 'France did not emancipate herself from scholasticism in order to fall straight away under the tyranny of Protestant Puritanism.'[1] The ground tilled by humanism would not prove very favourable to Calvin's seed.

The predominant tendency in France was much more that of 'Christian humanism,' which had had its precursors in Italy, in the persons of Marsilio Ficino and Pico della Mirandola, and whose theses seemed to be summed up in Erasmus's phrase: 'the philosophy of Christ.' There were very few real unbelievers, atheists; and in France their number long remained small, probably far smaller than in Italy. A few Paduans, e.g. Pomponazzi and Vicomercato, taught in certain colleges, and Vicomercato was for a time on the staff of the Collège de France. One curious Bohemian, Jerome Cardano, who proclaimed himself 'the false-hearted and envious detractor of religion,' certainly taught an astonishing astrological brand of theology which explained the Incarnation by the conjunction of Saturn and the sun. None of this went very far. The one disturbing antichristian group was that at Lyons, centred around *Étienne Dolet*, a native of Orleans, who had come to the banks of the Rhone in 1534 to work in Sebastien Gryphe's printing and publishing business. His *Commentarii linguae latinae*, which was set out like a dictionary, attacked the dogmas of the Church and the doctrines of Erasmus as well, for the latter were far too conformist in the eyes of this determined atheist.

These very attacks of Dolet are proof of the Christian character of authentic humanism, of the humanism professed by Guillaume Budé and the Estiennes, and even by Clément Marot and other great literary minds of the period. The dream they cherished was very close to that

[1] Brunetière's *Manuel de littérature française*.

developed by Erasmus. In 1516 Thomas More expressed it through the pleasant fiction of *Utopia*: it consisted of taking one's stand upon human nature, relying on the divine spark, the aspiration to Beauty and Truth, which it contained, 'entering into grace' by way of it, and thus realizing a gracious, receptive religion—perhaps one that was excessively so. The apparent contradiction between faith and life was much reduced; but this was to some extent achieved at the cost of dogmatic integrity. Christian humanism in the period prior to 1535 contained a number of disturbing elements which could, almost unconsciously, pave the way to heresy, but which were still no more than vague tendencies and veiled ambiguities.

As in Germany and Italy, the French humanists were 'reformers' in the broadest sense of the term. In other words, although they had not the slightest desire to break with Rome and the Church, they longed for a number of fundamental changes within the framework of Catholicism itself. Following the example of their teacher Erasmus, all violently criticized the vices and scandals of which ecclesiastical society provided far too many examples. Above all they complained of that perversion of piety, which too often substituted for true inner spirituality a religion of formalism embedded in parrotry. This excessively vehement criticism, however, threatened to shake the very foundations of the Church. The problem in France was the same as in the empire and everywhere else in the Christian world.

From this point of view nothing is more significant than the case of Rabelais,[1] the former Franciscan, who became a Benedictine at Ligugé, then canon of Saint-Maur, and finally parish priest of Meudon. He has often been presented as a blatant blasphemer, naturist and pagan, but Lucien Febvre's masterly exposition has made it impossible any longer to accept the superficial portrait of Rabelais as atheist and antichristian. We know that there was much that was thoroughly Christian in this mocking satirist, who was capable, even while he joked about them, of pronouncing the most terrible condemnation of all future rationalism and materialism: 'Knowledge without conscience is merely spiritual ruin.' Every Christian must be grateful for the wise counsel given by Gargantua to his son: Serve, love and fear God, and 'be united with Him by faith born of charity in such a way that you may never be separated from Him by sin.' But there is no question at all that the bitter criticism, often in the coarsest taste, which he showered upon the clergy, and the treacherous ridicule with which he riddled several Catholic dogmas, helped to fill the arsenal of the Church's enemies,

---

[1] See Lucien Febvre's absorbing work *Le Problème de l'incroyance au XVIᵉ siècle: la religion de Rabelais*, which is quoted in the Select Bibliography at the end of this volume. Paulette Lenoir's refutation of this book, *Quelques aspects de la pensée de Rabelais* (Paris, 1953) is unconvincing; the author makes Rabelais a pre-Marxian Marxist. The thesis of Rabelais's atheism has been more seriously expounded by Abel Lefranc.

whether Protestant or atheist. Dolet, for example, published Rabelais in a clandestine version, editing him to suit himself and using him to sow seeds of discord among the faithful.

Moreover the Church in France was no more and no less free from reproach than anywhere else in Christendom. There were universal complaints about the unworthiness and greed of the upper clergy, and the ignorance and immorality of the ordinary priesthood. These were excessive in the sense that they easily lent themselves to abusive generalizations, but they were only too well founded. The system of commendam, aggravated in 1516 by the concordat which made ecclesiastical benefices dependent on the king, was at least as wide-spread in France as in Germany:

> Petits enfants qui sont à peine nés
> Ont évêches, dignités, c'est la guise. . . .
> Et leur suffit d'être bien prévendés
> Sans dire messes, Heures, Vêpres, Psaultiers. . . .[1]

So had sung the mocking Gringoire. His words were no less true on the threshold of the sixteenth century, and there is little point in once again cataloguing these abuses here. The most serious aspect of the situation lay in the fact that the indifference of the greater commendatories resulted in a general lowering of standards among the junior clergy, which in turn led to a decline in faith and practice in many parts of France. In 1553 the Jesuit Broët wrote that in the neighbourhood of Bordeaux 'the divine cult and doctrine are hidden in the shadows' and that the people 'live like beasts of burden.' As for the regular clergy, the cruel shafts of Rabelais were not altogether undeserved. While edifying communities existed at Cluny, Fontevrault, Saint-Germain-des-Prés and elsewhere, the spectacle in far too many houses was much less deserving of respect. In this field too the system of commendam had many unfortunate consequences: at St Benignus, in Dijon, a boy of eleven was nominated prior and pantler of the abbey, that is to say, he was put in charge of the monks' material and spiritual nourishment. Criticisms of the clergy as expressed in the little booklets peddled about by Protestant agents were not without foundation.

Thus in many ways, albeit much less distinctly than in Germany, the Reformation might have been expected to find the ground in France fairly well prepared. Yet it did not suceed there. Why? What were the obstacles to its development? The most common, and indeed the simplest answer, can be found in two words: the king. It is true that, by virtue of all the tradition and loyalty which it represented, the

---

[1] 'Tiny children who are scarcely born possess dignities and bishoprics—for that's the fashion; it is enough for them to be loaded with livings, without having to say Masses Hours, Vespers, Psalms. . . .'

'Most Christian' crown of St Louis's descendants was infinitely more closely bound to the Church than those of the petty German princes. Also, and even more important, it is clear that from the time of the concordat of 1516 the French sovereign had not the slightest interest in rejecting an ecclesiastical system of which he himself was an integral part, and from which he derived extensive profit. The regalian, Gallican policy of Chancellor Duprat and Louise of Savoy was based on this evidence.

However, it would be wrong to say that France failed to become Protestant simply because her monarchs were unwilling to do so. The fundamental truth of the matter lies in this, that the French people themselves did not wish to change their faith. Cardinal Baudrillart writes: 'While the masses almost everywhere else in Europe let themselves be conquered and received the Reformation from the avid and brutal hands of their leaders, out of indifference, surprise or fear, the mass of the French people did not allow itself to be either seduced or subdued. It defended its faith against every enemy, by every means at its disposal, and even imposed it on its king.' [1] And the cardinal rightly concludes: 'This is one of the most glorious pages in a history rich in glory.'

But why did the French people fight against heresy in this way? Possibly because it sensed that the Catholic faith was most intimately linked with its national consciousness. The hold which religion had on man from the time of his birth, and retained until the moment of his death, making itself felt in every aspect of his private existence, in his work, as well as in his public life, was probably no stronger in France than in Germany, but it went far deeper. Save in the Rhineland and Bavaria, Christianity had been superimposed on the ancient tribal and pagan Germanic base and had not become an integral part of the German soul. In France Christian traditions were so firmly rooted in the popular mind that when the first examples of Protestant hooliganism occurred it was the Catholic masses themselves which reacted with such violence against the iconoclasts. Despite all its faults and limitations, piety in France was very much alive, and Protestant attacks, so far from weakening it, caused it to grow even stronger. Men's souls were exalted by the use of the Rosary and the Stations of the Cross, by devotion to the Passion and to the Immaculate Conception of the Virgin Mary—the latter being a devotion greatly encouraged by the Sorbonne. These sentiments must be taken into account when assessing the resistance which Protestantism encountered in France when it tried

---

[1] *L'Église catholique, la Renaissance, le Protestantisme.* This comment is true in a general sense, but the case of Geneva raises certain reservations. Here, for reasons which will be studied later in this chapter, the free citizens really seem to have desired Calvin's return and dictatorship.

to persuade the devout masses to cast aside their beloved saints, their pilgrimages and their ancient works of piety.[1]

One final point should be noted: the Frenchman felt none of that sullen, racial fury towards Rome and the Italian Church which could be observed in Germany. Unquestionably the Gallican Church had opposed the pontiffs on several occasions. Louis XII had even dared to pursue the adventure of schism against Julius II [2]; and this constant desire for independence, a prefiguration of Gallicanism in the age of Louis XIV, was so engrained in the national conscience that while the Wars of Religion were at their height, in 1568 when the league was strongest, the assembly of the French clergy talked of suppressing a papal bull because the nuncio's intervention infringed the privileges of the Gallican Church. But all such disputes and quarrels took place within the framework of a more fundamental loyalty. Even when they rebelled against papal authority the Catholics of France had no real wish to shake its foundations. 'The fact is that there is no nation in the world which demands more dispensations, privileges and other authorizations from the Holy See,' commented one shrewd Venetian ambassador.

In short, France was not really favourable soil for the Reformation. Despite some glaring faults in the clerical world, she was not to turn Protestant. If she let Protestantism gain a certain amount of ground, this was due to the inertia usual in the case of well-established majorities which are over-confident of their own system—their legal forces, their government—and which are invariably more or less taken by surprise by audacious minorities. But the fundamental reaction of the national conscience was to resist the expansion of heresy. Events in France followed a pattern exactly opposite to that which had occurred in Germany, where Lutheranism and Lutheranism alone had been able

[1] This was not so true in the case of the middle class, particularly so far as its wealthier and more educated elements were concerned. In general the middle class supported a reasonable, broader religion—a Christian humanism—but its numbers also included atheists and Catholics whose belief was only very half-hearted. As for the aristocracy, the vast majority of the nobles were loyal to the traditional faith. It was only later that the aristocracy provided recruits for heresy, and then for reasons in which politics were often deeply involved.

[2] The Pragmatic Sanction of Bourges was in abeyance. It was like a rusty tool, which was brought out and polished up from time to time. When his ally Julius II betrayed him, Louis XII made great play of the instrument which his more subtle predecessors had used only to scare Rome. He applied it thoroughly. He broke off relations with the Pope and asked the nuncio (a well-meaning, conciliatory man) to leave the realm. In 1510 assemblies of the clergy and the universities met at Tours and Orleans; these were violently hostile to the Pope. A series of edicts re-established the 'Holy' Pragmatic Sanction in all its severity, which proves that it had meanwhile fallen into abeyance. Hired writers supported royal policy: some (Le Maire de Belges and Bouchet, for example) by writing learned (and heavy) treatises, others, such as Gringoire, by composing frivolous and pointed satires. Louis XII convened a 'reforming' council at Pisa; it suspended the Pope, who died shortly afterwards.

to give a shapeless and chaotic mass a collective soul. The French form of Protestantism, created by a Frenchman according to ideological criteria of logic and universalism which were profoundly French, would be found capable of taking root outside France; but in France herself it gained only limited acceptance.

AN EVANGELICAL HUMANISM: LEFÈVRE D'ÉTAPLES AND THE MEAUX GROUP

The little circle of French intellectuals working to acclimatize humanism to their country consisted of pious, serious men, very different from such Italian pagans as Laurence Valla or Panormizio. About 1515 their unanimous and affectionate admiration was centred upon an old priest, a short, slight man with pointed mouse-like features, whose spirituality seemed to dominate even his outstanding intellectual qualities. His name was *Jacques Lefèvre*, and he had been born in 1455 at Étaples, in Picardy. From early youth Lefèvre had devoted himself unceasingly to the pure joys of learning. Every branch of knowledge had fascinated him, particularly mathematics, but he was also interested in ancient philosophy. Then, little by little, he had turned from the profane sciences to others of a more lofty and elevated kind. 'I was,' he used to say, 'long devoted to human studies, and my lips had scarcely brushed the edge of the divine; for they are majestic studies, and ought not to be rashly approached. But a distant light of such brilliance struck my eyes that human doctrines seemed but shadows in comparison with the divine, while the latter seemed to exude a perfume whose sweetness nothing on this earth could equal.' In order to devote himself more completely to inhaling this wonderful perfume, Lefèvre had eight years since retired to the monastery of Saint-Germain-des-Prés, on the outskirts of Paris, which had been reformed by Abbot Briçonnet, one of Lefèvre's own pupils.

The influence of this timid, stunted little man, who smilingly referred to himself as *homunculus*, was prodigious. The finest minds of the day came to visit him, among them some very eminent persons: the great scholar Guillaume Budé; the hebraist Vatable; the impetuous Guillaume Farel from Dauphiné; José Clichthove, who travelled expressly from the Low Countries; the famous preacher Gérard Roussel (chaplain to Marguerite, the most intellectual of the princesses of the blood); Pierre Caroli, Michel d'Arande, and even the king's own confessor, Guillaume Petit. All these would gather in a circle around the tiny figure of 'Faber Stapulensis,' hunched in his cassock, to listen to his teaching. It is known that the great Erasmus held him in high esteem; but although the two men exchanged frequent letters, they did not always agree with each other's views. The Dutchman reproached the Norman for putting too much emphasis on monastic asceticism and mystical speculation. Lefèvre retorted that Erasmus wasted overmuch time studying the classics, and that his excessively bitter irony was unworthy of a true Christian.

For Jacques Lefèvre of Étaples was Christian right to the marrow of his being. The living symbol of all those anxieties which were tormenting the souls of his contemporaries, he dreamed of a rejuvenated, pure faith, welling up in men's hearts spontaneously, drawn from living sources which would renew everything in a Church that sorely needed rejuvenation: but never for one moment did he contemplate infidelity to that Church. Lefèvre was an enthusiastic reader of the Fathers, particularly of St Ignatius of Antioch and St Polycarp; but he also enjoyed the medieval Victorines for whom 'love always goes further than reason,' and Ruysbroeck, and the two visionaries Mechthild and Hildegard. The essential of his spiritual doctrine was easily summed up by quoting St Paul's celebrated aphorism: 'With Christ I hang upon the Cross, and yet I am alive; or rather, not I; it is Christ that lives in me!' In practical terms he advocated a reformation to be effected inside the Church and by the Church, an intellectual reformation which would replace a now degenerate scholasticism by a positive theology based on the study of Scripture and the Fathers, and also a moral and disciplinary reformation which would put a stop to flagrant abuses. This reformation was to be achieved by bringing the faithful Christian back to the truth of Christ, by making the Gospel permeate the mind of each and every believer. Long before the days of Luther, Lefèvre d'Étaples reposed his hope of the essential task of rejuvenation and renovation in Holy Scripture, the Word of God. In 1509 he had edited the Psalms, in 1512 the Pauline Epistles. This *Evangelicalism* of scholars and humanists put its trust simultaneously in redeemed human nature and in the inexhaustible power of Christ's message.

Lefèvre and his disciples were given the chance to try out their ideas. In 1516 one of the group's leading members, *Guillaume Briçonnet*, was appointed Bishop of Meaux. Son of a minister of Charles VIII, he had taken holy orders on the death of his wife, obtained the archbishopric of Rheims, then the Red Hat, not to mention a good half a dozen other rich livings. He was, however, more interested in souls than in prebends. At Lodève, his first bishopric, and then at Saint-Germain-des-Prés, he had applied the highest principles. During a stay in Rome he had made contact with the Oratories of Divine Love, and he was acquainted with those working under the leadership of Carafa and St Gajetan to forge new weapons for the Church. Briçonnet was a man of exceptional nobility and purity, whose piety and eloquence are comparable with those of St Francis of Sales. He possessed the most elevated conception of his office. 'The episcopal ministry is entirely evangelical,' he used to say. 'The bishop is an angel sent from Christ, entrusted with His message, and he performs an angel's task—purging, illuminating and restoring souls to perfection.'

Briçonnet therefore undertook the vigorous 'purging' of his mediocre diocese. Its two hundred parishes were grouped into twenty-six sectors or 'stations'; a preacher was allocated to each, specially charged with the duty of tilling a soil that had so long lain fallow. Dances and public games, the occasions of frequent debauchery, were prohibited. Priests who were leading unexemplary lives or neglecting their flocks were sharply called to order. Certain Franciscans, who begged more skilfully than they preached, were expelled from the diocese. Measures of this kind were not to everyone's liking. Denunciations from high places began to rain down on this over-enterprising bishop.

Led by Lefèvre d'Étaples, the little group moved from Saint-Germain-des-Prés to Meaux. In 1523, knowing that his master was in difficulty with the Sorbonne, Briçonnet invited him to serve as his Vicar-General. Gèrard Roussel became treasurer of the cathedral chapter. Pierre Caroli, a canon of Sens, and Martial Mazurier, former head of a college in Paris, threw themselves enthusiastically into the task of reviving Christian theology. The *Meaux Group* became a community emanating piety and apostolic fervour—something like Port-Royal later on, or La Chesnaie in the days of Lamennais. Its influence extended far beyond the diocesan boundaries, and the movement was supported by many other bishops: the Du Bellays at Paris and Lemans, Lenoncourt at Châlons, and Sadolet at Carpentras. Through his sister Marguerite and his mother, Louise of Savoy, Francis I was in close touch with Briçonnet,' who was their intimate friend, and with the rest of his circle. They begged the king to fill all vacant sees with zealous bishops sympathetic to the new crusade.

Yet this noble and generous evangelicalism contained certain suspect and disturbing tendencies. Some of its formulas were ambiguous, and there was a certain vagueness in its theological bases. In 1523 Lefèvre d'Étaples published his highly successful French translation of the New Testament; the preface contained these remarks: 'The time has come when Our Lord Jesus Christ, the only Sun, the only Truth and the only Life, desires His Gospel to be clearly preached by everyone, so that men shall no longer be misled by other foolish additions or inventions or by any other human traditions, none of which can save them.' Such principles were acceptable enough to every Catholic. But there could hardly be equal agreement upon counsels such as the following, which appeared in his Commentary on the Epistles of St Paul, written in 1512: 'Expect salvation only through faith in Christ. Your salvation derives not from your works, but from the works of Christ. You cannot save yourself; Christ will save you. The Cross is not yours but His!' This is at once reminiscent of another reformer who upheld very similar theses singularly eight years later and in quite a different perspective. Likewise, when Lefèvre denounced the 'foolish piety' which was taught to ordinary people instead of doctrine, when he criticized the poor quality of certain prayers and devotions, or when he asked what good more Lenten fasting would do him, he was, albeit unintentionally and probably unconsciously also, linking up with a current which elsewhere was forcibly tearing men's souls from their devotions, their traditional prayers, their fasts, and many other things besides. And what ground are we on when we read such words as these: 'If you believe that Jesus Christ died for you, for the redemption of your sins, this is enough. . . .'?

The doctrine of Lefèvre and his circle, though doubtless Catholic in spirit so far as concerned the minds that first conceived it, was none the less pregnant with danger. Not least it tended to promote a wholly personal religion, in which the Church, as it were, had no part. Such a religion was probably capable of satisfying lofty souls, but not of giving simple, firm directions to a whole nation which longed anxiously for answers and reforms. In a more peaceful age *Fabrism*, or evangelical humanism, might have served a useful purpose, somewhat analogous to that performed by Salesianism later on; but at this grave turning-point of history it surely constituted a real peril.

It was easy for those opposing Lefèvre, Briçonnet and their friends to use the ambiguities of their own doctrine in order to attack them. As usually happens in such cases, the members of the group were not tackled on the essential, on the equivocal character of their theological theses, but on subsidiary issues: the suppression of alms and stipends for Masses; the use of vernacular in the Liturgy (the Epistle and the Gospel were read in French at Meaux); and above all their criticism of deviations in the cult of saints. The offensive was led by the Sorbonne, an institution which, though lampooned so wittily by Rabelais in his early books, included among its members more than such harmless buffoons as 'Master Janotus de Bragmardo,' with just enough intelligence to bid Gargantua return the bells of Notre Dame, which he had hung round his mare's neck. The head of the theological faculty at this time was *Noel Beda* (or Bedier), a former principal of the austere college of Montaigu,[1] who has been accurately [2] described as a 'self-willed, savage man, of personal moral integrity, insensitive to attack, and indifferent as to what weapons he himself used.' Soundly

[1] See p. 377.
[2] Pierre Gaxotte, *Histoire des français*.

established on theological bases which he regarded as beyond question, he hated everything, whether from near or far, which hinted at innovation. He had violently castigated Lefèvre d'Étaples for the first time in 1518, when the humanist had ventured to write that the Mary of Magdala, Mary the sister of Martha, and the woman whose sins were forgiven were three different persons, not one and the same, as tradition was said to aver. From the moment that the Meaux group's influence became apparent, Beda and his colleagues at the Sorbonne, and all the 'dabblers in theology,' swore to put an end to it.

In fact, matters came to a head very swiftly. Lutheranism had begun to penetrate France by about 1520, and its vocabulary was remarkably like that of the Missions of Meaux. The famous but anonymous author of the *Journal of a Paris Merchant* noted with some exaggeration that 'most of Meaux is infected with Luther's false doctrine, and the man called Fabry [*sic*] is the cause of the said confusion.' From 1521 onwards the royal tribunal, half of whose members were clerics, encroached on the preserves of the Parlement. It was no less determined than the Sorbonne to prevent the advance of heresy, and at the same time to check these evangelists from Meaux who seemed to give every indication of being Luther's harbingers. Rifts occurred within the group itself: Clichthove, the biblical scholar, left it after a violent argument in which he upheld against Lefèvre the idea that 'the sublime meaning of the Holy Scriptures cannot be understood without assistance from the commentaries of orthodox doctors.' A number of unfortunate incidents occurred, as when cards bearing prayers to Our Lady and the saints were torn to pieces in the churches of Meaux. Briçonnet became uneasy. The Parlement announced that publication of any religious work without official authorization was prohibited. The era of repression was about to open. It coincided with those years of tribulation during which the king was taken prisoner at Pavia and the regent, Louise of Savoy, looked for support to the Parlement and the Sorbonne, the two forces of order left in the kingdom. An overbold Dominican was arrested; a Franciscan was executed at Grenoble; and at Paris an Augustinian, Jacques Pavannes, who claimed to be a follower of Lefèvre d'Étaples, was put to death. When denounced by the Franciscans, in 1525, the aged evangelist did not wait for the Sorbonne's warrant of arrest; he fled to Strasbourg with Roussel, and returned to France only when the king, who had been informed of events by his sister, sent orders from Madrid that all persecution must be suspended.

This was the end of the Meaux group. A bull of Clement VII attacked the unwary evangelists, and Briçonnet made his submission. Lefèvre became the king's librarian for a time, and even taught the royal children. Then he retired to Nerac, to the court of his protector

N

Marguerite, where he died at the age of eighty-two, protesting that he had never wished to separate himself from the Church, but nevertheless continuing to preach his views until the hour of his death. The destiny of his followers varied. Some remained faithful to the Church: Clichthove; Roussel, who became Bishop of Oloron; and Michel d'Arande, who obtained the see of Saint-Paul-Trois-Châteaux. But Farel and Vatable went over to Protestantism; the former was to play a notable part therein. After flirting with Calvinism, Caroli returned to the Catholic faith.

Thus ended an attempt to effect a reformation within the Church by peaceful means, side by side with Luther's movement. It had possessed many admirable features, but some disturbing ones also. Humanist evangelicalism had failed. Possibly this was because its leaders were only self-effacing intellectuals, ill equipped to stir the enthusiasm of ordinary people. None of them was remotely comparable with the vigorous, aggressive Augustinian whose popular fire was rousing all Germany; nor had they anything in common with the blade of sharp, cold steel which Calvin would prove himself to be. This was no longer the time for subtle arguments or mystical aspirations. The moment had now come for command and firm resolution.

Is it possible to claim that this 'Pre-reformation'—the reader should remember that it was in fact anterior to Luther's movement—marked the beginning of Protestantism in France? Certain Protestant writers [1] have tried to represent Lefèvre and the Meaux group as their advance-guard on French soil; but their claim runs expressly counter to the views of Calvin himself, and even those of Guillaume Farel, neither of whom ever considered the 'Fabrists' as precursors of their Church. One Protestant historian [2] very rightly states that 'an impartial examina-tion of Lefèvre's writings compels us to reject as part of tendentious legend whatever has been put forward in favour of Lefèvre's genuine adherence to the Reformation and its principles.' However, in these 'confusions' to which the Paris merchant refers, perhaps evangelical-ism had unwittingly worked for other doctrines: it had opened the door to them.

The First French Reformation

The new doctrines, which were soon to supplant the gentle reform-ing mysticism of Meaux, came from the East. 'The key of heresy is made of fine German steel,' said the words of a farce played in Rouen in 1535. This is not entirely true, for Master John Calvin's French key

[1] Doumergue in particular.
[2] François Wendel, *Calvin*.

would soon turn a singularly heavy lock; but there is no doubt at all that
'Fabrism' could never have exercised much influence on the religious
destinies of France but for the existence and proliferation of the
doctrines of Zwingli and Luther.

The Lutheran theses began to penetrate France in 1519, immediately
after the 'Disputation of Leipzig' [1] between Johann Eck and the
Augustinian. It is intriguing to note that the rebel's earliest writings
reached Paris through the most official channels, inspired by the best
intentions in the world. As the Sorbonne had been chosen as one of the
universities which should judge them, her scholars examined them with
great care, so much so that some of their number became fascinated
by them, among whom was Louis de Berquin, the friend of Lefèvre
and Briçonnet.

Soon the troublesome theses were being spread by other means.
Pedlars arrived from Frankfurt, Basle, Nuremberg or Strasbourg, their
baskets bulging with subversive literature. 'We have sent six hundred
copies to France and Spain,' wrote Froben, the leading publisher at
Basle. 'They are being sold in Paris; even the doctors of the Sorbonne
are reading and approving them.' At this time Luther was being
discussed, but had not yet been condemned. Once judgment had been
given this roaring trade became sacred contraband in Paris as well as
in Rome. Little pamphlets, bearing the name neither of author nor of
printer, and propagating the doctrine of Wittenberg, were passed
from hand to hand secretly, and sold under shop counters. In 1523 the
first French translation of a Lutheran work, the *Summa of Holy
Scripture*, which had been printed by Wolf at Basle, was circulating
throughout France. Rather than dogmatic treatises, however, the
propagandists of the new doctrines preferred to distribute pamphlets
'against the authority of the Pope and the ordinances and ceremonies
of the Church,' to quote the words of the famous anonymous merchant
whose *Diary* relates the whole of this episode. Luther's *Babylonian
Captivity* and his sermons *Against Indulgences* were avidly read by
French anticlericals.

The first to be affected by these new ideas were the humanist friends
of Erasmus and Lefèvre d'Étaples, among whom the treatises on *The
Liberty of a Christian Man*, on *Servile Will* (Luther's reply to Erasmus)
and many others were the subject of heated discussion. Truly pious
souls, too, enjoyed the heretic's *Book of True and Perfect Prayer* and
Exposition of the Magnificat. In this way the essential of Lutheran
thought trickled through almost unnoticed. We need only peruse
Rabelais's early books to detect the 'Lutheran whispers' which they
contain: Gargantua declares that 'all real Christians pray to God, and
the Spirit prays and answers for them all,' while Pantagruel snorts

[1] See Chapter V, p. 301.

contemptuously in reply to Grandgousier's inquiry as to whether the monks are not of service to the world by their prayers, 'Anything but!' The author would certainly appear to have read the German Master of the Reformation; indeed Gargantua's mammoth letter to Pantagruel, in the second book, contains one passage lifted just as it stands from a Lutheran sermon.

Very soon, however, these little groups of educated Lutheran sympathizers were joined by others recruited from humbler circles. For these latter the second wave of Protestantism, in the form of more radical Zwinglianism, soon reinforced the revolutionary and anarchical elements found in Lutheranism. Numerous poor clerks and artisans, whose doctrine was somewhat shaky but whose religious sentiment was deeply offended by the sight of so much disorder in the Church, found answers to their many problems in the new teaching. In the morbid atmosphere of Christianity, as it existed during the fifteenth century, many such folk had become obsessed with the idea of expiation, of necessary purification; and when they learned of the dogma of justification by faith they were stirred by a sombre passion. Others, less disinterested, interpreted the Lutheran theses after the style of Karlstadt or the Anabaptists, discovering in them arguments for shaking off the tutelage of clergy and aristocracy, for ceasing to pay tithes and for demanding a share-out of monastic lands. The common people in the towns were especially affected by the Reformation: the 'gens meschaniques'—woolcarders, weavers, printers, day labourers of various kinds—were already being ground under by the evolution of capitalism and irritated beyond endurance by the constant rise in the cost of living. The peasants, on the other hand, were loyal to the cult of their saints, and scarcely allowed themselves to be ensnared by the new doctrines. Among the lower clergy there were some elements anxious to create a more living faith and a purer religion, together with innumerable priests and monks of uncertain vocation who were only too glad to find some excuse for taking a woman. The first to do this was a certain François Lambert, a Minorite from Avignon, who in 1522 flung his habit into the Rhône and went as far as Wittenberg to get married.

About 1530 Catholic France seemed to be riddled with little groups of 'Lutheranizers.' Paris contained a 'reformed' Church, with its focal point in the Latin Quarter. We have already studied Meaux in Lefèvre's time: it became contaminated soon after his departure. In Picardy there were heretics at Noyon and Amiens; in the north-east, at Metz, Bar-le-Duc, Châlons-sur-Marne and Vitry; in the south-east was an area where Waldensian communities still existed, and where Guillaume Farel was to carry on his apostolate. Protestants could be found at Lyons, Grenoble and in the valleys of the Mateysine and Champsaur.

To the west Normandy and the vicinity of Alençon formed 'a regular little Germany,' as Bucer claimed with rather too much enthusiasm; and in the south-west, the ancient territory of the Albigensians, there were various heretical groups in the area between Castres and Nîmes, and, needless to say, in the kingdom of Navarre. Before the situation clarified these were all points where the 'evil-thinkers' of the Reformation could be found. Brittany and the Auvergne contained none at all.

Things, however, remained utterly confused. In the first place the confusion affected those who were studying this ferment from outside. In 1533 Johann Sturm was still writing from Paris to Bucer: 'No distinction is made between Erasmians, Lutherans and Anabaptists.' And the first 'Protestant' of note to perish at the stake, Louis de Berquin, was condemned in the name of Erasmus, not of Luther. Those in the camp defending the new ideas were no clearer. No one really knew which doctrine to claim as his own: there was no choice between Luther, Zwingli, Bucer, Erasmus, Oeclampadius or Lefèvre; no Protestant 'Credo' existed at this time. Attitudes to the Church varied a great deal, from a rather naïve evangelical reformism, in the Meaux style, to Anabaptist violence and iconoclasm. These people simply referred to themselves as 'good Christians,' better Christians than those Catholics who fawned over relics and bought indulgences and whose conduct was often so unedifying. Each man virtually formulated his own personal doctrine, and this situation was to continue for many years to come. There was general agreement on certain points. The Bible alone contained the truth of Revelation, 'everything else is lies'; the ultimate interpretation of Holy Scripture belonged to ordinary laymen, 'poor, uneducated sinners, just as the Apostles were'; all ecclesiastical regulations, fasts and indulgences were 'inventions of the devil'; the Mass was, in Zwingli's words, 'a horrible blasphemy.' These negative convictions hardly comprised a body of doctrine capable of imposing itself on a whole country.

However, a few men realized that it was necessary to adopt different methods if the Reformation was to triumph in France. The most remarkable of these was undoubtedly *Louis de Berquin*, a young professor at the Sorbonne, who had taken so much interest in the Lutheran theses that he had been converted by them and had translated his new master's pamphlet in reply to the papal bull. De Berquin was an advanced Erasmian, trained to handle ideas, and an excellent publicist. Little is now known of his philosophy, for all his books were destroyed; but it is possible that he might have succeeded in creating the synthesis between Lefèvre's mystical evangelicalism, Erasmus's critical humanism, Zwingli's administrative genius and Luther's theological aspiration, thus producing a truly French form of Protestantism. As will be seen, his premature death put an end to any such dream.[1] Another outstanding figure was the impetuous, vehement and aggressive *Guillaume Farel*, who, though trained in Lefèvre's little group, had soon left it to throw himself into more violent battles. He flirted with Anabaptism, and extolled Karlstadt and Zwingli. He also took part on several occasions in sacrilegious demonstrations, throwing a shrine into the river, tearing down a chapel cross, and going so far as to snatch a consecrated Host from a priest's hands. But he was a far-sighted thinker and a good organizer, and in 1524 he had written a first French 'confession of faith' and later a set of liturgical rules. At this particular time Farel's influence in France was insignificant. Disturbed by the reaction to his conduct, and little inclined to martyr-dom, he fled to Neuchâtel, and thence to Geneva, where he cleared the way for Calvin.

Such was the first French Reformation. Imbart de la Tour observes that 'it had undoubtedly led to an individualist Christianity, stripped of an over-rigid dogmatism, which was bound sooner or later to fall apart in the diversity of its beliefs or the imprecision of its formulas. Common danger reunited it. It felt the simultaneous need to defend and define itself, and, like an army scattered in enemy territory, it had to provide itself with both a centre and a leader.' That leader was John Calvin.

THE ERA OF EQUIVOCATION

For over fifteen long years then the Reformation was able to in-filtrate into France without any opposition from the Crown. Francis I did not become aware of the danger immediately, or grasp that, in his position as leader of the established Church, with all the privileges allowed him by virtue of the concordat, it was not in his interest to permit the triumph of these 'evil-thinkers' who no longer recognized a Catholic hierarchy. In his defects as well as his good qualities Francis was a typical man of the Renaissance, possessing a smattering of humanism, professing a certain contempt for the masters at the Sorbonne and the 'dabblers in theology,' and delighting in elevating fine literary figures like Guillaume Petit or Jean du Bellay to the episcopate. Moreover he was too absorbed in international politics to take much interest in matters which seemed to him to be of secondary importance. Finally, in 1524, he had allied himself with the German Lutheran princes. So he preferred to wait. For what? No doubt for

[1] Hauser and Renaudet, in their *Débuts de l'âge moderne* (Peuples et Civilisations), seem to have been the only historians to note the real importance of this little known and most attractive personality. There is, however, an excellent note on him in the *Diction-naire de biographie française*, vol. iv, col. 139.

some event which would enable him to remain true to his own natural generosity—the wanderers' return to wisdom perhaps or a council. This equivocal situation continued for fifteen years.

On the one hand was a party advocating resistance to the new doctrines. It consisted of the vigilant Sorbonne with its terrifying professor, Noel Beda; of an anxious Parlement; of all who chose to rely on papal support in the struggle against the Hapsburgs—Clement VII had already been obliged to draw Francis I's attention to the perilous progress of heresy in France—of Chancellor Duprat, whose sole principle was the wellbeing of the State; and, finally, of such well-intentioned men as Briçonnet, who found that 'reformation' was leading into strange byways. The king's mother, *Louise of Savoy*,[1] a remarkable woman whose intelligence and strength of purpose were more notable than her aimiability or tenderness, and whom her son worshipped a great deal and feared not a little, rallied later to this party (though not without some hesitation), because the difficult situation seemed to make it imperative for her to rely on the forces of law and order.

The other faction, the party of those holding advanced views, and which included humanists and over-daring reformers, was also headed by a woman. This was *Marguerite of Navarre* (1492–1549) the king's own sister, a very different kind of person from the formidable queen-mother. It might be said that all the charm of the period was summed up in this one young woman, who was gracious rather than pretty, and whose expressive face concealed a subtle and intelligent mind. A true daughter of the Renaissance, of the Italian as much as of the French, passionately interested in Plato, Erasmus and Marsilio Ficino, and yet at the same time aglow with genuine mystical spirituality, the princess whom the poets called 'the Marguerite of all Marguerites' seemed to typify in her own crowded existence the confusion of the age. Marguerite was successively Duchess of Berry and of Angoulême, and in 1527 she married Henry d'Albret, King of Navarre.[2] Her sole passion was to surround herself with intelligent people of inquiring and independent outlook, but whose main preoccupation was religion. Humanists, Erasmians, Fabrists and Lutherans were all equally dear to her. Many great figures of the age benefited from her open-handed support and protection: Budé, de Berquin, Dolet, Vatable, Ambroise Paré, the printers Estienne, Bernard Palissy, the famous musician Goudimel, the sculptors Jean Goujon and Ligier Richier. The courtly Marot seemed to be one of her favourites. All this was generous, but highly ambiguous. Marguerite gathered her friends together at her

---

[1] Paule Henry-Bordeaux's book on Louise of Savoy (Paris, 1954) contains the most recent account of this subject.

[2] Her daughter, Jeanne d'Albret, was Henry IV's mother.

little court at Nerac, 'like a good mother-hen sheltering her chicks beneath her wings.' There the days were spent listening to some learned Hebrew scholar commenting on Job or Proverbs, or to one of the new-style preachers talking about salvation through faith, or to the queen reading one of her own pious poems:

> Aimez donc Dieu qui est si très aimable
> San rien avoir en Vostre cœur que Lui. . . .[1]

. . . but at night, when the air was heavy with the scent of myrtle, and the only sound was the gentle plash of the palace fountains, the company indulged in quite different pastimes, of a kind made popular by the *Heptameron*, and which Marguerite herself has chronicled. Though she had never any intention of adopting Lutheranism herself, and indeed always refused to do so, the Queen of Navarre made a habit of gibing at monks and priests, criticizing dogmas and ridiculing Catholic practices. This charming and restless creature exercised considerable influence over her brother; intellectually she was what he would have liked to be. She signed herself 'Your very humble and obedient subject and sweetheart' in the delightful and frequent letters which she wrote him; but she undoubtedly emphasized the 'sweetheart' in order that the 'subject' might be pushed as far into the background as possible.

The religious policy of Francis I was delicately poised for a long time between these two opposing tendencies. In 1521 the Sorbonne denounced to the Parlement all those 'booksellers, printers and other folk' who were disseminating throughout the country writings suspected of heresy. In 1523 it returned to the assault and condemned Melanchthon. As the king was then pursuing a glorious dream in the plains of Italy, the rigorists struck hard: the decisions of the Faculty of Theology were confirmed by royal edicts. It was now that the Meaux group received those blows which were directed primarily at the 'Lutheranizers,' that adventurous reformers (e.g. Pierre Piefort, who specialized in desecrating the sacred Host) were sent to the stake here and there, and that Louis de Berquin was arrested for the first time. Berquin's crimes consisted of having translated Hutten and Luther, and of having set all France laughing with his *Farce des Théologastres*. Pavia, the royal captivity and Madrid were so many trump cards in the game of the theologians and the various Orders, to whom the regent Louise referred as 'those hypocrites in robes of white and black and brown and dun and every colour of the rainbow.' She had little love for them, but she allowed them a free hand. Then, however, Francis I returned, and negotiated a vital alliance with the Lutheran princes; the wind was blowing in favour of indulgence, and Marguerite was in the

---

[1] 'Then love God, who is so loving to you, having nothing save Him in your heart.'

ascendant. Louis de Berquin, who had been arrested a second time, was released on the personal order of his friend the king, who sent 'his captain and the archers of his own bodyguard' to fetch the reformer from jail. The Protestant extremists now went too far: at Paris they smashed a highly venerated statue of the Blessed Virgin, and, despite the thousand crowns' reward offered by the angry monarch, the perpetrator of this sacrilege was never apprehended. The Church was not slow to react. In 1528 four important provincial councils were held at Bourges, Paris, Rheims and Lyons, which foreshadowed to some extent the work of the Council of Trent. They issued a lucid definition of the Protestant theses and condemned them. Foolhardy de Berquin, who had carried his audacity so far as to denounce Noel Beda as a heretic, was now arrested for the third time. This was the end: he was promptly burned (1529) before the king, who was then at Blois, had time to intervene.[1] The Meaux group scattered. But this incident did not herald the beginning of methodical repression. Francis was very loath to be severe; his beloved 'royal lecturers,' for whom he had just opened his college (1530), included several who looked with favour upon the new ideas, and he had no desire to seem a barbarian in his sister's eyes. A fresh mutilation of the Madonna was allowed to go unpunished, as that of 1528 had done. Moreover the Sorbonne was making a fine bundle of rods for its own back. Beda was so enraged by the sight of Marguerite's chaplain, the highly suspect Gérard Roussel, preaching before the court a Lenten fast after the style of the 'evil-thinkers' that he made no bones about saying, rather too loudly, that the whole of the king's *entourage* was infected with heresy. A royal decree condemned him to exile twenty leagues from Paris. The following year the Sorbonne believed it had found an opportunity to be revenged, and condemned a book of anonymous poems, *Le Miroir de l'âme pécheresse* (The Mirror of the Sinful Soul), which was all the rage in Paris. But the illustrious name of its troublesome author was well known to everyone; Francis would not allow his beloved 'sweet-heart and subject' to be touched, and the Sorbonne clique, to whom he referred as 'meal-worms,' were commanded to retract. In truth, confusion was complete. Why were these wretched people arrested and burnt for professing the very faith to which Queen Marguerite of Navarre apparently adhered? More vexed than ever, the Sorbonne smelt heresy everywhere; it even went so far as to pronounce sentence on Cardinal Cajetan and his Commentary on the Psalms. 'We theologians are going to end by condemning the Pope,' murmured Jean du Bellay

[1] Francis I actually demanded that the tribunal charged with judging de Berquin should be composed of laymen, some of whom were chosen by himself. De Berquin, sentenced to life imprisonment, was so unwise as to appeal, and the judges of the superior court increased the penalty.

sarcastically. At Marseilles Francis I was about to meet Clement VII, to sign an alliance with him against Charles V and marry his second son (the future Henry II) to Catherine de' Medici, the Pope's own niece. Bulls against the heretics were promulgated in France, calling on the 'evil-thinkers' to make their submission; and the young rector Nicholas Cop, master at the Sorbonne though he was, had to flee to escape persecution for having given too bold a lecture. There was panic in the 'reformed' party. Once more, however, Francis I intervened; he had just signed a secret treaty with the Landgrave of Hesse, and Noel Beda was packed off into exile afresh. Rumour had it that the king wished to invite Melanchthon to France—Henry VIII had just broken with Rome. . . . Nothing was settled yet. . . .

This game of battledore and shuttlecock might have lasted still longer had not the provocative attitude of the 'Protestants' exasperated public opinion. Accordingly as the Reformation seemed to gain ground, so the more moderate and conciliatory spirits were superseded by violent extremists. *The Placard Affair* (1534) alarmed the king so much that it threw him conclusively on the side of the repressionists. During the night of 17th–18th October—the account of the incident must be read in the racy *Merchant's Journal*—a placard was nailed up 'in the public squares and thoroughfares of Paris,' and also in the provinces at Orleans, Rouen, Tours, Blois and even at the castle of Amboise, where the king was in residence. The announcement was written in a 'trenchant and withering' style, fulminating against 'the honour and truth of the Blessed Sacrament and the Saints.' Its author dismissed as liars and blasphemers 'the Pope and all his verminous rabble of cardinals, bishops, monks and priests.' The Mass was insulted, since Christ could not be present 'in a box or a cupboard.' Everything pertaining to Catholic cult was shockingly derided—'chimes, screeching, caterwaulings, empty ceremonies, lights, censing, fancy costumes, all manner of magic practices.' And the conclusion of this scurrilous document said of the Catholics: 'Truth is attacking them, threatening them and persecuting them; in short, Truth is about to destroy their rule for all eternity.'

The author was a Frenchman named Antoine Marcourt, a Zwinglian who had taken refuge at Neuchâtel; but to have pulled off a feat of this kind he must have had many accomplices in France. Public opinion, led by the king, smelt conspiracy here. At this date the public mind was full of stories about the Anabaptists, who were causing such a sensation in almost every part of Germany and Holland: John of Leyden [1] had recently made Münster the capital of a revolutionary movement with supposedly biblical and communist affiliations, and it was said that the heretics in France wished to imitate Münster. Certain

[1] See Chapter V, p. 349.

people were not slow in claiming that the king's weakness was the real cause of the scandal; among these was Beda, who, as the result of his indiscretion, was dispatched forthwith to Mont-Saint-Michel, where he died. Francis I took fright. The police hurriedly rounded up a goodly number of suspects, the Parlement instituted a 'Court of Fire' (Chambre Ardente) to try the heretics, and about forty 'evil-thinkers' were burned at the stake. They included a wealthy merchant, a humble mason, a weaver, the printer of *The Mirror of the Sinful Soul*, a schoolmistress and even a paralysed cobbler. The rest were 'stripped naked and beaten with rods.' For several weeks the atmosphere resembled that of St Bartholomew's Eve nearly forty years later. The edict of 29th January 1535 decreed the exterminaton of the heretics; but this did not prevent the royal hand which signed it from drafting a memorandum addressed to his German allies in order to explain that he was merely taking legitimate measures against enraged revolutionaries, seditionists and other Anabaptists. 'I have never understood the words of the Psalm better than now: "the heart of the king is in the hand of God,"' wrote Johann Sturm to Bucer. This tolerant prince, this royal humanist, had just promulgated an astonishing edict prohibiting all printing of books in his realm 'under pain of the gallows.' At long last he had chosen his path. On 21st January 1535 he walked, bare-headed and carrying a burning torch, from Saint-Germain-l'Auxerrois to Notre Dame, followed by the queen, the cardinals and the bishops, the whole Parlement and all the colleges. The expiatory procession threaded its way along the icy streets. The era of equivocation was ended.[1]

JOHN CALVIN AT THE AGE OF TWENTY-FIVE

During the winter months of 1534–5 the roads leading to Strasbourg and Switzerland were crowded with travellers whose haste to reach their destination appeared as great as their extreme anxiety not to be recognized. Among those apparently making for Alsace was a tall, feverish young man with dry lips, a long, thin nose and glowing eyes, whose older companion treated him with considerable attention and affection. Both men had the refined air of scholars and aristocrats; the thin one was timid and reserved, the other more solid and well built. John Calvin was fleeing from Paris, where his friend Étienne de la Forge had just perished at the stake. His travelling companion was du Tillet.

[1] But this 'White Terror' had gone too far. Francis I quickly revoked the ordinance prohibiting the printing of books, and twelve booksellers were authorized to print. Pope Paul III criticized this 'horrible law,' and after Chancellor Duprat's death the Edict of Coucy, in July 1535, offered heretics the chance of an amnesty if they abjured. In fact, however, this backward step did nothing to alter the situation fundamentally. The dice were cast.

The man whom history remembers under the latinized form of his name, 'Calvinus' or *Calvin*, was at this time known only to a small circle of humanists who had a high opinion of his commentary on Seneca's *De Clementia*. He was twenty-five years old, having been born on 10th July 1509; but his life had already been a full one, and he had had wide experience of both men and ideas. Calvin had first seen the light of day in that strange land of Picardy where mundane realism was so curiously mingled with aspirations towards idealism or adventure, and where outward placidity concealed much secret violence. It was the home not only of Peter the Hermit, Grand Ferré and Lefèvre d'Étaples, but also of the Communes and the *Jacquerie*, and, in days to come, of Camille Desmoulins and Gracchus Babeuf. Noyon—Holy Noyon, as it was sometimes called, because of its large number of churches and relics—was Calvin's native town, the capital of a diocese whose bishop was extremely powerful. In fact Calvin's father, Master Gerard Chauvin, drew a comfortable income from clerical sources. He was notary apostolic, episcopal secretary, and procurator-fiscal of the chapter; for a cooper's son, whose brothers were locksmiths and blacksmiths, this little lawyer had done pretty well for himself. Master Gerard had six children, four sons and two daughters, whom he had had to bring up single-handed, for his wife, Jeanne Lefranc, had left him a widower quite early in life. Of them all he considered his second child, John, to be the most outstanding. From his mother the child had inherited his natural distinction and mysterious charm; but no one knew whence he derived the brilliant intellect, the capacity for assimilating and remembering everything he was taught, which had made him outstanding, even among his teachers, while he was still a small boy at school. By the time he was twelve years old, Calvin's character had become what it was to remain for the rest of his life— cold and resolute, reserved, but capable of terrible violence and as severe to others as he was to himself.

Following the custom of the age, his father had taken advantage of his important ecclesiastical connections to have a cathedral chaplaincy bestowed on young John. Later he secured him a parish, which he subsequently exchanged for one that was more lucrative, that of Saint-Martin at Marteville. This was simply the contemporary way of giving 'bursaries' to gifted boys. John Calvin had been a brilliant student, pursuing his studies with the same seriousness that he devoted to everything. He was friendly with the sons of the noble house of Hangest-Montmor, the bishop's nephews, and before he was fifteen had accompanied them to Paris, where, at the Collège de la Marche, he worked under Mathurin Cordier, the eminent Latinist, for whom he retained a respectful affection all his life. Then, at the instance of his friends' 'ludicrous' tutor, he was obliged to leave the learned pedagogue to fall under the sway of the terrifying Maître Tempête, Noel Beda's successor as principal of the celebrated Collège de Montaigu, who thoroughly deserved the nickname given him by his pupils—'horrida tempestas.' He derived much profit from the five years spent in this austere place which, at least so far as its scholarship was concerned, was quite the reverse of 'the poverty-stricken hole' lampooned by Rabelais. 'So much theology is brewed there,' said Erasmus, 'that the very walls are impregnated with it.' The curriculum at Montaigu was excellent, consisting of philosophy, literature, and the Latin and Greek Fathers studied in the original texts; and the young Norman from Noyon emerged with a fair smattering of everything.

He now experienced that insatiable thirst for knowledge which fires all really great minds in their early twenties. Calvin was connected with a number of intelligent men, such as his cousin Pierre Robert Olivétan, the future humanist. He also managed to win the friendship of such mature figures as Fourcy de Cambrai, a teacher at the Sorbonne, and Guillaume Cop, who came from Basle and was the king's principal physician. He was also on close terms with Guillaume Budé. Thus he found himself plunged into the midst of that wonderful circle where classical literature and the Bible were equally important subjects of discussion, and where the works of Erasmus, Lefèvre d'Étaples, Luther and Melanchthon were read with impassioned interest. Closeted for long hours in his room, worn thin with study, and his brain at fever heat, he had sailed through his examinations with the ease of a racehorse, becoming master of arts in 1528 and obtaining his law degree in 1532. What lay ahead? Calvin himself was inclined towards literature or theology, but his father, being a practical Norman, opted for the more remunerative profession of law. So the young man set to work to study laws, Digests and Pandects, without pleasure but to much purpose, first at Orleans with Pierre l'Estoile, to whom he was later referred as the 'undisputed prince' of juridical sciences, and then at Bourges, where the somewhat showy style of the Milanese Alciazzo disappointed him. His taste for illustrious acquaintances once more asserted itself at Bourges: here he met Master Rabelais, whose fame as a humanist had preceded the publication of his books. The learned Melchior Wolmar, a German supporter of Luther, had taught him the rudiments of Hebrew and introduced him to the Greek New Testament edited by Erasmus. Wolmar had made no secret of his view that the young scholar was taking the wrong direction in aiming at some legal office, and that his true vocation lay in theology, 'the mistress of all the sciences.' But of this John Calvin was not yet fully aware.

In May 1531 Calvin's father died, and the son was master of his own destiny. Master Gerard's death took place in painful circumstances which made a great impression on Calvin. Some years earlier the apostolic notary had become embroiled with the chapter concerning some complicated matter of liquidation, and had been promptly excommunicated. At his death, therefore, his sons were obliged to negotiate with the religious authorities a belated absolution. Young John returned to Paris, where he avidly resumed his literary studies, attending Pierre Danès's Greek courses at the new Collège des Lecteurs Royaux and learning Hebrew under Vatable. Then, during an interval of hesitation and vacillation, he spent two years gallivanting between Paris, Noyon, Orleans and Bourges, lodging for a few months at the Collège de Fortes, opposite the Montaigu. It was at this period that he published, though without commercial success, his commentary on Seneca, which contained many irreverent attacks on the established order, the Church and scholasticism. These were the final years of preparation, and there emerged from them the humanist who associated classical learning with the Christian Gospel. No one who saw him then would have thought that this extremely gifted young man would ever be anything more than a distant disciple of Erasmus or Guillaume Budé!

No one was more convinced than John Calvin that he had been born to accomplish a great mission, and he made this so clear that people considered him overweening and presumptuous. At Orleans he had been nicknamed 'the accusative' because of his extreme readiness to censure others. His best friends, however, recognized his fine inner qualities, and whenever he spoke of such intimates as Pierre Robert Olivétan, Nicolas Duchemin or François Daniel, he did so with brotherly affection. No one could really claim to understand him properly. He had made people laugh with his high dudgeon at the failure of his first book, but he was none the less sincere when he proclaimed in tones of stoical pride that all things were vain, and that he despised the things of this world. His pallid face revealed nothing of his secret, inner conflicts. There was a mystery about this young man, something cold and terrifying.

He was to guard his mystery most jealously on the very subject which interests us most: his spiritual evolution. How did he become 'reformed'? How was the Calvin of history born? Everyone knows how St Paul and St Augustine were suddenly struck by the Divine Light and personally summoned by God. The dark night of Pascal's spiritual struggle is equally famous; while Luther proclaimed his drama to the whole world. 'I don't like talking about myself,' said Calvin; 'I have always preferred obscurity.' Several not ignoble reasons may be the explanation of this reserve: his aristocratic disdain of intimate confidences; his proud determination to be the master of his own destinies; or his belief that man counted for nothing in this type of affair. 'I keep silent, O Lord,' he said again, 'because this work is Yours.'

We do not even know for certain when he became converted to the new ideas. 'There is no means whatsoever of guessing when the spiritual battle began, or when it ended . . .' says Abel Lefranc. The evidence of a letter from Calvin to Bucer was for many years regarded as proof that he adopted Protestantism as early as 1532, but the date of this letter is contested. In August 1533 Calvin actually attended a session of the chapter at Noyon, when it was decided to organize a religious procession against the plague. There is no indication at all that he raised the slightest protest against a manifestation of piety which he subsequently considered idolatrous. However, while he may not have yet considered himself explicitly Protestant, it seems probable that he had been slowly evolving in this direction for many years past. After all, he had heard the new ideas extolled or condemned at La Marche and Montaigu; and as a student moving in humanist circles he had undoubtedly glanced at the works of Lefèvre, Luther and Melanchthon. Guillaume Cop, who was a friend of both Erasmus and Reuchlin, must have discussed in his presence many of the problems which were common topics of conversation among thinking people at that time. In addition, a number of direct influences can hardly have failed to affect him; for example, that of his cousin Pierre Robert Olivétan, who had adhered to Protestantism and decided to leave France in order to be allowed to think freely, and his German teacher Wolmar, who had so often told him that he was born to be a theologian. Recent scholarship also considers that a sustained and systematic reading of Luther had a direct bearing upon his intellectual evolution. It was probably long drawn out, prepared in the subconscious of the soul, before being brought to sudden completion by a phenomenon of crystallization as so often happens in this kind of affair.[1]

Such is the impression given by those sparse and succinct documents in which Calvin elaborates on his 'conversion' to Protestantism. Some historians have considered them contradictory; it is more true to say that they seem complementary. In a passage to his *Letter to Sadolet*, on the one hand, he clearly states that his decision was preceded by lengthy preparation: 'The more closely I looked at myself, the more sharply my conscience was pricked; so much so that neither solace nor

---

[1] The sight of all the abuses and errors in the established Church does not appear to have played much part in his evolution. He scarcely mentions them. At most the painful incidents attending his father's death may have contributed to his abandonment of Catholicism, but they were not decisive. The traditional picture, showing the Protestant Reformation as something provoked by the scandals of Catholicism, no longer holds good where Calvin is concerned. Since the *Treatise on Relics* does not appear to be the fruit of a belated hunger for polemics, we can assume at most that he reflected on this subject. (In contrast, this factor played a major part in determining Farel's attitude.)

comfort remained to me, save to lose myself in self-oblivion. But, since nothing better was offered me, I continued to pursue the course I had begun, even though quite a different kind of doctrine had arisen. This did not deviate from the Christian faith, but rather reduced it to its true shape, and restored to it its purity, cleansed of all the dirt that sullied it. But this novelty offended me. I had little desire to listen to it, and indeed I confess that at the beginning I resisted it valiantly and courageously.' The obstacles he encountered at this time, he says, were the routine which binds men to accepted ideas and the reverence which he wished to retain towards the Church. Thus the evidence is clear: here is a slow evolution, slowed down by conflicts of conscience but at the same time driven forward under the lash of new doctrines, particularly those which presented the Reformation as a return to a purer kind of Christianity.

Nevertheless some of Calvin's other statements show that there was a decisive shock towards the end of this evolution. In his *Commentary on the Psalms* (1557) he wrote: 'Because I was so stubbornly devoted to papist superstitions that I could not be dragged from this deep and miry pit except with much difficulty, God overwhelmed me and restored my soul to its rightful obedience.' Elsewhere he expressly declares: 'God compelled me to alter course abruptly. Like a sudden flash of lightning, I saw into what a pit of falsehood I was plunged. . . .'

We must not for all this conclude too readily that Calvin's decision can be explained by mere intellectual progress culminating in one blinding moment of resolution. It is hardly credible that, as one historian claims, 'logic alone led him to break with Rome,' and that he 'made his decision without the anguish experienced by many others.' [1] Calvin does not seem to have felt the pain of separation which tormented Luther, and Melanchthon even more so. But it seems improbable that he journeyed into heresy by way of logical demonstration alone, particularly when we recall that his discovery of the answer to his one great problem (man's ultimate fate) was expressed in the dreadful theory of Predestination and drew from him the terrible admission: 'I confess that this statement is quite horrible.' But on the fundamentals of his spiritual progress the icy genius is silent.

The moment of final decision must have taken place between autumn 1532 and spring 1534. In September 1532 Calvin went to live at Paris, in the house of a wealthy Walloon cloth merchant, Étienne de la Forge, a convinced 'Protestant' who spent his fortune in almsgiving and in having thousands of copies of the Gospel printed in French. There John Calvin made contact with a miniature underworld of refugees from Flanders, Germany and Italy: smiths, cobblers, former prostitutes and even reformed bandits. Though by nature

[1] P. Jourdan.

'timid, weak and pusillanimous,' as he himself admitted, he discovered
in this circle the kind of courage possessed by humble folk inspired by
burning faith. At their secret meetings these enthusiastic supporters of
the condemned doctrines snapped their fingers at Morin, head of the
government police, at his armed spies and at his torturers. Their
exaltation must have resembled that of the early Church in the time of
St Paul.

The situation, however, had deteriorated. Through all the fluctuations of royal policy the hour of decision was evidently fast approaching; one day a choice would be inevitable. On 1st November 1533 the
newly elected rector of the university, a young man named *Nicholas
Cop*, son of the king's physician, had given the opening lecture of the
term in the church of the Mathurins. Two Franciscans were present,
and immediately denounced him to Morin. The theme of the address
was the Sermon on the Mount, and Cop had used it as a vehicle for
some unorthodox ideas. He had revealed his contempt for the sophists
who reduced theology to scholastic exercises. He had opposed to them
a form of Erasmianism, proclaiming Christ as 'the only mediator'
(which made him suspect on the grounds of despising Our Lady and
the saints) and preaching a return to the Gospel alone. There was no
reference to Tradition, and some of his remarks hinted at justification
by faith. Now Nicholas Cop was a close friend of Calvin, and it was
rumoured, as it is still rumoured today, that the sermon had been
written by Calvin himself. The text—whether draft or copy is uncertain—was found among Calvin's papers at Geneva; so it has never
been possible to disprove the allegation. Moreover the discourse
contained some passages taken almost literally from Erasmus's preface
to the New Testament and one of Luther's commentaries on St
Matthew's Gospel. In the eyes of a policeman it was of very little
importance whether or not Calvin was responsible for the address;
sufficient that he was a friend of Cop. The latter, summoned to appear
before the Parlement, made his escape by night and fled to Basle;
Calvin was warned in time to save himself. Taking refuge with a
vine-grower, a 'brother evangelist' who lived in the same district,
Calvin donned workman's clothes and, with sack on back and pick on
shoulder, left the capital. Shortly after his departure Étienne de la
Forge was arrested.

Was this the turning-point? Was it this event that established the
young scholar in the camp of the 'evil-thinkers'? It is hard to tell. For
a few months he lived quietly with his friend Louis du Tillet (parish
priest of Claix, and later of Angoulême), calling himself Charles
d'Espeville and devouring the treasures of a well-stocked library. Then
he pushed on to the court at Nerac, where Marguerite had just welcomed the aged Lefèvre d'Étaples, who, weeping with joy rather in the

manner of Simeon, prophesied that he saw in Calvin the emissary of Heaven. Dissatisfied with the extraordinary mixture of courtly eroticism and mystical piety that existed at Nerac, and also much disturbed to hear that he had been denounced, Calvin retraced his footsteps. At this time he may well have taken part in the secret meetings held in a cave near Poitiers, where the Lord's Supper was celebrated in the style of Primitive times. He spent the whole of 1534 constantly on the move. On one occasion he revisited Paris and met Michael Servetus, his future victim; he stayed for a while at Orleans, where he wrote a treatise against certain Anabaptist theses; then he took refuge again with his friend du Tillet at Angoulême. He was safe nowhere. The storm was about to break.

Meanwhile in May he had made an honest gesture. He was disgusted by the double life he had been leading for so long—a Protestant in his heart, but outwardly a Catholic in his appearances: theoretically chaplain of Noyon, supposedly parish priest of Pont-l'Évêque and a respected beneficiary for whom the canons of his city had offered to secure appointment as judge of the ecclesiastical court. He therefore returned to Noyon, and instead of asking to receive holy orders, which would have been necessary had he wished to make a career in the Church, he resigned all his benefices. This decision marked his break with the past. As a rejection of hypocrisy it compels our admiration. Calvin had deliberately placed himself in the camp of the schismatics, of those condemned as heretics. A few months later the Placard Affair unleashed the tide of royal repression, and launched him along the road to exile.

BASLE AND THE LATIN VERSION OF THE 'CHRISTIAN INSTITUTION'

When he was obliged to flee from France Calvin quite naturally went eastwards towards those Rhenish territories where bold religious experiments had been in progress for more than fifteen years. He reached Strasbourg by way of Metz, but made only a brief stop there. The town which attracted him was Basle, city of Oeclampadius, pulse of the Reformation, one of the movement's spiritual capitals. The memory of Erasmus was still very much alive there: Pierre Viret, Karlstadt, Caroli, Bullinger, Platter the printer, Oporinus, Ruch and Winter (publishers of the *Christian Institution*) made up a small cosmopolitan society in which anything and everything was discussed. He could imagine no more satisfactory climate.

The months spent by Calvin at Basle were among the most productive in a life devoted entirely to work. He settled in the Faubourg Saint-Alban, at the house of Catherine Klein, a worthy widow.

Perhaps with a view to securing peace and quiet, or perhaps as a measure of prudence, he again took a pseudonym after the manner of students and called himself Martianus Lucianus (an anagram of 'Calvin.') His friend Nicholas Cop had reached Basle somewhat earlier, and he introduced Calvin to enthusiastic groups of Protestants. Very soon, as had been the case in France, this frail young man with the firm, meditative air was looked up to as a teacher and a leader. 'I was quite surprised that all those desirous of a pure instruction should come to me at a time when I myself had scarcely begun to learn,' he confessed. He would come to meetings with his big felt cap pulled well down over his ears, and would remain silent for a long time, gently stroking his beard—the typical attitude of one who was 'a rather unsociable and bashful person, who liked peace and quiet.' But whenever he did interrupt, his authority was absolute, and he saw that it was imposed. However, he spent most of his time attending the lectures of famous professors, and, above all, reading and writing in his room. He set to work learning Hebrew with Sebastian Münster, one of Reuchlin's pupils. Theology was his prime concern. This was a branch of knowledge about which he knew very little, and he worked at it day and night, absorbing everything from the Greek Fathers to Luther. At the same time he was corresponding with other Protestant thinkers, notably the two leaders at Strasbourg, Capitanus and Bucer, who made a profound impression upon him. And he was writing.

In June 1535 he supplied a lengthy preface to the new translation of the Bible which his cousin Olivétan was then issuing. The tone of this was solemn, but the author displayed a lively irony in respect of certain errors, and asserted his principles firmly. 'Without the Gospel,' he says, 'we are useless and vain; without the Gospel wealth is poverty, wisdom is folly before God, strength is weakness. But through the power of the Gospel we are made children of God.' Already we see the real Calvin.

This was but a small beginning. For a long time past he had been considering a fuller and more personal work. According to Florimond de Rémond, who published the first complete history of *The Heresy of this Century* in 1623, Calvin had completed the formulation of his project during visits to his friend du Tillet, amid the comfort of the latter's splendid library. There he had 'started weaving the fabric of his *Institution*, in order to surprise all Christendom.' At all events when he wrote his little treatise on *Psychopannychia* (The Sleep of Souls) at Orleans soon afterwards, in order to refute an Anabaptist error, he certainly possessed the kernel of his thesis, for it contains a number of sentences almost exactly parallel with those of the *Institution*; for example, 'We acknowledge no other unity save in Christ, and no other love save that of which He is the bond; consequently the best way of preserving love is for our faith to remain whole and inviolate.' Theodore Beza states that it was the sight of the persecutions unleashed in France which determined Calvin to write and publish his book. He wished to provide the king, and if possible the whole world, with a defence and illustration of Protestantism. This little manual, however —*breve enchiridion*—later acquired the character of a manifesto and plan of action.

According to the date which closes the 'prefatory letter' to King Francis I, the *Christian Institution* must have been finished in *August* 1535 (the 1st or 23rd, the figure varied from edition to edition). One of the principal book fairs was held on 7th September, and Oporinus, Calvin's publisher, hoped to have the work out by then; he failed to do so, but it was ready for the Easter fair in March 1536. This early form of the *Institution* was written in Latin, and was very much shorter than the French volume which appeared five years later with the same title. Nevertheless it contained about 520 small octavo pages, and measured about 3 by 4½ inches. It consisted of six chapters, of which the first four dealt with the Law, the Faith, the Sermon and the Sacraments. The original draft was confined to these four chapters, but at the last moment Calvin added a chapter on False Sacraments and another on the Christian's Relationship with the State. Here already was a complete exposition of what it is convenient to call 'Calvinism.' The prefatory letter to the king is a magnificent piece of eloquence, firm and measured in its inspiration, written by an excited, tense hand. Its author considered it a skilful plea. 'Through this work, Sire, I should like to serve France. Seeing that countless folk in this realm hunger and thirst after Christ, but that very few know Him; seeing also that the fury of some iniquitous persons has been raised in your realm . . . and that every way is closed to righteous teaching, I should like this book to confess the faith of the persecuted believers.'

The book caused a sensation as soon as it appeared. By January 1537 the first edition was out of print; it was read with enthusiasm by all who were concerned about such problems. It is interesting to speculate whether the *Christian Institution* was that 'laudable object' which Marguerite of Navarre sent her brother, with instructions to read it for 'the universal wellbeing of everyone and the augmentation of the honour of God.' Between February and April 1536 Francis I was staying at Lyons, not very far from Basle, and he may have received a copy from the publisher. 'A number of minor mysteries surround the beginnings of this work. One suspects, for instance, that a French edition may have appeared in 1537, for in October 1536 Calvin stated that he was busy preparing one 'in all his moments of leisure.' There is, however, not the slightest doubt that the publication of this book, and the widespread interest that it caused, placed Calvin among the leading Reformers. Until now he had been regarded simply as a talented young man, capable of serving the cause well. But this soundly reasoned, firmly written treatise convinced many Protestants that they now possessed their code, their catechism, the fundamental exposition of the new doctrine. From this date, 1536, Calvin became, in Bossuet's phrase, 'the second patriarch' of the Reformation.

Several years, however, would elapse before he could translate his ideas into deeds; nor was this accomplished at Basle, a city strongly organized upon bases which were not his own. For a time it seemed that the event might take place in Italy, at the court of Ferrara, whither he was invited by the duchess, Renée of France, cousin of Francis I. Lefèvre d'Étaples had converted Louis XII's daughter, and this sad, gentle woman with beautiful deep blue eyes found in pious meditation the sole consolation she could hope for from the joyless existence forced upon her by her husband, Ercole d'Este, in whose veins ran Borgia blood. But as things turned out Calvin's stay at Ferrara had no other result but the formation of a *sancta amicitia* between the great lady and the young prophet, which was to endure for the remainder of their lives. Compelled to disguise himself as a Catholic priest in order to deceive the officials of the Inquisition, and seeing some of his co-religionists arrested, 'Lucianus' preferred to take to the road again. He never fancied the stake.

During his absence his authority in France was growing. Calvin himself dared to talk, or rather to write, more authoritatively. From Ferrara he sent several of his friends and relations letters in the form of stern rebuke. A number of actual or near Protestants appeared to be wavering: Duchemin, Gérard Roussel and even du Tillet. Calvin admonished them as though they were his subjects. Duchemin, who was talking of taking holy orders, received a vehement epistle in which he was invited to 'flee all papal superstitions,' and not to simulate a faith he no longer possessed: 'If Our Lord is God, follow Him.' Gérard Roussel, who had just obtained the bishopric of Oloron, was likewise taken to task: Donning the mitre? Was he going to take his place among the 'false prophets and hypocrites,' among those 'little thieving, stealing villains' of priests?

His youthful authority was seeking an outlet. But where? and how? One final act proves that Calvin had made up his mind to devote his whole being henceforward to the service of what he believed to be the truth. Taking advantage of the Edict of Toleration (July 1535) which temporarily suspended persecution of 'evil-thinkers,' he returned to France, went to Noyon, disposed of his share of his father's estate and persuaded his brother Antoine and one of his sisters to follow him into foreign exile. He was contemplating a return to Basle, or rather of settling in Strasbourg, when, according to the pattern decreed for him by the law of Predestination, his life was suddenly given quite a new direction.

IN THE GENEVA OF THE 'HUGUENOTS'

War had broken out again for the third time between Francis I and Charles V; all the roads in Lorraine were crowded with troops and were none too safe. Calvin was therefore obliged to take the route south, through Savoy and Geneva, where his destiny awaited him.

At this period Geneva was an imperial city, a small independent state, all the more jealous of her liberty in that she saw it threatened by her formidable neighbour, the Duke of Savoy, whose territories, along with le Bugey, the Vaudois and the Valais, completely encircled her. In recent times Geneva had been governed by her bishop and her citizens. The latter expressed their wishes in a General Council, or Assembly, which in turn delegated its authority to three subsidiary Councils, each restricted to its own particular function: the Little Council, the 'Sixty' or Senate, and the 'Two Hundred' or Great Council. This hybrid system repeatedly gave rise to friction, for the Genevans suspected their bishop of taking sides with the Duke of Savoy, since his diocese extended into the latter's territory.

The infiltration of Protestant ideas into Switzerland had done nothing to alter the situation. The Protestants had gained much ground in the country, despite the defeat of the German-Swiss Zwinglian cantons at Kappel in 1531. Inspired by Bullinger, Zwingli's successor at Zürich, and by three audacious preachers—Guillaume Farel, Pierre Viret and Antoine Froment—they had made inroads at Morat and Neuchâtel. Berne, which had been converted to Protestantism, now threw her considerable political forces into the balance. Along with Freiburg, which had remained Catholic, and Geneva, she had formed the League of Confederates—*Eidgenossen, Huguenots* [1]—to save their common liberty. At this juncture the new doctrines, which had already conquered the people of Berne, rapidly permeated Geneva. In 1532 Protestant posters had appeared in the town on the occasion of a

[1] Here, it seems, is the origin of the word 'Huguenots,' which was used to describe the Protestants in France. 'Huguenot' appears to be the distortion of *Eidgenossen*, due to confusion with the word *Hugues* (from Hugues Besançon, the leader of the Swiss patriots). It is amusing to study the fantastic etymologies which have been suggested for this word. Étienne Pasquier claims that the folk of Touraine believed in a nocturnal devil named Hugon, and that they called the Calvinists 'Huguonneaux' because the latter held their meetings at night. Castelnau asserts that 'the huguenot' was a bronze coin of Hugues Capet; to say 'They are Huguenots' was equivalent to saying 'They are not much good.' De Brieux's explanation is even more bizarre. He states that one Calvinist preacher stuttered the first words of a sermon which began with this Latin quotation: 'Huc nos venimus,' whereupon the crowd began to chant 'Huc, Huc, Huguenot.' In Condé's memoirs we read that the Protestants had 'usurped' the name of 'aignos,' which is fairly accurate, since there were Catholic Freiburgers in the political league of the Eidgenossen.

preaching of indulgences ordered by Clement VII. The Catholic authorities had attempted to react. But two years later the bishop had become even more unpopular and had to flee the city; whereupon the democratic Councils, now in sole charge, showed their defiance by leaving the field wide open to the ministers of the Reformed religion. A great public 'disputation' was arranged between Protestants and Catholics in which the former won the day, at any rate in the opinion of the judges. The Catholics were so enraged at seeing the Mass prohibited that they invoked the aid of the Duke of Savoy and their bishop, who had taken refuge at Annecy, in order that the rebel town might be reduced by force. This minor war ended in victory for Geneva. Helped by the citizens of Berne and by Francis I—whom the Duke of Savoy had just deserted to ally himself with the emperor—the free townsfolk repelled the enemy with heavy losses. This triumph (1535) had also ensured the success of Protestantism in the city, for reasons which, as can be seen, were political rather than religious.

The man who had taken the most active part in all these affairs, and who had proved himself a tireless preacher, a gallant military leader, a source of constant inspiration and an excellent organizer, was *Guillaume Farel* (1489–1565). A native of Dauphiné, he was a former disciple of Lefèvre d'Étaples, and had come to Geneva after an unsuccessful attempt to introduce Protestantism at Montbéliard. Farel was a strange little man, rather like a red gnome with a face raddled with scarlet pimples, bloodshot eyes and enormous lips. Whether he was talking to a large crowd or to a single listener, his voice was always sharply pitched; the veins in his neck would swell, and he gave the permanent impression of haranguing or censuring. He was also highly intelligent: he gauged his own limitations with perfect accuracy, and desired for himself only the humble but necessary place of John the Baptist alongside a new Messiah. In Geneva which was divided between rival clans—for the Catholics were still powerful—Farel had tried to lay the foundation-stones of an 'evangelical' city, to organize a regular cult and recruit a clergy, but he was well aware of the meagre results of his effort. His real value was that he saw in Calvin the man who would give reality to his dreams.

It was du Tillet, still a 'Protestant' at this time, who brought the two men face to face. He was staying at Geneva when Calvin arrived there to spend one night at an inn near the Cornavin Gate. Du Tillet passed the news to Farel, whereupon the latter hurried to the inn. There a most extraordinary scene took place, of which Calvin retained painful memories for the rest of his life. Shouting, gesticulating and waving the wide sleeves of his gown, Farel called upon Calvin in the name of God to remain in Geneva, to undertake the task which he, God's messenger, would indicate to him. The prudent Norman tried to evade the summons; he had 'a number of particular studies to pursue, for which he desired to keep himself free.' But the little red gnome refused to listen; his neck swelled with fury, his beard quivered angrily, and he told his hearer that if he refused to apply himself to the essential work, he, Farel, would ask God to destroy the tranquillity of his studies. This imprecation 'terrified' Calvin, who yielded to Farel's request. His journey therefore ended at Geneva.

Calvin was nominated 'reader in Holy Scripture in the Church of Geneva,' and was soon entrusted with the additional task of delivering sermons and concerning himself with religious organization in the town. He placed his eminent gifts of French logic and severity at the service of the Reformed community. The situation which he found at Geneva was not particularly encouraging. Later on he described it thus: 'There was virtually nothing in this Church. Preaching was all there was to it. Everything was in a state of muddle and confusion.' Since the Genevans' basic reason for turning Protestant had been political, they were little interested in religious matters. Master Calvin's sermons at St Peter's Church met with little success. However, when entrusted with the task of arguing his cause at Lausanne, where yet another 'disputation' was being held between Catholic and Protestants, and then at Berne, where an attempt was made to reach agreement between Lutherans and Zwinglians, he proved himself to be an outstanding controversialist and a telling orator. His influence in Geneva increased considerably. He then set to work to put into practice the three-point programme he had drawn up with Farel: to replace the Catholic cult by a Protestant one, to formulate a body of doctrine which could be imposed on all the citizens, and to exert control over the life and morals of the city. In November 1536 the *Articles on Ecclesiastical Discipline* attained the first objective: the churches, now known as 'temples,' were stripped of their ornaments, statues and pictures were destroyed, and even crosses—'the insignia of papal devilry'—were condemned; divine service was reduced to prayers, a sermon and the singing of psalms. Calvin would have liked fairly frequent celebration of the Lord's Supper, probably at monthly intervals, but under the influence of the Bernese he was forced to agree that it should take place only three or four times a year. A few months later, in February 1537, the *Instruction and Confession of Faith*, a kind of catechism taken from the *Christian Institution*, tackled the second objective: the Council of Two Hundred decreed that all citizens must adhere to this formulary under pain of banishment; a few harmless Anabaptists and Caroli, the French pastor who was daring enough to say that Calvinism seemed to him like a brand of Arianism, were exiled.

Things began to go awry when Calvin and his followers tried to attain their third objective, the reform of morals of which they asserted that the townsfolk stood in urgent need. The Genevans considered that they had not expelled their bishop and defeated the Savoyards simply in order that a clique of Frenchmen should tell them how to run their lives. But the terrifying young man declared from the pulpit that 'the Church's strength is in her discipline, and the strength of her discipline lies in her power of excommunication.' He therefore called for the creation of an organism which would be entrusted with the task of forbidding the Lord's Supper to loose-living citizens. Violent reaction ensued. A party of the friends of liberty, or 'Libertines' as they were called, was formed round a few eminent citizens who had played a leading part in the struggle against the Savoyards. Derisive jingles directed at the masters of the day were sung in the streets:

> 'Diable roux
> Démon noir!
> Maître Guillaume
> Maître Jean!' [1]

At night peaceful Geneva, which had never before witnessed such scenes, was disturbed by wild sarabands of mummers, who came singing indecent songs and shouting blasphemies under the very windows of Farel and Calvin. Finally, at the elections in 1538, the majority passed to the reformers' enemies on all the Councils. In order to embarrass the Frenchman the Grand Council decreed that the Eucharist should be given in the Bernese fashion, which was virtually Lutheran in style, with unleavened and not ordinary bread as required by Calvin; a subsequent edict forbade 'any preacher from interfering in the affairs of the State.' This was clearly directed at Calvin, who protested; he was thereupon stopped from preaching at all. Rioting followed. Calvin's supporters resisted; their opponents advanced, shouting 'Into the Rhône with them!' and waving firearms.

Calvin prepared his answer in conjunction with his friends Florel and Courand. On Easter Day 1538, despite the ban, he mounted the pulpit in St Peter's Cathedral, protested vehemently against the Council's decisions and announced that he refused to distribute the Lord's Supper to such a dissolute, sacrilegious and blaspheming people. He excommunicated the entire city. Despite the many threats against his life, and the swords that were unsheathed, he refused to go back on his astounding decision. Bloodshed was only just avoided. Next day, however, the citizens banished the preachers from Geneva. 'Capital!' declared Calvin. 'If we were serving-men this would be poor recompense; but we serve a far greater Master, and He will be able to reward us well.' [2]

---

[1] 'Red devil, black demon, Master Guillaume [Farel], Master John [Calvin]!'

[2] This sentence is, to say the least, unexpected, springing from the lips of a theologian who did not believe in the efficacity of good works.

STRASBOURG, BUCER AND THE FRENCH VERSION OF THE 'CHRISTIAN INSTITUTION'

Calvin felt immensely relieved on quitting the shores of Lake Geneva; it troubled his conscience to distribute the Eucharist to unworthy Christians. Very soon, however, that same conscience began to reproach him. Was his departure from Geneva not likely to weaken the cause of the Reformation? Had his own severity and excessive demands made him partly responsible for the rupture? Would not God call him to account for these souls whom he had not been able to love as much as he ought? This remorse was so strong (and Farel was likewise afflicted) that Calvin felt an urge to go to Zürich, where a synod of Swiss pastors was in session, and confess his sins in public. He did so, and to such effect that several of his hearers wrote to the Genevans advising them to take back their apostle. A categorical refusal confirmed the decree of banishment.

Where should he go? While Farel established himself at Neuchâtel,[1] Calvin decided to return to Basle and resume his studies. But two years earlier, while in Berne, he had met Bucer, the leader of the Strasbourg Protestants, and this clear-sighted man had divined the strength of the bold young prophet with his trenchant views. He now suggested that Calvin should settle near him and act as pastor to the numerous French exiles in Strasbourg. Calvin hesitated for some months, dreading to shoulder a new burden. Bucer insisted and, 'remonstrating and protesting very much as Farel had done before him,' reminded his correspondent of the terrible example of Jonah, who, when summoned by God to carry the Word to the Ninevites, had tried to shirk the task and had thereby brought upon himself an awful fate. Calvin confessed himself 'terrified' of being swallowed by the whale. And he resolved to leave for Strasbourg.

Strasbourg had been for several years past one of the leading centres of Protestantism, comparable with Wittenberg and Basle. It was an imperial city, virtually free, its political affairs controlled by an outstanding leader called Jakob Sturm, while its principal theologians were two eminent scholars, Capito and, most important of all, *Bucer*.[2] Thanks to these two men Strasbourg had succeeded in carving herself an original niche within the Protestant fold: the Church of Strasbourg, though it had adhered to the Wittenberg Agreement ever since 1536, had nevertheless preserved its own confession of faith, 'the tetrapolitan,'[3] which it had upheld against that of Augsburg. Bucer, a

---

[1] Where he was to remain until his death in 1565, save for a brief stay in Metz between 1542 and 1543, when he unsuccessfully tried to make that city a second Geneva.

[2] See Chapter V, p. 336.

[3] See Chapter V, p. 338.

shrewd, broad-minded man, preached a reasoned and moderate theology which steered a middle course between Lutheranism and Zwinglianism; he had organized his Church in the most stable fashion with the help of a council of elders and a college of higher education founded by Sturm. The civil and ecclesiastical authorities in the city worked hand in hand, and the feeling of communion with the universal Church was stronger there than anywhere else in the Protestant world. Calvin was to learn a great deal from his contact with this vigorous body.

Strasbourg therefore constituted the final stage in Calvin's formation, and it was a stage which he had the good fortune to clear in company of a master whose lessons he readily accepted. Bucer was eighteen years older than Calvin. 'If I do not come up to your expectations on any point whatsoever, you know that I am in your hands,' wrote the younger man to the older. 'Scold, chastize, do whatever a father is permitted to do to correct a son.' And Bucer answered his pupil with moving affection: 'You are my heart and my soul.' Thanks to the former Dominican, Calvin had the corners rubbed off his character during his stay in Strasbourg, and, as Bucer himself told him, 'learnt to let people make mistakes sometimes.' His philosophy, as well as his character, reached completion at this time.

He stayed in Strasbourg for three years, acting as pastor of the French parish of Saint-Nicolas-des-Eaux and teaching theology at a salary of a florin a week. His success was considerable; his little community was fervent and many Anabaptists left their sect to ask for baptism from the young French pastor. He very wisely abandoned all those aspects of his ministry which had failed so badly at Geneva—the over-stringent demands and excessively categorical orders. The cult he practised here was little different from the Lutheran; what did it matter? For instance, he tolerated bell-ringing. Following Bucer's example Calvin went to much trouble to improve church music, writing some hymns in French, and also using a translation of the Psalms which had been recently completed by Clément Marot and set to music by Mathias Greiter, the Strasbourg organist. This warm friendly little parish gave Calvin great happiness, and later on he tried to use it as his model at Geneva.

In 1539 and 1540 Calvin did two decisive things. Firstly, he sought and obtained citizen rights at Strasbourg. Before granting this privilege the law required that he register his name with one of the trade guilds (in this case the tailors), and also pay an entry fee of twenty florins, which seemed enormous for his slender purse. Secondly, he married; or rather, he allowed himself to marry. Why? Certainly Calvin's reasons were very different from Luther's; the weight of the flesh did not press so heavily upon the gaunt Norman as upon the full-blooded

German. He may have been influenced by the fact that his health, which had never been good, was rapidly deteriorating; bad food at Montaigu, excessive study during his youth, the anxieties and fears that had beset his wanderings and the terrible experience at Geneva had all contributed to make him extremely delicate. He suffered from head-aches, dizziness, catarrh, stomach trouble and, later, haemorrhoids. Gradually his whole life became a constant Calvary, which was further aggravated by a semi-physical, semi-metaphysical anguish. 'I don't know whether I shall ever marry,' he said a few months before he made his decision; 'and if I were to do so, I would do so in order to be able to devote my time to the Lord, by being freer of day to day worries.' But this was not the sole reason for Calvin's marriage. Much more fundamental was his desire to follow Bucer's advice, and 'fulfil the Law.' In principle he condemned clerical celibacy, and he was setting a poor example by remaining celibate himself. The woman he chose, after two unsuccessful attempts, was the widow of an Anabaptist whom he had converted. Her name was *Idelette de Bure*. She was pretty, elegant and refined, well suited to the reformer's aristocratic tastes. 'Woman's sole beauty for me lies in her chastity, decency, modesty and attention to her husband's needs.' Idelette responded perfectly to her husband's definition. Her existence at Calvin's side was one of self-effacement. She died long before him (in 1549) and bore him only one son, who did not survive infancy. Unlike Luther, the austere Norman felt no need to leave posterity any intimate details about his married life.

Was he permanently settled in Strasbourg? All the evidence seemed to point that way as the months slipped by; Bucer associated him ever more closely with his own projects and activity. In February 1539 Calvin was a member of the delegation from Strasbourg which took part in the Congress of Frankfurt. This had been convened by command of Charles V, to try to put an end to the confusion in the Church. There he met Melanchthon, with whom he became close friends. He accom-panied Bucer as the latter's deputy to the subsequent meetings at Haguenau and Worms, which dragged on through 1540 and 1541. At Ratisbon, where the final attempt at pacification [1] took place, he was one of the three official delegates from Strasbourg, the other two being Jakob Sturm and Bucer. This contact with the German Churches resulted in confirming Calvin in his resolve to follow a different path, to avoid the mistakes he saw committed there, notably in the Churches' submission to the princes. His personal authority was so great that Marguerite of Navarre, with whom he still corresponded, led him to intervene on behalf of the Protestants in France.

It was in fact this youthful notoriety—which the publication of the

---

[1] On all these meetings see Chapter V, p. 354.

French edition of the *Christian Institution*, as we shall see, was bringing to its height—that resulted in his abandonment of that full, well-balanced life which he was leading at Strasbourg. Delegates from Geneva visited him there, just as they had done at Haguenau, Worms and Ratisbon, begging him to return to their city and once again take up his mission among them. What exactly had happened in Geneva? The Council itself admitted that the departure of the two preachers had been 'a great misfortune.' Ever since they left; the city had been plagued by 'internecine conflicts, denunciations, murders and disorders of every kind. . . .' Having retrieved their liberty, the citizens had taken advantage of it to the great prejudice of morality. The town was divided among rival factions. There was division even among the Protestants: the 'Guillermins,' who supported the ideas of Master Guillaume Farel, and the 'Articulants,' who favoured those of Berne, had fought to the point of banishing one another in turn. On the other hand, with the encouragement of Pope Paul III, the Catholics had raised their heads again, and had met at Lyons to consider what steps should be taken to restore their faith in Geneva. *Cardinal Sadolet* had just sent the Genevans an extremely diplomatic letter in which Calvin's faults and the dissensions which had apparently been caused by Protestantism were skilfully exploited. Eventually, by an overwhelming majority, the popular assembly had passed a motion beseeching Calvin 'to return and be its evangelist.' But when he received this petition the minister of Saint-Nicolas-des-Eaux felt himself more than ever devoted to his tranquil parish and to the good work he was peacefully carrying on there. 'I would rather suffer a hundred deaths than bear this cross,' he declared. When Farel added his prayers to those of the Genevans he confessed that 'the very word "recall" makes me shudder with horror. The further I go the more clearly I behold the pit from which the Lord delivered me.' But could he continue to ignore these supplications, when they too invoked the interest of God? After all, when Jonah emerged from the whale he had decided to carry the divine message to the Ninevites.

Nevertheless his years in Strasbourg had been astonishingly fruitful. In addition to four sermons a week, lectures and a vast correspondence, Calvin worked furiously at his books. It was here that he wrote his *Commentary on the Epistle to the Romans*, his *Short Treatise on the Lord's Supper* and his famous *Letter to Cardinal Sadolet*, in which he explained why he had become what he was. Above all, however, Strasbourg marked a stage of capital importance, not merely in the life of the reformer and the history of the Reformation, but in the religious history of the whole world and the literary history of France as well. This stage was marked by the publication of the French version of the *Christian Institution*.

Why? This translation on which, as we have seen, Calvin had been working in all his leisure moments ever since his days in Basle, was clearly intended to reach a much wider public than the Latin version had done. At the same period Dolet was publishing his *Manière de bien traduire* (The Style of Good Translation), in which he showed how advantageous it was for an author to have his works read in French, which was already the most exact language of the day. So in 1539 Ribel's printing-presses in Strasbourg produced a large, impressive book measuring some twelve and a half by eight inches, and comprising 436 thick pages, which was obviously intended for teachers and students, for university work. But Calvin was not yet satisfied; there should also be a copy which could be hidden in the bottom of a pocket. This was the edition which he prepared for the Genevan printer Jean Gérard, who had just published his revised version of the Bible (1540). As the reformer returned to Geneva his book was just coming off the presses there. It was tiny, measuring about seven by four inches, and consisting of 822 pages of very close type—a little volume that would spread its author's ideas throughout the world.

But it was no longer the Latin *Institution* of Basle; the work had grown enormously between times. This 'summa of piety and of almost everything that is essential in the doctrine of salvation' henceforward contained seventeen chapters. And this was only a half-way stage: later editions were to be even fuller, going so far as to include eighty chapters and more than eight hundred pages. The thing was no longer an expanded catechism, but a genuine manual of dogmatic theology. Every topic was thoroughly and systematically studied. Gaps were filled in, and the vocabulary studiously cleared of all over-academic words, together with any relics of scholasticism. Wendel accurately observes that 'the memory of the author's own experiences and of his recent conversations with the theologians of Strasbourg is evident on almost every page.'

The work became widely known very soon after its appearance. Pedlars travelling through Switzerland, the Low Countries and the valleys of the Vaud brought many copies of it into France. Proof of its success can be inferred from the haste shown by the Faculty of Theology at Paris to refute it (1543). Before long the *Institution* had been translated into German, English, Italian, Spanish, Hungarian and even Greek. No other book was more widely read during the sixteenth century, because it provided that essential and long-awaited element without which Protestantism could not hope to establish itself as an effective rival of the Catholic Church, and also because it was the work of a very great writer.

The Author of the 'Christian Institution'

Calvin was indeed an excellent writer, the first in time of the masters of modern French literature. No account of the reformer is possible without paying him the homage he so richly deserves in this field. Catholics, Protestants and free-thinkers, writers from Brunetière to Brunot, from Petit de Julleville to Morçay, from Lefranc to Plattard or Pannier—all who have studied his style are unanimous in assessing the considerable contribution which he made to a language which was soon to be used by St Francis de Sales and Montaigne, by Pascal and Bossuet.

The *Christian Institution* occupies pride of place among Calvin's literary work. But it constitutes only a relatively small part of the whole —one-quarter of his French work, which in itself was only about one-fifth of the total, for this great writer was prolific to a degree, particularly in Latin. His letters, treatises and pamphlets are of obvious interest for the study of his life, his way of thinking and his influence. The essential of his doctrine, however, the decisive testimony which he had to bear to the world, as well as the complete perfection of his literary style, are found in the *Institution*. Calvin first wrote this book when he was twenty-four years old; he continued to take it up again, remodel it and add to it until the end of his life.

If ever the completion of a work conformed exactly to its author's original purpose it is indeed this treatise, where everything seems clearly calculated to instruct, contend, prove and judge. The first thing which strikes the reader is its simplicity—the bareness of its vocabulary, which is the very antithesis of the pedantic intricacies of decadent scholasticism. The words of the *Institution* are those which artisans, housewives, pedlars and peasants could understand. There is an abundance of skilfully introduced and striking formulae, with a wealth of meaning. Important words are properly stressed. This sober, direct style placed a personal philosophy of persuasive logic within the grasp of ordinary people, and herein lay its very considerable threat to Catholicism. All was deliberate; the author said so himself on more than one occasion: 'Everyone knows my capacity for pressing an argument, and the accurate brevity of my writing.'

'Pressing an argument'—this could not be better stated. Of course 'argument,' 'counter-argument,' 'foreclosing' and 'demanding' are his obvious intentions; he is pleading a case as much as expressing his ideas. Hence the geometrical order of his developments, the sure, logical plan, the sound dialectic of the argumentation. Calvin never goes astray or wanders even when—as, for example, in his discussion of the Lord's Supper—his thinking is not very clear in his own mind.

Unlike Rabelais, who writes like a budding tree, throwing off leaves and branches in all directions, Calvin goes straight to the point, without allowing anything to deflect him. He excels in the play of ideas. Whereas medieval philosophy usually had recourse to successive deductions, enshrined in a number of short propositions, he knew the secret of constructing his sentences so that all their parts were arranged round the central idea to denote cause, consequence and conditions— all the connections, briefly, which constituted a complete thought. French, which had until his time been primarily narrative after the pictorial style of the illuminators, owed to him its new-found feeling of composition and perspective, becoming the art-form of the period which grasped the mind in its entirety. All this was magnificently new.

The defects of Calvin's style are the counterparts of his outstanding qualities: he risks being dry, dull and monotonous. His style is without sparkle. 'A more melancholy style,' Bossuet called it, comparing it with Luther's and yet recognizing it to be the 'more coherent and polished' of the two. Is this a fair assessment? Vivid imagery is not lacking to hold the reader's attention; there are plenty of proverbs and diverting comparisons. Calvin does not disdain to use familiar and even vulgar words: his work includes several plain-speaking Norman expressions, as well as much legal jargon. Needless to say he presents a colourless picture compared with that of Rabelais, his truculent contemporary. But if some of his paragraphs—those, for example, in his dedicatory letter to the king—are set beside those describing Gargantua's efforts, his superiority is striking. Force and beauty are on Calvin's side.

'The style is the man.' Ever since Buffon uttered this axiom men have tried to get to know the author through the pages of his book. There are few literary works which reveal as much of their writer's character as the *Christian Institution*; it also fixes his limitations. Severe, logical, expansive and strong as it is, this literary art remains that of a great intellectual, who is very little of a poet—though Calvin had once believed himself such—and who is interested only in the perfect play of ideas. There is no feeling here of that happy thirst for knowledge which makes Rabelais such a delight to read. There is not a single indication that the reformer was at all interested in the scientific discoveries which were beginning to excite men's minds—for example, the findings of Copernicus in 1530 on the rotation of the earth, of which Calvin was still ignorant in 1560. Neither is there very much indication that he loved his fellow men, in all their misery and weakness, with that warmth of brotherhood which alone moves human hearts. Luther doted on flowers, birds and children. Calvin never let himself descend to such weaknesses; nevertheless it is painful and shocking to find him describing children as '*petites ordures*.' The only time when he becomes exalted in tone is when he speaks of God, of His glory, honour and might; at these moments he is, it must be admitted, quite superb. And these flights of fervour succeed in giving meaning to the whole work; they remind us of the terrible doctrine served by this sonorous style, austere and pure as the duty it is intended to impose.

CALVINISM

The doctrine set out by Calvin is nowadays known as 'Calvinism.' [1] The accuracy of this nomenclature has been questioned. Some distinguished Protestants—Karl Barth, for example, the greatest non-Catholic theologian of modern times [2]—have protested against the use of the word. 'Calvinism is a concept that we owe to modern historians,' they say. 'There is no more any such thing as Calvinism than there is such a thing as "Lutheranism," and perhaps even less.' Within Calvin's perspectives, where, as we shall see, the Word of God is regarded as the sole source of truth and principal of action, it would be impossible to accept a body of doctrine, a categorical dogmatism imposed on man by an authority exercised through men, as is the case with Catholicism. 'A true disciple of Calvin has only one path to follow: he must obey not Calvin, but Him who was Calvin's Master.' [3]

So be it. Nevertheless it remains true to say that Calvin's philosophy presents itself to us as a complete and remarkably coherent system, despite certain flaws. In the sense in which one speaks of 'Platonism' or 'Cartesianism,' there is undoubtedly such a thing as 'Calvinism.' It is equally certain that in practice—and far more clearly than Luther had ever done—in order to establish his work in Geneva, Calvin was led to give his doctrine the character of an imperious dogmatism which in substance it refused to be. Once these reservations have been made, the edifice created by the Picard genius is extremely impressive. It is harmoniously constructed and powerfully presented. It seems to have been the fruit of one single inspiration, following which it merely had to grow and expand itself; from the first Latin edition of the *Institution* in six chapters, down to the final French version in eighty (to which, however, it is clear that various less gifted disciples made some contribution), there is not a single deviation or broken sequence of

[1] Translator's Note.—In view of the author's following comments it is interesting to note that in English-speaking countries the principal Churches deriving from Calvin are nowadays known as *Presbyterian*, rather than as *Calvinist* Churches, thus taking their name from the ecclesiastical organization supplied by their founder, rather than from the founder himself. The Calvinistic Methodist Church of Wales is an exception to this statement.

[2] This argument is taken from the preface of Charles Gaguebin's *Textes Choisis de Calvin*, produced for the collection 'Le Cri de France,' Paris, 1948.

[3] This justifies in advance the subsequent multiplication of doctrines and divisions into different sects—what Bossuet calls the 'variations' of Calvinism.

thought. The influence which it exerted on so many minds is quite understandable.

Calvin's philosophy is no more original than those of great creators usually are. Men of his stature sustain their work with anything that seems to them useful, without fear of being thereby diminished. 'Those who fear the influence of others, and avoid them, tacitly admit the poverty of their own souls,' says André Gide. Calvin belonged to the second generation of Protestantism. He followed in the footsteps of Luther, Melanchthon, Zwingli and Bucer, and he did not consider all the effort of his predecessors to be null and void. He borrowed from them the early material of his vast enterprise. It is clear, for instance, that his concept of human nature and of the role of faith owe a great deal to Luther's catechisms and *Servile Will*; that he must have arrived at the systematic exaltation of God from certain remarks of Zwingli's; that Melanchthon's *Loci communes* counted for something in his doctrine of the Lord's Supper, and that he would not have developed his own particular theology of the Church had he not witnessed the work of Martin Bucer at Strasbourg. It is even more evident that, no matter what idea he might encounter, he pushed it to extremes, pressing it home right to its logical consequences, taking care at the same time to remedy such errors or defects as he might find in it. He achieved a perfect synthesis of all those elements culled from his predecessors, by stamping it with the seal of a strong and genuinely original philosophy.

Calvin sought his fundamental inspiration, however, not from other human works, but from one that was divine—from the Book of Books, the text written at God's dictation. On this point too he was the direct disciple of Luther, who had centred the whole of the Reformation upon the Bible. 'The one veritable authority of Protestant Christians,' says Karl Barth, 'is the Word—the Word that God pronounced, still pronounces, and will pronounce for all eternity through the testimony of His Holy Spirit in the writings of the Old Testament and the New.' To listen to the Word of God and nothing else, to sweep away all that might be considered 'human commandments'—such was the intention (or pretension, according to the view taken) of all the supporters of the Reformation; they were sometimes known as 'Christaudins,' meaning 'listeners of Christ.' No one was more convinced than Calvin that this was the prime, indeed the sole, duty of the believer. God had made His Word comprehensible to men in Holy Writ, before which all else must efface itself. 'Neither antiquity nor customs, nor laws, nor edicts, nor decrees, nor councils, nor visions, nor miracles' must be set against the one unique text, the authentic message of the Most High. Authentic? On this point a Catholic is bound to raise a serious objection: who is to guarantee this authenticity? For him the guarantor is the Church and her infallible authority. 'I would not believe in the Gospel if I did not believe in the Church,' says St Augustine. Calvin rejects this guarantee: it is man's own conscience, his own mind, enlightened by the Holy Spirit, which discovers the true meaning of the Word. 'With a Bible in his hand every Protestant is his own Pope,' says Boileau. This thorough-going biblicism allows extraordinary freedom of judgment to the individual, a freedom which Calvin himself violently opposed in the cases of Castellio, Bolsec and Michael Servetus. But what pure scriptural perfume his work owed to this constant, loving association with the sacred text; and what brilliance he gave his style by means of apt quotation from the Old and New Testaments!

Thus inspired by the Word, Calvin conceived a whole system of the universe, a complete explanation of human destiny. The triple point of departure here is clearly provided by Luther. Original sin is the first and most irrefutable of evidences. 'We are products of unclean seed, we are born tainted with the infection of sin.' 'Man is an *ape*, a *wild* and *savage beast*, an *excrement*.' He tends 'necessarily to evil,' but 'what is most noble and valuable in our souls . . . is not corrupted; something worthy glimmers there.' Consequently human nature is corrupted 'from the understanding to the will, from the soul to the body': nothing at all can be understood if this has not first been fully admitted.

The load of sin is so heavy and decisive that man can only submit to it. He has no way whatsoever open to him of trying to rid himself of it. For he is not a free agent: the Calvinist 'servile will' is just as rigorous as that of Luther. Our nature as constituted can lead us only to evil, because 'the root is wicked and vicious, rotten through and through.' We are even forbidden to struggle: 'repentance is not at our disposal.' Man is the slave of that fatality which imposes upon him his very condition: he possesses no liberty of any kind by virtue of himself.

But this fundamental slavery carries within itself a hope. 'The more feeble you are in yourself, the better God receives you.' God can grant us the salvation we cannot attain by our own efforts, on one condition: we must have faith in Him. Calvin preaches justification by faith just as clearly as does Luther. 'He who is justified is not deemed a sinner, but a righteous man. God considers us righteous in Christ, however great our unrighteousness in ourselves. The justice of Jesus Christ is imputed to us.' To believe in Christ is to cling to Him in some way, in order that He may redeem us from all our unworthinesses and our taints, and enable us to escape the otherwise inevitable punishment due to us by our corruption. Such therefore is the first and almost the only duty of the Christian soul; it is also the Christian's comfort and certitude. 'Here then is our trust! Here is our only consolation! Here is all the foundation for our hope!'

Luther had discovered through inward experience these three fundamentals as answers to the questions he had asked himself during his spiritual conflict. He had felt personally corrupted and tainted; he had felt himself wholly and completely in the hands of God, the slave of a supernatural and implacable will; and he had not found peace until the day when he discovered that the other name of Justice is Love,[1] and threw himself into the arms of Christ. In Calvin's view the essential did not lie here. He did not sacrifice free will for any personal or psychological reason; he did so because he had the most elevated conception of the grandeur and 'honour' of God. In this he was indeed a true disciple of the Old Testament, a son of the nation which in all circumstances declared: 'To Thee alone, O Lord, be the sole honour and glory!'

Two men at this time were proclaiming with equal assurance the stirring message that everything on earth must be accomplished *ad majorem Dei Gloriam*: Calvin and St Ignatius. But whereas the Jesuit allowed their rightful function to the faculties of the human soul, which had been created in God's image, and employed them, as freely chosen instruments, to proclaim that glory, Calvin thought and taught that to acknowledge the slightest merit in man would 'obscure the glory of God and amount to rebellion against Him.' He stood poles apart from his contemporary humanists, who, whether Christians or not, founded their whole conception of the world on man. His insistence on magnifying the power and sovereignty of God, which was admirable enough in itself, had as its corollary a kind of sadistic pleasure in trampling roughshod over human nature. God was everything, man was nothing: this principle would brook no modification of any kind.

From this theodicy there emerged the thesis of *Predestination* which is generally regarded as Calvinism's most characteristic feature. The Lutherans had been aware that predestination was part of the logic of their system, and that it followed naturally upon the rejection of man's free will; but, being disturbed by its unpleasant and formidable features, and far less concerned with logic than the Frenchman, they had played it down, and Melanchthon had removed all mention of it from the Confession of Augsburg. Calvin's reasoning was more implacable. 'The Lord attributes all power to Himself.' His power 'is not . . . vain, idle and almost dormant, but eternally watchful and efficacious.' This God, whom man is fundamentally incapable of understanding and imitating, governs everything in the world and in life itself. Consequently man can believe nothing, want nothing or do anything that has not been determined by God from all eternity. And as to that goal which is most important to each and every human being,

[1] See p. 284 et seq.

namely, salvation, it depends solely on the will, the 'free decision' of God.

Here then is the central idea of all Calvin's doctrine. 'We mean by predestination the eternal counsel of God, by which He has decided what He must make of each and every man. For He does not create them all in a like state, but ordains some to eternal life and others to eternal damnation. . . . According to what the Scriptures clearly show us, therefore, we declare that God has constituted, once and for all, in His eternal and immutable counsel, those whom He desires to save and those whom He wishes to let perish. We declare that those whom He calls to salvation receive this benefit by virtue of His mercy freely given, without any account whatsoever being taken of their own merit. On the other hand, the gateway into life is barred to those whom He wishes to deliver unto damnation, and this is ordained by His secret and incomprehensible judgment, righteous and equitable as it is.'

Calvin himself asserted that this was a terrifying doctrine. 'I admit that this decree must strike terror into us,' he said. It was an inflexible law, nothing escaped it. 'Whatever the machinations of men, or even of devils, God is always at the helm.' It is God Himself who 'forces the reprobates to do what He desires of them.' This is the absolute anti-thesis of the Catholic doctrine of the goodness of God, of the Divine Justice which rewards each man according to his efforts and his merits, even if those efforts are puny and absurd by comparison with the Almighty. Only a few are chosen. Why? We do not know. And if we murmur 'I do not understand this,' Calvin is there to retort sarcasti-cally: 'What kind of creature are you, after all? If all the greatest doctors in the world tried to apply their minds to it they would not be able to find the answer.'

And if we complain of merciless injustice Calvin tells us to descend into our own souls and consider our abjection, in order to understand that we have deserved nothing better than Hell. Is this doctrine so inhuman then that it must plunge man into fatalistic resignation, total ataraxia? No, because there are some who are 'chosen,' because, if I have faith, I am predestined to salvation. It was from this stern con-viction of being wholly and completely in the hands of God that Calvin and his followers derived the grounds for their heroism. The soul which felt the ineffable testimony of its election could scarcely yield to discouragement or weakness. Here is a motivating force of the first order, the very root of all fanaticism. Far from being a source of impotence to Protestantism, Calvin's Predestinationism became an uplifting and compelling force.

No doubt; but suppose I am not saved? Suppose I am not among the elect? Am I to be held responsible for crimes which have been ordained for me, and linked with my destiny from all eternity?

According to the logic of his doctrine, Calvin acknowledged that 'evil enters into God's plan.' 'The first man chose evil because God so desired it. Why He desired it we do not know. We know only that He would not have desired it had He not foreseen that His glory would be increased thereby.' And likewise, 'in creating those whom He foreknew would be lost, God did so because He desired so to do.' Surely this argument provides an excuse for the worst kinds of behaviour. After all, the real responsibility for the evil I commit is not in myself, but in God, who forces it upon my feeble will. This was the argument which the 'Libertines' of Geneva were to use against Calvin; the French preacher Bolsec developed it forcefully; and Melanchthon, for his part, sought a middle road: 'If God creates the good in us . . . man alone sins by his own fault, and damns himself by his own sin. When we succumb, therefore, let us accuse our own will, and not seek the cause in the counsel of God.' Calvin himself rallied to this kind of division of responsibility. After railing against those 'wild beasts, baying hounds, swine that mistake their own snouts' who claimed to justify their dissolute life by the will of God—by which they proved themselves damned—he appealed to the testimony of conscience, which knows perfectly well that when it commits evil it does so not *through* God, but *against* Him. 'Therefore,' he declared, 'when I confess a hundred times over that it is true that God is the author of their damnation, they do not thereby efface their own crime in the slightest. This crime is engraved on their conscience and stares them in the face on each occasion it is committed.' It is impossible to deny that the gravest flaw in the system lies in this obligation to re-establish liberty in the moral order while rejecting it in the theological. Responsibility and liberty, as well as the basic principles of moral psychology, make the wholly unilateral doctrine of Calvin shiver into fragments. As Dom Poulet has stated so profoundly: 'Moreover who cannot see that this divine glory, to which he desired so fiercely to sacrifice everything, as to Moloch, would never have more brilliance than in a free soul, free to refuse but also free to give itself?'

Calvin's doctrine had one aspect which was not without value: it preserved a sound morality, which Luther had not done. Man must conduct himself properly. Why? Not *in order to be* saved, but *because he is* saved. Sanctification and justification are inseparable if I bear myself like a saint. I prove my faith and, in consequence, my election. Among the most elevated souls, this resulted in a remarkable moral aspiration, such as we find among that fairly widespread type of austere Protestants who are sincerely desirous of the glory of God and of their own moral improvement, but who are also ready moralizers. 'We are the Lord's: let us live and die for Him! We are the Lord's! May His will and wisdom preside over all our actions!' declared Calvin.

This is the kind of language to which every believer must listen. The average Christian would behave more modestly, and, without going to the lengths of these mystical demands, would devote himself to worldly activities with sobriety, equity and piety. Since he was convinced that he had been placed in his terrestrial position by divine decree, he would have no need to give up his worldly wealth—renunciation after the style of St Francis is fundamentally unknown to Calvinism. It was enough for him to use his wealth with moderation, while blessing God for having enabled him to profit from it. Anyone who succeeded in life, and who was loaded by God with prosperity, was surely—and this is also very much an Old Testament echo—being visibly protected by Him.[1]

As tokens of vocation, therefore, good works were essential; and on this point Calvin is nearer to Catholicism than Luther. But they had no meaning save as marks of the one decisive sign which is faith. For Calvin faith is truly and wholly a gift of God, one which man does nothing to deserve and which bears no relation whatsoever to any efforts of his own. I believe because 'God works within me.' This Calvinist faith is just as demanding as the Lutheran, but it does not proceed from the same source. Crushed beneath the weight of his misery Luther had flung out his cry of faith like an appeal from the very depths of the pit of despair: 'Lord, save me; I believe in you!' Calvin, on the other hand, was fascinated by God's splendour and transcendence, of which Holy Scripture gave him certain confirmation, and he sought to adhere to them through the action of the Holy Spirit. And for him—far more than for Luther, who had come round to this idea slowly and hesitantly, held back his feeling of unworthiness and degradation—the act of believing, that is to say, adhering to God, meant that one was already saved.

In such a theological system, where salvation comes from within the man, what room is left for anything that claims to bring it from without? The sacraments are not rejected: 'they are,' said Calvin, 'of immediate assistance in sustaining and confirming faith, like the preaching of the Gospel.' Moreover they are signs of the justification obtained through that faith. But in themselves they have no efficacity whatever. Calvin objected violently to all who, whether Zwinglians or Catholics, 'attribute I know not what kind of secret virtue to the sacraments,' for this 'insults the Spirit of God,' whose Grace has no need of signs in order to communicate itself to men. Any admission that 'the sacraments justify and confer grace' is in his eyes a 'wholly diabolical' opinion, since 'it twists conscience into confusion.'

---

[1] Here is an indication of the kind of relations which existed right from the beginning between middle-class capitalism and Calvinism. In this sense Calvin was very much a man of his times.

Furthermore Calvin showed himself more radical than Luther in retaining only two sacraments; like Zwingli, he believed he could find none but these in the Gospels: Baptism and the Lord's Supper. But he defined them in his own way. Baptism is 'the token of our Christianity and the sign whereby we are received into the society of the Church. It has been given us by God firstly to help our faith towards Him, and secondly to help our confession of our faith towards our fellow men. This does not mean 'that it is merely a mark,' a kind of badge which distinguishes the baptised from the rest; it is indeed 'the sign of the remission of sins,' but it is only the sign; it is not the baptismal water in itself which effects this remission; and the Holy Spirit may well operate our union with Christ outside the baptismal rite.[1]

As for the Eucharist, which Calvin called the Lord's Supper, a comparative reading of the successive editions of the *Institution* makes it quite obvious that this was a subject with which the author became increasingly preoccupied. He sought a middle way between the Lutherans and the Zwinglians. Like Zwingli, he was opposed to Luther who, as has been seen, admitted a Real Presence of Christ in the Host through *consubstantiation* (and not *transubstantiation* like the Catholics), and he interpreted the word 'is' in the formula 'This is my body' in the sense of to signify. 'The bread and the wine are visible signs.' Unlike Zwingli, however, he asserted that the Lord's Supper was more than a commemoration of Our Lord's last meal on earth, that the communicant gained far more than a mere symbolic union of his soul with Christ. There was a real union here, even though it was 'of spiritual substance.'[2] The bread and wine of the Eucharist were not, as they are for Catholics, the Body and Blood of Christ; but the glorified body of Christ was 'actually' communicated to the soul of the predestined, giving him 'unquestionable confidence in the life eternal.' In short, this is a complex and rather confused doctrine, which, as Wendel admits, 'leaves many obscurities imperfectly outlined.' It is alas rather touching to note that the explanation of this confusion lies probably in Calvin's own piety. On this point he was incapable of carrying his system to its logical conclusion, for he wished to retain the consoling certainty of Christ's presence in the bread.

Needless to say a doctrine which hinges entirely on the Holy Spirit's action upon the soul leaves only very limited room for the practice of a cult. The sacrifice of the Mass no longer had any meaning. Divine

---

[1] Calvin's views on confession seem to have been ambiguous. He undoubtedly understood the psychological value of personal and auricular confession, even though he did not regard it as a sacrament.

[2] The phrase 'spiritual substance' (Calvin actually said 'the spiritual substance of the Body of Christ') is obviously full of ambiguity. This is one of the points where Calvinist logic seems to break down. Protestant theologians have argued interminably over the word 'substance': cf. Helmut Gollwitzer, *Coena Domini*, Munich, 1937.

service was reduced to the hearing of the Word, in other words, to preaching, prayers and the singing of psalms. The Communion, which the Lutherans still retained, while of course removing from it the Catholic idea of sacrifice, was separated from the divine service. It was celebrated only a few times a year (four times at Geneva), and the whole community of the faithful then took part in it. This cult insisted on the most rigid simplicity. Statues, pictures, sacred ornaments and organs were prohibited as idolatrous; inner fervour and the exaltation of faith must suffice to compensate for the apparent coldness of a religion which asked nothing of human aids. Needless to say, like Zwingli and Luther before him, Calvin rejected the cult of the saints and of the Blessed Virgin: he naturally regarded them as exemplary figures, even though he scarcely ever mentions them. But they could scarcely assume that mediatory role close to the Divine Master which Catholicism assigned to them, when the essential of the religious act was effected in the solitude of the individual conscience, by direct contact with the Spirit.

As can be seen, this is all very much further removed from the Catholic Church than the positions adopted by Luther. On five capital points Calvin formulated theses with which Catholics are bound to be in total disagreement: firstly, that the Scriptures as interpreted by the Holy Spirit's dictation are the sole authority, that of the Church being non-existent; secondly, that man is fundamentally corrupt and incapable of finding the slightest hope of salvation in his own nature; thirdly, that God determines each individual's destiny as He pleases, and that man is quite incapable, by his own merits, of altering in the slightest degree the fate that awaits him; fourthly, that faith alone is the sign and means of salvation, and moral effort is only its corollary; fifthly, that the sacraments are mere symbols, stripped of all their efficacity. This French logician took up the theories which Luther, Zwingli, Bucer, Oeclampadius and so many others before him had all understood reasonably clearly, but had never dared take to their ultimate conclusions. He completed them, carried them through to the end and, albeit unintentionally, erected them into dogmas. This was a work of genius, and its historical influence was to be of decisive importance. It is questionable, however, whether this would ever have been the case had not Calvin also approached the final problem, that of authority, on which Luther had foundered so painfully.

Calvin set the seal on his doctrine by his definition of the Church. At the same time he fixed its essential relationship with the State. For Calvin—particularly for the youthful Calvin of 1536, as for Luther— the true Church was invisible, consisting of the community of the predestined. As his experience increased, however, he laid stress on a second aspect, that of the visible Church, comprising 'the multitude of men and women who make one like profession of honouring God and Christ Jesus.' His theological justification of this Church was far superior to Melanchthon's: it had been instituted by God; the treasury of Christ had been committed to its care; it was a just and sacred institution, to which the Christian owed obedience, and which had the right to impose its discipline, notably upon those who, 'by their turpitude, disgrace and dishonour Christendom.' This is very far indeed from that spiritual anarchism which Luther retained as his ideal throughout his life. After seeing Protestantism at work in Germany, Calvin had realized that if the forces of the Reformation were to organize themselves, and be ready to defend themselves against their enemies, something more than voluntarily accepted 'formularies of faith' were needed. . . .

There followed the question of this visible Church's attitude to the State. In Calvin's view, as in Luther's, human institutions were essential, having been willed by God. Civil society must organize men's collective life in a material sense. But whereas Luther had left the Church at the mercy of the secular authority, by asking the princes to apply the professions of faith; and whereas Zwingli had attempted to merge Church and State, Calvin's solution was more radical. He remembered the perfect way in which things had worked in Strasbourg, and he charged his Church to collaborate with the State while, at the same time, controlling it from above. Here is the most decisive difference between Luther and Calvin. It is a difference which makes the first into a religious reformer, the second into the founder of a Church. Religion at this juncture escapes from the bondage of the secular authority; it escapes too from the limitations forcibly imposed on it by the states in their own national interests; it becomes, like Catholicism, universal. Standing quite separate from the State, the Calvinist Church was to provide itself with a strong structure [1] under the direction of one supreme authority, the *Consistory*. This was something very different from the Consistory which Luther had eventually accepted, and which was dependent on the rulers. Calvin's Consistory was completely free of State interference, and was strong enough to command the obedience of the State. Thus 'drawn up,' as Calvin liked to say, the Church he had brought into being could assert itself and assume that historical role for which he knew it to be predestined. It now remained for him only to confirm the theory of his doctrine by subjecting it to practical test. Geneva provided him with the chance to do so.

---

[1] But it was not centralized, at least in theory; there were no hierarchies between the servants of a Church, and no subordination of one Church to another. There was merely a federation, whose leader was Christ, and whose law was the Bible.

'MARVELLOUS BATTLES'

On the morning of 13th September 1541 all the city magistrates of Geneva, preceded by a herald-at-arms, rode out of the Cornavin Gate and made for Versoix. They were going to meet the man whom they had expelled from their town three years earlier, and who had had to go into exile through the same gate and along the same road: Master John Calvin. The city archives still retain the record of that memorable meeting in which the Great Council had decided 'to beg him whole-heartedly to come and live here, and to go and send for him, with his wife and household.'

Calvin had yielded to their solicitations, though not without doubts and hesitation. He was torn between his two duties: that of saving the Genevan Church which he held all the more dear because of the suffering it had caused him, and that of continuing his extremely useful work in Strasbourg. On several occasions the messengers sent to suppli-cate him had seen him burst into bitter sobs; but he had recalled 'that he did not belong to himself,' and that the Lord was summoning him to take the straight and narrow way. At once this 'marvellous per-plexity' had ceased, and he had agreed to return to Geneva. Pale and almost silent, happy yet still anxious, he entered the town, to be met by a crowd which was also on the whole well pleased but rather uneasy. On the following Sunday St Peter's Cathedral was full to capacity. Calvin mounted the pulpit, and after a short prayer resumed his commentary on the Scriptures at the very spot where he had been forced to leave off four years earlier, as if the interruption had lasted only a brief moment.

He would live in this city until his death. He would make it his masterpiece, his City-Church, the practical realization of all his ideas. His own position was somewhat extraordinary. As professor of theology and city preacher he was in theory only an ordinary teacher and minister among all the rest, 'the servant of Geneva.' He often declared that he wanted to be this and nothing else. However, the city installed their servant in a house in the Rue des Chanoines which was comfortable rather than simple, and set in the midst of a splendid garden. It paid him a salary of five hundred gold florins, double what it gave any of his colleagues; but it did not offer him any official title, nor did he demand one. This man to whom a whole people delivered up its soul was a passing visitor, 'a traveller on this earth.' Calvin himself certainly derived pleasure from being merely a nonentity, quite satisfied at having claimed and obtained a limitless authority for God.

Calvin was thirty-two years old when this most important chapter of his life began. To us with our modern and stubbornly gerontocratic ideas, he might seem rather young to play the role of a leader and manager of men. In fact, he was exceptionally mature. His haggard, often pallid face and the deep steady gaze of his eyes betrayed that 'very great majesty' of which one member of Geneva's Little Council was to make mention in Calvin's funeral oration. Everything about him exhaled cold determination, indomitable energy and the courage to confront any opposition. When they saw him hurrying swiftly and discreetly through the streets of their city, his thin body wrapped in a thick overcoat, his cap pulled well down over his ears, his beard quivering in the wind, the Genevans, who had read St Paul at his command, were not long in saying that he had come among them, in the words of the Epistle to the Corinthians, more 'with the sceptre than with the spirit of tenderness.'

However, this frigid, energetic exterior was a mask, or rather the result of a perpetual battle. In order to be what his duty demanded of him, John Calvin had to battle constantly. First of all he had to fight his own body, which was increasingly prone to sickness and disease, to the point of making him on occasion almost an invalid, half maddened by headaches and pains in almost every limb. There is no doubt at all that his health was a matter of great concern to him; he often refers to it in his letters with a kind of shameless naïveté, going so far as to keep the Duchess of Ferrara informed about his haemorrhoids. But his poor physical state never prevented him from doing what he had resolved to do. Men of this kind, 'neurotic arthritics' in medical jargon (Richelieu was another), are capable of overcoming their bodily weaknesses by sheer force of will-power.

Far more serious was the battle he had to fight against his own fundamental inclination to risk everything, tackle anything and command everyone. There is no doubt that Calvin was quite sincere in his frequent assertions that 'I am naturally timid and pusillanimous.' But he knew how to conquer this timidity, and his energy was all the greater for being the result of a mastered weakness. 'This man is like a burning brand, snatched from the flames,' Theodore Beza said of him. He has often been accused of being hard. Here again his character was a mass of contradictions. The same Beza, who lived close to Calvin for sixteen years, also wrote: 'He seemed hard at first, but on closer contact there was no more tender man than he.' And numerous witnesses testify to what he himself called 'the softness, not to say weakness, of his soul.' It is inconceivable that this angular old man, with the neat beard, and face frozen into the severe expression which his engraving has made famous, would have had such enormous influence had he not also possessed that mysterious power to conquer souls which is never totally divorced from sensibility—even though, in his case, that sensibility might be held under and repressed.

Goethe refers to that *demoniac force*, 'that mysterious force which everyone feels but no one can explain . . . which manifests itself in the most diverse of circumstances . . . which is always positively creative.' . . . and which, he goes on to say, 'seizes most readily on great men, and has a fondness for the twilight centuries.' Merejowsky has rightly observed that this Faustian power is exactly like Calvin's. Calvin's authority was composed of audacity and reserve, arrogant pride and humility. He was overwhelmingly certain that he had been divinely invested with his mission, like the Old Testament prophets, or St Paul, or Mohammed. He was capable of terrible violence of a more calculated and atrocious kind than that of Luther, but he also excited a kind of magnetic charm over his fellow men. Add to this forceful character an intellect of the most alert kind, excellently fitted to dominate any discussion of ideas, an almost limitless capacity for work, and a keen sense of discipline, or, as he called it 'good order,' and there emerges the portrait of a quite outstanding leader. But such a personality need only be placed at the service of one great idea and it becomes the perfect type of fanatic. Calvin belonged to that family of terrifying and sublime men who, like Savonarola and Robespierre before and after him, dream of creating man's salvation or happiness without them, despite them, and even against them.

This great idea was an integral part of Calvin; he had expounded it in all his arguments in the *Christian Institution*. No sooner had he set foot on Genevan soil once more than he set to work to put it into practice. On the very morrow of his arrival in the city he asked the Councils to arrange for a Commission to prepare the *Ecclesiastical Ordinances* on which the religious constitution of the town should be based. In actual fact he drafted them single-handed. On 20th November the assembly of the people was convoked in the Plain of Molard by trumpet call. It unanimously passed a decree establishing 'a government in accordance with the Gospel of Our Lord Jesus Christ.' The reign of God was proclaimed at Geneva—as it had been at Florence in Savonarola's time, and also, in a rather more bizarre fashion, in John of Leyden's Münster. 'There is no authority save God, who is King of Kings and Lord of Lords. . . .' So Calvin was to murmur on his deathbed. For twenty-three years he was to devote all his energy and intelligence to making this precept not only a religious reality, but a moral, social and political reality as well. The idea of theocracy has never been more thoroughly applied than in Calvin's Geneva.

The establishment of the reign of God presupposed a twofold task for Calvin: on the one hand he must organize the Christian community of Geneva according to his theories—'draw up the Church'— and on the other he must make the whole life of the city subject to the commandments of God, to the Gospel—or rather to his own

interpretation thereof. It must not be thought that this twin labour could
be accomplished without opposition. Although the Genevans had re-
pented and were full of good intentions, they would not allow the
halter to be put around their necks without lashing out in protest. It
was not going to be easy to make the Church guide and censor of the
State, and it was even more difficult to force a people who had just
tasted to overflowing the various delights of liberty into a life of total
austerity. Calvin's first twelve years at Geneva, therefore, were anything but peaceful. 'I have survived some marvellous battles here,' he
said shortly before his death, in a farewell letter to the pastors of Geneva.
'The poor timid student' was committed to some curious adventures.

   The atmosphere in Geneva during these astonishing years almost
defies the imagination. It was that of a regime of 'public safety' in the
most complete and rigorous sense of the term. Calvin saw the little
community of which he had taken charge threatened on every side.
Firstly, there were the material dangers. The King of France's soldiers
were only forty minutes' march away, and the city was menaced also
by the Duke of Savoy, by its former bishop, by the Catholics and by
the Bernese, whose relations with Geneva had now deteriorated. A
town whose defences were insecure, and which was so vulnerable on
the lakeside, was a poor place in which to await attack. But this peril
was as nothing compared with the spiritual danger. The most terrible
enemy with whom battle must be joined was that ancient adversary,
the Fallen Angel, who was striving to separate the faithful from God's
Kingdom. The essential task which Calvin set himself, therefore, was
the prevent the Evil One from taking possession of his City-Church:
and it was indeed a dreadful conflict.

   In order to wage this war on two fronts, every weapon was legitimate: all that mattered was the work of salvation, the preservation of
public safety. Just as when republican France was invaded more than
two centuries later, so now a reign of terror was established; but in
Geneva its horror was aggravated by the fact that it was founded on
religious principles. This people which had consented to its own
servitude included countless men and women who thoroughly
approved of Calvin's regime, who collaborated with him, who denounced all suspects to the 'guardians' and applauded the repression.
But there were also many who rejected it, and their number might
increase if the terrifying leader displayed the slightest sign of weakness.
Some of these disliked Calvin because he was a Frenchman and a
foreigner; others felt their pleasures threatened by him; others again,
though theoretically in agreement with his principles, found his
practice often too extreme. There were also some who would not
accept his theology; and their hatred was no less intense, because
religion and public life were closely connected in his system.

Moreover these twelve years of conflict took place in the climate typical of the age, where superstition exacerbated collective passion. Less than two years after Calvin's return to Geneva there was an outbreak of the plague, and Geneva lived through some terrible weeks. The citizens accused one another of being 'plague spreaders,' alleging that they went out by night and smeared the door latches with an unguent made from the corpses of the victims. Witchcraft made enormous inroads: on all sides there were rumours of black magic, spells and men taken up into the sky by demons. His critics saw the hand of Calvin behind every one of these horrors. 'The calumnies which Satan loaded upon him in those days can scarcely be imagined,' says Theodore Beza; 'for the blame for everything which had come to pass in Geneva was laid at his door.' It is essential to remember this if the rigidity and apparent cruelty of his theocratic dictatorship are to be properly understood. Dogs set by street urchins at the reformer's breeches were of no importance, nor yet the gibes of Mistress Perrin, the captain-general's wife, who amused herself by making his horse shy; what was so terrifying for a man like Calvin was the feeling that he alone bore on his shoulders the sole responsibility for this people whom God had confided to his care, and who, without him, would certainly relapse into eternal death.

Under such circumstances he would feel bound to crush all opposition ruthlessly, no matter whence it came. The first resistance encountered by Calvin came from the pastors, who, in the words of Farel, were 'indifferent, intemperate, coarse and quarrelsome creatures'; in particular they had committed the crime of not being wholly subservient to Calvin, and of occasionally seeking to apply the doctrine of free inquiry to their own teaching. The most important of these was Sebastian Castellio, a Savoyard, who had at one time been in charge of the École de Genève. He publicly questioned the canonicity of certain sections of the Bible, and also interpreted certain lines of the Calvinist Credo in a different way from Calvin. He was forcibly dismissed from office, and then expelled the town. There followed a purge of the pastors, and gaps in their ranks were filled by French Protestant refugees, of whose loyalty there was no question.

After fighting for religious authority Calvin had to contend for political power. If the Church was to control public life he could not leave supreme power in the hands of the popular assembly, where opinion might always swing away from him. The Councils—Great and Little, Sixty and Twenty—were entrusted with application of the laws. They had a right to offer the people a list of candidates from which they could elect their own officials, so that the democracy of Geneva was firmly muzzled. There was, however, a good deal of opposition. When the secular authorities gave the Genevan pastor

Trolliet permission to preach, the religious flew into a fury and had the licence revoked. *Pierre Ameaux*, a merchant and member of the Little Council, whose trade in playing-cards had been severely affected by the new moralist measures, publicly criticized Calvin, calling him 'that evil and ambitious man from Picardy, the preacher of false doctrine.' Calvin raged and fumed, and announced that he would never again ascend the pulpit until this outrage had been avenged, and Geneva was amazed by the spectacle of an important counsellor parading through the streets bare-headed, wearing a penitent's shirt, carrying a burning torch and loudly begging God to forgive him his grievous sin. The more affluent citizens took this incident badly; the 'Libertines' began to stir. Their members included a number of excellent Protestants who were just as good Christians as the Calvinists. Some of them were even former friends of Calvin, such as Ami Perrin, who had been one of the most active instruments of his return. But such people had afterwards found that the reformer was going too far; they did not agree with this ecclesiastical annexation of their city. Calvin was quick to retort; his attack was aimed at the *Favre* and *Perrin* family. The aged François Favre, Perrin's father-in-law and a former Syndic, was condemned on a charge of 'libertinage.' His daughter Penthesilée was accused of being too fond of dancing. Her only answer was to laugh and, worse still, call the Minister of Justice a 'lump of filth.' She was promptly clapped into jail, and, as she was suspected of having friends among the warders, the entire prison staff was changed; but this did not prevent her from escaping. As for her husband, an opportune diplomatic mission in France kept him away for a while.

Tragedy began with the affair of *Gruet*. Three days after Mistress Perrin's flight, there was found nailed to the pulpit in St Peter's a notice containing threats against the clergy: 'when so much has been borne revenge is sweet.' Its author was traced: his name was Jacques Gruet. He was a kind of free-thinker, a fairly well-educated man, of dubious morals. Gruet's house was searched, and one of Calvin's books was discovered bearing the impious words 'All rubbish!' in its margins, together with some notes criticizing the Consistory's ecclesiastical ordinances, and even the draft of a letter to the King of France begging him to come and re-establish the ancient order in Geneva. After being arrested, tortured and condemned to death, Gruet was decapitated and his head nailed to the pillory.

As can be imagined, events such as this caused a considerable stir in Geneva. Opinion was divided. People were either for or against Calvin. His power was in actual fact very insecure: a single election could alter the majority on the Councils. Indeed in February 1548 'Libertines' and 'Calvinists' were equally balanced. Ami Perrin, who had now become a Syndic, started a reaction against the reformer. As the persecution unleashed in France by Henry II was causing large numbers of Protestant refugees to flock to Geneva, there to be welcomed by Calvin with open arms, the 'Perrinists' suggested that a law be passed stipulating twenty-five years' residence as the qualification for citizenship. This was a blow directed against Calvin himself. Simultaneously his opponents circulated one of Calvin's earlier letters, in which he expressed himself in harsh terms on the subject of the city's government. For some weeks Calvin feared that he might soon be obliged once again to go into exile. But the projected law was dropped just in time. Would Calvin now be able to rely for support on the French refugees, and establish his work on sound foundations?

Not yet; for a number of these same immigrants now protested against his theology, which was very far from being accepted by all the French Protestants. The most vehement of these objectors was a former Carmelite, *Jerome Bolsec*, who had settled as a doctor at Veigy, within Genevan territory. Because he was passionately interested in theology, Bolsec often attended those Friday 'Congregations' at which the most learned members of the reformed community discussed dogma and doctrine. He rebelled against the absolute character of Calvin's Predestinationism. To accept Calvin's thesis, argued Bolsec, was 'to make God into a tyrant or a Jupiter'; he added that this inhuman idea was never mentioned by St Augustine, although Calvin claimed to have derived it from him. Although arrested and subjected to much ill treatment in prison, Bolsec stood his ground, and went so far as to denounce his enemy as a heretic, and the author of doctrines contrary to the Scriptures. Touched on the raw, Calvin defended himself with equal violence, and sought the opinions of the Churches of Berne, Basle and Neuchâtel. Any toleration of anti-Predestinationism on his part would surely result in the demolition of the whole basis of his theological structure. But he failed to obtain the condemnation he had hoped for. While Farel of Neuchâtel supported him, Basle and Berne sent less explicit replies. The Little Council had no desire to send Bolsec to his death: it confined itself to banishing him.[1] No one had any illusions: this had not been one of Calvin's successes.

The winter of 1552-3 marked the decisive turning-point. Many people were wondering whether the reformer was not about to be expelled from Geneva a second time. Calvin himself declared that he would rather be relieved of his office than suffer so much in it. Trolliet,

[1] Bolsec took refuge first in Berne, whence he continued to launch furious attacks upon Calvin. Later he returned to France, renounced Protestantism and, having returned to the bosom of the Catholic Church, wrote a biography of Calvin which contained the most damaging accusations. Anti-Protestant polemics were to draw abundantly from this arsenal of calumnies, of which history has made short work. For example, no one any longer accepts Bolsec's assertion that Calvin had been convicted of homosexuality in his youth,

whom Calvin had forbidden to preach, revived the theories of Bolsec and stirred up public opinion. Denounced before the Council, he was lucky enough to have the charge against him dismissed. The 'Libertines'—friend of the Perrin and Favre party, innkeepers whose taverns had been closed by Calvin, women who liked dancing, men who enjoyed drinking, and many others—allied together for the purpose of ending the Picard's dictatorship. At the elections in 1553 the majority passed to the anti-Calvinists. Pastors were excluded from the Councils and refugees who had not yet received the right of citizenship were subjected to vexatious restrictions. This might have been the end of Calvin's career in his City-Church had not the whole situation been suddenly reversed by one tragic incident. The affair of Michael Servetus is so horrible and so moving that in order to be understood it must be examined in the light of the atmosphere of those months.

MICHAEL SERVETUS AT THE STAKE

On 13th August 1553 a stranger passing through Geneva, who had signed the register as 'Miguel Villanova, Spanish doctor,' was arrested. Some said he had been apprehended in a bedchamber at the Rose Tavern, others during divine service in St Peter's. The police of the little republic were vigilant, and beneath the traveller's pseudonym they recognized an individual in whom the Consistory was deeply interested: *Michael Servetus*. Servetus was a fair-haired, distinguished-looking man with a lively but muddled mind, a humanist who was interested in everything and passionately devoted to theology. He was born in 1511, at Tudela in Navarre, of an Aragonese family which came originally from Villanueva-de-Sigena. After a brilliant scholastic career [1] at Saragossa and Toulouse, he had led an undistinguished public life, being successively secretary to Charles V's confessor and a junior imperial official at the time of the Diet of Augsburg. Later he had worked as a printer and subsequently as a physician; in the latter capacity he had joined the household of the Archbishop of Vienne, in Dauphiné. This had clearly not been enough to make him well known; but he had also published several books which had been widely debated in theological circles.

Servetus had met Melanchthon at Augsburg, and, incessant traveller as he was, had encountered Oeclampadius and Capito at Basle and Strasbourg. Under their influence he had become an enthusiastic student of the Scriptures, or, to put it more accurately, a biblicist run riot. Following his master's example of 'free inquiry,' he had set himself to examine the sacred texts on his own, fully convinced that the Holy

---

[1] It is believed that he had been castrated in childhood in order to preserve his beautiful soprano voice.

Spirit would act as his guide. Since he did not discover in the Bible the Nicaean dogma of the Trinity, Servetus determined to purge his fellow Christians of such a manifest error; in 1531 and 1532 he published at Haguenau two treatises on this theme. Oddly enough his wild effusions were taken quite seriously. The solemn reformers of Strasbourg and Basle took the trouble to oppose them as if the little Spaniard had revived the ancient 'Monarchianist'[1] heresy. Servetus left Alsace and established himself in turn at Lyons, Charlieu in Forez and then Vienne, pursuing his medical studies and scriptural speculations simultaneously, and associating the two together in a most extraordinary way. Thus, having read in the Bible that the human soul resides in the blood, and having a rare gift of scientific divination, he investigated that precious liquid and concluded that arterial blood came from the lungs, where it was regenerated by the air inhaled. This was the starting-point of Harvey's great discovery of the circulation of the blood half a century later. It was at this period, about 1548, that Servetus published in secret his major work whose title alone indicates its audacious purpose: *Christianismi restitutio*.[2] He argued that, because Christian doctrine had early been falsified by the Catholic Fathers of the Church and no less by the Protestant reformers, it was his personal task to restore it to its pristine purity. How? By linking it with Platonism, with which he was momentarily intoxicated. He taught therefore that Christ is Reason, the Idea which conceives and assumes the essence of the world; all creatures are degraded emanations of the divine, and original sin is nothing other than this separation of man from his divine origin. In short, Servetus advocated a brand of Gnosticism,[3] into which Christian faith fitted as best it could.

Servetus had met Calvin in the past, and knew him slightly. Did he cherish the naïve hope of converting him to his own views? He sent Calvin an advance copy of his book before its publication. The reformer was furious. 'This man is certainly a son of Satan!' he cried. He called down the wrath of God upon the heretic and wrote to Farel (13th February 1547) these words: 'He [Servetus] asserts that he will come here if I wish. But I do not intend to give him my word, for if he comes, provided my authority prevails I will not suffer him to return home alive!'[4] There were several good reasons for Calvin's

---

[1] This was a heresy professed at the end of the second century and during the third, notably by Praxeas and Noetas, who maintained that the Three Divine Persons were only 'points of view' for considering God. It was fought by Tertullian and St Hippolytus.

[2] This book was burned at Geneva and elsewhere, and only one copy remains, which was itself damaged by the flames. It can be seen at the Bibliothèque Nationale in Paris.

[3] On Gnosticism see the author's *Church of Apostles and Martyrs*, p. 297 et seq.

[4] However, this did not prevent him from maintaining with the Spaniard a correspondence which was so significant that, when Servetus published his book, he was able to add to it (without permission, needless to say) twenty-three letters which he had addressed to Calvin.

fury. The theories of Servetus ran directly counter to the exaltation of the divinity of Christ, which constituted the basis of Calvin's theology and piety. Besides, when he himself had published the first (Latin) edition of his *Christian Institution* his own ideas on the Trinity had still not been very clearly formulated; he had been sharply criticized by certain other Protestants, notably Caroli, who, as we have already seen, had accused him of being an Arian and of denying the divinity of Christ at the time of his first stay in Geneva. It was therefore vitally important to Calvin to prevent the least possibility of any confusion between Servetus's aberrant speculations and his own position. Hence his violence—the violence of a theologian touched on the raw.

At the beginning of 1553 an episode occurred of which the least that can be said is that it does Calvin precious little credit. Protestant historians refer to it with embarrassment.[1] Among the French Protestant refugees in Geneva was a young man from Lyons, Guillaume de Trie, whom Calvin had made his secretary and whose relatives bitterly reproached him for embracing the Reformation. De Trie wrote a reply to one of them, Claude Arneys, observing that people in France had had the audacity to accuse him of heresy while tolerating the presence there of a heretic of the stature of Servetus, whose book thoroughly deserved 'to be burnt wherever it is found.' Was Calvin aware of this letter? We do not know; nor do we know whether he disapproved of the denunciation it contained. For denunciation it was. Arneys immediately took the letter to the judge of the ecclesiastical court at Lyons, who, after making some inquiries, discovered the author's identity: the book had been written by the Bishop of Vienne's physician. The legal department of the latter diocese was then apprised of the affair and had Servetus arrested; he categorically denied that he was the 'Villanueva' who had signed his name to the *Restitutio*. 'There was insufficient evidence to convict.'[2] So, at his relative's request, de Trie handed over various manuscripts. Among these were some letters which Servetus had addressed to Calvin, and which the latter had certainly not passed back to de Trie without considerable hesitation. Nevertheless it remains a fact that Calvin did in the end part with these compromising documents, and that he could not possibly have been ignorant of the use to which they were going to be put. Michael Servetus was haled before the Inquisition, where he found himself in an extremely dangerous situation. But he had been a good doctor and had many friends, and the authorities at Vienne were not particularly anxious to have a member of their bishop's *entourage* sent to the stake. Servetus was therefore allowed to escape under cover of

[1] Wendel, in particular, and Benoît, and even Doumergue.
[2] This material is taken from Wendel, p. 65.

darkness, and his accusers contented themselves with burning him in effigy, together with five large bundles of copies of his treatise.

The escape was made on 7th April, and in August, after four months of wandering, Servetus arrived at Geneva, where he was apprehended by the police. Why had he been guilty of such imprudence, after having originally decided to lie low in Naples? 'A fatal madness encouraged him to throw himself headlong into Geneva,' Calvin said later. His words have become the generally accepted explanation for Servetus's extraordinary behaviour. Perhaps the answer is not really so simple. The Spaniard's character undoubtedly contained something of the naïve braggart. Certain Genevans may have told him of Calvin's present somewhat critical position in the city, and it is quite conceivable that he imagined that his sole presence there would suffice to overthrow the reformer.

In fact, another incident had just occurred in the City-Church, which placed Calvin's authority in grave jeopardy. Its coincidence with the affair of Servetus explains the haste and cold fury with which the Frenchman set to work to destroy the Spanish heretic. *Philibert Berthelier*, one of Geneva's leading citizens and controller of the Mint, was the son of a patriot who had given his life in the cause of his city's freedom. A notorious member of the Perrin and Favre faction, he took advantage of the reversal of majorities on the Councils to conduct a skilful attack upon Calvin and the Consistory. When excommunicated for 'libertinage,' in other words, for making some rather bold remarks, he appealed to the Little Council for permission to take part in the Lord's Supper. Now if Calvin refused to give Berthelier Communion, the reformer would be setting himself up as a rebel against the Council; if he agreed his authority, and that of the Consistory too, would be shattered. The importance of the Servetus affair, breaking out as it did at this particular moment, is abundantly plain. The Spaniard was arrested on Calvin's complaint—to comply with the law one of the reformer's disciples had given himself up so that this complaint might be considered—and accused of heresy and blasphemy. Would he be condemned or not? As Pastor J.-D. Benoît accurately declares: 'Had Servetus been acquitted Calvin himself would have been morally condemned and his work destroyed. Hence the relentless character of the conflict.'

Now, given the present atmosphere of Geneva, the Spaniard's chances of acquittal were considerable. Three days after his arrest, Philibert Berthelier intervened before the Councils on his behalf with a legal objection. He contested the Consistory and the pastors' right to judge this foreigner who had been apprehended in the city, and he persuaded the Little Council to take over the suit. Servetus, however, lost his case. Why? Maybe because the theological absurdities sustained by his book were so outrageous that even indifferent Christians were offended by them. But perhaps the strongest reasons of all were psychological. In the eyes of the placid Genevans this swaggering, insolent, obviously paradoxical Spaniard must really have seemed like the devil's henchman, as Calvin had described him. The trial was soon over. This time evidence to convict was not lacking: to make quite sure of things contact was established with the Catholic authorities at Vienne, so that use could be made of the documents collected there by the officials of the Inquisition![1] In addition Servetus defended himself very clumsily. Knowing, or believing that he was supported by 'certain important people,' he put on great airs and went so far as to write to his judges, the members of the Little Council: 'I demand that my false accuser be punished likewise, and that he be detained as I am until the matter is settled by the death of either him or me'; which was simply bringing the supreme penalty down on himself. The unfortunate creature did not realize that each camp, Calvinist and Libertine, might use his case to prove to its rival its own perfect orthodoxy, and that he was in danger of being the victim of this process of outbidding. The terrible insults which he hurled at Calvin from the depths of his jail were recoiling upon himself: 'Who can believe that such a torturer and murderer as this can be a servant of the Church of God? . . . Or do you still hope to deafen the judges with your baying? You lie, you torturing monster. . . .' Calvin sensed the situation turning in his favour. On 20th August he wrote to Farel: 'I hope that Servetus will be condemned to death, but I should like him to be spared the worst part of the punishment,' meaning the fire. He resisted the 'Libertines,' who continued to intrigue against him with added vigour; when the Little Council gave Berthelier permission to take part in the Lord's Supper, Calvin protested and announced that he would deny him Communion. All the other pastors supported him and in the end he obtained his desire: the Council recognized the independence of the religious authority—the Consistory. Calvin was on the point of triumphing over all his enemies.

The opinions which had been sought from the four other Swiss Reformed Churches of Zürich, Basle, Berne and Schaffhausen supported his case against Servetus. They reached Geneva on 18th October; the Spaniard's theses were utterly condemned. Eight days later, on 25th October, Calvin learned that the 'Libertines' intended going to St Peter's the next day to attempt to force him to give Berthelier Communion. 'I would rather die than throw a sacred object to the dogs!' Calvin declared. On the following morning he mounted the pulpit amid total silence and announced that 'if any one of those excommunicated approached the Holy Table,' he would kill himself rather than

[1] Wendel, footnote to p. 66.

give them the bread. The crowd was deeply impressed and made not a move. 'Everything passed off with such calm and solemnity that one might have believed the Majesty of God was present in the house,' wrote Theodore Beza. The truth of the inseparability of these two issues is demonstrated by the fact that a few hours after this incident, the Council voted Servetus's death sentence. The register of the Genevan pastorate states that on 27th October he was to be 'taken to Champey and burnt alive.'

The punishment took place on the day arranged and in the way arranged—by burning—despite the leniency for which Calvin had undoubtedly asked. There is no reason to think that he was lying when he repeated in one of his letters that he had begged in vain for the penalty to be eased. It was a cool, drizzly morning when the Spaniard was led to the stake, preceded by the city judge and grand herald, and escorted by musketeers, 'without showing the slightest sign of repentance.' Calvin's observations on this appalling death make horrifying reading: 'The depraved should not glorify their hero's obstinacy in terms of a martyr's constancy. He showed the dumb stupidity of a beast. . . . He went on bellowing over and over again, in the Spanish fashion: "*Misericordias! Misericordias!*"' Other witnesses, however, assert that Servetus had only cried, undoubtedly with that 'awful Spanish' accent which so amused the Frenchman, 'I do not fear death in such a righteous cause.'[1]

'Servetus's death, for which Calvin bears much of the responsibility,' writes Wendel, 'marked the reformer with a bloody stigma which nothing has been able to efface.' In the following year he himself felt the need to defend his actions, for he published a treatise *Against the Errors of Servetus*, in which he said: 'Many people have accused me of such ferocious cruelty that (they allege) I would like to kill again the man I have destroyed. Not only am I indifferent to their comments, but I rejoice in the fact that they spit in my face.' This attitude of terrifying severity has appeared so appalling to later generations, particularly to those of modern times, that in 1903 the honest Calvinists of Geneva felt constrained to erect an expiatory monument to Servetus, upon which, as 'respectful and grateful sons of Calvin,' they condemned 'a mistake which was that of his age.' It is certainly true to say that the 'mistake of the age' provides a partial explanation for Calvin's violence in this affair. Where religious matters were concerned the men of his epoch showed no indulgence: Melanchthon, gentle humanist though he was, warmly applauded the Genevan Council's decision to execute the 'blasphemer,' an attitude which sets him poles apart from the tolerant ideas of his master Erasmus. But it is not certain that this tragedy would have gone so far as its atrocious finale had Calvin not

[1] Cf. Henry, III. p. 168.

been fully aware that judgment brought for or against the heretic was in reality an implicit condemnation or approval of him and of his work. His fanaticism in this affair seems to have been at least as political, in the most fundamental sense of the term, as it was religious and theological. As Michelet observed, he believed he was saving 'religion and his city, the European revolution,' the true faith, and the Church itself. The twentieth century is well placed to understand the depths of horror to which men can go when they believe that they alone possess the truth and hold the future of humanity in their hands.

THE TRIUMPH OF 'GOD'S STEWARD'

After the execution of Michael Servetus, Calvin was regarded by the Genevans as the defender of the Word of God, the saviour of the faith. His authority, which had been so recently contested, was now established on unshakable foundations. By supporting the Spanish blasphemer, his opponents had undoubtedly condemned themselves! The final efforts of the 'Libertines' against him were mercilessly punished. A drunken conspiracy resulted in savage repression; the brothers Comparet, two humble boatmen, were executed and pieces of their dismembered bodies nailed on the city gates; a Berthelier implicated in the affair was beheaded; all the other leaders of the party took flight and were sentenced to death in their absence.

From now onwards until his death Calvin's rule over Geneva was absolute. His mastery lasted more than ten years. The elections of February 1554 reversed the majority in his favour: three of the four Syndics were his friends, and the fourth came over to his side a few weeks later. Henceforth the government of Geneva worked in complete agreement with its 'evangelist.' The Consistory's right to determine the admittance of any member of the faithful to the Lord's Supper was recognized, and the Councils were forbidden to tamper with this right in any way whatsoever. But while Calvin had succeeded in preserving the religious authority from any political interference, the reverse was certainly far from true; under pretext of seeing that morality was respected, the Consistory intervened in many fields proper to the secular power. 'We are the stewards of God,' Calvin openly informed his colleagues; with such a title they naturally sought to make the divine law universally applied. In addition, in order to make more sure of the electorate, Calvin gave Genevan citizenship to all the French refugees. He himself modestly waited six years before allowing citizen rights to be offered him at Christmas 1559; his power had no need of this paper backing. Even on the international plane the situation favoured him. The growing threat of Duke Emmanuel Philibert of Savoy, victor of St Quentin in 1557 and friend of Philip II

of Spain, united all the patriots around their religious leader; it even
led the Bernese to abandon the 'Libertines' and sign an alliance with
Geneva. Henceforward nothing could prevent God's steward from
practising his theocratic principles.

The Church 'drawn up' by Calvin was remarkable for its organization. The ecclesiastical government comprised four orders: the
pastors (or ministers), the doctors (or teachers), the elders and the
deacons. Of these the first were the most important. They were not
priests in the Catholic sense of the term; and they married and lived in
exactly the same way as the rest of the faithful, but they nevertheless
possessed a very distinct religious character, and they were most carefully trained. Their functions were threefold: (1) They must proclaim
the Word of God, in other words, preach, instruct, exhort and ad-
monish; every Sunday there were at least two sessions of instruction in
each temple, and one session three times a week; at St Peter's there was
one daily. (2) They must administer the sacraments, namely, baptize
and preside over the Lord's Supper four times a year. Finally (3), they
must comfort the sick; none of the faithful was to remain confined to
his bed for more than three days without being visited by his pastor.
Once a week all the pastors met together in 'congregation' to study the
Scriptures, to decide on their common action, and also to censure one
another whenever the need arose. The doctors did not, properly
speaking, exercise any ministry; they were the intellectuals of the
Church, who had the task of maintaining purity of doctrine and who
educated the young people in the schools and the Academy. The
elders were the representatives of the Christian community, chosen
by the Councils from among the wisest and the best. Finally, the
deacons were entrusted with material duties, notably work connected
with the poor and the sick. This well-constructed edifice was surmounted by the Consistory composed of twelve elders chosen by the
Councils and six pastors elected by their colleagues; it met each week
on Thursday, and its function was to ensure the unity of the faith, to
supervise church attendance and to control morals. It possessed
vigorous and effective weapons: admonition, which obliged its
recipient to do public penance; excommunication, which in practice
cut off the victim from the life of the community; and lastly denunciation to the civil authority. The ordinances which had established this
religious constitution also fixed the spirit in which the authority of the
Consistory was to be exercised: 'Let all be done so moderately that
none be treated with severity. Likewise, correction must be no more
than medicine to subdue—that is to say restore—sinners to Our
Lord.' This is a touching ideal, but its application was rather less
delicate and gentle.

For, since men were 'bestial savages' and sinners by nature, it was obvious that doctrinal integrity and moral probity could be preserved only by force: 'It is necessary to procure their good despite themselves.' In this respect it must be conceded that the Genevan Consistory procured a great deal of good for those in its charge. To put the matter plainly, Geneva at this period experienced a moral dictatorship such as has scarcely a parallel in history. It had begun at the time of Calvin's return in 1541, but it went on perfecting itself all the time. The police or 'guardians' watched everything, even the most intimate details of men's private lives. Anyone thinking evil thoughts or doing evil things was punished with brotherly ferocity. Let the reader judge for himself! [1]

There was prison for those who liked dancing, prison for those who enjoyed drinking in the taverns, prison for card-players. Anyone found reading the *Golden Legend* or the great *Amadis of Gaul* in the privacy of his own fireside was forthwith clapped into jail. Women who braided their hair too elaborately or indulged in leg-of-mutton sleeves and fashionable shoes were induced by a heavy fine to turn from these evil ways, which 'much offended' God. Barbers were forbidden to tonsure priests passing through the city, and jewellers prevented from fashioning chalices. Both these offences were punishable by hanging. It was regarded as a confession of blasphemy and heresy to murmur *requiescat in pace* over the grave of a dear departed, as bad as daring to say that the French refugees held too important a place in the town or, even worse, pretending that the Pope might after all be an honest fellow. The humming of a satirical song against Calvin was a crime, falling asleep during his sermon a grave misdemeanour. One young woman was sent into exile for having remarked 'What Jesus Christ said is quite enough for us,' and a cowman was arrested for calling his bulls 'horned beasts,' this being an epithet that the pastors reserved for the devil. No one escaped this supervision: two small children were beaten with rods for having eaten two rounds of cake on leaving church, and another young ragamuffin was nearly beheaded because he returned a box on the ears given him by his mother. Excesses were such that they amounted on occasion to actual retrogression, e.g. an attempt to replace taverns by 'abbeys' in which the sole distraction allowed was reading of the Bible, or the effort to substitute ordinary Christian names by Esau, Jacob, Rebecca, Abraham and so forth. The extent of Calvin's own responsibility for this regime is hard to define. It was clearly shared by his colleagues in the Consistory and by the city magistrates, whose intransigence rivalled his own. And the case is quoted of a woman who, after being imprisoned for publicly insulting him, was pardoned at his personal request. It is, however, inconceivable

---

[1] All the facts cited above are taken from Protestant historians, notably Henry, Walker Koehler, Wendel, Doumergue and Benoît.

that he can have been ignorant of these vexatious attentions by the police; in one year alone three hundred people were questioned on charges of behaving badly during his sermons.

Moreover this *de facto* dictator, the 'steward of God,' did not consider it beneath his dignity to 'procure' material as well as spiritual benefits for his people. Geneva certainly owed to Calvin's efforts some admirable hospitals, doss-houses and work-houses. It was he who introduced into the town the wool and silk industries, both of which resulted in great wealth. The economic organization of the city under Calvin merits a study on its own. The anti-inflationary laws were Draconian but effective; in practice all products were taxed. One edict commanded under pain of imprisonment that all stale food be thrown into the Rhône. It remains astonishing nevertheless to see Calvin writing to the magistrature to secure a decree ordering all property owners to bar the windows of their houses, so that small children should no longer fall out. It is even more astonishing to hear him demanding *ex cathedra* that care should be taken to ensure 'the cleanliness of the public lavatories and of those things of which modesty prevents any mention.' But it is common knowledge that dictatorships inevitably end by seeking to regulate every single thing.

The most remarkable aspect of the whole story is the fact that the Genevans accepted this regime for so many years. They were sustained by a singular feeling of exaltation, a conviction of being the advance guard of the army of God, the Holy City among all the rest. It was not merely the police who prevented any serious protests being made; it was public opinion too, influenced partly by fear no doubt, but also by its own fanaticism. On countless occasions those condemned to death would, at the very moment of execution, thank God and their judges for having permitted them to expiate their offences and thus possess the hope of obtaining eternal salvation. Men vied with one another in their exaltation, and this tended to increased severity: one husband whom the Council had sentenced to imprisonment for having committed adultery was unwise enough to appeal against this verdict to the popular assembly, which immediately condemned him to death.

Such then was Geneva, the City-Church, in the days of the triumphant Calvin. His thin, pallid figure dominated the whole of this population which could pursue its way of life only at his direction. He was hardly ever seen in the streets; he scarcely went out at all except to preach, to take part in the pastors' 'congregation,' or to visit a few sick folk. Although wakened at dawn, for he slept very little, his health was so poor that he would stay in bed nearly the whole morning. He ate only one meal a day, and that very quickly. When it was over he would take a short stroll for about half an hour in his room or garden, depending on the weather.[1] Occasionally he would indulge in a game of quoits or keys [2] with some close friend. Nearly all his time was devoted to his duties; his capacity for work was unaffected by his illnesses and physical discomforts. He would write for ten or twelve hours a day, which explains the dimensions of a literary output filling fifty-nine octavo volumes and almost forty thousand pages. Theodore Beza relates that on average Calvin preached two hundred and eighty-six times a year, and that during the same period he would hold as many as one hundred and eighty conferences. To all this must be added his gigantic correspondence, correction of books, and frequent consultations. What gifts this prodigious activity reveals: a flawless memory, blinding lucidity, perfect ease of expression and incomparable speed! All these qualities appear the more extraordinary because their instrument was a sickly body—'more a symbol than a body,' as one of his friends said—withered and wasted by premature old age and suffering. The head seemed balanced almost awry on the neck that receded into the narrow shoulders: his face had the pallor of a corpse, with its pointed nose and long, curling beard, which was now also white. Only his eyes seemed alive, with the penetrating stare which no one could meet for long.

A very small group of close friends and loyal followers gathered close around him. After his wife's death Calvin derived precious little satisfaction from his own family: his sister Marie was a nonentity; his brother Antoine, who was one of his secretaries, is famous only for his marital misfortunes; as for his stepdaughter, the child of Idelette's first marriage, she caused scandal after scandal. Calvin recognized his real family not in ties of blood, but of friendship. This is the only aspect of his life in which his austere soul allows itself to give way to tenderness. With Bucer, Farel, Melanchthon, Renée of Ferrara and several other friends, he maintained a correspondence whose confidential character is rather surprising in a man of such reserve. Many of his ardent supporters made their residence close to his house in the Rue des Chanoines, in order that they might be nearer him. The most ardent of all were the French refugees, who had given up everything for their faith and could conceive of no greater happiness than that of living beside their master. These included such men as the Norman Laurence, Calvin's intimate friend, the sons of Guillaume Budé and even Guillaume de Trie who played such a painful role in the affair of

[1] As can be seen, this was a simple life and shows no trace of luxury. Nevertheless certain historians, founding their theses on Bolsec's calumnies, have claimed that Calvin was an avaricious miser. His estate at his death amounted to 200 crowns, which is not very much for a man who had been master of Geneva and spiritual director of half Europe for some twenty years.

[2] This harmless little game consisted of pushing a key from one side of the table to the other, without colliding with that of one's competitor.

Servetus. The most famous of them all was *Theodore Beza* (1509–1605), Calvin's junior by ten years, to whom the reformer awarded a leading place in his City-Church.

Beza was a Burgundian from Vézelay, a nobleman who had fallen upon hard times. As a student at Orleans he had first met Calvin at Wolmar's lectures, at a time when the future reformer was still seeking to find his true self. But it had taken Beza many years to rejoin him. He was too passionately interested in literature and philology, too busy studying law, writing poems—of a very advanced character more-over—frequenting the elegant world of Paris and indulging in amorous intrigues. In 1548 a serious illness led to his 'conversion'—in other words, Beza adopted the austere life recommended by his teacher, Melchior Wolmar. And thus it was that in the following year he came to ask Calvin to receive him into his Church. Beza settled in Lausanne to earn his living. He taught Greek while also writing theatrical pieces and translating the Psalms, which he did extremely well; but he visited Geneva frequently. He settled there for good in 1558, and was made a pastor and a citizen of the town. Henceforth he was rather like Mel-anchthon to Calvin's Luther, though he showed far more doctrinal loyalty than Melanchthon had done. Beza proved himself an infinitely devoted aide to Calvin. He was more skilled than his leader at winning men's hearts, more inclined to palliate excessive severities, and at the same time he was Calvin's most affectionate commentator and bio-grapher. He succeeded Calvin at Geneva, and during his forty years of religious leadership he established the Genevan Church on lasting bases. The reformer himself had chosen Beza for this important office by making him the head of what he considered to be both the keystone and the crown of his work.

This was the *Academy of Geneva*. Ever since the rupture with Sebastian Castellio higher education at Geneva had languished; Mathurin Cordier, formerly master of the Collège de la Manche, was virtually the only person now making it his concern. Calvin felt the need for improvement here. He was primarily preoccupied with the question of the education of his pastors and doctors, but he also con-sidered it essential to provide an excellent spiritual sustenance to all those young men who were flocking to the City-Church as to a living source, from France, England, Scotland, the Low Countries and even from places as far afield as Poland. Calvin looked back with envy at the college founded by Sturm at Strasbourg. So on 5th July 1559 the Calvinist University, whose foundation is one of the reformer's most creditable and glorious achievements, came into being. Theodore Beza was made its first rector and was to prove himself an outstanding teacher. Its picturesque building still stands with its high, double flight of steps, its lofty, red-tiled roof and its pointed bell-turret. A most thorough education was given at the university, both humanist, scriptural and theological. Hebrew received particular attention, but not the natural sciences, *diabolica scientia*, whose study Calvin regarded with fear as 'imprudent curiosity and rashness.' By 1564 the Genevan Academy contained no less than twelve hundred pupils in its ordinary schools, and over three hundred specialist students. Its role was undoubtedly considerable: to it Protestantism owes the fame of having very rapidly constituted a pastoral body provided with a high level of culture. Geneva became the nursery that Wittenberg had never been, it was a centre where missionaries of the Reformation could be trained and also a university for the Protestant *élite*. The only places that were to rival the quality of its teachers and its methods were the Jesuit colleges. (It should be emphasized that the model for the latter, the 'German College' at Rome—which is today known as the Gregorian University—had been founded in 1551, and therefore the Catholic foundations owe nothing to Geneva's example.) This marvellous establishment contributed not a little to glorifying the man who had brought it into being, and to making his city one of the beacons of the West.

The astonishing influence which Geneva very rapidly acquired was due not only to her doctrinal and institutional coherence, nor even to the quality of her masters. As we have seen, universalism was one of the axes of Calvin's thought. He had never considered that his work would be adequate if it was confined within the walls of his city, or even restricted to the Switzerland, in the way that Luther had allowed Lutheranism to become enclosed within its Germanic framework. Calvin was perfectly well aware of the danger which the Reformation ran if it presented itself in extended order in the inevitable battles that lay ahead. Consequently, although so intransigent in Geneva itself, he showed a conciliatory attitude in his dealings with outsiders. Like Bucer, he was much concerned with the problem of Protestant unity, and in 1540 he had signed the Confession of Augsburg, in which Melanchthon had modified the definition of the Lord's Supper. He had behaved with courtesy in the bitter 'sacramentary' controversies between the Lutherans and Zwinglians, and, contrary to current practice, had refrained from insulting his opponent. Union to him was important not merely for tactical reasons; he believed that, since the Church was the Body of Christ, all the various Protestant churches claiming the Lord's authority ought to agree to their differences, like separate members of one organism. He worked hard to establish ties with other Protestant leaders. After ten years of negotiations with Bullinger, Zwingli's successor, Calvin managed to sign an agreement with the Church of Zürich, to which those of Basle, Neuchâtel, Bienne, Berne and Schaffhausen subsequently adhered, this *Consensus Tigurinus* (from the Latin name of Zürich) sealed the union of the Swiss reformed communities around the Calvinist conception of Christ's real but always spiritual presence in the Lord's Supper.

Was it possible to go even further? Calvin certainly wished to do so; an agreement with Lutheranism seemed to him essential. Although he was not ignorant of the arrows which the German hypochondriac had sometimes directed at him towards the end of his life, he nevertheless talked of Luther with admiration: 'The excellence of his gifts, the constancy of his soul, are unforgettable . . . what flexibility and doctrinal strength he showed in his battle with Antichrist! Were he to call me the devil, I should always render him this homage of acknowledging him as a servant sent from God.' And in his old age Luther himself had declared that he 'rejoiced that God had sent man such as Calvin upon earth, to deal papism the final blow and finish the work he himself had begun.' All the same, despite the undoubted desire for a *rapprochement* evinced by Melanchthon and several other Lutherans, union could not be achieved. On the very morrow of the *Consensus* a fiery minister from Hamburg, one Westphal, did all he could to emphasize that the doctrine of the Lord's Supper as expressed in the agreement was quite contrary to the teaching of Luther. A petty war of pamphlets then ensued, in which several fools, and even ranting extremists (e.g. Tileman Hesshusius of Heidelberg), took part, and vulgar quarrels resulted. Nothing could persuade the fanatics from Wittenberg to come to any understanding with those whom they regarded as defenders of the abominable sacramentary errors. Nevertheless Calvin did not abandon his efforts to reunite all Protestants; supported by Farel and Beza, he continued his endeavours. In 1552 the Archbishop of Canterbury, Thomas Cranmer, proposed to him, and likewise to Melanchthon and Bullinger, that common agreement should be reached on the doctrines of salvation and the Lord's Supper. The attempt came to nothing. Again, in 1557, Melanchthon agreed that representatives of the two principal Protestant confessions should meet at Worms, but Luther's conciliatory successor was himself hotly criticized by his coreligionists. Nothing at all emerged from the conference; the divergencies on the Real Presence and Predestination (which, as we know, Melanchthon had removed from the Lutheran Credo) were, if anything, accentuated. So, although considered by many as the leader of Protestantism, Calvin did not succeed in meeting Protestant unity; there was to be not one Reformation but many, and all tended to split up into sects. While Calvinism embodied the expansionist force of Protestantism, it proved itself incapable of disciplining the whole, or of forcing it into subjection to itself. Possibly this is because the true genius of the Reformation lay in its conception of religion as a purely personal affair, the private dialogue between the sinner illuminated by the Spirit and his omnipotent Creator, and because this message, the essence of the new Christianity, had been carried to the world not by Calvin but by Luther.

Nevertheless it remains true that Calvin's influence and that of his City-Church was exerted in many vast areas won over to Protestantism, and that it alone constituted an element of unity among those adhering to the new ideas. Geneva has been called the *Protestant Rome*. The expression is only partially valid. Calvin himself would undoubtedly have rejected it, for he thought merely that Geneva ought to be 'the ark on the mighty waters of the flood'; and Karl Barth has protested forcefully against this 'cream of sentimental rhetoric,' this tendency 'to vest the *Christian Institution*, the ecclesiastical ordinances and the very person of Calvin with a prophetic and apostolic authority. Assuredly Protestant Rome has never existed, save in caricature, whether well intentioned or otherwise.' It is quite certain indeed that Geneva is not, and never has been, for Calvinists all that Rome is for Catholics—at once the motherland of all their spiritual loyalties, the centre from which all legitimate authority flows, and the place where, from St Peter to the present Pope, a sacred presence offers a visible representation of Christ. In a looser sense, however, during the reformer's residence there, and while so many anxious souls looked towards it, Geneva did assume the role of a spiritual capital.

It is essential to note this influence when making any assessment of Calvin's historical role. The crushing weight of correspondence which he forced himself to maintain, and which, despite the assistance of several secretaries, became a heavier burden to him with every day that passed, spread his influence throughout the world. Nearly six thousand of his letters have been published, addressed to 507 correspondents and dealing with every subject from morality to politics, from exegesis to theology, and even on many practical matters too. Some of them might be described as circulars sent to several communities simultaneously, almost like encyclicals. Calvin's correspondence shows that he was both spiritual director and head of his Church.

Even more moving are the numerous testimonies we have concerning those men and women who abandoned all they had and went to Geneva in order to live close to the man who in their eyes possessed the Word of God. Florimond de Rémond, the first Catholic historian of Protestantism, tells of having known a man who assured him that he had felt the Holy Spirit descend upon him and sing the name of Calvin in his ear. Straight away he had taken the road to Geneva 'as joyously as that worthy and religious knight Godefroy de Bouillon going to Jerusalem.' Shortly before he died Calvin received a visit from a humble widow who had just arrived from France. She had waited thirty years before being able to make the journey, but had not wanted to die without having seen him.

Right to the last Calvin himself, squatting in his modest city like a tiny spider, followed with impassioned interest the progress of that gigantic web he had spun. He watched it spreading out in all directions. Sometimes he had disappointments. In Germany and Scandinavia his ideas collided with the powerful Lutheranism of the princes; in Italy his friend the Duchess of Ferrara, after many vacillations, remained loyal to the Catholic faith; in England, despite his connections with Cranmer and Somerset, the situation did not evolve as he had wished. But he also had moments of great joy: his ideas penetrated into several countries. In Switzerland they were gradually to absorb Zwinglianism altogether; in Hungary and the Palatinate his doctrines replaced those of Wittenberg; in the Low Countries his beloved disciple Guy de Bray made it triumph over all other faiths, that of Luther as well as that of the Anabaptists; finally, in Scotland, Calvinism in its Presbyterian form attained a degree of perfection at least equal to that of Geneva, thanks to yet another disciple, *John Knox*. The influential radiance of a doctrine which in itself possessed so little inherent radiance, and so much that was tyrannical, may seem to us strange and surprising: a phrase of John Knox explains its success. To him, as to so many other deeply religious people, Calvinism was 'the most perfect school of Christ that has ever existed on earth since the time of the Apostles,' and Calvin could be proud of having been the master of this school.

CALVIN AND FRANCE

The reformer of Geneva devoted sustained attention to one country more than to any other. This was France, his native land, which he had left in order the more surely to bring her the truth from beyond her frontiers. France had been particularly in his thoughts when he translated his *Christian Institution* into French (1541) and published it in popular form. With France also his ties were constantly renewed by the twofold current of arriving refugees and departing missionaries. The work of inspiring and organizing Protestant propaganda in France was certainly one of the sections of Calvin's immense task to which he devoted most time and enthusiasm. He wrote letters of encouragement and advice to all those whom he knew to share his doctrine; in like manner, on his orders, the French refugees in Geneva sent letter after letter to their families and friends who had remained in France. It was he too who inspired and directed those wonderfully courageous teams of clandestine messengers who would slip secretly back into the kingdom in order to bear the master's latest thoughts to

P

the reformed communities there, and who would often stay to become
pastors of this or that community. Were such men captured they were
certain of being burned, as happened to five young ministers who were
stopped and searched, quite by chance, at Tamié in Savoy, and who
perished at the stake some weeks later. This was a skilful, effective
kind of propaganda, which did not shrink from cunning. Thus Calvin
hit on the idea of publishing booklets which passed for Catholic ones,
such as *The manner of praying in French churches*, which bore the words
'Printed in Rome by order of the Pope' on its cover, but which had
actually been printed at Strasbourg and written by himself.

Calvin could follow the joyful progress resulting from this propaganda. News reached him from all four corners of the realm, announcing the establishment of fresh Calvinist communities;[1] distributors of
Bibles were opening up shop there, obtaining their supplies from
Lyons, the centre for pedlars from Germany and Geneva, which were
the wholesalers of this kind of merchandise. The printing of the
Christian Institution in France was prohibited, but whole sackfuls of
copies were smuggled in. From his office in Geneva Calvin controlled
all the threads of this action with detailed care.

His effort was directed not only at enlarging this potential harvest.
He was no less interested in using diplomacy and patience to forge
solid links which would bind these little cells of converts closely to one
another. Since the establishment of his City-Church at Geneva his
fame had become immense throughout the French Protestant world,
and this enabled him to talk authoritatively and be sure of a hearing.
He told each one of these communities to establish close relations with
its neighbours, so that they might together study the problems facing
them and arrive at joint decisions. As Theodore Beza wrote, Calvin
demonstrated 'the evils which could occur, leading to doctrinal as
much as to disciplinary quarrels, in churches which were not bound
together and drawn up under the same yoke of authority and ecclesiastical order.' His policy of unity triumphed in 1559, when the *First
Calvinist Synod* was held in Paris, at the very height of the persecution.
There the French pastors met to decide on a common confession of
faith and organization for the whole kingdom, which was divided into
sixteen provinces. Possibly this undertaking was rather too bold and
ambitious, for a few years later its scope had to be slightly reduced.
Nevertheless it proves how, thanks to Calvin's logical inspiration,
the desire for strong organization was replacing the anarchical indi-
vidualism which had marked the beginnings of French Protestantism.

The news from France, however, was not all so happy. Since the
days when Calvin himself had fled eastwards, following the Placard
Affair, events had moved swiftly. The era of relatively favourable

[1] The progress of Calvinism in France is studied in the following chapter, p. 484 et seq.

equivocation had been succeeded by one of repression—a repression which was restrained whilst Francis I still lived, but which, under Henry II, soon became systematic and formidable. Henceforth the pace was set by the forces hostile to Protestantism, led by the Parlement and the Sorbonne. Messages reached Geneva from every part of the realm telling the same sorry tale: arrests, imprisonments and, all too often, burnings at the stake. The massacre of the Waldenses [1] of Provence, the destruction of the Protestant community at Meaux, and the execution of its principal members, followed one after the other. Then, when Henry II ascended the throne, there came news of the institution of the new *Chambre Ardente* and the promulgation of the Edict of Châteaubriant, which denied all Protestants the right of appeal. 'This is an atrocious edict!' cried Calvin, 'the right which, until now, has been freely accorded to poisoners, forgers and thieves, and is still accorded them, is being snatched away from good Christians. The relatives of accused persons in danger of death are forbidden to intervene on their behalf, under pain of being regarded as supporters of heresy themselves. A third of the condemned person's goods are reserved for the creature that denounced him.' All this was true, and much else more terrible besides. In 1557 the Edict of Compiègne had forbidden the judges of the terrible *Chambres Ardentes* to impose any penalty other than death. This was an appalling situation, and there is no doubt at all that Calvin was sorely afflicted by it, though his feelings were somewhat divided. Each day he wrote new letters, exalting the courage of those who were risking their lives for the cause. 'The times demand that we sign our faith in our blood, that faith which we have testified by word of mouth or in pen and ink. . . .' But often too he was seized by terrible anguish and wondered if his duty did not require him to return to France forthwith and risk his life there, testifying to his faith by his own martyrdom.

Thus the last years of Calvin's life were darkened by the knowledge that his Church in France, which he foresaw as leader of all the rest, was suffering so terrible an ordeal. Flames from the stakes were rising everywhere: Anne du Bourg, a member of the Parlement of Paris itself, had just perished at one of them. The Conference of Poissy convened at Catherine de' Medici's instigation in 1561, and to which Calvin had sent Beza as his representative, had yielded no results. The very character of Protestantism in France was changing. Originally an exclusively religious force, it was gradually evolving into a political one, due to the arrival on the scene of several important aristocrats who had been converted to heresy and were determined not to let it be destroyed. And Calvin, who had so recently written 'Better that we all perish a hundred times than let the name of Christianity and the

[1] All these events are dealt with in the following chapter, pp. 487 and 488.

Gospel be exposed to such shame'—the shame of bloodshed—now gave way to the insistent pleas from France and finally declared insurrection to be lawful. So, convinced that they were fighting for the Christian faith, and at the same time determined to further a policy which, if it succeeded, would make them masters of France, the leaders of the new 'Protestant Party' opened the battle. As he lay dying the tireless reformer must surely have wondered whether he was not leaving the Church born of his efforts leaderless at the very moment when it had most need of him.

The Death and Fame of John Calvin

On Christmas Eve 1559 Calvin had to strain his voice in order to make himself heard when he preached in St Peter's, which was packed to overflowing. The following day he was seized by spasms of violent coughing and began to spit blood. His doctor diagnosed pulmonary tuberculosis; there was at this period nothing that could be done to arrest or cure such a complaint. Calvin was only fifty years of age, his case might not have been desperate had not his whole system—ravaged for many years by so many other ills, and worn out by work and worry—been that of a prematurely old man. Roused by this fresh malady, all the old familiar ills rushed to join the attack: lungs, kidneys, intestines, brain, even his arms and legs were affected. Very soon every part of his body was the source and seat of dreadful agony.

Calvin endured this ordeal for five years with admirable physical courage and spiritual fortitude. Though tortured by colic, fever and gout, he nevertheless continued to carry on with all his tasks, his correspondence and his books. He even preached, though this demanded a superhuman effort. On days when he was unable to stand he preached sitting down, and when he was too weak to walk he had two friends carry him to church in a chair. Sometimes, however, the pains were so severe that people would hear him murmuring words which sounded very like a supplication for deliverance: 'How long, O Lord, how long?'

As he faced death Calvin remained what he had always been: lucid, steadfast and reserved. He never once showed the slightest fear or weakness. He made his will according to a plan drawn up with his customary logic, and received the corporate bodies of the town in audience, one by one, from the Little Council to the pastors. To the latter he addressed a long and detailed discourse, in which he summed up all his work in a number of striking formulas, with that mixture of sincere humility and tranquil pride which were so typical of him. He invited his colleagues to show themselves firm and vigilant towards this 'perverse and wicked nation' which he was confiding to their care, and he ended by declaring that his sole desire on earth had been to serve the glory of God. It was as if he were dictating his spiritual testament.

Death, however, granted him yet one more respite, and Farel was able to come and visit him for the last time. Even now the dying man, who already looked more like a corpse than a living being, put forth one supreme and quite extraordinary burst of energy. Realizing that, according to the ecclesiastical legislation he himself had established, the next occasion of the quarterly 'censures' was fixed for 19th May, he ordered that he should be carried there in order to join for the last time in this ceremony of fraternal confession. He humbly subjected himself to censure first of all, castigating his own defects—'anger, obstinacy, cruelty and pride'—and then, in a halting voice constantly broken by fits of coughing, he spoke on for another two hours, putting each of his listeners on his guard against his own evil inclinations, and then, little by little, rising to important principles, commenting on the Gospel in impassioned terms.

This was Calvin's last public act: the effort had killed him. On the following day he began again to spit more blood. He no longer left his bed and scarcely spoke at all, save to murmur prayers. Thus he was heard to say several times: 'O Lord, you are crushing me sorely, but it is enough that I am in your hand.' His end when it came was so peaceful that no one actually saw him give up the ghost on 27th May 1564, towards eight o'clock in the evening. In accordance with the instructions given in his will, Calvin's body was sewn into a large plain Holland sheet, and placed in a pine coffin exactly like those used for the poor; and without sermon or hymns an immense crowd escorted it to the graveyard of Plainpalais. No monument was erected over his tomb, not even a cross or a plain stone. This was how he had wished to return to dust, anonymously and in silence. Today no one can point with certainty to the spot where John Calvin lies.[1]

Few men have left behind them so deep an impression. No one can deny Calvin's greatness. He spread many important ideas, he carried out many great achievements and he determined many great events. Had he never lived, thought and acted with all his implacable drive and will-power, history would have been quite different. Today some fifty million Christians claim authority from him. Of these forty-one million belong to the Reformed and Presbyterian Churches, while some five million are Congregationalists; and there is probably not a sector of Protestantism which does not owe something to him. It is quite another matter whether Calvin himself would acknowledge all

---

[1] The stone marked 'J. C.' which the visitor is shown in the cemetery of Plainpalais was put there by a Dutch Calvinist in 1830, but the siting of it is the subject of some argument.

those who profess to continue his message, but who have virtually abandoned the theory of Predestination which he regarded as more important than life itself, and who have in many cases allowed his fiery teaching to become a kind of egalitarian and moralizing sentimentality. Yet of the decisive nature of his influence, even in the development of capitalism, democracy and Socialism there can be not a shadow of doubt. He unquestionably belongs to that tiny band of master-craftsmen whose hands, in the course of centuries, have fashioned the destinies of the world.

Such a man is not easily judged. Only He who sounds the secrets of all our hearts and minds can do that. Moreover Calvin has always been the subject of widely differing opinions. Michelet was too ardent an admirer of his work of 'liberation'; Renan regarded him as hard-working and ambitiously self-seeking, but as otherwise unexceptional. We can join with his supporters in exalting his genius, his acute understanding of great problems, his capacity for synthesis and organization. We can even admit that kind of frigid attraction which emanates from Calvin as from all great minds which possess a taste for the long and careful study of ideas as well as for their perfect expression. And it would be grossly unfair not to recognize his ardent zeal for God, his passion to win souls, that tragic seriousness with which he always regarded his vocation, and his unfailing sense of duty. But it is equally impossible not to observe that this outstanding personality lacked two essentially Christian virtues which would have set the seal upon his greatness. First, true humility, not only before God, but before men also, the kind of humility which later impelled St Vincent de Paul to fall on his knees before a peasant who had struck him in the face. Secondly, true goodness, which knows how to love men despite their abjection, and indeed because of it, and which is always ready to pardon any fault. It seems that though Calvin read his Gospel so thoroughly, he had not understood its two noblest precepts: that it behoves us to be the least important at the table end, and that we ought to love our enemies.

Opinions regarding Calvin's historical role are also conflicting. 'Calvin was the principal destroyer of genuine Protestantism,' says one historian.[1] 'Calvinism saved Lutheranism,' says another.[2] Both are correct. Calvin undoubtedly led Protestantism far from its original bases, and directed it towards ends which Luther had not desired; but the ways which Luther had in mind led to one of two impasses—anarchy or the subjection of religion to the State. Protestantism owed to Calvin its order, its common faith, its clergy, its methods, and also that solemn face which we know so well, a face that is often more respectable than lovable. In short, it owed him a new type of believer.

[1] J. Dedieu.   [2] Doumergue.

Calvin was, however, first and foremost the man who sealed the final rupture, and on this point more than on any other a Catholic cannot look upon him but with horror. He set himself to build an impassable wall, or an abyss, between the Church which had given him baptism and that which he wished to 'draw up': and he did this far more thoroughly than Luther had done, and with a kind of devilish severity.[1] It is true that, dialectically speaking, his role, like that of his German predecessor, could in the last resort be considered favourable to the ultimate designs of Providence, for the terrible blow he dealt Christendom was the cause of her reawakening; but this does not lessen the extent of his sin. After Calvin all hopes of repairing the rent in the Seamless Robe vanished for centuries to come. Such in brief is the significance of this man's life; such was the success of John Calvin.

---

[1] And without engaging in any of those violent polemics in which Luther was involved throughout his career.

CHAPTER VII

FROM RELIGIOUS REVOLT TO POLITICAL PROTESTANTISM

MYSTIQUE AND POLITICS

'EVERYTHING begins with mystique and ends in politics.' Péguy's famous phrase invariably springs to mind whenever one considers the history of the Protestant Reformation and the evolution that occurred therein. In the poet's special vocabulary, of course, 'mystique' is the impulse of generosity and enthusiasm which leads man to sacrifice himself unreservedly for an ideal, without taking into account calculation or self-interest. Politics is exactly the opposite, the less conscious determination to safeguard individual and group interests in the train of the ideal and its demands, to put the latter to the service of the former. What angered Péguy was the fact that politics, the force of degradation, always ended by winning the day, destroying mystique at the very moment when the latter's triumph seemed assured and in exact proportion to the extent of that triumph. The poet saw in this phenomenon a proof of man's 'baseness,' and even referred to his 'sin.'

Man must realize that he is a free Christian, sustained by faith and adhering firmly to his God in the knowledge that this faith justifies and saves, thanks to the gratuitous gift of love, the incomprehensible grace which sinful man in no sense deserves. He becomes aware of its presence in a private spiritual colloquy between himself and his Creator. He reads the Bible, the book of the Word, with the eyes of faith, in order to receive spiritual illumination without the assistance of any intermediary whatsoever. . . . Such was the message of spiritual liberation which Martin Luther had enunciated and repeated all his life, absolutely certain of possessing a truth so sound that no force on earth could make him abandon it. And this cry from a single conscience had awakened such powerful echoes all over Christian Europe that countless souls had responded to it. They were fervent souls, willing to sacrifice everything for the doctrine which revealed them to themselves, what Péguy would have called full of 'mystique.'

But less than ten years after that crucial feast of All Saints in 1517, when the famous protest against indulgences had been found on the door of the Schlosskirche at Wittenberg, the picture had changed considerably. Naturally many convinced and exalted enthusiasts still existed, but politics had now intruded in a number of different ways into the religious issue. Luther had originally addressed his message to everyone able and willing to listen to him, but although his strong feeling of national solidarity had not restricted its propagation, he had none the less bound it so closely to the concepts and sentiments of his 'beloved Germans' that it had lost much of its force. At the same time circumstances had obliged him to entrust the lot of the liberated Christian communities to the authority of secular rulers. He realized that the success of his doctrine was henceforth dependent upon a political structure which he was forced to support even in its wrong-doings and which was generally more concerned with practical interests than with spiritual freedom.

This phenomenon had been repeated everywhere. The religious movement of reform was taken over by political forces which hence-forth controlled its development. The free cities and small republics of the Rhineland and Switzerland offered different but equally striking examples of this. At Basle under Oeclampadius, at Zürich under Zwingli, and at Strasbourg under Sturm and Bucer, the intervention of the civil authority may not have been the first element of the Reformation, but it was assuredly the most decisive. The new doctrines were imposed wherever the local magistrate was converted, even in places where the people's acceptance of them was far from complete. Berne had actually taken up arms at Zürich's side in an effort to rally a majority of the cantons to the new faith; and this would undoubtedly have been the outcome had not the defeat at Kappel shattered their project. We have already seen what a vital role the counsellors of Geneva played in Calvin's triumph, notably when they recalled the exiled reformer for reasons which were far from exclusively religious. The secular power's increasingly obvious responsibility for spiritual reform was a momentous fact; but Calvin himself had no desire to change the situation. Quite the contrary. While he had reversed the relationship between the religious authority and the secular, by giving the former the right to control the latter, he had in fact made each more interdependent on the other; and by freeing·religious reform from the narrow cage of nationalism in which Luther had imprisoned it, the author of *The Christian Institution* had given to the world his theo-cratic formula, in which religion and politics were completely merged.

The period between the affair at Wittenberg in 1517 and the death of Calvin in 1564 witnessed a similar evolution taking place all over Christian Europe. While the Reformation launched attack after attack against the ancient Catholic structure, the same political problem affected Calvinism, which was more logical and better organized. There was not a single country in which religious impulse alone, the genuine 'mystique,' was sufficiently powerful to implant the heretical Reformation; the social, economic and religious motives which are often put forward to explain certain limited successes do not provide the reason for the final triumph. Where this victory was achieved it was due to the intervention of the civil authority. Recourse was had to politics in order that the State might impose the religious revolution with its customary weapons, violence and deceit.[1] This was true in England, Scandinavia and several other places. Conversely, however, it should be remembered that in areas where Protestant expansion was halted, this too was largely due to the action of political forces which undoubtedly combined support of Catholic truth with the furtherance of various material interests.

'Everything begins with mystique and ends in politics. . . .' It is this political intervention which bears so heavily upon the whole history of the Reformation and gives it its tragic character. The drama of souls is mingled with the antagonism of ambitions and interests; and this coalition of fanaticisms would involve Christendom in more than a century of bloody conflict.

THE LUTHERAN WAVE GAINS GROUND IN THE EAST AND THE NORTH

The Lutheran wave began to break very soon after the impassioned young monk had set it in motion. As we have already seen,[2] it swept first across Germany, affecting the peasantry, artisans and the landless knights, as well as scholars and middle-class merchants. The printing-press, invented by the German Gutenberg, played a considerable part in this early expansion, in which worldly motives were already mingled with religious ideals—the appetites of the petty squirearchy and the serfs. The former were fired with national pride, the latter with desire to win their freedom. Then, at the very moment when the social repercussions of the reformed doctrine were producing a series of crises in which it might well have foundered, the nobility intervened, taking over from the heresiarch's first allies, and the movement thus passed on to quite a different plane. Faced with the threat of anarchy, Luther handed back to the temporal rulers the task of ensuring law and order, and of organizing the religious society born of his efforts. 'The Gospel alone is not enough, we need the law and the hangman too.' Imprisoned within each separate state, whose ruler became both Caesar and Pope, the Church linked her destiny with that of the great feudatories, who at once saw the advantages of the situation. The

[1] This idea is brought out particularly well by Cardinal Baudrillart in *L'Église Catholique, la Renaissance, le Protestantisme*.
[2] See Chapter V, pp. 299 et seq.

prince who responded to the reformer's call could secularize Church property, exercise stronger authority over his subjects and, through the ministers of religion, control all religious life in his domains. Thus delusively but effectively the faith of Wittenberg was imposed on almost the whole of Germany, with the exception of the Rhineland and Bavaria. Albert of Brandenburg, by secularizing the possessions of the Teutonic Knights, of whom he was the Grand Master, and forming them into the hereditary duchy of Prussia, appeared to set the seal on this process in a spectacular manner. Refractory Catholic priests were hounded out of the country; altars, statues and pilgrimages were forbidden. Shortly afterwards Livonia and Courland, which also belonged to the Order, were forcibly converted to Protestantism by other less important but equally ambitious dignitaries.

Once set in motion the wave rolled forward to attack the borderlands of Germany. Bohemia, the native land of John Huss, was rapidly affected, for the Hussite crisis which he had provoked had left some tragic after-effects.[1] The Christians of Bohemia were divided into three groups. There was a small but courageous minority of Catholics. Then there was a majority of *Utraquists*, or former moderate Hussites, who had been officially recognized by the *Compactata* in 1436 and granted the right of communicating in both kinds (whence their name), and whose status had been confirmed by the agreements signed in 1485 and 1512. Finally, there were the *Bohemian* or *Moravian Brethren*, heirs of the Hussite extremists, the now pacified Taborites; they still longed to do battle with Rome and Catholicism, and their adherents included some of the nobility. Of these only the Utraquist Church, which commanded two-thirds of the population, could have campaigned effectively against the new doctrines; but it was devoid of original theology, possessed of an intolerant and mediocre clergy, was interested primarily in ritualistic details and provided little spiritual sustenance for its members. When Luther's teaching crossed the Böhmerwald (*c.* 1520), carried thither by travellers from the neighbouring duchy of Saxony, the Bohemian and Moravian Brethren rallied to it at once. *John Augusta* became their leader, and in 1538 he drafted a 'Confession' which was approved by Luther. The nobility immediately began to secularize the possessions of the Church; the Utraquists clung to their privileges and offered but a token resistance; only the Catholic minority stood its ground.

From this new bastion the Lutheran tide flowed eastwards. Silesia, an autonomous duchy under Bohemian suzerainty, was a Catholic area in which the Hussites were only a minority, but its clergy was decadent. Here the Reformed preachers were welcomed by great lords such as Frederick of Liegnitz, and by such towns as Breslau which were on

[1] See Chapter III, section: 'John Huss.'

bad terms with their bishops. Their success had its now habitual corollary: expropriation of priests and monks, confiscation of all their property and expulsion of recalcitrants. When Ferdinand of Austria inherited the duchy he was anxious to restore the Catholic faith there, but he soon realized that it was too late.

Crossing the Hapsburg territories of Upper and Lower Austria, both of which had been contaminated by heretical ideas, Lutheranism followed the course of the Danube and infiltrated into Hungary. It converted the settlements of German miners, the Saxon colonies in Transylvania, the cities which were permeated by Germanic elements, and the aristocracy which had received its education in the imperial universities. The new doctrine at first encountered a number of obstacles, for the Hungarians hated the Germans. But the disastrous defeat at Mohacs in 1526,[1] in which Louis II, six bishops and the flower of Hungary's youth perished, modified the situation. In those parts of the country controlled by them the Turks favoured the Reformed communities; for since these possessed no hierarchy, they were less capable of welding together national resistance to the Infidel. In the region which still remained free there were two rival candidates for the throne: the Archduke Ferdinand, heir by virtue of his wife's right, and John Zapolya, who had been elected by the nobility. The Reformed clergy skilfully played off this antagonism between two faithful sons of the Catholic Church, and they were abetted by the aristocracy, who, on the morrow of Mohacs, had appropriated the estates of the dead bishops. Consequently a Germano-Hungarian Lutheran Church was established, which adopted the Confession of Augsburg.[2] However, in the interval prior to the Catholic reaction at the beginning of the sixteenth century,[3] Calvinism rapidly overwhelmed the Lutheran influence in Hungarian Protestantism.

In north-east Europe the enormous kingdom of Sigismund I, which stretched from the Baltic to the Carpathians, and which at this time comprised a union of Lithuania and Poland, was exposed to every prevailing influence; it occupied a plain which had no natural frontiers, and its population was very mixed. The common people possessed a genuine, ostentatious faith, easily given to superstition: crowds flocked to the great pilgrimages, such as that to Our Lady of Czestochowa. The nobles were often idle and penniless, and were fast becoming religiously indifferent. They regarded the higher clergy, which was wealthy and depraved, with lustful anger, and despised the ordinary priests, who were extremely ignorant. At the beginning of the fifteenth

[1] See Chapter V, p. 322.
[2] See further on in this chapter, p. 498.
[3] See *The Catholic Reformation*, Chapter III.

century the Hussite doctrines had held some attraction for the Poles; a century later a great many of them were impressed by the appeals of Luther. The king watched with anxiety as the new doctrine gained ground in his Prussian cities. In 1520, before he had learned of the papal bull of condemnation, Sigismund issued the Edict of Thorn forbidding the introduction, sale or reading of the writings 'of a certain Augustinian brother, Martin Luther,' as injurious to the Holy See and a dangerous threat to public order; and in 1523 he announced that anyone contravening these regulations would be punished by death. The constant progress of the heresy made Sigismund even more stringent. In 1526 Danzig, where the Reformed communities were very numerous, was severely punished; in 1534 all Polish and Lithuanian noblemen were ordered to recall without delay any of their sons who might be studying in Germany (there were many Poles at Wittenberg). In future no Pole would be allowed to visit heretical countries, and courts for the trial of heretics were set up at Cracow. These brutal but unco-ordinated measures merely proclaimed the government's impotence. The Reformation went forward all over the country. Polish humanists, among whom were several bishops, deluded themselves into regarding Luther as a pupil of their beloved Erasmus. The nobility, determined to gain political power, was anxious to flout the king; consequently many aristocrats gave asylum to the Reformed preachers. For example, Gorka, vaivode of Poznan, welcomed an unfrocked Dominican, Andrew Samuel, and his companion John Seklucyan, and allowed them to celebrate the Lutheran office in his castle. The neighbouring Baltic territories accepted Protestantism: Riga and the urban Estates-General of Estonia in 1524, and the Livonian cities in 1539. The Catholic Church, which contained some of Queen Bonna Sforza's most unsavoury favourites—she was in fact responsible for bringing the most disreputable features of the Italian Renaissance to Poland—seemed to be falling to pieces. When the aged Sigismund died in 1548, the most powerful families, comprising about one-sixth of the nobility, threw off the mask and openly embraced the Reformation. Bonna's son, Sigismund II, Augustus, told his subjects: 'I am your king; I am not sovereign of your conscience.' A Lutheran Church was established in Poland proper, and Prince Radziwill had the Wittenberg Bible translated into Polish. Heresy seemed to have won the day. But this was only an illusion: the vast mass of the Polish people remained loyal to Catholicism, and when all the other Protestant sects—Calvinists, Moravian Brethren, Anabaptists and so on—demanded a place in the sun, Lutheranism was speedily weakened and the Roman Church was able to resume the offensive.[1]

Prior to England, whose methods were slightly different, the most

[1] See *The Catholic Reformation*, Chapter V.

striking instance of political action being used to detach whole nations
from the Catholic Church is provided by the Scandinavian kingdoms.
The Protestant historian Schoell admits this unreservedly: 'In Sweden
the Reformation was directly attributable to politics; it was summoned
and introduced against the inclination of a large part of the population
by a monarch who looked upon it as a means of consolidating his
power, and who spent his entire reign fighting the reluctance of his
subjects to renounce the faith of their fathers.' At the beginning of the
sixteenth century, in accordance with the terms of the Union of Kalmar,
the kingdoms of Denmark, Sweden and Norway were grouped
together under the same sovereign; it was a tenuous union, however,
which had been shattered and rebuilt many times, and which was
perpetually threatening to fall apart. Sweden, which was governed by
royal regents, longed for independence. But the Catholic prelates, who
were in continual conflict with the regents and the nobility, preferred
the authority of the King of Copenhagen. In 1520 Gustav Trolle,
Archbishop of Upsala, besieged by the regent Sten Sture in his castle
on the outskirts of Stockholm, appealed for help to King Christian II,
persuading the latter that his enemy was both a traitor and a heretic.
When it came Danish intervention was savage: the Swedish Army was
scattered on the ice of Lake Asunden, and Sten Sture expired in the
sledge which was carrying him to safety. At the archbishop's instigation
a court was convened, which falsely condemned some fifty of the
regent's followers as heretics, and handed them over to the king. He
added about thirty of his personal enemies to their number, and thus
eighty-two victims were left dangling from the ropes of a score of
gibbets. This odious ferocity of a Catholic king, and senseless religious
repression—for the Swedes were hardly concerned at all with religious
problems and ecclesiastical reform—resulted in Sweden acquiring an
implacable hatred for the Danish ruler and, in consequence, for Rome
also. *Gustav Vasa* (1523–60), a nobleman who was not yet thirty years
of age and whose father had been executed, put himself at the head of
a rebel army, defeated the Danish forces and had himself proclaimed
king by the Diet of Strengnaes (1523).

Now that he was master of Sweden, the young leader found himself
in a difficult position. Spiritually his country needed a national conscience; on the material plane the war had been costly and the new
regime began its career weighed down by debt. Now Gustav Vasa had
already encountered Lutheranism during a stay in Lübeck. Upsala
University too had some knowledge of the humanism of Erasmus and
other great figures of the age. But the decisive factor at this stage was
the return from Wittenberg of Olaf and Laurence Petersen, sons of a
blacksmith. Together with some German traders living in Sweden the
Petersens preached the Lutheran ideas to a race who were not much

concerned with theological subtleties. Swayed partly by personal convictions, and partly by a desire to find herein a solution to his serious political problems, Gustav Vasa decided to join the Reformation. In 1524 the break with Rome was finalized. Laurence Petersen was made Archbishop of Upsala, while his brother Olaf became the leading preacher in Stockholm. The Swedish Church became a State Church, and entrusted its destinies to the king. Haloed in the glamour that always surrounds a national liberator, Gustav made Luther's doctrine obligatory on all his fellow countrymen at the Council of Orebro in 1529. Chancellor Laurentius Andreae, a humanist who had translated the Bible into Swedish, gave his sovereign vigorous help in this task. A well-organized, closely supervised episcopal hierarchy was retained under the control of the king and the primate of Upsala. The Diets of 1532 and 1540 conferred upon Vasa what in practice amounted to complete spiritual authority. Finland, then annexed to Sweden, followed the latter's example: Peter Sarkilahti, who had listened to Luther's lectures, and Bishop Michael Agricola, the father of Finnish literature, introduced the same kind of State Lutheranism there, and in the end, slowly but surely, the people accepted it.

The most curious part of the whole affair was provided by Denmark. Her brutal 'Catholic' intervention had caused the whole tragic sequence of events, yet she herself was very soon following the path of heresy. Christian II regarded himself as a humanist; he had met Erasmus in 1521, and joined him in deploring the abuses in the Roman Church. Above all, financial difficulties had encouraged him to cast a longing eye upon the estates of his clergy, and to consider the example of his German neighbours who enriched themselves with such ease by becoming Lutherans. Christian, however, had married the sister of the Emperor Charles V, and it was therefore not easy for him to break with the Catholic party; but in 1523 he was deposed. King Frederick, who was of German origin, was well disposed towards the idea of a State Church; his chaplain, Hans Tausen (another ex-student from Wittenberg), persuaded the Diet of Odensee (1527) to allow the free practice of the Lutheran faith, and the Diet of Copenhagen (1530) adopted the Reformed doctrine and liturgies. Catholicism, which was now considerably weakened, was used as an instrument of opposition by enemies of the monarchy; it foundered in their defeat. In 1535 Christian III conceded only one Church in Denmark—the Lutheran; and the hierarchy was suppressed and replaced by 'superintendents' introduced by the German Lutheran Bugenhagen.

Denmark's political subordinates underwent an analogous revolution. In 1531 the former monarch, Christian II, tried to reconquer Norway, but in vain. Later still Olaf Engelbrektssön, Archbishop of Trondhjem, tried to resume the struggle but he was arrested, together with all his suffragans, and the Lutheran faith was extended over the whole country. Nevertheless it took at least a generation for Protestantism to change from a sign of Danish subjection and become part of Norway's national patrimony. Lutheranism managed to spread as far afield as Iceland. The doctrines of Wittenberg had been introduced by traders from Hamburg at a very early date. Oddir Gottkalsson and Gissur Einarson, both of whom had studied at German universities, developed the new theses, and in 1539 the governor of the island adopted the Reformed faith. One courageous prelate, John Aresen, Bishop of Itolar, stubbornly opposed the introduction of heresy, and after Lutheranism had been proclaimed the official religion he was captured and executed. By 1540 Catholicism in Iceland had been virtually wiped out and Gissur translated Luther's Bible into Icelandic.

Thus northern and eastern Europe offered easy access for the Protestant flood-tide in its Lutheran form, and several countries were completely overwhelmed. Others, although not yet seriously threatened, gave the impression of being able to put up no more than a token resistance. One of the states in this category was Scotland, a kingdom independent of England, although the latter's immediate neighbour. Once England had separated from Rome, Scotland rapidly succumbed to the same influences. Lutheranism was carried there by Hanseatic and Scandinavian traders, and it found a soil ready to receive it. As the Catholic Council of 1549 admitted unequivocally, 'the two fundamental causes of the evils which result in troubles and heresies are, firstly, moral corruption—the impure lives led by ecclesiastics of almost every rank; and, secondly, their appalling ignorance of learning and the arts.' Satirical writers ridiculed the clergy on both these counts: in his pamphlet, *Franciscanus*, the humanist, George Buchanan, heaped sarcasm upon the monks, sneering withal at the Papacy 'which opens the purses of simpletons rather than the gates of hell.' Catholicism probably seemed to be still firmly established in the kingdom of the faithful *Stuarts*, where the eight-day-old *Mary* had succeeded her father in 1542. Since 1525 the propagation of Lutheran ideas there had been forbidden by Act of Parliament. One young fanatic, Patrick Hamilton, who had brought them over from Wittenberg, had been burned at the stake in 1528. Hostilities between Scotland and England, which were almost continuous until 1550, resulted in the profession of Reform being considered in Scotland as an act of treason, since her neighbour and enemy was adopting the doctrines of the Reformation in an increasingly pronounced form. Yet various incidents occurred which showed that Protestantism was on the way. Hamilton had his disciples: one after another they mounted the stake, but more always appeared. In 1543 the Earl of Arran himself, who was Regent in Mary Stuart's name, allowed the English Bible to be printed in Scotland. The iconoclasts entered the lists; a statue of St Francis was publicly 'hanged' in Perth, and the religious houses in Dundee were ransacked. George Wishart, a notorious Lutheran who had been hounded from the country in 1538 and who subsequently travelled in England, Germany and Switzerland, returned to his native land in 1544 to begin a vehement 'evangelical' campaign. In 1546 he was arrested and executed, calling down divine punishment upon his executioner. Three months later Cardinal Beaton, Archbishop of St Andrews, who had been responsible for Wishart's death, was attacked in his palace by a mob of young noblemen and done to death in cold blood. Scotland seemed ripe to fall into the jaws of heresy when one determined leader set himself at the head of the forces of attack. His name was *John Knox*.

THE TIDE ENCOUNTERS OBSTACLES IN THE WEST AND SOUTH

The achievements of Lutheranism were undeniably impressive, but in some directions they were less extensive. As has been seen,[1] it seemed to gain ground fairly quickly in France; it penetrated intellectual circles, which were in the throes of a renaissance and which had already received their initiation in scriptural exegesis from Lefèvre d'Étaples, as well as the class composed of artisans and small business men, especially in Paris, Meaux and Lyons. It took advantage of the fluctuations in royal policy to implant itself in several localities; but its growth was still sporadic, without any organization or overall plan; and even before 1534, when the Placard Affair forced the authorities to take up a definite position in the matter, it was obvious that the forces hostile to Lutheranism in Francis I's kingdom were so great that the doctrine's expansion was bound to meet with violent opposition sooner or later.

The Lutheran tide had already encountered this barrier in the Low Countries, the 'Seventeen Provinces' which owed direct allegiance to Charles V. Although some differed considerably from the rest—the seven northern provinces were mainly seafaring and spoke Flemish-Dutch, while the ten in the south depended principally upon agriculture and spoke French—they nevertheless possessed many features in common, which they owed to their geographic position as a corridor between the rest of the continent and the sea. Antwerp was the greatest commercial centre in north-west Europe at this time; its wealthy and enterprising middle class stimulated the intellectual life of Flanders and Brabant and controlled an important trade which ranged across the whole of the North Sea. Receptive to every influence, and lavish patrons of the arts, the moneyed classes of the Low Countries who had

[1] See Chapter VI, section: 'The First French Reformation.'

doted on the Virgins of *Memling* (1433–94), admired the exciting luxury of *Quentin Matsys* and the truculence of *Hieronymus Bosch*, which foreshadowed that of the *Elder Breughel* (b. 1525), and encouraged the efforts of the humanists. At Antwerp Peter Giles, the town clerk, prided himself on being a friend of Erasmus. The latter was installed at Louvain, where he was inspiring an intellectual movement which was just as active as the expansion in the economic field. Moreover the Church in the Low Countries was suffering from the same abuses as elsewhere: the badly educated clergy lacked both enthusiasm and prestige; there were only four bishops for all seventeen provinces, and these were more preoccupied with worldly interests than with the salvation of souls. The devotional influence exerted by the fifteenth-century mystics had considerably declined in the motherland of the *Imitation*, and the Beguine houses were in the grip of internal crises. The new ideas had little difficulty in infiltrating into Flanders. They were propagated by printers, and, above all, they were disseminated by converted Jews who took advantage of the Erasmian tolerance of the Brussels administration. The intellectuals and the textile workers were rapidly permeated with the views of two rival heresies, Lutheranism and Anabaptism.

Charles V, however, reacted violently against this. While he realized that his authority was doubtful in the Empire he could talk in quite a different tone in the Low Countries. When he saw that Antwerp was becoming a centre of heretical propaganda—the Augustinian prior, Jacobus Praepositus, was one of Luther's friends—and that Tournai and Lille, on the one hand, and Holland on the other, were infected with the new doctrines, he issued a number of Draconian decrees. The Inquisition was re-established in the Low Countries, with judges chosen by the king. The papal nuncio was summoned to Antwerp and, in his presence, Luther's books were confiscated and publicly burned.[1] Louvain University, in the persons of Jacobus Latomus and Eustace de Sichem, refuted the Lutheran theses in 1521. It was now that Erasmus sought refuge in Basle, and that Dürer, who had been converted to the new ideas, left Antwerp. In 1523 two Augustinian monks were burned at the stake in Brussels. In 1529 and 1530 the death penalty was decreed not merely for heretics alone, but also for those who knew them and failed to denounce them. The Inquisitors were given authority to have recourse to the secular arm in all cases. Lutheranism was abruptly halted. It took refuge in the large towns in the west, where clandestine presses continued to print Bibles, canticles, small tracts and pamphlets. Because it was poorly supported by Wittenberg this Flemish Protestantism henceforth tended to seek its inspiration

---

[1] It will be remembered (see p. 303) that Luther replied to this by burning the papal bull.

from the sacramentaries of Strasbourg and Basle, until the emergence of Calvinism radically transformed the situation.

In the south the check was even more complete. All the same, even the Mediterranean lands had been affected by the contagion of the new doctrines. From 1519 onwards editions of Luther's tracts reached Bologna and Venice from Basle, hidden away in sacks of linen or bales of silk. At the same time heretics in the Low Countries were translating them into Castilian, and although Charles V ordered his police to search all ships, this contraband literature was smuggled into the Spanish peninsula. In Naples people sympathetic to the new ideas grouped themselves around the Spaniard *Juan de Valdes*, the viceroy's secretary, and the poetess Vittoria Colonna. There were Reformed groups in Turin, Pavia and Venice also. At Venice copies of Melanchthon's *Loci communes* were printed; at Florence Antonio Bruccioli translated the Bible into Italian; and at Ferrara, as will be remembered, Renée of France, Louis XII's daughter, gave asylum to many people suspected of adhering to the new dogmas.

However, most of those who were attracted by the appeal of an evangelical religion were not resigned to breaking with the Catholic Church, to which the mass of the common people remained faithful. Juan de Valdes, who found endless mystical inspiration in the doctrine of justification by faith, did not abandon orthodox Catholicism. In Spain the position was even more clear cut: the small Erasmic groups, which were by no means all Protestant, were persecuted by the state police and the Inquisition. It was now that Juan de Valdes decided that Naples was preferable to his native Castile, that Juan Diaz fled to Geneva and Strasbourg, and that Franco Euzinas, who had translated the Wittenberg Bible into Spanish, was obliged to leave the country, and, after making his home in Brussels for a short time, finally sought refuge in Basle. Less important refugees made for Italy. Shortly after 1540 there was a brief upsurge of Protestantism there, more Calvinist than Lutheran in inspiration, which was no real danger to Catholicism. Once the ancient Church took herself in hand, reformed her discipline and put an end to flagrant scandals, the Italian masses, who remained attached to their popes even while they derided them, and the ruling classes, who had countless links with the ecclesiastical system, would be ready to take the counter-offensive. As for Spain, where Cardinal *Ximenes* (*d.* 1517) had laboured energetically to reform the Church,[1] she rejected the Protestant virus in an even more radical manner: the vigilant Inquisition there arrested one hundred and eighty-two suspects; nearly half of these perished at the stake under the regime of Philip II.

---

[1] See *The Catholic Reformation*, Chapter I, section 2.

ENGLAND ON THE EVE OF THE REFORMATION

If ever there was a country in which politics seems to have been the decisive factor in determining the passage of a whole nation from Catholicism to Protestantism, that country is unquestionably England, which had been ruled since 1509 by the handsome, ambitious and ruthless King Henry VIII. Nevertheless when the first appeals of Luther reached his shores, they received no welcome from the king. In 1520 Erasmus, who had several devoted friends in influential quarters in England, had to intervene personally in order to obtain the revocation of an order commanding the burning of Luther's books. The sovereign himself, who was extremely proud of his knowledge of theology, was horrified to read, in Luther's treatise on *The Babylonian Captivity*, that there were only three valid sacraments. With his own hand he drafted quite an erudite treatise on the *Seven Sacraments of Orthodox Doctrine*, a pious work for which Pope Leo X awarded him the magnificent title 'Defender of the Faith.' [1] And it was to this worthy monarch that Erasmus dedicated his treatise on *Free Will* (1524), which was answered by the Lutheran tract on *Servile Will*.

Consequently the new doctrines made very slow progress in England. A few small Lutheran groups sprang up somewhat belatedly; there is little evidence of their existence prior to 1525, and they had a negligible membership. The only gathering of any significance was a small body of Cambridge students. They met at the White Horse Tavern, nicknamed 'the Germany' by their hostile fellow undergraduates. Moreover the doctrine of these early reformers was very vague, and their desire for changes in the Church was not particularly strong. For one William Tyndale (who fled to the Continent rather than renounce the heretical faith and published a New Testament in English at Cologne) scores of the first English Protestants abjured the new ideas as soon as the ecclesiastical courts obliged them to give an account of their opinions!

Taine was entirely wrong when he wrote: 'When five million people are converted, it is because five million people wish to be converted.' The English kept up an active religious life within the framework of the old Church. While strongly resenting certain abuses, and only grudgingly accepting Roman surveillance, they would never have embraced the Reformation had the initiative of their ruler not first cut them adrift from the Papacy. To discover how and why one man, in whom the thirst for power and sensual appetites were strangely combined, could play upon the contradictory sentiments of a whole

---

[1] Translator's Note.—A title which the English sovereigns have continued to hold ever since!

nation, and in one single blow produce a change of direction of incalculable significance upon its historical future, is certainly one of the most fascinating and original out of all the many tragic problems which the sixteenth century sets the historian.

In the first place, however, it is essential not to regard the England of Henry VIII through twentieth-century eyes. The little Tudor kingdom was very far from being an important industrial nation, the possessor of gigantic commercial and financial power, or the head of a worldwide community of peoples. In the sixteenth century the wealthy and mighty states were Spain, in process of building herself a vast overseas empire; France, which had been restored by her kings, and was now prosperous and populous; Italy of the merchants and artists; and Germany of the great bankers. With her paltry five million inhabitants, England's population was only half as numerous as that of Poland. Her economic resources were modest. For a long time she had been a predominantly agricultural country, engaged in arable and pastoral farming. For the past one hundred years she had heard the call of the sea: the *Society of Merchant Adventurers* dated from 1404, but so far she was only interested in the North Sea, and certainly none of her undertakings compared with the audacious enterprises of Spain and Portugal. The Tudors, her new rulers, encouraged their sailors, gave bonuses to naval shipbuilders, and sent the Venetian *Cabots* to discover Labrador in 1497. But these were still no more than tentative beginnings, the premonitory signs of a great future.

The Tudors themselves, however, sensed the approach of that future in their blood. They were an upstart, adventurous dynasty. Force had brought them to power, and force might easily cast them out again; their neighbours in Scotland threatened them perpetually, but they were well able to defend themselves. The centralized, absolute government which Henry VII had imposed was asserted with increasing force by *Henry VIII* (1509–47), the founder's son. Royal officials controlled every county of England in the king's name; administration of justice was in their hands and, to some extent, in those of the landed gentry, who comprised the bulk of the magistrates.

The English had given the Church many saints, and they remained deeply loyal to her. Their spiritual requirements were enormous. It is noteworthy that of 349 works printed between 1468 and 1530 (the complete list can be found in the catalogue of the British Museum), 176 were liturgical collections, manuals of devotion or edifying books. Englishmen were extremely fond of lives of the saints, so rich in both excitement and example. *The Golden Legend*, enriched by seventy chapters, was reprinted no less than six times between 1483 and 1537. Our Lady was the object of real filial piety. Her Office was printed twenty-eight times within the space of forty years, seven times in 1530 alone. Few sailors ever went to sea without first going to pray at the shrine of Our Lady of Walsingham, who was believed to protect her pilgrims against shipwreck. Dozens of collections of sermons intended for preachers poured from the printing-presses, and for anyone desiring to die a good death there were countless pious tracts which were veritable guide-books to Paradise. Every foreign visitor noticed how many of the faithful filled the churches, prostrating themselves before the Blessed Sacrament exposed for all to see, venerating the relics which existed in profusion everywhere, and enriching the Church treasuries with their gifts. None of these things indicated the slightest desire to break with the old traditions.

The English clergy, which existed to satisfy this fervour, was no worse and no better than that of any other Christian country at the time. Here, as everywhere else, bishoprics were distributed to the Crown's most important servants. In 1530 only four out of a total of thirty bishops resided in their own dioceses. In many collegiate churches and cathedrals there was no longer more than one canon out of four present to sing in the choir and recite the Office. The country contained over eight hundred religious houses, which, in the vast variety of their observances, recalled the whole of England's religious history. But their abbots, who were nominated by the king, had often scarcely anything religious about them save their title; and their walls, some of which had been ruined during the Wars of the Roses, now housed only a small, badly disciplined body of monks. As for the lower clergy, which was recruited without discrimination, extremely ignorant and left largely to its own devices, the least that can be said is that it was unequal to the importance of its task. Despite its 10,000 seculars and 5,000 regulars, the human machinery of the Church in England was inefficient and somewhat rusty.

The clergy themselves were aware of this. A number of Benedictine and Cistercian monasteries had made a valiant attempt to return to a stricter way of life: the 'Observance' movement had something of a rejuvenating influence upon the Franciscans. William Selling, the Benedictine Prior of Christchurch, Canterbury, had revived the study of classical literature. At Cambridge colleges where future priests could learn theology had been founded. These are certainly interesting symptoms of revival, but they are nevertheless very modest and isolated in character.

The humanist scholars were more definite and zealous in their desire for reform. For there was an English humanism, known as the 'New Learning,' in exactly the same way as there was an Italian, German and French humanism. In the main it possessed the same fundamental characteristics as did they, but it also had features peculiar to itself. It was in order to provide English humanism with a further means of expression that Cardinal Wolsey, the king's chief minister, endowed Cardinal College [1] at Oxford, very soon after the foundation of the Royal College in Paris by the monarchs of France. Three men dominated this little group of far-sighted intellectuals. The first was *John Colet* (1467–1519), son of a Lord Mayor of London, who had brought the philological methods of Laurence Valla back from Italy in 1496, and had applied them so authoritatively at Oxford that his pupil Erasmus said of him: 'Whenever I hear him I seem to hear Plato himself speaking.' The second was *Thomas More* (1478–1535), the future Chancellor, whose brilliant intellect and calm yet steadfast character were equally impressive and whose *Utopia* (1518) delighted all great minds. The third was none other than *Erasmus* himself, the great Erasmus of Rotterdam, the Dutchman whose thin, sharp face we have already encountered at several crossroads during this period, in both Germany and France. Erasmus had studied at Oxford. He had written his famous *In Praise of Folly* in the home of his friend Thomas More, and his translation of the New Testament was highly esteemed by English scholars. [2]

All three 'Oxford reformers' were devout Christians. English humanism had a more noticeably Christian flavour than that of any other land. It was anxious to effect a sensible fusion between the new cultural assets and the old traditional religious basis, in order to bring about the latter's revival. What these reformers wanted—and their desire was shared by many other great minds, such as Linacre, Tunstall, Gardiner, Bishop John Fisher of Rochester and Archbishop Warham of Canterbury—was a simple, pure religion, sustained by an accurate knowledge and constant meditation of the Scriptures, and at the same time enlarged by a vast philosophic culture founded on the classics. It would be a receptive religion, tolerant in all things save in the matter of abuses, psittacism and superstition, which would be rigorously suppressed.

It was on this final point that the influence of these three men of goodwill might be somewhat dangerous. Colet had followed Savonarola's sermons enthusiastically in Florence, and he made no bones at all about repeating the impetuous Dominican's criticisms in England. On one occasion, when he was entrusted with the task of making the opening speech at a synod convened to destroy the last vestiges of Lollardry, he delivered such a radical diatribe in favour of reform that he was henceforth forbidden to preach. Erasmus's mordant irony in his *Praise of Folly*, which was directed against popes, priests, monks and theologians, not to mention the cult of statues and relics, could easily have an untoward effect upon those whose faith was weak. And

[1] Translator's Note.—Later refounded by the Crown and renamed Christ church.
[2] On Erasmus see Chapter V, p. 328.

when even Thomas More, the future saint, announced that in his ideal kingdom of Utopia the faithful of all religions would meet in the same temple to celebrate a cult common to them all, he was scarcely helping to strengthen the position of the One Church. In England as elsewhere Christian humanism unthinkingly and unwittingly prepared the way for the Reformation by its own only too well founded criticism.

Moreover their strictures accurately reflected the opinion of a whole nation which, though faithful to Catholicism, had little love for the face which the Church presented to the world at this period. The centralized monarchy headed by the Pope of Rome, the taxes levied by Rome, the courts whose system of appeals led eventually to Rome, the Church's preoccupation with Italian politics—all these were things which English Catholics found extremely repugnant. In addition their attitude had a very ancient history; it can be traced back to the disputes between Henry II and Alexander II in the twelfth century, and between John Lackland and Innocent III in the thirteenth, to the antipapal teaching of William of Ockham and to the indictments of Wyclif. The Avignonese exile, the Great Schism and the conciliar crisis had done nothing to strengthen the Papacy's prestige in the eyes of Catholics in England. People from one end of the social scale to the other distrusted it.

The Church was not only at fault in being too Roman. The privileges which she had been granted to prevent her from being engulfed in the feudal world, and the enormous possessions which she had then accumulated, seemed out-dated and scandalous now that feudalism was so enfeebled and the State was becoming increasingly aware of its own prerogatives. This was particularly the view held by the middle class, which, though sincerely religious, had a markedly practical attitude to life. The middle class was now making its voice heard in the lower chamber of Parliament, the House of Commons, which henceforth had a quite distinct existence from the House of Lords. In 1512 Parliament had removed the 'privilege of clergy,' i.e. the right of being answerable only to the ecclesiastical courts, previously enjoyed by anyone who had taken the tonsure and who might not be even a deacon. More than one Member of Parliament, sick and tired of the increased taxes demanded by a government that was always short of money, turned his thoughts to the possessions of the Church with the same solicitude displayed 250 years later by the 'Constituants' in France. The 'gentry,' the ambitious squirearchy, were casting an equally greedy eye towards the wealth of the clergy. Henry VIII would not have to bully his Parliament or the opinion of his loyal subjects should he decide to confiscate the properties and revenues of the Church.

Besides, such an operation could easily be related to the movement which John Wyclif [1] had promoted one hundred and fifty years before. Had not the Oxford scholar rejected the authority of Rome, justified the civil power's seizure of Church possessions, and made appeal to the one and only authority of the Scriptures? Although his doctrines were condemned, and he himself banished from the university, 'the morning star of the Reformation' had managed to end his days peacefully in a pleasant country parish. The Lollards, his quasi-disciples, with their popular preachers and advocates of social revolution, had been savagely repressed following the bloody rising of Wat Tyler, though evidence of any direct connection between Lollardry and the Peasants' Revolt is entirely lacking. In fact, by the beginning of the sixteenth century the number of Lollards had declined so greatly that for all practical purposes they had ceased to exist at all, save to enable a few preachers to launch furious diatribes against them from time to time. But Wyclif's disciples and the Lollards had been too much a part of recent English life not to have left some mark upon men's minds.

As can be seen, the English scene was a somewhat complex one. The popes themselves realized that this geographically isolated kingdom needed delicate handling. It was no doubt to please the king, a king of such dogmatic purity, that Leo X conferred the style and prerogatives of legate in England upon *Cardinal Wolsey* for life; but the gesture in itself had been of capital importance. An Englishman, nay better, a royal minister, now possessed papal powers throughout the realm; he was to hold them from 1518 until 1529. He had authority to inspect all ecclesiastical institutions, was the sole intermediary between the English clergy and Rome, and had the task of keeping a watch on the purity of faith and dogmas. Even before it became schismatic the Church in England was already a national Church, and to a large extent the latter fact explains the former. Who exactly was the man to whom the Papacy had granted such considerable powers? He was a royal favourite, the son of an Ipswich butcher, who had risen to become a canon of Windsor, court chaplain, wealthy prebendary, Bishop of Winchester and Durham, and Archbishop of York—all this by the express will of Henry VIII, who found him intelligent and straightforward. Although he was promoted chancellor at the same time that he was made cardinal and legate, and even aspired to the papal throne on two occasions (1522 and 1523), Thomas Wolsey was not equal to such an important function. He was not lacking in either scholarship or political intelligence, and in religious matters he actually favoured disciplinary reform and Erasmian humanism. But he was ambitious and totally devoid of scruples, a man without morality, who maintained a regal *entourage* of eight hundred servants, kept a concubine, and concentrated all the revenues he could squeeze from

[1] See Chapter III, pp. 155 et seq.

the benefices in the hands of his family. In short, Wolsey was not at all the kind of man the Church in England needed as its leader if its resistance to its king's future excursions into the realms of theology was to succeed.

HENRY VIII's DIVORCE AND THE ANGLICAN SCHISM

On 22nd June 1527 Henry VIII confronted his wife, Catherine of Aragon, and commanded her to leave his court forthwith in order to put an end to the state of mortal sin in which the couple had been living for the past eighteen years. The argument upon which the royal theologian founded the case against his queen was as follows. On his accession to the throne at the age of less than eighteen years, he had already, in deference to his father's wish, asked for the hand of the daughter of the 'Catholic Sovereigns,' aunt of the future emperor Charles V. Now Catherine had previously been married to Henry's elder brother Arthur, who had died at the age of fifteen, less than six months after the wedding ceremony. This first union constituted a canonical impediment to any subsequent marriage between Catherine and Henry. But Henry VIII, who was anxious to lose neither Catherine's dowry nor the alliance with Spain, had asked the Pope for the necessary dispensation. Julius II had readily granted this, all the more readily since his anti-French policy made the friendship of England essential to him. Since that time no query of any kind had been raised about the union.

The marriage itself, however, which had been based entirely upon political convenience, had not been a great success. Although there were no spectacular quarrels, the household limped along. Husband and wife were so different. According to the Venetian ambassador, Catherine, who was seven years Henry's senior, was 'short and plump, with a frank, open face. She was pleasant, fair-minded and extremely good.' She was very devout and possessed high moral standards. Obviously this was scarcely the ideal wife for a young husband whose own bearing and temperament predisposed him for the role of a Don Juan. Everyone who saw him in his youth, when he was very different from the famous, awe-inspiring portrait painted by Holbein many years later, agreed that Henry VIII was an outstandingly handsome man. 'He is more handsome than any other king in Christendom, even the King of France,' said one observer. 'His face is more than merely handsome, it is angelic,' said another; 'he has Caesar's head, serenely majestic.' He had grown a beard after the style of Francis I of France, and this 'sparkled and glinted like gold.' In addition Henry possessed great charm, was highly educated and had genuine musical talent. When he was tired of showing his prowess in sport, particularly on the tennis-courts, he could shine just as well in intellectual exercises. He believed and declared himself a perfect Christian, 'often hearing three and even five Masses a day (which seems a little excessive), and reciting Vespers and Compline into the bargain.' Thomas More, whom the king was later to cut down, praised his chastity, his mercy and his justice. In fact, his character was based upon pride and sensuality; he would tolerate no opposition either to his royal powers or to his carnal desires. Whenever he encountered resistance of any kind he would use any means at his disposal to crush it. His green eyes betrayed a latent violence and a kind of feline ferocity.

But nature had raised one derisive barrier across the path of this well-endowed monarch: he lacked a legitimate male heir. The problem of the succession had been uppermost in his mind ever since 1514 and it tormented him sorely. Of the five children whom Catherine had brought into the world only one survived, a daughter named Mary. The queen did not seem capable of conceiving again. Although no Salic Law existed in England, the succession of a woman seemed fraught with difficulties. The importance of this question cannot be overestimated when it is remembered that Henry VIII was the son of a man who had had to establish his claim to the throne by force, and that a crisis over the succession would undoubtedly have plunged England into another bloodbath like the recent Wars of the Roses.

The king sought a solution to this problem. He was vaguely considering legitimizing one of the bastards he had had by his various transitory mistresses when the devil, who, as is well known, often chooses the prettiest faces to lead men from the straight and narrow way, brought him face to face with *Anne Boleyn*. She was the sister of one of his short-lived lights o' love—a haughty brunette with sparkling black eyes, who had received her courtly training in France, in Queen Claude's *entourage*, and who was in addition a sly hussy. Her elder sister, who wished to keep the royal favours in the family, presented her to the king, and Anne at once perceived the impression that she made upon him. Acting on the advice of her uncle, the Duke of Norfolk, she cunningly made Henry pay dearly for every favour granted. The passing fancy became a passionate love-affair, and this passion was to cause a dramatic turn of events that was both political and religious in character.

It is not certain who first provided Henry VIII with the canonical argument that would enable him to obtain a perfectly legal separation from Catherine. Probably it was the French ambassador, Grammont, Bishop of Tarbes; what a splendid diplomatic success a divorce between the crowns of England and Spain would be for France! Bishop Longland, the king's confessor, supported the plan for reasons which are rather obscure, but possibly from genuine conviction.

Henry VIII was confronted with the eighteenth chapter of Leviticus, in which it is written: 'Thou shalt not uncover the nakedness of thy brother's wife, for it is thy brother's nakedness,' and also (Chapter xx) 'if a man takes his brother's wife, it is an unclean thing . . . they shall be childless.' Such texts naturally overjoyed the king, who had been asking himself whether he might have to beg the Pope to allow him to commit bigamy in order to marry Anne. With the Book of Leviticus in hand he could henceforth proclaim null and void the dispensation granted by Julius II, and, by the same token, his union with Catherine was null and void also. In fact, had he read his Bible rather more carefully, Henry would have seen that his case, so far from falling under the condemnation of the law, was actually considered exemplary. The Book of Deuteronomy orders the brother of any husband who has died childless to marry his widow in order to provide the dead man with an heir. Thus the patriarch Judah commanded his second son, Onan, despite the latter's lack of enthusiasm, to marry Thamar, the widow of his brother Her. But the main advantage of quotations has always been their ability to support any argument. In the play which he devoted to Henry VIII, Shakespeare wittily pointed the moral of this affair. 'It seems,' says the Chamberlain, 'the marriage with his brother's wife has crept too near his conscience.'—'No,' replies Suffolk, 'his conscience has crept too near another lady!'

The course it was decided to take to settle 'the king's great matter' was as follows: instead of asking the Pope to annul the dispensation which his predecessor had granted, the king petitioned him to renounce his part in the affair altogether, even as a court of appeal, and entrust the entire business to his legate, Wolsey. This was a clever move, and its timing well chosen. A month before Henry VIII strode into the queen's chamber to announce that he intended divorcing her, Clement VII had watched the Constable de Bourbon's soldiery sacking Rome with all manner of barbarity and he himself had been besieged in the Castle of Sant' Angelo. One third of Europe had been undermined by the teaching of Luther and seemed on the verge of foundering into Protestantism. What could the unfortunate pontiff do? He knew very well that if he acceded to Henry VIII's desire he would be authorizing him to violate the law of the Church. On the other hand, in a position as perilous as his, he could scarcely afford to fall out with one of his supporters. So he became involved in a complex game which was admittedly somewhat 'Florentine' in character, in which he attempted to safeguard dogma without prejudicing his own interests. He agreed to renounce his supreme jurisdiction on condition that Cardinal Wolsey examined the case in conjunction with an Italian, Cardinal Campeggio. Clement advised the latter to make the proceedings as long drawn out as possible; this would allow time for the royal passion to burn itself out. There is also the very remarkable history (which has never been fully explained) of a bull which Campeggio had among his papers, ready to produce at the right moment, and which the Pope eventually ordered him to destroy; it may well have accorded the king all he asked for. Nothing is clear cut in this affair where the intrigues of love and politics are inextricably intertwined, and where principles and interests come to terms with one another far too often.

Campeggio realized straight away that Henry VIII was determined on divorce. He himself was undoubtedly loyal to the Pope, but his left hand ignored what his right was doing, and was readily accepting royal subsidies and the revenues of a fat English bishopric. He was prepared to evade the main issue. Catherine must renounce the crown herself and withdraw to a convent, where she would take the vow of chastity. But the proud Spanish princess absolutely refused to follow his advice. She was almost alone, supported by no one except Chapuys, Charles V's ambassador, whom she could only see in secret, and by the courageous bishop John Fisher. All the other prelates turned a deaf ear to her entreaties; 'Indignatio principis mors est,' commented one of them. Nevertheless when the case opened in 1529 Catherine stood her ground. She delivered a firm but dignified protest against the outrage which had been done to her, and then left the hall with the announcement that she was appealing to the Pope in advance of the legates' decision. By this time the political climate had changed. Clement VII and Charles V were reconciled; there was no longer any question of producing the secret bull or of sacrificing the emperor's aunt, any more than there was of acting contrary to dogma. When Campeggio was urged to settle the case he adjourned the court. Shortly afterwards it was learned that Clement VII had cancelled the legates' jurisdiction and revoked the whole affair to his own authority. It would be pleasant to be able to believe that his was done solely in the interests of the Church, and that politics played no part in the decision.

The Pope's intervention precipitated the downfall of Cardinal Wolsey. Although he was reasonably in favour of a separation between Catherine and the king, he had never been well disposed towards Anne Boleyn; he would have preferred another political marriage, with a French princess, for example. When he was swept from office he tried to appease his master by handing over to him all his immense wealth, and the 'affianced couple,' as they were politely called, spent several weeks counting their spoils. However, although he was relegated to his archbishopric of York, the crafty cardinal continued his intrigues, plotting new combinations with France and the emperor, and spreading the rumour of an impending royal excommunication. His Italian physician betrayed him, and he was arrested and summoned to London; death overtook him on the journey (November 1530) and undoubtedly spared him the humiliation of the scaffold. 'If I had served God as diligently as I served the king,' he murmured on his death-bed, 'He would not have deserted me in my old age.'

Now that the leading exponent of a policy of temporization had disappeared from the scene, Henry VIII became more determined. Henceforth he would rely on Parliament, the voice of the English nation, in his struggle against the Pope. Wolsey had convened Parliament only once since 1516, in order to make it vote new subsidies. Such a scandalous state of affairs could not be permitted to continue! Norfolk, who had become the king's chief minister (the Great Seal was entrusted to Thomas More), was commanded by the king to summon Parliament. An important section of the Commons, led by the middle-class squires and merchants, was openly hostile to the clergy. In the Lords the protests of a handful of bishops and abbots were drowned by the loyalist acclamations which were strengthened by a number of newly created peers. Because he was quite certain of his instrument, as well as cunning enough to proceed by easy stages and rush nothing, Henry was able to ignore the reticence of the ancient aristocracy, the humanists and the common people, and listen only to the bold voices of his new advisers.

Two men were the principal agents of this policy. One was *Thomas Cranmer*. He was a faithless priest, whose enforced first marriage had led to his temporary dismissal from his fellowship at Jesus College, Cambridge, and who afterwards married the niece of Osiander, the German Lutheran preacher. Cranmer had no respect for the discipline of the Church. He suggested that the king should consult the principal universities of England and the Continent as to the validity of his marriage with Catherine. Cambridge, Oxford, Paris, Orleans, Angers, Toulouse, Ferrara and Pavia, duly forewarned by envoys whose pockets had been well lined with pounds sterling,[1] decided that Julius II's dispensation had exceeded his authority, and as such was null and void, and that Henry VIII had never had the right to marry his brother's wife; a number of bodies, however, added the proviso 'presuming the first union to have been consummated,' a presumption which Catherine vehemently denied. Fortified by these views, Henry VIII sent the Pope a threatening letter, which he followed up with a petition signed by the most illustrious men in England. The situation was extremely grave. When told of it by Jean du Bellay, his ambassador in London, Francis I actually informed the Pope that an English schism was not merely possible, but highly probable, and that this was scarcely the right moment to separate a new mass of Christians from

---

[1] The catalogue of payments can still be seen in the British Museum. It is clear that theologians were paid in proportion to their authority; certain unimportant monasteries were bought for a few shillings.

the Church. But Clement VII could hardly allow his authority and that of the most sacred principles of the Christian faith to be flouted with impunity, especially as Charles V had just offered him the agreement (subsequently signed in Barcelona) whereby his own family, the Medicis, were to be re-established in Florence. He therefore continued his policy of procrastination, confining himself to forbidding the king to marry anyone for the present, and confirming that the final decision would be made by him alone.

It was now that the second decisive figure in the English tragedy came upon the scene. His name was *Thomas Cromwell,* and he had once been Wolsey's secretary. Cromwell was a self-made man, the son of a blacksmith, who had served as a mercenary in France and Italy. In addition he was gifted with a marvellously practical understanding and was totally devoid of scruples. With his small, shifty eyes and thin, pinched lips, there was something almost Mephistophelian about him. He claimed to take the rules of conduct from Machiavelli's *Prince,* preaching that the courtier ought to apply himself to satisfying all his master's caprices (in fact, he was the provider of the king's pleasures over a period of several years) and that the ultimate aim was to give political motives the appearance of virtue. To such a man deceit, trickery, blackmail and crime became perfectly legitimate weapons from the moment that they helped increase the ruler's power. As for the Church, in Cromwell's view she ought to be an instrument controlled by the sovereign, and the State should have the right to dispose of her possessions.

There already existed a very simple way of putting the clergy at the mercy of the king: they could be accused of having broken the laws of the realm, of violating, among others, the Statute of *Praemunire* of 1353, which forbade recourse to foreign courts of law. The clergy of the provinces of Canterbury and York met in *Convocation* in 1531. They were under accusation of high treason, and the threat of confiscation of their fortunes hung heavily over them. They offered subsidies to the king; but he wanted their submission. On 11th February the 'Convocation of the South' accepted the formula drawn up by Warham, Archbishop of Canterbury, which recognized the king as supreme head of the Church of England. John Fisher managed to add the proviso, 'so far as the law of Christ allows.' On 18th May the 'Convocation of the North' accepted the same conditions.

By voting for Fisher's reservation the prelates had eased their consciences and made it clear that they hoped that the storm-cloud would pass. After all, Henry VIII was still negotiating with Rome and had actually told the nuncio that he had no intention of challenging the Pope's authority 'provided that His Holiness deals with him justly.' Charles V's ambassador, Chapuys, was more far-sighted. He observed:

'The matter which has just been settled to the Pope's disadvantage is that the clergy has been forced to accept the king as head of the Church. This is in fact equivalent to declaring the king to be Pope of England. It is true that the clergy appended a proviso to the declaration stating that it accepted this title only in so far as the law of God allowed; but so far as the king is concerned the position is exactly the same as it would be if there were no reservation at all, for no one in future will dare to argue with the king regarding its extent.'

Henry exploited his advantages: Parliament abolished annates, a payment made to the Curia from the annual income of all benefices conferred by the Pope; at Cromwell's instigation it drafted a 'petition against the Ordinaries,' which was a comprehensive list of objections and grievances concerning ecclesiastical jurisdiction. On 15th May 1532 the 'Convocation of Canterbury' renounced all its legislative powers and agreed that a government commission should examine the canons of the English Church, to find out whether or not they infringed the royal prerogative. Things seemed to be moving towards a withdrawal of obedience. Thomas More resigned office on 18th March 1532. On 22nd August the king suggested that Cranmer should occupy the primatial see of Canterbury in succession to Warham who had recently died and Clement VII agreed. The Pope was either blind to the true character of the new archbishop, or else he still cherished a hope that the king would not resort to measures of an irreparable nature.

The rupture, however, was now very near. It was no longer possible to postpone the decision concerning the divorce. 'Nan Bullen,' who had been created Countess of Rochford, was treated at court as the rightful queen, while the wretched Catherine languished forgotten in some remote apartments. 'The only thing lacking now is a priest to bless the ring,' jeered the enraged Chapuys bitterly. At the opportune moment the cunning temptress had yielded to the royal passion; she was pregnant, and the astrologers swore that her child would be a boy. On 25th January 1533 the king married Anne in secret. On 5th April Parliament prohibited any appeals from English courts to Rome. This meant that the pronouncement of divorce made by the docile Cranmer on 23rd May was absolute and final, despite all Catherine's last desperate protests. Five days later the archbishop announced the validity of the union between the king and his mistress. There followed a week of the kind of splendid festivities which the merry monarch loved so well: the new queen made her way to the Tower in Catherine's own royal barge, escorted by two hundred other vessels, amid the tumult of salvoes and fanfares—exactly as her successor would do three years hence, while Anne lay in prison awaiting execution. She was crowned at Westminster Abbey in June. In September she gave birth to a daughter, who was called Elizabeth. The 'Act of Succession' disallowed the claims of Mary, Catherine's daughter, and decided that Anne's posterity should inherit Henry's throne after his death.

Rome's answer to this scandalous state of affairs was quite un-equivocal. On 11th July 1533 Henry VIII was excommunicated. In an interview at Marseilles Francis I tried to reconcile England and Rome, and Jean du Bellay made similar efforts; but they were all in vain. Even more meaningless was the English king's indication to the Pope that he was going to appeal against the excommunication to the Council of the Church. This damp squib entirely failed to explode. Now that the rebel had been cast out of the Catholic community, what was he going to do? Unless he wished to see his authority undermined, only one solution remained: he must set up a national Church which was independent of the Pope and subject to him. This is exactly what he did. During 1534 he enacted a whole series of measures to establish this new organization. The *Act of Supremacy* commanded that the king be recognized as 'the one supreme head on earth of the Church of England,' and the scope of royal power was defined as 'power and authority from time to time to visit, repress, redress, reform, order, correct, restrain and amend all such errors, heresies, abuses, offences, contempts and enormities, whatsoever they be, which by any manner spiritual authority or jurisdiction ought or may be lawfully reformed.' A subsidiary clause, which was not to be forgotten, provided that all the moneys previously sent to Rome be henceforth paid to the royal exchequer. Bishops were to be nominated by the king. In January 1535 Thomas Cromwell was given the title of 'Vicar-general of religious matters.' The English schism was complete. Never before in history, not even in Lutheran Germany, had the State engineered such a total confiscation of spiritual authority to its own advantage.

CATHOLIC RESISTANCE: THE MARTYRDOM OF ST JOHN FISHER AND ST THOMAS MORE

It only remained to make the English nation accept this substitution of power. The clergy were ordered to preach on the theme of royal supremacy for several Sundays in succession. Fully alive to the importance of printing as a means for disseminating his views, Henry VIII had a stream of books and pamphlets published on the subject; there was something for everyone—an abbreviated edition of the *Defensor Pacis* by Marsilio of Padua; an adaptation of the *Dialogue between a Clerk and a Knight*, an ancient piece of French antipapal propaganda dating back to Philip the Fair's conflicts with Boniface VIII; selections of documents collected by Foxe; and treatises by Gardiner and Sampson. Each of these publications proclaimed that his

Q

subjects owed the king obedience in everything; their arguments even went to the lengths of quoting the Caesaro-Papism of the Byzantine emperors as an example.

Such propaganda, however, was slow to bear fruit. There were several signs of popular discontent. Whenever Catherine appeared in public she was enthusiastically acclaimed. Now that praise of the Pope had become an implied criticism of the king, the Papacy was referred to more favourably than it had ever been in the past. Various prophecies were whispered from mouth to mouth, alleging that Anne would meet her end at the stake. An imminent intervention by the 'good Emperor Charles,' to restore the rights of 'faithful wives,' was also freely predicted. But there was no organized opposition to Henry. The vast majority of the English clergy were probably not fully aware of the significance of the actions required of them; and so impressed were they by the king's prestige that they bowed to his will. Very few Englishmen refused to take the oath of loyalty to the new laws of the State. But these isolated opponents were still far too numerous in the eyes of Henry VIII and his satanic henchman Cromwell; and they decided to deal with them severely.

Thus began what Green, the great Victorian historian of the English nation, called 'the English Terror' and compared with that of Robespierre's dictatorship in France. For the next ten years the gallows and the scaffold were regular instruments of government. No social class was spared. The first victims were members of the regular clergy, who, in the main, showed more steadfastness than the seculars. Heading the list was a strange visionary called Elizabeth Barton, who was known as the 'Nun of Kent.' She was believed to possess prophetic and thaumaturgical gifts, and many important people had been to visit her, including Wolsey, Fisher and More. Found guilty of having fulminated against 'the shameless king' and of predicting his imminent downfall, she was arrested, pilloried and finally executed with her alleged accomplices, all of whom were priests. Next it was the turn of the Franciscan Observants. Their most famous preacher, William Peto 'the new Micah,' actually dared to condemn 'the illegal marriage' before the king himself. When threatened with being sewn in a sack and thrown into the Thames he replied: 'Man can reach heaven by water just as well as by land.' The Order's seven houses were closed, and their members scattered or sent into exile; about fifty of them perished in prison. But the penalties inflicted on the Carthusians were even more terrible. When asked to take the Oath of Supremacy, the Carthusians categorically refused. A most atrocious persecution followed: three of their priors were arrested and brought to London. After being dragged to execution bound to wooden horse-drawn hurdles, they were hanged from the gallows, their hearts and bowels torn out while they still breathed, and their bodies then plunged into boiling pitch. Their mutilated remains were subsequently exposed on the Tower or City gates.[1] Other more fortunate monks were simply hanged or decapitated, and several more still died in prison from cold or starvation. Thus did the new head of the English Church establish the law of Christ in his kingdom.

These frightful episodes broke the spirit of the English. Nevertheless two important humanists were still to move the hearts of all Europe by their self-sacrifice and heroic resistance to the royal tyranny. *John Fisher* (1459–1535) was unquestionably the most outstanding representative of that tiny English episcopal *élite* which was anxious to reform the Church from within, and he had put his principles into practice without waiting for outside assistance. His episcopal palace at Rochester was said to resemble a cloister in its regularity of observance, and a university in its love of knowledge. Fisher was a humanist of wide tastes. He had revived the classics at Cambridge and was passionately fond of Greek, which he had learned at the age of forty-seven. His temperament was that of a saint; nobility and gravity blended delightfully with an impish gaiety. As Queen Catherine's confessor, John Fisher at once took her part against Anne Boleyn, whom he detested. He was first arrested in 1530 for disapproving of the laws concerning ecclesiastical benefices, and in 1532 he was arrested again after publicly criticizing the royal divorce. However, his prestige was so enormous that the authorities hesitated to destroy him. It was the Act of Supremacy which finally brought about his ruin. Although imprisoned a third time, and deprived of the most elementary comforts, though he was almost eighty years of age, John Fisher held his ground and refused to take the oath. Possibly Henry VIII might have eventually relented and spared his life, had not Paul III, either out of ignorance of the violent opposition between bishop and king, or because he hoped thereby to save him, made him a cardinal. This action aroused the despot to a state of blind fury. 'He will have no head for his cardinal's hat!' he jeered. Fisher was brought before a special court, found guilty of high treason and condemned to death after one of those travesties of justice which Macaulay has described as 'assassinations preceded by a few mummeries.' To the very end the old man's bearing was like that of a martyr of the Early Church. He dressed for execution as carefully as for a wedding-day, and joked with his distracted servant. His final words were those of the Psalmist, '*In te Domine speravi*,' as he laid his head willingly on the block. In London it was rumoured that Anne Boleyn had had the bishop's bleeding head brought before her in order to insult it.

[1] The three Carthusian priors were joined by a Brigittine monk and the old and venerable vicar of Hales.

Fisher's execution took place on 22nd June 1535. Two weeks later, on 6th July, another great Englishman, *Thomas More* (1478–1535), mounted the steps of the same scaffold. By a singular coincidence this was the eve of the translation of the relics of St Thomas Becket, who, like More, was a Londoner, a former royal chancellor, and a martyr for the liberty of the Church and the primacy of the Apostolic See. More had been made chancellor at the end of a career whose brilliance was entirely due to his own merits; he had been in turn lawyer, member of Parliament and deputy sheriff of London. He knew the king to be fickle and changeable, and he had advanced in royal favour almost against his will, regarding worldly honours as onerous burdens, and the heaviest duties as the purest joys in God. When he was made lord chancellor in 1529—a most unusual promotion for a layman and a commoner—More had no illusions about the uncertain character of his good fortune. 'If my head were worth a French castle to the king it would not remain long on my shoulders,' he remarked in reply to his son-in-law's congratulations. He knew his master well, and he had quickly foreseen the tragedy which the 'King's great matter' held in store.

Thomas More was a delightful person, one of the simplest and most human saints in the calendar. There was nothing stiff or severe or morose about him. He radiated the joyous tranquillity and spiritual goodness of a man who, having once resolutely opted for heaven, is able to offer the world below a never-ending peace of mind. In the magnificent portraits by Holbein—the one at Florence is the finest— we can see him exactly as his friends saw him, with smiling face, laughing grey-blue eyes and lips poised ready for prompt repartee. 'He would make me dance the tight-rope,' said Erasmus. At the same time he was the perfect type of humanist, his mind and soul packed with noble thoughts; a man well abreast of all the discoveries of his age, and passionately interested in new ideas. His love of knowledge and the arts took him to the lengths of turning his own house into a miniature Platonic Academy, where sons, daughters, sons-in-laws, friends and relations rivalled one another in the brilliance of their scholarship. But this dazzling personality drew its support from the soundest of spiritual foundations, and confronted the temptations of success and the ordeals of failure with equal steadfastness of purpose. St Thomas More had been preparing for the grandeur of his death in prayerful meditation and silence all his life. 'Man is a prisoner waiting in the condemned cell for the final moment,' he was fond of saying; but he said it with the smile of the true Christian. This is the saint we love so well, and whom we long to resemble.

His religion corresponded with his noble character. He was tolerant towards his fellow men, completely free from dogmatism, but resolute in his principles. Christian humanism, in the tradition of Marsilio Ficino, Pico della Mirandola, Guillaume Budé and Erasmus, had no more accomplished representative than More. Though he had no illusions about human nature, he did not consider it irrevocably tainted and perverse, but believed that, given Divine Grace, it could develop the twofold blessing of reason and brotherly love. His *Utopia*, published in 1515, had won rapid fame. It contained a neat exposition of More's doctrine by describing life in an imaginary country where the monarchy was elective, all property was commonly owned, the clergy was chosen by the faithful, and the law consisted of the Gospels. The absence of dogmatism from these pleasant pages is so marked that More's doctrine can be held to verge dangerously close to Lutheran reformism. At the beginning More, like Erasmus, had viewed the great stir and commotion at Wittenberg with a certain amount of amused delight. But it was not very long before the utterances of Luther shocked and disgusted him; in 1529 he had condemned them in his spirited little masterpiece, *Dialogue on Heresies*; then, in his *Supplication of Souls*, he pointed out the falsehood of the Lutheran view of monastic vows and indulgences. He had sustained a lively argument against the Protestant propaganda of Tyndale, in which he had shown that the alleged return to primitive doctrine was a false enticement to the unwary, and that Tradition was simply the adaptation to changing kinds of society of one single, fundamental message.

A man of this stamp was obviously not made to participate in the king's game and accept the wholly personal reasons which had led Henry VIII to disobey the laws of the Church. By making him chancellor, his royal master may have believed he was robbing More of his intellectual authority. How wrong he was! However, unlike Fisher, More did not break with Henry straight away. So long as his own conscience was not threatened he kept silence, disapproving of the divorce in his own heart, but not wishing to do anything which might allow his attitude to be construed as treachery to the king or an encouragement to popular rebellion. When the choice between Church and king became compulsory and the 'Act of Succession' was made a part of English law, thereby forcing all important persons in the realm to connive at the illegal marriage, Thomas More slipped quietly from the public scene. He resigned the chancellorship on the grounds of ill health, preferring to seek the peace and tranquillity of his Chelsea home.

Unfortunately his enemies in the Boleyn party were watching his every movement. When ordered to swear to the Act of Succession, he tried to evade the issue; but the king's soldiers came to arrest him, and on 17th April 1534 he was sent to the Tower. For fourteen months he remained in prison, displaying a serenity and nobility of spirit to

which his letters and last writings bear striking witness. He meditated
on the *Passion of Our Lord* and composed a treatise called the *Dialogue
of Comfort*. When his wife and daughter asked him why he did not
copy the example of so many other good men and submit to the king,
so that he might return to the pleasures of his beloved library, More
waved his arm round his dungeon and replied: 'Surely this place is near
heaven too?' His possessions had been confiscated; his wife had to sell
her clothes to pay for his food. What rare discernment this man
possessed, to defend, almost single-handed, not the petty ruler of
Rome but the basic principle of the primacy of Peter and the Unity of
the Church, against king, Parliament, the majority of the clergy and
even his own family! Not a single doubt crossed his mind in the
moment of decision. In vain Cromwell himself visited him in prison,
to invite him to agree to the Act of Succession and submit to Henry.
On 1st July 1535 he was condemned to death in Westminster Hall
where he had so often dispensed justice in the past.

Now there was no longer any need to dissemble or to hang back for
fear of seeming disloyal. Thomas More rose to his feet, very calm, and
told this court of flunkeys and time-servers why he was going to his
death. 'Seeing that I see ye are determined to condemn me (God
knoweth how), I will now in discharge of my conscience speak my
mind plainly and freely touching my indictment and your Statute
withal. And forasmuch as this indictment is grounded upon an Act of
Parliament directly repugnant to the laws of God and His holy Church,
the supreme government of which, or of any part whereof, may no
temporal prince presume by any law to take upon him, as rightfully
belonging to the See of Rome, a spiritual pre-eminence by the mouth
of Our Saviour Himself, personally present upon earth, only to St
Peter and his successors bishops of the same see, by special prerogative
granted; it is therefore in law amongst Christian men insufficient to
charge any Christian man.' 'What!' remonstrated Audley, the new
chancellor. 'Do you consider yourself wiser and more conscientious
than all the bishops and nobles in the kingdom?' 'My lord, I have for
every bishop of yours, above one hundred; and for one Council or
Parliament of yours (God knoweth what manner of one) I have all the
Councils made these thousand years. And for this one kingdom, I have
all other Christian realms.' 'We now plainly perceive that you are
maliciously bent,' interjected Norfolk. 'No,' replied More, 'very and
pure necessity, for the discharge of my conscience, enforceth me to
speak so much. Wherein I call and appeal to God, whose only sight
pierceth into the very depth of man's heart, to be my witness . . . the
Church is one and indivisible, and you have no authority to make a
law which infringes Christian unity.' Only the executioner could reply
to words like these. The last word was his. However, Henry VIII was

merciful enough to commute the penalty which the tribunal had fixed for treason—hanging, drawing and quartering—to beheading in the case of his former servant. And the head of 'the noblest of all the English,' to quote the words of Reginald Pole, rolled on the scaffold.

This judicial murder provoked the strongest reactions throughout Europe. Only three weeks after the martyrdom [1] one of the saint's last letters had been translated into French, Latin, Spanish, German and Dutch, and was in general circulation. The Pope talked of deposing Henry VIII, but neither Francis I nor Charles V was in favour of a sensational act of this kind. Reginald Pole, the friend of both More and Fisher, and like them opposed to the schism, tried in vain from his Venetian refuge to organize some kind of European intervention. The despot took his revenge by sending Pole's brother Montague, his uncles, and even his aged mother, the Countess of Salisbury, to the scaffold. All protests were of no avail against an autocrat like Henry. He confined himself to telling other rulers that he had merely punished traitors, and had fourteen Anabaptists burned at the stake to demonstrate his own religious zeal. But what did he really think at the bottom of his heart? Stapleton relates how Henry was brought the news of More's execution while he sat at a game of dice, and how he sprang to his feet, quite pale, overcome by an absurd remorse. Looking blackly at Anne Boleyn, he shouted: 'You are responsible!' The blood of this new John the Baptist was soon to spill over the Tudor Herodias. A year later, to the very day, she too would mount the scaffold steps.

THE CHURCH OF ENGLAND UNDER ROYAL CONTROL

Henceforth the Church of England was well and truly separated from Rome and under royal control. Such an operation needed to be a paying proposition. The time had now come to perform an operation whose prospect had undoubtedly, albeit tacitly, been one of the motives behind the breach with the Papacy, the proclamation of royal supremacy and the willing acquiescence of the Commons. I refer to the secularization of all monastic wealth. It was all very well to criticize Luther and his following; the example of the Lutheran princes was a good pattern in this respect, and an institution whose international character most obviously conflicted with the nationalization of the Church disappeared at one fell swoop. The idea of appropriating the wealth of the religious houses was a very old one. In 1414, at the height of the Hundred Years War, all 'foreign' priories, in other words, those owing allegiance to mother houses on the Continent, had been suppressed; but Henry V had used their wealth to endow various

---

[1] John Fisher and Thomas More were canonized in 1935, together with about fifty of the victims martyred under Henry VIII.

charitable institutions. Between 1524 and 1528 Wolsey had exceeded his powers as legate in order to dissolve twenty-nine establishments. Thomas Cromwell, who nursed a really Machiavellian hatred towards the monks, was entrusted with the task of major dissolution. Faithful to Henrician tactics, however, he proceeded by easy stages, and under cover of 'reform' royal commissioners began visiting the monasteries in 1535. They inquired into the houses' incomes, tried to persuade monks who were under twenty-five to renounce the monastic habit on the grounds that they had taken their vows too young, tempted the religious with tales of the joys of life in the outside world, and disorganized monastic administration. In their report (which dealt with less than half the English monasteries and convents) they particularly exaggerated a few examples of immorality which had come to their notice.

In February 1536 Parliament passed an Act dissolving all the smaller monasteries whose incomes were less than two hundred pounds sterling, on the grounds that they were places of licentious living. The reason is a surprising one: dissipation must have found a far easier entry into the larger, wealthier establishment. But the essential thing was to disorganize any possible monastic resistance by giving the leading abbots, who had seats in the Lords, the impression that they at any rate were not to be disturbed. In the first year of the Act's operation three hundred and twenty-seven religious houses were dissolved in this way; fifty purchased their survival; and the rest provided the Crown with £32,000 from their annual revenues.

The northern provinces had so far submitted passively to the royal policy whose complications were far from clear to their rugged, poor but devoutly religious inhabitants. However, when they saw the priory gates closing for ever, and the monks leaving the land, they rose in open revolt. In these areas the religious houses owned a great deal of the land; their tenants had few complaints about them, but after the Dissolution many were evicted. The local nobility supported the movement which set Lincolnshire afire in October 1536; the king quelled it with a lavish spate of promises and flattery. But the flame broke out again in Yorkshire, Cumberland and Westmorland. Led by Robert Aske, a lawyer, and marching behind banners bearing the name of Jesus, some thirty-five thousand yeomen seized York and made for London. This was, they declared, 'the Pilgrimage of Grace.' A delegation of the 'pilgrims' was received by Henry VIII at Windsor. Simultaneously agreeing to summon a new Parliament and threatening to have them all burned alive by his soldiers, he persuaded the insurgents to return to their homes. Subsequently he was able to put to death the leaders, who had trusted his word of honour for their safety, without arousing any opposition.

This disturbing upsurge of rebellion probably decided the government to precipitate the closure of the five hundred monasteries still in existence. No mass confiscation was made, but each superior was ordered to hand his establishment over to the king. In less than three months fear of imprisonment and the offer of pensions or honours had done their work. The abbots of Reading, Colchester and Glastonbury, who stood their ground, were executed for having dared to disobey the sovereign. On 23rd March 1540 Waltham, the last religious house in England, was surrendered to the king.

Parliament had sanctioned the Crown's acquisition of all monastic properties; needless to say the promise to make some contribution to charitable and educational works was honoured only in part. Anything which had a market value was confiscated by the royal agents and sold at bargain prices; the Exchequer profited by a million and a half pounds. The monastic buildings were abandoned; people living near by removed the lead, iron, bronze and woodwork; the delicately carved choir-stalls were used as firewood. Two-thirds of the lands (the income from the whole seems to have represented not more than one-tenth of the national revenue, contrary to certain allegations) were sold for ridiculously small sums to people whose loyalty the Crown was anxious to ensure—merchants, lawyers and civil servants. Courtiers were presented with monastic property free of charge: Suffolk collected thirty monasteries. There were enough new property owners to guarantee the permanence of the schism. Unlike to what had occurred in Germany, only one-third of English monastic property actually reverted to the Crown. The mass of the peasantry and yeomanry received nothing. The new owners, shopkeepers, bankers or needy noblemen, had no attachment to the rural past, and they exploited their lands in a spirit that was solely business-like. Rents were increased, arable land converted to pasture and large areas enclosed. Thousands of unemployed farm hands were thrown on to the streets. Social distinctions became accentuated and pauperism increased in an alarming fashion.

The cult of saints and the practice of pilgrimage were both attacked at the time of the suppression of the monasteries. Certain statues which were the object of popular veneration were burned. The shrine of St Thomas Becket was destroyed and his remains scattered; after all he was a saint who had dared to resist a king! Because he was intent on choosing prelates devoted to his cause, Henry VIII invested a number of men who supported reformed ideas with episcopal sees from 1535 onwards. Latimer went to Worcester, Shaxton to Salisbury and Edward Foxe to Hereford. Cromwell set about having the Bible translated into English, but the former Augustinian monk, Miles Coverdale, whom he chose for this task, was an old collaborator of

* Q

Tyndale. While Coverdale took the Vulgate as his starting-point he planned his translation round those of Luther and Bucer, rather than going back directly to the Greek and Hebrew. The English Bible, which was finally published under the fictitious name of Thomas Matthew, used Tyndale's version for the New Testament and the first books of the Old, and Coverdale's translation for the rest.

There was, however, not the slightest doubt that the king intended to preserve Catholic orthodoxy. But the Church whose master he now was suffered perpetually from the effects of his policy, and its character was influenced by both the support he needed within his kingdom and the alliances which he made outside it. From January 1534 onwards relations were established with the German Lutheran princes. In 1535 Foxe and Heath met Martin Bucer at Strasbourg before going on to visit the members of the Schmalkaldic League; but the reformers insisted that an understanding must be reached regarding dogma before any common action could be contemplated. Melanchthon suggested the articles of Wittenberg; Henry VIII rejected them, but the Ten Articles of the Confession of Faith agreed upon in 1536 by the English clergy mentioned only three sacraments—Baptism, Penance and the Eucharist —without making any reference at all to the four others. Nevertheless the Real Presence was acknowledged, the cult of saints and prayers for the dead were retained on condition that no abuses were engendered thereby, and there was no question of accepting the doctrine of justification by faith alone.

None of the German delegations which came to England between 1536 and 1538 succeeded in shaking the king's doctrinal principles. Melanchthon begged him to accept the Reformation in full, but his pleas were all in vain. Indeed matters actually went into reverse. After the risings in Yorkshire and Lincolnshire a commission of bishops and theologians met under Henry's personal supervision and produced the Confession of Faith (1537) known as the 'Bishop's Book,' which explicitly retained all seven sacraments. Owing to the divergences of view and practice between traditionalists and innovators in the episco- pate, the king judged it prudent to bring in the 'Act for the Abolition of Diversity of Opinions' (1539), whose Six Articles were regarded as 'the whip with six tails' by those of heterodox opinions. Henry did not forget that he had once refuted Luther; he insisted on transubstantia- tion, clerical celibacy, the observation of the vow of chastity even by the religious who had been expelled from the monasteries, private masses and auricular confession; he turned down Communion in two kinds. Anyone defying one or other of these stipulations was im- prisoned, deprived of his property and hauled before a special com- mission. Cranmer had to send his second wife back to Germany in order to avoid falling into disgrace. Shaxton and Latimer preferred to resign their sees. It was now that Thomas Cromwell, who had remained strongly in favour of a Lutheran alliance, arranged a marriage between Henry and the Protestant Anne of Cleves. But the new queen was not to Henry's liking; Cromwell was accused of having propagated errors concerning the Eucharist, and on 29th July 1540 it was his turn to climb the steps of the scaffold. No one mourned his passing.

By the time he was fifty Henry VIII had grown into the man depicted in Holbein's famous portrait now at Windsor Castle. He was enormously fat (his stomach was supported by an iron corset) with a huge, puffy face, bloated features and clumsy, podgy fingers. In this portrait his cloth-of-gold doublet with its slashed sleeves, and his purple cloak, edged with ermine, are both covered with precious stones. His right hand toys with the courtier's gloves, while the left grips an assassin's dagger. At this stage all the sensitivity of his youth had vanished for ever, having yielded place to a calculated cruelty guided by pride and sensuality alone. After the frivolous Anne, who had gone to her death in a helpless peal of hysterical laughter, four other wives had occupied the royal bed, each slipping into her predecessor's place before it was yet cold: Jane Seymour, who had died giving birth to a son, the future Edward VI; Anne of Cleves, 'the Flanders mare,' who was repudiated after a few weeks; Catherine Howard, who met the same end as Anne Boleyn after a similar accusation of adultery had been made against her —albeit with rather more justification in this case; and Catherine Parr, who had been already twice widowed when Henry married her in 1543. She was the only bride to survive this crowned Bluebeard.

The further Henry went the more he prided himself on being the 'Defender of the Faith.' Nothing was going to make him deviate from the strictest orthodoxy! In March 1543 he wrote a preface to *A Necessary Doctrine and Erudition for any Christian Man*, which he imposed on his Church like a kind of catechism, and whose doctrine was sound enough to be accepted, at any rate provisionally by Cardinal Pole during the reign of Henry's daughter Mary Tudor. One peer testified: 'No prince ever showed himself more wise, more learned or more Catholic than the king in this Parliament.' The prayers of the Mass were recited in English, but the Book of Ceremonies used the traditional liturgy. Stephen Gardiner conducted the religious argument with the continental reformers with considerable skill and talent.

And the blood flowed faster and faster. Why? Sometimes the reason was religious, sometimes political; no one really knew how to distinguish the two any more. *Beheaded!* This little word marked the abrupt end of many lives. Apart from the two queens 'with their accomplices,' Henry VIII's list of kills comprised cardinals, bishops, abbots, priests, scholars, peers, knights, middle-class citizens and many women of gentle birth: the sum total ran into hundreds. The persecution was universally applied, striking down both Protestants and Catholics alike. Foxe preserved the memory of the first in his *Book of Martyrs*. Those who denied the Real Presence were burned at the stake in Calais, London and Windsor, on the express orders of that most excellent theologian, the king. The most famous Protestant martyr was Anne Askew. Her insolent answers to her inquisitors resulted in her being tortured on the rack with such ferocity that she had to be carried to the stake in a chair. But those who denied the royal supremacy were hanged from the gallows just as zealously. 'Merciful God!' declared one foreign visitor to England. 'What a way these people live! They hang Papists on one side of the street, and burn antipapists on the other!'

ONE HAPPY EXCEPTION: ANABAPTISM BECOMES A PACIFIC RELIGION

Thus the break-up of Christian unity resulted in violent reactions all over Europe, reactions for which politics bear as much responsibility as religion. Soon the very extent of the Reformation was to force all the states to take definite sides on the matter one way or the other. There was one exception to this process: a sect whose numerical importance was not particularly great, but whose attitude gave it enormous significance.

Here we are faced with an historical paradox: these non-violent reformers, who made no attempt to enforce their doctrines by political means, were the heirs and descendants of men who, in Melchior Hoffman's time, had seemed bent on shaking the very foundations of society; they were also in the direct tradition of John of Leyden, who had tried to establish the most rigid dictatorship ever known anywhere.[1] In fact *Anabaptism* had undergone a complete change of character after the bloody catastrophe of 1535, in which the 'Republic of Saints' met its downfall. Even while the corpses of John of Leyden and his disciples were being picked bare by the ravens in the iron cages where they had been hung from the cathedral belfry of Münster, the adherents of the doctrine of the Second Baptism abandoned the idea of imposing by force the religious, social and political anarchism which

---

[1] See earlier in this book, pp. 332 and 349. Heirs and descendants . . . : this at least is the view generally accepted. Recent scholarship supports a new thesis, and rejects the usual theory, namely, that the movement evolved through the Peasants' War and Münster, reaching Menno, who gathered up its remains, after the catastrophe. In this new view true Anabaptism arose at Zürich, 1523–5, as a branch of Zwinglianism. It was completely pacific in character, and had nothing in common with the Münster movement. Lastly, the Dutch sect, although a kind of offshoot of Münster, was always pacific and non-violent, while remaining extremely apocalyptic. (Cf. the works of Blanke, Bende, and van der Zijtt.) The author is indebted to John Yoder of Basle for this information.

they advocated. There were certainly still a few violent tremors, such as Jan Van Geelen's uprising at Amsterdam, or Jan Van Batenburg's at Steewijk and Overijssel. Where Anabaptism survived—for in a number of places, notably in Germany and Switzerland, it soon merged in the official Lutheran and Calvinist Churches—it became, in the main, peaceful and respectable. In Hungary, Bohemia, and to some extent in Sweden, small Anabaptist communities continued to exist, practising a harmless, quasi-communist evengelicalism. Not a single important nobleman or prince belonged to their sect or tried to impose their doctrine on his realm.

Anabaptism underwent its most significant expansion in the Low Countries. This started at Amsterdam with *David Joris*, Van Geelen's successor, an upright individual whose intentions were generous enough, but whose mind was fogged by apocalyptic ideas. Then the movement spread to Friesland, where a former Catholic priest, *Menno Simons*, devoted his tireless enthusiasm and administrative genius to making Anabaptism into a coherent system for the first time, a system which was extremely well suited to the religious aspirations and social conditions of the humble folk to whom he addressed his message. Thanks to Menno Simons, the doctrine has survived to the present day, and some modern Anabaptists are still called *Mennonites*. This ill-educated, indifferently intelligent man possessed real goodness and piety, and had a profound love for his fellow men. For him the essential of religion was an inner peace, an indifference to all worldly cares and a belief in universal brotherhood. His dogmas were simple: he accepted original sin, but did not consider it transferable, and this led him to refuse baptism to children and to regard only adult baptism as valid. He believed in the remission of sins through the merits of Christ, rejecting the Lutheran dogma of justification by faith, and teaching that the only faith which ensured salvation was that which was present in love. His Church, the community of the righteous, elected its own pastors democratically, and they were then confirmed in their office by the laying on of hands; they were strictly enjoined to take all their teaching direct from the Bible. Only two sacraments were recognized: Baptism and the Lord's Supper. Menno retained a few of his predecessors' extreme ideas; for example, the belief in the imminent end of the world (which is still found today among his distant spiritual descendants, the Seventh-Day Adventists), and the refusal to obey the laws of civil societies, which he regarded as sinful institutions running contrary to the laws of God. He forbade his followers to appear in courts of law, to take oaths of any kind, or to serve as soldiers or civil servants. This gentle anarchism did not beget a spirit of violence; when the Mennonites were persecuted they allowed themselves to be punished for their faith, and made no attempt to defend themselves.

And persecuted the Anabaptists certainly were. The antisocial character of these sects disturbed the Lutherans just as much as the Catholics. Charles V legislated against them most rigorously. Of 877 names which appear in the Protestant martyrologies for the Low Countries, 617 are those of Anabaptists. Numerous executions took place at Louvain, Ruremonde, Maastricht, Liège, Antwerp and Bruges; the men were burned and the women buried alive. But this did not prevent Mennonism and other kindred types of Anabaptism from gaining ground. There were 1,500 Anabaptists at Liège c. 1560, and more than 1,000 at Maastricht; Friesland undoubtedly contained tens of thousands of them. An organization had been set up whereby the Low Countries were divided into circuits, with a bishop in charge of each. Slowly but surely this extremely simple form of Christianity, with its elementary dogmas, continued to spread. It was soon found in Prussia, in the duchy of Holstein, in southern Russia and in England.[1] Crossing the Atlantic, it reached North America, and it still exists in all these countries today.

CALVINISM TAKES OVER FROM LUTHERANISM

By 1535–40 Lutheranism had become an important political force. It dominated Germany and had been forcibly imposed on Scandinavia. In England Henry VIII, although no Lutheran, had cut himself off from Rome in a most violent fashion. The situation was hardly favourable for the Catholic Church; but it was scarcely any better for the Reformation, in the sense in which the ex-monk of Wittenberg had conceived it. The Churches which had separated from Rome were now controlled by secular rulers. In Germany and Scandinavia such rulers imposed the doctrine laid down in Melanchthon's *Loci communes*. The English Church, under the leadership of a deplorable monarch—'a very swine, a second Herod,' to quote the words of Luther himself— claimed to retain traditional orthodoxy. Elsewhere, in areas where State control was not complete, a multiplicity of religious groups sprang into being, ready to degenerate into as many different sects. This was a sorry ending to that clarion call of freedom which Luther, drunk with his discovery of the truth, had made to the world some twenty years before.

Luther would occasionally reveal his own bitterness and anxiety about the future. There was his prophetic conversation with his beloved Master Philip in 1538, when he expressed his ardent desire that a council should meet and fix a dogma and a discipline, in order to

[1] Where it merged to a large extent with one of the 'independent' sects, to give rise to the 'Baptists.' These subsequently underwent an immense development in the United States, where they now number more than ten million.

prevent 'enormous scandals.' [1] In fact, it was the Catholic Church which was about to undertake this effort of unification. It was an effort which would leave Luther and his followers completely outside its scope and run counter to all their beliefs. The rupture was complete, the hour for compromise was past. Rome no longer desired anything save total submission from the reformers. All the negotiations which in 1540 and 1541 took place under the aegis of Charles V, at Haguenau, Worms and Ratisbon between the exponents of the two confessions collapsed on the questions of the sacraments, the nature of the Eucharist and the authority of the Holy See. Paul III approved the constitution of the Society of Jesus, and these shock-troops of the impending counter-attack were placed under his immediate protection. John Peter Carafa pressed on with the re-establishment of the Roman Inquisition, modelled on that operating in Spain. The oecumenical council which would reassert the force of Catholicism in the face of the heretical Reformation was on the point of meeting at Trent. These were disturbing symptoms in the eyes of Luther.

Success and failure balanced one another very neatly in Luther's achievement. He had touched off a formidable movement; countless individuals, cities and states had followed his example and shaken off the old religious tutelages. His disciples had spread his teaching from the mouth of the Scheldt to the Vistula, from the Baltic to the Mediterranean. In the space of twenty brief years the Roman Church had lost positions which she had held for centuries. But Luther was no longer capable of keeping this flame alive. The over-accommodating Melanchthon busied himself balancing out the formulae of a mediocre kind of orthodoxy. Wittenberg was not an important centre of learning, even less a breeding-ground for missionaries. These 'liberated' souls had in theory been left to their own devices, but they were in fact at the mercy of the secular rulers' whims. Their position, and that of the religious essence of the Reformation too, was a most perilous one. The danger was equally great on the intellectual plane; Lutheranism was totally divorced from the scholastic trends of the times and the humanists rejected it. In this they were following the example of Erasmus, who had died in 1536, but whose philosophy, which favoured 'Free Will,' remained efficacious against the protagonists of 'Servile Will.'

True the reformers' enthusiasm was unflagging. Their numbers grew; they preached and wrote and spent their energies with a lavishness and self-sacrifice that compel our admiration. Luther's correspondence is known to number some 4,000 letters. But there are also extant 1,200 of Zwingli's, 2,000 of Vadian's, the evangelist of Saint Gall, 7,500 of Melanchthon's, and as many as 12,000 belonging to Bullinger, who succeeded Zwingli at Zürich! One of Bullinger's letters

[1] See p. 353.

actually describes the feverish tempo of his life. 'I am overwhelmed with the task of continuous and arduous preaching, and there are also lectures to be given. I have to devote several hours to this or that friend, now writing letters, now giving advice to someone who has come specially to see me. As well as this I want to preach the message of Christ to people who are far away, and to explain the Scriptures to all those who are prevented by some difficulty from visiting me. This is why I am preparing some Commentaries for printing—another crushing labour. There is little time left for eating, sleeping and refreshing the body and the soul.' Bullinger maintained this strenuous existence for forty-five years, working single-handed at his task: a splendid example of the Herculean labours undertaken by the great Protestants.

Yet all such efforts were in grave danger of coming to nothing. They lacked the one factor necessary to a successful revolution—the security of a sound doctrine and the coherence of a strong organization. Bucer, the Protestant apostle of Strasbourg, was well aware of this. In 1530 he had drafted a confession of faith which he believed to be generally acceptable, and this had been signed by four cities.[1] Then in 1536 he had adhered to the 'Wittenberg Agreement' and suggested the idea of one Germanic Church which should be entirely separate from the Papacy. But the sacramentaries of Zürich and Basle remained aloof from these attempts at unity. Luther himself, who was primarily concerned with the question of the liberation of the individual soul, evinced little interest. Moreover a compromise would not avoid for Protestantism the twofold danger of disintegration and secularization. What the movement needed now was new determination and new blood. Certain people believed that Zwinglianism might perform this function: its logical simplicity was attractive. 'I would be quite happy with this very simple faith,' said Myconius; 'I could live my life with it, the transcendent means nothing to us.' However, Zwinglianism's lack of metaphysic was almost too complete; it was really little more than a religious rationalism. 'Zwingli says almost nothing about Christian sanctity,' said Melanchthon. 'He simply follows the Pelagians, the Papists and the philosophers.' What was wanted was a really coherent religion, firmly established on strong bases of its own, which would possess both genuine fervour and a rigid organization. But that seemed scarcely conceivable. It was at this point that Calvin took over.

In 1541 he triumphantly established himself at Geneva, and set about converting the city into an archetype of Protestant society. His contribution to Reformation Europe was enormous. Although his basis was common to all the reform movements—reliance on the authority of the Scriptures alone and rejection of Tradition; justification by

[1] Hence his title 'Tetrapolitan.' (See p. 338.)

faith and the omnipotence of Divine Grace; denial of the Catholic concept of the sacraments, cult of the Saints and the Virgin Mary; and condemnation of clerical celibacy and monastic vows—he provided the Reformation with so many completely new elements that his seal is indelibly impressed upon it. His book, the *Christian Institution*, had such logic, style and compulsive force that it came to be regarded both as a *Summa* of philosophy and as a manual of action. His theological concept of *predestination*, i.e. man's total dependence upon God, produced disciples whose will was utterly indomitable, since this will was the very seal set by God Himself upon each one of them. Lutheranism, albeit unintentionally, had undermined the bases of morality; Calvinism re-established it upon unshakable foundations, for although it did not regard good works as a means of salvation, it proclaimed them to be none the less a sign and token thereof. Refusing to subject the Church to the secular authority Calvin decided that the whole of civil society must be permeated to some extent by faith, and that on this account the religious authority should exercise control over it. A very strong, close-knit organization, whose central element was the consistory, preserved the community of the elect from all possible encroachments by the civil power. Instead of handing over its destinies to some unworthy prince, this community freely elected its own ministers (in this respect Calvinism is a part of the great individualist movement which was manifesting itself in the world at this period). In appearance and in its theories Calvinism was no less violently hostile to the philosophers and humanists than Lutheranism had been. It regarded them as sceptics and treated them with deep suspicion; it did indeed, as has often been said, 'effect the divorce between the Renaissance and the Reformation.' In a more fundamental sense its doctrine remained an almost unconscious humanism. After all, it sought the support of reason, desired to reach God by way of reason and not merely to reach Him by means of a mystical impulse, and was convinced that knowledge could lead men to the divine. Thus, far from separating itself from the intellectual current of the times, Calvinism actually participated in it, albeit at the cost of some confusion and ambiguity, and benefited enormously in consequence. It readily assimilated the newest and most modern political and economic ideas, coinciding with the nascent tendencies towards democracy and capitalism. Finally, by refusing to be confined within the narrow, national and feudal framework which enclosed German Lutheranism, Calvinism proved itself a universalist force, which gave it an affinity to humanism, even though it was neither Roman nor Catholic. This summary alone is sufficient to measure the importance of Calvin's role in history. He undoubtedly altered the character of Protestantism, but he saved it from some mortal dangers. And what powerful influence he placed at the service of this coherent and fruitful mass of doctrine! Hencefor-ward Geneva, with its famous academy, training ground of the mission-aries of the Reformed faith and centre of Protestant propaganda, outshone Wittenberg. After 1541 it became the European capital of the Reformation.

From now onwards the tide of Calvinism came to the assistance of Lutheranism, and even ousted it in many places. But by stepping up opposition to Catholicism it aggravated tension in a most tragic manner and provoked a number of bloody countermeasures.

THE TRAGEDY IN FRANCE BEGINS TO TAKE SHAPE

No sooner had Calvinism been formulated than it spread rapidly into France. The Latin edition of the *Christian Institution* enjoyed a cultured public as early as 1536, the year of its publication. But it was primarily the French edition, published in 1541, that attained a wide popularity wherever people were interested in this type of problem. The pro-hibition and suppression of the work by the Parlement of Paris in the following year is sufficient to show the importance with which it was regarded by the Catholic authorities. These measures hindered Calvin-ist propaganda to some extent, but were unable to prevent it entirely; enforced secrecy probably helped to make it more effective.

Geneva, which Calvin had formed into the living hub and model of the Reformation, exercised a decisive influence over all the small, varied and scattered communities which made up French Protestantism at that date: Biblians, Evangelicals, Fabrists, Christaudians and Lutherans. Within the space of fifteen months the Calvinist brand of Protestantism had imposed itself on all of them, and the name 'Cal-vinists' was universally applied. Henceforth those persecuted for their religion in France sought refuge in Geneva. From Geneva there flowed a constant stream of religious messengers of every conceivable sort, salesmen of pious contraband literature and fanatical missionaries who had received their training in the academy. The Rhône, an ancient artery of trade, now spread this new kind of merchandise along its banks, depositing it in the Alps and Cévennes, as well as in the towns through which it flowed. Then, pushing on by way of Nîmes and Albi, the Genevan heresy conquered the entire Midi, finally veering north-wards through Bordeaux, Angoulême, Poitou and Saintonge. The course of this insidious wave could almost be followed on the map.

This penetration of France by the most harsh and rigid type of Protestantism coincided with a stiffening in royal policy. As the reader will recall,[1] an ambiguous and vaguely uneasy indulgence had existed as late as 1535. After the Placard Affair the situation had changed

[1] See p. 376.

completely. Francis I made one final bid for peace. On 16th July 1535, still hoping to arrange an amicable solution, and much disturbed by the violence of the Catholic reaction, he issued the Edict of Coucy, which accorded a general amnesty. This was to be the last measure of clemency for a long time to come. The king had come to regard heresy with suspicion. He was quite willing to encourage it in the territories belonging to Charles V, or to help the Genevan Protestants against the Duke of Savoy, but he looked upon it as a potential source of weakness in his own kingdom. If he ever read the letter which Calvin addressed to him in August of that year, in the dedication to his *Christian Institution*, Francis had certainly not been convinced by its suggestion that he ought to abandon 'the Mass, Purgatory, pilgrimages and all the other useless rubbish.' He had actually reproached certain bishops, who, he wrote, 'had not been careful enough to make provision for such important matters touching the honour of God.' Perhaps he had received information concerning the heresy's progress in France. Or perhaps the lawyers at his court had persuaded him that the only formula which could ensure the stability of his state was that of 'one King, one Law, one Faith.' At all events, from 1538 onwards, having signed the ten-year Truce of Nice with the emperor, Francis I became quite clearly committed to a policy of repression.

Thus the stage was set for the French tragedy, and over the next sixty years its episodes unfolded in sorrowful succession. The country was divided into three camps, and it was now that the protagonists in this melancholy and long-drawn-out affair took up their positions. On the one side stood the Protestants, increasingly organized and inspired by Calvin. As always happens, persecution simply strengthened their faith and resolution. On the other were the advocates of a policy of rigid repression, led by Parlement and the Sorbonne. They were supported by a section of the episcopate, including Cardinals Jean de Lorraine and De Tournon, convinced now that indulgence was synonymous with weakness, and also by certain courtiers who were enamoured of absolutism and the policy of Rome. Among the latter were the Guise faction and the Constable de Montmorency. Between these extremes stood a third party composed of moderates, intellectuals, magistrates and many of the bishops, e.g. *Cardinal Sadolet*, who believed in religious pacification and general conciliation. Francis I's personal sympathies were with this latter party: while he condemned the heretics he also distrusted the right-wing extremists, to whom he referred as 'Conspirators.' But the situation had become so grave that royal clemency was no longer acceptable. The hour for the great policy of tolerance that was to be the glory of Henry IV had not yet sounded. The teams were lined up for a contest in which much blood would flow.

In December 1538 the Edict of Coucy was revoked. Eighteen

months later the Edict of Fontainebleau formulated positive legislation against the heretics; the courts were ordered to prosecute them, even if they were priests. All the judges were commanded to play their part in this repressive policy 'under pain of grave punishment,' and this secular control of the struggle against heresy even provoked protests from the clergy. The Sorbonne established a Catholic 'formulary of faith' which all teachers and graduates had to sign, and at almost the same time issued an Index of evil-thinking, forbidden books, in which the names of Luther, Melanchthon, Calvin, Dolet and Marot figured prominently. The trumpets sounded in the streets of Paris, ordering anyone possessing these works to hand them over to the Parlement record office immediately. The bookseller Antoine le Noel had to make honourable amends in the square before Notre-Dame for having sold the *Christian Institution*, and a copy of this work was publicly burned by the executioner. No one dared publish it in France before 1562. The wave of repression rolled across the whole country from Langres to La Rochelle, from Picardy in the north to Provence in the south, with all the excesses usually found in this kind of operation. At Orleans the royal inquisitor was so zealous that he even arrested the bishop's aide and theological adviser.

Such chastisement made Protestantism more active and violent. The clandestine pedlars from Strasbourg and Switzerland grew in number; their business prospered. Agitation in the universities increased. At Toulouse the students met together to read the Bible and the forbidden books; at Montpellier they acted an openly anti-catholic 'morality play.' Various polemic works circulated secretly. The most comic of these was the *Confession of Noel Beda*, which was written by Marcourt (author of the Placards in 1535). He pictured the fiery theologian exiled by the king and eventually confessing his errors and adhering to the new faith. There were also countless edifying treatises, inspired by Protestant teaching, which were passed from hand to hand. Everywhere people were either violently for or against the subversive ideas; they frequently passed from diatribes to blows. Youthful Protestants beat up religious and loyal Catholics in several places. At Bordeaux in 1545, 'to avoid being insulted or annoyed, devout women were obliged to have Masses said in secret at the Franciscan convent and elsewhere, and to hide the candles which they were accustomed to offer beneath their gowns.' Sermons were interrupted by demonstrations almost everywhere, and sometimes fanatical Protestants would creep out at night to smash the statues of the Blessed Virgin and the saints on church fronts or street niches, which were so highly venerated by ordinary folk. This stupid iconoclasm did much to provoke severe countermeasures. Religious ferment was fast turning to anarchy. The State was about to strike even harder.

The final years, 1545–7, of Francis I's reign, were marked by a number of violently repressive acts. In 1545 he had just signed the Peace of Crépy with the Emperor Charles V, who was attempting to crush the German Lutherans, and the two Catholic sovereigns may well have agreed to carry out a simultaneous operation against the heretics. The most painful episode of all occurred at Meaux, where a number of executions had already taken place twenty years earlier.[1] Pierre le Clerc, brother of one of the victims of 1524, had been elected pastor and had organized a small Protestant Church of about fifty members which made rapid progress. On 8th September 1546 the police surrounded the community while its members were celebrating the Lord's Supper according to the Calvinist rite, and all, or almost all of them, were arrested, taken to Paris in tumbrils and tried in the most summary fashion. After being sentenced to death the fourteen leading members of the community were sent back to Meaux, exactly a month later, to be executed there; and lest any of them should take the last opportunity to preach their views, their tongues were torn out before they were burned at the stake. A terrible chapter had just been added to the Protestant *Book of Martyrs*, which Crespin was soon to write.

This repression affected not only the small Protestant communities, which contained a mixture of Lutherans, former Fabrists, Zwinglians and Calvinists. Once set in motion the ponderous governmental machine crashed down on others who were hard to distinguish from the Protestants. This was how the Waldenses of Upper Provence perished, in circumstances so appalling that they were to leave a memory of horror in the land for many years to come. These remote heirs of Pietro Valdo were the descendants of medieval heretics. They had taken refuge in the Alpine valleys, and there they lived austere, peaceful lives, giving little offence to anyone. Protestant propaganda, however, had led them to discard their usual tranquillity; among them too there was an outbreak of iconoclasm and sacrilege. In 1540 the Parlement at Aix had reacted by sentencing to death ten leading Waldenses; but their bishop, who was none other than Sadolet, had strenuously opposed their execution. He wrote a letter to Rome, which is one of the most generous-minded documents of the age. In it he protested strongly about the use of force against the heretics: 'Terror and punishments are futile. Only truth and the utmost exercise of mercy will make them confess their errors, not merely with their mouths, but with their hearts also. I am the shepherd of these people's souls, and not a mercenary. No one is more indignant against the wrongdoers than I am, but my compassion for them is even greater still.' Alas! that brutal age could scarcely understand such noble

[1] See p. 378.

Christian sentiments. Five years later the Waldenses established relations with Geneva and iconoclasm broke out amongst them once more. Oppède, first president of the Parlement of Aix, took advantage of the bishop's absence in Rome to persuade the king to authorize a fresh persecution. What followed was sheer butchery. The troops of Paulin de la Garde, who were crossing Provence on their way to Piedmont, were set loose on a score of unfortunate villages and practised the excesses customary among soldiers at that time. Merindol and Cabrières were almost totally destroyed, and all male prisoners were sent to the galleys.

Francis I responded to his sister Marguerite's cry of anguish and opened an inquiry into the killings. This ended in the condemnation of some of those responsible. But at least eight hundred corpses made up the frightful catalogue of this first major military operation, which foreshadowed that of the Wars of Religion.

One famous victim of Francis I's repression came from a very different quarter. He was *Étienne Dolet*, humanist, sceptic and publisher, whose books from Lyons disseminated subversive ideas all over France. Taking advantage of the Protestant ferment, he had increased his publications very considerably, borrowing quite shamelessly from the texts of Marot and Rabelais, and re-editing Calvin's translation of the Psalms and a Bible in the vulgar tongue. Moreover all these things were very well done. When the publisher was denounced by his rivals and arrested for the first time, he escaped the stake, thanks to some influential protectors. But he was then foolish enough to try to sell clandestinely the works he had promised to destroy. He was arrested once more and brought to Paris, where he was burned at the stake in the Place Maubert two years later, though it seemed that the approach of death had brought some improvement in his views.

Dolet's execution, the Waldensian massacre, the destruction of the Protestant church at Meaux, and last but not least the publication of the general Index of forbidden books, all showed very clearly that those in high places at the end of Francis I's reign were determined to deal severely with all heretics. Although the repressive measures had been largely ineffective against Protestant propaganda taken as a whole, they had made the realities of the situation crystal clear. This becomes very apparent when we consider the attitude of the intellectuals. A few adhered quite openly to the Reformation: the jurist Hoffman, Ambroise Paré, Ramus and Jean Goujon. But all the waverers, the men who had toyed with the new ideas without becoming deeply committed to them, immediately steered towards calmer waters. Rabelais, who had flirted with Protestantism until this date, and had several times incurred suspicion as a result, hastily paid his respects to the established order. Henceforth, whenever his early books were reprinted, he modified his attacks against the Sorbonne professors and the theologians, and in his fourth book—the one in which he had bitterly mocked the 'Papimanes'—he now shot some fiery darts at the 'devilish Calvinists, the impostors from Geneva.' It must be added, however, that the Genevan reformer awarded him a prominent place in his *Treatise on Scandals*. As for Marot, who had done more than merely touch the fringe of Protestantism, and who had had several of his translations condemned, he was overjoyed at having managed to escape 'hell' not just once, but twice. He hurried to explain in splendid verse that he was very far from being a heretic, and returned very humbly to the bosom of the Catholic Church. The time for prevarication was definitely past.

This became abundantly clear on 31st March 1547, when *Henry II* (1547–59) ascended the throne of France. This narrow-minded man, who disliked all innovation and was fiercely jealous of his own authority, was surrounded by a clique which prided itself on a doctrinal intransigence that would today be regarded as integrism of the worst kind. The members of this clique were Diane de Poitiers, his former mistress, whose faith was more orthodox than her morals; Anne de Montmorency, who had been on bad terms with the late king; and, most important of all, the *Guises*, the notorious 'Lorrainers,' who were to be in the forefront of events for many years to come. At his coronation the king was told by Cardinal Charles de Lorraine (another Guise): 'Act in such a way that posterity will say of you "But for the reign of Henry, King of France, the Roman Church would have been utterly destroyed."' And the king replied 'I will.'

In October 1547 a special criminal court had been constituted for the trial of heretics. It soon became known as 'la Chambre Ardente,' the Court of Fire. Two years later a second edict commanded the closest co-operation between ecclesiastical and secular judges, granting the civil courts competence to try all cases of heresy which were considered a public scandal. Countless suspects were hauled before these secular tribunals: the Chambre Ardente of Paris alone awarded 500 sentences between December 1547 and January 1550. The king seemed to think these measures sufficient warning for the present. He now returned the heretics to the ecclesiastical courts, which did not condemn their victims to the stake. Soon after this, however, realizing that Calvinist propaganda was just as active as before, he signed the *Edict of Châteaubriant* (27th June 1551), which co-ordinated all previous measures taken against the heretics. The publication or sale of books on the general Index was forbidden; all candidates for public office had to produce a certificate of orthodoxy; and the Edict even went so far as to pronounce that there could be no appeal from any sentence involving heresy. In 1557 the Edict of Compiègne confirmed these degrees, and even increased their severity. When Calvin heard of the measures whereby Protestants were denied the legal guarantees accorded to poisoners and forgers he was understandably appalled.[1] The Edict of Châteaubriant had publicly proclaimed that he and his propaganda were largely responsible for these decisions. Geneva was named in it more than ten times; it was actually decreed that all heretics who sought refuge in Geneva would have their goods and chattels confiscated, and that any friend or relative who agreed to look after their property in their absence would be treated as their accomplice. All these strictures prove what an important factor Calvinism had become in French Protestantism.

France now experienced some years of real anti-Protestant terror. It was virtually impossible to earn a living as a publisher or bookseller there. Robert Estienne sought refuge in Geneva. Men and women went to the stake in every corner of the land, and their executions were often accompanied by atrocious refinements. If they would not promise to refrain from addressing the bystanders (those who did were strangled before being burned) their tongues were cut off or torn out; in several places the victim was hung from a chain attached to a pulley, so that he could be pulled up and down and thus burn more slowly.

All Catholics must acknowledge that the French Protestants almost always faced these terrible penalties with truly admirable courage. The number of abjurations was very small indeed. Cardinal Baudrillart has written of them: 'Although mercilessly persecuted, they endured with unwavering constancy horrible punishments no less terrible than those which the last pagans inflicted on the early Christians.' Their souls were sustained by an extraordinary exaltation, kept alive by letters and messages which trickled through from Geneva. These wretched people died happily, in the firm belief that their sacrifice would bring them eternal salvation. On the morning of his execution one Protestant pointed towards the glorious dawn and declared that very soon, 'when I am raised on high,' he would see a sight still more wonderful. And quite often the stakes would echo with the verses of one of the Psalms which the Protestants loved to sing in their own churches:

'Quand mon corps sera tréspassé
Mon âme ne sera pas morte.'[2]

Here, above all, it is necessary to recall St Augustine's observation that it is not his suffering but his cause which makes the martyr: *causa non poena martyrum facit*.

These heretical martyrs affected the society which killed them exactly as those of Primitive Christian times had done. 'Their blood

[1] See p. 437.
[2] 'Though my body perish, my soul will not die.'

brought new converts to Protestantism and confirmed in their errors many whom gentler persuasion might have restored to the bosom of the Church.' Baudrillart goes on: 'The stake was a magnet that attracted and held fast the noblest souls and most generous minds.' This was also Bossuet's view. And Agrippa d'Aubigné afterwards wrote a moving paraphrase of Tertullian's famous remark:

> 'Les cendres des brulés sont precieuses grains . . .
> Tant de sang que les rois épauchent à ruisseaux
> S'exhale en douce pluie et en fontaines d'eaux. . . .'[1]

In fact the results of this persecution were extremely disappointing. Tiepolo, the Venetian ambassador, wrote: 'It is an astonishing thing that although someone is burned almost every week the flame of heresy remains alight.' Police reports showed that heresy was making considerable progress in places such as La Rochelle, Orleans, Bourges and Grenoble. This rapid growth of Protestant communities all over the country has been almost totally ignored by historians, for the documentary evidence is so rare. We have only an indistinct picture of the life of the first Calvinist church in Paris, with its nocturnal celebrations of the Lord's Supper held at deliberately irregular intervals, its different meeting-places and passwords, and the hurried exits through cellars and windows which were made at the slightest hint of danger. No doubt the rest had a very similar kind of existence. But the result is quite definite: by the end of Henry II's reign the only parts of the kingdom which were without Protestant communities were probably an area in the north and the eastern half of Brittany. In some places, e.g. Normandy, Brie and around Viviers, the bishops had unintentionally prepared the ground for Calvinism; in others—Saintonges, for example—a powerful landowner—in this case Antoine de Pons, who had known Calvin at Ferrara—made his estates a centre from which the Protestant doctrine could be disseminated far and wide. Elsewhere the first seeds had been sown by a college or university, or by printers and booksellers on the look-out for new material; and in other places the Waldensian tradition of the Alps or the free-thinking humanism of Marguerite of Navarre were responsible. However the heresy originated, it was always the missionaries from Geneva who completed the work. But it is not easy to assess this progress in numerical terms. The First President of the Parlement of Paris, Lizet, wrote to Montmorency, Constable of France, as follows: 'The sickness in this kingdom has gone so far and is so deeply rooted in many places that it is impossible to wipe it out without recourse to entirely new measures.' Cardinal de Lorraine, who was undoubtedly exaggerating in order to assist his own

[1] 'The martyrs' ashes are precious seeds. . . . The rivers of blood set in spate by the kings bring down gentle rain and living fountains. . . .'

cause, proclaimed that two-thirds of France had succumbed to heresy. And Pastor Macar wrote to Calvin in grandiloquent terms: 'The fire is kindled throughout the entire kingdom, and all the waters in the ocean would not suffice to extinguish it.' In fact the most accurate assessments enable us to conclude that about one-sixth of the French population was affected by Protestant doctrines: between two and three million people.

Such then was the result of the Calvinist flood-tide *c.* 1557. But alongside this material result (Protestant expansion) was another: the fundamental modification which the Reformed communities had undergone. Calvin's logical genius as an organizer was now apparent everywhere. His translation of the Bible had replaced that of Lefèvre d'Étaples, and although his *Christian Institution* was a forbidden book it had been distributed all over France. Very soon Theodore Beza had not sufficient ministers to send to all the French churches who were demanding one. By 1555 the churches strictly following the Geneva model numbered 34: and there were probably 72 of them by 1559. 'During 1555-6 and the years following,' says Crespin, in his *Book of Martyrs*, 'the heritage of the Lord began to be set in good order.' Paris, Meaux, Poitiers in 1555; Bourges, Issoudun, Blois and Tours in 1556; Orleans, Sens, Dieppe and Rouen in 1557; La Rochelle, Saintes, Cognac and Toulouse in 1558; Chartres, Castellane, Evreux and Vire in 1559. The movement was irresistible. And there were all the unorganized churches too, which were no less fervent than the rest. It is hard to tell whether or not Coligny was yielding to excessive enthusiasm when he claimed that there were 2,150 Calvinist communities in France in 1561. Rouen certainly contained 10,000 Protestants. Such figures as these make it easy to understand why the State was soon led to increase its repressive measures still further in its efforts to face a danger that was undoubtedly very real indeed.

EDWARD VI's ENGLAND TURNS TO CALVINISM

Although the first part of Francis I's reign had appeared to promise the triumph of humanism and moderate reform in the Church, the Valois had come round to a policy of repression—albeit one that remained disappointing in its results. Meanwhile Tudor England was evolving rapidly towards the official adoption of Calvinism, now that the Roman observance had been withdrawn. Henry VIII died on 28th January 1547. He was succeeded by his son by Jane Seymour, *Edward VI* (1537-53), a boy of only nine years old. His father had made provision for a council of regency. Almost at once, however, the predominant role was assumed by the maternal uncle of the boy-king, Edward Seymour, Earl of Hertford, subsequently *Duke of Somerset*, who conferred on himself the title of 'Protector.' Somerset was a competent and cautious politician. While he was very far from despising the rewards of power, he realized that violent tactics were fraught with risks, and he therefore opted for compromise solutions. In the matter of religion, as in everything else, he was guided by two preoccupations. Firstly, he must keep content the nobility, which had been enriched by the spoliation of the monasteries and which feared that a reconciliation with the Papacy might be purchased by the abandonment of these recent acquisitions. This anxiety obviously encouraged him to deepen the ditch dug by Henry VIII between Rome and the English Church. Secondly, it was difficult for him to remain deaf to the counsels of those increasingly numerous voices which urged him to adopt the Reformation. Foremost among these was that of Cranmer, Archbishop of Canterbury, who translated Luther's catechism into English in 1548. From now onwards the kingdom afforded asylum to a whole clan of Protestant refugees whose influence was far from negligible: the Italian Vermigli, better known as Peter Martyr, a former Augustinian who had taken a wife: his compatriots Tremellio and Ochino, an ex-Capuchin; and, most important of all, Martin Bucer, whom Charles V had expelled from Strasbourg because of his hostility to the Interim, and who was to spend the last years of his life in England. Such *émigrés* were well provided with prebends and university chairs—Peter Martyr taught at Oxford, Bucer was given a government pension—and all of them regarded the Protector as their friend. Calvin actually dedicated to him his Commentary on the First Epistle to Timothy, and wrote the duke an extraordinarily clear-sighted letter pointing out that if Somerset failed to provide his people with a religious faith and discipline, he would see it sink into anarchy. The lesson was understood.

The new master's first steps were to put an end to the penal laws of Henry VIII. 'High treason' was defined more modestly, and it was no longer possible to send anyone to the scaffold at will. Both Catholics and Protestants ceased to be persecuted. But at the same time there was a gradual slide towards Protestantism. To be sure this was a slow process, carried out with considerable circumspection and even ambiguity. The 'Injunctions' of July 1547 apparently left the traditional liturgy untouched, but they ordered priests to obtain for themselves Erasmus's *Paraphrase*, together with the New Testament in English and Latin, and to read the *Homilies* of Cranmer, which Convocation had rejected as suspect in 1543. The royal visitors entrusted with the task of seeing that these measures were properly applied, were carried away by their zeal and considerably exceeded their duties. They ordered that statues be removed from the churches and their walls covered with whitewash. Two of the bishops, Gardiner and

Bonner, protested and were promptly imprisoned. As regards clerical celibacy, Parliament passed an Act which was a model of cunning ambiguity: so far from abolishing it, the Act actually stated that celibacy was desirable 'for the priest's good name and reputation,' but married laymen were authorized to assume sacerdotal functions. Protestantism was silently worming its way forward. A few fanatics blasphemed the Eucharist. Both Parliament and Protector brought them sharply to task, but the *Order for Holy Communion* was very close to the Lutheran Lord's Supper, not merely because it recognized Communion in two kinds, but also because it robbed the Mass of its sacrificial character. The *Book of Common Prayer* of 1549—'the Book of Common Prayer and Administration of the Sacraments and other Rites and Ceremonies of the Church,' generally called the *Prayer Book*—confirmed these Protestant tendencies, although they continued to be veiled in ambiguity. The Mass became a simple thanksgiving service entitled 'The Lord's Supper, or Holy Communion'; the prayers of oblation were omitted. Baptism was administered in the Lutheran fashion; auricular confession became optional; English was recognized as the official religious language, but the framework of the liturgy was allowed to remain as it was. *The Act of Uniformity*, which was passed in 1549, made these regulations compulsory as from Whitsunday of that year.

This was the position when an unforeseen political event brought about its rapid development. Somerset fell from power. The risings which occurred simultaneously in north, west and eastern England during the summer of 1549 were not fundamentally due to the peasantry's dislike of the trend towards Protestantism. The small farmers and landowners were rebelling in an attempt to put a stop to 'enclosures' —a curious and completely English phenomenon, which was leading the high and mighty to create vast areas of pasturage—veritable latifundia—at their expense. It is significant, however, to note that the rebels in Devon and Cornwall had drawn up Sixteen Articles containing a number of purely religious requests, among them the re-establishment of private Masses and the restoration of Latin in place of the present 'Christmas mummeries.' The revolt was a serious one. A certain Robert Kett commanded as many as 16,000 rebels, and Somerset committed the mistake of entrusting its repression to his principal rival in the Council, John Dudley, *Duke of Northumberland* and *Earl of Warwick*. With the help of some German mercenaries Northumberland scotched the rising with considerable bloodshed, and having done so his most urgent task was to rid himself of the Protector.

This outstanding aristocrat was a fine soldier and a shrewd diplomat, but so arrogant that his contemporaries nicknamed him 'the new Alcibiades.' He was possessed of unbridled ambition and was totally

unscrupulous. In religious matters he was personally inclined to con-
servatism, or was at all events 'Henrician' in his convictions. But in
order to safeguard his authority it was necessary for him to provide
himself with a devoted following. A short time previously an opportune law had put all the colleges, pious foundations and wealth of the
religious guilds at the disposition of the Crown. Northumberland
applied it recklessly, and there was sufficient to quieten many greedy
scruples. Church property was filched; several bishops gave up a part
of their incomes, either voluntarily or under duress; and the class of
new incumbents was prepared to accept any dogmas it was offered,
provided its possessions were left intact. No one really knows what the
young monarch thought of these developments. It seems difficult to
attribute responsibility in this matter to a boy of thirteen; Edward VI
had been brought up in an atmosphere of Anglicanism and hatred of
Rome, and in any case he could scarcely have opposed his counsellors'
actions.

At this stage the English Reformation swung towards Calvinism,
and even assumed an almost Zwinglian radicalism, a further proof of
that exhaustion of Lutheranism observed earlier in this chapter. Souls
who had abandoned Roman dogma sought their logical satisfaction in
the formulae of Geneva and Zürich. Cranmer was in continuous
contact with Bullinger and corresponded with Calvin.

Ever since its publication the Prayer Book of 1549 had been attacked
by Protestant extremists; the leader of the critics was Hooper, a
former monk, who had now married and been made Bishop of Gloucester. Cranmer therefore assembled a commission of theologians, in
which Bucer exercised a profound influence (even after his death,
which occurred in 1551), and this body undertook to revise the
religious blueprint of England. As a result a new Prayer Book was
issued whose use was also made obligatory by a fresh *Act of Uniformity*.
War was declared on altars, which were replaced by plain tables that
stood in the centres of churches stripped bare of their statues and
paintings. Meanwhile the dogmatic evolution towards Calvinism was
nearing completion. Everything which suggested the Real Presence
was omitted from the new Prayer Book. At the Consecration the
celebrant henceforth spoke as follows: 'Take and eat this in remembrance that Christ died for thee, and feed on Him in thy heart by faith
with thanksgiving. . . . Drink this in remembrance that Christ's Blood
was shed for thee, and be thankful.' The Ordinal of 1550 had abolished
all minor orders and the subdiaconate; the priest was no longer the
agent of sacrifice, but a preacher and pastor, who presided at the Lord's
Supper in his white surplice. At his ordination the bishop would
present him with a Bible, a chalice and some bread, and would say to
him: 'Take thou Authority to preach the Word of God, and to

minister the holy sacraments in the Congregation.' At this juncture the declaration that clerical marriages were now legal followed naturally enough. The *Ave Maria* disappeared from the Book of Hours, and the Catechism taught the doctrine of justification by faith alone. However, the 42 Articles of 1553, to which all ecclesiastics had to subscribe, were content to make do with imprecise and often conciliatory formulae on several controversial questions. This foreshadowed the intermediary character which was to distinguish the Anglican Church of the future.

Such measures had their opponents. Quite a number of bishops were unwilling to go beyond the limits reached by Henry VIII; the more stubborn of them were imprisoned and replaced by creatures of the government. Gardiner and Bonner told their judges that they were much saddened to see 'heretics authorized to preach and deny that the Body and Blood of Christ are present in the Sacrament of the Altar.' They were ready (a little late in the day) to acknowledge that without the existence of an independent and superior spiritual authority the royal authority was powerless to guarantee orthodoxy. The law dealing with high treason was brought back again, in order to crush the opposition which the government was now facing. Executions of Papists and 'fantasticals' (Protestants who wished to carry the present trend to its extreme limits) recommenced, and John Foxe, author of the English *Book of Martyrs*, called Northumberland 'a cruel hangman.' Even the king's elder half-sister, Mary, found herself subjected to various indignities because of her rigid attachment to Catholicism. The government went so far as to persecute her own chaplains, and these harassments were at least partially responsible for the hatred with which she subsequently regarded Protestantism in all its forms. Should she have resisted Northumberland's innovations more seriously? It is hard to say. On 6th July 1553, a few weeks after the publication of the second Prayer Book, Edward VI died and *Mary Tudor* succeeded him.

Calvinism Mounts its Attack

Calvinism was not content with its impressive progress in France and its quasi-triumph in England. It mounted its attack on all sides with a vigour and enterprise that deserve the highest respect. Its declared enemy was Catholicism, but in fact, by devious ways, it came into conflict with Lutheranism and with all the other forms of Protestantism which had preceded it; for their desire for power soon proved weaker than that of the Genevan heresy. The Calvinist attack took many different forms and produced some very unequal results.

In many instances it was a case of slow transformation. Penetration ended in substitution. This was exactly what happened in *Switzerland*. Although Bullinger, Zwingli's son-in-law and successor, was outstandingly active and devout, he did not possess such a vigorous personality as that of Zwingli himself. He very quickly bowed to Calvin's ascendancy, notably on the question of the Eucharist, where he discarded the pure symbolism of Zwingli and adopted the compromise position of Geneva. During 1548–9 negotiations took place which resulted in the doctrinal understanding known as the *Agreement of Zürich* or the *Consensus Tigurinus*.[1] Fundamental differences of organization and discipline still existed between the Calvinist and Zwinglian Churches, but in practice Zürich ceased to exert any external influence. Even within its own walls the Zwinglian nucleus was gradually encircled by Calvinist groups, and it shrank so much that today it is but a tiny minority of the Protestant whole.

The faith that was henceforth common to Zürich, Geneva, Berne and Basle travelled down the Rhine to conquer Zweibrücken, the Palatinate and several other areas of the Rhineland, where Lutheranism was for all practical purposes eliminated. Heidelberg University became the centre of the new doctrine, and it spread its message far and wide, so that before long it was accepted in places many miles from the Rhine valley. The Palatinate adopted Calvinism in 1562, Nassau in 1578, Bremen in 1584, the duchy of Anhalt in 1595, Lippe in 1602, Hesse-Cassel in 1605; even Brandenburg, a fief that owed its creation to the Wittenberg reform, was converted to the ideas of Geneva in 1614. Towards the Danube Calvinism established itself at Ulm, Ratisbon and Passau, although here it lacked legal status.

In the *Low Countries* Charles V's severe repression had combined with Anabaptist propaganda to hinder the spread of Lutheranism very considerably. It was apparent that the Reformation had there entered a second phase from 1543 onwards. This was first noticeable in the south-west, at Lille, Tournai and Valenciennes; next it swept along the seaboard of Flanders, breathing new life into the sorely tried Protestant communities of Antwerp, as well as that of Ghent, which had almost been annihilated in the repression following the social crisis of 1539; and finally it spread into Holland and Zealand. It had its origins not only in Geneva, but also in Strasbourg and England. But Geneva's influence soon became predominant. After preaching at Lille and Ghent, *Guy de Bray*, one of Calvin's disciples, became head of the Protestant community at Tournai, and in 1561 he drafted a confession of faith which was wholly Genevan in style. Such churches were visited only by transitory ministers, and were maintained for the rest of the time by elders and deacons. They led a precarious but fervent existence, calling themselves by such symbolic names as 'Palm,' 'Vine' or 'Sword.' After 1560 they held their heads high again, no longer meeting only in the homes of citizens, but in the open air as

[1] See p. 432.

well. These 'hedge sermons' left behind them a vivid memory. The democratic organization of Calvinism was well suited to such industrious and intensely critical people. The educated middle classes read the *Christian Institution* with admiration; Anabaptism had prepared the proletariat of the ports and the cloth towns for a doctrine more radical than that of Luther. In the Low Countries the Calvinist Reformation encountered a following possessed of revolutionary instincts, which an aristocracy weary of Hapsburg authoritarianism was strongly tempted to join. The way was being made ready for a crisis of terrible violence.[1]

The faith of Geneva took over from that of Wittenberg in the eastern part of Christian Europe in exactly the same way. *Hungary* had suffered severe dismemberment after the westward advance of the Turks. Lutheranism had benefited there from the annihilation of the Catholic hierarchy after the disaster of Mohacs and the presence of numerous German colonies in the country; but the Magyar element now adopted Calvinism in preference to it. Hungary's Calvinist apostle was Pastor Juhasz, who adopted the name of *Melius*; his stronghold was Debreczen. The *Confessio Czengerina*, which 'Pope Melius' drafted in 1557, was the charter and catechism of what was known as 'the Hungarian Church'; a revised version by Theodore Beza became obligatory in 1563. The existence of Calvinist groups in Transylvania was recognized simultaneously.

The same process can be observed in *Bohemia*. Here, however, Protestantism found its path more difficult on account of official opposition. The strict evangelicalism of Calvinism and its structural independence of the civil authorities had a particular appeal for the Bohemian Brethren, descendants of the Taborites and the Hussites. When Ferdinand of Hapsburg harshly persecuted them, the Bohemian Protestants closed their ranks around the rigid doctrine of Geneva. After the imprisonment of John Augusta, apostle of the Lutherans, his 'Confession of Faith,' which Luther himself had approved, rapidly lost its influence. 'The unity of the Brethren' was re-established in semi-secrecy, and this, despite an important emigration of many of its members to the indulgent Poland of Sigismund Augustus, set about constituting an organization on the Genevan model, and adopted many doctrines very close to those of Calvin, particularly those concerning the Eucharist. About 1555 the entire Czech nation seemed doomed to slide into the most rigid kind of Protestantism.

For a moment it appeared possible that, in the firm hands of Calvin, the heresy might gradually come to dominate all Europe. But this was not to be. In certain quarters Calvin was to suffer partial and even complete failure. He had set great hopes on Poland. In 1554 he outlined a programme of action to her feeble monarch, but he failed to

[1] See *The Catholic Reformation*, Chapter III.

understand the complexity of the religious situation in a country that was paralysed by chronic anarchy. The common people remained loyal to Catholic principles, while the German middle class in the towns adhered to Lutheranism; but Calvinism had won over a section of the nobility, and it could boast some spectacular conversions, such as those of Nicholas Radziwill and several other families who had formerly belonged to the Russian Orthodox rite. A Protestant majority existed in the Chamber of Notables; but there were swarms of differing sects, and each detested all the rest. The Diet of 1556 authorized the nobility to practise the cult of their choice. *Jan Laski*, who belonged to the magnate class, had broken with Catholicism, then been reconciled to it, and finally—possibly disappointed because he had not been recompensed with a fat benefice—had embraced the doctrines of the sacramentaries. In 1549 he was preaching to a cosmopolitan community of *émigrés* in London. In 1556 Calvin entrusted him with a regular mission, and he returned to his native land. His activity and success among the aristocracy of Lithuania and the region around Cracow were enormous; he dreamed of uniting all the Protestants of the realm in one single Confession, even the Bohemian Brethren, who had been flocking there in large numbers ever since 1548; but he was an authoritarian and rather muddle-headed character, his efforts were doomed to failure, and he did not even manage to hold together the Calvinist groups. Lelio Sozzini, a Sienese, who stayed for a time at Cracow during the course of a wandering existence, introduced his somewhat wild ideas there; he took his criticism to the lengths of rejecting the idea of God in three Persons and inspiring an anti-Trinitarian or 'Unitarian' movement which was little more than Deism. The hour of the Catholic counter-attack was now very near at hand.

This then was one setback for Calvin. He suffered a number of others in several parts of *Germany*, where the Lutheran rulers were firmly established in religious positions which assured them substantial political and financial advantages, and where they controlled their subjects sufficiently closely to prevent the introduction of theses which were far too democratic for their taste. The same thing happened in *Sweden*, where the Lutheran Church had implanted itself solidly under the wise direction of its episcopal hierarchy. Eric IV, son of Gustavus Vasa, was converted to Calvinism by Denis Beureé, a Frenchman, and attempted to introduce the new faith into his kingdom. Then his brother, John III, who was married to a Polish Catholic, tried to restore the Catholic faith. Neither of them succeeded in shaking the Lutheran bastion.

Calvinism had no greater success at the other end of Europe. In Spain, where the barrier against heresy had been very strong from the

· R

beginning, the Genevan theses penetrated even less than those of Luther. There are some slight traces of them in the writings of Montanus, a former Dominican who was expelled from Spain and found asylum for a time on the shores of Lake Geneva. Cardinal Carranza, Archbishop of Toledo, who was suspected of possessing Calvinist sympathies on account of his *Commentary on the Catechism*, spent seventeen years in prison—the Inquisition, as we can see, had no respect for titles—but it was never possible to convict him of heresy. Italy, which had also proved hostile to the Lutheran heresy, was not much beguiled by Calvinism either. Renée of Ferrara, who had received the future reformer at her court in his youth, and had subsequently made him her spiritual director, eventually slipped from his influence. In 1560 she was in retirement at Montargis, preparing to die a good Catholic death. Only a few isolated individuals rallied to the faith of Geneva, but some of them were none the less remarkable. There was *Bernardino Ochino*, General of the Capuchins, a mysterious personage whose motives have never been properly elucidated. In 1542 he forsook his young Order and the entire, horrified Catholic world, to go off with a woman. He went first to Geneva, then to England, and never returned to Italy, despite all the charitable approaches of St Ignatius of Loyola. There was Pietro Vermigli—Peter Martyr—Vicar-General of the Augustinians, who was also to play an important role in the English Reformation. There was the famous and unfortunate Dominican *Giordano Bruno*, whose death at the stake would cause so much ink to flow, and who was moreover more of a Pantheist than a Calvinist.[1] These were not sufficient to make a Church. The little semi-evangelical, semi-Calvinist groups which managed to remain alive in Venice, Piedmont, Emilio, Tuscany, Campania and Sicily were totally without organization.

But the most impressive example of a whole nation's resistance to the influence of the Reformation was provided by *Ireland*. Ireland had been since the twelfth century subject to the English Crown, whose authority, however, it suffered with considerable impatience. It was also prey to particularist passions which resulted in many feuds between the various clans or 'Septs,' and the Irish Church was beset by serious disorders (it was commonplace to see candidates for bishoprics settling the matter by the sword); but when there was a question of fighting for her faith, the ancient land of St Patrick united her forces and held firm. Henry VIII easily obtained the Irish Parliament's approval of the schism—it was in fact largely composed of English colonists—but when he tried to make the episcopate and the people accept it he found he was wasting his time. Even though he appointed a number of complaisant clerics to some of the sees, the king could not wear down

[1] See the Index to *The Catholic Reformation*.

this resistance. Lord St Leger's efforts during the reign of Edward VI to impose the Prayer Books were equally futile; Dowdall, Archbishop of Armagh, preferred to leave Ireland altogether rather than see 'the holy Mass outraged.' Thanks to Northumberland, Bale, a former Carmelite who was nicknamed 'the foul-mouthed,' was made Bishop of Ossory. He began a thoroughly violent anti-Catholic campaign. The statues in many of the churches were smashed, sacrilegious plays were enacted by the young, and the English rite and the writings of Calvin were circulated far and wide; but the only result was to stir up rebellion among his flock. Hunted down on all sides the Irish Catholics began to write that glorious page which they were to sign with their own blood in the days of Elizabeth.

IN THE EAST THE GREEK AND RUSSIAN CHURCHES REJECT PROTESTANTISM ABSOLUTELY

The most curious defeat suffered by Protestantism in its effort to conquer the Christian world occurred in the East. This is a fact of great importance, and one that every Catholic who desires to see the fraternity of all the baptized sealed anew one day cannot ignore. The Eastern Church, commonly called the 'Orthodox' Church, remained quite impervious to all Protestant influences in whatever form.

It might have been thought that the common hatred which both Orthodox Christians and Protestants bore towards Rome would have drawn them together. Nothing of the kind occurred. In 1559 Melanchthon sent a Greek translation of the *Confession of Augsburg* to the Patriarch of Constantinople, Josaphat II. The Patriarch never so much as answered him, but privately uttered fulsome imprecations against this heretic. Shortly afterwards some professors from Tübingen had occasion to enter into relations with the Patriarch Jeremiah II, and they suggested to him that their churches should unite on the basis of the Reformed doctrines. This time a reply was indeed received, but it was scarcely in conformity with the desires of the German theologians. Constantinople haughtily rejected the Lutheran theses on the Eucharist and the ecclesiastical hierarchy, and invited her correspondents to cease their useless efforts. The Calvinists in their turn sought a *rapprochement* with the Eastern Church, notably through the mediation of the German colonists in Transylvania and a few Venetian traders who had been converted to the new ideas. Their failure was equally manifest. At the beginning of the seventeenth century it actually verged on the tragic. The Patriarch of the period, Cyril Lukaris, allowed himself to be converted to the faith of Geneva and published a *Confession of Faith* in which he extolled predestination and interpreted the Communion in the Calvinist fashion. But his clergy and people rose up against him in indignation; a council deposed him and denounced him to the Turkish authorities, who were determined to maintain religious peace among their subject peoples and hastened to have him strangled. In this way despite her enslavement and her decadence, the Greek Church preserved her faith.

As for the Russian Church it is scarcely correct to say that she rejected Protestantism: she was impervious to it. A few German merchants, who frequented the fairs at Novgorod and elsewhere, talked about the new ideas in the inns, but with little result: the mass of the Russian people ignored them. Besides, the Church in Moscow was moving towards that spiritual nationalism which was henceforth to be its salient characteristic. The Patriarch of Moscow, heir to the monarchical Romano-Byzantine tradition, obtained his autonomy of the four other Patriarchates in 1589. He exercised an increasingly absolute authority over the whole of the immense territory of Russia, sanctioning the fusion of nation and State in one religious ideal. At the end of the fifteenth century it was he who had led the struggle against two heretical sects, the *Strigolviki* (the folk with shorn locks), who showed tendencies which were vaguely rationalist and certainly anticlerical, and the *Judaizers*, who rejected the Trinity, the cult of saints and the sacraments. *Maximus the Greek*, a former monk from Athos who had been summoned to Moscow, fought the Judaizers successfully on the intellectual plane, and *Joseph of Volokolamsk* opposed them with the first Russian theology; but the State also intervened, and fires were kindled to burn the leaders of both sects. Obviously the climate did not favour the sort of propaganda which could only remind the Russian faithful of their own anticlericals and insulters of the saints. At a time when Holy Russia was glorying in the possession of her most important mystic, *St Nilus Sorsky* (*d.* 1508), whose *Ustav* (the Rule), a treatise on asceticism, brings to mind the *Imitation of Christ* and the *Exercises of St Ignatius*, she was scarcely likely to yield to a doctrinal movement which was so alien to her temperament.

THE DECISIVE YEARS: CHARLES V's FAILURE IN GERMANY

But the resistance which Protestantism encountered in many quarters should not inspire the reader with any illusions. The situation was a tragic one for Catholicism. Whole walls of the Church's edifice were crumbling away: two-thirds of Germany, Scandinavia and England were all lost; Bohemia, Hungary, Poland, Scotland and France were seriously contaminated; Protestant propaganda fell on ready ears everywhere. Was all Europe destined to pass under the sway of the heresiarchs? Encumbered by its Italian policy, and held responsible for the disasters now affecting the Church, the Papacy seemed incapable of galvanizing the forces of resistance and reversing the situation in its own favour.

The fifteen to twenty-odd years in the middle of the sixteenth century, spanning roughly the period between the death of Luther and that of Calvin, were decisive years, in which the destiny of Christendom was decided. The ancient Roman and Catholic Church rallied her strength to effect a recovery which many had believed she could no longer make. She reorganized herself, boldly confronted her enemies, counter-attacked them and eventually retrieved part of the ground she had earlier lost. Meanwhile, in one furious effort, the Protestants overwhelmed a number of new positions, and won some victories that were to be their last. And the one result of this twofold hardening process was to leave the Church of Christ permanently wounded and divided.

The most sensational episodes in the conflict between the two opposing forces took place in Germany. In 1546 the Catholic outlook there seemed very black. All the Lutheran rulers were allied in the *Schmalkaldic League*.[1] Taking advantage of Charles V's many difficulties, they were gaining ground all the time and converting new areas of the Empire to Protestantism by force. In fact, all was not lost for the supporters of the Roman faith. The Lutheran, like all coalitions, were slow to act, and were unable to attack their enemy at the opportune moment. Once the Peace of Crépy had freed Charles V from the threat of France he turned his attentions to Germany, firmly resolved to crush those whom he regarded as rebels against his sovereign authority.

Charles came to terms with *Duke Maurice*, the head of the junior branch of the ruling house of Saxony and the natural rival of his cousin, the Protestant Elector John Frederick. In July 1546, on his own sole authority, the emperor put the Elector of Saxony and the Landgrave of Hesse under the ban of the Empire on the grounds that they had violated public peace. Pope Paul III sent him a contingent of troops under the command of his grandson, Ottavio Farnese. The summer was spent in limited operations in the region of the upper Danube, but in the autumn Maurice of Saxony, who had taken care to lull his cousin's vigilance, hurled his troops on the Electorate. John Frederick deserted the Schmalkaldic army in order to repulse this aggression against his own territory and his discomfited allies scattered. Free to move as he pleased, the emperor forced the Duke of Württemberg to submit; he deposed the highly suspect Archbishop of Cologne; he made his appearance as master in Ulm, Augsburg, Frankfurt and Strasbourg, all of which had previously adhered to the Schmalkaldic

[1] See Chapter V, pp. 345 et seq.

League. The Protestant princes no longer possessed any allies; within the space of a few weeks, at the beginning of 1547, both Henry VIII and Francis I disappeared from the scene. However, the Elector of Saxony regained the initiative over Maurice, and Charles V hurried to the rescue of his ally. On 24th April the imperial troops crossed the Elbe unexpectedly, swept down on the camp at *Mühlberg*, and carried off John Frederick's banners and artillery almost without loss to themselves. Wittenberg capitulated; Luther had now been dead for fifteen months. John Frederick surrendered to Charles V, who declared him a traitor to the Empire and bestowed his Electorate upon Maurice. Deserted by all his allies, the Landgrave Philip of Hesse joined the Saxon ex-Elector in prison; both men were to remain there for five years. Bohemia, which had refused to send contingents to the emperor's aid, was severely punished by Ferdinand of Hapsburg.

The emperor's power was at its height. He had shattered the political and military might of the Protestants; from now on he intended to regulate the religious question. He had fought the Schmalkaldic War in his capacity as head of state, hammering the rebels, but he had assiduously avoided setting himself up as an enemy of the heretics. The Elector of Saxony and the Landgrave of Hesse had been condemned for stealing territories from the Duke of Brunswick, but not for their religious views; and when Charles reduced to submission the urban republics of the south-west, he had promised to respect certain rites and secularized property. He was undoubtedly aiming to reconstitute religious unity; but for this it was not possible to rely upon the Council, whose preliminary sessions had just taken place. Not only had the sources of faith, justification and the sacraments been defined in a fashion fundamentally incompatible with the reformers' ideas, but Charles V himself was at loggerheads with the Pope, who reproached him for trying to manage religious affairs and for levying excessive taxes on Church property in Spain. When the Council moved to Bologna, on account of an epidemic which had attacked the imperial city of Trent, Charles looked upon its action as a challenge. He resisted the establishment of Pietro Luigi Farnese, son of Paul III, at Parma and Piacenza, and his governor of Milan had some part in Pietro Luigi's assassination.

Since Germany was at his mercy, Charles decided to give her a provisional religious settlement. He had it prepared by three theologians, two Catholics, Pflug and Helding, and one Protestant, John Agricola. Duly set out in twenty-six articles, the *Interim* was proclaimed by the Diet of Augsburg on 15th May 1548. The liberties and advantages which the Protestants had gradually obtained were annulled, while juridical guarantees were given to Catholics living in the territories of Protestant rulers, and the Church's traditional doctrine on the cult of the saints and the seven sacraments was re-affirmed. Nevertheless the emperor's personal intentions were made perfectly clear in the authorization accorded to married priests to continue their ministry, and in the concession of Communion in two kinds. Paul III realized that the conqueror of Mühlberg was disowning the Council, and he suspended it.

Events, however, very soon caused Charles V bitter disappointment. It was admittedly difficult to apply the Interim; no one was satisfied with it; Maurice of Saxony himself refused to impose it on his subjects. Prematurely aged, tortured by gout, visibly weary—just as he appears in the portrait by Titian, which was painted at this period—the emperor was completely incapable of adopting a firm line. Sometimes he used severity. He besieged Magdeburg, for example, and at Stras-bourg he expelled Bucer, who sought refuge in England. Sometimes he shut his eyes to legal distortions, as in the case of Brandenburg, where the Margrave Joachim showed no respect for the Interim, and of Saxony, where Maurice had the Augsburg stipulations adapted by a group of theologians which included Melanchthon. The document which emerged from this made no allusion to the authority of either pope or bishops. This new draft, which was known as the *Interim of Leipzig*, had the same fate as its predecessor. Charles V was being visibly outflanked throughout the Empire. Pamphlets violently attacking the provisional settlement were in common circulation.

Above all, the emperor was unaware that the princes were not so humbled that they would never again take arms against him. German opinion was on their side: people intensely disapproved of the intro-duction of foreign troops into the Empire, and they were anxious about a current rumour—though without foundation—that Charles V in-tended bequeathing the imperial crown to his son Philip, a Spaniard whose intransigence was well known, rather than to his brother Ferdinand. The northern rulers secretly reformed their ranks and sought the support of France. They could now count on Maurice of Saxony. Maurice was a ruler of the true Machiavellian pattern, who furthered his own interests and ambitions with a dexterity and skill which have often been compared with those of Frederick II and Bis-marck. He had no wish to consolidate imperial authority any further, and, although he did not yet desert Charles V, he let the Protestants know that he shared their views and would be able to take his place as their leader at the proper time. Moreover the emperor was about to be faced with fresh international problems. The cool, prudent Henry II was now King of France, and Marshal de Vieilleville had convinced him that he would be better advised to strengthen his Lorraine frontier rather than pursue adventure in Italy. On 15th January 1552 the French monarch signed the Treaty of Chambord. In return for his financial assistance and a military operation in the Rhine area, Henry II obtained the right to occupy the three bishoprics of Metz, Toul and Verdun, where French was the language spoken. A manifesto issued from Fontainebleau represented the king as defender of Germanic liberties. Maurice threw off his mask: while the other rulers set off on the march, while the French invaded Lorraine and thrust forward as far as the Rhine, he occupied Augsburg so as to deprive Charles V of the bankers' financial aid, and hurled his forces on Innsbruck. The emperor had to rise from a sick-bed and flee in the middle of the night. Maurice was only three or four days' march from Trent, where the Council had resumed its labours, and where even a few Protestant delegates were present. The session was suspended once more.

After vainly attempting to recapture Metz, which was superbly defended by Francis de Guise, Charles V retired to Brussels to be near his sister, Mary of Hungary. He left his brother Ferdinand to negotiate the Treaty of Passau with the Protestants. The Diet which was destined to bring peace to Germany was delayed by fighting in the course of which Maurice of Saxony died, and it did not open at *Augsburg* until *5th February 1555*. By 26th September the treaty was ready, and Ferdinand signed it on 3rd October. It recognized the right of every ruler—Catholic and Lutheran alike—to regulate the religious affairs of his own state, and to impose his own religion on his subjects. If the latter would not submit to his ruling they risked being brought before the courts and sentenced to exile or even to death, unless of course they had already taken the precaution of fleeing to an area where their faith was the official one. The prince thus became ruler of his people's souls; this was the principle *cuius regio, huius religio*—'whoever has the kingdom controls the religion'—which formed a completely new basis of Germanic law, and consecrated the triumph of politics in the sphere of religion. So far as concerned the secularization of ecclesiastical property, it was laid down that all property secularized before 1552 should be retained by its present owners. Nevertheless, taking advantage of the full powers accorded him by his brother, Ferdinand insisted on the insertion of the special clause of 'ecclesiastical reservation' (*reservatum ecclesiasticum*), which debarred any bishop or abbot who might in future go over to Protestantism from retaining the possessions which he had administered by virtue of his office. Since the Protestant princes, who knew from their own experience what a large part self-interest had played in securing adhesion to the faith of Wittenberg, were not likely to enforce the other provisions of the peace, Ferdinand expressly agreed that for a principality of the Church to abandon Catholicism all that was required was a decision by the nobility and the towns in that principality, in other words, the legally represented 'Orders' of society there.

Thus did the Reformation in Germany receive its political constitution. By confirming the piecemeal partition of the country, the Peace of Augsburg contained within it the seeds of fratricidal conflicts, and provided the cause for the terrible Thirty Years War which broke out in the following century. It also illustrated the impotence of imperial authority. Agreement had been reached at the principality level. There was no question of recognizing liberty of conscience; the beliefs of his subjects were at the mercy of each individual ruler, and as the allies of Schmalkald had adopted the Lutheran form of Protestantism, the choice of faith was limited to Rome and Wittenberg. Calvinism, which, as has been seen, was permeating the Palatinate, had received no legal recognition.

Charles V's failure was crushing. He who had dreamt of assuming responsibility for the whole Christian world, and of guiding the Catholic Church along new paths, was forced to admit that in Germany, in the very heart of his vast domains, heresy had free play. Protected by the rulers and embodied in official churches, it was imposed on several millions of his subjects. He had assumed the crown two years after Luther's theses had been nailed to the church door in Wittenberg; twenty-six years later he had succeeded in preserving for Roman Catholicism only Westphalia, most of the Rhineland, the bishoprics of Main, Austrian Swabia and the northern side of the Alps. Henceforth Germany was cut in half along the line of the old Roman *limes*.

Charles V himself never again returned to his imperial territories after Maurice of Saxony's treacherous offensive; he was physically broken and morally spent. Perhaps he felt the burden of the scattered realms which he possessed in the four corners of the world become too heavy for his shoulders; or perhaps he read a heavenly warning in the collapse of his most cherished dreams. With solemn ceremony he divested himself of all his titles, all his offices and all his domains. In the Great Hall at Brussels, where the Emperor Maximilian had proclaimed him of age forty years earlier, and given him his fabulous inheritance, Charles first took off the collar of the Golden Fleece, and then, one by one, all the insignia of temporal power. His brother, Ferdinand I, Duke of Austria and King of Hungary and Bohemia, received the Empire; his son Philip was allotted Spain, the Italian territories, the Low Countries, Franche-Comté and the vast lands beyond the seas. The man who had seemed master of the world was henceforth interested only in his personal salvation. He took ship for Spain, resolved 'to do penance in reparation and amends for all the serious offences he had committed against God.' For a while he lived on, in the humble monastery of the Hieronymite Fathers at Yuste, on the slopes of the Estramadura, tormented by gout and beset by bouts

* R

of shivering which chilled him from head to foot, devoting himself entirely to prayer and meditation. He died on 21st September 1558, having left precise instructions for his obsequies. His last words were: 'The moment has come.' He had decided that his body should be buried in the monastery, under the high altar in the church. It was to be placed partly beneath the actual table, and partly outside it, in such a way that when the priest celebrated Mass, he would stand on the emperor's breast and head, in token of Charles's eternal humiliation.

The Decisive Years: French Protestantism Becomes a Political Party

While Lutheranism was establishing itself on solid foundations in Germany, French Protestantism, which was henceforth almost wholly Calvinist, was preparing to decide its destiny. Ever since the Genevan reformer had acquired control of it, it had spread insidiously and with increasing rapidity throughout the kingdom. Far from striking terror into men's hearts, the 'martyrs'' stakes had fired their enthusiasm. The printed page and the picture spread the fame of these unfortunate people. All Protestant communities revered the memory of those five brave young students from Geneva who had been arrested at Lyons, and who, after converting a malefactor imprisoned with them, had died in the flames, singing their joy to the last. Rather less touching incidents of iconoclasm were taking place all over France: statues of the Blessed Virgin were found decapitated, and the saints on the altar were run through with sacrilegious daggers. Social unrest assisted the expansion of Protestantism. One such example was the bloody uprising in Aunis and Saintonge on account of the *gabelle*, or salt-tax. But so far the royal government showed no reaction.

Two incidents made Henry II aware of the full extent of the danger. On the night of 4th or 5th September 1557 some students from the Collège du Plessis surprised a Protestant congregation which was holding a service in a house adjoining the Sorbonne and rented by a young lawyer belonging to the Parlement. The watch arrested one hundred and thirty people, who were taken to the Châtelet and it was discovered that about thirty of these, mostly women, belonged to the upper nobility. Some months later, in May 1558, processions consisting of several thousand people assembled on the Pré-aux-Clercs, outside the city walls on the left bank of the Seine, which was a place commonly used by students for games and recreation. These processions were escorted by armed horsemen, and Psalms were chanted. The Parlement prohibited all such demonstrations, and the king ordered an inquiry to be made; it was found that Antony de Bourbon, King of Navarre and

a prince of the blood, had taken part in them, and that the man responsible for the processions was François d'Andelot, nephew of the
Constable de Montmorency and brother of the future Admiral Coligny.
These were enlightening glimpses for the king, who was a slow but
stubborn man. He confessed that he had always regarded Protestantism
as a matter involving unimportant people: the presence of aristocrats
—armed, so it was said—at Protestant meetings filled him with
horrified amazement and anxiety.

The fact was that Protestant membership had changed a great deal
during the years preceding these incidents, and now affected social
classes very different from those which it had penetrated at the beginning. About 1540 'Evangelicalism' had been characteristic of intellectuals, then the new ideas had spread among the common people,
affecting workmen and artisans. When they became irreconcilable with
the Catechism, many educated people abandoned them. The mendicants and parish priests, who had originally shown some sympathy
for the new dogmas had mostly returned to the bosom of the Church.
All these half-hearted supporters and renegades had fully merited
Calvin's bitter pamphlet, *Apologies to the Nicodemites*. Of the early
Protestants, only the 'gens meschaniques' (workmen) had remained
loyal and increased in number. Gradually, however, they had been
joined by some not unimportant members of the aristocracy. There is
no doubt that the landed nobility, which had been a victim of monarchical centralization, of monetary devaluation and of the peace of
1559 which had brought it back to hearth and home, regarded the
Reformation as an excellent opportunity to attack the autocracy of the
Crown, and it may even have had the conscious idea of restoring its
own finances by secularizing the wealth of the Church. Other important people were of course converted to Calvinism for reasons of
genuine conviction, but their decision was influenced also by a desire
to oppose the ultra-Catholic faction, whose power at court was much
too great. In this way people of considerable authority slid gently
towards the Protestant camp. The three brothers Chatillon (Cardinal
Odet de Chatillon, Admiral Gaspard de Coligny and General François
d'Andelot); two of the king's cousins, Antony de Bourbon, King of
Navarre, a descendant of St Louis and Marguerite's son-in-law, and
his brother Louis de Rohan, founder of the house of Condé and one of
the best generals of the age—all these were certainly Protestant sympathizers, although they did not openly proclaim themselves Protestants. Jeanne d'Albret, Antony's wife, who was converted in her turn,
became a vigorous propagandist for the Reformed faith. The age of
the humble and pure in heart, whose eyes shone with fervour and
innocence even at the stake, was drawing to a close. Now came the
dawn of political Protestantism, whose leaders were to place their

swords, their ambitions and their rancour at the service of their faith. Their real aim was to seize political power, gain control of the monarchy and impose their doctrine on France. 'Do they seek then to snatch the crown from my head?' cried the angry king not unjustly.

After the incident in the Pré-aux-Clercs, which had caused enormous scandal in Paris, Henry II resolved to act. His own attempt to persuade d'Andelot to submit convinced him that there was nothing to be hoped for from such obstinate people. 'I solemnly swear that if I can settle my external affairs, I will make the streets run with the blood of this infamous Lutheran rabble,' [1] he told the Duke of Modena.

He did indeed settle his external affairs shortly after this. Perhaps his desire to have his hands free to deal with the Protestants explains his imprudent eagerness to abandon Savoy, Bresse and Bugey by the treaty of *Cateau Cambrésis* which he concluded with the Spanish monarchy on 3rd April 1559. This brought to an end the wars in Italy, which had started in 1494, and the conflict with the house of Austria, which had been in progress since 1519. France renounced all her efforts and ruinous adventures in Italy. As a result there was a regrouping of Catholic forces under the direction of the King of Spain; an offensive policy against heresy replaced the struggle for hegemony; this was tacitly recognized as belonging to the kingdom of Philip II, who had been able to protect himself from the Protestant contagion with the greatest success. On 2nd June 1559 the *Edict of Ecouen* defined the French Government's line of conduct; in order that heresy might be extirpated, the law was ordered to persecute without mercy those adhering to the false doctrines. On 10th June the king held a *lit de justice* in order to register the edict with the Parlement of Paris; a small group of counsellors had recommended that the law be applied with moderation, that the death penalty should not be applied for offences concerning religion, and that it would be best to wait for the Council to correct 'the Roman abuses.' The counsellors du Faur and du Bourg dared to repeat these proposals in the king's presence; the enraged Henry had them arrested on the spot with two of their colleagues and all were executed. But on 10th July Henry II died from wounds received at a tournament given in honour of his sister's marriage with the Duke of Savoy.

This happened just when French Protestantism was organizing itself into a separate Church. On *25th May 1559* the representatives of all the Reformed communities had held their *first synod* in Paris, under the chairmanship of Pastor Morel. There were three delegates representing Calvin. La Roche-Chandieu reached agreement with them on the wording of a Confession of Faith comprising forty articles. It was

---

[1] At this date, as is obvious, the distinction between the various forms of Protestantism was not yet complete.

decided that the ministers would be elected by consistories, and that all the Churches should be equal and autonomous, but that they should meet together regularly in provincial synods and eventually in a national synod. This meant that French Protestantism had established itself on the Genevan model as a fully fledged Church, which had no connection whatsoever with the traditional Church of France. It should, however, be emphasized that none of these ministers and theologians had the slightest intention of erecting it into a state against a state. The synod had very humbly assured the king of the loyalty of his Protestant subjects, and had begged him to study their doctrine more closely so that he might see for himself that it contained nothing subversive. But the underlying design of many of the ambitious leaders of the 'Protestant party' was probably quite different.

The political antagonism was soon apparent. Three powerful families aspired to the most important role in the kingdom. The Bourbons, descendants of St Louis, were princes of the blood royal. Antony, the eldest, a weak, indecisive character who had become King of Navarre by virtue of his marriage to the fiery Jeanne d'Albret, and the third brother, Louis, the ambitious and turbulent Prince de Condé, had gone over to Protestantism, while the second brother, Charles, remained Archbishop of Rouen and a cardinal of the Church. The Montmorencys, descendants of the aged Constable who had been the favourite of Francis I, were also divided in their religious allegiance; the direct branch remained Catholic, but its nephews were none other than the three Chatillon brothers, who, as we have seen, had become Calvinists. Confronting these two powerful dynasties was a third, which was capable of standing up to all the rest entirely alone: the *Guises*, who derived from Lorraine—that is to say, they were half foreign—but who had a Bourbon mother, and whose estates were mostly in France proper. The elder brother, François de Guise (1519–63), was a magnificent soldier, who had acquired fame by his defence of Metz and recapture of Calais; Charles, the younger, was Cardinal of Lorraine, Archbishop of Rheims, and commendatory abbot of Saint-Denis, Cluny, Noirmoutiers and Fécamp. It has been said of the Guises that 'their Catholicism went hand in hand with vast political designs.'[1] By posing as mortal enemies of Protestantism, and by taking their stand on Rome and the Pope, they would be satisfying their family ambitions quite as much as their religious convictions.

Now the new king *Francis II*, a boy of fifteen, had married a niece of the Guises, who was none other than Mary Stuart, Queen of Scotland, his elder by several years. Mary dominated her young husband and left his uncles 'in charge of everything.' For a few months the persecution of the Protestants continued with redoubled violence;

[1] Lucien Romier, *Origine politique des guerres de religion.*

it was at this time that Counsellor Anne du Bourg was hanged and burned. But the very ferocity of the persecution and the unpopularity of the Guises and their greedy following was sufficient to make the Protestant princes answer back in kind. A conspiracy was hatched to abduct Francis II and remove him from Guise influence. Its nominal leader was an ordinary gentleman, La Renaudie, but its real head was the Prince de Condé. When Calvin learned of the plan he condemned it, accurately foreseeing that 'from this one drop of spilt blood whole rivers will inundate France.' All in vain. The Guises had taken the king to the castle of Amboise, to ensure his security, and the conspirators had assembled in the nearby forests when they were denounced by a traitor. Reprisals were savage; all who were captured were drowned, beheaded or hanged. Shoals of corpses floated down the Loire and there were so many rotting bodies on the castle battlements and in the city streets that disease broke out. These atrocities called for revenge, and pamphlets threatening death to the Guises were passed from hand to hand. The failure of the *Conspiracy of Amboise* (1560) marked the beginning of the tragedy that was to rend France in twain. The Guises made immediate reply to the threats against them. They had Condé himself arrested and condemned to death; only the young king's death saved him.

One person was preparing to profit from this 'great tumult': *Catherine de' Medici* (1519–89), widow of Henry II, mother of the dead boy-king and of his brother Charles XI (1560–74) who succeeded him. Catherine was a typical Medici, a woman of great personality and political ability. The dull stare of her prominent eyes, and the plain face whose waxen pallor was enhanced by the widow's white collar, gave no indication whatsoever of the feelings which they hid. But these feelings were firm and resolute. Catherine had a very exalted idea of the State; she retained a wonderful memory of Francis I, her father-in-law, and, like him, she intended to command without let or hindrance. She was passionately fond of power, but acutely conscious of the realities of the situation. Above all, she detested the dominance of the Guises, and regarded the Protestant aristocracy as a useful counter-weight. She was determined to plot in her own interest between the factions whose fanaticism she herself was incapable of sharing. As from 8th March 1560 the trial of heretics was removed from the jurisdiction of the Parlements and handed back to the ecclesiastical courts. On 30th June Catherine appointed as her chancellor Michel de l'Hôpital. De l'Hôpital was a humanist who had retained his Erasmic moderation, a jurist who proposed to strengthen the authority of the crown, and a prudent Catholic who refused to hound the Protestants from the bosom of the Church as long as the Council was still in session. The accession of Charles XI, a sickly boy of nine, meant that Catherine became regent, and this enabled de l'Hôpital to put his policy to the test.

Michel de l'Hôpital made his famous entreaty to the States-General at Orleans: 'Let us get rid of these diabolical words—these names of parties, factions and seditions—Lutherans, Huguenots, Papists. Let us not corrupt the name of Christian!' In order to restore the dignity of episcopal prómotion, election by the chapters was re-established, and the Queen-Mother wrote to Pope Pius IV, who had just convoked the Council for a third series of sessions, to arrange some liturgical changes in order to show her good faith. Protestant persons and property were preserved from violence, and placed under the protection of the law. Feigning ignorance of the Council of Trent's preliminary decisions, the failure of all Charles V's efforts and the rigidity of the Roman attitude, Catherine and her chancellor hoped that a conference, at which representatives of the different Christian confessions might express their opinions clearly and freely, would engender a *rapprochement*, or at least a truce. This conference was held at *Poissy* in the autumn of 1561. The Protestant communities within the kingdom had chosen twelve delegates. Calvin sent Theodore Beza, who put his case with moderation, but who, in explaining the Genevan thesis on the Eucharist, maintained that the Body and Blood of Christ were as far removed from the consecrated bread and wine as the highest heaven from earth. The aged Cardinal de Tournon protested that this was blasphemy. After recalling the Catholic catechism, Cardinal de Lorraine skilfully argued a case to prove how varied were the Protestant Churches, by showing that, so far as the Real Presence was concerned, the Calvinists were no more capable of coming to an agreement with the Lutherans than with the Catholics. Finally two emissaries from the Curia arrived in the persons of Cardinal Ippolito d'Este and Lainez, General of the Jesuits. The latter flew into a violent rage, calling the Protestants 'wolves, serpents and assassins.' This harshness was undoubtedly both deliberate and calculated. Realizing how such excesses displeased the queen-mother, Cardinal de Lorraine suggested inviting the German theologians to the meeting. Beza announced that he did not agree with their doctrine, and the conference ended without result.

The old antagonisms were accentuated afresh. François de Guise came to terms with the Constable de Montmorency, who had an enormous feudal following at his disposal, and with Marshal de Saint-André. This 'triumvirate,' which knew it could count on the support of the majority of Catholic France, and particularly the peasantry, decided that it would not tolerate any increase of heresy in the future. Encouraged by the Parlement of Paris and the King of Spain, it was determined to oppose the policy of conciliation. On the other hand, the

Bourbons, who regarded Michel de l'Hôpital simply as a politician and nothing more, were not averse to the idea of upholding the cause of Calvinism by force of arms.

However, the royal government stubbornly continued to look for compromise solutions. Catherine de' Medici, who was deeply impressed by the success of the Reformation in Europe, and also moved by the courage of Jeanne d'Albret who had come to live with her at Saint-Germain, where she regularly attended Calvinist services, was intent on defining the limits within which Protestants in France could be permitted freedom of worship. The edict of 7th January 1562, known as the *January Edict*, granted them this freedom anywhere except inside fortified towns, and even within the walls of such places they were allowed to meet in the houses of specially designated persons.

This policy of moderation had not the slightest chance of succeeding. Acts of violence occurred on all sides: at Montpellier the Protestants killed fifteen Catholics in the cathedral itself. On 1st March an affray in Champagne precipitated civil war. The Duke of Guise was returning from Saverne, where he had held a meeting with the Lutheran Duke of Württemberg, probably with the intention of preventing the German rulers from supporting the French Huguenots. At *Vassy*, not far from the family estates which the Lorraines owned at Joinville, the duke's army came upon a Protestant meeting: about a thousand people were spilling out into the streets, listening to a sermon there. The city was a fortified one, yet the service had the character of a public meeting. François's men wished to pass; the duke advanced, to be met by a hail of stones. His followers immediately charged and hacked a bloody passage for their convoy.

This was the signal for the tragedy to begin. Within a few weeks the whole realm was in a state of tumult. The Guises took charge of the young king and his mother; Condé set up his headquarters in Orleans and proclaimed himself 'defender of the French crown.' Massacres, looting and pitched battles laid waste the provinces. The *Wars of Religion* had started: they were to last for thirty-six years.

THE DECISIVE YEARS: IN ENGLAND MARY TUDOR MAKES CATHOLICISM HATED

Thus in both Germany and France politics was taking precedence over properly religious intentions. What of England, where a king's political decision alone had been enough to cause the breach with Rome? The situation there was one of extreme complexity, oscillating between Anglican, Calvinist and Catholic intransigence. Under Henry

VIII and Edward VI the personality of the sovereign (or, in the latter case, of his regents) had played a decisive part in determining the nation's religious inclinations; and this pattern of behaviour was to be repeated yet again under the queen whom the order of succession now called to the throne (6th June 1553). Her name was *Mary Tudor*.

Mary was the daughter of Henry VIII by Catherine of Aragon. Though no longer young, she was still unmarried. She was a sour-faced, tight-lipped woman, who lacked not goodness, but charm. In many ways she was a typical Tudor. She had her father's deep voice, wonderful eloquence and innate sense of authority, and she came to the throne absolutely determined to carry out certain operations of capital importance. She made no secret of her preferences. 'I would far rather lose ten crowns than put my soul in peril,' she said. Mary had been brought up in the Spanish-tinted Catholicism of her mother, and had demonstrated her courage during the period of the Schism and the triumph of heresy. Her semi-captivity and sufferings had given her an aura of glamour. The English nation accepted her willingly. Northumberland attempted to oppose her by putting Lady Jane Grey, one of Henry VIII's young nieces, on the throne. All to no purpose: he was executed for his pains.

The first acts of the new reign were a clear indication that it was Mary's definite intention to bring her country back to the Catholic faith. Although the queen exhorted her subjects to live together 'in peace and love, shunning those devilish new words, papist and heretic,' she freed bishops Bonner and Gardiner, who had accepted the Henrician schism. But she refused to bow to Calvinism, and sent to the Tower Thomas Cranmer, Archbishop of Canterbury, who had inspired the religious policy in the years preceding her accession. While she allowed Edward VI's funeral rites to be celebrated in the Anglican fashion, she herself was not present. Instead she preferred to hear a Requiem Mass for her deceased half-brother, and she asked the Pope for permission to be crowned at Westminster Abbey in accordance with ancient custom. At the end of the year Parliament annulled all the religious laws which had been passed under Edward, while the Convocation of Canterbury acknowledged 'the Real Presence of Jesus Christ in the Sacrament of the Altar' and thrust aside the Genevan catechism.

Mary was full of good intentions, but she was naïve and clumsy in her methods. In order to gain her ends she would have needed infinite tact and prudence. The advice she was given was not always of the best. Her beloved uncle, Charles V, advised her not to show 'over-zealous haste' and to confine herself to practising in her private life those Christian virtues—that ardent piety and fasting—which were the admiration of her *entourage*. These were wise counsels, but they lost

much of their weight when the emperor caused his niece to commit a
blatant political mistake. The most influential figure of the reign was
Reginald Pole (1500–58), who had protested strongly against the
martyrdom of St Thomas More, and who, from his Italian refuge, had
even tried to provoke foreign intervention to avenge his friend's death.
Pole was the new queen's cousin, a man of monastic piety and meditation, but at the same time a notable humanist whose courage and
eloquence had won him high prestige. He had lived in Italy since
Henry VIII's divorce, when royal attempts to win him over had called
forth a vigorous treatise in reply, the *Pro Ecclesiasticae unitatis
defensione* in which Pole had advised the rebel to repent and submit to
the Pope. Despite his protests at the thought of the 'manifest peril' in
which such an elevation would place his family, Pole was created
cardinal by Paul III. Since 1537 he had borne the title 'Legate of
England,' as the result of which Henry VIII had set a price on his head.
Reginald Pole was a far from violent man. In Italy, where he had
helped Cardinals Sadolet and Contarini to prepare an agenda for the
future Council, intransigents like Cardinal Carafa had considered him
far too half-hearted; and having refused to apply certain repressive
measures within his bishopric of Viterbo, and having tried in vain to
persuade the Council of Trent to accept his views, he had retired to
the Benedictine monastery of Maguzzano, on the shores of Lake Garda.
He was still there when a papal summons, requested by Mary Tudor
and confirming his legation, entrusted him with the task of reconciling
his native land to the Roman Church. This shrewd, gentle humanist
might well have succeeded in this mammoth task had his action not
been obstructed by his sovereign's ill-advised severity. At Mary's
accession Pole had written her a letter naïvely comparing her with the
Blessed Virgin! Such an exalted personage could obviously not be
crossed.

But even before Pole arrived in England, Charles V's intervention
had fatally compromised the situation. The emperor was extremely
anxious to marry his niece to his own son, the Infante Philip, in order
to put England fairly and squarely in the Hapsburg military and
political camp. His ambassador, the aptly named Simon Renard, one
of the many natives of Franche-Comté whose services the emperor
used, arranged the matter with considerable skill. Titian's portrait of
the Spanish suitor (which can be seen in Madrid today) easily convinced the virgin queen that this handsome young man with the
prominent chin would make an excellent husband. In the meantime, as
the result of detailed inquiries, Renard was advising his master not to
link the Anglo-Spanish alliance with the queen's cherished religious
operation. But it was quite impossible to prevent public opinion from
believing that the return to Roman obedience was to be the most

important clause in this alliance. The consequences were to be enormous. This Spanish marriage ran counter to all the national feeling, suspicious insularity and independence of the English nation, and for centuries to come it was to bring discredit upon Catholicism, which was henceforth regarded as an alien faith.

Thus Mary Tudor's tragedy can be summed up in a few pitifully simple facts: a queen whose personal choice dictated the religion of her kingdom, who would have needed a long life and consummate skill to restore spiritual peace, but who was endowed only with blind courage and frail health; a legate who understood the susceptibility of the English completely, and who was determined to use moderation and patience, but who was occasionally carried away by his own mystical fervour and embarrassed by the action of the queen and her supporters; a husband and father-in-law who belonged to the most powerful Catholic family in Europe, and whose origin alone made them suspect to the English nation; a people which was in the main willing to return to the fold of the ancient Church to which it remained attached in its heart of hearts, but anxious on the score of national independence, hostile to the Curia and ready to protest at the least sign of foreign influence. The rebels of the winter of 1553–4 were well aware that the confusion of national honour and religious faith was an effective way of retaining England in the Protestant camp. They protested against the 'invasion of the realm by foreigners,' and attempted to place on the throne Henry VIII's daughter by Anne Boleyn, who was considered to have Protestant sympathies. Thomas Wyatt, a Kentish squire, brought his followers to the very gates of London, but Mary surmounted the crisis; the rebels were crushed and then beheaded (including the wretched little Jane Grey, an innocent pawn of sixteen, daughter of the Duke of Suffolk, one of the leaders of the affair). Elizabeth, Mary's half-sister, was clever enough to prevent any personal intervention on her part from being discovered. She was not executed, but was kept under restraint for a few months at Whitehall, then in the Tower, and finally relegated to the royal manor at Woodstock. On 25th July on the feast of St James, Spain's patron saint, the Queen of England married Prince Philip of Spain in Winchester Cathedral. The Spaniard sacrificed his personal feelings in the interests of his country; he was a joyless bridegroom.

One important question remained unresolved: the fate of all the ecclesiastical possessions which had been given away or sold since 1537. As in the case of those who acquired national property during the French Revolution, a whole class of property owners was an interested party in the Schism, which had afforded it an opportunity of doing some profitable business. Charles V was kept accurately informed of the situation by Renard. The emperor was not in the habit of stinting the Holy See, but he considered that in this case restitution was impracticable, a view later taken in France by Napoleon I when negotiating his Concordat with the Pope. Charles was determined that the reconciliation between England and Rome should be arranged in accordance with his personal views. He let the Pope know that he would allow the legate to travel to England provided only that Pole was given sufficient authority to acknowledge the permanent alienation of the properties of the English Church. Dominated by a clique of rigorists, Julius III tried to gain time by employing the legate on a mediatory mission between the emperor and the King of France. But the legate was growing impatient, and the pontiff admitted that since the Church could dispose of her goods in order to ransom prisoners, she was even more justified in sacrificing them for the salvation of an entire kingdom. The English Parliament then agreed to Pole's mission, and the legate landed at Dover on 21st November 1554. On the 24th he sailed up the Thames to London, followed by a triumphal procession. Mary and Philip welcomed him at Whitehall, the king-consort at the door, the queen at the head of the stairs. On the 27th Pole reminded Parliament of its country's ancient loyalty to the Roman faith, and of the limits beyond which the temporal authority might not go. On the 30th the assembly begged its sovereigns to acquaint the representative of the Apostolic See with the fact of its repentance, and solicit his pardon. Lords and commons knelt while the cardinal pronounced the words of solemn absolution, first in Latin and then in English, over the prostrate figures of Philip and Mary. The *Te Deum* rang out. All the Catholic glories of the past blazed into life once more. The following day twenty-five thousand worshippers packed St Paul's and its precincts, falling on their knees to receive the Apostolic Blessing. On 3rd January 1555 all the legislation which had been enacted against the Church by Henry VIII and Edward VI was annulled.

The House of Commons, which had just been elected, was at this juncture rather like the French 'House of Peers' at a later date. It was passionately anxious to punish all who had been party to the Schism, and Mary's second error was her failure to restrain these blind avengers. The laws enacted against the Lollards in days gone by were revived. Pole thought it wise to entrust judgment in this matter to a commission of bishops. The bishops, however, who had accepted Henry VIII's breach with Rome in the past, were anxious to be forgiven their own fall from grace. They showed no mercy of any kind towards those who rejected reconciliation, and were especially hard on anyone with Calvinist connections. The fires were lit once more. Philip intervened and, through his own chaplain, condemned the excessive violence. The man who was to show himself implacably opposed to any tolerance in

Spain counselled clemency in England. Thanks to his representations, Elizabeth enjoyed a less strict regime; Philip preferred that she should succeed his wife rather than the Queen of Scotland, Mary Stuart, who was affianced to Francis, the Dauphin of France. But in August 1555 Philip was summoned to Brussels to be present at his father's abdication. He was away for twenty months, and his absence was to have unfortunate consequences.

The persecution was redoubled. Now perished most of the 277 victims whose trials and executions are related by John Foxe in the *Book of Martyrs*. This work was read almost as much as the Bible in English households during the next two centuries, but it contains a number of exaggerations. The queen became known as 'Bloody Mary'; the nickname was to stick. Those bishops who had been willing participants in the Schism perished. At Oxford, Latimer, Bishop of Worcester, spoke his celebrated words to Ridley, Bishop of London, to whom he was chained: 'Be of good cheer, Master Ridley, and show yourself a man. By God's grace we shall today light a candle in England that I am confident will never be put out.' Although excommunicated and degraded, Cranmer attempted to save his life by signing no fewer than six abjurations in which he recognized papal supremacy; but on 21st March 1556, when asked to address the people before the torch was set to the stake, he showed one last spark of honour. He disowned everything he had been inspired to do by fear of death, and held his right hand steadily in the flames so that, as he said, it would be the first to suffer for his shameful retractions.

Meanwhile Pole was reorganizing the English Church. Having been appointed Archbishop of Canterbury and Primate, he had a council prepare a body of measures known as the *Reformatio Angliae*. The parish clergy were showered with a collection of homilies and a general exposition of the Catholic faith, in order to provide for the most urgent necessities of preaching; a detailed ruling laid down the age, studies and qualities essential to clerics; pluralism was prohibited; residence in the benefice was strongly recommended; bishops were urged to visit their dioceses and instruct their flocks. Simultaneously with the prudent disciplinary reform thus proposed for the seculars, the monks returned. But although Pole kept the universities under strict surveillance, he resisted the introduction of the Roman Inquisition and he declined Ignatius of Loyola's suggestion to send some young English priests to Rome to join the Society of Jesus.

Alongside these developments in England, the Irish Catholics obtained the recognition of the rights which they had so zealously defended. Archbishop Dowdall returned to his see of Armagh and became primate once more. All the heretics' work was destroyed and the faithless bishops deposed. A provincial council started reforming the Irish Church, following the pattern set by the Council of Trent. The Irish would have had nothing but praise for Mary Tudor had she not, at the very same time, made a serious attempt to anglicize their island, which she had persuaded the Pope to elevate into a kingdom. She established far too many English colonists there, thus allowing national antagonism to subsist, and even increase, after religious antagonism had disappeared.

The accession to the Papacy of Paul IV, leader of the intransigent party in Rome, and the vicissitudes of her European policy, inclined Mary and her advisers towards measures of severity. The Neapolitan Pope, anxious to free the kingdom of Naples from Spanish tutelage, formed an alliance with France and declared war on Spain. Philip II forced his wife's kingdom to lend him assistance despite the opposition of the Privy Council. The angry Paul IV, considering him too weak, deprived Pole of his powers as legate *a latere*, replaced him by an aged Franciscan, William Peto, and even summoned him to appear before the Holy Office in Rome. Mary Tudor detained the cardinal, who raised an indignant protest; and it must be admitted that this was a strange way to treat a prelate who had restored a whole kingdom to the Papacy. But on the Continent Guise's French troops were occupying Calais, England's last foothold in France. Had England implored the Pope's forgiveness in order to endure humiliation such as this? Rumbles of anger could be heard throughout the kingdom: Catholicism and loyalty to Rome were becoming synonymous with treason and defeatism. Distressed by her husband's constant absence on the Continent, Mary was mortally stricken by the news of the disaster in France. 'Were my heart opened,' she murmured, 'Calais would be found engraved upon it.' She died on 17th November 1558, and on the selfsame day, as if he and his sovereign were indeed one heart and one soul, Cardinal Pole too gave up the ghost. Both had served the Church selflessly, faithfully and courageously, but an implacable combination of errors had rendered all their work worthless. Catholicism in England had lost many of the roots which it had still retained five years earlier. The ground was well prepared for Elizabeth—whom Philip II recognized out of hatred for Mary Stuart, Dauphine of France—and, with her, for Protestant Anglicanism.

ON THE BRINK OF ATROCIOUS CARNAGE

Thus, by about 1560, towards the close of those decisive years in which determinant positions had been taken, the fate of the Reformation everywhere no longer rested on the result of a spiritual debate, but was dependent upon governments and political parties. Right from the very beginning Luther's spiritual revolt had let loose material greed. The German rulers, the Scandinavian monarchs and Henry VIII of England had all taken advantage of the break from papal tutelage to appropriate both the wealth and the control of their respective Churches. It is significant that the very word which described the sort of Christianity, 'Protestantism' (albeit at the price of a translator's error![1]), originated with an event which was essentially political, not religious—a protest by the princes and free cities against the emperor's change of tactics at Spires in 1529. The deterioration of 'mystique' into politics was abundantly clear. And it is hard to recall that these profane calculations had been authorized by the disinterested quest of spirits seeking for the truth, and that the success of the Reformation had in the first place been the adhesion of millions of Christians to a faith which was exciting precisely because it was stripped of worldly taint.

But accusations are fruitless. This evolution was inevitable. Unless they resigned themselves to being destroyed, sooner or later, the heretics were bound to form alliances with one another, organize and defend themselves. The role accorded the secular authorities in the Wittenberg system had been the logical consequence of a situation which threatened to plunge the whole of Germany into anarchy. By adopting a political structure the German Reformation saved itself from mortal danger, but at the same time it gave birth to an antagonism which the Thirty Years War was to make tragically apparent many years later. Likewise, when Calvinism was threatened by the established authorities, it could hardly rest content with the heroic protests of its martyrs, under pretext that the Master of Geneva had enjoined respect for these selfsame powers. Surely it was by virtue of no secret and suggestive law of correspondence that the struggle of the Protestant coalition against the Catholic emperor broke out in Germany a few weeks after Luther's death. And why, when Calvin died, was England on the point of passing from Catholic orthodoxy to that of Geneva, while in France the Catholic party and the Calvinist party were polishing their swords in readiness for a frightful civil war? The spiritual revolution, which had burst forth like a flame in the soul of Martin Luther, was henceforth to be at the mercy of intrigue, alliances and ordeal by battle. And that 'atrocious carnage' which Erasmus had foreseen as the logical consequence of the rebellion was about to drench the whole Christian world in blood.

Naturally, in the last resort, face to face with God, the decisive option is taken in the sanctuary of each individual conscience, since the

---

[1] A translator's error, for the expression in the Spires manifesto, '*Protestati sumus*,' should correctly be translated as: 'We testify. . . .' Many Protestants have deplored the continued currency of a word which seems to give their doctrine a negative meaning. (Cf. Wilfrid Monod, Raoul Stéphan.)

price of a soul is worth more than the domination of the universe. And it would be wrong to regard all those who were to support the cause of heresy, even at the sacrifice of their own lives, as nothing but ambitious schemers. But the historian is sadly limited to the facts that are self-evident; and henceforth his account of the religious history of divided Christian Europe returns again and again to alliances, battles and treaties, rather than to theology, mysticism and spiritual adventure. Protestantism would join battle as a political force, and this collision would be all the more terrible in that the Catholic Church, having at last recovered possession of herself, had in the meantime regrouped her forces, restored her discipline and united around her leader. The stakes had been cast for the final game.

CHRONOLOGICAL TABLE

FOURTEENTH CENTURY

DATE	HISTORY OF THE CHURCH	POLITICAL AND SOCIAL HISTORY	ARTS, LITERATURE AND SCIENCE
50		The Turks set foot in Europe. John the Good, King of France (1350–63).	Boccaccio (1313–75).
52	Innocent VI (1352–62).	The Golden Bull does away with all papal participation in imperial elections. Battle of Poitiers.	
60		Treaty of Bretigny. Murad I, Sultan (1360–89).	
61	Death of Tauler (b. 1290).		
63	Urban V (1362–70).	Charles V, King of France (1363–80). In Russia, Prince Dmitri of Moscow (1363–81).	Guillaume de Machaut's *Mass* (1300–77).
64			Foundation of Cracow University.
65	Death of Henry Suso (b. 1295).		Foundation of Vienna University.
66		The Count of Savoy's crusade.	
69		Death of Peter de Lusignan, King of Cyprus.	
70	Gregory XI (1370–8).		
73	Death of St Bridget of Sweden (1302–73).		
74			Death of Petrarch.
77	*Return of Gregory XI to Rome, end of the papal exile in Avignon.*	Richard II, King of England (1377–99).	
78	*Beginning of the Great Schism in the West.* Urban VI, Pope of Rome (1378–89). Clement VII, Pope of Avignon (1378–94).		
80	Death of St Catherine of Siena (b. 1347).	Charles VI, King of France (1380–1422). The Mongols defeat Dmitri's Russian armies at Kulikovo.	
81	Birth of St Colette. Death of Ruysbroek (b. 1293).	Peasants' Revolt in England.	
82	Condemnation of Wyclif (b. 1328, d. 1384).	Flemings crushed at Roosebeke.	
84	Death of G. de Groote (b. 1340); formation of Brethren of the Common Life.		
86		Swiss victory at Sempach.	Foundation of Heidelberg University.

DATE	HISTORY OF THE CHURCH	POLITICAL AND SOCIAL HISTORY	ARTS, LITERATURE AN SCIENCE
1387	The canons of Windesheim.		
1389	Boniface IX, Pope of Rome (1389–1404).	Serbs defeated by the Turks at Kossovo. Bajazet becomes Sultan (1389–1402).	
1390	Foundation of the Hierony- mites.		P. de Mezières's *The Drean the Old Pilgrim.*
1391		Manuel II, Emperor of Byzan- tium (1391–1425).	
1392		Madness of Charles VI of France.	
1394	Benedict XII, Pope of Avi- gnon (deposed 1417; *d.* 1422).		
1396		Death of Emperor John V Palaeologus (1341–96). *Defeat of the Crusade at Nicopolis.*	Claus Sluter (1360–1406)
1399		Accession of the House of Lancaster in England, Henry IV (1399–1413).	Thomas à Kempis (138 1471).

FIFTEENTH CENTURY

DATE	HISTORY OF THE CHURCH	POLITICAL AND SOCIAL HISTORY	ARTS, LITERATURE AN SCIENCE
1400			*The Imitation of Jesus Chr*
1401		Tamberlane defeats Bajazet at Ankara.	*Flamboyant Art* in France 1400–20, the manuscripts the Duc de Berry. Jean de Béthencourt sails the Canaries.
1402	Birth of Denys the Carthusian (*d.* 1471).		
1404	Innocent VII, Pope of Rome (1404–6).		
1405	John Huss (*b.* 1368) preaching in Bohemia.		
1406	Gregory XII (Pope of Rome; deposed 1417).		Brunelleschi (1377–144 architect of the cupola St Mary's cathedral, Fl ence. Ghiberti(1378–145 Fra Angelico (1378–145
1409	Council of Pisa: three popes now in office at once. Alex- ander V, Pope of Pisa (1409–10).		Foundation of Leipzig U versity.
1410	John XXIII, Pope of Pisa (deposed 1415, *d.* 1419). St Bernardino of Siena (1380–1444).	Sigismund, King of Germany, crowned emperor 1432, *d.* 1437. Polish victory at Tannenberg.	Poggio (1380–1459). Pie d'Ailly's *Mirror of World.*
1413		Henry V, King of England (1413–22).	
1414	Council of Constance (1414– 1417). Execution of John Huss.		

TE	HISTORY OF THE CHURCH	POLITICAL AND SOCIAL HISTORY	ARTS, LITERATURE AND SCIENCE
4			Henry the Navigator (1394–1460) established at Sagres. Donatello (1386–1466). The Portuguese reach Cape Bojador.
7	*End of the Great Schism, election of Martin V (1417–1431).*		
9	Death of St Vincent Ferrer (*b.* 1357). St Antoninus (1389–1459).	Beginning of the Hussite Wars (first defenestration of Prague).	The Portuguese in Madeira.
0		Treaty of Troyes.	Death of Pierre d'Ailly (*b.* 1350).
2		Charles VII, King of France (1422–61). Henry VI, King of England (1422–61).	
	St John Capistrano (1393–1456).		
5		John VIII, Emperor of Byzantium (1425–48).	
9		Capture of Orleans by Joan of Arc. Coronation of Charles VII at Rheims (17th July).	Death of John Gerson (*b.* 1363).
0			Death of Christina of Pisa (*b.* 1367). Luca della Robbia (1400–81).
1	*Eugenius IV (1431–47).* Council of Basle.	*Death of Joan of Arc, burnt at Rouen (31st May).*	
4		The Medicis at Florence.	
6	Foundation of the Oblates by St Frances of Rome.		Alberti (1466–70).
8	Felix V, the last antipope (1438–43).	Pragmatic Sanction of Bourges.	The first complete manuscript of Plato reaches the West.
0		The epic stand of John Hunyadi against the Turks. In Germany, Frederick III of Hapsburg (1440–93).	
4	Death of St Bernardino of Siena (*b.* 1380).	Christian defeat at Varna.	
5			The work of Alain Chartier (1390–1450). The Portuguese reach Cape Verde. P. della Francesca (1416–92). Creation of the Vatican Library.
7	Nicholas V (1447–55). Death of St Colette.	St Francis of Paola (1416–1507).	
8	Concordat of Vienna.	Constantine XI, last Emperor of Byzantium (1448–53).	
0			*Invention of the Printing Press.* *The Passion* of Arnould Gréban. Benozzo Gozzoli (1420–97).
1		Mohammed II, Sultan (1451–1481).	Platina (1421–81) and the Roman Academy.

DATE	HISTORY OF THE CHURCH	POLITICAL AND SOCIAL HISTORY	ARTS, LITERATURE AND SCIENCE
1453		*Capture of Constantinople by the Turks. End of the Hundred Years War* (battle of Castillon).	
1454		League of Lodi.	
1455	Callixtus III Borgia (1455–1458).	In England, the Wars of the Roses (1455–85). Belgrade liberated by John Hunyadi.	
1456	Rehabilitation of Joan of Arc.		
1457		Christian naval victory of Metelina.	
1458	Pius II (Aeneas Sylvius Piccolomini) (1458–64).		
1460			The work of François Ville (1431–6?).
1461		Louis XI, King of France (1461–83).	Bellini (1430–1516). Scho gauer (1430–91). Ma tegna (1431–1506).
1462		In Russia, Ivan III (1462–1505).	
1464	Paul II (1464–71).		Marsilio Ficino (1433–99 Memling (1433–94). Dea of Nicholas of Cusa (1401). Verrocchio (143 1488).
1469		Marriage of Ferdinand of Aragon and Isabella of Castile.	
1471	Sixtus IV (1471–84).	Turkish advance guards in the West (at Otranto in 1480).	The Portuguese cross t Equator.
1472		Ivan III marries Sophia, heiress of the Palaelogues.	
			Bramante (1444–1514). *Bo ticelli* (1444–1510).
1477	St Catherine of Genoa (1447–1510).	End of the House of Burgundy (death of Charles the Bold).	
1478	Bull instituting the Inquisition in Spain.	Assassination of Giulio de Medici in Florence.	
1480		End of Mongol domination in Russia.	Signorelli (1450–1523). Hi ronymus Bosch (1450 1516).
1481		Death of Mohammed II, rivalry of Bajazet II and Djem.	
1483	Birth of Luther at Eisleben.		*Leonardo da Vinci* (145 1519).
1484	Innocent VIII (1484–92). Franciscan mission to the Congo.		
1485		Accession of Henry VII Tudor in England. In Florence, striking domination of Lorenzo the Magnificent.	Carpaccio (1455–1526 Reuchlin (1455–1522).

DATE	HISTORY OF THE CHURCH	POLITICAL AND SOCIAL HISTORY	ARTS, LITERATURE AND SCIENCE
1487			Bartholomew Diaz reaches the Cape of Good Hope.
1488	Codification of measures against witchcraft and sorcery.		
1490			Mathias Grünewald (1466–1528).
1491	Appearance of the Blessed Virgin at 'The Three Ears of Corn.' Birth of St Ignatius.	The Capetian Crown annexes Brittany: end of the great fiefs in France. Charles VIII, King of France (1491–1498).	
1492	*Alexander VI Borgia.*	*Capture of Granada by the Catholic Sovereigns of Spain.*	*Christopher Columbus discovers North America.*
1493		Alexander VI divides the New World between Spain and Portugal. Beginning of the wars in Italy.	Pico della Mirandola (1463–1494).
1494		Battle of Fornovo.	*Erasmus (1466–1536).* Quentin Matsys (1466–1538). Guillaume Budé (1467–1540).
1497			Cabot discovers Labrador.
1498	Savonarola executed at Florence.	Louis XII, King of France (1498–1515).	Vasco da Gama discovers the maritime route to India.
1499			*Bramante is summoned to Rome to rebuild St Peter's.*

SIXTEENTH CENTURY

DATE	HISTORY OF THE CHURCH	POLITICAL AND SOCIAL HISTORY	ARTS, LITERATURE AND SCIENCE
1500		Birth of Charles V.	Machiavelli (1469–1527). *Albert Dürer (1471–1528).* Lucas Cranach (1472–1553).
1503	Pius III (Sept.–Oct.). *Julius II (1503–13).*		
1504	Bartholomew Las Casas (1474–1566) begins his apostleship.		Amerigo Vespucci in 'America.'
1508		League of Cambrai.	*Michelangelo (1475–1564). Titian (1477–1574).*
1509	Birth of Calvin.	French victory at Agnadello. The Holy League against the French. *Henry VIII, King of England (1509–1547).*	
1511	Luther's visit to Rome. Creation of the diocese of San Domingo in the Antilles.		Erasmus's *In Praise of Folly.*
1512	Publication of the Polyglot Bible. Opening of the 5th Oecumenical Lateran Council (1512–17).	Victory and death of Gaston de Foix at Ravenna.	

DATE	HISTORY OF THE CHURCH	POLITICAL AND SOCIAL HISTORY	ARTS, LITERATURE AND SCIENCE
1513	*Leo X (1513–21).* Creation of the first diocese in America (Darien in Panama).		*Raphael (1483–1520).*
1515		*Francis I, King of France (1515–47).* Victory of Marignano.	
1516	Concordat of Francis I.	Perpetual peace between France and Switzerland.	
1517	*The Affair of the Indulgences* (31st October). At Rome, development of the Oratory of Divine Love.		
1518	*Zwingli (1484–1531)* in Switzerland. Leo X consecrates Henri, the first Negro bishop, in the Congo.		
1519		*Charles V, emperor.*	Magellan sails round world (1519–22). Fernando Cortez conqu Mexico.
1520	*Luther breaks with Rome.* Bull 'Exsurge Domine.'	Solyman the Magnificent (1520–66).	
1521	Luther translates the Bible at the Wartburg.		
1522	*Adrian VI (1522–3).*	Marguerite of Navarre (1492–1549) exercises great influence in France.	Luis Vives (1492–1540).
1523	*Clement VII (1523–34). Lefèvre d'Étaples* and Briçonnet: the Meaux group. St Ignatius at Manresa.	Gustavus Vasa, King of Sweden (1523–60).	Paracelsus (1493–1541).
1524	Oeclampadius at Basle. Bucer at Strasbourg. Sweden passes to Lutheranism. Creation of the Theatines.		*Corregio (1494–1534).* E mus's *Free Will.*
1525	Luther's marriage. The Meaux group is dispersed. St Louis Bertrand in Colombia.	Battle of Pavia. Francis I taken prisoner. Peasants' War in Germany.	Luther's *Servile Will.* Ra lais (1495–1553).
1526	Foundation of the Capuchins.	Albert of Brandenburg secularizes the estates of the Teutonic Knights. Battle of Mohacs, capture of most of Hungary by the Turks.	Clément Marot (1496–15
1527		The sack of Rome.	Melanchthon (1497–15 *Veronese (1528–88).*
1529	The 'Protestants' in Germany. In France, execution of Louis de Berquin.	Diet of Spires.	
1530	*Confession of Augsburg.* Protestantism penetrates France.		
1531		War of the Swiss cantons. Death of Zwingli. In Germany, the Schmalkaldic League.	

TE	HISTORY OF THE CHURCH	POLITICAL AND SOCIAL HISTORY	ARTS, LITERATURE AND SCIENCE
32		Peace of Nuremberg between the emperor and the German princes.	First book of *Gargantua*. Pizarro and Almagro in Peru.
33	Henry VIII of England breaks with Rome. Calvin is converted to Protestantism. Foundation of the Barnabites. In India, creation of the bishopric of Goa.		
34	*Paul III* (1534–49). *The Placard Affair in Paris*. St Ignatius at Montmartre.	The 'Capitulations' assure France's position in the Middle East.	Jacques Cartier in Canada. Primatizzio (1504–70).
35	The Anabaptist tragedy in Münster. Calvin at Basle. Denmark becomes Lutheran. Martyrdom of St Thomas More.		Melanchthon's *Loci communes*.
36	Calvin publishes the *Christian Institution* in Latin. First period in Geneva (1536–8).	New war between Charles V and Francis I. Francis I allies with the Turks.	
37	*St Ignatius of Loyola founds the Society of Jesus.*	*Ivan IV the Terrible is 'Tsar' of Russia* (1537–84).	
38	Calvin at Strasbourg, where he prepares the French translation of the *Christian Institution* (published 1541).	Truce of Nice between Charles V and Francis I.	
40	Foundation of the Brethren of St John of God. Paul III authorizes Society of Jesus. *St Francis Xavier* (1506–1552) sets off on his mission.		Jean Goujon (1510?–1568). Pierre Lescot (1510–76). Bernard Palissy (1510–1590). Goudimel (1510–1572).
41	Calvin at Geneva again.	Charles V's defeat before Algiers. Interim of Ratisbon between Charles V and the princes.	
42	Creation of the *Roman Inquisition*.		
44		Peace of Crépy between Charles V and Francis I.	
45	*Council of Trent* (13th December, first session).		Philibert Delorme (1515–1570).
46	Death of Luther (18th February). Massacre of the Waldenses in Provence.	Charles V fights the German Lutheran princes.	
47		*Henry II, King of France* (1547–59). Edward VI, King of England (1547–1553).	Ambroise Paré (1517–90).
49	The first 'Prayer Book.' England glides towards heresy. St Francis Xavier goes to Japan.	Beginning of the 'Reductions' in Paraguay.	
0	*Julius III* (1550–55).		
1		Edict of Châteaubriant.	
2	Suspension of the Council of Trent. Deaths of St Ignatius and St Francis Xavier.		Joachim du Bellay (1522–1560).

DATE	HISTORY OF THE CHURCH	POLITICAL AND SOCIAL HISTORY	ARTS, LITERATURE AND SCIENCE
1553	Calvin secures the condemnation of Michael Servetus at Geneva. The 'Conversion of St Teresa of Avila.'	Mary Tudor, Queen of England (1553–8).	
1555	Marcellus II (April). *Paul IV* (1555–9). Defeat of Mary Tudor's attempt to restore Catholicism in England.		Ronsard (1524–85).
1556		Charles V retires to Yuste. *Philip II* (1556–89), King of Spain. Ferdinand in Austria, then emperor.	*Palestrina's* masterpiece (1526–94).
1557	Calvinism triumphs in Hungary.	French defeat at St Quentin.	
1558	The Index.	*Death of Charles V. Elizabeth I, Queen of England* (1558–1603).	Paul IV has the nudes of Michelangelo's fresco veiled.
1559	*Pius IV* (1559–65). In France, rigorous measures against the Protestants, who hold their first Synod. John Knox in Scotland.	Treaty of Cateau-Cambrésis. Francis II, King of France (1559–60).	
1560	The Oratory is constituted around St Philip Neri.	Protestant conspiracy of Amboise. Charles X, King of France (1560–74), regency of Catherine de' Medici.	La Boétie (1530–63).
1561	Failure of the Conference of Poissy.		
1562	Guy de Bray introduces Calvinism into the Low Countries. New meeting of the Council of Trent. *St Teresa* (1515–82) founds the first reformed Carmelite house.	The riot at Vassy starts the Wars of Religion in France.	
1563	Close of the Council of Trent (4th December). In England, the Thirty-Nine Articles.		*Montaigne* (1533–92)
1564	Death of Calvin (27th May).		Death of Michelangelo.

SELECT BIBLIOGRAPHY

SELECT BIBLIOGRAPHY

It is hoped that the following selective list, which has been taken from M. Daniel-Rops's much more extensive bibliography in the French edition of his work, will be of value to French-speaking readers who wish to study aspects of the period described in greater detail from some of the author's own sources. Where possible, English translations are given. A further short list of English and American books on the period is added as an Appendix.

GENERAL WORKS (applicable to Chapters I—VII)

A. *Primarily secular.*

Peuples et civilisations: vol. vii, *La Fin du moyen âge* (in 2 parts); vol. viii, *Les Débuts de l'Âge moderne, la Renaissance et la Réforme,* by A. Renaudet.

Final volumes of the *Cambridge Medieval History.*

First volumes of the *Cambridge Modern History.*

Histoire générale des civilisations: vol. iv, by R. Mousnier, 1954.

J. Burckhardt: *The Renaissance in Italy,* 1875.

J. Huizinga: *The Waning of the Middle Ages,* 1924.

P. Renucci: *L'Aventure de l'humanisme européen au moyen âge,* 1953.

A. Hyma: *Renaissance and Reformation,* 1951.

R. Schneider and G. Cohen: *La Formation du génie moderne dans l'art de l'occident,* 1936.

B. *Primarily religious.*

L'Histoire de l'église, ed. A. Fliche and V. Martin: vol. xv, *L'Église et la Renaissance,* by R. Aubenas and R. Ricard; vol. xvi, *La Crise religieuse du XVIe siècle,* by E. de Moreau, P. Jourda and P. Janelle.

F. Mourret: *Histoire générale de l'église:* vol. v, *La Renaissance et la Réforme,* 1920.

L. F. A. von Pastor: *History of the Popes since the End of the Middle Ages* (Eng. trans., 1891–1938).

Cardinal Baudrillart: *L'Église catholique, la Renaissance et le Protestantisme,* 1905–28.

J. B. Bossuet: *L'Histoire des variations des église protestantes,* 1688.

CHAPTER I. A CRISIS OF AUTHORITY: THE SCHISM AND THE COUNCILS

E. DE LAGARDE: *La Naissance de l'esprit laïque au déclin du moyen âge*, vols. ii and iv, 1934 and 1942.

G. MOLLAT: *Les Papes d'Avignon*, 1949.

L. MIROT: *La Politique pontificale et le retour du Saint-Siège à Rome en 1376*, 1899.

G. SCHNÜRER: *L'Église et la civilisation au moyen âge*, 1935.

E. GILSON: *La Philosophie au moyen âge*, 1942.

R. FOLZ: *L'Idée d'Empire en Occident du V⁰ au XIV⁰ siècle*, 1953.

E. PERROY: *L'Angleterre et le Grand Schisme d'Occident*, 1933.

M. DE BOUARD: *France et Italie au temps due Grand Schisme*, 1935.

There are lives of St Catherine of Siena by J. Jörgensen, 1924, A. Lemonnyer, 1934, and A. Levasti, 1953.

Bishop Ameilh's rhyming account, *Le Voyage de Grégoire XI ramenant la Papauté d'Avignon à Rome*, has been translated into French, and commented upon, by Pierre Ronzy, 1952.

CHAPTER II. A CRISIS OF UNITY: CHRISTENDOM DISINTEGRATES AND LOSES THE EAST

R. PERNOUD: *Les Villes marchandes au XIV⁰ et XV⁰ siècles*, 1948.

B. VOYENNE: *Petite histoire de l'idée européene*, 1952.

G. SCHLUMBERGER: *Le Siège, la prise et le sac de Constantinople par les Turcs en 1453*, 1915.

BRIAN-CHANINOV: *L'Église russe*, 1924.

E. KRAKOWSKI: *L'Histoire de Russie*, 1954.

See also general histories of France, Germany, Italy and England.

There are lives and studies of Joan of Arc by P. Ayrolles, 1890, L. Petit du Julleville, 1900, and R. Pernoud (Eng. trans.: *The Retrial of Joan of Arc*), 1955.

CHAPTER III. A CRISIS IN THE SOUL: CHRISTIAN FOUNDATIONS BEGIN TO TOTTER

FATHER DENIFLE: *La Désolation des églises, monastères et hôpitaux de France pendant le guerre de cent ans*, 1897.

F. VERNET: *Spiritualité médiévale*, 1929.

E. BAUMANN: *L'Anneau d'or des grands mystiques*, 1924.

P. DE JAEGER: *Anthologie mystique*, 1933.

Life of St Colette by J. Goulven, 1952.

Life of Henry Suso by J. A. Bizet, 1946.

Life of Ruysbroeck by J. A. Bizet, 1946.

There are studies of the general body of Flemish mystics by E. Brugge-man, 1928, and P. Groult, 1926.

The *Imitation of Jesus Christ* has been translated into English and pub-lished by Dent/Dutton in the Everyman's Library series. See also: M. Lewandowski, *L'Auteur inconnu de l'Imitation*, 1940; H. Daniel-Rops, *Des Images de grandeur*, 1950.

A. FOREST, F. VAN STEENBERGHEN and M. DE GANDILLAC: *Le Mouvement doctrinale du IXᵉ au XIVᵉ siècle*, 1951.

E. MÂLE: *La Fin du moyen âge*, 1908.

L. LEFRANÇOIS-PILLON: *L'Art en France au XIVᵉ siècle*, 1954.

There are studies of Wyclif in English by R. L. Poole, 1911, and H. B. Workman, 1926.

There are lives (in German) of John Huss by Loserth, 1925, and F. Strunz, 1917. See also E. Denis, *Huss et la guerre des Hussites*, 1930.

Chapter IV. THE RENAISSANCE POPES

P. MONNIER: *Le Quattrocento* (new edition), 1936.

J. GUIRAUD: *L'Église et les origines de la Renaissance*, 1902.

F. HERMANS: *Histoire doctrinale de l'humanisme chrétien*, 1952.

G. SORANZO, *Studi intorno at Papa Alessandro VI Borgia*, 1951.

There are lives of Savonarola by G. Ridolfi, 1952, and O. Ferrara (in Italian), 1952; by M. Brion (in French), 1948.

There is a study of Machiavelli by M. Brion, 1948.

A. LEROY: *L'Histoire de la peinture religieuse*, 1954.

Chapter V. THE TRAGEDY OF MARTIN LUTHER

H. STROHL: *La Substance de l'évangile selon Luther*, 1934.

L. CRISTIANI and H. DANIEL-ROPS: *Luther tel qu'il fut*, 1955.

A. JUNOT: *Le Développement de la pensée religieuse de Luther jusqu'en 1517*, 1908.

IMBART DE LA TOUR: *Les Origines de la réforme* (revised edition), vol. ii, 1944.

G. TAVARD: *À la rencontre du Protestantisme*, 1954.

L. Cristiani: *Luther et la question sociale*, 1912.

E. Vermeil: *Réforme luthérienne et civilisation allemande*, 1924.

Catholic lives and studies of Luther include those by Father Denifle, 1904–6, Father Grisar, 1911–12, and L. Cristiani, 1908 and 1911.

Protestant lives and studies of Luther include those by A. von Harnack, 1917, and O. Scheel, 1930 (both in German), and J. Mackinnon, 1925–30 (in English). In French see Henry Strohl, *Luther, sa vie et sa pensée*, 1954, and also an independent Catholic work, L. Febvre, *Un destin, Martin Luther*, 1928.

There is a life of Zwingli by J. Courvoisier, 1953, of Bucer, by J. Erber, 1954 (in *Annuaire de Selestat*), and of Bullinger by A. Bouvier, 1940.

G. Walter: *Thomas Münzer et les luttes sociales a l'époque de la réforme*, 1937.

G. d'Aubarède: *La Révolution des saints*, 1946.

There are lives and studies of Erasmus by A. Renaudet, 1936, and J. Huizinga, 1955.

Chapter VI. THE SUCCESS OF JOHN CALVIN

P. Gaxotte: *L'Histoire des Français*.

L. Febvre: *Problème de l'irréligion au XVIe siècle*, 1942.

A. Renaudet: *Préréforme et humanisme à Paris pendant les premières guerres d'Italie*, 1916.

Imbart de la Tour: *Les Origines de la réforme* (revised edition), vols. i—iv, 1944.

N. Weiss: *La Chambre ardente*, 1887.

There are lives and studies of Lefèvre d'Étaples by J. Barnaud, 1936; of Marguerite of Navarre by A. Lefranc, 1900, and P. Jourda, 1930; and of Étienne Dolet by R. Coplet Christie (in English), 1886.

For Calvin's works see *Textes choisis*, ed. C. Gagnebin for *Le Cri de France*, with preface by Karl Barth, 1948.

L. Christiani and H. Daniel-Rops: *Calvin tel qu'il fut*, 1955.

There are studies of Calvin by E. Doumergue, 1899–1927, F. Wendel, 1950, J. D. Benoit, 1947, H. Bois, 1919, and E. Choisy, 1926. Some of these, notably Doumergue's work, have a marked anti-Catholic bias.

G. Goyau: *Genève, Ville-Église*, 1907.

A. Lefranc: *La Jeunesse de Calvin*, 1888.

J. Pannier: *Calvin écrivain*, 1936.

F. Wendel: *L'Église de Strasbourg*, 1942.

A. Favre-Dorsaz: *Calvin et Loyola*, 1951.

A. Hollard's study of Michael Servetus, 1945.

Chapter VII. FROM RELIGIOUS REVOLT TO POLITICAL PRO-TESTANTISM

E. G. Leonard: *Histoire du protestantisme*, 1950, and *Le Protestant français*, 1953.

L. Romier: *Les Origines politiques des guerres de religion*, 1913–14, and *Le Royaume de Catherine de Médicis; La France à la veille des guerres de religion*, 1922.

H. Hermelinck and W. Maurer: *Reformation und Gegenreformation*, 1931.

J. Lertz: *Die Reformation in Deutschland*, 1939–40.

J. Hoffman: *La Réforme en Suède et la succession apostolique*, 1945.

E. Rodocanachi: *La Réforme en Italie*, 1920–1.

Father de Moreau: *Histoire de l'église en Belgique*, vol. v.

Abbé G. Constant: *La Réforme en Angleterre*, vols. i and ii, 1930–9.

J. Gairdner: *The English Church in the XVIth Century*, 1924.

W. Schenck: *Reginald Pole, Cardinal of England*, 1950.

The outstanding life of St Thomas More is that by R. W. Chambers (in English), 1932. There are French lives by H. Brémond, 1920, and L. Lemonnier, 1948. St Thomas More's *Utopia* and *Dialogue of Comfort* are published by Dent/Dutton in the Everyman's Library series.

APPENDIX

Father P. Hughes: *A History of the Church* (2nd edition), 1948.

C. Dawson: *The Making of Europe*, 1932.

J. Atkins: *The Renascence*, 1957.

M. Deanesly: *A History of the Medieval Church*, 1925.

O. Gierke: *Political Theories of the Middle Ages* (Eng. trans.), 1900.

H. F. M. Prescott: *Jerusalem Journey*, 1954.

G. Bullett: *The English Mystics*, 1950.

Life of St Catherine of Siena by Sigrid Undset in *Saga of Saints*, 1934.

Lives of St Joan of Arc by A. Lang, 1908, H. Belloc, 1929, and V. Sackville-West, 1936.

M. Creighton: *A History of the Papacy*, 1897.

M. de la Bedoyère: *The Meddlesome Friar* (a study of Savonarola and Alexander VI Borgia), 1958.

J. Mackinnon: *The Origins of the Reformation*, 1939.

The Oxford History of England (vols. vi and vii).

H. Maynard Smith: *Pre-Reformation England*, 1938.

Sir F. M. Powicke: *The Reformation in England*, 1941.

T. E. Bridgett: *The Life of Blessed Thomas More*, 1891.

Lives of Henry VIII and Cardinal Wolsey by A. F. Pollard, 1905 and 1929; of Wolsey by H. Belloc, 1930; of Anne Boleyn by P. Sargeant, 1934; of Catherine of Aragon by G. Mattingly, 1942; of Thomas Cranmer by A. C. Deane, 1927, and H. Belloc, 1932; of Mary Tudor by B. White, 1935, and H. F. M. Prescott, 1940; and of Elizabeth I by J. E. Neale, 1934.

L. Baldwin Smith: *A Tudor Tragedy*, 1961.

C. H. Smyth: *Cranmer and the Reformation under Edward VI*, 1926.

A very fine fictional representation of the Henrician Reformation in England is contained in H. F. M. Prescott's *The Man on the Donkey*, 1952, a portrayal of Rober Aske and the Pilgrimage of Grace.

J. Maritain: *Three Reformers* (Eng. trans.), 1948.

R. E. Davies: *The Problem of Authority in Continental Reform*, 1946.

H. W. Kramm: *Theology of Martin Luther*, 1947.

Abbé G. Constant: *The Reformation in England*, vols. i and ii, 1934–41. (Already given in French, p. 537.)

Mgr P. Hughes: *The Reformation in England* (3 vols.), 1950–4, and *A Popular History of the Reformation*, 1957.

Fr Bede, O. P Jarrett: *A History of Europe*, 1929.

Hilaire Belloc: *How the Reformation happened*, 1928.

New Cambridge Modern History, vol. ii, *The Reformation*, *1520–1559*. [Published 1958.]

INDEX OF PRINCIPAL NAMES

*s

INDEX OF PRINCIPAL NAMES

(Main references are shown in heavy numerals)